THE YALE EDITION

OF

HORACE WALPOLE'S

CORRESPONDENCE

EDITED BY W. S. LEWIS

VOLUME THIRTY

HORACE WALPOLE'S CORRESPONDENCE

WITH

GEORGE SELWYN
LORD LINCOLN
SIR CHARLES HANBURY WILLIAMS
HENRY FOX
RICHARD EDGCUMBE

EDITED BY W. S. LEWIS
AND
ROBERT A. SMITH

NEW HAVEN
YALE UNIVERSITY PRESS
LONDON · OXFORD UNIVERSITY PRESS
1961

ADVISORY COMMITTEE

LIST OF SUBSCRIBERS

H. M. QUEEN ELIZABETH II

AGNES SCOTT COLLEGE LIBRARY, Decatur, Georgia
ALAMEDA FREE LIBRARY, Alameda, California
ALBERTUS MAGNUS COLLEGE LIBRARY, New Haven, Connecticut
ALEXANDER TURNBULL LIBRARY, Wellington, New Zealand
ALLEGHENY COLLEGE, THE REIS LIBRARY, Meadville, Pennsylvania
ALL SOULS COLLEGE LIBRARY, Oxford, England
LLOYD V. ALMIRALL, Esq., New York, New York
JOSEPH W. ALSOP, JR, Esq., Washington, D. C.
FRANK ALTSCHUL, Esq., Stamford, Connecticut
THE AMERICAN ACADEMY IN ROME, Rome, Italy
AMERICAN INTERNATIONAL COLLEGE LIBRARY, Springfield,
   Massachusetts
AMERICAN UNIVERSITY LIBRARY, Washington, D. C.
AMHERST COLLEGE, Converse Memorial Library, Amherst, Massa-
   chusetts
F. D. ANDERSON, Esq., Indianapolis, Indiana
W. ARMYTAGE, Esq., Moyvore, Eire
THE ATHENÆUM CLUB, London, England
ATLANTA UNIVERSITY LIBRARY, Atlanta, Georgia
HUGH D. AUCHINCLOSS, Esq., McLean, Virginia
AUCKLAND UNIVERSITY COLLEGE, Auckland, New Zealand
THE REVEREND ALBAN BAER, Portsmouth, Rhode Island
RICHARD B. BAKER, Esq., Saunderstown, Rhode Island
BANGOR PUBLIC LIBRARY, Bangor, Maine
Sir T. D. BARLOW, K.B.E., London, England
W. D. BASTON, ESQ., Morpeth, England
BATH MUNICIPAL LIBRARY, Bath, England
BAVARIAN STATE LIBRARY, Munich, Germany
BEDFORD COLLEGE FOR WOMEN, London, England
C. F. BELL, Esq., London, England
BERKELEY COLLEGE LIBRARY, Yale University, New Haven, Con-
   necticut

BEVERLY HILLS PUBLIC LIBRARY, Beverly Hills, California
THEODORE BESTERMAN, Esq., Geneva, Switzerland
BIBLIOTECA NACIONAL DE PERÚ, Lima, Peru
BIBLIOTHÈQUE DE L'UNIVERSITÉ, Bordeaux, France
BIBLIOTHÈQUE DE L'UNIVERSITÉ, Caen, France
Mrs NORMAN H. BILTZ, Reno, Nevada
BIRMINGHAM PUBLIC LIBRARY, Birmingham, England
BOSTON ATHENÆUM, Boston, Massachusetts
BOSTON COLLEGE LIBRARY, Chestnut Hill, Massachusetts
BOSTON PUBLIC LIBRARY, Boston, Massachusetts
BOSTON UNIVERSITY, COLLEGE OF LIBERAL ARTS LIBRARY, Boston,
  Massachusetts
BOWDOIN COLLEGE LIBRARY, Brunswick, Maine
BRANDEIS UNIVERSITY LIBRARY, Waltham, Massachusetts
BRISTOL PUBLIC LIBRARY, Bristol, England
WALLACE BROCKWAY, Esq., New York, New York
BROOKLYN COLLEGE LIBRARY, Brooklyn, New York
BROOKLYN PUBLIC LIBRARY, Brooklyn, New York
BROOKS SCHOOL, North Andover, Massachusetts
RALPH S. BROWN, JR, Esq., Guilford, Connecticut
BROWN UNIVERSITY, JOHN HAY MEMORIAL LIBRARY, Providence,
  Rhode Island
BRYN MAWR COLLEGE LIBRARY, Bryn Mawr, Pennsylvania
JOHN N. BRYSON, Esq., Oxford, England
BUCKNELL UNIVERSITY LIBRARY, Lewisburg, Pennsylvania
BUFFALO AND ERIE COUNTY PUBLIC LIBRARY, Buffalo, New York
BUTLER UNIVERSITY LIBRARY, Indianapolis, Indiana
LYMAN H. BUTTERFIELD, Esq., Boston, Massachusetts
CALHOUN COLLEGE LIBRARY, YALE UNIVERSITY, New Haven, Con-
  necticut
CALIFORNIA STATE LIBRARY, Sacramento, California
CAMBRIDGE PUBLIC LIBRARY, Cambridge, England
CAMBRIDGE PUBLIC LIBRARY, Cambridge, New York
CANISIUS COLLEGE LIBRARY, Buffalo, New York
CARDIFF PUBLIC LIBRARY, Cardiff, Wales
CARNEGIE LIBRARY OF PITTSBURGH, Pittsburgh, Pennsylvania
RALPH E. CARPENTER, JR, Esq., Scarsdale, New York
CATHOLIC UNIVERSITY LIBRARY, Washington, D. C.
Mrs RALPH CATTERALL, Richmond, Virginia

CHICAGO PUBLIC LIBRARY, Chicago, Illinois
CINCINNATI PUBLIC LIBRARY, Cincinnati, Ohio
CLAREMONT COLLEGES LIBRARY, Claremont, California
CLEVELAND PUBLIC LIBRARY, Cleveland, Ohio
SCOTT CLIFFORD, Esq., Indianapolis, Indiana
COE COLLEGE LIBRARY, Cedar Rapids, Iowa
COLBY COLLEGE LIBRARY, Waterville, Maine
COLGATE UNIVERSITY LIBRARY, Hamilton, New York
COLLEGE OF THE CITY OF NEW YORK, New York, New York
COLLEGE OF NEW ROCHELLE LIBRARY, New Rochelle, New York
COLLEGE OF ST CATHERINE LIBRARY, St Paul, Minnesota
COLLEGE OF ST THOMAS, St Paul, Minnesota
COLLEGE OF WOOSTER LIBRARY, Wooster, Ohio
COLORADO COLLEGE, COBURN LIBRARY, Colorado Springs, Colorado
COLUMBIA UNIVERSITY LIBRARY, New York, New York
COMMONWEALTH NATIONAL LIBRARY, Canberra, Australia
CONNECTICUT COLLEGE, PALMER LIBRARY, New London, Connecticut
CONNECTICUT STATE LIBRARY, Hartford, Connecticut
REGINALD G. COOMBE, Esq., Greenwich, Connecticut
Mrs FRANK COOPER, Albany, New York
CORNELL UNIVERSITY LIBRARY, Ithaca, New York
HUGH B. COX, Esq., Alexandria, Virginia
CREIGHTON UNIVERSITY, Omaha, Nebraska
E. C. CULL, Esq., Dorking, Surrey
DARTMOUTH COLLEGE, BAKER MEMORIAL LIBRARY, Hanover, New
    Hampshire
DAVENPORT COLLEGE LIBRARY, YALE UNIVERSITY, New Haven, Con-
    necticut
FRANKLIN DAY, Esq., Allendale, New Jersey
DENVER PUBLIC LIBRARY, Denver, Colorado
DES MOINES PUBLIC LIBRARY, Des Moines, Iowa
DETROIT PUBLIC LIBRARY, Detroit, Michigan
DEUTSCHE STAATSBIBLIOTHEK, Berlin, Germany
Mrs ROBERT CLOUTMAN DEXTER, Belmont, Massachusetts
CHARLES D. DICKEY, ESQ., Chestnut Hill, Philadelphia, Pennsylvania
DICKINSON COLLEGE LIBRARY, Carlisle, Pennsylvania
Mrs FRANK F. DODGE, New York, New York
Mrs NELSON DOUBLEDAY, Cleft Road, Oyster Bay, New York
E. H. DOUGLAS-OSBORN, Esq., Barnt Green, Worcestershire

Miss BLANCHE HARVEY, Cleveland, Ohio
HENRY E. HUNTINGTON LIBRARY AND ART GALLERY, San Marino, California
RICHARD A. HERZBERG, Esq., Whippany, New Jersey
HOBART COLLEGE LIBRARY, Geneva, New York
C. B. HOGAN, Esq., Woodbridge, Connecticut
E. C. HOHLER, Esq., Aylesbury, Buckingham, England
MAJOR T. S. HOHLER, Aylesbury, Buckingham, England
HOLLINS COLLEGE, CHARLES L. COCKE MEMORIAL LIBRARY, Hollins College, Virginia
HOTCHKISS SCHOOL, Lakeville, Connecticut
HOUSE OF COMMONS LIBRARY, London, England
HOUSE OF LORDS LIBRARY, London, England
W. H. HUGHES, Esq., London, England
DR K. HUIBREGTSE, Haarlem, Holland
HUNTER COLLEGE LIBRARY, New York, New York
Miss HUNTINGTON, Henley-on-Thames, England
INCARNATE WORD COLLEGE LIBRARY, San Antonio, Texas
INDIANA STATE LIBRARY, Indianapolis, Indiana
INDIANA UNIVERSITY LIBRARY, Bloomington, Indiana
THE INSTITUTE FOR ADVANCED STUDY, Princeton, New Jersey
THE INSTITUTE OF HISTORICAL RESEARCH, UNIVERSITY OF LONDON, London, England
JACKSONVILLE PUBLIC LIBRARY, Jacksonville, Florida
OLIVER B. JENNINGS, Esq., Coldspring Harbor, Long Island, New York
JEWISH NATIONAL AND UNIVERSITY LIBRARY, Jerusalem, Israel
JOHN CARTER BROWN LIBRARY, Providence, Rhode Island
JOHNS HOPKINS UNIVERSITY LIBRARY, Baltimore, Maryland
Mrs DOUGLAS JOHNSTON, Hazel Green, Alabama
JOINT UNIVERSITY LIBRARIES, Nashville, Tennessee
KANAWHA COUNTY PUBLIC LIBRARY, Charleston, West Virginia
KANSAS STATE UNIVERSITY LIBRARY, Manhattan, Kansas
KENYON COLLEGE LIBRARY, Gambier, Ohio
THE RIGHT HONOURABLE LORD KENYON, Gredington, Flintshire, Wales
WILLARD L. KING, Esq., Chicago, Illinois
KING COLLEGE LIBRARY, Bristol, Tennessee
KING'S COLLEGE LIBRARY, Cambridge, England

MINNEAPOLIS ATHENÆUM, Minneapolis, Minnesota
THE MITCHELL LIBRARY, Glasgow, Scotland
MOUNT HOLYOKE COLLEGE LIBRARY, South Hadley, Massachusetts
MOUNT UNION COLLEGE LIBRARY, Alliance, Ohio
THE MOUNT VERNON LADIES' ASSOCIATION OF THE UNION, Mount Vernon, Virginia
MUHLENBERG COLLEGE LIBRARY, Allentown, Pennsylvania
MERRILL CALVIN MUNYAN, ESQ., Ashland, Virginia
NATIONAL GALLERY OF ART, Washington, D. C.
THE RIGHT HONOURABLE LORD NATHAN OF CHURT, London, England
THE NATIONAL CENTRAL LIBRARY, London, England
NATIONAL LIBRARY OF IRELAND, Dublin, Eire
NATIONAL LIBRARY SERVICE, Wellington, New Zealand
A. E. NEERGAARD, Esq., M.D., New York, New York
NEWBERRY LIBRARY, Chicago, Illinois
NEW HAMPSHIRE STATE LIBRARY, Concord, New Hampshire
NEW HAVEN PUBLIC LIBRARY, New Haven, Connecticut
THE NEW SOUTH WALES LIBRARY OF PARLIAMENT, Parliament House, Sydney, Australia
NEW YORK PUBLIC LIBRARY, New York, New York
THE NEW YORK SOCIETY LIBRARY, New York, New York
NEW YORK STATE LIBRARY, Albany, New York
NEW YORK UNIVERSITY LIBRARY, New York, New York
NORFOLK PUBLIC LIBRARY, Norfolk, Connecticut
NORTH TEXAS STATE TEACHERS COLLEGE LIBRARY, Denton, Texas
NORTHERN ILLINOIS STATE TEACHERS COLLEGE, DeKalb, Illinois
NORTHWESTERN UNIVERSITY LIBRARY, Evanston, Illinois
OBERLIN COLLEGE LIBRARY, Oberlin, Ohio
OHIO STATE UNIVERSITY LIBRARY, Columbus, Ohio
OHIO UNIVERSITY LIBRARY, Athens, Ohio
OHIO WESLEYAN UNIVERSITY, CHARLES ELIHU SLOCUM LIBRARY, Delaware, Ohio
OKLAHOMA AGRICULTURAL AND MECHANICAL COLLEGE LIBRARY, Stillwater, Oklahoma
ASHLEY W. OLMSTED, Esq., Buffalo, New York
R. HUNT PARKER, Esq., Roanoke Rapids, North Carolina
PASADENA PUBLIC LIBRARY, Pasadena, California
PEABODY INSTITUTE LIBRARY, Baltimore, Maryland
PEMBROKE COLLEGE LIBRARY, Cambridge, England

PENNSYLVANIA STATE COLLEGE LIBRARY, State College, Pennsylvania
PENNSYLVANIA STATE LIBRARY AND MUSEUM, Harrisburg, Pennsylvania
PHILLIPS ACADEMY, OLIVER WENDELL HOLMES LIBRARY, Andover, Massachusetts
PHILLIPS EXETER ACADEMY, DAVIS LIBRARY, Exeter, New Hampshire
THE PIERPONT MORGAN LIBRARY, New York, New York
Miss PORTER'S SCHOOL, Farmington, Connecticut
PORTLAND PUBLIC LIBRARY, Portland, Maine
L. F. POWELL, Esq., Oxford, England
PRINCETON UNIVERSITY LIBRARY, Princeton, New Jersey
PROVIDENCE ATHENÆUM, Providence, Rhode Island
PUBLIC LIBRARY OF NEW SOUTH WALES, Sydney, Australia
PUBLIC LIBRARY OF VICTORIA, Melbourne, Australia
PURDUE UNIVERSITY LIBRARY, Lafayette, Indiana
QUEENS BOROUGH PUBLIC LIBRARY, Jamaica, New York
QUEENS COLLEGE LIBRARY, Flushing, New York
QUEEN'S UNIVERSITY OF BELFAST LIBRARY, Belfast, North Ireland
RANDOLPH-MACON WOMAN'S COLLEGE LIBRARY, Lynchburg, Virginia
READING UNIVERSITY LIBRARY, Reading, England
JOSEPH REATH, ESQ., M.D., Wayne, Pennsylvania
REDWOOD LIBRARY AND ATHENÆUM, Newport, Rhode Island
REED COLLEGE LIBRARY, Portland, Oregon
REFORM CLUB, London, England
RICE INSTITUTE LIBRARY, Houston, Texas
Mrs CARL P. ROLLINS, Hamden, Connecticut
ROOSEVELT UNIVERSITY LIBRARY, Chicago, Illinois
C. G. ROSENBERG AND CO. LTD., London, England
THE RIGHT HONOURABLE LORD ROTHSCHILD, Cambridge, England
THE ROYAL LIBRARY, Stockholm, Sweden
THE ROYAL UNIVERSITY LIBRARY, Upsala, Sweden
RUTGERS UNIVERSITY LIBRARY, New Brunswick, New Jersey
JOHN RYLANDS LIBRARY, Manchester, England
SAGINAW PUBLIC LIBRARIES, Saginaw, Michigan
ST ANDREWS UNIVERSITY LIBRARY, St Andrews, Fife, Scotland
ST BONAVENTURE COLLEGE, FRIEDSAM MEMORIAL LIBRARY, St Bonaventure, New York
ST JOHN'S UNIVERSITY LIBRARY, Brooklyn, New York
ST JOSEPH'S COLLEGE FOR WOMEN LIBRARY, Brooklyn, New York

ST LOUIS PUBLIC LIBRARY, St Louis, Missouri

ST LOUIS UNIVERSITY LIBRARY, St Louis, Missouri

ST MARY'S COLLEGE LIBRARY, Notre Dame, Indiana

ST MARY'S COLLEGE, Strawberry Hill, Middlesex, England

ST OLAF COLLEGE LIBRARY, Northfield, Minnesota

ST PAUL PUBLIC LIBRARY, St Paul, Minnesota

ST PAUL'S SCHOOL, Concord, New Hampshire

ST PETER'S COLLEGE LIBRARY, Jersey City, New Jersey

Mrs JAMES SALLADE, Ann Arbor, Michigan

SAN BERNARDINO VALLEY JUNIOR COLLEGE LIBRARY, San Bernardino,
     California

SAN FRANCISCO PUBLIC LIBRARY, San Francisco, California

SAN JOSÉ STATE LIBRARY, San José, California

SEATTLE PUBLIC LIBRARY, Seattle, Washington

ERIC H. L. SEXTON, Esq., Camden, Maine

THE SIGNET LIBRARY, Edinburgh, Scotland

SKIDMORE COLLEGE LIBRARY, Saratoga Springs, New York

RICHARD SMART, Esq., London, England

SMITH COLLEGE LIBRARY, Northampton, Massachusetts

WARREN H. SMITH, Esq., Geneva, New York

P. H. B. OTWAY SMITHERS, Esq., Alresford, Hampshire, England

SOMERVILLE COLLEGE LIBRARY, Oxford, England

SOUTH AFRICAN PUBLIC LIBRARY, Cape Town, Union of South Africa

SOUTHERN ILLINOIS UNIVERSITY LIBRARIES, Carbondale, Illinois

SOUTHERN METHODIST UNIVERSITY, FONDREN LIBRARY, Dallas, Texas

SOUTHWESTERN COLLEGE LIBRARY, Memphis, Tennessee

SOUTHWESTERN LOUISIANA INSTITUTE, STEPHENS MEMORIAL LIBRARY,
     Lafayette, Louisiana

STANFORD UNIVERSITY LIBRARIES, Stanford, California

STATE LIBRARY OF WESTERN AUSTRALIA, Perth, Western Australia

STATE UNIVERSITY OF IOWA LIBRARIES, Iowa City, Iowa

JAMES STRACHEY, Esq., London, England

STRATFORD LIBRARY ASSOCIATION, Stratford, Connecticut

Miss L. STUART SUTHERLAND, Lady Margaret Hall, Oxford, England

SWARTHMORE COLLEGE LIBRARY, Swarthmore, Pennsylvania

SWEET BRIAR COLLEGE, MARY HELEN COCHRAN LIBRARY, Sweet Briar,
     Virginia

SYRACUSE UNIVERSITY LIBRARY, Syracuse, New York

HENRY C. TAYLOR, ESQ., Coldspring Harbor, Long Island, New York

UNIVERSITY OF DELAWARE LIBRARY, Newark, Delaware
UNIVERSITY OF DENVER, MARY REED LIBRARY, Denver, Colorado
UNIVERSITY OF DURHAM LIBRARY, Durham, England
UNIVERSITY OF FLORIDA LIBRARY, Gainesville, Florida
UNIVERSITY OF GEORGIA LIBRARIES, Athens, Georgia
UNIVERSITY OF HULL LIBRARY, Hull, England
UNIVERSITY OF ILLINOIS LIBRARY, Urbana, Illinois
UNIVERSITY OF KANSAS CITY, Kansas City, Missouri
UNIVERSITY OF KANSAS LIBRARY, Lawrence, Kansas
UNIVERSITY OF KENTUCKY LIBRARY, Lexington, Kentucky
UNIVERSITY OF LEICESTER LIBRARY, Leicester, England
UNIVERSITY OF LIVERPOOL LIBRARY, Liverpool, England
UNIVERSITY OF LONDON LIBRARY, London, England
UNIVERSITY OF MANCHESTER LIBRARY, Manchester, England
UNIVERSITY OF MARYLAND LIBRARY, College Park, Maryland
UNIVERSITY OF MASSACHUSETTS LIBRARY, Amherst, Massachusetts
UNIVERSITY OF MELBOURNE, Melbourne, Australia
UNIVERSITY OF MICHIGAN, DEARBORN CENTER LIBRARY, Dearborn, Michigan
UNIVERSITY OF MICHIGAN LIBRARY, Ann Arbor, Michigan
UNIVERSITY OF MINNESOTA LIBRARY, Minneapolis, Minnesota
UNIVERSITY OF MISSISSIPPI LIBRARY, University, Mississippi
UNIVERSITY OF MISSOURI LIBRARY, Columbia, Missouri
UNIVERSITY OF NEBRASKA LIBRARY, Lincoln, Nebraska
UNIVERSITY OF NEVADA LIBRARY, Reno, Nevada
UNIVERSITY OF NEW HAMPSHIRE, HAMILTON SMITH LIBRARY, Durham, New Hampshire
UNIVERSITY OF NEW MEXICO LIBRARY, Albuquerque, New Mexico
UNIVERSITY OF NORTH CAROLINA LIBRARY, Chapel Hill, North Carolina
UNIVERSITY OF NORTH DAKOTA LIBRARY, Grand Forks, North Dakota
UNIVERSITY OF NOTRE DAME LIBRARY, Notre Dame, Indiana
UNIVERSITY OF OKLAHOMA LIBRARY, Norman, Oklahoma
UNIVERSITY OF OMAHA LIBRARY, Omaha, Nebraska
UNIVERSITY OF OREGON LIBRARY, Eugene, Oregon
UNIVERSITY OF OSLO LIBRARY, Oslo, Norway
UNIVERSITY OF OTAGO, Dunedin, New Zealand
UNIVERSITY OF PENNSYLVANIA LIBRARY, Philadelphia, Pennsylvania
UNIVERSITY OF PITTSBURGH LIBRARY, Pittsburgh, Pennsylvania

University of Rhode Island Library, Kingston, Rhode Island
University of Richmond Library, Richmond, Virginia
University of Rochester Library, Rochester, New York
University of Santa Clara, Varsi Library, Santa Clara, California
University of Sheffield Library, Sheffield, England
University of Southampton Library, Southampton, England
University of South Carolina, McKissick Memorial Library, Columbia, South Carolina
University of Southern California Library, Los Angeles, California
University of Sydney, Sydney, Australia
University of Tennessee Library, Knoxville, Tennessee
University of Texas Library, Austin, Texas
University of Toledo Library, Toledo, Ohio
University of Toronto Library, Toronto, Canada
University of Tübingen Library, Tübingen, Germany
University of Utah Library, Salt Lake City, Utah
University of Vermont, University Libraries, Burlington, Vermont
University of Virginia Library, Charlottesville, Virginia
University of Washington Library, Seattle, Washington
University of Wichita Library, Wichita, Kansas
University of Wisconsin Library, Madison, Wisconsin
University of Wyoming Library, Laramie, Wyoming
Vassar College Library, Poughkeepsie, New York
Vermont State Library, Montpelier, Vermont
Villanova University Library, Villanova, Pennsylvania
Virginia State Library, Richmond, Virginia
A. P. Vlasto, Esq. King's College, Cambridge, England
George Wahr, Esq., Ann Arbor, Michigan
Mrs Christopher Ward, Greenville, Delaware
Washington State College Library, Pullman, Washington
Washington University Library, St Louis, Missouri
A. J. Watson, Esq., Shoreham-by-Sea, Sussex
Wayne University Library, Detroit, Michigan
M. E. Weatherall, Esq., South Clifton, Guernsey
Wellesley College Library, Wellesley, Massachusetts
Wells College Library, Aurora, New York
Wesleyan University Library, Middletown, Connecticut

WEST VIRGINIA UNIVERSITY LIBRARY, Morgantown, West Virginia

WALDEMAR WESTERGAARD, Esq., Los Angeles, California

WESTERN COLLEGE LIBRARY, Oxford, Ohio

WESTERN KENTUCKY STATE TEACHERS COLLEGE LIBRARY, Bowling Green, Kentucky

WESTERN RESERVE UNIVERSITY LIBRARY, Cleveland, Ohio

WESTERN STATE TEACHERS COLLEGE LIBRARY, Kalamazoo, Michigan

WESTMINSTER PUBLIC LIBRARY, Westminster, England

WHEATON COLLEGE LIBRARY, Wheaton, Illinois

WHEATON COLLEGE LIBRARY, Norton, Massachusetts

HENRY WADE WHITE, ESQ., Boston, Massachusetts

PETER A. WICK, Esq., Boston, Massachusetts

WILLIAM AND MARY COLLEGE LIBRARY, Williamsburg, Virginia

WILLIAMS COLLEGE LIBRARY, Williamstown, Massachusetts

THE HENRY FRANCIS DU PONT WINTERTHUR MUSEUM, Winterthur, Delaware

WITTENBERG COLLEGE LIBRARY, Springfield, Ohio

YALE CLUB LIBRARY, New York, New York

YALE MEDICAL LIBRARY, New Haven, Connecticut

YALE UNIVERSITY LIBRARY, New Haven, Connecticut

MAURICE F. YORKE, Esq., Green Craig, Aberlady, East Lothian, Scotland

WILLIAM ZIMMERMAN, Esq., Arlington, Virginia

TABLE OF CONTENTS

LIST OF ILLUSTRATIONS

INTRODUCTION

This volume and the following show the variety of Walpole's friendships: from Lord Lincoln to Hannah More. We read in his first letter to Lincoln about 'millions of pretty women' at Genoa in 1739, and in the last letter to Hannah More, written fifty-seven years later, about the failure of Fanny Burney's *Camilla*. The correspondents in these two volumes, who were poles apart in their interests and conduct, are linked by Walpole's desire to please and entertain them: the word that connects these two very dissimilar casts of characters is 'friendship.' Madame du Deffand concluded her 'Portrait' of Walpole: 'Vous avez des amis, vous leur êtes entièrement dévoué, leurs intérêts sont les vôtres, et tous vos discours et tous vos raisonnements contre l'amitié ne persuaderont pas que vous ne soyez l'homme du monde qui en est le plus capable.'[1]

The most striking feature of this volume is the new light that it throws on Walpole in his twenties. His 'new' letters to Lincoln and the many unpublished letters to Charles Hanbury Williams from Henry Fox and others of the younger Whigs fill in many gaps during the six-year period after his return from the Grand Tour. In this volume we have the young man whom Gray called 'the friend of London.'

Because we know so much about Walpole in his later days we tend to think of him in terms of his portrait by Dance and to see him as the Abbot of Strawberry Hill or entertaining dowagers at cards. Now, thanks to Lord and Lady Cholmondeley, we can see him at the age of twenty-three in the Rosalba that gives us a magnificently dressed young man with a very intelligent and lively countenance, a young man who is thoroughly enjoying his very fortunate position in life. Most of his new friends in the Young Club at White's were politicians whose primary concerns were money and power and who accepted venereal disease and the

1. DU DEFFAND vi. 73.

duns of creditors as routine. These are the friends we meet in this volume. Many more, such as Winnington, Hans Stanley, 'Gilly' Williams, and Rigby, are heard off-stage. After describing to Hanbury Williams the unhappy consequences of his association with Polly Henley, Rigby goes on, 'Hori, who you intend to use your interest with to invite me to Houghton, has already done it in the most obliging manner, he is most extremely civil and there is hardly a day passes that we don't spend some time together. I am fond of his company beyond all things.'[2] Rigby, then only twenty-two and already a cold-blooded politician, doubtless wrote this and many similar protestations of friendship for Walpole, confident that they would reach him, yet while he and the rest wished to secure whatever benefits old Lord Orford at Houghton might still be able to confer, it is clear that they liked Horace Walpole for himself.

The tone and quality of this circle are indicated in Walpole's account of Sir Charles Hanbury Williams (*post* pp. 311–23), which is printed now for the first time. Walpole defends his friend against unfair charges of peculation while admitting that Williams 'had innumerable enemies; all the women, for he had poxed his wife, all the Tories, for he was a steady Whig, all fools, for he was a bitter satirist, and many sensible people, for he was immoderately vain.' A page farther on we read how Lord Hervey tricked Henry Fox into making love to the Duchess of Manchester 'in order to betray this amour to rich Mrs Horner, who kept Mr Fox,' etc., etc. Walpole was carried away for a time by the flattering attention of these opportunists, a circumstance noted by his older friends. Conway wrote to him, 'By the way, I hear you have sold yourself body and soul to [Sir Charles Hanbury Williams]; . . . your old friends complain they never see you.'[3] To which Walpole replied, 'You have seen (I have seen you have) that I am fickle, and foolishly fond of twenty new people: but I don't really love them.'[4] The later defection of many of these new friends inspired, in part, his tirades against

2. Rigby to Hanbury Williams 21 July 1744, unpublished; MS at Farmington.
3. Conway to HW 1 July 1744, unpub-
lished; MS in private hands in Ceylon.
4. HW to Conway 20 July 1744.

friendship. Although his quickness and gaiety and flair for political intrigue might have made him well suited for the life they led, he was too thin-skinned and emotionally vulnerable for it. Instead of ending up a suicide or a bankrupt he outlived all of these men and became the centre of a large and affectionate circle.

The letters to Lincoln are printed here for the first time. We have hitherto known him chiefly as the amorous young man who accidentally saved Walpole's life at Reggio and the person whom Walpole tried to defend in the scuffle at the opera.[5] Now, although we still lack his side of the correspondence, we discover that he was one of Walpole's most intimate early friends. There is in Walpole's letters to him an effusiveness, even an obsequiousness, that does not appear to anything like the same degree elsewhere. That Lincoln finally snubbed him is clear, but Walpole had the last word. In his *Memoirs* he wrote: [Lincoln's] 'exceeding pride kept him secluded from the world, and rarely did he appear either at Court or in Parliament. . . . [his] avarice was as unbounded as his haughtiness.'[6] However, four years after writing this he urged Mann to be attentive to Lincoln's son. 'The Duke [Lincoln had succeeded his uncle as Duke of Newcastle] and I have been intimate from our school-hood, and I should like to have him find that I have been zealous about his son.'[7]

Walpole's early letters to him are written in such extravagant high spirits that they could mislead those modern readers who are quick to suspect homosexual relationships, but eighteenth-century men were less afraid of showing their feelings than men are today and they frequently wrote and acted in a way we should consider effeminate. There is no proof that Walpole had any affairs with men or women. The line

Untossed by passions and in arts reposed,

which was written of him on his nineteenth birthday by an Eton and King's contemporary[8] refers to sexual passion and is applicable to him throughout his life.

5. HW to Mann 29 April 1742, MANN i. 411–12.
6. *Mem. Geo. III* i. 164–5.
7. HW to Mann 26 July 1770.
8. By Sneyd Davies, in John Nichols, *Literary Illustrations*, i. 591.

His relations with Henry Fox (who was twelve years his senior) are so complicated that we have thought it advisable to summarize them in an appendix. Walpole went from his youthful wholehearted eulogy in the 'World Extraordinary' to his mature conclusion that Fox 'was cruel, revengeful, daring, and subtle.'[9] Fox counted on Walpole's unwavering support in politics, and when Walpole did not vote for his proposals for the Peace in 1762 Fox stopped payment on one of his most lucrative places, yet in his unavailing struggle to get an earldom Fox turned to Walpole for help, and Walpole did all he could do to get it for him.

This is not the pleasantest volume of the *Correspondence*. The man who comes out best in it—apart from Walpole himself—is Selwyn. Frivolous, undependable, cynical, the wit of wits, he remained a good friend. When he died Walpole wrote to Lady Ossory, 'His end was lovely, most composed and rational. From eight years old I had known him intimately without a cloud between us; few knew him so well, and consequently few knew so well the goodness of his heart and nature.'[10] None of Walpole's correspondents in this volume could write so feelingly.

I have to record the deaths of two more members of the original Advisory Committee.

My friendship with Sir Lewis Namier began in 1933 when, at the suggestion of R. W. Chapman, he wrote to ask if I would let him see Walpole's account of the House of Lords debate on November 13th, 1761. His acknowledgment of the photostats that I sent him fills six fascinating pages. From then until his death he called my attention to new letters and other unique Walpoliana, and read our proofs with special attention to the subject that he had made his own; that is, he accepted the Yale Walpole into full partnership from its start. His wholehearted cooperation is illustrated in the present volume by the 'new' letters to Lincoln. When Mr A. N. Newman of the History of Parliament Trust discovered them in the Nottingham University Library, Namier

9. *Mem. Geo. III* iv. 84.   10. HW to Lady Ossory 28 Jan. 1791.

encouraged him to report them to me at once. Their appearance here is Namier's final contribution to this edition of which he was an unwavering supporter during its first twenty-seven years.

The first letter that I had from R. W. Chapman was written in 1926. He had discovered that the *Additional Lives* in the *Anecdotes of Painting* is a bibliographical puzzle and could I solve it for him? I could not, but our correspondence continued more and more briskly until by the time of his death it had reached hundreds of letters on both sides. I have described in *Collector's Progress* the major part that he played in the launching of this edition and the thoroughness with which he read and corrected our proofs. It was he who gave me the convincing illustration that I used in the Preface to Cole (p. xxxv) to show the advantages of publishing by correspondences rather than giving the letters in chronological sequence and also why we should 'normalize' the text (although he privately wished we would not do so). His bringing Namier and me together is an example of how unobtrusively and skilfully he managed introductions—whether or not they would ultimately benefit the Clarendon Press. Many American scholars are in his debt, but none, I think, are more so than myself.

W. S. L.

MANUSCRIPTS AND BIBLIOGRAPHY

There are 152 letters in this volume. Of the 132 from Walpole, fifty-six are printed here for the first time. Four of the twenty to Walpole are 'new'; two others to him are first printed in full. Most of the unpublished material is to be found in the correspondences with Lincoln and Selwyn.

The correspondence with Lincoln consists of twenty-seven letters, twenty-five of them from Walpole, all 'new.' One of the two notes from Lincoln is also printed for the first time. Walpole's letters to Lincoln were kindly reported to us by Mr. A. N. Newman when the Newcastle family papers were placed on loan in the Nottingham University Library by the Trustees of the Newcastle Estates.

All but one of the sixteen letters in the correspondence with Sir Charles Hanbury Williams are from Walpole; twelve derive from Williams's papers at Pontypool House, Newport, Monmouthshire, three, printed here for the first time, from the larger collection of Williams's papers at Coldbrook.[1] The letters from Pontypool were given to the Newport Public Library before 1925, when Dr Toynbee printed them in his third supplement. The letters at Coldbrook were sold with the other Williams MSS there to Sir Thomas Phillipps in 1841. They were eventually acquired by Messrs W. H. Robinson, who sold them to W. S. Lewis in 1949. The one letter from Williams that has been found was left by Mrs Damer to the first Sir Wathen Waller and is now at Farmington.

Only two letters from Edgcumbe have been recovered, both now at Farmington from the Waller Collection. One of these is printed in full for the first time.

The correspondence with Henry Fox consists of forty-seven letters. Of the thirty-two from Walpole, two are now printed

---

1. The history of Williams's papers is given by Lord Ilchester in the introduction to his *Life of Sir Charles Hanbury Williams*, 1929, pp. 12–17.

for the first time; three of Fox's letters are also printed for the
first time and a fourth is first given in full. Twenty-four of Walpole's letters remained among Fox's papers at Holland House;
twenty-three of these were first printed by the late Earl of
Ilchester in his *Letters to Henry Fox*, 1915; the twenty-fourth is
now first printed. The remaining eight became separated from
the main body of the correspondence and are in various collections. The originals of at least twelve of the fifteen letters from
Fox remained in Walpole's possession and are now also scattered.

The correspondence with Selwyn consists of sixty letters, all
of them Walpole's; twenty-six of these appear here for the first
time. In addition, we have, from sales catalogues, dateable abstracts of two letters that differ from all recovered letters, and
we also have references to four more that cannot be connected
with the provenance of any known letter. Doubtless still other
letters to Selwyn will eventually turn up. The chief repositories
of them that are known to us are those at Farmington (15), the
Cely Trevilian Collection at the Society of Antiquaries (11),
and Sir John Murray's collection (10).

The history of the Selwyn papers is obscure and uncertain,
but it seems probable that most, if not all, of the letters from
Walpole were in the two boxes of Selwyn's papers that were over-
looked by his executors at the Office of Woods in Whitehall and
not rediscovered until about 1840.[2] John Heneage Jesse began the
publication of them in *George Selwyn and His Contemporaries*
in 1843–4, but the enterprise was brought to an abrupt end by
the intervention of the then Earl of Carlisle. The boxes again
disappeared until 1900, when the officials of the Office of Woods
turned them over to the Carlisle family, in whose possession
they still are at Castle Howard. During the interval several hundred letters had been removed and given away or sold.

Our editorial method has been that described in the earlier
volumes of this edition with two minor exceptions. Sources for
our French identifications have usually been omitted where notes

2. S. Parnell Kerr, *George Selwyn and*   of these boxes.
the Wits, 1909, pp. vii–ix, gives the history

merely repeat information given in the Du Deffand correspondence, and in a few cases we have corrected these silently on small
points from material supplied by the *Dictionnaire de biographie
française,* 1933–   . We have also occasionally corrected silently minor errors and omissions in our cited authorities and
our previous biographical notes on Members of Parliament from
a mimeographed list kindly given to us by the late Sir Lewis
Namier. Dates before September 1752 are Old Style except
where distinguished by NS.

W. S. L.
R. A. S.

ACKNOWLEDGMENTS

OUR first acknowledgments are to the following institutions and private owners who have kindly permitted us to print manuscripts in their possession: the British Museum; Mrs Colin Davy, Heckfield Place, Basingstoke, Hants; the R. G. Shaw Library-Theatre Collection, Harvard College Library; the Roberts Collection, Haverford College Library; Mr and Mrs Donald Hyde, Somerville, New Jersey; the late Earl of Ilchester; Sir John Murray; the Trustees of the Newcastle Estates and Mr A. N. Newman; the Newport Public Library, Newport, Monmouth; the Henry W. and Albert A. Berg Collection, New York Public Library; the Nottingham University Library; the Hon. Mrs Clive Pearson, Parham Park, Sussex; the Carl H. Pforzheimer Library of New York; the Society of Antiquaries; the Earl Stanhope; the late Dr Roderick Terry; the Forster Collection, Victoria and Albert Museum; and the Earl Waldegrave.

The following members of the Advisory Committee have very kindly read the proofs of this volume: the late Sir Lewis Namier and Messrs Erskine, Hazen, Hilles, Ketton-Cremer, Pottle, and Sedgwick, all of whom made many valuable suggestions and additions and helped us to solve several complicated problems. The proofs were also read by Dr Warren H. Smith in New Haven who has assisted at every stage in the preparation of the volume. The late Charles H. Bennett gave much counsel and assistance in the early stages of preparing the Fox correspondence.

The annotation has been verified by Miss Emma H. E. Stephenson and Mr Joseph W. Reed Jr; Mr Jeffrey L. Sammons of the Yale Graduate School has assisted with the preparation of the texts and index. As usual we have received much assistance from Mr A. J. Watson, formerly of the British Museum, and from Miss Julia McCarthy at Farmington. The staff of the Yale Library have continued to render invaluable assistance as have members of the staff of the British Museum, the Harvard College Library, and the New York Public Library.

The following student assistants on bursary appointments from Yale College have performed many important tasks: George A. Baradel, Michael J. Clifford, William N. Free, J. Lee Grove, Marsh Leicester, Henry W. Powell, Jeffrey L. Sammons, Ernst W. Schoen-René, Gary K. Taylor, and Laurence R. Veysey.

We also wish to thank the following for various kindnesses and assistance on particular problems: Professor A. R. Bellinger, Yale University; Dr Eugene C. Black, Brandeis University; Dr Theodore V. Buttrey, Yale University; the late R. W. Chapman, Oxford; Professor Lewis P. Curtis, Yale University; Mr David F. Foxon, London; Professor Robert Halsband, Hunter College; Mr Hugh Honour, London; Mr William A. Jackson, Houghton Library, Harvard; Mr S. Parnell Kerr; Dr George L. Lam, Yale University; Mr W. R. LeFarris, Royal Company of Surgeons, London; Sir Shane Leslie, Bt; Mr Herman W. Liebert, Yale University; Professor Maynard Mack, Yale University; Dr Robert F. Metzdorf, Yale University; Mr Robert Olson, Yale University; Mr James M. Osborn, Yale University; Dr Robert L. Patterson, Castleton, Vermont; Mr H. K. Percy-Smith, London; Miss Gladys Scott Thompson, Edinburgh; Professor E. R. P. Vincent, C.B.E., Corpus Christi College, Cambridge; Mr John Warner, formerly borough librarian of Newport, Monmouth; Professor Robert Warnock, University of Connecticut; Mr Francis J. B. Watson, Wallace Collection, London.

W. S. L.

CUE-TITLES AND ABBREVIATIONS

BERRY . . . *The Yale Edition of Horace Walpole's Correspondence: The Correspondence with Mary and Agnes Berry,* New Haven, 1944, 2 vols.

BM Add. MSS . . Additional Manuscripts, British Museum. Film in the Yale University Library.

BM Egerton MSS . Egerton Manuscripts, British Museum.

'Book of Materials' . Three manuscript volumes, the first two entitled by Walpole 'Book of Materials,' the third entitled 'Miscellany,' begun in 1759, 1771, and 1786 respectively, now in the possession of W. S. Lewis.

Chatham Corr. . . William Pitt, Earl of Chatham, *Correspondence,* ed. W. S. Taylor and J. H. Pringle, 1838–40, 4 vols.

CHATTERTON . . *The Yale Edition of Horace Walpole's Correspondence: The Correspondence with Thomas Chatterton . . . ,* New Haven, 1951.

Coke, Lady Mary, *MS* Photostats of unpublished journals (1775–91)
Journals . . . of Lady Mary Coke in the possession of Lord Home.

COLE . . . . *The Yale Edition of Horace Walpole's Correspondence: The Correspondence with the Rev. William Cole,* New Haven, 1937, 2 vols.

Collins, *Peerage,* 1812 . Arthur Collins, *The Peerage of England,* ed. Sir Samuel Egerton Brydges, 1812, 9 vols.

Cunningham . . *The Letters of Horace Walpole, Earl of Orford,* ed. Peter Cunningham, 1857–9, 9 vols.

Daily Adv. . . . *The Daily Advertiser,* 1731–95. Film in the Yale University Library from the file in the Library of Congress.

DALRYMPLE . . . *The Yale Edition of Horace Walpole's Correspondence: The Correspondence with Sir David Dalrymple . . . ,* New Haven, 1951.

'Des. of SH,' *Works* ii .   Horace Walpole, 'A Description of the Villa of Mr Horace Walpole at Strawberry Hill near Twickenham,' in Vol. II of *The Works of Horatio Walpole, Earl of Orford*, 1798, 5 vols.

DNB .   .   .   .   *Dictionary of National Biography*, ed. Leslie Stephen and Sidney Lee, reissue, 1908–9, 22 vols.

DU DEFFAND .   .   *The Yale Edition of Horace Walpole's Correspondence: The Correspondence with Mme du Deffand*, New Haven, 1939, 6 vols.

Foster, *Alumni Oxon* .   Joseph Foster, *Alumni Oxonienses; 1500–1714*, Oxford, 1891–2, 4 vols; *1715–1886*, Oxford, 1887–8, 4 vols.

GEC .   .   .   .   George Edward Cokayne, *The Complete Peerage*, revised by Vicary Gibbs *et al.*, 1910–59, 13 vols; *The Complete Baronetage*, Exeter, 1900–9, 6 vols.

GM .   .   .   .   *The Gentleman's Magazine.*

GRAY .   .   .   .   *The Yale Edition of Horace Walpole's Correspondence: The Correspondence with Thomas Gray, Richard West, and Thomas Ashton*, New Haven, 1948, 2 vols.

Grenville Papers .   .   *The Grenville Papers, being the Correspondence of Richard Grenville, Earl Temple, K.G., and the Right Hon. George Grenville, their Friends and Contemporaries*, ed. William James Smith, 1852–3, 4 vols.

Hardwicke Corr. .   .   Philip C. Yorke, *The Life and Correspondence of Philip Yorke, Earl of Hardwicke*, Cambridge, 1913, 3 vols.

Hazen, *Bibl. of HW* .   Allen T. Hazen, *A Bibliography of Horace Walpole*, New Haven, 1948.

Hazen, *Cat. of HW's Lib.*   Allen T. Hazen, *A Catalogue of Horace Walpole's Library*, New Haven (in preparation), 4 vols.

Hazen, *SH Bibl.* .   .   Allen T. Hazen, *A Bibliography of the Strawberry Hill Press*, New Haven, 1942.

Hist. MSS Comm.   .   Historical Manuscripts Commission.

HW	Horace Walpole.
Ilchester, *Hanbury-Williams* . . .	Earl of Ilchester and Mrs Langford-Brooke, *The Life of Sir Charles Hanbury-Williams,* 1929.
Ilchester, *Henry Fox* .	Earl of Ilchester, *Henry Fox, First Lord Holland,* 1920, 2 vols.
Jesse, *Selwyn* . .	John Heneage Jesse, *George Selwyn and His Contemporaries,* new edn, 1882, 4 vols.
Journals of the House of Commons . .	[Great Britain, Parliament, House of Commons], *Journals of the House of Commons . . . Reprinted by Order of the House of Commons,* 1803, 51 vols.
Journals of the House of Lords . . .	[Great Britain, Parliament, House of Lords], *Journals of the House of Lords,* [ca 1777]–1891, 123 vols.
Judd, *Members of Parliament* . . .	Gerrit P. Judd, *Members of Parliament 1734–1832,* New Haven, 1955.
La Chenaye-Desbois .	François-Alexandre Aubert de la Chenaye-Desbois and —— Badier, *Dictionnaire de la noblesse,* 3d edn, 1863–76, 19 vols.
Leinster Corr. . .	*Correspondence of Emily, Duchess of Leinster,* ed. Brian Fitzgerald, Dublin, 1949–57, 3 vols.
Letters to Henry Fox .	*Letters to Henry Fox, Lord Holland,* ed. Earl of Ilchester, Roxburghe Club, 1915.
MANN . . .	*The Yale Edition of Horace Walpole's Correspondence: The Correspondence with Sir Horace Mann,* New Haven, 1954– .
MASON . . .	*The Yale Edition of Horace Walpole's Correspondence: The Correspondence with William Mason,* New Haven, 1955, 2 vols.
Mem. Geo. II . .	Horace Walpole, *Memoirs of the Reign of King George the Second,* 2d edn, ed. Henry R. V. Fox, Lord Holland, 1847, 3 vols.
Mem. Geo. III . .	Horace Walpole, *Memoirs of the Reign of King George the Third,* ed. G. F. Russell Barker, 1894, 4 vols.

MONTAGU . . . *The Yale Edition of Horace Walpole's Correspondence: The Correspondence with George Montagu, New Haven, 1941, 2 vols.*

MORE . . . *The Yale Edition of Horace Walpole's Correspondence: The Correspondence with Hannah More . . . , New Haven, 1961.*

MS Commonplace Book of Verses . . . Horace Walpole, 'A Common Place Book of Verses, Stories, Characters, Letters, &c. &c. with some Particular Memoirs of a Certain Parcel of People,' MS in the possession of W. S. Lewis.

MS Poems . . . Horace Walpole, 'Poems and Other Pieces by Horace Walpole, Youngest Son of Sir Robert Walpole, Earl of Orford,' MS in the posession of W. S. Lewis.

MS Political Papers . Horace Walpole, 'Political Papers Written by Horace Walpole son to Sir Robert Walpole Earl of Orford,' MS in the possession of W. S. Lewis.

NBG . . . . *Nouvelle biographie générale,* ed. Jean-Chrétien-Ferdinand Hoefer, 1852–66, 46 vols.

OED . . . . *A New English Dictionary on Historical Principles,* ed. Sir James A. H. Murray *et al.,* Oxford, 1888–1928, 10 vols.

P.C.C. . . . Prerogative Court of Canterbury.

Scots Peerage . . *The Scots Peerage,* ed. Sir James Balfour Paul, Edinburgh, 1904–14, 9 vols.

SH . . . . Strawberry Hill.

sold SH . . . *A Catalogue of the Classic Contents of Strawberry Hill Collected by Horace Walpole,* 25 April – 21 May 1842. The roman and arabic numerals which follow each entry indicate the day and lot number in the sale.

S.P. . . . . State Papers. Film in the Yale University Library from the MSS in the Public Record Office in London. The class numbers (98 or 105) are followed by the volume numbers in arabic numerals.

Toynbee . . . *The Letters of Horace Walpole*, ed. Mrs Paget Toynbee, Oxford, 1903–5, 16 vols.

Toynbee *Supp.* . . *Supplement to the Letters of Horace Walpole*, ed. Paget Toynbee, Oxford, 1918–25, 3 vols.

Venn, *Alumni Cantab.* *Alumni Cantabrigienses*, Part I to 1751, compiled by John Venn and J. A. Venn, Cambridge, 1922–7, 4 vols; Part II 1752–1900, ed. J. A. Venn, Cambridge, 1940–54.

Vict. Co. Hist. . . *The Victoria History of the Counties of England* [with name of county].

Williams MSS . . A collection of Sir Charles Hanbury Williams's manuscripts and correspondence owned by W. S. Lewis. The citations are to volumes and folios or pages.

Williams, *Works* . . *The Works of the Right Honourable Sir Chas. Hanbury Williams, K.B. . . . with Notes by Horace Walpole, Earl of Orford,* 1822, 3 vols.

Works . . . *The Works of Horatio Walpole, Earl of Orford,* 1798, 5 vols.

Wright . . . *The Letters of Horace Walpole, Earl of Orford,* ed. John Wright, 1840, 6 vols.

WSL . . . . W. S. Lewis.

Toynbee	The Letters of Horace Walpole, ed. Mrs Paget Toynbee, Oxford, 1903-5, 16 vols.
Toynbee Supp.	Supplement to the Letters of Horace Walpole, ed. Paget Toynbee, Oxford, 1918-25, 3 vols.
Venn, Alumni Cantab.	Alumni Cantabrigienses, Part I to 1751, compiled by John Venn and J. A. Venn, Cambridge, 1922-7, 4 vols; Part II 1752-1900, ed. J. A. Venn, Cambridge, 1940-54.
Vict. Co. Hist.	The Victoria History of the Counties of England [with name of county].
Williams MSS	A collection of Sir Charles Hanbury Williams's manuscripts and correspondence owned by W. S. Lewis. The citations are to volumes and folios or pages.
Williams Works	The Works of the Right Honourable Sir Charles Hanbury Williams, K.B. . . . , with Notes by Horace Walpole, Earl of Oxford, 1822, 3 vols.
Works	The Works of Horatio Walpole, Earl of Oxford, 1798, 5 vols.
Wright	The Letters of Horace Walpole, Earl of Oxford, ed. John Wright, 1840, 6 vols.
WSL	W. S. Lewis.

LIST OF LETTERS

The dates of the letters to Walpole are printed in italics. Missing letters are marked by an asterisk after the date. Letters printed here for the first time are marked by a dagger (†); those printed in full for the first time are marked by a double dagger (‡). Page references to earlier editions are given in the preliminary notes to the letters.

LETTERS BETWEEN WALPOLE AND
HENRY FOX (LORD HOLLAND)

LETTERS BETWEEN WALPOLE AND
SIR CHARLES HANBURY WILLIAMS

HORACE WALPOLE'S CORRESPONDENCE

To LINCOLN,[1] Saturday 21 November 1739 NS

Printed for the first time from a photostat of the MS deposited in the Nottingham University Library by the Trustees of the Newcastle Estates. Confusing and frequently misleading endorsements in an unidentified hand have been omitted from all the Lincoln letters.

Genoa,[2] Nov. 21, 1739.

My dear Lord,

THANK you: this word is short, but as I feel it, contains a vast deal: it contains all I owe you for your civilities to me at Turin,[3] and for your company, which you know I am fond of; I wish you were here, that I might thank you better. You can't imagine how well I would do the honours of Genoa; do, come and see; try if I have not learned of you. Here are a thousand inducements; a glorious town, delightful situation, a dear Doge,[4] a French play, and an English Lord Granby;[5] millions of pretty women beside, which my Lord can tell you more of.

Except to Mr Spence,[6] I won't trouble you with any compliments; he is so much in the way of Mr Hume,[7] I am quite fond of him; you

1. Henry Fiennes-Clinton (after 1768 Pelham-Clinton) (1720–94), 9th E. of Lincoln; nephew of the 1st D. of Newcastle, whom he succeeded in 1768. HW describes him as 'a very dark thin young nobleman, who did not look so much of the Hercules, as he said he was himself' (*MS Poems*, p. 99). He plays a prominent part in HW's 'Patapan, or the Little White Dog,' printed below, Appendix 1.

2. HW and Gray arrived at Genoa 20 Nov. 1739 NS and stayed a week (GRAY i. 9 n. 50).

3. HW and Gray had been at Turin 7–18 Nov. (ibid. i. 188 n. 1, 190–1; Gray to West 16 Nov. 1739 NS, Thomas Gray, *Correspondence*, ed. Toynbee and Whibley, Oxford, 1935, i. 127–9). Lincoln and his tutor, Joseph Spence, had been at Turin since 11 Oct. NS and remained until 15 Sept. 1740 NS (GRAY i. 191 n. 23; BM Egerton MSS 2235, f. 79).

4. Costantino Balbi (d. 1740), Doge of Genoa 1738–40 (Michael Ranfft, *Genealogisch-historische Nachrichten*, Leipzig, 1739–52, ii. 74; Vittorio Spreti, *Enciclope-*

dia storico-nobiliare italiana, Milan, 1928–36, i. 475, 476). HW and Gray had seen him that morning at a festival 'in his robes of crimson damask, and a cap of the same'; Gray describes him as 'a very tall, lean, stately, old figure' (Gray, *Correspondence*, ed. Toynbee and Whibley, i. 130–1).

5. John Manners (1721–70), styled M. of Granby; eld. son of 3d D. of Rutland; army officer; M. P. Grantham 1741–54, Cambridgeshire 1754–70.

6. Rev. Joseph Spence (1699–1768), author, friend of Pope; professor of poetry at Oxford 1728–38; regius professor of modern history, 1742; HW's occasional correspondent; at this time Lincoln's tutor.

7. Rev. John Hume (1703–82); Bp of Bristol 1756–8, of Oxford 1758–66, of Salisbury 1766–82 (S. H. Cassan, *Lives . . . of the Bishops of . . . Salisbury*, Salisbury, 1824, iii. 320–5; John LeNeve and T. Duffus Hardy, *Fasti ecclesiæ Anglicanæ*, Oxford, 1854, i. 219–20, ii. 316, 450, 508, iii. 366; Philip Morant, *History . . . of Essex*, 1768, ii. 362; Foster, *Alumni*

know that is thinking all with me; if you will, you may give my service to Chetwyn[8] in dumb show.[9] Mr Gray is much your Lordship's humble servant, but nobody so much as my dear Lord

Yours most sincerely,

HOR. WALPOLE

PS. Just coming out of Turin, I met with an epitaph, which you will be so good as to communicate to Mr Spence;

Here lies L—— L——n; Death had wondrous luck
To overtake him,—*for he was a buck.*

I forbear writing the name at length, because the person is living on whom the epitaph was made. Goodnight, my dear Lord.

From LINCOLN, ca Saturday 24 December 1740 NS

Missing, written from Rome; received by HW after he had finished his letter of 27 Dec. (see postscript to that letter in which HW quotes a line from Lincoln's letter). It took about three days for letters to go from Rome to Florence (MANN i. 2, 6, 21, 27).

Oxon.). He had begun life in the Duke of Newcastle's household and had been at Cambridge with Lincoln as a sort of tutor-companion; see his letters to Newcastle 1737–9, BM Add MSS 33065 *passim.* For his relations with Newcastle, see also Norman Sykes, *Church and State in England in the XVIIIth Century,* Cambridge, 1934, pp. 164, 180–1, 278–82, 437–9; and idem, 'The Duke of Newcastle as Ecclesiastical Minister,' *English Historical Review,* 1942, lvii. 77–81.

8. Also mentioned almost immediately after HW and Gray in Spence's MS list of persons met at Turin (BM Egerton MSS 2235, f. 94). Probably Walter Chetwynd (1710–86), fellow of King's College, Cam-

bridge 1730–86, after whom the present Chetwynd's Court of the College is named (*Eton College Register 1698–1752,* ed. R. A. Austen-Leigh, Eton, 1927, p. 69). 'He was one of the earliest visitors to the Valley of the Chamouni in Switzerland in 1740, and the names of two of his companions, Pocock and Wyndham, painted on a rock by the side of the Mer de Glace, still show where the party slept' (H. E. Chetwynd-Stapylton, *The Chetwynds of Ingestre,* 1892, p. 173). Of the several Chetwynds living in 1739, he is the only one recorded as being on the continent at about this time.

9. HW describes him to West as 'a man that never utters a syllable' (GRAY i. 191).

To Lincoln, Tuesday 27 December 1740 NS

Printed for the first time from a photostat of the MS deposited in the Nottingham University Library by the Trustees of the Newcastle Estates.

Florence, Dec. 27, 1740 NS.

My Lord,

I WAS really uneasy till I heard by Mr Spence, that you had escaped all those torrents.[1] We had calculated your being on the road, just as we were swimming in the Arno.[2] You saw Florence in a bad time for the company; if you were to see it now for itself, no Brentford or Cambridge were ever half so foul. The horses go up to their middle in mud in all the quarter of Santa Croce and about Collins's.[3] One has great apprehensions of an epidemical disease, and one has fetched down from the mountains a miraculous bit of terra cotta called our Lady of the Impruneta.[4] She is a woman that is famous for making waters pass; and curing what nothing else can cure. She lives about seven miles off, and has not been here since the plague of Marseilles.[5] She was found many hundred years ago[6] in the lands of the Buondelmontis.[7] Some people were plowing and of a

1. Lincoln and Spence had left Florence (where they had been since 21 Oct. NS) for Rome 24 Nov. NS (Spence's travel notes, BM Egerton MSS 2235, f. 79). Spence describes their trip in a letter to his mother as 'a journey that was bad enough, by being so deep in the year, and made a great deal worse by the rains, which have fallen most part of the forty days last past. . . . When we were got within three mile of this place [Rome, where they arrived 5 Dec. NS], we found that the Tiber was overflown; and was got all over the road we were obliged to pass. . . . There has not been such an inundation here for several years' (8 Dec. 1740 NS, BM Egerton MSS 2234, f. 227). Spence had also written to his mother from Florence, 7 Nov. NS, 'We have got Mr Walpole here again, and dine with him almost every day' (ibid. f. 223).

2. There had been a severe flood at Florence on 3 Dec. NS (Gray i. 237 and n. 2; Giuseppe Conti, *Firenze dopo i Medici*, Florence, 1921, pp. 196–9).

3. John Collins, 'owner of the best inn in Florence' (Janet Ross, *Italian Sketches*, 1887, p. 137).

4. The Madonna dell' Impruneta, a miracle-working Byzantine bas-relief of the Virgin kept in the church of Santa Maria dell' Impruneta, on a hill about seven miles south of Florence, and carried in procession at Florence in time of calamity ([Raffaello del Bruno], *Ristretto delle cose più notabli della città di Firenze*, Florence, 1745, pp. 196–8; *Enciclopedia italiana, sub* Impruneta).

5. 1720–1. An account of a successful earlier visit is in Francesco Rondinelli, *Relazione del contagio stato in Firenze, l'anno 1630 e 1633, con un breve ragguaglio della miracolosa immagine della Madonna dell' Impruneta*, Florence, 1634.

6. An inscription in the church erected in her honour gives 1054 as the date of its consecration (*Enciclopedia italiana, sub* Impruneta); this is approximately confirmed by the surviving parts of the original structure.

7. A Florentine noble family of great antiquity, hereditary patrons of the

sudden the oxen fell down on their knees and remained several days fasting and praying; at last one struck his horn into the ground and tossed up my Lady. She was naked, and cried, 'Cover me'; and they covered her; and she cried, 'Cover me more,' and they put on another veil; in short she screamed for coverings till she had got seven veils on: since which time she has never been seen but by one priest who was in the odour of sanctity; his companion who was not quite so fragrant, lost his sight. She came hither by torch-light on Christmas night, and lay at Santa Felicita;[8] yesterday morning she was escorted to the Dome in the most solemn procession, by the Council, Senate, Cavalierhood, and religious orders;[9] and there remains wonder-working for eight days.[10] Just before her walked the Senator Buondelmonti[11] with his two sons the Abbé and Peter,[12] as lords of the manor.

My dear Lord, I must beg you to say a great deal for me to Mr Spence; as Mr Mann[13] writes to him tonight, I would not give him the trouble of a second letter. Will you give him this epigram for me; 'tis spick and span new out of Mr Pope's shop[14]—

To Sir R. W.

Walpole, be wise, let each man play his part,
You mould the state, let others judge of art;
What though by either Andrew[15] often bit,

church of Santa Maria dell' Impruneta (Pompeo Litta *et al.*, *Famiglie celebri italiane*, Milan, Turin, and Naples, 1819–98, i. *sub* Buondelmonti, *passim;* Conti, op. cit. 202) Accounts of the discovery of the image, differing somewhat in detail from HW's, are in Raffaello del Bruno, op. cit. 196–7; and Frances, Countess of Hertford and Henrietta Louisa, Countess of Pomfret, *Correspondence*, 1805, ii. 216–8. See also Gray to Philip Gray 12 Jan. 1741 NS (Thomas Gray, *Correspondence*, ed. Toynbee and Whibley, Oxford, 1935, i. 180–1).

8. A description of this procession is in Conti, op. cit. 200–1. See also Hertford and Pomfret, op. cit. ii. 218–19.

9. This procession is fully described in Conti, op. cit. 201–2.

10. Bad weather kept the image at Florence until the second week in January (Conti, op. cit. 205; see also *post* 3 Jan.

1741 NS and Gray, *Correspondence*, ed. Toynbee and Whibley, i. 180).

11. Francesco Gioachimo Buondelmonti (1689–1774), senator, 1736 (Litta, op. cit., i. *sub* Buondelmonti, table xii).

12. Litta gives them as Giuseppe Maria Buondelmonti (1713–57), abbé and author (see also Gray i. 231–2 and n. 10); and Giangualberto Buondelmonti (1715–60).

13. Horace Mann (1706–86), cr. (1755) Bt; British diplomatic representative at Florence 1738–86; HW's correspondent.

14. This epigram does not appear in any edition of Pope's poems. HW also quotes it in his *MS Commonplace Book of Verses*, p. 26, with explanations of the allusions, and says that 'Pope made the following epigram to Sir R.W. in the year 1740 when the war with Spain had not had so great success as had been expected.'

15. Most of HW's explanation of this

You scarcely know a Jervas from a Tit;[16]
Blush not, great Sir, you cannot know it less,
Than we (God help us) if it's war or peace.

How do you like Rome, my Lord? The Coliseum and the Princess Borghese;[17] the Tiber and the Prince Borghese?[18] The two first are fine ruins, the two last nasty foul things.[19] I hear you have a fine opera;[20] we are not in likelihood to have one: the country is ruined, the government poor, and the people cross. Our conversation[21] is grown the best of our diversions; we have all the good company.

There is to be a fine opera in England next year; Lord Middlesex[22] the chief undertaker; they are to have the Viscontina,[23] Monticelli,[24] and, if they can Amorevoli;[25] with fine dances.

Adieu, my dear Lord, I have told you all I know; you know, don't you? how much I am

Your faithful humble servant,

HOR. WALPOLE

allusion is cut away in the MS; he begins: 'Sir Andrew Fountain, one of the persons here mentioned, was formerly vice-chamberlain to Queen Caroline when Princess of Wales, but disgraced for having. . . . .' He was Sir Andrew Fountaine (1676–1753), Kt, 1699; collector; friend of Swift and Leibnitz; according to HW, 'Annius' in *The Dunciad* iv. 347–70 (CHATTERTON 153 n. 90).

16. 'Jervase [Charles Jervas (ca 1675–1739)], another painter, having one day copied a picture of Titian, he placed the original and copy together, and in ecstasy of his own work, cried out, "Poor little Tit, if he was alive now, how he would stare!"' (HW's *MS Commonplace Book of Verses*, p. 26). HW repeats the story in *Anecdotes of Painting, Works* iii. 410.

17. Agnese Colonna (1702–80), m. (1723) Principe Camillo Borghese (MANN i. 12 n. 51). The Président de Brosses, writing from Rome in the winter of 1740, describes her house as 'le rendez-vous ordinaire des Anglais' (Charles de Brosses, *Le Président de Brosses en Italie*, ed. R. Colomb, 2d edn, 1861, ii. 213).

18. Camillo (1693–1763), Principe Borghese (GRAY i. 210 n. 16).

19. 'La princesse est aimable, enjouée,

spirituelle, galante, et d'une figure agréable. Monsieur son époux est assez bien aussi de figure . . . mais le dit seigneur n'est pas si gracieux que sa femme, qu'il trouve un peu trop avenante, ce dont il fait souvent la mine, sans qu'il en soit ni plus ni moins' (De Brosses, op. cit. ii. 213).

20. Spence's letter to his mother 13 Jan. 1741 NS contains a description of the Roman opera that winter (BM Egerton MSS 2234, ff. 237–8).

21. Mann's Monday night assembly; see *post* 3 Jan. 1741 NS, n. 1.

22. Charles Sackville (1711–69), styled E. of Middlesex 1720–65; 2d D. of Dorset, 1765; M.P. East Grinstead 1734–42, 1761–5, Sussex 1742–7, Old Sarum 1747–54.

23. Caterina Visconti, called 'Viscontina,' soprano (MANN i. 72 n. 21).

24. Angelo Maria Monticelli (ca 1710–64), soprano; sang with the opera in London 1741–6 (MANN i. 141 n. 7; Sir George Grove, *Dictionary of Music and Musicians*, 5th edn, ed. Eric Blom, 1954, v. 859).

25. Angelo Amorevoli (1716–98), tenor, sang in London during the 1741–2 season (ibid. i. 140; MANN i. 80 n. 16). HW met them all at Calais on their way to England in Sept. 1741 (*post* 13 Sept. 1741 OS; HW to Mann 11 Sept. 1741 OS, MANN i. 141).

PS. Since I wrote my letter, I received your Lordship's. You make me extremely happy with letting me think that my endeavours to please you were not lost, and that you saw I had the inclination if I had not the power. 'Twould have been a great satisfaction to me to have kept you longer here; my dear Lord, wherever I ⟨am⟩[26] you will always command my affections; I did not love you without thinking; and not believing you will alter, I never shall.

Now you are absolutely and irrecoverably gone from Florence, I am sorry I prophesied so truly of the dullness of Rome: indeed I did not give you so strong an idea of the Princess Borghese, as you seem to have contracted. I did not imagine *she would even surpass what you could have the assurance to hope for.* I knew your merit, and thought on some occasions you would not want assurance; and her benevolence and penetration have been known. I only hope that the presence of the Prince did not confine her good nature to under the pharaoh table. I should laugh to see a scene I can figure; your eyes fixed, and Boccapaduglio[27] crying, 'My Lord, you lose the ten; *grazie infinite!'*

I am astonished at the Duke Mattei's[28] rudeness; he was extremely civil to Lord Hartington.[29]

Mr Mann and Gray are extremely your humble servants; I won't fail to make your compliments to the Pomfrets;[30] the *Adorable*[31]

26. The corner of the MS is torn.

27. The faro banker at the Borgheses'. The Président de Brosses characterizes him: 'C'est un maudit Boccapaduli, que nous appelons, en haine de son métier et de sa main harpie, *Bocca Paludi,* bouche de marais: effectivement, c'est un abîme sans fond où tout se perd. La peste! sa profession doit lui valoir bien de l'argent dans son hiver; avec cela on le tromperait tant qu'on voudrait, sans qu'il pût l'empêcher' (De Brosses, op. cit. ii. 214).

28. Probably Girolamo Mattei (d. 1753), Duca de Giove (MANN vi. 115 n. 5).

29. William Cavendish (1720–64), styled M. of Hartington 1729–55; 4th D. of Devonshire, 1755; M.P. Derbyshire 1741–51. He was at Rome when HW was there in April 1740 (MANN i. 7–8).

30. Thomas Fermor (1698–1753), 2d Bn Leominster, cr. (1721) E. of Pomfret; m. (1720) Hon. Henrietta Louisa Jeffreys (ca 1700–61). They and two of their children, Lady Sophia and Lady Charlotte, were at Florence from 20 Dec. 1739 NS to 13 March 1741 NS (GRAY i. 227 n. 18; MANN i. 4 n. 18). See HW's character of Lady Pomfret in GRAY ii. 247–8.

31. Lady Sophia Fermor (1721–45), m. (1744) John Carteret, 2d Bn Carteret, 1st E. Granville, 1744. HW describes her in his *MS Commonplace Book of Verses* p. 29, as 'very beautiful and graceful; much prejudiced in favour of her own person, but not to the prejudice of any-one that liked it.' Lincoln had fallen in love with her at Florence. He confessed his attachment to his uncle, the Duke of Newcastle, from Rome in April: 'My Lord I own to you I love Lady Sophia more than words can express . . . but I can most faithfully assure you nothing can ever be capable of making me forget what I owe to your Grace, or ever so much as to think of entering into the least engagement without your approbation and the rest of my friends. . . . In short, my Lord, I am most sincerely to

has been ill of a fever and swelled face, but is recovered; she had a whole dish of chocolate flung over her last night, and I wished for your Lordship to take the same trouble in washing her gown that Mr D——[32] did; he was vastly busy about it, but not thanked so kindly as perhaps you would have been; I only mean you could not have been less. Lord Lempster[33] is here; and a charming sister[34] of Madame Suarez;[35] all our beauties are in bloom, and ⟨in sh⟩ort I would you were here; do, wish a little so too!

My dear Lord, I have wrote you a horrid long letter, but you won't be angry with me for it.

Compliments to Mr Pit[36] etc. etc.

To Lincoln, Tuesday 3 January 1741 NS

Printed for the first time from a photostat of the MS deposited in the Nottingham University Library by the Trustees of the Newcastle Estates.

Florence, Jan. 3d 1741 NS.

I WRITE to you, my dear Lord, for poor Mr Mann, and should be glad of the occasion, if it did not arise from his violent head-

be pitied, for the greater the sense I have of my Lady Sophia's merit, consequently the loss of her, if it should happen, as I greatly fear [it] will, must make me the more miserable, for I do but too plainly see, my Lord, the many obstacles that must necessarily arise from such a proposal. I am but too well acquainted with the many incumbrances upon my estate, and that marrying without a fortune would be reckoned very imprudent, for you know my Lady Sophia has nothing which the world calls fortune, though more qualifications than one could ever expect to find in any one person; never did I want to be rich before, nor ever did I despise riches in comparison of real merit so much as I do at present' (BM Add. MSS 33065, f. 406). Lincoln made similar remarks to HW on their way back to England (MANN i. 91).

32. Presumably Samuel Dashwood (?1717–93), later of Well, Lincs (R. C. Dudding, History of . . . Alford, [Horncastle], 1930, p. 44; MANN ii. 451 n. 28). 'Mr Dash-

wood' is frequently mentioned in Lady Pomfret's letters to Lady Hertford from Italy; HW subsequently describes him as 'Lady Carteret's [i.e. Lady Sophia's] quondam lover' (MANN i. 125 n. 12; ii. 451).

33. George Fermor (1722–85), styled Lord Lempster 1722–53; 2d E. of Pomfret, 1753. He remained at Florence until 27 Feb. (Hertford and Pomfret, op. cit. ii. 277).

34. Maria Cristina di Valvasone (1705–47), m. (1721) Marchese Orazio Francesco Pucci (MANN i. 39 n. 26). See the following letter for HW's opinion of her.

35. Maria Anna di Valvasone (1697–1773), m. (1716) Balì Baldassare Suares de la Concha (MANN i. 39 n. 24).

36. George Pitt (1721–1803), of Stratfield-Say, Hants; cr. (1776) Bn Rivers; M.P. Shaftesbury 1742–7, Dorset 1747–74. He had been at Florence during October and had fallen in love with Lady Charlotte Fermor (GRAY i. 233–4 and n. 25; MANN i. 468 and nn. 17, 19; Hertford and Pomfret, op. cit. ii. 116, 160).

ache. I fear the conversation brings it, for after every Monday night,[1] he is out of order: I shall insist upon its being laid aside, though 'tis now grown extremely agreeable, and not confined to two families.[2] The addition to that of Suarez is not my only reason for thinking it improved; and so I am in love, my Lord, am I? Madame Pucci is charming, but not so irresistible as you have been told. Her eyes are delightful, her skin and her air; she is very tall, and very lean; she has an ugly mouth with fine teeth, and a large nose: she has not the life, but much of the circumstantial faculty of her sister. Here are good circumstances and bad; here are charms and antidotes: here are grounds enough, if you insist on believing me in love; and here are reasons why I have not a mind to be so. The council declare her lovely, but the pope being so meagre himself, has no thoughts of propagating scraggy cardinals.

The extreme bad weather has stopped the last post from England;[3] and the return of my Lady to the Impruneta.

Lady Sophia bids me tell you, you remember her a long while, that you are a parlous man and she did not think it had been in you.

I hear the master of the house where Lady Mary[4] lodged at Rome,[5] complains he did not imagine so old a woman could have spoiled his bed with her flowers: she is most extraordinary in all her concerns,

—cui non certaverit ulla
Aut tantum fluere, aut totidem durare per annos.[6]

All conversation turns upon the Emperor's obsequies;[7] Buondelmonti[8] makes the oration, and a paltry Lorrainer[9] the catafalque: it

1. 'Every Monday Mr Mann . . . has a select set, and a sixpenny faro table' (Lady Pomfret to Lady Hertford 20 Nov. 1740 NS, Hertford and Pomfret, op. cit. ii. 176–7).

2. I.e., the Pomfrets and Mann's house-guests.

3. 'The weather has been so extremely bad of late, that, though two days beyond the usual time have elapsed, the post is not arrived yet' (Lady Pomfret to Lady Hertford 1 Jan. 1741 NS, ibid. ii. 216).

4. Lady Mary Pierrepont (1689–1762), m. (1712) Edward Wortley Montagu.

5. Lady Mary had been at Rome for a month from 19 Oct. 1740 NS (Robert Halsband, Life of Lady Mary Wortley Montagu, Oxford, 1956, pp. 207–8). Her

lodging, which had been recommended to her by Sir Francis Dashwood, is described in her Letters and Works, ed. Lord Wharncliffe and W. Moy Thomas, 3d edn, [1861], ii. 77.

6. Virgil, Georgics ii. 99–100: 'Which none may match, either in richness of stream or in lasting through many years.'

7. Charles VI (1685–1740), Emperor 1711–40, had died 20 Oct. 1740 NS at Vienna. His public obsequies at Florence were performed in the church of San Lorenzo 16 Jan. NS (Giuseppe Conti, Firenze dopo i Medici, Florence, 1921, p. 206; Hertford and Pomfret, op. cit., ii. 236–7).

8. The Abbé Buondelmonte (ante 27 Dec. 1740 NS, n. 12).

9. Jean-Nicolas Jadot (1710–61), Baron

has already tumbled down three times. There is no telling you the absurdities this creature has said and done upon the occasion, and the old-fashioned inventions he has trumped up by way of decorations;[10] for which instead of Monsieur *Jadeau,* they call him Jadis. He desired of the Abbé to know the subjects of the oration, that he might paint them; the Abbé bid him draw the Pragmatic Sanction;[11] he set about it. T'other day he sent to Dr Lami[12] to complain that the distichs were too long for the places he designed them, and that he begged they might be retrenched. Here's an epigram made on that too;

> Disticha longa nimis, Lami, tua qui putat; illum,
> Unius versus disticha velle puto.[13]

Good night, my dear Lord! I hope Mr Spence is as busy as a bee about gods and goddesses.[14] I left off compliments when I began loving you, and am now only

Yours most sincerely,

HOR. WALPOLE

From LINCOLN, ca Saturday 28 January 1741 NS

Missing; answered in the following letter.

To LINCOLN, Tuesday 31 January 1741 NS

Printed for the first time from a photostat of the MS deposited in the Nottingham University Library by the Trustees of the Newcastle Estates.

de Ville-Issey; made a Florentine nobleman for his services on this occasion (MANN i. 75 n. 11).

10. 'In the middle [of San Lorenzo] was erected a vast pile of pasteboard, painted like marble, with several gilt figures as large as life representing the virtues of the deceased' (Lady Pomfret to Lady Hertford 22 Jan. 1741 NS, Hertford and Pomfret, op. cit. ii. 237); it is illustrated in Conti, op. cit. 207.

11. The settlement, promulgated in 1724, by which the Emperor had provided that all his hereditary kingdoms and lands should pass to his daughters in default of direct male heirs.

12. Giovanni Lami (1697–1770), writer and antiquary (NBG).

13. 'He who thinks your distichs too long, Lami, I think wants distichs of one verse.'

14. For his *Polymetis,* 1747.

Florence, Jan. 31, 1741 NS.

I AM too well persuaded of your goodness for me, my dear Lord, to think you slight me when you don't write. I trust to your heart and not to your pen: whenever I hear from you, it gives me pleasure; and if I do not, I please myself with thinking that you are better amused. Write when you have an inclination, but make me no more excuses: you will spoil me if you do. Believe that I love you sincerely, and that I think you deserve it. I will never change, unless you give me more real occasions than letting slip a few posts.

I did not doubt but Lady Mary would be glad of having you flesh of her flesh, but did not imagine she would try to bring it about by making you of her blood;[1] of her poxed, foul, malicious, black blood! I have gone in a coach alone with her too,[2] and felt as little inclination to her as if I had been *her son*.[3] She is a better specific against lust than all the bawdy prohibitions of the Fathers. She comes up to one of Almanzor's rants in a play of Dryden—

The thought of me shall make you impotent![4]

1. Lady Mary returned to Rome from Naples 12 Jan. 1741 NS (Halsband, op. cit. 209). Lincoln wrote to his uncle, the Duke of Newcastle, 21 Jan.: 'Well! my Lord, we have at last Lady Mary Wortley at Rome, who is as extraordinary as my imagination had fancied her (which by the by is not saying a little). I am so happy as to be mightily in my kinswoman's good graces for you must know she claims a relation, which I own I did not in the least suspect. She takes a sure way to be well with me, for she flatters me so much as to tell me that I am extremely like your Grace, not only in person but in my ways' (quoted ibid. 210 from BM Add. MSS 33065, f. 392). Lady Mary was correct about the relationship: she and Lincoln's mother were second cousins through descent from the Hon. William Pierrepont. A note attributed to HW on Sir Charles Hanbury Williams's obscene 'Ode to Lord Lincoln' states that 'the postilion of Lady W. Montagu, a lad of sixteen, said, "I am not such a child, but that I can guess something whenever my Lord Lincoln comes to my Lady; she orders the porter to let in nobody else, and then they call for pen and ink, and say they are going to write history"' (Williams, *Works* ii. 35). This anecdote appears (except for the proper names) in HW to Montagu 8 Nov. 1759 in a context where it apparently relates to Mrs Elizabeth Montagu and Lord Lyttelton (MONTAGU i. 255 and nn. 12, 12a). Many of the notes attributed to HW in Williams, *Works* are quotations from his letters selected by the editor (see below, p. 159, n. 5), and it seems probable that this identification of the persons in the note about Lincoln and Lady Mary is merely a misinterpretation of the anecdote in the Montagu letter. Professor Robert Halsband supports us in this view.

2. Presumably during her visit to Florence 22 Aug.–16 Nov. 1740 NS; the account of this in Halsband, op. cit. 201–5 mention frequent social encounters between them.

3. Edward Wortley-Montagu (1713–76), with whom Lady Mary was on bad terms.

4. *Almanzor and Almahide, or, The Conquest of Granada*, Pt I, V. ii.

I hear there is a Genoese abbé[5] declared her cicisbeo in all the forms; poor man! He must be in the same situation with Mr Southcote,[6] when my Lady Townshend[7] figured him in the body of old Cleveland,[8] like Van Trump,[9] lost in an ocean neither side nor bottom!

Mr Mann and Mr Gray are vastly yours: the poor former is dying every other day of the headache; I suffer extremely to see him suffer so much.

Is Mr Spence enough at liberty among his antiquities to think of me? I deserve it a little, for I have a vast esteem for him. Do you hear, Mr Spence, though I naturally love anyone that has so real an esteem for Lord Lincoln, yet I hope you won't put all my friendship to his account. When we meet in England, I hope we shall be vastly well together, without any other consideration. I design to visit the Virgil you tell me of,[10] but for getting it, I have no hopes. If I could steal it roundly, I would without any scruple, but for procuring it from so thorough a rogue as Stosch[11] without paying double its value, I despair. He told me t'other day a most ridiculous accident; he corresponds with a learned man[12] at Perugia, and seals his letters with an antique horse's head, round which in small Greek characters is the graver's name, Mithridates.[13] The Inquisitor[14] stopped the letter,

5. Lady Mary, in a letter to Lady Pomfret 15 Feb. [1741] NS mentions amongst her acquaintance at Rome 'a Genoese abbé, who has both wit and learning in a very ugly form, and who on a disagreeable adventure is resolved never to return to Genoa' (Lady Mary Wortley Montagu, *Letters and Works*, ed. Lord Wharncliffe and W. Moy Thomas, 3d edn, [1861], ii. 88).

6. Philip Southcote (d. 1758), 'first designer of the *ferme ornée*' at his seat, Woburn Farm, Chertsey, Surrey; see COLE i. 44 n. 2, ii. 275 n. 15.

7. Etheldreda (or Audrey) Harrison (ca 1703–88), m. (1723) Charles Townshend, 3d Vct Townshend.

8. Anne Pulteney (1663–1746), m. 1 (1694) Charles Fitzroy, 2d D. of Cleveland; m. 2 (1733) Philip Southcote.

9. Cornelis Tromp (1629–91), Dutch admiral, rumoured to have been drowned in a naval battle with the English 2–3 June 1665. The allusion is doubtless to a ballad celebrating the English victory.

10. Probably the engraved cornelian gem later in the Prussian royal collection (from Stosch's collection) described as a youthful head with long hair, under it a cricket playing a seven-stem shepherd's pipe and on each side of it a shepherd's crook and an ear of corn, therefore undoubtedly a portrait of Virgil when young (E. H. Toelken, *Erklärendes Verzeichniss der antiken vertieft geschnittenen Steine der Königlich Preussischen Gemmensammlung*, Berlin, 1835, p. 324).

11. Baron Philipp von Stosch (1691–1757), collector; British secret agent at Florence (MANN i. 9 n. 31).

12. Not identified.

13. The seal is described in Toelken, op. cit. 406, who accepts the stone itself as genuine, but the inscription, M I Θ, as later, though ancient. Other authorities, however, describe it as 'a doublet made to Stosch's order from a wax model'; see C. W. King, *Handbook of Engraved Gems*, 2d edn, 1885, p. 277.

14. 'Padre Maestro Paolo Antonio Ambrogi, della Serra a San Quirico nella Marca d'Ancona' was Inquisitor at Flor-

and sent word to the person that he should take care how he corresponded with such dangerous friends. That he knew the horse's head
and those *strange* characters contained the whole secret and mystery
of freemasonry.[15] Was ever such a holy blockhead?

My dear Lord, I am glad you acquit me of love to Madame Pucci.
There is another face from which I should not be so secure, if it
were not engaged: you lost the most charming sight in Florence by
not seeing Madame Grifoni.[16]

I will make all your compliments, general and particular. As the
post is going out, I shall not have an opportunity today: as a friend
of mine, and no ill-wisher to the fair subject, I will trust you with
a little sonnet composed by Prince Craon.[17] You will see he has all
the gallantry of an old Frenchman, and that a certain pair of eyes
have charmed more pairs than one. Be so good as not to give any
copy of it: here it is quite a secret, and would disoblige him if it
were seen: for though he is gay enough to write it, he is sensible
enough to know that it would not be proper to appear as his.

Sonnet

Nous vous voyons, belle Sophie,
Dans l'âge heureux où les plaisirs
S'offrant en foule à vos désirs
Doivent bannir de votre vie
Et la tristesse et les soupirs.
Les jeux, les ris, les agréments
Compagnons de votre jeunesse,
Semblent vous garantir sans cesse
La durée de votre printemps.
Défiez-vous de si belle promesse,
Mettez à profit vos beaux jours;
Vous auriez enfin votre tour,
Et sentirez des vôtres la puissance ennemie.
Défiez-vous, belle Sophie,
De l'homage flatteur que tout le genre humaine
Rend aux beautés qu'en vous nous voyons réunies;

ence until July 1741 (Giuseppe Conti,
Firenze dopo i Medici, Florence, 1921,
pp. 180–2).

15. For Ambrogi's persecution of free-
masons (which included an attempt to have
Stosch exiled in 1739), see Conti, op. cit.
Chap. XVI, and Janet Ross, *Italian
Sketches*, 1887, pp. 145–51.

16. Elisabetta Capponi (1714–80), m.

(1732) Cavaliere Pietro Grifoni; HW's ci-
cisbea at Florence (MANN i. 33 n. 7). See
also the references to her below, Appendix 1.

17. Marc-Antoine de Beauvau (1679–
1754), Prince de Craon; President of the
Council of Regency to the Grand Duke of
Tuscany 1737–49 (MANN i. 9 n. 27).

Qu'alliers il chercherait en vain,
Et qu'à vos yeux cache la modestie:
Qui vous laisse ignorer tant de dons précieux,
Qu'à pleins mains sur vous ont répandu les dieux;
Mais quand ils vous rendent accomplie,
C'est pour nous éblouir, non pour vous rendre heureux.

If you have a mind to sing it, the three first stanzas go to the tune of the "Black Joke," and the two last to that of "Patient Grisel."[18] Now I talk of the "Black Joke," make *grazie infinite* for me to the Princess Borghesi, for the honour of her remembrance. Adieu, my dear Lord,

Yours ever,

H. W.

To Lincoln, Tuesday 18 April 1741 NS

Printed for the first time from a photostat of the MS deposited in the Nottingham University Library by the Trustees of the Newcastle Estates.

Florence, April 18, 1741 NS.

My dear Lord,

I DON'T know [how] long it may appear to you, but to me it seems an age since I heard from you. I should have told you so sooner, if I had known you fixed,[1] or if I had been fixed myself; but I have been this month or two on the wing fluttering and fluttering,[2] and not yet flown. Well, next week I go certainly;[3] I have been cooking up

---

18. One version of the 'Black Joke,' which took its name from a set of obscene lyrics, is in [Charles Coffey], *Songs in the Opera called the Beggar's Wedding*, 2d edn, [1724], p. 17; see also Sabine Baring-Gould, *English Minstrelsie*, Edinburgh, 1895–?, viii. pp. x–xi, 80–1, for further notes on the tune and two other versions of it. The ballad of 'Patient Grissel' is described as 'one of our most antique songs' in *A Collection of Old Ballads*, 1723–5 [reprint ca 1871], i. 252, where it is said that it was sung to the tune of 'The Bride's Good-morrow.'

1. Lincoln had been at Rome since 5

Dec. 1741 NS except for an excursion to Naples 5–19 March (BM Egerton MSS 2235, f. 79), but HW may have known that he was being pressed by his uncle, Newcastle, to return to England as soon as he 'conveniently' could (Newcastle to Lincoln 16 March 1741 OS, BM Add. MSS 33065, f. 398).

2. HW had received instructions from his father in February to 'leave Italy as soon as possible' because of the probable arrival of Spanish troops (HW to Spence 21 Feb. 1741 NS).

3. HW and Gray left Florence 25 April NS (MANN i. 31 n. 1).

a resolution so long, that at last 'tis scarce worth taking. 'Tis with infinite reluctance I leave Florence without the hope of returning—my dear Lord, you have had of these reluctances,[4] have you not? if you have, pity me, me who at most can carry away but a picture to England.[5] I have indeed made a most agreeable party to go to the fair of Reggio;[6] if they will go; if one of the ladies[7] will, I shall easily content myself for quitting Florence. But I own, I scarce flatter myself that the only one for whom I have made the party, will determine to continue it. As I do not go till tomorrow sennight, if you can find time from your better pleasures to write me a line, it will find me here, and give me vast satisfaction. I do not ask you how you like Rome, for now I know you like it; and knowing you do, I will not be so selfish as to wish to meet you at Venice:[8] in England we must see one another—hum!—would it were to be anywhere else!

We have had an opera for this fortnight, good for nothing but keeping the theatre open. There is a great Saletti,[9] that tries to imitate Farinelli,[10] but is like him only in what one would not wish to resemble him. The first woman[11] has no voice, but is pretty: the second woman had a mind I should think her so too. She came into our box one night when the Tesi[12] was with me. She calls herself Rosa Costi,[13] and is short, crooked, humpbacked, shrill, painted and

---

4. Lincoln had postponed leaving Rome because of Lady Sophia Fermor; see his letter to Newcastle 8 April 1741 NS, quoted *ante* 27 Dec. 1740 NS, n. 31.

5. A portrait of Mme Grifoni by Ferdinand Richter, which he kept the rest of his life in his bedroom at SH ('Des. of SH,' *Works* ii. 452).

6. The party was broken up (*post* 29 April 1741 NS), but HW, Gray and several others went nevertheless, arriving at Reggio about 4 May NS. HW and Gray quarrelled there and separated a few days later (Mann i. 36; Gray i. 9–10 and n. 59, 241–2 and n. 1).

7. Presumably Mme Grifoni.

8. HW and Lincoln met at Reggio in May and again at Venice in early June and travelled together to Paris.

9. Probably Lorenzo Saletti, castrato, who sang at Venice in 1735 when he was described as 'virt. di S.A.S. la Princ. di Toscana' and 'virt. della Princ. Eleonora Gonzaga di Toscana' (Taddeo Wiel, *I teatri musicali veneziani del settecento*, Venice, 1897, pp. 117, 120, 122). He sang

in Spain in 1738 (M. N. Hamilton, *Music in Eighteenth-Century Spain*, Urbana, 1937, p. 115).

10. Carlo Broschi (1705–82), called Farinelli; soprano; sang in England 1734–7; favourite of Philip V of Spain (Sir George Grove, *Dictionary of Music and Musicians*, 5th edn, ed. Eric Blom, 1954, iii. 23–5).

11. Not identified.

12. Vittoria Tesi (1700–75), m. (ca 1743) ———— Tramontini, a barber; contralto (Grove, op. cit. viii. 401–2). She had returned to Florence from Spain in the spring of 1740 but did not sing there that year (Benedetto Croce, *Un prelato e una cantante*, Bari, 1946, pp. 82–8; A. Ademollo, 'Vittoria Tesi,' *Nuova antologia di scienze, lettere ed arti*, Rome, 1889, cvi. 315). HW heard her at either Bologna or Reggio in May (Mann i. 40).

13. Presumably the Rosa Costa who sang at Venice in 1742, 1757 (when she is described as 'virt. di S.A. Elet. di Colonia'), and 1777 (Wiel, op. cit. 142, 215, 325–6).

stinking, in short she has all the acquired deformities of Lady Mary, added to considerable ones of nature. For want of other discourse, I asked her how many songs she had in the last act; she said, 'Only one'; 'Lord,' says I, 'that's a pity'; *'si,' dice, 'perchè non vien trovarmi a casa?'* and I, unbred, squeamish wretch, have never gone to find her in the only place where she ought ever to be.

The Marquise Rinuncini[14] is going to Loreto[15] to get a son;[16] one would think when women go to the Virgin on such a purpose, it should be to learn to get a son without their husband; but she drags her lawful moiety of procreation[17] along with her, and they are to knead their human dough together under the inspection of the Lady Mary.

I must trouble you, my dear Lord, with my compliments to Lord Pomfret and his family;[18] I hope Rome answers the expectation of one so capable of being pleased with antiquity and erudition as my Lady. For Lady Sophy, 'tis impossible the antique world should delight her so much, as she must the modern. I hope Lady Charlotte[19] does not give up the Tuscan language for the Roman, especially as the Florentines look on her as the brightest foreigner that has honoured their Crusca.[20]

I am extremely the humble servant of any of the English that honour me with their remembrance, especially of Mr Spence, whom I would not forgive forgetting me.

Adieu, my dear Lord, may you always be happy, and may I sometimes contribute a little, however little, to your being so!

Yours most sincerely,

HOR. WALPOLE

14. Camilla Aldobrandini (1718–83), m. Marchese Folco Rinuccini (MANN i. 473 n. 14).

15. To the miracle-working Madonna in the Santa Casa at Loreto in Ancona.

16. The pilgrimage was successful; her son Carlo Maria Giuseppe Rinuccini (1742–90) was born in July 1742 (Mann to HW 8 July 1742 NS, MANN i. 473 and n. 15).

17. Marchese Folco Rinuccini (1719–60), chamberlain to the Grand Duke Francis, 1737 (MANN ii. 169 n. 12).

18. Who had left Florence for Rome 13 March, where they arrived 17 March and remained until 18 May (Frances, Countess of Hertford and Henrietta Louisa, Countess of Pomfret, *Correspondence*, 1805, ii. 284, 290; iii. 153).

19. Lady Charlotte Fermor (1725–1813), m. (1746) Hon. William Finch (MANN i. 4 n. 23).

20. The Accademia della Crusca, founded at Florence in the 16th century to preserve the purity of the Italian language. HW told Conway 5 July 1740 that Lady Charlotte was 'the cleverest girl in the world; speaks the purest Tuscan, like any Florentine.'

From LINCOLN, ca Saturday 22 April 1741 NS

Missing; received at Florence and forwarded by Mann immediately after HW's departure, 25 April (Mann to HW 25 April 1741 NS, MANN i. 31).

To LINCOLN, Saturday 29 April 1741 NS

Printed for the first time from a photostat of the MS deposited in the Nottingham University Library by the Trustees of the Newcastle Estates.

Bologna,[1] April 29, 1741 **NS.**

My dear Lord,

I AM so much upon the wing that I scarce know what or where I write, but I would not fail to thank you for your letter, and to obey you in answering it; but really for my motions they are so uncertain, that I cannot tell you when I may hope to meet you. I go tomorrow to Modena, and thence to Reggio, but fear I cannot be at Venice by the Ascension.[2] If I should be so unlucky as to miss seeing you there, I trust we shall meet soon in England, and that you will then give me leave to be sometimes of your company: you will never meet any man more sincerely desirous of your friendship; you have promised it me and I do not doubt of it.

I pity you extremely for the separation you mention,[3] but yours can be but for a short season: mine[4] may be endless! Our party was broke by the illness of a mother,[5] and I obliged to come away! I found Lord Elcho[6] here who goes directly to Venice; Mr Chute[7] and Whitehead,[8] and Mr Hervey[9] came at the same time with me from Florence, and we shall all be at Reggio together.

1. HW and Gray expected to arrive at Bologna on the 27th and stay 'for a few days, to hear the Viscontina sing' (Thomas Gray, *Correspondence*, ed. Toynbee and Whibley, Oxford, 1935, i. 182; MANN i. 31 n. 5).

2. Which fell on 11 May NS in 1741, when the traditional espousal of Venice and the Adriatic was celebrated. Neither HW nor Lincoln reached Venice by that date.

3. From Lady Sophia Fermor.

4. From Mme Grifoni.

5. Perhaps Maria Maddalena Corsi (d. 1754), m. (1707) Roberto Domenico Capponi; Mme Grifoni's mother (Pompeo Litta *et al, Famiglie celebri italiane*, Milan, Turin, and Naples, 1819-98, ii. *sub* Capponi, table xxi).

6. David Wemyss (1721-87), styled Lord Elcho until he was attainted for his part in the '45; titular 6th E. of Wemyss, 1756.

7. John Chute (1701-76) of the Vyne; HW's correspondent.

8. Francis Whithed (formerly Thistlethwayte) (1719-51), M.P. Hampshire 1747-

I beg my compliments to the Pomfrets and to Mr Spence: if you are so good as to let me know your journey[10] by a letter enclosed to Mr Mann, I will endeavour to make my motions square with yours. I am, my dear Lord,

Your sincere humble servant,

HOR. WALPOLE

Lincoln and Spence found HW seriously ill at Reggio 'of a kind of quinsy' late in May. They probably saved his life by sending for Dr Cocchi from Florence ('Short Notes,' GRAY i. 10 n. 62). *HW joined Lincoln at Venice 9 June* (MANN i. 54 n. 1), *and they agreed to return to Paris together* (ibid. i. 61). *After some talk that Lincoln would abandon HW to pursue Lady Sophia Fermor through Germany, they set out for Paris 12 July. HW describes one of the first stages of their journey in a letter to Mann from Genoa 19 July:*

'You will laugh to hear how we shortened the tediousness of the last day; as Lord Lincoln rode, Mr Spence and I went together in the chaise; and employed ourselves the whole day in counting the number of loaded mules etc. that we met on the road: they amounted to eight hundred forty-seven. . . . Lord Lincoln, I told you, rode most of the way, *pour se dissiper:* he is quite melancholy, and one day that we went together, talked to me the whole time of Lady Sophia. He says he is determined not to engage with her again on his return, unless he can settle his affairs so as to marry her. He is resolved to try all ways to have her, for, says he, nobody can say she wants anything but fortune: and added, "till now I never wished for riches." I pity his determination of marrying much more than his present pain' (ibid. i. 91).

HW was not without complaints of his travelling companions. Mann had warned him that they might be 'very dull' (ibid. i. 86), *and it is clear from Mann's replies to his missing letters that HW found them so. Lincoln was brooding over Lady Sophia Fermor and Spence was dull by nature:*

'I comprehend perfectly well what you say of your fellow travellers [in HW's missing letters of 2 and 7 August] and I am sorry to see my Lord's passion so deeply rooted. Spence, I take it, will always be a fellow of a college; that is with all their classical learning extreme tiresome. It is a

51; Chute's cousin and travelling companion (MANN i. 42 n. 50).

9. Hon. George William Hervey (1721–75), 2d Bn Hervey of Ickworth, 1743; 2d E. of Bristol, 1751; diplomatist. He was on

his way back to England; see MANN i. 34 n. 17.

10. Lincoln did not leave Rome until 15 May (BM Egerton MSS 2235, f. 81).

character extreme difficult, I have observed, to lay aside. But how few people there are one can bear to be locked up with!' (Mann to HW 21 Aug. 1741 NS, ibid. i. 107).

To Lincoln, Saturday 16 September 1741 NS

Printed for the first time from a photostat of the MS deposited in the Nottingham University Library by the Trustees of the Newcastle Estates.
Address: To the Right Honourable the Earl of Lincoln. These.

Above Stairs,[1] Sept. 16, 1741 NS.

My dear Lord,

IT is an age since I saw you, and above three months since I had a letter from you. By your silence I am afraid you have received none of mine, for I will not think you have forgot me. I should have wrote to you above a quarter of an hour ago, but I did not know in what room you was; and was unwilling to have my letter fall into other hands, especially in the present situation of affairs, when it is scarce safe to write from one storey to another. I heard some time since you were at Paris, by the noise you made under me; and should have immediately waited on you, if I had not had something else to do— but I flatter myself that we shall meet soon in England or at dinner. I have no news to tell you, for I have not seen a soul, having been a good deal confined upon the couch by Mr Patapan's[2] having been asleep in my lap. There is great talk of a peace between the King of Prussia[3] and the Queen of Hungary,[4] and of a most extraordinary suit of clothes that has been made by a certain person of our acquaintance; 'tis said, but I don't know how to believe it, that the coat is crimson, lined with scarlet, and turned up with cherry colour, and

1. In the Hôtel de Luxembourg, Rue des Petits Augustins, in Paris, where HW and Lincoln had arrived ca 30 Aug. 1741 NS ('Short Notes,' GRAY i. 11 n. 68).
2. HW's dog, given to him by Mme Grifoni.
3. Frederick II (1712–86), the Great; K. of Prussia 1740–86.
4. Maria Theresa (1717–80) of Austria;

Empress 1745–80; Q. of Hungary. The reports of the peace were widespread but premature; the secret convention of Kleinschnellendorf, providing for the gradual suspension of hostilities, was not concluded until 9 Oct. 1741 NS; see MANN i. 121 and n. 23, 134 and n. 18, 144 and n. 5, 154 and n. 13.

the waistcoat purple and silver with a pink and gold fringe—but this must be stretched. You know our friend has a very bad taste, but he can never be so extravagant as that.

My dear Lord, I won't keep you any longer from your breakfast, or myself from my own, having before me some charming bread and butter, of which you know nobody is so fond as, my Lord, your Lordship's

Very humble servant and sincere friend,

CAPTAIN ROLLS[5]

PS. Mr Lampridge, Cosin Tameridge, Mrs Strowell and Dr Dickison beg their compliments to your Lordship and Mr Spence.

If you favour me with a line, please to enclose it to Mr Selwin,[6] Banquier à Paris.

To LINCOLN, Sunday 13 September 1741 OS

Printed for the first time from a photostat of the MS deposited in the Nottingham University Library by the Trustees of the Newcastle Estates.

Sittinbourn, Sept. 13 OS, 1741.

My dearest Lord,

MIND 'tis Sunday night and I am not yet got to London; two days and a half did I stay at Calais in expectation of a fair wind[1]—'twas not quite bad, for there I found the Viscontina, Amorevoli and Monticelli, whom some English women[2] in my packet-boat call *the Creature*. Then there was the Barberina[3] whom Dashwood[4] had overtaken five posts from Paris, and brought all the way in his

5. Doubtless a character they had encountered, together with the others mentioned in the postscript, on their travels.
6. Charles Selwin (ca 1716–94), banker in Paris (GRAY i. 239 n. 12).

1. HW describes his delay at Calais to Mann 11 Sept. 1741 OS (MANN i. 140–1).
2. HW told Mann in the second part of the above letter, written at Sittingbourne, Kent, on the 13th, that he 'came over in a yacht with East-India captains'

widows' and a Catholic girl (ibid. i. 142).
3. Barbara Campanini (1721–99), called the 'Barbarina,' dancer; born in Parma; m. (ca 1748) Karl Ludwig, Freiherr von Cocceji, from whom she was divorced a few years later; cr. (1789) Gräfin Campanini in her own right. For further details of her career, see MANN i. 141 n. 8, and *post* 17 July 1744.
4. Presumably Samuel Dashwood (*ante* 27 Dec. 1740 NS, n. 32). He had been at Paris while HW was there (MANN i. 125).

chaise; pretty faces to him are more contagious distempers than the woman's looseness at Uzerches:[5] but she is pretty, vastly pretty. In the packet-boat came with me an Irish priest, who says, for two years he studied medicines, and for two years he studied *learning*.[6]

I came to Canterbury the day after a review of Horton's regiment[7] by Churchill.[8] I had much rather a day after than a day before.

My dear Lord, I shall not get to London till tomorrow night which is the moment the post goes out, but I would write to you—it was not because I promised you, for that would have gone for nothing, if I had not liked to keep it, but I have a pleasure in writing to you— as you will find, if you stay long behind me. I hear there is great opposition making to Lord Middlesex by a Mr Sergison,[9] who is determined to spend ten thousand pounds, to make them spend twenty. This is the first bit of madness I have heard; by next post I shall have more plenty to send you.

I have a vast deal of paper before me, which I could fill up with compliments, but if you have a mind to make any for me, I have given orders to Mr Selwin, and he will let you have any that you

5. Where HW and Lincoln had been 24 Aug. (Spence's itinerary, BM Egerton MSS 2235, f. 81).

6. HW repeats this to Mann the same day (Mann i. 142).

7. Presumably the 56th (after 1748, the 45th) Foot of which Daniel Houghton became the first colonel 11 Jan. 1741 OS. He was later Col. of the 24th Foot, 1745; Brig.-Gen., 1746; and died in the autumn of 1747 (Charles Dalton, *George the First's Army*, 1910, i. 306 n. 4; H. C. Wylly, *History of the Sherwood Foresters (45th Foot)*, i. 1–7; C. T. Atkinson, *The South Wales Borderers (24th Foot) 1689–1937*, Cambridge, 1937, pp. 109–10, 483; information kindly supplied by Mr David Erskine). See also *post*, Fox to HW 9 Oct. 1746, 30 Oct. 1747.

8. Charles Churchill (ca 1679–1745), Lt-Gen., 1739; Col. 1st Foot 1709–13, 16th Dragoons 1713–17, 10th Dragoons 1723–45; governor of Chelsea 1720–2, of Plymouth 1722–45; M.P. Weymouth and Melcombe Regis 1701–10, Castle Rising 1715–45; natural son of Gen. Charles Churchill (1656–1714), brother of the 1st D. of Marlborough (DNB *sub* Charles

Churchill [1656–1714]; Judd, *Members of Parliament* 151; GM 1745, xv. 276).

9. Thomas Sergison (formerly Warden) (1701–66), of Cuckfield, Sussex; M.P. Lewes 1747–66. He had unsuccessfully opposed the Pelham interest at Lewes at the general elections of 1734 and 1741, but took the Newcastle 'livery' in 1747 and remained thereafter a faithful supporter of the Duke (Sir Lewis Namier, *The Structure of Politics at the Accession of George III*, 2d edn, 1957, pp. 22–3 and n. 3; *Sussex Archæological Collections*, 1873, xxv. facing p. 84; Judd, *Members of Parliament* 330). He was now challenging Lord Middlesex (already returned for the Sackville family borough of East Grinstead at the general election of 1741) in a by-election for the county of Sussex occasioned by the death of James Butler, one of the sitting members, 17 May 1741. Sergison abandoned the contest in December and Middlesex was returned without a poll, 12 Jan. 1742. The campaign is described in a forthcoming essay by L. P. Curtis, 'Chichester Towers. A Sussex Comedy of the Eighteenth Century.'

shall draw for. Only to Mr Spence ten thousand; and a competent sum to Mrs Hayes,[10] Lady Lambert,[11] and the married Mashams.[12] My dear Lord, you mentioned having an inclination to know Madame de Matignon.[13] I take the liberty to send you a letter for Lady Pen,[14] which I give you my word I would not have wrote, but that you may have an opportunity of visiting her. If you do not care for it, burn the letter; it is of no other consequence than as I thought it might please you, which I own I love to do.

Forgive my not writing more, or my writing at all, when I had nothing to say, but that I am ever by inclination and by gratitude for all your goodness to me, my dearest Lord,

Yours sincerely,

HOR. WALPOLE

PS. A woman on the point of marriage was prayed for lately, *as going to take a great affair in hand.*[15] Blot out *lately,* if this is an old story.

If you do see Madame de Matignon, my dear Lord, tell her how much one night has made me her admirer and humble servant. Don't laugh at admirer, till you have seen her one night too.

10. She may have been connected with the Walpoles through the marriage of HW's uncle Galfridus (1684–1726) to Cornelia, 'daughter of Mr. Hays of London' (Collins, *Peerage*, 1812, v. 653); she was intimate with the entire family at this time; see HW's account of a later visit to her in his letter to Lady Suffolk 16 Oct. 1765. Spence's list of people met in Paris in 1741 includes 'Mrs Hayes and her niece' and 'Hayes' (BM Egerton MSS 2235, f. 94).

11. Anne Holmes (d. 1794), m. (ca 1728) Sir John Lambert, 2d Bt, banker in Paris.

12. Probably Samuel Masham (1712–76), 2d Bn Masham, 1758; m. (1736) Henrietta Winnington (d. 1761). They are mentioned in Spence's list of people met in Paris (loc. cit.).

13. Edmée-Charlotte de Brenne de Bombon (ca 1700–56), m. (1720) Marie-Thomas-Auguste de Goyon-de-Matignon, Marquis de Matignon; lady of the Palace to the Queen of France 1725–41 (MANN i. 140 n. 11). For the little that is known of HW's connection with her at this time, see Mann's comments on a passage from HW's missing letter of 17 Sept. 1741 NS (MANN i. 140, 152).

14. Lady Penelope Barry (ca 1707–86), m. Hon. James Cholmondeley. Her husband's brother had married HW's sister (MANN i. 152 n. 38). HW's letter is missing.

15. HW repeats this to Mann the same day (MANN i. 142). It also appears among HW's notes on the cover of Conway to HW ?11 July 1741 OS.

To LINCOLN, Friday 18 September 1741 OS

Printed for the first time from a photostat of the MS deposited in the Nottingham University Library by the Trustees of the Newcastle Estates.

Friday, Sept. 18 OS, 1741.

My dearest Lord,

I AM very unfortunate; the first moment I got my clothes unpacked, I went to wait on Lady Lucy Clinton,[1] and found her gone to Claremont.[2] She has been some time at your Uncle Pelham's[3] in Spring Garden, who has never lived at Whitehall since the loss of his children.[4] I sent the head and ruffles the moment I arrived. I am really quite sorry I missed your sister, for, my dear Lord, I wanted to see her, and talk to her of you, a topic she would have loved. I have so many obligations to you, and so much love for you, that I shall talk of nothing else to all your relations.

My King[5] does not come to town till Monday, so I have been to no public places, nor to Court. The Princesses[6] are in town, and have Drawing-Rooms Sundays and Thursdays. The town is absolutely empty. I trust it will be a little gayer in the winter, for sure now 'tis the dirtiest of dismal places. I have seen so few of the few that are in it, that I know nothing, but that what we used to say in jest I find realized—all England is mad! Lady Cowper,[7] Mr Skinner,[8] Lord

1. (1721–63), Lincoln's eldest sister (Collins, *Peerage*, 1812, ii. 213).
2. The Duke of Newcastle's seat in Surrey.
3. Hon. Henry Pelham (?1695–1754), M.P. Seaford 1717–22, Sussex 1722–54; first lord of the Treasury and chancellor of the Exchequer 1743–54.
4. His two sons, Thomas (1729–39) and Henry (1736–39) had died of 'an epidemical sore throat' within a day of each other; one of his daughters, Lucy (ca 1729–40), died two months later; and another, Dorothy, an infant, at the same time (Collins, *Peerage*, 1812 v. 520–1; Arthur Collins, *Historical and Genealogical History of the . . . Family of Pelham*, 1755, p. 565; HW to Mann 20 Jan. 1760).
5. His father, Sir Robert Walpole.

6. Amelia Sophia Eleanora (1711–86); Caroline Elizabeth (1713–57); and Louisa (1724–51), m. (1743) Frederik V of Denmark; the unmarried daughters of George II.
7. Lady Henrietta Nassau d'Auverquerque (d. 1747), m. (1732) William Cowper, 2d E. Cowper. Lord Hinton told Charles Hanbury Williams in Oct. 1739 that he heard she had been 'mad of a moping madness' though she was now better; and Mrs Delany in a letter of Dec. 1740 mentions her being 'much worse than she was' but does not specify that she was mad (Williams MSS lxviii, f. 20; *Autobiography and Correspondence of . . . Mrs Delany*, ed. Lady Llanover, 1861–2, ii. 136).
8. Possibly Matthew Skinner (1689–1749), prime serjeant, 1734; chief justice

George Graham,[9] and Tom Hervey[10] are shut up—besides numbers that have bespoke their apartments in Bedlam for next November—but of all the mighty mad, was Sir Will. Keyte,[11] a Glocestershire baronet, who last week assembled all his linen and clothes in one room, drove his family out of the house with pistol in hand, and then burned himself with his whole habitation. As strange as this will sound to you, who have been so long absent; here people don't think it very particular.

The town talks of nothing but the Neutrality which is said to be signed;[12] it occasions the greatest discontent— They say 'tis absolutely contradictory to the last speech in Parliament.[13]

I have been much asked about a dear Lord and a charming Lady! I always deny there being any thing in it;[14] several say they are mar-

of Chester 1738–49; M.P. Oxford city 1734–8 (MANN iii. 282 n. 18). There is no evidence, however, that he or any of the others mentioned by HW were confined at this time.

9. (1715–47), son of the 1st D. of Montrose; Capt. in the navy, 1740; M.P. Stirlingshire 1741–7 (*Scots Peerage* vi. 266).

10. Hon. Thomas Hervey (1699–1775), eccentric pamphleteer; M.P. Bury St Edmunds 1733–47.

11. Sir William Keyt (1688 - Sept. 1741), 3d Bt; M.P. Warwick 1722–35. 'Gloucester, September 12. This week the seat of Sir William Keyte, Bart, at Norton, in the parish of Mickleton, in this county, was entirely consumed by fire, and he himself wilfully perished in the flames, notwithstanding the utmost endeavours of his servants to save his life; which is a glaring proof that he was disordered in his senses. 'Tis said he set it on fire himself' (*Craftsman* 19 Sept. 1741; *London Magazine*, 1741, x. 464).

12. The secret convention between George II, as Elector of Hanover, and France guaranteeing the neutrality of the Electorate in return for promises to prevent the Hanoverian troops from joining the Austrian and to vote for the Bavarian Elector as Emperor, was not signed until 27 Sept. NS; however, a report from The Hague 19 Sept. NS that it was already concluded reached London in the Dutch mails on the 14th OS (MANN i. 133 n. 10; *Daily Adv.* 15 Sept. 1741). Suspicion that

such negotiations were under way was already causing consternation in the English ministry; see *Hardwicke Corr.* i. 268–74.

13. The King's Speech, 8 April 1741, promising effectual support to Maria Theresa to prevent the subversion of the House of Austria and to maintain the 'liberties and balance of power in Europe' (*Journals of the House of Commons* xxiii. 702–3). The neutrality was attacked on these grounds in *Common Sense* 31 Oct. 1741.

14. HW apparently did not know that Lincoln had already abandoned hopes of marrying Lady Sophia. He had written to his uncle, Newcastle, from Paris 14 Sept. 1741 NS: 'The result of my thoughts in relation to my Lady Sophy (and I have now had a good deal of time to think of it) is that it would be unhappy both for myself and her to carry that affair so far as I might otherwise have wished, and as that is the case I would for her sake and my own avoid any occasions of meeting. The reason I before wanted to stay longer out of England was not to be at the Birthday where I could not have avoided it; and I was unwilling too to come to England about the same time they did because that might increase a report which I hear is but too much put about town already. Were I to set out in a few days 'tis very probable I should meet Lord Pomfret at Calais. . . . The coming into England so together might justify the

ried. I will write you word next post if the Duke[15] mentions it to me
or Mr Pelham. But don't tell Mr Sp[ence] I said anything of it. You
may tell him, that I found four verses in the gazette[16] on Rollin's
death,[17] which I will believe are his;[18] if he does not prove the contrary— They are said to be by an English gentleman now at Paris (a
Protestant), who going to make a visit to Rollin met the corpse and
said as follows—

> Charmed with thy truth and by thy learning fired,
> I ran to tell how much I both admired,
> When lo! thy bier and a long weeping train—
> Ye noblest things of earth alas how vain!

The most curious observation I have made since my arrival was a
writing under a sign—'Good Snuff and Beer sold here.' After such
nonsense, I will send you a pretty epigram; 'tis Pultney's[19]

> Two able physicians as e'er prescribed physic,
> On *Burlinton's*[20] illness were sent for to *Chiswick;*
> Each took my Lord's pulse and most solemnly felt it,
> Then called for his urine, viewed, tasted and smelt it.
> On sight of the water *Mead*[21] cried out, ' 'Tis plain
> That my Lord has a fever and must breach a vein.'
> 'You are right, Brother *Mead*, and besides,' *added Sloane,*[22]
> 'Who voided this water, no doubt had a stone.'
> 'You are out,' quoth the nurse, 'and have both of you missed it,
> For 'twas not my Lord, but my Lady[23] that pissed it.'

There are lately come out two volumes of letters, a correspondence
between Lord Bolinbroke, Swift, Arbuthnot and Pope,[24] with the life

town in such a report; might do hurt to
her' (BM Add. MSS 33065, f. 457).

15. Thomas Pelham-Holles (1693–1768),
2d Bn Pelham; cr. (1715) D. of Newcastle-
upon-Tyne.

16. The verses have not been found in
any of the available newspapers.

17. Charles Rollin (1661–14 Sept. 1741
NS), historian.

18. There is no evidence that Spence
wrote the verses.

19. William Pulteney (1684–1764), cr.
(1742) E. of Bath; M.P. Hedon 1705–34,
Middlesex 1734–42.

20. Richard Boyle (1694–1753), 3d E. of
Burlington; architect.

21. Dr Richard Mead (1673–1754), M.D.,
1695; physician to the King, 1727.

22. Sir Hans Sloane (1660–1753), cr.
(1716) Bt; physician.

23. Lady Dorothy Savile (1699–1758), m.
(1721) Richard Boyle, 3d E. of Burlington.
Her uncle described her in 1736 as 'the
wickedest mischievous jade upon earth. I
can easily pardon the lady her coqueting
and her intriguing . . . but lying and
making mischief, abusing everybody, im-
posing upon her husband and exposing
him only to show her own power does
deserve some correction and some whole-
sale severity such as sending a lady down
into the country' (GEC ii. 433 n. a).

24. *The Works of Mr Alexander Pope,
In Prose, Vol. II*, published 16 April 1741,
in both folio and quarto (R. H. Griffith,
Alexander Pope: A Bibliography, Austin,

of Martin Scriblerus; they are much commended, especially the letters of the first, but I have not yet seen them.

I have this moment been told another epigram, that will divert you, I don't tell you 'tis said to be Lord Chesterfield's,[25] because everything is his of course first—'tis on Lord H——[26]

Dum dubitat natura marem[27] etc.

While Nature H——'s clay was blending,
Uncertain what her work would end in,
Whether a female or a male,
A pin dropped in, and turned the scale.

My dear Lord, I wish to hear you are coming to England—quite for my own sake, not a bit for yours, for though I shall be happy I can't believe you will be so— I find England much duller and disagreeable even than I expected—today I went to church and heard a sermon! for my encouragement to frequent it, one of the first sentences that blundered out of the mouth of the parson, was, how then can we take *complacency* in a vicious life—I that have been abroad two years and a half can talk better English than that—I take no *complacency* in sermons.

My dear Lord, I must beg a favour; I have been much teased to send to France for some Saxon ruffles; if you will be so good to bring me half-a-dozen pair, you will oblige me vastly.

Adieu, my dearest Lord—I wish I could execute any commands for you here before you come—you know how it would please me, for you know how much I am

Yours most faithfully,

Hor. Walpole

Texas, 1927, i pt ii. 426–30). There was only one volume published at this time.

25. Philip Dormer Stanhope (1694–1773), 4th E. of Chesterfield; wit and letter-writer. There is no evidence that the epigram is his.

26. John Hervey (1696–1743), summoned to Parliament as Bn Hervey of Ickworth, 1733. The epigram is printed in *The New*

Ministry, 1742, p. 32, and *The Foundling Hospital for Wit, Part I*, 1743, p. 53.

27. From the epigram, sometimes attributed to Ausonius:
Dum dubitat natura, marem feceretne puellam:
factus es, o pulcher, paene, puer.
('While nature was in doubt whether to make a boy or girl, thou didst become almost a girl, my handsome boy.')

From LINCOLN, ca Sunday 1 October 1741 NS

Missing, written from Paris; acknowledged 1 Oct. 1741 OS.

To LINCOLN, Thursday 1 October 1741 OS

Printed for the first time from a photostat of the MS deposited in the Nottingham University Library by the Trustees of the Newcastle Estates.

London, Oct. 1, 1741 OS.

My dearest Lord,

I HAVE had the pleasure of your letter, and should have wrote
to you last Monday, but I have been at Swallowfield[1] for four or
five days and out of the way of hearing anything. 'Tis a most charming place; but lies in a bottom; the country round it, is beyond anything on earth. I am sure Mr Spence would kiss me on both sides my
face, if he saw how I was pleased with it. I wish I could say as much
for London: but sure 'tis the dirtiest of old rubbishes! I went to the
play t'other night for the first and last time. Such actors, such an
audience, such a noise! How would you be surprised my dear Lord,
to see the Gossein[2] or Dangerville[3] pelted, and desire leave to ha-
rangue the pit, as Mrs Clive[4] did that night I was there. 'Hear her!
Hear her!'—'Gentlemen, they have flung an halfpenny at me; it
might have cut out my eye, and I can't stand to bear that.'—You will
be so sick of this, and to see all the world turned bluecoat boys.[5]

I was to wait on the Duke of Newcastle this morning, but he was
gone out; tomorrow I shall go again to your Uncle Pelham. He was
excessively pleased with all the *white truths,* which I could not help
telling him of you—Dodd[6] says I talk of nothing but Lord Lincoln.—

1. In Berks, about six miles south-east
of Reading; the seat of HW's friend John
Dodd (Constance, Lady Russell, *Swallowfield and its Owners,* 1901, p. 226).

2. Jeanne-Catherine Gaussem (1711–67),
called Gaussin; actress (NBG).

3. Marie-Anne Botot (1714–96), called
Mlle de Dangeville; actress (*Enciclopedia
dello spettacolo,* Rome, 1954– , iv. 65;
NBG). They were the leading French ac-
tresses of the day.

4. Catherine Raftor (1711–85), m. (1732)
George Clive; actress; later a friend of
HW and the occupant of Little SH
('Cliveden').

5. I.e., behaving like the schoolboys of
Christ's Hospital, London.

6. John Dodd (1717–82), of Swallowfield; HW's contemporary at Eton and
King's; M.P. Reading, 1740, 1755–82 (Constance, Lady Russell, op. cit. 226–44;

Oh, I forgot to tell you about Mrs Dodd:[7] she is vastly pretty, and one of the most agreeable women on earth; I am sure you will like her as much as I do.

Lord Euston[8] was to be married to Lady Dorothy Boyle[9] today, but it is again put off;[10] nobody will believe yet, that he will have her.

The King comes next week,[11] the Duke[12] is at Mr Poyntz['s][13] so I have not been presented to him. Princess Louisa is grown so fat and like the Queen,[14] has such a monstrous pair of flummey bubbies, that I really think it indecent for her to live with her f[ather]. Princess C. and Lord H.[15] are, I believe, less well than usual; Mrs Horner[16] is said to cuckold her. Lady Emily[17] goes on as usual, and as usual

Quintilium perpetuus sopor urget.[18]

COLE ii. 299 and nn. 7 and 8, 303; HW's letters from John Whaley).

7. Jane St Leger (1719–44), m. (1739) John Dodd (Constance, Lady Russell, op. cit. 229, 232 and genealogical table facing p. 230).

8. George Fitzroy (1715–47), styled E. of Euston; eldest son of the 2d D. of Grafton; M.P. Coventry 1737–47.

9. (1724–42), m. (10 Oct. 1741 OS), George Fitzroy, styled E. of Euston; she 'was reckoned the handsomest woman of this time' (HW's note in his MS Poems, p. 53).

10. It was rumoured that Euston wanted to marry his sister-in-law, Lady Augustus Fitzroy; see MANN i. 175 and nn. 24, 25. HW implies, post 13 Oct. 1741 OS, that Euston was also considering a 'Miss Adams.' The wedding had been repeatedly postponed since the winter of 1740 (Frances, Countess of Hertford and Henrietta Louisa, Countess of Pomfret, Correspondence, 1805, ii. 162–5).

11. He finally arrived in London 20 Oct. OS (London Gazette No. 8059, 17–20 Oct. 1741).

12. William Augustus (1721–65), D. of Cumberland.

13. Stephen Poyntz (1685–1750), diplomatist; governor to the Duke and later his secretary. The Duke had gone to his estate at Midgham, Berks, 6 Sept. and did not return to London until 10 Oct. (Daily Adv. 7 Sept., 23 Sept., 12 Oct. 1741).

14. Caroline (1683–1737), m. (1705) George II of England.

15. Princess Caroline and Lord Hervey. For their intimacy, see John, Lord Hervey, Memoirs, ed. Sedgwick, 1931, i. p. l; Mem. Geo. II iii. 83.

16. Susanna Strangways (1689–1758), m. (1713) Thomas Horner; Stephen Fox's mother-in-law (Ilchester, Henry Fox i. 31–3, 44–6, ii. 105–6). For her friendship with Hervey at a slightly earlier period see Lord Hervey and His Friends 1726–38, ed. Earl of Ilchester, 1950, pp. 233, 256–7 (with HW's note), 260–1, 264–6, 269, 274; and HW's character of Hanbury Williams, below Appendix 3. It was also reported, falsely, on Hervey's death that he had 'ordered his eldest son, immediately after his death, to carry away his eldest unmarried daughter to Mrs Horner' (Fanny Russell to Lt-Col. Charles Russell 26 Aug. 1743, Hist. MSS Comm., Frankland-Russell-Astley MSS, 1900, p. 285). See also D. M. Stuart, Molly Lepell, Lady Hervey, 1936, p. 120.

17. Apparently the Princess Amelia, from the context. HW may be referring to her long flirtation with the Duke of Grafton; see Mem. Geo. II i. 182.

18. Horace, Odes I. xxiv. 5–6 ('The sleep that knows no waking lies heavy on Quintilius'). This could refer to Grafton; HW comments on the 'great slowness in his delivery' (Mem. Geo. II i. 181), and Lord Hervey satirized him as 'Awake he can't hurt and is still half-asleep' (MANN ii. 82).

I am obliged to Lady Pen[19] much for her good will, and her letter. I will answer it very soon. I beg a thousand compliments to all my friendships, particularly Mrs Hayes; Lord Cholmley[20] is out of town, or I should have executed her commands to him.

My dear Lord, I long to see you; will you not be here for the Birthday?[21] I wish the Duke[22] would give me orders to send for you. My love to Mr Spence in the character of (which after all the treason I have wrote will be convenient) his and my dear Lord

Your affectionate humble servant,

CAPT. ROLLS

To LINCOLN, Tuesday 13 October 1741 OS

Printed for the first time from a photostat of the MS deposited in the Nottingham University Library by the Trustees of the Newcastle Estates.

London, Oct. 13, 1741.

My dearest Lord,

AT last this mighty marriage is over, and Lady Dorothy Boyle, not Miss Adams,[1] is Lady Euston. They were married on Saturday; he does not see company, she did last night and does tonight. Her face is vastly fine but a little cloudy; her person, what Denoyer[2] the dancing-master said to the Queen of the Duke;[2a] *nous sommes un peu clumsy.*

Lord Pomfret and his family are arrived:[3] Lady Sophia has been out of order with a fatigue and a cold, but is recovered, and looks as much handsomer than the bride, as she used to do than all other

19. Lady Penelope Cholmondeley; her letter to HW and his reply are missing.

20. HW's brother-in-law, George Cholmondeley (1703–70), 3d E. of Cholmondeley.

21. The King's birthday, 30 Oct. 1741 OS (MANN i. 165 n. 12). Lincoln was intentionally delaying his return to avoid it; see *ante* 18 Sept. 1741 NS, n. 14.

22. Of Newcastle.

———

1. Not identified. Vcts Howe told the Cts of Huntingdon 1 April 1740 OS that it was said that Euston had 'certainly been married to Miss Adams these three years, but I daresay it is not true' (Hist. MSS Comm., *Hastings MSS*, 1928–47, iii. 29).

2. ?Philip Dunoyer or Desnoyers, a French dancing-master, confidant of the Prince of Wales and at the same time welcome in the royal household (MONTAGU i. 29 n. 29).

2a. Of Cumberland.

3. About 8 Oct. 1741 OS; HW had called on them on the 10th (MANN i. 165 and n. 5, 169 and n. 1).

women. She asked extremely after a Lord at Paris; I was very sorry I could not tell her we were likely to see him before the Birthday. I have begged much that at least on that day she would let people see what it is to be well-dressed and nobly genteel, not gim[3a] and smart like a dairy-maid. She will dress her head French, but that charming shape is condemned to be bound up in an English manteau, till it looks like a wasp ready to break in the middle.[4]

You have heard of Admiral Vernon's[5] new conquests;[6] he has killed a little fort in Cuba, taken a small town which he named the Cumberland, and dispersed seventeen hundred horse, who retired out of prudence; but the chief success is having made himself master of a vast river twenty-five miles[7] long where his fleet can harbour during the winter months. Don't think these words are my own; they are the style of my court, who love to lessen all he does.[8] People are persuaded that he has done more, but till he has done all, will not give notice of it, lest it fail like Carthagena.[9] There have been great riots at Rochester, where the sailors of a ship just returned from Vernon, have pulled down all the signs in the town that bore his head;[10] mem. he is hated in the fleet—as I hear.

Sir Robert has been dying, but is quite well again[11]—the King sets out today from Hanover.[12]

I must tell you an old story, which I fancy will be new to you— last session on some great question, Churchill came to vote though

---

3a. Smart, spruce; now obsolete (OED).

4. HW makes similiar comments to Mann 13 Oct. 1741 OS (MANN i. 170).

5. Edward Vernon (1684–1757), Vice-Adm., 1739; Adm., 1745; dismissed, 1746; M.P. Penryn 1722–34, Portsmouth 1741, Ipswich 1741–57.

6. Inaccurate reports of these, coming in a roundabout way from Jamaica, were printed in the *Daily Adv.* 8 Oct. 1741, and, more fully, in the *Craftsman* and *Common Sense* 10 Oct. All the facts HW mentions are in the published accounts. The news was not officially confirmed until the *London Gazette* No. 8061, 24–27 Oct. 1741. See also HW to Mann 22 Oct. 1741 OS (MANN i. 175 and n. 26). The expedition, which never proceeded beyond occupying the vicinity of Guantánamo Bay, was withdrawn in November; see H. W. Richmond, *The Navy in the War of 1739–48*, Cambridge, 1920, i. 126–30.

7. Guantánamo Bay, near the south-east corner of Cuba.

8. Vernon was an outspoken opponent of Sir Robert Walpole.

9. Vernon had attacked Cartagena 9 March 1741, but after considerable initial successes, had to raise the siege and retire at the end of April (Richmond, op. cit. i. 111–25).

10. No other reference to these riots has been found. HW apparently discussed them in a missing letter to Chute ca 13 Oct. 1741 OS; see Chute's reply ca 11 Nov. 1741 NS.

11. Sir Robert had been taken ill 4 Oct. and was 'in great danger' from 'an ague and looseness,' but was recovering by the 8th (HW to Mann 8 Oct. 1741 OS, MANN i. 164–5).

12. An express to this effect is mentioned in the *Daily Adv.* 10 Oct. 1741.

lame on crutches. The Prince of Wales[13] met him—'So, Mr Churchill, I see even the lame and the blind come to vote'—'Yes, Sir, the lame of our side, and the blind of theirs.'[14] Was it not admirable?

In return for the mighty pretty sonnet you sent me, my dear Lord, I will tell you an epigram of Dr Munro's;[15] Hulse[16] had let drop some too free expressions, which he thought to get clear of, by carrying about a nephew clergyman[17] in his chariot—

> When *Hulse* for some trifling unorthodox jests,
> As unchristian was censured by bigots and priests,
> The politic doctor t'avoid the reproach
> Was seen with a parson six months in his coach.
> When *Cheselden*[18] saw the device had success
> He conceived in some sort it might suit his own case;
> So to take an unlucky damned censure away,
> He contrived to be seen with a wit ev'ry day:
> And with *Pope* by his side in the pride of his soul,
> 'Now damn ye,' says he, 'now d'ye think I'm a fool?'

My dear Lord, I have read over ten times your history of Madame de Matignon's supper; you can't think how it diverted me; but I cannot find words to answer the kind things you say to me in another part of your letter. I only hope that you know how sincerely and how very much I love you and consequently how happy your goodness makes me; indeed, my Lord, it does—excessively! and I shall always endeavour to deserve an affection and friendship that can make me so. 'Tis hard to be reduced to say this on paper, when I wish so much to see you; but what can I do; how can I persuade you to come? not by the promise of much diversion to be found here, I am sure. I could invite you by a card to come and play at whisk every night as everybody does: but would you play? The operas begin the last of this month,[19] but whether they will go on, is a question; parties are

13. Frederick Louis (1707–51), cr. (1729) P. of Wales; a partisan of the opposition to Sir Robert Walpole.

14. HW also includes this anecdote in *MS Poems*, p. 35.

15. James Monro (1680–1752), M.D., 1722; physician to Bethlehem Hospital (for the insane) in London. HW sent a copy of the verses to Mann 8 Oct. 1741 OS (MANN i. 168). They are also printed, with some verbal differences, from a MS note-

book of epigrams, etc. in Hist. MSS Comm., 12th Report, App. ix, *R. W. Ketton MSS*, 1891, p. 190.

16. Sir Edward Hulse (1682–1759), M.D., 1717; cr. (1739) Bt; physician to George II.

17. Not identified.

18. William Cheselden (1688–1752), surgeon and anatomist.

19. They were scheduled to begin 31 Oct., and apparently did so (MANN i. 165, 183 n. 3, 186 n. 30).

making against them already, though not one of the performers have sung yet even in private; but you know here 'tis enough to displease people, to mean to please them.

I have been in a little disgrace at my court for these two days for not being inveterate enough to hold my tongue, when a very clever man was abused unjustly. At dinner t'other day Lord Chomley was very eloquent (*alii legunt* virulent) against young Bohun,[20] and said he was amazed at his assurance in adopting a reputation from two speeches which he did not make himself—this from one so notorious for having his speeches given him, made me blurt out, 'Is that so very uncommon, my Lord?' He replied in vast confusion, 'Why yes really, to be entirely given; one may have instructions—'

My dear Lord, you are vastly obliging, but I have no more commissions to trouble you with—bring but yourself, and you will infinitely please

Yours most sincerely and ever

H. W.

P.S. A thousand compliments to dear Mr Spence.

———————————

Lincoln finally returned to London early in November; HW describes his reception to Mann:

'He is come over, and met her [Lady Sophia] t'other night: he turned pale, spoke to her several times in the evening, but not long; and sighed to me at going away. He came over all alive; and not only his uncle-duke, but even Majesty has fallen in love with him. He talked to the King at his levee, without being spoken to—that was always thought high treason —but I don't know how, the gruff gentleman liked it; and then he had been told that Lord Lincoln designed to have made the campaign, if we had gone to war—in short, he says, *Lord Lincoln is the handsomest man in England*' (23 Nov. 1741, MANN i. 210).

20. A 'Mr Bohun' is mentioned as speaking for the Opposition in the debate on the Convention of the Pardo 8 March 1739 in three letters printed in William Coxe, *Memoirs of . . . Sir Robert Walpole*, 1798, iii. 517–19. One of the writers admits uncertainty as to the spelling of his name and states that he had formerly been a fairly steady supporter of the Court. Since no Bohun sat in Parliament during the 18th century, it seems likely that this form of the name is a phonetic version of Boone and that the person intended is Daniel Boone (1710–70), of Rook's Nest, Surrey; M. P. Luggershall 1734–41, Grampound 1741–7, Stockbridge 1747–54, Minehead 1754–61, a supporter and later a member of the household of the Prince of Wales; he became commissary-general of the musters in 1742 (MANN i. 494 n. 19; J. B. Owen, *Rise of the Pelhams*, 1957, p. 322).

HW's letters to Mann during the next few months contain frequent references to Lincoln, including an account of a 'scuffle' at the opera in April:

'We had a great scuffle t'other night at the opera, which interrupted it. Lord Lincoln was abused in the most shocking manner by a drunken officer, upon which he kicked him, and was drawing his sword, but was prevented. They were put under arrest, and the next morning the man begged his pardon before the Duke of Marlborough, Lord Albemarle, and other officers, in the most submissive terms. I saw the quarrel from the other side of the house, and rushing to get to Lord Lincoln, could not for the crowd: I climbed into the front boxes, and stepping over the shoulders of three ladies, before I knew where I was, found I had lighted into Lord Rockingham's lap—it was ridiculous!' (HW to Mann 29 April 1742, ibid. i. 411–12).

HW also reports the gradual decline of Lincoln's attachment to Lady Sophia Fermor; by 17 December 1741 he was 'sure' that Lincoln would not marry her, but as late as June 1742 he still saw indications that 'the Earl is not quite cured' (ibid. i. 248, 468). He also witnessed, together with Thomas Ashton, Lincoln's grant of £100 per year to Joseph Spence on 28 April 1742 (MS in the Osborn Collection).

To LINCOLN, Monday 23 August 1742

Printed for the first time from a photostat of the MS deposited in the Nottingham University Library by the Trustees of the Newcastle Estates.

Houghton,[1] Aug. 23d 1742.

My dear Lord,

I INTENDED not to write to you, till I had something to say— but I have waited so long for that something to no purpose; that I must write without it—only to ask you how you do? or if you have any commands for me. I unluckily missed the pleasure of seeing you the day before I came into the country—but if you want me at any time, and will send me a line, I will immediately wait on you.

I go to Holkam[2] tomorrow for two or three days: I wish we could

1. HW had been at Houghton with his father since ca 7 Aug. and remained there until 25 Oct. (MANN ii. 25, 88).

2. Holkham, Norfolk, seat of Thomas Coke (1697–1759), cr. (1728) Bn Lovel and (1744) E. of Leicester, a steady supporter of Sir Robert Walpole. HW was presumably going there to visit his friend, Lord Lovel's son, Edward Coke (1719–53), styled Vct Coke 1744–53. He was back at Houghton by 28 Aug. (MANN ii. 31).

persuade you thither and to Houghton—I will not tell you how little diversion I have here, unless I find you absolutely determined not to come.

Sir Robert has found out, he says, that I love hunting—after that, I shall not be afraid of his finding out anything I would not have him.

I see myself unfortunately in print,[3] and what is more provoking with large additions, none of my own. Indeed the author[4] has imitated the style of Scripture better than I did, for his chapter is quite Billinsgate.

If I am very good, and learn my *patois* well, I am promised that I shall go to the Mayor's feast at Lynn[5]—there's joy!

Mr Hervey[6] and Mr Ellis[7] have been here four or five days[8]—except them, and swarms of natives of the country, we have had no company. We have heard nothing of my Lord Townshend,[9] but that he drinks very hard three times a week with his tenants. I am not sure that the people that told me this, did not mean it as a commendation of him.

Adieu! my dear Lord; I am

Yours most sincerely and ever,

Hor. Walpole

3. HW's *The Lessons for the Day. Being the First and Second Chapters of the Book of Preferment.* Printed for W. Webb, 1742. It was published 5 Aug. Only the 'Second Chapter' was by HW; see HW to Mann 14 July 1742 OS (Mann i. 491–3 and notes) and Hazen, *Bibl. of HW* 19–22.

4. Not identified.

5. HW apparently complained of this prospect to Conway as well; see Conway to HW 15 Sept. 1742 NS.

6. Probably Hon. George William Hervey, later 2d E. of Bristol (*ante* 29 April 1741 NS, n. 9).

7. Welbore Ellis (1713–1802), cr. (1794) Bn Mendip; politician; M.P. Cricklade 1741–7, Weymouth and Melcombe Regis 1747–61, 1774–90, Aylesbury 1761–8, Petersfield 1768–74, 1791–4.

8. HW mentions a visit from them, together with Lord Edgcumbe, 'in their way to Coke's' in his letter to Mann ca 9 Aug. 1742 (Mann ii. 25).

9. Charles Townshend (1700–64), 3d Vct Townshend. His seat was at Raynham, near Houghton.

To Lincoln, Saturday 18 September 1742

Printed for the first time from a photostat of the MS deposited in the Nottingham University Library by the Trustees of the Newcastle Estates.

Houghton, Sept. 18, 1742.

My dear Lord,

DON'T be angry with me for writing to you again so soon, but one is always most troublesome when one has nothing to do: I am sure you have found me so a thousand times. I own I am desperate and take any method to divert myself. Indeed writing letters is of great service to me; I do it to keep up my English; I should forget it else at this distance from all language—I try indeed to learn the noises by which the people about me convey their minds to one another—but I don't make great progress; and am constantly forced to use the country interpreter, the bottle, when I have a mind to converse with any of my neighbours. Reading is indeed a great resource, and I have been recommended to a very pretty little book, called Rider's *Almanack;*[1] it teaches one when to sow parsnips, kill bees and let blood. Another great part of my diversion is the dress of the natives: the women come to visit my sister in bob-periwigs of all colours without powder, which they call frontlets.[2] Do tell me if you pass your time half so well as I do!

I am just going to write to Florence to congratulate Prince Craon on the great escape which the Great Duke[3] has had in not taking Prague![4] Who knows what danger he might have run amongst those giddy Frenchmen, who might have taken his Royal Highness for a German and knocked him on the head in a moment! I hope our Master[5] will follow this prudent example, and not be so rash as to go and besiege Dunkirk[6]— There is no good comes of those sieges:

1. Rider's *British Merlin*, begun in 1656 by Cardanus Rider and continued until at least 1840, was issued with the *Court and City Register* and similar publications.

2. Usually called 'fronts': 'a band or bands of false hair, or a set of false curls, worn by women over the forehead' (OED sub 'front' 9.c; cf. 'frontlet' 1.d).

3. Francis I (1708–65), Grand Duke of Tuscany 1737–65; Emperor 1745–65; at this time in command of the Austrian army before **Prague**.

4. The Austrians had been besieging the French in Prague since 1 July, but on 12 Sept. 1742 NS most of the Austrian army was withdrawn and the siege converted into a blockade. The news had just reached England (Mann i. 466 n. 4, ii. 58 and nn. 1–3, 61 and n. 9b).

5. George II.

6. The King had been planning to go to Flanders since the beginning of September to assume personal command of the army assembled there; it was generally

wise men grow tired of them; Adm. Vernon and the Great Duke found out in time that it was better not to take Carthagena and Prague. But I am talking like a country gentleman, quite ignorant of the *carte du pays:* perhaps in London it may be the fashion to think quite otherwise of sieges, campaigns, and expeditions to Ghent[7]— do write me word, if the French are vastly frightened with the Duke of Marlbro's name being in Flanders?[8]

Adieu! my dear Lord, you see I want to draw a letter from you— If I don't hear of you, I shall make some excuse to go and look for you—I am

Yours most faithfully

HOR. WALPOLE

In February 1743 HW transcribed for Mann a 'Persian letter' he had presented to Lincoln (MANN ii. 166–8):

'I must tell you an amusing scene I had with him [Lincoln] last week. You know he is just made lord of the Bedchamber; and you must know too that his general style of talking is the vigorous— T'other night at supper at the Duchess of Richmond's, he said to Lady Albemarle, "but why won't Lord Bury write to wish me joy?" "Why," said she, "to be sure he does not know it." "Pho, not know it, why all the world must know it!" The next night happened to be the masquerade night: we were all to go together from the Duchess's. I dressed myself in an Indian dress, and after he was come thither, walked into the room, made him three low bows, and kneeling down, took a letter out of my bosom, wrapped in Persian silk, and laid it on my head: he stared violently! They persuaded him to take it: it was a Persian letter from Kouli Kan, and was written on a long sheet of red Indian paper—here it is:

Thamas Kouli Kan Schah Nadir
to Henry Clinton Earl of Lincoln.

Highly favoured *among women*

Yesterday's sun brought us the glad tidings of the high post to which thou hast been advanced by our brother the Sultan of the Western Isles.

believed that the immediate object was to attack Dunkirk (J. B. Owen, *The Rise of the Pelhams,* 1957, pp. 138–9; HW to Mann 11 Sept., 25 Sept. 1742, MANN ii. 48 and n. 10, 61 and nn. 5, 8). The journey was finally postponed in early October until the following spring (ibid. ii. 69; Owen, op. cit. 139). HW's concern arose

from the presence of his cousin, H. S. Conway, with the army in Flanders.

7. Where the 'Pragmatic Army' was assembled.

8. Charles Spencer (1706–58) 2d D. of Marlborough, was with the English forces in Flanders as Col. of the 2d Foot Guards.

We congratulate thee thereon, and wish thee a long continuance of health and prosperity in the eye of thy Lord.

We have heard prodigious things of thee: they say, thy vigour is nine times beyond that of our prophet; and that thou art more amorous than Solomon the son of David. Yet they tell us, that thou art not above the ordinary stature of the sons of men: are these things so?

We would know of thee what is the nature of thy new post. Does thy admission to the bedchamber of thy Lord give thee access to his women? Or are they veiled from thy sight as ours in Persia?

Most potent Lord, we have sent thee as a mark of our grace fifty of the most beautiful maidens of Persia, fifty more of Georgia, and fifty of the most chosen of Circassia. Moreover, having heard that there are no eunuchs in thy country, but a few which you buy in a neighbouring kingdom at an excessive price, and considering what occasion thy magnificence must have for them to guard the prodigious number of women in thy seraglio, we have sent thee a thousand black eunuchs.

Adieu! happy young man! May thy days be as long as thy manhood, and may thy manhood continue more piercing than Zufager, that sword of Hali which had two points: and when thou art full of years, may Azraël the angel of death conduct thee to those fields of light, where the favourites of the Prophet taste eternal joys in the arms of the beautiful houris!

From the Seraglio of Ispahan, the first
of the month Regeb.'

The original 'Persian letter' is now WSL; *its conclusion is illustrated here.*

To Lincoln, Wednesday 22 June 1743

Printed for the first time from a photostat of the MS deposited in the Nottingham University Library by the Trustees of the Newcastle Estates.

Houghton,[1] June 22d 1743.

My dear Lord,

YOU see how easily I get rid of all my haughty resolutions, when you desire it— Indeed I tell myself that I only write to you to know how you do, as you were not well when you went away

1. HW had been at Houghton since the end of May (Mann ii. 236).

to London[2]—I am so anxious about your health, that I believe I should even have wrote if you had not desired me.

If I don't express myself with as much love as I used to do, and as you know I have for you, don't wonder—Dick[3] is here, and as he has twice perused the superscriptions of my letters, I am not sure he would not open one directed to so particular a friend of his as you are. Now, after your way of dealing with him, if he should find me very fond of you, God knows what he might suspect! He would at least burst the waistband of his breeches with the glee of the discovery—and, my dear Lord, I would not for the world wrong your bed— As irresistible as he is, he shall never injure you with me. You will stare at my coldness, when I assure you I am happy that he goes away tomorrow. He comes into the library, and when I am reading and won't answer him, he talks to his book, as he did to his cards. Then he is so inquisitive! Miss Leneve[4] says he has asked her every question in the world but *the* question.

I go to Holkam tomorrow for two or three days— Will you think of us? We shall talk much of you. I have the comfort of not having it the first time of my being there, and so need not be dragged to see clumps, nor sailed over the lake, nor drove two miles into the sea when the tide is down. I know no clumps I would give sixpence to see, but those in Grosvenor Square—

Adieu, my dear Lord—I don't ask you to write, but merely to tell me you are quite well again—I am

Ever and most sincerely yours

H. Walpole

From Lincoln, ca Saturday 25 June 1743

Missing.

2. Lincoln had visited Houghton earlier in the month (ibid. ii. 248).

3. Hon. Richard Edgcumbe (1716–61), 2d Bn Edgcumbe, 1758; M.P. Plympton Erle 1742–7, Lostwithiel 1747–54, Penryn 1754–8; friend and correspondent of HW. HW also mentions his being at Houghton

in his letter to Mann 4 June 1743 (ibid. ii. 245).

4. Elizabeth Le Neve (1720–before 13 March 1759), m. (between 1743 and 1748) Hugh Pigot, later Adm.; niece of 'Mrs' Isabella Le Neve (ibid. ii. 36 n. 35).

To LINCOLN, Saturday 2 July 1743

*Printed for the first time from a photostat of the MS deposited in the Notting-
ham University Library by the Trustees of the Newcastle Estates.*

Houghton, July 2d 1743.

My dear Lord,

SURE as I am that you are mortified at not having contributed the
thunder of your arm to the victory at Dettingen,[1] I did not write
to wish you joy of our success. I say ours, for we are all Dukes of
Marlborough: chance sent Lord Stair,[2] the Duke of Richmond[3] and
Lord Albemarle[4] to the Rhine, and left you in the arms of Peggy
Lee,[5] and planted me here in the wilds of Siberia—but had we been
there, and had his Grace been where we could guess,[6] Lord Albemarle
where we can't[7] and Lord Stair in the wilds of Scotland, the victory
had been equally certain. Don't you feel that? Mr Wright,[8] the parson
of Euston, is not more sensible of the *genius of England,* than I am.
For my part, as no mortal will doubt the prowess of every individual
Englishman, I am very well content to have beat the French by proxy.

I am much obliged to you, my dear Lord, for your thinking of me
about Mr Conway.[9] I am really concerned he was not in the battle;
at least I will not tell him I am not.[10] The next victory he gains, I
shall expect he send over two or three French officers to kiss Patapan's

1. 27 June 1743 NS; the news reached
England 23 June OS (MANN ii. 258 n. 1).

2. John Dalrymple (1673–1747), 2d E. of
Stair; diplomatist and field-marshal; com-
mander-in-chief of the allied forces in
Flanders.

3. Charles Lennox (1701–50), 2d D. of
Richmond; M.P. Chichester 1722–3.

4. William Anne van Keppel (1702–54),
2d E. of Albemarle; commanded the 3d
Troop of Horse Guards at Dettingen,
where he had his horse shot from under
him (MANN ii. 261 and n. 26).

5. Lincoln's mistress, by whom he had
a daughter, born about Nov. 1743. HW
celebrated the event in 'Little Peggy. A
Prophetic Eclogue in Imitation of Virgil's
Pollio' (MS Poems, pp. 119–22; printed
below, Appendix 2).

6. In the arms of his wife; see *post* 27
Dec. 1743 and Wednesday ?1743–1744.

7. Not explained.

8. Rev. John Wright (ca 1699–1768),
rector of Euston 1729–68 (Venn, *Alumni
Cantab.*). HW had presumably met him
when he had visited the Duke of Grafton
at Euston about two weeks before (MANN
ii. 254).

9. Hon. Henry Seymour Conway (1719–
95), statesman and field-marshal; M.P.
Higham Ferrers 1741–7, Penryn 1747–54,
St Mawes 1754–61, Thetford 1761–74, Bury
1775–84; HW's cousin and correspondent;
at this time Lt-Col. in the 1st Foot
Guards.

10. HW's letter to Conway on Dettingen,
written 25 June, is missing; see Conway
to HW 27 July 1743 NS.

foot; who, like another Dulcinea, will perhaps be found by those polite captives, winnowing corn.[11]

I have been three or four days with Mr Coke at Holkam, where we grew prodigiously upon the victory, he a foot taller, and I half a yard in the waist—so by the end of the campaign, we shall probably be somebodies.

Adieu! my dear Lord, I am ever

Most faithfully yours

John Duke of Marlborough[12]

To Lincoln, Thursday 25 August 1743

Printed for the first time from a photostat of the MS deposited in the Nottingham University Library by the Trustees of the Newcastle Estates.

Houghton, Aug. 25, 1743.

My dearest Lord,

I KNOW not how to express my joy for your uncle's success,[1] or how to distinguish it from the general congratulations you will receive: but if you have always found my love the same, if you always knew me as glad of your good fortune when we had the Treasury, as I am now you have it, I hope you will think my friendship attached to you, not to that office. One difference indeed there is, that if ever you lose it, you will find me much more concerned, than you will remember I was, when it went from us.

I would not put you in mind of what is past, but that I would have you keep this letter for a memorandum of a friend you have in reserve against you shall miss all the new ones of this week—when they fall off, I shall be very happy to take my old place again.

This is a formal letter, and therefore it shall be a short one: indeed I have still used too many words to tell you what you know so well;

11. *Don Quixote*, Pt I, Chap. XXV.
12. HW also uses this signature in his letter to Chute 25 June 1743.

1. A messenger arrived from the King at Worms on the evening of 23 Aug., after a long delay, with a warrant appointing Henry Pelham first lord of the Treasury (J. B. Owen, *The Rise of the Pelhams*, 1957, pp. 165–72; Mann ii. 299 n. 9).

that I am happy at your being so, which I am sure you are, for you are too just not to rejoice when virtue and merit have their proper rewards and honour.

Adieu! my dear Lord—I am not the least more than I always was

Yours,

H. Walpole

To Lincoln, Tuesday 27 December 1743

Printed for the first time from a photostat of the MS deposited in the Nottingham University Library by the Trustees of the Newcastle Estates.

Arlington Street, Dec. 27, 1743.

My dear Lord,

THOUGH I am bound to write to you by promise and inclination, both which in this age are equally and religiously fulfilled; yet I could almost violate both, were I not afraid of being particular; and particularity you know I have all my life most cautiously avoided.

I have no news for you— Bawds though subject to some common circumstances of mortality, do not die every day;[1] common whores are not every day brought to bed;[2] such things as Sandys[3] are not every day made peers—and though Lord Carteret[4] is drunk every night, yet that is not new.

I might flatter you; but I have been too nearly related to a minister myself, not to know that even panegyrics can have nothing new in them. Has ever anybody surprised you with a virtue, which you had not discovered in yourself, before it was mentioned to you? I who

1. Probably an allusion to the recent death (11 Dec.) of 'the noted Mrs Haywood, who for many years kept the bagnio in Charles Street, Covent Garden, a lady well known to the polite part of the world, said to have died worth £10,000' (*London Magazine*, 1743, xii. 621; GM 1743, xiii. 668).

2. As Peggy Lee had recently been of Lincoln's daughter.

3. Samuel Sandys (1695–1770), cr. (1743) Bn Sandys; M.P. Worcester city 1718–43;

chancellor of the Exchequer 1742–3; prominent opponent of Sir Robert Walpole. His patent is not dated until 20 Dec., but his promotion was known by the 11th; see Mann ii. 357–8 for HW's satirical verses to the House of Lords on the occasion.

4. John Carteret (1690–1763), 2d Bn Carteret; 1st E. Granville, 1744; at this time secretary of state for the northern department and virtually first minister despite Henry Pelham's position at the head of the Treasury.

was youngest son, and consequently had much fewer excellencies to my share, than my two brothers,[5] have been wearied with praises—what must you be, who have no rival in perfection—except Mr Carteret![6]

It may proceed from my partiality to you, but, my dear Lord, in my opinion, you are the more accomplished young man of the two: though he is very hopeful—I myself was exceeding hopeful too, till about February the ninth one thousand seven hundred and forty-two[7]—and then, I don't know how it happened, but I certainly have never been very promising since. Several that I took for my best friends, for they used to commend me excessively, have seemed to have no more hopes of me— This mortified me for some time, as I did not perceive the least alteration in my own merit, but in my own eyes was every way as charming as I used to be—the only comfort I feel, is that you my dearest Lord, are just as clever, as handsome, as well-made and as vigorous now, as I was till within these two years: and what gives me more satisfaction, is, that when you lose these, as they are not qualities for life, but perquisites, you have enough merit of your own, to supply their room.

This is so good a period, and so proper a place to set my name to it, that I don't know why I don't conclude— Two sides are very handsome, when writing to you at all, is pure generosity—'tis like lending Lord Gage[8] a guinea, which one never expects to have returned—all I beg, is, that you won't give my letter to Mr Heath at White's,[9] and bid him answer it; it would not be pleasant to me to appear in the magazine, which I certainly should do, since the world and Dr Etoffe[10]

5. Robert Walpole (1701–51), cr. (1723) Bn Walpole, 2d E. of Orford, 1745; and Edward Walpole (1706–84), K.B., 1753; M.P. Lostwithiel 1730–4, Great Yarmouth 1734–68.

6. Hon. Robert Carteret (1721–76), styled Lord Carteret 1744–63; 2d E. Granville, 1763; M.P. Yarmouth (Hants) 1744–7. See the accounts of him, all unflattering, collected in GEC vi. 91 n. a.

7. HW is two days out on Sir Robert Walpole's resignation. He resigned on the 11th.

8. Thomas Gage (ca 1695–1754), cr. (1720) Vct Gage; M.P. Minehead 1717, Tewkesbury 1721–54 (Judd, Members of Parliament 202). For his financial difficul-

ties, see HW to Mann 24 Dec. 1741 (MANN i. 255 and n. 37).

9. A Mr Heath became a member of White's in 1743 and figures prominently in the club's betting books between 1744 and 1750; see [W. B. Boulton], The History of White's, 1892, ii pt i. 5–20 passim; ii pt ii. 45. One of these entries mentions his house in Sussex, so he is perhaps Richard Heath (ca 1706–52) of Hatchlands, East Clandon, Surrey, and (later) of Newhall, Sussex; M.P. Bossiney 1747–52 (Judd, Members of Parliament 225, and references there cited; Vict. Co. Hist. Surrey iii. 344–5; Court and City Register, 1748, p. 23).

10. Rev. Henry Etough (ca 1687–1757),

are of opinion that the Walpoles write pretty letters. It was very hard upon my father to meet that fate, who wrote in the security of his heart to Mr Churchill,[11] who he knew could not transcribe his letter.[12]

I have seen nothing since you went but a tide of old ladies at the Duchess of Richmond's[13] who sees company in form.[14] She looks so pretty; and her children round her are so pretty, I don't wonder the Duke makes as many of them as ever he can.

Adieu! my dear Lord!

Yours ever

H. W.

PS. Williams[15] has just told me a kind of rebus, that was sent to Lord Lovel t'other day in a penny post letter, as he was at dinner with the Duchess of Manchester[16]—

> To Chester's town prefix a man;
> Then, Lovel, win her if you can;
> But would you make a virgin yield,
> To Chester's town subjoin a field.

rector of Therfield, Herts 1734–57, a preferment he owed to Sir Robert Walpole. He also officiated at Sir Robert's marriage to Maria Skerrett in 1737 or 1738 (GRAY ii. 42 n. 58; John Nichols, *Literary Anecdotes of the Eighteenth Century*, 1812–15, viii. 261–4). HW eventually quarrelled with him in connection with the Nicoll affair; see HW to Etough 12 Oct. 1751; GRAY ii. 56, 58.

11. A letter from Lord Orford to Gen. Churchill, Houghton, 24 June 1743, was printed in the *London Magazine* for Sept. 1743 (xii. 456). The MS and a copy (of which there seem to have been many made) are now WSL. It is also printed (from a MS copy) in Hist. MSS Comm., *Denbigh MSS*, 1911, p. 242. The letter is on the charms of the inanimate world at Houghton. The connection of Heath and Etough with the publication is unknown.

12. HW wrote of Churchill: 'For his illiterateness, it will be only necessary to quote himself and his works; he professed never having read a whole book through in his life, and his letters were so ill-wrote

and so ill-spelled that Sir R. Walpole used to keep them unread till he saw him, and then he often could not read them himself' (*MS Poems*, p. 95).

13. Lady Sarah Cadogan (1706–51), m. (1719) Charles Lennox, 2d D. of Richmond.

14. After the birth on 24 Nov. OS of her tenth (fifth surviving) child, Lady Louisa Augusta Lennox (1743–1821), m. (1758) Thomas Conolly (Brian Fitzgerald, *Lady Louisa Conolly*, 1950, pp. 11, 17).

15. Charles Hanbury Williams (1708–59), K.B., 1744; politician, diplomatist, wit and poet; M.P. Monmouthshire 1735–47, Leominster 1754–9; HW's friend and correspondent. See HW's account of him, printed below, Appendix 3.

16. Lady Isabella Montagu (d. 1786), m. 1 (1723) William Montagu, 2d D. of Manchester; m. 2 (1743, secretly) Edward Hussey (after 1749, Hussey-Montagu), cr. (1762) Bn and (1784) E. of Beaulieu. Her friendship with Lovel is also celebrated by Williams in his 'Isabella; or The Morning' (Williams, *Works* i. 85–9).

To Lincoln, Wednesday ?1743–1744

Printed for the first time from a photostat of the MS deposited in the Nottingham University Library by the Trustees of the Newcastle Estates.

The letter is written in the character of one of Lincoln's mistresses. Its date is uncertain, although the reference to Lady Sophia Fermor suggests a date between Lincoln's formal renunciation of marrying her, which HW mentions to Mann 15 Nov. 1742 (MANN ii. 103) and her marriage to Lord Carteret 14 April 1744. The reference to Lady Townshend as living in Upper Grosvenor Street also confirms a terminal date before the end of 1744, since she left her house there preparatory to moving to her new house in Whitehall early in the autumn of that year (Hist. MSS Comm., *Denbigh MSS*, 1911, pp. 180, 183, 257; Rigby to Williams 21 July 1744, Williams MSS lxviii, f. 65; *post* 17 July 1744).

Wednesday night, twelve o'clock.

To the dear man
Whom folly pleases, and whose follies please.[1]

I HAVE changed my mind: instead of desiring you to have done loving me, I am going to ask something much more difficult for you to comply with—pray continue to love me: I like it vastly. I could never have imagined there were half so many *agréments* in having a lover. You can't conceive how I regret the time I have lost. How strangely dull you was never to think of it before—though I can't blame my fortune, for to be sure out of the millions that there are of both sexes, it was a vast chance that it did not come to my turn these twenty years. Now, though I am persuaded that I shall be just as agreeable twenty years hence as I am now (for indisputably my charms don't consist in youth, bloom or beauty) how can I tell that you will be as lovely then as you are now?—now! why nothing under the sun is so charming as you! you have all the tenderness, all the attentions of a lover in a romance, and all the dear indiscretion of a lover out of one. 'Tis amazing how little real anger I feel at the moments that I ought to hate you the most—when you expose me to the greatest dangers!

In short, whether 'tis my vanity, or my heart that is pleased, I must have you continue to love me—I won't pretend that I feel vast tenderness and passion when I expect to meet you, but it cer-

1. The concluding line (327) of Pope's *Second Epistle of the Second Book of Horace, Imitated*.

tainly gives a spirit to all I do, which is equivalent in pleasure to something softer.

Women generally try to persuade men to constancy, in return for their loving them—now my reason for desiring yours, is from the direct contrary. My satisfaction arises from your passion, not from my own. So you see, 'tis absolutely necessary you should continue to love me; for if you don't, I have no resource! I have no love and fidelity that is proof to ill-usage, to comfort me, and to make me support my ill-stars with dignity: I shan't be able to tell my heart, that spite of all your perjuries and broken vows, I love you still. No, if you are fickle, I am undone— 'Tis no passion of my own, but yours that diverts me; and do but think how cruel it would be to deprive me of such an amusement, for to be sure, for all the little ridicules of an affair, nothing can come up to you. You have all the whims and follies that can entertain one, without any of the lamentable languishings and insipidness that consume three parts of the time of other lovers. Therefore do tell me, what it is can secure you to me: point out—if you can guess, what sort of turn and behaviour could fix you—if that time can ever come! and I assure you, there is no part I won't act to keep you. Thank my stars, I have not passion enough to blind me; and if it is in the power of art to preserve your heart, it shall be mine! I own, I will try all arts, for I have not seen so little of the world, as to believe that merit or beauty ever kept a man three weeks: besides if they could—why, I won't declare my reasons for not depending on them. At least, neither of them, had the least share in gaining you!

I will still own farther; I have studied and endeavoured to find out what sort of person could fix you. I have recollected all I remember of you; *though as I never expected to have the use for it I have,* your actions did not always make a lasting impression on me. All I can remember, is, that you have loved so many and such various people, that I cannot trust to any hints collected from my memory. I then consulted others— I asked Lady S. F.[2] what was most likely to keep you? She replied with a charming grace (but without blushing) that all she knew, was, that beauty and sense could *not* keep you.—Mem. I was not shocked at this answer. I then consulted Fanny M——.[3] She pertly replied; smartness, forwardness, and half-

2. Lady Sophia Fermor.
3. Apparently Frances Macartney (d.
1789), m. (1748) Fulke Greville; poetess;
the 'Fanny' of HW's 'The Beauties'

a-dozen French songs with double entendres would rivet any man alive— To be sure, this was convincing! but however I tapped at her sister's[4] door, and put the same question to her. I now believed I should come at the truth, for she rolled her eyes with all the convulsions of an inspired prophetess, and with the finest circumflexion of every muscle, told me, that sentiments and a well-made naked body were perpetual chains.—The two ingredients sounded oddly together; and meeting Os——o[5] on the stairs, I only thought of the last words, *perpetual chains.* I then slipped on my French cloak, whipped into a hack, and drove to Peggy Lee's. I asked her, what was the best receipt for keeping a man? She replied with all the naiveté of her profession, that she knew no other way of keeping a man, but by being kept oneself by some very rich one— I smiled and went away determined to examine no more common women—but one, Lady Townshend, so drove to Upper Grosvenor Street. There I found a woman old enough to give young women any instructions, but so loathsome in her person, that one could hardly believe any man had ever given her any. However the room was filled with men, who like the description of sinners in the Psalms,[5a] seemed to run headlong into the broad way, rather than enter in at the straight way that leads to life everlasting. One was an elderly officer, G. Campbell,[6] who was languishing by her with all the politeness of the old Court— Another, Mr Winnington,[7] a rough gentleman, who, I should have thought, had never seen a court, but from his own account of his morals and

(BERRY i. 47 n. 41; *post* 19 July 1746 and Appendix 4). Fanny Rudman (ca 1729–78), called Fanny Murray, courtesan, is also possible, but she did not become well-known until about 1746 and had no sisters (Horace Bleackley, *Ladies Fair and Frail*, 1925, pp. 3–49).

4. Fanny Macartney had three sisters, Alice (living in 1789); Catherine (living in 1789); and Mary (d. 1765), m. (1761) William Henry Lyttelton, cr. (1776) Bn Westcote and (1794) Bn Lyttelton (John Lodge and Mervyn Archdall, *Peerage of Ireland*, 1789, vii. 91). The one most likely intended is Alice, who later had an evil reputation as a troublemaker; see *Leinster Corr.* i. 176–7, 187–9; iii. 168, 176, 186, 210.

5. Cavaliere Giuseppe Osorio-Alarcon (ca 1697–1763), Sardinian ambassador to England 1730–49, to Aix-la-Chapelle 1748; minister to Spain 1749–50 (references cited in MANN i. 186 n. 20). HW told Mann 2 Nov. 1741 that 'scandal, who I believe is not mistaken, lays a Miss Mccartny to his charge' (ibid. i. 186).

5a. More correctly Matthew 7.13–14.

6. Probably Gen. John Campbell (ca 1693–1770), 4th D. of Argyll, 1761; M.P. Buteshire 1713–5, Elgin burghs 1715–22, 1725–7, Dumbartonshire 1727–61. Williams planned to include 'Jack Campbell' among Lady Townshend's admirers in a projected poem about her in the autumn of 1743; see Ilchester, *Hanbury-Williams* 121–2.

7. Thomas Winnington (1696–1746), M.P. Droitwich 1726–41, Worcester city 1741–6; paymaster general of the Forces 1741–6; intimate friend of Williams, Fox, and the younger supporters of Sir Robert Walpole; 'declared cicisbeo' to Lady Townshend (HW to Mann 22 Oct. 1741, MANN i. 173 and n. 6a).

honesty, which seemed imbibed from the most profligate courts that ever existed. This latter the lady of the house used as insolently as if she had kept him, not he her— Indeed it seemed as if they kept to each other, for fear of having the most wicked enemy alive; for except each, nobody else could be shameless enough to tell what each does every day. When the male was gone, I asked the female, by what secret she had kept the most inconstant, most unfeeling man alive— but she gave me so many infamous receipts, that I was charitable enough to believe that there was no more truth in this, than in all the rest she says.

Resolved to make but one inquiry more, I drove to the other end of the town,[8] where I heard lived a constant couple—I found a man and woman, Duke and Duchess of Richmond, both handsome enough to have been tempted to every inconstancy, but too handsome to have ever found what they would have lost by the exchange. I begged this happy charming woman to tell me by what art she had for twenty years together made herself beloved; and that I was persuaded from that air of heavenly good nature in her countenance that she would tell me, when she knew my happiness depended upon it. She coloured with a sort of mild indignation that made her ten times more beautiful, and replied, she knew not what I meant by art—that she had always obeyed, been virtuous, and loved her husband; and was it strange he should return it?—I sighed at the words, *virtue* and *husband* and envied her for not knowing that love does not always produce love.—In short, I am melancholy about it, and so mortified, that I think I could love you, only you, and you unboundedly—if I had any hopes that that would do to keep you mine—

Adieu!

P. P.[9]

PS. What an enormous letter, when I had no occasion but to transcribe you the enclosed song![10] One would think I had no pleasure but in seeing you or writing to you!

8. To Richmond House, Privy Garden, Whitehall.

9. We do not know which of Lin-coln's mistresses these initials represent.

10. Missing.

During the spring and early summer of 1744, HW informed Mann of the final scenes in the long romance between Lincoln and Lady Sophia Fermor, on the occasion of her marriage to Lord Carteret.

'Lincoln is quite indifferent [to the approaching marriage], and laughs. . . . I am really glad of it [the marriage], for her beauty and cleverness did deserve a better fate than she was on the point of having determined for her for ever. How graceful, how charming, and how haughtily condescending she will be! How, if Lincoln should ever hint past history, she will

> Stare upon the strange man's face,
> As one she ne'er had known!'
> > (to Mann 22 March 1744, MANN ii. 424).

'What is ridiculously lucky, is, that Lord Lincoln goes into waiting today, and will be to present her [to the King on her marriage]!' (to Mann 15 April 1744, ibid. ii. 431).

'She [Lady Sophia] has not quite digested her resentment to Lincoln yet. He was walking with her at Ranelagh t'other night, and a Spanish refugee Marquis, who is of the Carteret court, but who not being quite perfect in the *carte du pays*, told my Lady that Lord Lincoln had promised him to make a very good husband to Miss Pelham. Lady Carteret with an accent of energy, replied, *"J'espère qu'il tiendra sa promesse!"* Here is a good epigram that has been made on her:

> Her beauty like the scripture feast,
> To which th'invited never came,
> Deprived of its intended guest,
> Was given to the old and lame'

> > (to Mann 22 July 1744, ibid, ii. 483).

To C. H. WILLIAMS, Saturday 16 June 1744

Missing. 'Hory Walpole . . . showed me the letter he sent to you last Saturday' (Rigby to Williams, Thursday [21] June [1744], Williams MSS lxviii, f. 57).

To C. H. WILLIAMS, Tuesday 26 June 1744

Printed from a photostat of the MS in the Newport Public Library, Newport, Monmouth. First printed, with an omission, Toynbee *Supp.* iii. 354–7. For the history of these letters, see above, p. xxxi.

Arlington Street, June 26, 1744.

AS Lady Caroline Fox[1] does not go to Cheltenham[2] I conclude I may venture this to Coldbrook.[3] I am told you have been very ill,[4] and fear you may date it from sitting to write by your cascade[5] with so great a cold. Let me hear you are quite recovered.

The King has had another determination for abroad since I wrote to you;[6] but yesterday it was again put off.[7] You will hate me for telling you, that I believe some news from Dunkirk,[8] were concerned in this last alteration of his scheme. My dear Williams, I am sure you will pray with me for the peace that is talked of.[9] The Dutch have sent over a plan very advantageous for the French:[10] grant Heaven! they accept

1. Lady Georgiana Caroline Lennox (1723–74), m. (secretly, at Williams's house in Privy Gardens, 3 May 1744) Henry Fox, cr. (1763) Bn Holland; cr. (1762) Bns Holland, s.j. (Ilchester, *Henry Fox* i. 107).

2. The Foxes had recently abandoned plans to meet Williams at Cheltenham because of Lady Caroline's pregnancy (Fox to Williams 21 June, 23 June 1744, Williams MSS xlviii, ff. 77, 81). Williams seems to have gone there nevertheless (*post* 17 July 1744).

3. Coldbrook House, Williams's seat near Abergavenny, Monmouth. It is described in Ilchester, *Hanbury-Williams* 26–8, and illustrated ibid., facing p. 178.

4. Williams told Henry Fox, in a letter which the latter received on 22 June, that he had been 'too much out of order' to write (Fox to Williams 23 June 1744, Williams MSS xlviii, f. 81).

5. Williams's 'Epistle to Henry Fox,' which he was writing at this time, refers to Coldbrook's 'limpid streams' (Ilchester, *Hanbury-Williams* 27, 123–6).

6. Presumably HW's missing letter of 16 June.

7. George II had been resolved for some

months to visit the war in Flanders. On 18 June he declared his intention of leaving the first week in July and ordered his equipage made ready, but on the 24th, he announced that he had changed his mind and would not go (*Hardwicke Corr.* i. 347–8; George Harris, *Life of Lord Chancellor Hardwicke*, 1847, ii. 90; Fox to Williams 30 June 1744, Williams MSS xlviii, f. 84; *Daily Adv.* 23 June; MANN ii. 456 n. 1).

8. The King explained his decision to remain in England to Lord Hardwicke by reading him a letter telling of the presence of 400–500 ships at Dunkirk and indications that the French were about to besiege Ostend. Henry Fox told Williams that he believed 'the French army [had] a great and English eloquence a very little share' in the King's decision (*Hardwicke Corr.* i. 348; Harris, op. cit. ii. 91; Fox to Williams 30 June 1744, Williams MSS xlviii, f. 84).

9. HW's concern was particularly for the safety of his cousin Henry Seymour Conway who was with the army.

10. 'On Wednesday night [20 June] arrived a special messenger from Holland, who we hear has brought a plan which the

it: a bad peace is better than a worse. In the meantime, I am wishing them away all Flanders: when once they have got it, our army must come home; and it grows the immediate affair of the Dutch, who leave it all to us,[11] while there is a foot of land between them and France to stick in an English soldier.

My father went the day before yesterday,[12] not quite well of his gravel,[13] but impatient to be clear of the absurdities and broils,[14] which he in vain endeavoured to compose and remedy. The world expects some great crack in the ministry every day.[15] I care not; it can't be worse, and I don't see how 'tis likely to amend. I don't send you the new poem on discord,[16] supposing you have had it:[17] besides 'tis too big for a letter, and not good enough to send all. The two characters of Craterus and Plumbosus are admirable;[18] especially the latter, who—is not a hero sure![19]

Have you heard of poor Fitz's[20] disgrace; of his fit on the wedding-day,[21] the deferring the espousals, and the disappointment of St

Dutch have settled for a general peace; which plan, if 'tis approved on here, as they flatter themselves it will, is to be carried immediately by M. Twickle to the French king . . . . and as this plan is very much in favour of the French, 'tis thought it will meet with no obstacle from that quarter' (*Daily Adv.* 22 June). There seems to have been no basis for the report.

11. The Dutch were being recalcitrant during June 1744 in sending promised reinforcements to the Allied army in Flanders and in providing ships to reinforce the English fleet in the Channel (HW to Conway 29 June 1744; *Daily Adv.* 27 June).

12. To Houghton.

13. He thought himself much better after reaching Houghton (Orford to HW 14 July 1744).

14. His situation had also been eased by securing, 19 June, his pension of £4000 per annum, which he had been promised when he went out of office in 1742 (MANN ii. 465).

15. Because of the friction between Carteret and the Pelhams.

16. *Discord: or, One Thousand Seven Hundred and Forty Four. By a Great Poet Lately Deceased,* 1744; advertised as 'this day is published' in *Old England* 23 June. The author of the poem is unknown, though Henry Fox thought it might be by

Whitehead (Fox to Williams 30 June 1744, Williams MSS xlviii, f. 83). HW describes it and quotes 24 lines in a letter to Conway 29 June 1744. HW's copy is Hazen, *Cat. of HW's Lib.,* No. 280.

17. Fox sent a copy to Williams on 21 June (Fox to Williams 21 June 1744, Williams MSS xlviii, f. 77).

18. HW quotes these two 'characters' in his letter to Conway 29 June 1744, supplying names for the blanks in the poem and slightly altering one line. Craterus (presumably from *cratera,* a vessel for mixing wine and water) represents Carteret; Plumbosus (leaden) is Henry Pelham. There are echoes of the 'character' of Plumbosus in Williams's lines on Henry Pelham in 'An Epistle to the Right Hon. Henry Fox,' although that poem was not completed until August 1745 (Williams, *Works* ii. 139–40; Ilchester, *Hanbury-Williams* 123–4).

19. The last line of the character of Plumbosus:
'An honest man,—but not a hero sure!'

20. William Fitzwilliam (1720–56), 3d E. Fitzwilliam; M.P. Peterborough 1741–2.

21. Fitzwilliam was to marry Lady Anne Watson-Wentworth (d. 1769), eldest dau. of Thomas Watson-Wentworth, cr. (1734) E. of Malton, and (1746) M. of Rockingham, on 21 June. Henry Fox describes

James's Market, by the unordering the provisions? However they were patched together next day; have feasted the whole sable race,[22] and been presented about in the japanese chariot.[23] I know no anecdotes of the wedding-night; Lincoln I believe does; but he is discreet, I suppose by compact.[24] The jewels he has given her, cost seven thousand pound: where then was Lambe?[25]—unless he sold them.

Ask me no more questions of *the Family;*[26] I am sick of them, and have done with them.[27] I don't know what diversion you might extract out of them, but I can't: they are too childish. George[28] in good downright quarrelling t'other day flung a bag of counters in my Lady's face; which she put up as quietly as if he had put his p——

what occurred: 'I saw Fitz on Thursday morning who was to go to dine in private at Malton House, have his wedding clothes brought him there, be married at nine, sit down to supper with eighteen people at ten, dine with twice as many at the same place yesterday, and bring his bride home as last night, when behold, about an hour after I left him, he falls down in a swoon which takes away his senses for a considerable time. Wilmot, Ranby, the Malton coach, all hurry to St James's Square, and the eight cooks got together in the Malton kitchen are in the utmost confusion. He recovers but the marriage put off till yesterday when I hear it was celebrated, and I hope no second fit prevented the consummation. He has literally been, as we told him he was, frightened out of his senses' (Fox to Williams 23 June 1744, Williams MSS xlviii, f. 82). See also Lady Townshend to Lady Denbigh 22 June 1744 (Hist. MSS Comm., *Denbigh MSS*, 1911, p. 249) for similar details.

22. The Finch family: Williams described them as 'the black funereal Finches' in his *A New Ode to a Great Number of Great Men Newly Made,* 1742 (Williams, *Works* i. 143). The bride's mother was Lady Mary Finch, dau. of Daniel Finch, 7th E. of Winchilsea and 2d E. of Nottingham.

23. Lady Townshend describes it as 'a new equipage . . . made in the Chinese fashion being all over japanned' (to Lady Denbigh 22 June 1744, Hist. MSS Comm., *Denbigh MSS*, 1911, p. 249; see also Sarah Byng Osborn, *Letters,* ed. McClelland, Stanford University, 1930, p. 57).

24. Because of his own approaching marriage (*post* 26 July 1744, n. 4).

25. Probably Matthew Lamb (1705–68), of Brocket Hall, Herts, cr. (1755) Bt; attorney; M.P. Stockbridge 1741–7, Peterborough 1747–68. He was reputedly worth a million pounds at his death. Apparently Fitzwilliam was in his debt. Lady Townshend also mentions the jewels 'to the value of above six thousand pounds' which Fitzwilliam had given his bride (Hist. MSS Comm., *Denbigh MSS*, 1911, p. 249).

26. The Townshend family; neither this reference, nor a similar one *post* 14 Aug. 1744, is entirely clear. The 'my Lady' mentioned below is Lady Townshend, and 'George,' George Selwyn; George Townshend had gone abroad in 1742 and did not return until March 1745 (C. V. F. Townshend, *The Military Life of . . . George, First Marquess Townshend,* 1901, pp. 4–6; *Daily Adv.* 5 March 1745).

27. 'We are grown tired of the Family and don't troubles ourselves much about them: nothing remarkable has happened among 'em or I should have heard of it from George Selwyn' (Rigby to Williams, Thursday [21] June [1744], Williams MSS lxviii, f. 57).

28. George Augustus Selwyn (1719–91), wit and politician; M.P. Ludgershall 1747–54, 1780–91, Gloucester city 1754–80; HW's friend and correspondent. He was closely connected by marriage with the Townshends and more distantly with Williams.

into her hand.[29] But she abuses him behind his back. In short, they are too simple. Rigby[30] has taken George and Mr Fortescue[31] into Essex till Friday.[32] I like Rigby more and more;[33] but I have done with all the rest of my new acquaintance: even the gentle Mr Vezey[34] is a dead weight. Dick[35] is come back,[36] but I have not seen him; I hear I dine with him and Lincoln at White's today.

My Lady Bolinbroke[37] is come over, and has brought back the Pitt-Maid of Honour;[38] who was a wit long ago, and I suppose now will be the reigning fashion.

My Lady Townshend says the whole Hervey family have quarrelled with Mr Phipps,[39] on having caught him speaking truth. The delicate Lord[40] is come back from Stowe, where by his own account he shut himself up all day, and only walked out by moonlight. Was not

29. The last half of this sentence is printed for the first time.

30. Richard Rigby (1722–88), politician; M.P. Castle Rising 1745–7, Sudbury 1747–54, Tavistock 1754–88; later secretary to the D. of Bedford. HW's friendship with him remained close for several years, but eventually cooled.

31. Probably either William Henry Fortescue (1722–1806), cr. (1770) Bn, (1776) Vct, and (1777) E. of Clermont; or Matthew Fortescue (1719–85), 2d Bn Fortescue, 1751.

32. 'I go to Mistley [his seat near Manningtree, Essex] on Sunday for four or five days' (Rigby to Williams, Thursday [21] June [1744], Williams MSS lxviii, f. 59).

33. Rigby reciprocated the feeling; he and HW, he wrote to Williams, were 'grown as great together, as my Lady and her spouse. We spend all our evenings together' (Rigby to Williams, Thursday [21] June [1744], Williams's MSS lxviii, f. 57). A month later he wrote, 'there is hardly a day passes that we don't spend some time together. I am fond of his company beyond all things' (Rigby to Williams 21 July [1744], ibid. lxviii, f. 65).

34. Presumably Agmondesham Vesey (d. 1785), Irish politician and M.P.; husband of Elizabeth Vesey, the blue-stocking. Burke, in nominating him for the Club in 1773, described him as 'a man of gentle manners' (Boswell's Life of Johnson, ed. G. B. Hill and L. F. Powell, Oxford, 1934–50, iv. 28; Sir Joshua Reynolds, Letters, ed. Hilles, Cambridge, 1929, pp. 33–4).

35. Edgcumbe.

36. He had been in Somerset with Sir Charles Wyndham for a fortnight (Rigby to Williams, Thursday [21] June [1744], Williams MSS lxviii, f. 57).

37. Marie-Claire des Champs de Marcilli (1675–1750), m. 1 (1695) Philippe le Vallois, seigneur de Vilette, m. 2 (1720) Henry St John, cr. (1712) Vct Bolingbroke (La Chenaye-Desbois xix. 458–9).

38. Anne Pitt (1712–81), sister of William Pitt, 1st E. of Chatham; maid of honour 1733–7; keeper of the Privy Purse to the Princess of Wales 1751–72; subsequently HW's friend and correspondent. She had been living with Lady Bolingbroke in France since Sept. 1742 (Lord Rosebery, Chatham: His Early Life and Connections, 1910, p. 86; Basil Williams, Life of William Pitt, 1913, i. 48, 94). They arrived in London 20 June (Hist. MSS Comm., Denbigh MSS, 1911, p. 250).

39. Constantine Phipps (1722–75), cr. (1767) Bn Mulgrave, m. (1743) Lepell Hervey, dau. of John, Lord Hervey.

40. George William Hervey (ante 29 April 1741 NS, n. 9), who had succeeded his father as Bn Hervey the previous year. Lady Townshend wrote to Lady Denbigh 22 June 1744: 'Lord Hervey is come to town from Lord Cobham's and is to be two days at Lady Suffolke's at Marble Hill, and a Sunday intends going with Lady Hervey to Ickworth in Suffolk to pass the rest of the summer with Lord Bristol' (Hist. MSS Comm., Denbigh MSS, 1911, pp. 249–50).

that doing the honours of Stowe and his own flattery? It puts me in mind of his father,[41] who always took pains to ridicule to you the things he had intended to flatter, and was never easy till he had told everybody else that he was acting a part.

I have never seen Mrs Woffington,[42] but inquired and hear she lives at Teddington.[43] Rigby will have told you that Lord Darnley [44] is on the *tapis* again.

Adieu! my dear Williams! I am ever

Most faithfully yours,

Hor. Walpole

From C. H. Williams, ca Wednesday 4 July 1744

Missing. HW showed this letter to Rigby on 7 July (Rigby to Williams, Saturday [7 July 1744], Williams MSS lxviii. f. 68).

To C. H. Williams, Saturday 7 July 1744

Printed from a photostat of the MS in the Newport Public Library, Newport, Monmouth. First printed, Toynbee *Supp.* iii. 357–62.

Arlington Street, July 7th 1744.

I AM so obliged to you, my dear Williams, for writing to me at all, that I will never complain of your not being punctual. I will

41. John, Lord Hervey.

42. Margaret Woffington (ca 1714–60), actress. Williams had been enamoured of her since her London debut in 1740 and had written several poems to her, but she does not seem to have become his mistress until the winter of 1744. The affair, though ardent, was of short duration, for Williams discovered that she had 'betrayed' him shortly after he left town in June. He then wrote a satire comparing her to the Earl of Bath, though making it clear that he still loved her (Ilchester, *Hanbury-Williams* 50–2, 77–80; Williams, *Works* ii. 13–15). Williams seems to have arranged for Rigby to take his place with her during his absence (Rigby to Williams, Thursday [21] June [1744], Williams MSS lxviii, ff. 58–9).

43. 'She told me . . . that she was to go

out of town next day [17 June] to a house she has taken at Teddington, where she intended to live in the privatest and most retired manner' (ibid. f. 58).

44. Edward Bligh (1715–47), 2d E. of Darnley. He had been Mrs Woffington's 'protector' in 1741. As HW surmised, Rigby did tell Williams that Darnley was again in favour: 'Sir C[harles] W[yndham] by the way gave it me as his opinion that Darnley has got Woffington' (ibid. f. 59). 'I have seen nothing of her since the last opera and have heard only a confirmation of her former lover's having restored her to her former dignity' (Rigby to Williams, Saturday [7 July 1744], ibid. lxviii, f. 68). See also Fox to Williams 17 Aug. 1744, ibid. xlviii, f. 101; Thomas Winnington to Williams 28 July 1744, ibid. lxviii. f. 110.

only try to invite you to it, by never letting the correspondence drop on my side. What you promise to let me see,[1] is not my least inducement: you know the taste I have for your compositions. 'Tis no compliment to tell you I think you the only true poet in England now Pope[2] is dead. Why may not I say this to you, when I do assure you it has been said to me more than once of you?

I don't desire you to rebuild Dunkirk even in your map: but you may be perfectly at rest about it: Prince Charles[3] at the whole distance of France has quashed it more than ten Treaties of Utrecht could.[4] So much for my politics—you know I inquire no farther, when I am once satisfied there is to be no invasion.

The town has been entertained this week with Anson's[5] Aquapulca triumph:[6] I saw it in profile from my window: and a trumpery sight it was—I don't conceive anybody's being pleased with it, but, Sir John Heathcote[7] or my Uncle Horace,[8] who, as Mrs Chenevix[9] says

---

1. Possibly Williams's 'Epistle to the Right Hon. Henry Fox' (ante 26 June 1744, n. 5). Williams also wrote an 'Epistle from Clytemnestra to Sappho or Kitty to my Lady' in July 1744, which has disappeared (Ilchester, Hanbury-Williams 86–7).

2. Who died 30 May 1744.

3. Prince Charles-Alexandre (1712–80) of Lorraine; governor-general of the Austrian Netherlands. Information that he had crossed the Rhine near Stockstad with 50,000 men and that 30,000 more Austrian troops had crossed near Philipsburg between 30 June and 3 July NS reached England on 29 June OS (Daily Adv. 30 June; MANN ii. 466, n. 3). HW had also received a long letter on the subject from Conway, 6 July 1744 NS, which was probably sent by the messenger who brought the dispatches.

4. Article IX of the Treaty of Utrecht, 1713, provided for razing the fortifications of Dunkirk and for filling up the harbour.

5. George Anson (1697–1762), cr. (1747) Bn Anson; Rear-Adm., 23 June 1744; Vice-Adm., 1746; Adm., 1748; M.P. Hedon 1744–7; first lord of the Admiralty 1751–6, 1757–62. He had recently returned from his voyage around the world, reaching London on 18 June (Daily Adv. 19 June).

6. Anson captured the Spanish galleon Nuestra Señora del Cabadonga, bound from Acapulco to Manila, near Cape Santo Spirito, off Manila, on 20 June 1743. Its cargo included '1,313,843 pieces of eight

and 35,682 ounces of virgin silver and plate' (Anson to Newcastle 14 June 1744 OS, printed in extracts in Daily Adv. 18 June; see also Sir John Barrow, Life of George Lord Anson, 1839, pp. 74–5; W. V. Anson, Life of Admiral Lord Anson, 1912, pp. 55–9, 62–70). The treasure was carried through London in 'state' on 4 July: 'Passed through St James's Street, the Strand, Cheapside, etc. in their way to the Tower, 32 wagons from Portsmouth, with the treasure brought home by Admiral Anson; they were guarded by the ship's crew (which consisted of many nations) and preceded by the officers, with swords drawn, music playing and colours flying, particularly that of the Aquapulca prize' (GM 1744, xiv. 392). The procession is also described in a letter from Thomas Birch to the Hon. Philip Yorke, 7 July 1744, printed in Hardwicke Corr. i. 349.

7. Sir John Heathcote (1689–1759), 2d Bt; M.P. Grantham 1715–22, Bodmin 1733–41. His father, notorious for his avarice, was reported to be the wealthiest commoner in England (DNB sub Sir Gilbert Heathcote; HW to Mann 24 July 1749, MANN iv. 80–1 and nn. 13–15).

8. Horatio Walpole (1678–1757), cr. (1756) Bn Walpole of Wolterton; diplomatist and politician; M.P. Lostwithiel 1710, Castle Rising 1710–15, Bere Alston 1715–17, East Looe 1718–22, Great Yarmouth 1722–34, Norwich 1734–56; ambas-

when she would have you buy gold buckles preferably to Pinchbeck,[10] love the conscious pleasure of knowing it was gold. That evening I carried Rigby to my Lady Townshend's: they asked him what time the procession got to the Tower? He did not know, but imagined it would be good breeding to name some hour; so said half an hour after two. Unluckily it was two before it got through Pall Mall. This malapropos civility diverted us excessively—Lady Isabella Scot[11] who was at whisk and had laughed for half an hour, turned behind to me, and said, 'Pray Sir tell me what is trumps.' I replied, 'I believe, Madam, half an hour after two.' This laughing cured Rigby of politeness, and he set down to whisk, had Winnington for his partner, and was as charmingly brutal as my Lady[12] herself can think Winnington.[13] He turned my Lady and my Lord Stair out of the winning places, with as little ceremony as he would my Lady Bland[14] and Dick Edgcumbe. While all this was passing, and that was the whole evening, Lady Susan Keck[15] was haranguing Dr Shaw[16] on her palsy at the end of the room: we lost all patience, and wrote a card to her to know how she did.

I dined with my Lady and Lady Susan t'other day at my Lord Stair's. Scandal says, I drank every bumper my Lord Dumfries[17] filled me, and went home very sick. Don't believe this, for the two ladies sat as long as I, and were perfectly sober. I was mightily pleased with feeding by instinct a great fat dog that my Lord Stair calls Horace, from his loving dispatches. With his great good breeding he did not care I should know the dog's name; but he was as much pleased as I was, when he found how little I was shocked with the freedom he

sador to France 1724–8; HW frequently mentions his penuriousness.

9. Elizabeth Deard, wife of Paul Daniel Chenevix; 'a toy woman at Charing Cross, famous for her high prices and fine language' (HW's *MS Poems*, p. 229). She was the occupant of SH before HW took it. See Mann ii. 366 n. 12; Gray i. 17, 103 n. 11.

10. 'An alloy of about five parts of copper with one of zinc, resembling gold: used in clock-making, cheap jewellery, etc.,' named after the inventor, Christopher Pinchbeck (ca 1670–1732), a watch- and toy-maker in Fleet Street (OED).

11. Lady Isabella Scott (d. 1748) (*Scots Peerage* ii. 239; Collins, *Peerage*, 1812, ii. 552).

12. Lady Townshend.

13. For the 'attachment' between Lady Townshend and Winnington, see *ante* Wednesday ?1743–1744.

14. A slip or a joke; no one correctly styled 'Lady Bland' was alive at this time.

15. Lady Susan Hamilton (1706–55), youngest dau. of James, 4th D. of Hamilton, m. (1736) Anthony Tracy Keck, of Great Tew, Oxon, grandson of John, 3d Vct Tracy (*Scots Peerage* iv. 391, ix. 104).

16. Dr Peter Shaw (1694–1763), M.D.; author; editor of the works of Bacon and Boyle.

17. William Dalrymple-Crichton (1699–1768), 4th E. of Dumfries; 4th E. of Stair, 1760 (*Scots Peerage* viii. 155–6).

took with my uncle. I begged Horace and Patapan[18] might be acquainted; but I am afraid Horace will think Patapan a trifler; for the latter hates gazettes, and loves your odes.

Old Mark Kerr[19] was there. Certain it is he got most complaisantly drunk; and told most civil lies of his own courage ten thousand years ago. Particularly of his being shot in the mouth with a bullet, and spitting out the blood[20]—'fore Gad, I have got a most confounded toothache.

T'other morning I was sent for to see Lady Carteret[21] set for her picture:[22] old Countess Granville[23] came out to me: you know she affects old Marlborough.[24] À propos de rien, she began; 'I have been reading the history of Francis the First:[25] I don't like him: he was hot: he was giddy: he was rash: he was governed by a foolish mother'—Imagine all this said with a toss of the head and a snuffle through the nose: I was ready to burst at this family picture which she was drawing without knowing it.

I went t'other night to see *Hamlet* by Machlin's[26] company at the little Haymarket House, but could not stay above two acts. It would not do even for summer: they are neither good nor ridiculous. The King and Prince Hamlet were dressed in blue ribbands and stars: Dick[27] has found out by his sagacity in all points that relate to chivalry, that their mistake must have sprung from seeing Solenthall with his new blue ribband.[28] Polonius had a coat of Fitzwilliam's,

18. HW's dog (*ante* 16 Sept. 1741 NS, n. 2).

19. Lord Mark Kerr (1676–1752), 4th son of the 4th E. and 1st M. of Lothian; capt. in the Army, 1693; Gen., 1743; governor of Guernsey, 1740; governor of Edinburgh Castle, 1745 (*Scots Peerage* v. 478).

20. Perhaps at the battle of Almanza 25 April 1707, where he was wounded (ibid.).

21. Lady Sophia Fermor had married Carteret 14 April 1744.

22. Which was being painted by George Knapton, at whose studio HW met her on this occasion and asked leave to stay while she sat (HW to Mann 29 June 1744, MANN ii. 467).

23. Lady Grace Granville (d. 18 Oct. 1744), 2d dau. of John Granville, 1st E. of Bath; m. (1675) Sir George Carteret, Bt, cr. (1681) Bn Carteret of Hawnes; cr. (1715) Vcts Carteret and Cts Granville, s.j.

24. Sarah Jennings (1660–18 Oct. 1744), m. (1678) John Churchill, cr. (1702) D. of Marlborough.

25. François I (1494–1547), K. of France 1515–47. Lady Granville had probably been reading Antoine Varillas's *Histoire de François I*ᵉʳ, 1685, in one of its several editions.

26. Charles Macklin (ca 1697–1797), actor. Following a quarrel with Garrick and expulsion from Drury Lane, he gathered a set of 'raw recruits' and drilled them into a company which opened at the Haymarket Theater on 6 Feb. 1744 (E. A. Parry, *Charles Macklin*, 1891, p. 79).

27. Edgcumbe.

28. Baron Henrik Frederik Söhlenthal (ca 1672–1752), envoy from Denmark to Great Britain 1714–31; minister plenipotentiary and ambassador 1737–43; ambassador extraordinary 1744–50 (*Repertorium der diplomatischen Vertreter aller Länder*,

I suppose just given away upon his wedding.[29] Dick loses his daily twenty guineas[30] to the constant entertainment of Sir Charles Windham:[31] t'other day the latter was punting[32] for sixpences to plague him; and on losing a great card, struck his breast, as if he was in a passion of despair. Dick with real agony cried out, 'I'll show you how you should strike,' and gave himself on his naked breast three confounded blows. When we scolded him for it, he only replied, 'I wish I durst do it with something sharper.'[33] Sir Charles Windham is got into Henley's[34] advertisements:[35] you know he declaims upon all subjects within the newspapers and the bills of mortality:[36] today is given out a discourse on consecrating heathen temples at Ranelagh.[37]

Our friend the Speaker[38] has been publishing an abridgment of Middleton's[39] *Letter from Rome* on the Roman Catholic superstition:[40] he calls it *Popery Unmasked:*[41] the quotations are left out, the

Vol. II, ed. Friedrich Hausmann, Zurich, 1950, pp. 35, 36; Michael Ranfft, *Neue genealogisch-historische Nachrichten*, Leipzig, 1750–63, iii. 247–9; GM 1752, xxii. 44). He had been admitted to the Danish Order of the Elephant 4 Dec. 1743; its ribbon was light blue (Ranfft, op. cit. iii. 249).

29. See *ante* 26 June 1744, n. 21.

30. 'I am waiting here for Sir C. Wyndham, Boon, and Edgecumbe to supper, the latter having lost his twenty guineas, and consequently having nothing left to do but to be good company' (Fox to Williams 7 July 1744, Williams MSS xlviii, f. 85).

31. Sir Charles Wyndham (1710–63), 4th Bt; 2d E. of Egremont, 1750; M.P. Bridgwater 1735–41, Appleby 1742–7, Taunton 1747–50; secretary of state 1761–3.

32. That is, betting against the dealer in faro.

33. 'Dick is at present in a most distracted condition, his perpetual loss at play, and his violent love of the Kitten who he can't get at, make him continued uneasiness, which he carries I think much farther than he used to do' (Rigby to Williams 21 July [1744], Williams MSS lxviii, f. 65).

34. John ('Orator') Henley (1692–1756), eccentric London preacher.

35. No reference to Sir Charles Wyndham in Henley's advertisements in the *Daily Adv.* has been found.

36. Henley delivered a sermon every Sunday morning, an oration on some special theological theme in the evening and lectured on Wednesdays on 'some other science.' On Saturdays he advertised his next theme 'in mysterious terms' to draw a large audience (DNB).

37. Henley's advertisement in the *Daily Adv.* 7 July 1744 reads in part: 'List of Rt Rev. High Priests who have and are to preach, visit, absolve, ordain, and consecrate at the new heathen temples (near the town) of Belphegor, Asmodenus, Succoth Benoth, and Tammus; Dagon and Urimn and Thummim at Chelsea; Brother Wesley's Chapel in West Street, and the B. of L. and Dr G. at shuttlecock about it.'

38. Arthur Onslow (1691–1768), Speaker of the House of Commons 1728–61; M.P. Guildford 1720–7, Surrey 1727–61. HW had satirized him in 'Patapan, or the Little White Dog,' written in the summer of 1743 (*MS Poems*, pp. 94–112; printed below, Appendix 1). See also *post* 19 Sept. 1744, n. 8.

39. Conyers Middleton (1683–1750), D.D., author and controversialist; HW's correspondent.

40. *A Letter from Rome, Showing an Exact Conformity between Popery and Paganism: or, The Religion of the Present Romans Derived from That of their Heathen Ancestors*, first published 1729; 4th

print small and paper coarse, to adapt it to the lowest capacities, for he says it may be of great service in the present circumstances.[42] 'Tis so like good women that give away the week's reparation; those that buy six may have a seventh gratis.

I have strangely wandered into a fifth side of paper—but 'tis an awkward time of night, and I had nothing else to do but to write. Rigby and I have been to dine with Mrs Handaside[43] and the Dab[44] at Hammersmith: there was nobody else but Tom Hervey: they produced the old paralytic General;[45] and it was not pleasant. We sat them down at Ranelagh: tumbled over the Prince, Princess[46] and Duke,[47] and came away—

> He as his business or diversion led him[48]—
> But for my own poor part, I came to write[49]—

edn with a postscript and a long 'Prefatory Discourse,' 1741.

41. *Popery Unmasked. Being the Substance of Dr Middleton's celebrated Letter from Rome: demonstrating an exact conformity between Popery and Paganism. With an abstract of the Doctor's Reply to the objections of the writer of a Popish book, intituled, The Catholic Christian Instructed, etc.*, published by R. Manby and H. S. Cox, in 12mo, 1744. HW's copy is Hazen, *Cat. of HW's Lib.*, No. 1574.

42. Rigby also reported this anecdote to Williams: 'The Speaker has got a great number of Middleton's *Letters from Rome* printed of[f] with the quotations left out, to distribute in the country in these unsettled times to prevent people from turning Papists, and has styled 'em in the title-page *Popery Unmasked:* I saw one of 'em lay upon Hory's table this morning, and as soon as he gave me the account, longed to be first to give it you' (Rigby to Williams, Saturday [7 July 1744], Williams MSS lxviii, f. 69).

43. Susannah Bunbury (1700–64), m. William Handasyd; housekeeper at Windsor ca 1756–64, 'a fine place,' according to Lady Mary Coke, worth £600 a year (Lady Mary Coke, *Letters and Journals*, ed. Home, Edinburgh, 1889–96, i. 16). HW's affection for her is shown in his letter to Montagu of 10 Sept. 1750 (MONTAGU i. 111). Rigby wrote to Williams on 21 June that he and HW often spent their evenings with 'Mrs Handyside and her daughter.' In

another letter he mentions this particular dinner (Rigby to Williams, Thursday [21] June [1744], Saturday [7 July 1744], Williams MSS lxviii, ff. 57, 68).

44. Presumably Susannah Handasyd (b. ante 1734), mentioned in her father's will, dated 5 Feb. 1733/34 (P.C.C. 169 Seymour).

45. William Handasyd (d. 1745), Col. of the 31st Foot 1737–45; Brig.-Gen., 1743 (GM 1745, xv. 164; *Archæologia Æliana*, 3d ser., iv. 144; Richard Cannon, *Historical Record of the Thirty-First . . . Foot*, 1850, pp. 217–8; Robert Beatson, *Political Index*, 3d edn, 1806, ii. 149). There are some dozen recorded spellings of the family name (Northumberland County History Committee, *A History of Northumberland*, Newcastle-upon-Tyne, 1893–1940, xv. 471–2), but Gen. Handasyd spells it as above in his will (P.C.C. 169 Seymour).

46. Augusta (1719–72) of Saxe-Gotha, m. (1736) Frederick Louis, P. of Wales.

47. Of Cumberland. 'Last Saturday night [7 July] their Royal Highnesses the Prince and Princess of Wales, and the Duke of Cumberland, were at Ranelagh Gardens' (*Daily Adv.* 9 July 1744).

48. It also led him to write to Williams that evening the letter in Williams MSS lxviii, ff. 68–9.

49. 'You, as your business and desire
    shall point you,
. . . and for my own part,
Look you, I'll go pray'
        (*Hamlet* I. v. 129–32).

I must however see you stretch into a second sheet of paper, before I hold it decent for me to say every thing that comes into my head— At that rate I should be writing you journals of my life and conversation, instead of letters. And though to be sure all I do may be of most material consequence to me, it can be of none to you; so good night—

Yours faithfully,

Hor. Walpole

To C. H. Williams, Tuesday 17 July 1744

Printed from a photostat of the MS in the Newport Public Library, Newport, Monmouth. First printed, Toynbee *Supp*. iii. 362–6.

Arlington Street, July 17, 1744.

My dear Williams,

I SUPPOSE you will be returned from Cheltenham, before this arrives at Coldbrook: if you are not, it may wait; for I am sure there will be nothing in it, that will not be full as new a fortnight hence as today. There are not people enough left in town to make anything happen; or to propagate it, if it did: all communication is at an end between the several parts of the town: the few that remain in the several streets seem to live only in adjacent counties: I just know that the Duchess of Manchester lives in Dovershire;[1] and from thence to Upper Grosvenor Street, there is not an inhabited house. The house of our acquaintance there,[2] is only peopled by Scotch. My Lady was ill on Sunday: I went there only in the evening, and found nothing but old Mark Kerr and Lord Dumfries. Mr Mackensie[3] had dined there. You know he was sent away at short

1. Dover Street, Piccadilly.
2. Lady Townshend. J. de Pesters wrote to Lady Denbigh a few days later 'Lady T[ownshend] aura sa maison vuide. Elle est brouillée avec le sommeil depuis huit ou dix jours, et cette privation de sommeil provient de ce que son second fils a changé son fièvre contre le haut mal. . . . On l'a envoyé à Scarborough; cependent la bonne dame, qui croit aimer beaucoup ce fils, a pris cet air dolent qu'elle avait un jour que nous dînions chez elle' (26 July

1744, Hist. MSS Comm., *Denbigh MSS*, 1911, p. 182). Lady Townshend was about to leave her house in Upper Grosvenor Street, having just purchased a house in Whitehall; see *ante* Wednesday ?1743–1744 (heading).

3. Hon. James Stuart-Mackenzie (1719–1800), brother of the E. of Bute; M.P. Argyllshire 1742–7, Buteshire 1747–54, Ayr burghs 1754–61, Ross-shire 1761–80; keeper of the Great Seal of Scotland 1763–5, 1766–1800.

notice from Berlin at Lord Hyndford's[4] request;[5] for which I think he is most reasonably enraged at him.[6] If one's father is dead, I don't conceive any other friend or relation on earth interposing by force to hinder my marrying a Barberina. When I was in Italy, the Duke de St Aignan's[7] son[8] had actually married an opera girl: they got her seized and confined; sent him to Paris and dissolved the match, though consummated.

Mr Mckensie is very ill with his love and fatigues,[9] and spits blood; so perhaps the noble blood of the Campbells and Stuarts[10] may yet avoid pollution: he is going to Bristol with George Pitt. In short everybody is gone or going. I find I must go[11] after all; though it will

4. John Carmichael (1701–67), 3d E. of Hyndford; diplomatist; envoy to Prussia 1741–4.

5. Mackenzie had fallen in love with the 'Barbarina,' a ballet dancer (see *ante* 13 Sept. 1741 OS, n. 3), whom he planned to marry at Venice. However, his uncle, Archibald, Duke of Argyll, working through his friend Lord Hyndford and the Court of Berlin, had the Barbarina arrested by order of the Senate and sent under guard to Berlin where she had a previous contract to dance for the winter. Mackenzie followed her, but was frustrated by Lord Hyndford: 'On alighting from his carriage, he [Mackenzie] was saluted with a peremptory order to quit the King of Prussia's dominions in four-and-twenty hours; and a file of unpitying grenadiers forthwith escorted him beyond the frontier' (Lady Louisa Stuart, 'Memoir' of John, Duke of Argyll, in Lady Mary Coke, *Letters and Journals*, ed. Home, Edinburgh, 1889–96, i. pp. lii-lv).

6. Mackenzie sent a challenge to Hyndford 'who laughed, and put it in the fire' (Lady Louisa Stuart, op. cit. i. p. liv).

7. Paul-Hippolyte de Beauvillier (1684–1776), Duc de Saint-Aignan; French ambassador to Spain 1715–18, to Rome 1730–40; Governor of Bourgogne 1740–54 (*Dictionnaire de biographie française*, 1933–, v. 1220–1; MANN i. 12 n. 52).

8. Paul-Louis-Victor de Beauvillier (b. 1714), 4th son of the Duc de Saint-Aignan; abbé of Lagny, 1733 (La Chenaye-Desbois ii. 769; *Répertoire . . . de la Gazette de France*, ed. de Granges de Surgères, 1902–6, i. 290). HW's account of the incident,

which occurred in September 1739, shortly before he reached Italy, is slightly confused. The Abbé secretly resigned his benefices, eloped with a jeweller's daughter (whose mother had previously been his mistress), and married her at the first town on their flight from Rome. He was arrested at Florence on his father's order and confined until he could be sent back to France. The marriage was eventually dissolved on a technicality (Charles de Brosses, *Le Président de Brosses en Italie*, ed. R. Colomb, 2d edn, 1861, ii. 91–3; *Recueil des instructions données aux ambassadeurs . . . Rome*, ed. Gabriel Hanotaux, 1888–1936, iii. 76 n. 1; Maurice Boutry, *Intrigues et missions du Cardinal de Tencin*, 1902, pp. 145–6; Mann to John Courand 7 Sept. 1739 NS, Public Record Office, S.P. 98/42 f. 210; Florence newsletters 7 Sept., 12 Oct. 1739 NS, ibid. ff. 213, 244; John Walton's [i.e. Baron Stosch's] dispatch of 6 Sept. 1739, S.P. 98/41 f. 340).

9. According to Lady Louisa Stuart, Mackenzie 'committed every extravagance which love and rage could dictate, till the conflicts of his mind, overpowering his bodily strength, threw him into a dangerous fever' (Lady Louisa Stuart, op. cit., i. p. liv). Mackenzie's eventual recovery was accelerated by the discovery that the Barbarina had married someone else (ibid.).

10. Mackenzie's mother was Lady Anne Campbell, dau. of the 1st D. of Argyll; his father's family were descended from an illegitimate son of Robert II of Scotland.

11. To Houghton. Lord Orford had written to HW on 14 July urging him to come; HW decided to go for six weeks

be like what children call the parson and clerk[12] in burnt paper, the last spark of all. I will let you know before I set out,[13] and hope you won't forget your promise.[14]

All foreign news I think is gone out of town as well as domestic. Prince Charles's great passage of the Rhine seems to end in his having passed it;[15] one hears no more of it. The news Winnington sent you of his defeat[16] was not true. My Lord Carteret says this passage has gained *him* a reprieve for another year.[17]

Your friend Rigby and I made a little tour yesterday to see places. You know my laziness hates expeditions, and therefore I easily comfort myself when they don't answer. We went to Cannons:[18] did you ever see it? You know it was always the great standard of bad taste: 'tis now the ruins of it.[19] The garden is demolished, as if to contradict

(HW to Mann 22 July 1744, Mann ii. 481), but postponed his departure as long as possible, finally leaving London in mid-August.

12. The earliest quotation of this phrase in OED (*sub* parson 6) is from HW to Hannah More 22 Sept. 1788; see More 285 n. 3.

13. HW wrote three more letters to Williams (*post* 26 July, 7 Aug., 14 Aug.) before he finally left London.

14. To visit him at Houghton. Williams did not go (*post* 14 Aug. 1744).

15. Between 30 June and 3 July NS (*ante* 7 July 1744, n. 3). HW makes a similar comment in his letter to Mann 22 July 1744 (Mann ii. 481).

16. Winnington's letter to Williams, 7 July 1744, informing him that 'bad news is arrived from Paris and Dunkirk that Marshal Coigny has forced Prince Charles's lines at Weissenberg and defeated a great part of his army which I am afraid is too true though no accounts are arrived here of the battle' is in Williams MSS lxviii, f. 101. Fox explained a few days later, however, that the defeat, 'which was at that time both reported and believed generally . . . was founded only on that advantage gained at Weissenbourg, by Coigny, in taking what was disputed by one regiment only, with his whole army. He called it *déroute totale* and sent M. de Croissy his son-in-law to the King of France with the news. You'll see the Austrian account of it in the enclosed printed paper. However,

Coigny's march by which he joined his whole force together at Weissenbourg, and is since (having abandoned Weissenbourg) got to Haguenau, and so is between Straasbourg and Prince Charles, is reckoned a very masterly thing' (Fox to Williams 16 July 1744, Williams MSS xlviii, f. 87).

17. Carteret was under attack by the Opposition for his conduct of the war and was being intrigued against by his own colleagues who were jealous of his share of royal favour. He resigned in November 1744 after Orford advised the King to remove him. See especially J. B. Owen, *The Rise of the Pelhams*, 1957, Chap. VI.

18. Cannons Park, Little Stanmore, Middlesex, seat of James Brydges (1674 – 9 Aug. 1744), 9th Bn Chandos; cr. (1714) E. of Carnarvon and (1719) D. of Chandos. The house was built 1713–23 with the wealth Chandos acquired as paymaster of the forces 1705–13, at a cost usually estimated at £200,000; HW notes that bills to the amount of £170,000 were found in the house ('Book of Materials,' 1759, p. 4). The house was pulled down in 1747. It is described in detail by C. H. Collins Baker and M. I. Baker in *The Life and Circumstances of James Brydges, 1st Duke of Chandos*, Oxford, 1949, *passim*, esp. pp. 114–51, from expense accounts and inventories now in the Huntington Library.

19. The Duke's losses in stock speculation, beginning with the South Sea scheme, made it necessary for him to economize almost as soon as the house was completed

Pope's *Epistle*.[20] An old domestic[21] that showed us the house lamented extremely the evergreen hedges;[22] and told us a man had come from over the water and brought my Lord Duke a plan for laying it all open—and added the nobility are often drawn into those projects! He had lived seventeen years in the family and said he had passed many hours with the late Duchess:[23] by the way he never would mention the present.[24] His late lady was a great painter:[25] there is an admirable immense picture of her, drawing the Duke's portrait, by one Vandernime.[26] He is in a Roman habit with buskins and cerulean stockings. The last room we were carried into, was all patchwork;

(Collins Baker, op. cit. *passim*, esp. pp. 160–2).

20. The description of Timon's villa in Pope's 'Epistle to Lord Burlington' was generally believed to represent Cannons, but present-day scholars have shown that it was taken from other places as well (George Sherburn, ' "Timon's Villa" and Cannons,' *Huntington Library Bulletin*, No. 8, Oct. 1935, pp. 131–52; 'Timon and the Duke of Chandos,' Appendix B in Pope's *Epistles to Several Persons*, ed. F. W. Bateson, 1951, pp. 164–8). HW doubtless had in mind

'His gardens next for admiration call'

etc. (ll. 113 ff.) particularly the lines (which he later misquoted in his 'Essay on Modern Gardening,' *Works* ii. 525),

'Grove nods at grove, each alley has a brother,
And half the platform just reflects the other.'

21. Probably Richard Lund, Groom of the Chambers to the Duke of Chandos. He joined the family about 1727, and for several years one of his principal duties was showing the house to visitors, though after 1735 the task frequently lapsed to the Duke's housekeeper (Collins Baker, op. cit. 84, 181–2).

22. Iron balustrading rather than walls or hedges was used to form the divisions in the gardens at Cannons, but most of these had been removed several years before HW's visit (Collins Baker, op. cit. 160–1; J. R. Robinson, *The Princely Chandos*, 1893, pp. 67–8). Alexander Blackwell's name is the only one associated with planning the grounds, and he is only men-

tioned in passing in Collins Baker, op. cit. 152–62.

23. Cassandra Willoughby (1670–1735), m. (1713) James Brydges, 1st D. of Chandos (Collins Baker, op. cit. 422).

24. Lydia Catherine van Hatten (ca 1693–1750), m. (1) Sir Thomas Davall, Kt (d. 1714), of Ramsey, Essex; m. 2 (1736) James Brydges, 1st D. of Chandos. 'The Duke of Chandos's marriage has made a great noise; and the poor Duchess is often reproached with being bred up in Burr Street, Wapping' (Mrs Pendarves to Dean Swift 22 April 1736, in *The Autobiography and Correspondence of . . . Mrs Delany*, ed. Lady Llanover, 1861–2, i. 555); but for her family, see J. R. Robinson, *The Princely Chandos*, 1893, pp. 191–4; and Collins Baker, op. cit. 418–20.

25. Lord Wilton's description of Cannons, ca 1745, mentions 'a little closet belonging to the Duchess and most of the pictures are of the late Duchess's painting. One is Mrs Vincent late of Chelsea that was; and the late Bishop Robinson's lady' (quoted in Collins Baker, op. cit. 151).

26. Herman van der Myn or van der Mijn (1684–1741), born in Holland, who worked in England during the 1720's. The painting hung in the 'best dressing room' and was described by the Duke's grandson in 1745 as 'a picture of my Lady Duchess painting my Lord's picture. It is a fine piece but not like.' Van der Myn is reported to have received 500 guineas for it, but the Cannons inventory of 1725 values it at only £80 (Collins Baker, op. cit. 150, 164; Ulrich Thieme and Felix Becker, *All-gemeines Lexikon der Bildenden Künst-*

which as old Trifaldin[27] told us, was composed by my Lady Duchess out of the remnants of all the furniture—for says he, *as her Grace understood painting, it let her mightily into the upholstery-business.* We laughed excessively at this observation; and I beg you will remember it, for 'tis quite new. We saw Cashiobury[28] and More Park[29] —dined miserably at a miserable inn at Watford and came home tired. I'll go no more of these journeys; before I make my great one into Norfolk; they don't prepare me, but deter me.

How can you ask one for particulars of such a mob story as that about the Duke[30] and Lady Anne Montagu?[31] If I were at Houghton, I could excuse your imagining I knew anything of it. I dare say you will have heard it with numerous circumstances at Cheltenham: I believe it came from some waters originally.

With my narrow shoulders I heaved four people t'other night to Vauxhall—but alas! I am not fashionable! I am neither Duke of Richmond, to be agreeable from my royal blood,[32] nor Lord Cobham,[33] to be sensible for having some sensible nephews.[34] Who do

---

ler, Leipzig, 1907–50, xxv. 308; Michael Bryan, *Dictionary of Painters and Engravers*, ed. Williamson, 1903–5, v. 248; DNB.

27. The squire of the Distressed Duenna in *Don Quixote* Pt II, Chap. XXXVI.

28. Cassiobury Park, near Watford, Herts, seat of the Earl of Essex. HW paid another visit in Sept. 1761, described in his 'Journals of Visits to Country Seats,' *Walpole Society*, 1927–8, xvi. 37. The house is illustrated and described, among other places, in Charles Latham, *In English Homes*, 1904–9, i. 405–12; *Country Life*, 1910, xxviii. 392–400; and Llewellynn Jewitt and S. C. Hall, *The Stately Homes of England*, 1st ser., [1873], pp. 308–21.

29. Moor Park, near Rickmansworth, Herts, seat of the late Benjamin Styles (d. 1739). HW paid another visit there in July 1760 after Lord Anson had purchased the property (HW's 'Journals of Visits to Country Seats,' *Walpole Society*, xvi. 24; HW to Montagu 4 July 1760, MONTAGU i. 285). The house is illustrated and described in *Vict. Co. Hist. Herts* ii. 377–8, and Christopher Hussey, *English Country Houses, Early Georgian 1715–1760*, 1955, pp. 43–7.

30. Of Cumberland.

31. Probably Lady Anne Montagu (ca 1715–66), dau. of George Montagu, cr. (1715) E. of Halifax; m. (1750) Joseph Jekyll, of Dallington, Northants (George Baker, *History and Antiquities of the County of Northampton*, 1822–41, i. 132); see MONTAGU for several references to her. 'The Duke is fallen desperately in love with Lady Ann Mountague, and it is generally reported as well as universally believed that she has miscarried by him, her Ladyship being much in Miss Vain's style, seemingly very proud of the honour' (Lady Townshend to Lady Denbigh 22 June 1744, Hist. MSS Comm., *Denbigh MSS*, 1911, p. 250). 'Lady A's passion for the —— and his for her, I fancy, is now quite at an end. It has really made talk enough, and I hope, for her own sake, she will never let it come on again' (Fanny Russell to Lt-Col. Charles Russell 27 Aug. 1744, Hist. MSS Comm., *Frankland-Russell-Astley MSS*, 1900, p. 338).

32. Richmond was a grandson of Charles II.

33. Sir Richard Temple (1675–1749), 4th Bt; cr. (1714) Bn and (1718) Vct Cobham.

34. Including Richard Grenville (later Grenville-Temple) (1711–79), 1st E. Tem-

you think will go to a place because I go to it? Don't you consider that I am related to nothing but a disgraced Duke of Courland[35] that lives in Siberia? And though you will make journeys to the Northern Ocean to see such people; you will never find it grow a fashion: ask my Lord Chomley or Mrs Selwyn[36] if 'tis knowing the world to go anywhere, whither the Walpoles go! When it is, I will set up Vauxhall again. At present my Lady Carteret and my Lord Bathurst[37] go every night to Ranelagh. Adieu!

Yours ever

H. W.

From C. H. Williams, ca Monday 23 July 1744

Missing.

To C. H. Williams, Thursday 26 July 1744

Printed from a photostat of the MS in the Newport Public Library, Newport, Monmouth. First printed, Toynbee *Supp.* iii. 367–8.

Arlington Street, July 26, 1744.

I GIVE you a thousand thanks for your long letter, and that is all I shall give you in return today; for I know nothing to tell you, and besides have made it so late before I began writing, that I have not time.

It is mighty lucky for me, that it will be as convenient to you to

ple, 1752; George Grenville (1712–70); and George Lyttelton (1709–73) cr. (1756) Bn Lyttelton.

35. HW to Mann 29 June 1744 (Mann ii. 467) makes a similar allusion to Ernst Johann Biron (1690–1772), Duke of Courland, 1737, favourite of the Czarina Anne, after whose death he was exiled to Siberia by the Regent Anne, and recalled under Elizabeth only to be exiled again. Catherine II restored him to his duchy.

36. Mary Farrington (ca 1690–1777), m. (ca 1708–9) Col. John Selwyn; George Selwyn's mother; Bedchamber woman to Queen Caroline (Mann i. 339 n. 33). HW mentions elsewhere her lack of curiosity to see Raynham and Houghton after the retirement of Townshend and Walpole and her fondness for ministers 'while in power' (*MS Poems*, p. 127).

37. Allen Bathurst (1684–1775), cr. (1712) Bn and (1772) E. Bathurst. HW mentions him as one of Lady Carteret's 'constant gentleman ushers' in a letter to Mann 22 July 1744 (Mann ii. 483), and again as a member of her court 16 Aug. 1744 (Mann ii. 501).

go a week later to Houghton: if it had not, I should have put off everything to have met you there exactly at your time. I am so obliged to you for going there at all, that I should certainly have preferred it to any convenience of my own. I hear the Selwyns[1] are going there, but it is not fixed: I believe you would dislike their company as much as I do. When I know their determination, I will let you know. However regulate your own motions, as you please, and they shall direct mine. The only part I desire to govern, is your bringing all your books and papers. I am sure my Lord will be as happy with them as I shall—and you know how fond I am of everything you write. You must own 'tis very flattering for me, to be one of the few that see the works of the only man living that can write.

Rigby says positively he answered your last the very next day.[2] I hope my punctuality won't be so unlucky as his.

Adieu! my dear Williams; I am ashamed of writing you such a scrap—or rather, should not I be ashamed of the volumes I have sent you already?

Yours ever,

Hor. Walpole

PS. Hartington is in Derbyshire, Coke in Norfolk, Ellis in Ireland, and Lincoln will be in[3] Miss Pelham[4] the beginning of September.

From C. H. Williams, ca Sunday 5 August 1744

Missing.

To C. H. Williams, Tuesday 7 August 1744

Printed from a photostat of the MS in the Newport Public Library, Newport, Monmouth. First printed, Toynbee *Supp.* iii. 368.

1. Col. John Selwyn (1688–1751), George Selwyn's father (Mann i. 329 n. 9), and his wife.

2. Presumably Rigby's letter to Williams 21 July [1744], Williams MSS lxviii, ff. 64–5.

3. Printed '[with]' by Toynbee.

4. Catherine Pelham (1727–60), dau. of Henry Pelham, m. (16 Oct. 1744) Henry Fiennes-Clinton, 9th E. of Lincoln, 2d D. of Newcastle-under-Lyne, 1768. The marriage had been settled since June 1743 (Mann ii. 245). See also *post* 25 Aug., 5 Sept. 1744.

Tuesday Aug. 7.

Dear Williams,

YOU have given me great pleasure with your letter; for I am
ready for our journey: I believe the Selwyns don't go, but Jack[1]
will wait on you if you will be so good to give him a place in your
coach. I don't quite understand your regulation: you can't have this
till Friday; I can't have your direction till Monday, and yet you talk
of setting out on Saturday. If you cross the country, you will be got
much too far for me to overtake you: but I wonder you won't come
by London. Winnington tells me 'tis the best and shortest way you
can come, and advises you to it. Be that as you like; all I beg is, that
you will not set out till Sunday, instead of Saturday, if you don't come
to London, because I have business on Tuesday, and cannot set out
till next Wednesday. I would not ask this, but it is only the difference
of a single day. I am infinitely obliged to you for your company, and
shall wait for the time impatiently.

Yours ever,

H. WALPOLE

From EDGCUMBE, Friday 10 August 1744

Printed in full for the first time from the MS now wsl. First printed, with
omissions, Toynbee Supp. iii. 117–9. The MS passed from HW to Mrs Damer
and was bequeathed by her to Sir Wathen Waller, 1st Bt; sold Sotheby's 5 Dec.
1921 (first Waller sale) lot 119 to Maggs; sold again Sotheby's 5 April 1955
(Major H. T. H. Foley sale) lot 203 to Maggs for wsl.

Mamhead,[1] Aug. 10, 1744.

Dear Hory,

COMPLAINT is the relief of the afflic⟨ted,⟩ and who so proper
to complain to, as ⟨those⟩ who have some knowledge of the
cause of our distress? You see already whereabouts I am; but I promise you beforehand that, after this time, I will trouble you no more
with whining, though I propose to myself the pleasure of writing to

1. Perhaps John Selwyn (ca 1709–51)
the younger; M.P. Whitchurch 1734–51
(Venn, *Alumni Cantab.*; Judd, *Members
of Parliament* 330).

1. In Devon, 8 miles s. of Exeter, seat of
Thomas Ball (below, n. 4).

you now and then, if you permit. I do not choose you before all the
rest of my acquaintance only because I had rather talk to you than
anybody else, and upon a subject I love most, but because I think
you have more feeling, and will be more sensible of my present uneasiness. You will be going, or gone, into Norfolk, when this comes
to your hands. I know how unwillingly you leave London, and how
you will regret the common course of the ordinary pleasures of that
place. Judge then, by your own example, what I feel, who was forced
to quit the only perfect happiness I ever knew, as soon as I had obtained it. By this time you begin to laugh at me; and well you ma⟨y,⟩²
for who would have thought that I, ⟨who⟩ never cared for any past
sixteen, and who shuddered at the thought of a wrinkled belly,
should be mad for love of a little whore,³ after eight years acquaintance, and three or four children? But I want to know how you go
on with her, and whether you have been to see her. Pray, dear Hory,
do not refuse me an account of what you know concerning her since
I left London, as who appears with her at Ranelagh, if any except the
tailor. Who knows but I am now applying for intelligence to a happy
rival? I am sure, if her word goes for anything, it may be so. And to
tell you the truth, as I know she must and will do bawdy with somebody, I should be as little vexed to hear she had with you as anybody.
This is an amour that in its nature cannot admit of much delicacy;
and my chief jealousy is for the possession of my part of a whole
which neither I, nor any other will be able to keep entire. I cannot
help thinking that I am obliged to a piece of your advice to her, for
the success I have had, and that she made me happy only that I
should be the more miserable at leaving her, which was your counsel
one night, when she said she wished she knew how to plague me. But
'tis time now to have done with her.

You know what I have left; now hear what I am come to. After
four days living in a coach, we're at last arrived at Mamhead, the
seat of one Mr Ball⁴ (from whence I now write). If it was possible to

2. The rest of this sentence and the
five following are printed for the first
time.

3. The Kitten; not further identified;
d. April 1745 (*post* 25 June 1745). According to Fox, Edgcumbe had admired her
for nine years, but she did not become
his mistress until the end of July 1744
(Fox to Williams 2 Aug. 1744, Williams

MSS xlviii, f. 93). Other anecdotes are in
HW's *MS Commonplace Book of Verses*,
p. 43, and *ante* 7 July 1744, n. 33.

4. Thomas Ball or Balle (d. 1749); see
Richard Polwhele, *History of Devonshire*,
1793–1806, ii. 155–6 for a more favourable
portrait of him, with an emphasis on his
activity in planting the famous woods on
the estate.

give you any idea of the place and the owner of it, I would attempt a description. But to give you a general notion of it, you must know that our landlord is what is called a humourist, that is to say a mule of such a stubborn temper that he does no one thing that any other person would, or would have him do. For a specimen, he has an admirable good house; and because his friends have told him he ought to furnish it, for that very reason he chooses to have a dunghill in every room of it. I am now in as fine an apartment as ever you saw, the whole furniture of which is a bawdy-house table and three or four broken chairs. In my bedchamber there is but one; and all the floors are strewed with t—ds of dogs, who are much more reasonable beasts than their master. Yet this is the prime favourite of my father, who always passes two or three days with him both going and coming.

If Sir Charles Williams is with you, pray assure him of my respects; and tell him that I shall endeavour to make his instalment[5] a pretence for coming to town before my father. I know you will be merry with him over this letter, which you have my free leave to show him: and I shall be very glad to contribute any amusement to you in a country where you want it, being very truly and sincerely, dear Hory,

Your most obedient humble servant,

R. EDGCUMBE

My direction is to Mount Edgcumbe near Plymouth, Devon.

To C. H. WILLIAMS, Tuesday 14 August 1744

Printed from a photostat of the MS in the Newport Public Library, Newport, Monmouth. First printed, Toynbee *Supp.* iii. 369–72.

Arlington Street, Aug. 14, 1744.

MY poor Williams, how concerned I am you are ill![1] what a disappointment it is to me! I feared it would happen so when

5. Williams had been named K.B. 28 May 1744. The installation took place 20 Oct. (W. A. Shaw, *The Knights of England*, 1906, i. 169). See also *post* 10 Sept., 19 Sept. 1744.

1. Fox's letters to Williams indicate that the latter had been complaining of his health since the beginning of August: 'Your account of yourself, and your Cheltenham waters agrees so ill with what my brother told me was your intention,

I saw your letter to Winnington[2] wrote by your servant. I had proposed a great scene of pleasure in a place where I never have any. Don't expect I should bear the losing all this with my usual apathy. The hopes you had given me of tumbling over all your manuscripts, and your new pieces, which by the way I won't lose, made me figure my journey to Houghton without my usual reluctance. Then I had packed up volumes of plays, and in short, I don't know what you intended, but I intended to like it vastly. And now all this is not only knocked on the head, and I am still to go, but you are ill, which is most real concern to me. I insist upon the first well-lines that you can write yourself.

We are all in confusion, that is the ministry, which I don't know why I call *we*, for I am sure I am not of the *we;* this rascally King of Prussia has given such a checkmate to all our laurels![3] I don't understand his minister's[4] publishing by his own authority[5] that address to the people of England[6] against the King and the allies: though

and is Hory Walpole's daily expectation, that I don't know what to make of it. I am resolved however not to think that waters put off the Houghton journey, so as to let that disappoint, or retrench from Maddington' (Fox to Williams 6 Aug. 1744, Williams MSS xlviii, f. 97). But Fox thought, until he received another letter from Williams, that his illness was partly feigned: 'Shall I tell you the truth, that Winnington and I comforted ourselves a little with the hopes that to be excused from an ill-advised engagement with Hory Walpole [you] had a little heightened your account of your illness' (Fox to Williams 17 Aug. 1744, ibid. f. 101).

2. Missing. Williams had also had his servant write a letter to Fox (Fox to Williams 15 Aug. 1744, ibid. f. 99).

3. Frederick, alarmed by the successes of Austria in Alsace, had re-entered the war on the French side by invading Bohemia. The news of his move was publicly reported in London on 10 Aug. (*Daily Adv.* 10 Aug. 1744).

4. Jean-Henri d'Andrié (1693–1762), cr. (1749) Baron de Gorgier in the canton of Neuchâtel; Prussian minister to Great Britain 1738–47; legal counsellor in Berlin 1747–62 (*Dictionnaire historique et biographique de la Suisse,* Neuchâtel,

1921–33, i. 329; Michael Ranfft, *Fortgesetzte neue genealogisch-historische Nachrichten,* Leipzig, 1762–77, iii. 665; *Repertorium der diplomatischen Vertreter aller Länder,* Vol. II, ed. Friedrich Hausmann, Zurich, 1950, p. 297).

5. D'Andrié informed Carteret that he had special instructions from Frederick to have the 'Rescrit' and 'Exposé' justifying his master's action printed and distributed (*Preussische Staatsschriften aus der Regierungszeit König Friedrichs II,* Berlin, 1877–92, Vol. I., ed. Reinhold Koser, pp. 575–6).

6. Frederick's 'address' to the people of England, dated 8 Aug. NS, was presented to Carteret for George II 8 Aug. OS, and published almost immediately afterwards by J. Osborne, 16 pp., 8vo, with French and English parallel texts, under the title of *Rescrit de S.M. le Roi de Prusse . . . A Rescript of H.M. the King of Prussia to Mr D'Andrié . . . whereby H.M. Orders Him to Declare . . . the Motives which Obliged Him to Supply the Emperor with Auxiliaries.* The translation was also printed in GM 1744, xiv. 426–7. The 'Rescrit' was accompanied (pp. 17–31) by a manifesto entitled *Exposé des motifs qui ont obligé le Roi de donner des troupes auxiliaires à l'Empereur, An Exposition of the Motives which Obliged the King to*

by what I find there is to be no interruption given to the correspondence. I can't bear the coxcomb; I am sure the whole manifesto and exposé are his Majesty's own penning.[7] 'Tis such a political pedant, with such mistaken flimsy knowledge! Do but mind his stupid fancying he writes to the humour of the nation, when he talks about patriots, and that nonsensical case he puts about the Pretender,[8] which is no more to the purpose than the story of St George and the dragon.

We expect news every day of the destruction of the Brest squadron;[9] which Sir John Balchen[10] has followed to Lisbon: they can't get into that harbour, for five of our men of war actually lie there: our fleet consists of twenty-eight sail,[11] and theirs but of fourteen:[12] it is not talking too English to conclude the victory ours; is it?

The *Family*[13] are gone a second time to Tunbridge, to retrieve what they lost there the week before. I saw George Selwyn sitting in his window t'other day after dinner and stopped to go up. He called out aloud, 'they are playing at pharaoh.' So they were, and the parson[14] was tallying: they have never forgiven him this indiscretion.

My Lady Townshend has taken a room at Brumpton to sleep in the air.[15] After having had it eight days without having been there

Supply the Emperor with Auxiliaries; as Mentioned in the Above Rescript (MANN ii. 500 nn. 12, 15 and references there cited), also printed in GM 1744, xiv. 427–9, and *Daily Adv.* 13 Aug. HW's copies of the *Rescrit* and *Exposé* (Hazen, *Cat. of HW's Lib.*, No. 1608, vol. 39) are now WSL.

7. The documents were drawn up by Johann Gotthilf Vockerodt of the Prussian Foreign Office (*Preussische Staatsschriften aus der Regierungszeit König Friedrichs II*, Berlin, 1877–92, Vol. I., ed. Reinhold Koser, p. 441; *Politische Correspondenz Friedrich's des Grossen*, Berlin, 1879–1939, iii. 218–9).

8. Frederick argued that he looked at Austrian manœuvres in the Empire much 'as every true English patriot would look with indignation upon all such intrigues as should be carried on in his country towards making the now regnant family to descend from the throne, in order to establish the Pretender there, and would oppose all such practices with all his power' (*Rescrit*, p. 11).

9. HW based his expectations of an en-

gagement between the Brest squadron and Balchen's fleet on a premature rumour of the arrival of both forces off Lisbon (*Daily Adv.* 14 Aug.). Balchen did not find the French ships until 30 Aug., and then no engagement took place, since the Brest squadron retired to Cadiz before Balchen's superior forces; for the incident see H. W. Richmond, *The Navy in the War of 1739–48*, Cambridge, 1920, ii. 104–9.

10. Sir John Balchen (1670–1744), Kt, 1744; Rear-Adm., 1728; Vice-Adm., 1734; Adm., 1743.

11. A list of Balchen's fleet as of 25 July, printed by Richmond, op. cit. ii. 106, mentions 23 ships, 17 of them English and 6 Dutch. Only two more Dutch ships joined him before he sailed (ibid.), but HW is perhaps including the five ships already at Lisbon in his figure.

12. Only twelve ships were in the French squadron when Balchen sighted it on 30 Aug. (Richmond, op. cit. ii. 109).

13. The Townshend family, as *ante* 26 June 1744.

14. Unidentified.

15. 'Lady T[ownshend est] à une demie

within six hours of the evening, she set out t'other night with Dorcas,[16] and movables and household stuff, and unnecessaries enough to have stayed there a fortnight. Nightshifts, and drops, and her supper in a silver saucepan, and a large piece of work to do, four books, paper, and two hundred crow quills.[17] When she came there it was quite dark: she felt her way up to her bedchamber, felt she did not like it, and felt her way down again. All this before the woman of the house could get candles. When she came down, her coach was gone; but luckily Winnington who had happened by the greatest accident in the world to come over to make her a visit, not knowing but she had been settled there for some time, arrived in his chariot, into which she and Dorcas and all the luggage mounted, and returned to London: Winnington walked back. They told me this themselves. I must tell you an admirable thing he said t'other day. We were talking of Kitty Edwin's[18] and her Ladyship's quarrel—poor Charlotte[19] with all the shining innocence in the world, said, 'But, Ma'am, I thought you visited still!' 'Yes,' replied Winnington, 'or they could not keep up their quarrel.'—I don't know whether my Lord Chesterfield has so little wit as you think he has,[20] but I am sure Winnington has ten times more.

Now I'll tell you a bon mot of Chesterfield's, which I'll agree with you in liking as little as ever you please, not from the subject, but absolutely because I see no wit in it, though he does himself, and has repeated it every day for this week, and I know twenty people that will repeat it every day for this month. He is going to my Lord Leicester's:[21] he says, into Norfolk; you are to ask to whose house:

campagne. Elle couche à Brumpton et traule les rues de Londres le reste du jour' (J. de Pesters to Lady Denbigh 27 Aug. 1744, Hist. MSS Comm., *Denbigh MSS,* 1911, p. 182).

16. Lady Townshend's 'woman' until sometime before 1766; see *post* p. 224 n. 23 and Montagu i. 47. She is perhaps the 'Mrs Runnington' mentioned in HW to Lady Townshend 12 Sept. 1759.

17. HW discusses similar details of Lady Townshend's excursions to Brompton in his letter to her, 25 Aug. 1744.

18. Catherine Edwin (d. *ante* 1777), dau. of Samuel Edwin (Mann i. 438 n. 47). She had been Lady Townshend's 'inseparable friend and companion' until they quar-

relled at Tunbridge Wells in 1738 (Lady Mary Wortley Montagu, *Letters and Works,* ed. Lord Wharncliffe and W. Moy Thomas, 3d edn, [1861], ii. 33; Frances, Countess of Hertford and Henrietta Louisa, Countess of Pomfret, *Correspondence,* 1805, i. 5).

19. Probably Charlotte Dyve (ca 1712–73), m. (1762) Samuel Masham, 2d Bn Masham.

20. Williams wrote of Chesterfield, 'Upon all my conversations, which have been very long with him, I think him extremely affected, no wit at all, less judgment, and really a very weak man' (quoted in Ilchester, *Hanbury-Williams* 58).

21. Holkham.

he replies, not to my Lord Orford's.—I am sorry you are not going thither: I don't think we should be reduced to repeat such epigrams as that. Adieu! my dear Williams, at least let me have the pleasure of hearing you are recovered.

Yours ever,

H. W.

PS. Harry Fox[22] is just come in this moment and has delivered me —not of a child, but of a great boy; which I intended to sink but he insists on my telling it you, after telling you how concerned we both are for your illness. Well then, Mr Stanley[23] came from the army last Wednesday; Thursday morning and evening we passed together, Saturday he would dine with me at White's, and at night to Ranelagh. Sunday he went out of town, not to return till today, but returned yesterday; came directly; I was not well and would not see him; he left word, we should dine at White's today; I desired he would dine here as I did not go out: he came at one to know how I did, and again at three till half an hour after eight when Harry found him here. If you can crowd more assiduity into this compass of time, do. Harry says, I have made *une assez belle resistance,* which he is sure I must have done, or he could not have stayed so long—I think that an affront to charms so powerful as you see mine are. Lord! I am tired! all my antiquities and modernities, my lares and pagods[24] have stood me in great stead; we have talked them over all, and all parties, and all people, and all foreign affairs, and all pictures, and statues and architecture, and he has drawn me the plan of Mr Doddington's[25] house,[26] and—but I have no more room. Adieu!

22. Henry Fox (1705–74); cr. (1763) Bn Holland; politician; M.P. Hindon 1735–41, New Windsor 1741–61, Dunwich 1761–3; at this time a lord of the Treasury; HW's and Williams's friend and correspondent.

23. Hans Stanley (ca 1720–80), diplomatist and politician; M.P. St Albans 1743–7, Southampton borough 1754–80.

24. HW gives a similar description of his 'antiquities' in his letter to Mann 22 July 1744 (MANN ii. 481).

25. George Bubb Dodington (1691–1762), cr. (1761) Bn Melcombe; politician; M.P. Winchelsea 1715–22, Bridgwater

1722–54, Weymouth and Melcombe Regis 1754–61.

26. Eastbury, near Blandford, Dorset, a monumental pile designed by Vanbrugh, which Bubb Dodington completed between 1724 and 1738 at a cost of £140,000. HW describes it as a 'pile of ugliness' (HW to Mann 26 Sept. 1762). Most of the house was pulled down in 1795; a description, plans, elevations, and photographs of its remains are in H. A. Tipping and Christopher Hussey, *English Homes. Period IV. Vol. II. The Work of Sir John Vanbrugh and His School 1699–1736,* 1928, pp. 175–86.

To Lincoln, Saturday 25 August 1744

Printed for the first time from a photostat of the MS deposited in the Nottingham University Library by the Trustees of the Newcastle Estates.

Houghton, Aug. 25, 1744.

I WONDER I don't begin my letter, *dear Cousin;* for these three days that I have been here, I have heard nothing but the tender titles which familiarize near relations with one another, and which once prefaced, gives them a right to say every brutal truth afterwards that comes into their head. They would think it a sin to omit apostrophizing you with the degree of parentage but look upon it as no crime to tell you your nose is awry, or as my Lord Powlett[1] said to his brother,[2] 'Dear P. your breath stinks confoundedly.' I am in the midst of all this frankness and sincerity; have twenty uncles and cousins lowing round me; 'tis quite a patriarchal establishment, and if we had but Jacob's nostrum for making speckled cattle, we might drive our wives and our herds before us with all the opulence and show of that ancient Hebrew.

Tomorrow is my father's birthday; my Uncle Horace is here—in short the whole Walpole family are enjoying one another and their retirement, and reflecting with infinite satisfaction how little true happiness they ever knew in courts and power. My uncle is quoting all the old classic commonplaces in praise of the *felices agricolæ,* and wonders at me for loving London and the hurry of business. Indeed he does read the Dutch Gazette[3] with a little too much relish for a philosopher; and now and then drops a sharp sentence against the King of Prussia[4] even in the middle of a field of turnips: I am not even clear that a Congress in Holland[5] would not set the Norwich Assizes hard—but as this is mere conjecture, pray don't mention it.

—Oh! my dear Lord, you see how willing I am to divert myself

1. John Poulett (1708–64), 2d E. Poulett.
2. His twin brother Peregrine (1708–52), M.P. Bossiney 1737–41, Bridgwater 1747–52 (Collins, *Peerage*, 1812, iv. 13–14; Judd, *Members of Parliament* 310).
3. Probably either the *Gazette de Leyde* or the *Gazette d'Utrecht.*
4. For re-entering the war by invading Bohemia; see *ante* 14 Aug. 1744 and nn. 3–7.
5. Probably a reference to the rumour, current earlier in the summer, that the Dutch were attempting to negotiate a peace between England and France (*ante* 26 June 1744 and n. 10).

with anything that can turn my thoughts from their real object—
if I were to write what I feel, how little would my letters be filled
with the foibles of other people—I should indulge my own, but as
you are the person upon earth I would not have reflect on my weaknesses, I shall not give you any to consider over at your leisure—you
know but too many of them, and are infinitely too good to love me
with so many faults as you know I have. This is the last I will say
on this subject; you see how I am forced to struggle to avoid what
I should not say.

I am come here as you bid me; and have left Ranelagh and the
Duke's[6] jovial countenance, for the deserts of Siberia and the Mayor
of Lynn.

> Nunc mihi Sauromatæ pro Cæsaris ore videndi.[7]

You must observe that *Sauromatæ* has no determined signification;
sometimes it is taken for Goths and Vandals, sometimes for Croats and
Pandours;[8] and in this letter for Townshends and Hammonds,[9] who
are a sort of northern people, that talk a very barbarous inarticulate
dialect, much like what Ovid complains of in his *De tristibus*. But I
won't talk to you any more about myself— It will be more friendly
to give you some advice for your own conduct. Besides the grave duties
of the station into which you are going to enter,[10] and which I don't
doubt but those reverend pastors Mr Hume and Mr Spence have fully
explained to you, there is another point in civil life which is very material for you to consider; and the more nice as it is particular to yourself. Any slip in this may give the world a contemptible opinion of you
for the rest of your life— I own 'tis a difficult task— In short, my Lord
as you are going into Downing Street House,[11] you must consider

6. Of Cumberland.

7. 'At mihi Sauromatæ pro Cæsaris ore videndi' (Ovid, *Epistulæ ex ponto* II. ii. 93). ('But I must gaze upon the Sauromatæ in place of Cæsar's face.')

8. 'The name borne by a local force organized in 1741 by Baron Trenck on his own estates in Croatia to clear the country near the Turkish frontier of bands of robbers; subsequently enrolled as a regi-ment in the Austrian army, where, under Trenck, their rapacity and brutality caused them to be dreaded over Germany, and made *Pandour* synonymous in Western Europe with "brutal Croatian soldier"'

(OED). See also MANN i. 144 n. 4 and Con-way to HW 27 July 1743 NS.

9. HW's aunt Dorothy Walpole (1686–1726) had m. (1713) Charles Townshend, 2d Vct Townshend; and his aunt Susan Walpole (1687–1763) had m. (1707) An-thony Hamond. HW describes the be-haviour of some of his Townshend cousins during this family reunion in his letter to Lady Townshend 25 Aug. 1744.

10. Marriage; see *ante* 26 July 1744, n. 4.

11. Later No. 10, which Sir Robert Wal-pole had had annexed 'forever' to the office of first lord of the Treasury (GRAY i. 11 n. 74). Henry Pelham, now first lord,

whom you succeed! A man of the weight, abilities, address, politeness, magnificence and generosity of my Lord Sandys,[12] will set any other man in a very disadvantageous light, without very particular attention to his conduct. Besides he had a person whose great knowledge of the world contributed considerably to assist him in making the figure he did; and I fear Miss Pelham's great youth will prevent her doing the honours of your palace with half the grace of my Lady Sandys.[13] I beg pardon my dear Lord for taking this liberty, and will only add a private request to you, which I must insist on your not mentioning to Miss P[elham]. If you have any friendship for me, you will restrain the excess of your vigour—this is a very odd boon to ask, but I'll tell you the reason of it. When you mentioned the disposition of the apartments, I observed you intended lying in the room where the last mistress of the house died[14]—now my Lord I don't desire to see her come into play again, and I am sure your vigour if exerted, would reanimate her, though she has been dead these six years: don't shake that bed too violently!

Adieu! do love me; I do you to excess: and am ever

Yours

H. W.

From C. H. WILLIAMS, August 1744

Missing; a letter which HW mentions *post* 19 Sept. 1744 as having deferred answering.

did not choose to live there, but turned it over to Lincoln who occupied it 1745–53 (London County Council, *Survey of London*, xiv [Parish of St Margaret, Westminster, pt iii, 1931], p. 130).

12. Who had lived at No. 10 since July 1742 (MANN i. 494–5).

13. Laetitia Tipping (d. 1779), m. (1725) Samuel Sandys, cr. (1743) Bn Sandys. HW describes her in a note to his 'Dear Witches' as 'an ordinary woman, niece to Russell, Earl of Orford, which title she wanted her husband to have, and hated Sir Robert Walpole for taking. She grew

a constant courtier on the change' (*MS Poems*, p. 85).

14. HW's step-mother, Maria Skerrett (1702–38), m. (ca 1738) Sir Robert Walpole. 'Last' is a slip; Lady Sandys was the last mistress. In HW's annotated set of plans of No. 10 Downing Street (now in the Metropolitan Museum, New York) he identifies 'the Middle Room, West Front, Second Floor' as the 'Bedchamber in which Mrs Skerrit, Lady Walpole, died' (reproduced in the *Survey of London*, op. cit. xiv. plate 152).

From Lincoln, ca Saturday 1 September 1744

Missing.

To Lincoln, Wednesday 5 September 1744

Printed for the first time from a photostat of the MS deposited in the Nottingham University Library by the Trustees of the Newcastle Estates.

Houghton, Sept. 5th 1744.

I TOOK up t'other day in the library here a volume of Voiture,[1] whom I have not read since I was at Cambridge, and will use his style to answer your letter.

Monseigneur,

Though you have employed the finest words in the world in the letter you did me the honour to write me, yet there was something in it, that I was more intent upon, than those happy expressions. The five lines that you blotted out, gave me more pain, than the two most eloquent sides that ever were wrote, gave me pleasure. Certes 'tis the only way your pen can give pain, when it effaces what it has wrote itself. I took infinite trouble to discover what you had erased, for a simple or injudicious sentence of yours, would be a greater curiosity even than the beauties which all the world so much admire in your expressions. But if I could have deciphered your blot, I am persuaded, I should have been happily disappointed, and should in searching for a defect, have retrieved a treasure, which nothing but your modesty would have buried in oblivion. I was very inquisitive to discover how you could write anything, even extempore, which was not proper; but on reflection, I believe your diffidence of yourself is the only point in which your judgment can fail you; and I don't doubt but your pen erred in what it destroyed, not in what it had wrote——.

My dear Lord, I can't go on with this affected stuff, which makes me as sick to write as it will you to read; yet these civil periods and unnatural turns were the admiration of the age an hundred years ago. But with Voiture's leave, I who know you better than he did the Monseigneurs of his correspondence, can easily believe what you

1. Vincent Voiture (1598–1648), courtier and letter-writer. HW's copy of his *Œuvres*, 2 vols, 1729, is Hazen, *Cat. of HW's Lib.*, No. 955.

say, that you had wrote something childish and silly; you often say such things; why should not you write them? I have no patience with people that don't write just as they would talk: if you could say nothing simple, I might admire you more, but I am not sure I should love you so well; one don't love men so much above one. I only take it ill you should not let me see it. Do I ever hide any of my weaknesses from you? Don't I always send you the first nonsense that comes into my pen? Don't I even love any nonsense of yours? and was not there sense enough and tenderness for me in the rest of your letter to out-weigh even all the stupid things that my Lord Lempster or the absurd things that Admiral Vernon[2] could have crammed into five lines?

But I must thank you for so long a letter; I did not expect it; but you know how to make me happy, and always do.

I am excessively obliged to Lady Lucy Clinton for thinking of me; but I owe it to you. My dearest Lord, do make me quite well with her and Miss Pelham: you know how devoted I am to everything that belongs to you: pray convince them of it; and assure Lady Lucy, how happy I am for her recovery.

I am not at all surprised at your liking Mrs Frier and her husband Toby:[3] but I can only ascribe to that oddness which I have often told you of, your friendship for Mr Plunkett.[4] I know him perfectly, and begging your pardon, think there is as little amiable in him, as in most people; besides he is very unpopular. I don't wonder at his taking to you; by what I have heard him say, you are like a man, for whom he had the strongest friendship when he was in France: it was the Comte de Guiche.[5] His partiality might make him exaggerate the good qualities of his friend, but with some allowance for that, I can perceive a great resemblance in your manners: I will transcribe a sketch he once gave me of him:—

2. Mr Romney Sedgwick suggests that this may be a reference to Vernon's letter to Thomas Corbett, secretary to the Ad-miralty, 30 June 1744, printed GM 1744, xiv. 391–2, where it is described as hav-ing been 'handed about in MS and after-wards printed in the papers.' HW else-where describes Vernon as 'a very foolish, popular, noisy admiral' and 'a most silly noisy popular commander' (MS Poems, pp. 51, 109).

3. Not further identified; a Tobias Frere, Jun., described as 'of the Island of Barbados' 'died of the smallpox at his lodgings in Burlington Gardens' 26 March 1763 (London Chronicle 26–28 March 1763, xiii. 297; GM 1763, xxxiii. 146). A 'Mrs Frere' is also mentioned in HW to Mann 1 Sept. 1750, and, obscenely, in Sir William Maynard to Selwyn 24 Sept. 1748 (MS now WSL). HW's use of the name, however, may be part of a joke and not an allusion to actual individuals.

4. HW himself; 'Plunkett' is an unex-plained joke of HW's and Lincoln's.

5. What follows is a portrait of Lincoln.

Character of the Comte de Guiche.

The Comte de Guiche is tall and slender; neither so handsome nor so well-made as you would imagine by the women that have liked him or the men that have tried to imitate him; but his beauties being in and natural to his mind, throw a grace over his person which no art could acquire. His good-breeding serves him for genteelness, his good nature for ease. He is of so strict honour, that he is more afraid of carrying it to brutality and quarrelsomeness than of having it hurt; and could sooner forgive an affront than forgive himself for offering one. His parts are strong and lively, but with such a mixture of levity, that one is astonished it does not affect his virtues: but though he would not regard exposing his greatest qualifications, he never risks the least of his good qualities. One don't talk of his wit, because he never says an ill-natured thing; one don't observe his complaisance, because he never flatters; and one should doubt of his penetration, for though he immediately discovers everybody's foibles, he never seems to find out their faults. He is the only man I ever knew that could tease without vexing; but whenever he rallies, the person he laughs at, is always as much diverted as the persons he laughs with. He is as constant in his friendships, as fickle in his amours, though his fickleness is rather an affectation, for he naturally has as much friendship as love for his mistresses; and oftener counterfeits indifference than he does love. He is expensive, yet generous; for he only tries to please when he spends, but is pleased himself when he gives. He is alike free with his equals and inferiors, yet loves both should know he is their equal or superior; but will never think of being either, till the others forget he is so. He loves to be thought to have a taste for all fashionable pleasures, and to have a constitution equal to them; and is really more equal to them than one should imagine from his taking so much pains to make it believed. 'Tis impossible not to be pleased when he is in spirits; 'tis impossible not to be better pleased when he is out of spirits, for in the first he only discovers the goodness of his temper, but in the latter the goodness of his heart. In short, as other people's faults serve for foils to their merit, his foibles only tend to obscure his; for his follies and oddnesses are so agreeable that you are never obliged to have recourse to his virtues to counterbalance them.

Whom folly pleases and whose follies please.[6]

I will only add as to Mr Plunkett, that if you can get over his faults, you must love him, for where he professes a friendship, which is very seldom, he even carries it to excess.—He had a sister[7] that I knew

---

6. HW also applies this quotation (Pope's *Second Epistle of the Second Book* of *Horace, Imitated,* l. 327) to Lincoln, *ante* Wednesday ?1743–1744.

7. That is, Lady Maria (Mary) Wal-

too, but for private reasons I have made a vow never to mention her—

> Fair eyes and tempting looks which still I view,
> Long loved adored ideas, all adieu![8]

Adieu! my dearest Lord!

Yours ever,

H. W.

At this point HW's friendship with Lincoln was interrupted; why is not known.

From Edgcumbe, Monday 10 September 1744

Printed from the MS now wsl. First printed, Toynbee *Supp.* iii. 119–20. For the history of the MS see *ante* 10 Aug. 1744.

Mount Edgcumbe, September 10, 1744.

Dear Hory,

SURE, I am the unluckiest fellow in the world! A likelihood of obtaining a point, so material, at this time, as going a month earlier to London, no sooner appears, than the pretence of asking it vanishes. One post brought word, that Mr Carteret declined standing,[1] and the next, that the instalment is put off.[2] But as everything is not gospel, that one sees in the papers, I hope this is false. I desire you will certify me, as soon as possible. I have a further request to

pole (ca 1725–1801), m. (1746) Charles Churchill. This suggests that Lincoln may have been among the many who were talked of as her prospective husband.

8. Pope, *Eloisa to Abelard*, ll. 295–6, with 'still' substituted for 'yet' in l. 295.

---

1. Not fully explained, though it probably relates to negotiations for the forthcoming by-election for the county of Cornwall, necessitated by the recent death of Sir John St Aubyn. There had been rumours in the papers that the seat would be contested (*Daily Adv.* 22, 25 Aug. 1744), and young Carteret, whose family had great

estates in the county, would be a likely candidate. He did not stand, however, but was returned to Parliament, 14 Dec. 1744, at a by-election for Yarmouth, Isle of Wight ([Great Britain, Parliament, House of Commons], *Members of Parliament*, 1878, part ii, p. 91). The Edgcumbes, as managers of several Cornish boroughs, would be deeply involved in the county election as well.

2. Apparently a false report; the installation of the Knights of the Bath, scheduled for 20 Oct. since late June (Rigby to Williams [21] June [1744], 21 July [1744], Williams MSS lxviii, ff. 58, 65), was not postponed.

make you, in case it is not deferred, which is to provide tickets for
the several parts of the show from Sir C[harles] Williams for me.[3] He
promised them me last summer;[4] and I should not take this roundabout way of asking him, if I knew where to write to him, myself.
Though I should not fear a refusal in my own name, yet, I think,
it will be more secure to join it with yours.

This is about the time that the K[itte]n was to set out on her travels
into foreign parts, but, instead of that, I hear that she is very ill,
and in some danger. I do not know what to think of it; for there
is no believing anything that regards her, especially from herself, or
counsellors. It may be true, and, if so, I am heartily sorry for it. But
I am more apt to think that it is contrivance; and is to be a come-off
for not going abroad, which she never intended at all. If so, we shall
meet again; but, I am afraid, if we make peace (for we are now at
war) we shall not agree very long; for I will set out upon a new foot-
ing with the lady, and I much doubt whether she will conform.

Pray, write me word if Williams can and will furnish me in time,
that in case of failure there I may apply elsewhere. *Au pis aller*, I
am sure of the Duke of Montagu.[5]

If you and Rigby[6] strike out anything merry, I beg you will make
me a partaker. 'Tis a sad thing to have no conversation, but at three
hundred miles distance, yet such is the case of, dear Sir,

Your obedient servant etc.,

R. EDGCUMBE

From C. H. WILLIAMS, ca Saturday 15 September 1744

Missing.

---

3. HW passes this request on to Williams *post* 19 Sept. 1744.

4. Edgcumbe apparently means earlier
in the summer; Williams was not named
to the Bath until May 1744 (*ante* 10 Aug.
1744, n. 5).

5. John Montagu (1690–1749), 2d D. of
Montagu; grand master of the Order of
the Bath 1725–49.

6. Who was about to visit HW at
Houghton; see *post* 19 Sept. 1744.

To C. H. Williams, Wednesday 19 September 1744

Printed from a photostat of the MS in the Newport Public Library, Newport, Monmouth. First printed, Toynbee *Supp.* iii. 373–5.

Houghton, Sept. 19, 1744.

YOU are particularly good to me to send me so long a letter, when I had deferred answering your last; I fear all the people I am indebted to will not use me so tenderly: but I am at Houghton, where I do nothing worth mentioning and hear nothing worth repeating, which is the true reason of my silence. I can't set down to write, when it is to be all spun: if my letters can't write themselves, I leave them unwrote, for I love none of my friends so little, as to consider a moment what I shall say to them. They must excuse what I write and when I don't write. But I have been still more alone than even by the common being here, for my Lord[1] and the girls[2] have been all this week at Woolterton:[3] so I was left alone with Dame Isabel[4] and the lap-dogs. Rigby came to me but the day before yesterday;[5] I believe he will do extremely well here, for he talks all the language of turnips and foxhounds, only with an accent a little too distinct; but he will soon grow more inarticulate, and consequently more understood. I assure you I am in a very hopeful way: and though you despise my Muscovite way of walking,[6] don't make at all a bad figure here. I have found riding so necessary for my health, which was very poor when I came out of town, that I go a-coursing

1. Orford.

2. HW's half-sister, Lady Mary Walpole, and Elizabeth Le Neve (*ante* 22 June 1743, n. 4).

3. Wolterton Hall, Norfolk, seat of HW's uncle, Horatio Walpole.

4. 'Mrs Isabella Leneve [ca 1686–1759], a gentlewoman of a very ancient family in Norfolk, who had been brought up by Lady Anne Walpole, aunt of Sir Robert Walpole, with his sister Lady Townshend, and afterwards had the care of Sir Robert's daughter, Lady Maria, after whose marriage with Mr Churchill she lived with Mr Walpole to her death. She had an excellent understanding, and a great deal of wit' (HW's note to his letter to Mann 13 Dec. 1759). See also MONTAGU i. 62 n. 27 and MANN ii. 36 n. 37.

5. HW had invited him in July. 'Hori who you intend to use your interest with to invite me to Houghton, has already done it in the most obliging manner' (Rigby to Williams 21 July [1744], Williams MSS lxviii. ff. 64–5).

6. There was something odd about HW's gait. Years later he twice wrote to Lady Ossory (18 Aug. 1775 and 22 Aug. 1791) that Winnington said of him that he 'ran along like a pewet,' and in the first of these letters HW added 'my march at present is more like a dabchick's.' Miss Hawkins describes him walking with his 'knees bent, and feet on tiptoe, as if afraid of a wet floor' (Laetitia-Matilda Hawkins, *Anecdotes, Biographical Sketches and Memoirs*, 1822, i. 106). 'Muscovite' is unexplained.

constantly every morning and by letting nobody go with me but my own footman who knows no more of it than I do, I have imprinted a mysterious awe upon it, and pass for a whimsical gentleman that loves nothing but solitary country diversions. How I shall do tomorrow, when I begin hunting, I can't tell, for I can't make that a tête-à-tête affair! At least by this exercise I hope to make myself strong enough to go through a winter of Waller,[7] Admiral Vernon and the Speaker![8] I carried Rigby to Rainham[9] yesterday; we wanted my Lady excessively to do the honours! I showed the house to the housekeeper, who is a new one, and did not know one portrait; I suppose has never dared to ask my Lord. I would have put one of them upon her for my Lady's and so have defeated the end of my Lord's bonfire,[10] but it would have [been] cruel to the poor creature; and might have made her been pinched and turned away a fortnight sooner than she will otherwise.

I am to ask you from Dick[11] *for tickets for the several parts of the show.* These are his own words[12]— Don't you envy me? I am in a constant correspondence and confidence with him[13]— He vents all his woes about the Kitten upon me; don't you think

       —— Cato's a proper person
To trust a love-tale with?[14]—

Oh! but I have an elegy[15] from him too—and his leave to show it you: 'tis really very pretty. You shall take this for what you desire me to write—when I am be-kittened, perhaps I may—but till then I am in

7. Edmund Waller (d. 1771), M.P. Great Marlow 1722–41, Chipping Wycombe 1741–54; cofferer of the Household, 1744 (*Vict. Co. Hist. Bucks* iii. 159; GM 1771, xli. 239; Judd, *Members of Parliament* 367); member of the Secret Committee to inquire into Lord Orford's conduct. HW describes him as 'a dull obscure person, of great application to figures and the revenue, which knowledge he could never communicate. He spoke with a tone, which yet was the least cause of the unintelligibility of his speeches' (*MS Poems,* p. 97).

8. Arthur Onslow (*ante* 7 July 1744, n. 38). HW makes fun of his 'pompous rhetoric,' in 'Patapan, or The Little White Dog' (*MS Poems*, pp. 94–112; below, Appendix 1). He also apparently made similar complaints to Conway about On-

slow; see Conway to HW 7 Oct. 1744 NS.

9. Raynham Hall, Norfolk, seat of Lord Townshend.

10. Apparently Lord Townshend had burned his wife's portraits when they separated in 1741.

11. Edgcumbe.

12. See *ante* 10 Sept. 1744.

13. HW wrote 'me.' Only one other letter to HW from Edgcumbe survives, that of 10 Aug. 1744.

14. 'Cato's a proper person to entrust
    A love-tale with!'

    (Addison, *Cato* II. v.).

HW's celibacy was known by his friends, although Edgcumbe thought, *ante* 10 Aug. 1744, that HW might have succeeded him with the Kitten.

15. Missing, and not mentioned in either of his surviving letters to HW.

my senses enough to be content with your goodness in letting me see what you write.

I am much obliged to you for your concern at my disgrace;[16] 'tis too simple a story to enter into the detail of it—I was only sorry Miss E.[17] was innocently drawn into it by those two fools Lady Caroline Fitzroy[18] and Jenny Conway[19]—but when the first had given her so ridiculous a message, it was very natural for her or anyone to deliver it, if it was only to laugh at.

You do me great justice in thinking I am concerned to hear you are out of order: I really am, and wish you well-recovered by your installation,[20] for it is not a pretty ceremony in October for a man with an ague. I intend being in town by then, but without having an ague, shall not care for the Abbey at that time of year. I shall content myself with seeing you and Rigby in your robes:[21] you will both look so abominably pink and blooming; I would not advise you to show yourselves to my Lady Townshend!

After the catalogue of the company you have given me,[22] you will not wonder I much wish myself with you; and that I should be extremely happy to think Lady Caroline Fox would not dislike my being there— At least I hope her royal cousin[23] has not forbid *her* see-

16. The nature of HW's 'disgrace' is unknown. It perhaps grew out of the quarrel with Lady Caroline Fitzroy mentioned in HW to Conway 20 July 1744 and Conway to HW 5 Aug. 1744 NS.

17. Possibly Elizabeth Evelyn (1723–94), m. (1750) Peter Bathurst of Clarendon Park, Wilts, whose beauty HW subsequently celebrated in 'The Beauties' (*MS Poems*, p. 159, and below, Appendix 4; *post* 19 July, 24 July 1746; *Miscellanea genealogica et heraldica*, 1892, 2d ser., iv. 339).

18. (1722–84), m. (1746) William Stanhope, styled Vct Petersham, 2d E. of Harrington, 1756.

19. Hon. Jane Conway (1714–49), dau. of 1st Bn Conway by his second wife; half-sister of H. S. Conway (Mann i. 274 n. 32; *Miscellanea genealogica et heraldica*, 1890, 2d ser., iii. 58).

20. As Knight of the Bath.

21. Rigby was apparently to act as one of Williams's esquires (each knight and knight-elect was accompanied by three) in the ceremonial of the installation; see the descriptions of the procession and ceremony in GM 1772, xlii. 292 and *London Gazette* No. 12992, 20–24 May 1788. Like the knights, the esquires wore crimson garments ('Robemakers' Bill for one of Lord Heathfield's Esquires,' 1788, MS bound into the Yale University Library's copy of John Anstis, *Observations Introductory to an Historical Essay upon the Knighthood of the Bath, 1725*).

22. Williams was attending the 'Maddington Congress,' a meeting of the Foxes and their friends for a hunt, which took place every September on the family estate at Maddington on Salisbury Plain. In 1744 the company which assembled on 4 Sept. included Lord and Lady Ilchester, Henry Fox and Lady Caroline, Fox's sister Mrs Digby, her two sons, and Williams. Winnington arrived on the 6th, and a few days later 'Parson' Samuel Hill (Ilchester, *Henry Fox* i. 47, 54–5; Ilchester, *Hanbury-Williams* 85).

23. Probably Lady Caroline Fitzroy, who, like Lady Caroline Fox, was a great-granddaughter of Charles II.

ing me![24] As she forbid Miss E. and as Jenny Conway forbid my Lady
Yarmouth[25] and Nanny Wilson.[26]

Adieu! my dear Williams,

Yours ever,

H. W.

PS. Let me know if Dick can have his tickets.

To C. H. Williams, Thursday 30 May 1745

Printed from a photostat of the MS in the Newport Public Library, Newport,
Monmouth. First printed, Toynbee *Supp.* iii. 376–8.

Arlington Street, May 30, 1745.

THEY tell me you are ill at Gloucester, but as I have no mind to
believe it, I will direct my letter to Colbrook. If you are out of
order, why won't you come back? You see going out of town disagrees
with you: indeed there is no such thing as being well out of town. All
that system of health and spirits and I don't know what, being only to
be found in the country, is quite exploded: the modern philosophers,
like Copernicus, have discovered that the sun stands still in London—
Everywhere else 'tis damps, and vapours and darkness! Don't you
perceive that all your irregularity, late hours, whisk at seven in the
morning, and dozing till dinner, have but added to the vermilion of
your countenance—I only speak this as to health, for mind, I don't
think it becoming to look so well!—but 'tis so certain that the country is the source of sickness, that I should not wonder if my Lady[1]
herself were to drive to Rainham, instead of Mr Graham's,[2] to reduce
her person to the sentimental standard. I saw her yesterday; she has

24. As the Duke and Duchess of Richmond had forbidden their friends to visit
their daughter after her elopement with
Fox (Ilchester, *Henry Fox*, i. 107–8; Ilchester, *Hanbury-Williams* 81–2). 'For-
bidding' visitors to HW was doubtless a
result of the 'disgrace' referred to above.

25. Amalie-Sophie Marianne von Wendt
(1704–65), m. (1727) Oberhauptmann Gott-
lieb Adam von Wallmoden; cr. (1740)

Cts of Yarmouth, s.j.; mistress of George
II.

26. Probably the Duke of Cumberland's
mistress; see MANN iii. 52 n. 5.

1. Lady Townshend.

2. Daniel Graham (d. 1778), apothecary
in Pall Mall; see MORE 30 n. 6. HW
describes Lady Townshend's most recent
visit to him in a letter to Conway 27
May 1745.

brought up Frederic Campbell[3] by eye, as nurses do children by hand. He now fetches everything at the least look— Indeed he is not quite perfect, for yesterday as she was sending him to the cabinet, she happened to put a little too much softness into the orders, and he brought a Chinese machine,[4] instead of the bottle of salts.—When he is to fetch Mr Townshend's[5] picture, she looks at Lady Caroline.[6] Poor Lady Caroline! She is forced now to romp with Spitzer, the hussar-dog; for Sir John Bland[7] has hired Mr Young[8] to eat his toads. Sir John was most extremely drunk yesterday: he gave a vast dinner to Sir John Furness[9] at the King's Arms, in lieu of a thousand pound that he had forfeited to him by a tie at gaming.[10] Rigby was forced to carry him home and put him to bed. The rest of the company finished the entertainment with pelting the mob in Pall Mall with bottles and glasses, and the whole concluded with the solemn Mr Peachy's[11] beating an officer, to the great scandal of my Lady Brown's[12] Sunday, who honours a redcoat ever since the reign of Col. Macguire.[13] That happy Highlander[14] has gained immortal

3. Frederick Campbell (1729–1816), later Lord Frederick Campbell; M.P. Glasgow burghs 1761–80, Argyllshire 1780–99; keeper of the Privy Seal of Scotland, 1765; Lord Clerk Register 1768–1816; HW's executor. For Lady Townshend's attachment to him, see a letter from his father to Lady Townshend, 30 Sept. 1746, in Hist. MSS Comm., 11th Report, App. iv, *Townshend MSS*, 1887, p. 362; HW to Conway 5 May 1752.

4. It has been suggested that this was an artificial penis.

5. Hon. George Townshend (1724–1807), 4th Vct Townshend, 1764; cr. (1787) M. Townshend; soldier and politician; M.P. Norfolk 1747–64. He had recently left England to join the Duke of Cumberland as a volunteer in Flanders (HW to Conway 27 May 1745).

6. Lady Caroline Fitzroy. She was engaged in a flirtation with George Townshend at the time (ibid.).

7. (1722–55), 6th Bt, of Kippax Park, Yorks; M.P. Ludgershall 1754–5. Rigby reported in early August that Bland had 'carried Lady Catherine Hanmer off to Scarborough in his way home' (Rigby to Williams 7 Aug. 1745, Williams MSS lxviii. f. 66).

8. Not identified.

9. No other reference to a person of this name has been found; it is probably a slip for Henry Furnese (d. 1756), M.P. Dover 1720–34, Morpeth 1738–41; New Romney 1741–56 (Mann i. 384 n. 18). He was a considerable gambler; Rigby mentions his winning 1000 guineas in an evening (to Selwyn 12 March 1745, Jesse, *Selwyn* i. 58–9).

10. Bland was a notorious gambler. His losses ruined his estate and drove him to suicide; see HW to Montagu 20 Sept. 1755, Montagu i. 172–3 and n. 3; HW to Bentley 23 Feb. 1755.

11. James Peachey (1723–1808), 4th Bt, 1765; cr. (1794) Bn Selsey; M.P. Seaford 1755–68; groom of the Bedchamber to George, P. of Wales, 1751, and to him as King 1760–91; Master of the Robes 1792–1808.

12. Margaret Cecil (ca 1698–1782), m. Sir Robert Brown, 1st Bt. She was famous for her concerts on Sunday evenings.

13. Hugh Maguire (d. 1766), an Irish Catholic officer in the Austrian service who abjured his religion and became a Lt-Col. in the British army in 1742 (W. J. Hardy, 'Lady Cathcart and Her Husbands,' *St Albans and Hertfordshire Architectural and Archaeological Society Transactions*, i (n.s.), 119–28, esp. pp. 121–

honour with his Lady Cathcart,[15] who declares she never was *really* married before, though she has three times before gone through the ceremony.

Churchill[16] has had still more hard usage. He wrote to Sir Everard Falkener,[17] to tell the Duke[18] his father[19] was just dead, and that it was impossible for him to set out yet; that as his Royal Highness had indulged him so long, he could not pretend to ask farther leave, but could only offer up his commission.[20] The Duke took it! He intends going volunteer in a fortnight,[21] which is sure very handsome and alive, after such treatment!

I give you a thousand thanks, my dear Williams, for the cider: do remember another promise you made me, which I infinitely depend upon, a copy of your works; you never forget when you promise, and this I certainly can't forget.

Rigby tells me he hears George Selwyn is found out and to be expelled:[22] a foolish boy! I have no patience with him for such dirty tricks!

Adieu! Write to me soon, and tell me what you are about. Rigby would have wrote today, if I had not.

Yours ever,

H. W.

3, 126; MANN i. 420; GEC *sub* Cathcart; GM 1766, xxxvi. 247; 1789, lix pt ii. 766–7).

14. Correctly, Irishman.

15. Elizabeth Malyn (1691–1789), m. (1) James Fleet; m. 2 (ca 1734) Capt. William Sabine; m. 3 (1739) Charles Cathcart, 8th Bn Cathcart; m. 4 (18 May 1745) Hugh Maguire. Maguire carried her off to Ireland and kept her a prisoner for twenty years (Hardy, loc. cit.; GM 1789, lix pt ii. 766–7). They are supposed to have inspired two characters in Maria Edgeworth's *Castle Rackrent*.

16. Charles Churchill (ca 1720–1812), of Chalfont Park, Bucks; M.P. Stockbridge 1741–7, Milborne Port 1747–54, Great Marlow 1754–61; later (1746) husband of HW's half-sister, Lady Mary Walpole (GRAY i. 183 n. 18).

17. Sir Everard Fawkener (1684–1758), Kt, 1735; ambassador to Constantinople 1735–45; secretary to the D. of Cumberland, 1745; joint postmaster-general, 1745;

later (1747) Churchill's brother-in-law.

18. Of Cumberland, then commander-in-chief of the British forces in Flanders.

19. Gen. Charles Churchill (see *ante* 13 Sept. 1741 OS, n. 8). Young Churchill was his natural son.

20. He had been a captain in his father's (the 10th) Regiment of Dragoons (*Daily Adv.* 21 June 1745).

21. 'Charles Churchill, Esq., lately a captain in General Churchill's Regiment of Dragoons, is gone a volunteer to the Allied Army in Flanders' (ibid.).

22. From Hertford College, Oxford, for profaning the sacrament at a drinking party on 21 May; he was formally expelled on 29 July. The details appear in the records of the 'full Committee of the University of Oxford' which banished him, printed in S. P. Kerr, *George Selwyn and the Wits*, 1909, pp. 37–43. Several letters to Selwyn on the affair are in Jesse, *Selwyn* i. 69–99 *passim*. See also S. G. Hamilton, *Hertford College*, 1903, pp. 77–9. HW's

To C. H. Williams, Tuesday 25 June 1745

Printed from a photostat of the MS in the Newport Public Library, Newport, Monmouth. First printed, with an omission, Toynbee *Supp.* iii. 378–82.

Arlington Street, June 25, 1745.

TO the great astonishment of all Christian people I have stayed above a fortnight in the country[1] by choice! but you can't conceive how I suffer for it! I have in vain endeavoured to recover the dignity of affectation, but it won't do. I have played off *épuisements,* nerves, headaches, and aversions, all to no purpose: nay, I have been laid up two days with *a pain in my voice,* without having had one card to inquire how it did. I could not be treated upon a more robust foot, if I were to wear a pair of buckskin breeches, or half-a-dozen capes of different materials. Since this unhappy fortnight at Mistley, there is not a native that makes a scruple of asking me to go to a boxing match—I even expect that Ned Harvey[2] will send for his shirt to dress at my room, or go still farther and even inject there; or that the barber's boy will want to drive me in a chaise and pair to Epsom. In short I am quite undone; Sir John Bland is rose upon my fall,[3] and has darkened his dressing-room two shades beyond what I ever pretended to. I am not quite sure that if I had the honour of being acquainted with Lady Caroline Fitzroy,[4] whether she would not have a scruple of talking downright bawdy before me, as if I were of consequence. Lord Hervey who to be sure had better care taken of his education and *sentiments,* which to us, you know, are what *principles* are to other people, has lately given a happy proof that he will not deviate from his ancestors. Lady Caroline proposed his going about with her in her chaise; he replied, 'No, Madam, anything in a room with your Ladyship; but I have not constitution

report was a little premature, since this particular 'crime' had not yet been discovered by the University authorities. Selwyn was, however, under discipline for another offence, mentioned in the following letter, during the investigation of which the profanation scene was discovered.

1. HW had been visiting Rigby at Mistley Hall, near Manningtree, Essex, for 'near three weeks' (Montagu i. 14).

2. Edward Harvey (1718–78), 3d son of

William Harvey of Chigwell, Essex; Lt-Gen., 1772; Gov. of Portsmouth 1773–7; M.P. Gatton 1761–8, Harwich 1768–78 (*Record of Old Westminsters,* ed. G. F. Russell Barker and A. H. Stenning, 1928, i. 433–4; *Supplementary Volume,* p. 71). The allusion is not explained.

3. 'Bland is more frisky and alive than ever' (Rigby to Williams 27 June 1745, Williams MSS lxviii, f. 70).

4. HW was, of course, well acquainted with her.

enough to go about with you.' Put into this all the accents, delibera-
tion, and softness that you know he inherits, and you will pity me
who am quite barbarized by living a fortnight in the open sun among
open mouths! After so strong an instance of his Lordship's being
proper for a *confidente,* you will be surprised to hear Lady Caroline
has given the preference to Frederic Campbell. They were all at
Ranelagh one evening with Lord Kildare:[5] Mr Boyle[6] his friend
kissed Miss Anne,[7] who was so angry, that it set Lady Caroline into a
violent fit of laughter, which was attended with some very liquid consequences: this she imparted to Frederic in less delicate terms, than
are generally used to describe a river-goddess's oversetting her urn.

I like Mistley prodigiously; if it were not for the house, and the
walls and the avenues, which are all bad and *déplacées,*[8] it would
be a delightful place; I have built Roman porticos, Gothic spires,
and Chinese galleries in plentiful ideas there.[9] Indeed the river goes
to sea so often, that half the day one is inquiring for water: but when
Rigby has married some great City fortune, and got a taste, which
last is the consequence of t'other, he may make one of the finest seats
in England there: I don't propose his making his fortune in Parliament, which was to have been part of the foundation for embellishing
Mistley, because those schemes are all to be knocked on the head.
The University of Oxford knowing my brother's[10] attachment to the
Church and those seminaries of learning, and depending upon his
gratitude for all the good offices that so religious and politic a body
of men always endeavoured to do his father, have come to a resolution to write to Lord Orford to desire he will not choose Rigby for
Castlerising,[11] to punish him for his insulting the University, in the
person and face of their pro-proctor.[12] As this is a reasonable request,

5. James Fitzgerald (1722–73), 20th E. of
Kildare; cr. (1761) M. of Kildare and (1766)
D. of Leinster.

6. Perhaps Richard Boyle (1728–1807),
styled Vct Boyle 1756–64; 2d E. of Shannon, 1764.

7. Perhaps Hon. Anne Seymour Conway
(d. 1774), m. (1755) John Harris; HW's
cousin.

8. HW makes similar criticisms of
Mistley to Montagu 25 June 1745, where
he describes it as 'the charmingest place
by nature and the most trumpery by art
that ever I saw' (MONTAGU i. 14–15). The
house, now pulled down, is described in

François de la Rochefoucauld, *A Frenchman in England, 1784,* Cambridge, 1933,
pp. 162–9; it is illustrated in Thomas
Wright, *History and Topography of . . .
Essex,* 1836, ii. facing p. 780.

9. This appears to be HW's earliest
reference to his desire for romantic architecture. HW later (1750) designed a Chinese drawing-room for Mistley (MANN iv.
166 and n. 2).

10. Robert, 2d E. of Orford.

11. Rigby succeeded Gen. Churchill as
M.P. for Castle Rising in October 1745.

12. HW mentions this incident in his
'Mac‑Hack‑Shock‑Knock‑O‑Thunder‑

they will undoubtedly have as favourable an answer, as they would return the King, if he was to desire them not to choose any man, for being a Jacobite. I hear they intend you a deputation too;[13] is it arrived?

I saw George yesterday morning; he desired me to ask his pardon of you.[14] He diverted me excessively with the description of their consultations and accusations. One of the most grievous against him, is, his commending Rochfoucault's maxims to the young people, which the Vice-Chancellor[15] thinks will give them a bad opinion of mankind. Dr Newton[16] his Principal has lately wrote an octavo book

Blood, Late King of the Mohocks, To Richard Rigby,' 1748: 'We have heard . . . how courageously you overthrew with a crystal mace charged with Burgundy an *Oxonian* proctor—not wont to be so overcome; and how heroically after that victory you assumed the royal dignity of monarch of the Mohocks, and yourself declared your person sacred.' HW comments on this passage: 'Mr Rigby going with Sir Charles Williams into Wales, made a visit to Mr G. Selwyn at Oxford, where they supped at a tavern, and the riot here mentioned happened. The proctor threatened to commit Mr Rigby to prison, who told him he was a member of Parliament, and that his person was sacred' (*MS Poems*, pp. 175, 176; below, Appendix 5). Williams mentions the affair in a letter to Fox 9 June 1745: 'I suppose you have heard much of the riot at Oxford. I was ill, and had gone to bed hours before anything happened; but I hear Rigby tells his story very well, and I dare swear you have heard it' (quoted in Ilchester, *Hanbury-Williams*, 91). This riot played a part in Selwyn's expulsion from Oxford, but it seems to have had no connection with the episode of profaning the sacrament (*ante* 30 May 1745, n. 22); when that incident was only a rumour, Selwyn was under discipline for a disturbance at the 'Angel,' presumably the riot mentioned here (unpublished documents mentioned in S. G. Hamilton, *Hertford College*, 1903, pp. 77–9).

13. 'I hear you have . . . a most extraordinary visitor from Oxford; G. Selwin (my informer) came to town last night, and has been before the V. Chancellor and Heads of Houses almost every day since you saw him. They move heaven and earth to find matter sufficient to expel him, and revenge in his person the affront received from Rigby who thinks nothing of it' (Fox to Williams 13 June 1745, Williams MSS lxxii, pp. 118–9).

14. 'George Selwyn has at last found it advisable to take his name out of the College Books and has been in town. I saw him only one quarter of an hour. He lived chiefly at Sir William Maynard's in Essex, he told me. I understand he has wrote to you, I suppose to beg your pardon: though the little talk I had with him, he seemed much too jocular upon his usage of us both at Oxford. He is gone down to Oxford again, God knows for what' (Rigby to Williams 27 June 1745, Williams MSS lxviii, f. 71).

15. Euseby Isham (1697–1755), D.D., 1733; Rector of Lincoln College 1731–55; vice-chancellor of Oxford 1744–7 (Foster, *Alumni Oxon.*; *Vict. Co. Hist. Northants, Geneological Vol.*, 1906, p. 162).

16. Richard Newton (1676–1753), D.D., 1710; Principal of Hart Hall (after 1740 Hertford College) 1710–53. The liberality of Newton's conduct in the affair is indicated by his letter to Selwyn of 10 Dec. 1745 (Jesse, *Selwyn* i. 92–5) and three letters to Selwyn written in 1748, 1752, and 1753 (now WSL) in which it is clear that he had only the most amiable feelings for the expelled member of his college. An attractive account of him is given in John Nichols, *Literary Anecdotes of the Eighteenth Century*, 1812–15, v. 708–10.

in his own defence, for not letting ale be brewed in his own college, but sending for it out.[17] He professes no objection to that liquor, which he thinks very wholesome, but is afraid it is an obstruction to the Muses in a morning, when to be had in college.[17a] Dr King,[18] the Jacobite Latin poet, has ruined a poor man for accusing another Fellow of imitating two illustrious heads of houses, who have been expelled for loving to make the young Fellows tuck up their gowns behind.[19] Charles Lyttelton,[20] who thought George *a good creature*, has been very warm in his defence, till a story came out of his drinking out of an old popish chalice at a tavern;[21] but since that he has given him up.[22]

As I know you love anecdotes of Lord Bath,[23] I can tell you two new ones. A friend of mine lodges over against the side of his house.[24] Four years ago when his girl[25] was alive, she broke a lower pane of glass in the staircase window; the servants did not dare tell of Miss, and they themselves have pretended never to see it, so it remains stopped up with paper. Over the staircase is the maids' room, who go to bed publicly every night, because the Peer and Peeress[26] will not

---

17. Newton defends this practice in his anonymous *Expense of University Education Reduced*, first published in 1727; 4th edn, 1741, pp. 24–38.

17a. 'Ale is a liquor innocent, cheerful, useful; and . . . my intention is not to decry the use, but only to change the situation of ale. At present it is too near me. . . . I drink it in the morning, a time friendly enough to the Muses without this pretended aid' (ibid. 24–5).

18. William King (1685–1763), D.C.L., 1715; Principal of St Mary Hall 1719–63; head of the Jacobite party at Oxford until 1761.

19. The last part of this sentence from *expelled* is printed for the first time. The only known expulsion of the head of a house for such an offence is that of Robert Thistlethwayte (1690–1744), D.D., 1724; Warden of Wadham 1724–39; canon of Windsor, 1739. He was forced to resign in 1739 and went to France, where he died at Boulogne (Foster, *Alumni Oxon.; The Registers of Wadham College, Oxford,* ed. Rev. R. B. Gardiner, 1889, i. 432–3; Joseph Wells, *Wadham College,* 1898, p. 133; Sir Richard Colt Hoare, *History of*

Modern Wiltshire, 1822–44, v pt i. 46).

20. Charles Lyttelton (1714–68), antiquary; D.C.L., 1745; dean of Exeter 1748–62; Bp of Carlisle 1762–8; HW's correspondent.

21. See *ante* 30 May 1745, n. 22.

22. Selwyn had probably just received Lyttelton's letter of 23 June, which hardly shows Lyttelton ready to give him up: 'If you are entirely innocent of the tavern business, in God's name, come as soon as you will, and put it in the power of your friends (and myself in particular) to justify your character, in the manner we would wish when that of an absent friend is arraigned in every company' (Jesse, *Selwyn* i. 72).

23. Bath was the frequent subject of Williams's political satires.

24. In Piccadilly.

25. Anna Maria Pulteney (1727–42) (Arthur Collins, *Peerage,* 3d edn, 1756, iii. 642; HW to Mann 10 March 1742, MANN i. 363).

26. Anna Maria Gumley (ca 1694–1758), m. (1714) William Pulteney, cr. (1742) E. of Bath.

allow shutters, window- or bed-curtains.[27] You shall see both these circumstances when you come to town.

Adieu! my dear Williams—oh! I forgot to tell you, that Dick[28] says he has just quarrelled with the Kitten:[29] you will stare and cry, why she has been dead these two months![30] That is nothing; he has just discovered a deathbed infidelity of hers with my Lord Belfield.[31] The last quarrel he had with her, was the night before she died, about his or More's[32] paying for her burying.

I am impatient to see what you are about,[33] or rather to see it finished, for I know you never will let me see sketches. Adieu!

Yours ever,

H. W.

From C. H. WILLIAMS, ca Sunday 4 August 1745

Missing.

To C. H. WILLIAMS, Tuesday 6 August 1745

Printed from a photostat of the MS in the Newport Public Library, Newport, Monmouth. First printed, Toynbee *Supp.* iii. 382–4.

Arlington Street, Aug. 6, 1745.

I THOUGHT you had left me off, but to show you how little I should like it, I avoid taking so fair an opportunity of being angry with you, and answer your letter immediately. The only revenge I

27. The avarice of Lord and Lady Bath was notorious.

28. Edgcumbe.

29. Edgcumbe's late mistress; see *ante* 10 Aug. 1744, n. 3.

30. 'The Kitten is quite forgot, and he [Edgcumbe] is now most terribly smitten with a chambermaid of Lady Caroline Duncannon's, but having been a week in the house with her without having spoke one word though he owns having met her many times alone, I hope this passion

will have no bad consequences, and be only a pretence for a daily bumper at each meal' (Sir Charles Wyndham to Williams 9 July 1745, Williams MSS lxviii, f. 43).

31. Robert Rochfort (1708–74), cr. (1738) Bn and (1751) Vct Belfield; cr. (1756) E. of Belvidere.

32. Not identified.

33. Williams was working on his *Epistle to Henry Fox* at this time.

will take, is to frighten you out of your senses. The French are certainly coming;[1] the Pretender come—at least the Regency have offered thirty thousand pound for taking him,[2] and I suppose they don't mean to have him apprehended in France—yet the foolish scene they have played with Belleisle[3] should teach them to dread any more state prisoners: not but if they had him, I am persuaded the Duke[4] would want to give him a Cloe-dinner[5] at Claremont:[6] Murray[7] would tell him the night, without incurring the penalties of the Act,[8] and Stone[9]

1. Belief that a French invasion was imminent was wide-spread at the beginning of August 1745. HW discusses this possibility of an invasion in his letter to Mann 26 July 1745 (MANN iii. 78), and mentions that talk of the French coming is 'quite the fashion' in his letter to Montagu 1 Aug. 1745 (MONTAGU i. 23). A letter from Newcastle to the Duke of Argyll 1 Aug. 1745 also discusses 'undoubted intelligence' that France was going to 'attempt immediately' an invasion (quoted in A. C. Ewald, *The Life and Times of Prince Charles Stuart*, 1883, pp. 85–6).

2. HW apparently had not read the proclamation offering £30,000 for taking the Pretender's *son* when he wrote this letter. The Proclamation, though dated 1 Aug., was not issued until the 6th (*London Gazette* No. 8455, 3–6 Aug. 1745; *Daily Adv.* 7 Aug. 1745; *General Evening Post* 6–8 Aug. 1745; Winnington to Williams 1 Aug. 1745, Williams MSS lxviii, f. 123; *Hardwicke Corr.* i. 436).

3. Charles-Louis-Auguste Fouquet (1684–1761), Comte de Belle-Isle; Duc de Gisors, 1742; Maréchal de France, 1741 (La Chenaye-Desbois viii. 492; *Dictionnaire de biographie française*, 1933– , v. 1336–8). He had been captured in Hanover in Dec. 1744, brought a prisoner to England in Feb. 1745, and confined first at Windsor and later at Frogmore House. He was allowed great freedom, and was finally released in July in exchange for the British prisoners held by the French. He returned to France on 13 Aug. (HW to Mann 4 Jan., 28 Feb., 26 July 1745, MANN ii. 563 and nn. 16–20, iii. 18 and nn. 12a–15, 78 and nn. 4a, 5). HW makes similar comments about the conduct towards Belle-Isle in

his letter to Montagu 1 Aug. 1745 (MONTAGU i. 22).

4. Newcastle.

5. Monsieur Cloué, popularly known as 'Chloe,' Newcastle's French cook. According to HW, Cloué was turned away about this time 'at the instance of the Duke of Grafton for whom he was to dress a dinner for Marshal Belleisle [presumably the dinner on 30 July 1745 (GM 1745, xv. 387)], but he sent word he had tired himself with playing at bowls' (*MS Political Papers*, f. 1; MANN i. 485 n. 9). Newcastle's problems with his cook, including selections from their correspondence, are discussed in Romney Sedgwick, 'The Duke of Newcastle's Cook,' *History Today*, 1955, v. 308–16.

6. Where Newcastle had given a great dinner for Belle-Isle on 29 July (GM 1745, xv. 387).

7. William Murray (1705–93), cr. (1756) Bn and (1776) E. of Mansfield; solicitor-general 1742–54; Lord Chief Justice 1756–88; M.P. Boroughbridge 1742–56. The intimations of Jacobitism made by HW (and others) are unfounded, though Murray's family were Jacobites and his elder brother James (titular E. of Dunbar), minister to the Old Pretender; see particularly *Letters from George III to Lord Bute*, ed. Romney Sedgwick, 1939, pp. xxvii ff.

8. HW is probably referring to the act passed on 3 May 1744 making it treason to correspond with the sons of the Pretender and extending the forfeiture of the estates of those guilty of treason to the life-time of the Pretender's sons (*Journals of the House of Lords* xxvi. 380; *Journals of the House of Commons* xxiv. 680–1).

9. Andrew Stone (1703–73), under-secre-

—would he persuade him against it? Your friend Lord Bath went to Tunbridge the day he should have signed the proclamation;[10] one of the Princes of the Blood[11] was at his Chantilly,[12] and t'other,[13] 'God! My Lord, I dont love setting my hand'— He stretched it out, but I don't believe he signed.[14] Our whole prospect of safety lies in Vernon[15] with six ships only.[16]—The Prince trusting to the love he says the people in general have for him, is in no pain, and has sent a page to France for French songs.

Here end my politics—I don't like thinking of our situation; the danger is too great to let one laugh at the contemptible objects that are bringing it on: *a fly, a grape-stone, or a hair can kill.*[17]

Rigby and I are going to see Portsmouth and Wilton—we talk of stretching to Mount Edgcumbe,[18] but you will not believe my resolution great enough for that. He gave you a description of my picture very different from what it deserved: 'tis very ill-painted, and for the likeness, they say one don't know one's own face; I am sure I don't mine, if it is round and fair, and blooming, and about eighteen; all which ingredients the obliging Mr Robinson[19] has bestowed upon me, who used to think mine was long and yellow, and towards eight

tary of state and secretary to the D. of Newcastle; later (1751) tutor to George III when P. of Wales; M.P. Hastings 1741–61. HW's suspicions of him are unjustified; see Sedgwick, loc. cit.

10. 'A certain Earl, who was at the ordering of it [the proclamation], went out of town before the signing it, which is matter of observation' (Lady Hardwicke to the Hon. Philip Yorke 8 Aug. [1745], *Hardwicke Corr.* i. 436–7). HW commented in November that Lord Bath had 'absented himself whenever any act of authority was to be executed against the rebels' (MANN iii. 167).

11. The Duke of Richmond, grandson of Charles II.

12. Goodwood, in Sussex. Chantilly was the seat of the Princes of Condé. Richmond's absence had nothing to do with an unwillingness to sign the proclamation; see Newcastle to Richmond 3 Aug. 1745, printed in Lord March's *A Duke and His Friends*, 1911, ii. 465.

13. Charles Fitzroy (1683–1757), 2d D. of Grafton; grandson of Charles II.

14. Grafton did sign the proclamation.

15. He was appointed commander of

the western squadron on 7 Aug. (H. W. Richmond, *The Navy in the War of 1739–48*, Cambridge, 1920, ii. 168).

16. HW's description of the home fleet as containing some fourteen or fifteen ships (HW to Mann 26 July 1745, MANN iii. 79) is more accurate. The home fleet at the end of July actually consisted of 13 ships and 3 frigates and sloops under Admiral Martin (Richmond, op. cit. ii. 166).

17. Line 54 of Matthew Prior's 'An Ode Inscribed to the Memory of the Honourable Col. George Villiers' (Prior, *Literary Works*, ed. Wright and Spears, Oxford, 1959, i. 218).

18. Near Plymouth; seat of the Edgcumbe family. HW had been planning this expedition since late June (HW to Conway 1 July 1745).

19. John Robinson (1715–45). HW notices him briefly in *Anecdotes of Painting, Works* iii. 441. A copy of his portrait of HW, presumably painted for Lord Lincoln, is now at King's College, Cambridge, and is reproduced here. It was acquired by King's at Christie's 4 June 1937 (Clumber sale), lot 85.

HORACE WALPOLE, BY JOHN ROBINSON, 1745

and twenty. You shall see it, and if you think me so like one of the seasons, shall have a copy; pray let Rigby be drawn like autumn.

I don't like your talking of my staying for your works till they are in print; you promised me a manuscript edition. I insist upon it from admiring your writing so much, not to adorn my bookery,[20] which with due deference to the memory of my canary birds, is a more considerable article in my apartment than my aviary was. I thank you for the offer of inserting Lady O.'s[21] name in your satires,[22] but I think she is too vulgarly infamous to deserve any place but in a collection of bawdy trials.

Adieu! my dear Williams; I suppose you have all the news that comes under the article of divinity, which are, Rigby's boxing the parson on a Sunday;[23] and George's being expelled Oxford for profaning the sacrament.[24]

Yours ever,

Hor. Walpole

From C. H. Williams, August 1745

Missing.

20. This is the earliest mention of HW's library; at this time it consisted of perhaps 1000 volumes.

21. Margaret Rolle (1709–81), m. 1 (1724) Robert Walpole, 2d E. of Orford, 1745; m. 2 (1751) Hon. Sewallis Shirley; Bns Clinton, s.j., 1760.

22. She appears in 'An Ode Addressed to the Author of "The Conquered Duchess,"' probably written in 1746:

'Sprightly as Orford's Countess she,
And as the wanton Townshend free,
    And more than both discreet'
                (Williams, Works i. 96)

23. HW mentions this incident in his 'Mac - Hack - Shock - Knock - O - Thunder - Blood, Late King of the Mohocks, To Richard Rigby,' 1748: 'We have heard how you encountered and vanquished in single combat a brawny priest at the Ford of

Bristol' (MS Poems, p. 176; below, Appendix 5).

24. On 29 July (ante 30 May 1745, n. 22). By this time Selwyn was trying to get the sentence of expulsion reversed and taking the Attorney-General's opinion on it under pretence that the University could not pass so severe a sentence without giving him a fair trial. 'He is now grown to talk gravely and consequently foolishly about it, he is in a damned fright and does not know how to help himself, so is stupid enough to pay a lawyer [H. Brookes] for assisting him with advice that won't avail him a farthing. The sentence passed against him is expulsion from Oxford and five miles round, and expulsion for a gownsman that should speak to him in the town or within that distance of it' (Rigby to Williams 7 Aug. 1745, Williams MSS lxviii, f. 66).

To C. H. Williams, Saturday 7 September 1745

Printed from a photostat of the MS in the Newport Public Library, Newport, Monmouth. First printed, Toynbee *Supp.* iii. 385–6.

Arlington Street, Sept. 7, 1745.

DON'T blame me, my dear Williams, for not answering your kind letter sooner; I did not receive it till the night before last;[1] having ordered all to be kept till I came back.

I have found everything in—I was going to say, in confusion—but I can't say that, for though 'tis probable the rebels may be at London, in a fortnight, everybody seems as much unconcerned, as if it was only some Indian king brought over by Oglethorpe:[2] Tooanohowy,[3] the young prince, has vowed he will not change his linen till he lies at St James's; and King George is at Kensington[4] with as much indifference,[5] as if he were to lose nothing but St James's. I don't conceive what should hinder the Pretender from being immediately master of everything, except of what the French will reserve for themselves, who are every day expected from Dunkirk.[6] Nobody is ignorant of the progress of the rebels, for the Prince is so obliging constantly to tell all the news to everybody at Ranelagh. Did you hear that he and Briton,[7] went up to Bootle's[8] chambers, and left the

1. When he returned from his visit to Mount Edgcumbe (Mann iii. 101).

2. James Edward Oglethorpe (1696–1785), general, philanthropist and colonist of Georgia. He had brought a party of Cherokee Indians to England in June 1734 (L. F. Church, *Oglethorpe: A Study of Philanthropy in England and Georgia,* 1932, pp. 116–21; A. A. Ettinger, *James Edward Oglethorpe,* Oxford, 1936, pp. 144–6).

3. Tooanahowi, nephew or grandnephew (not son) and heir of the Cherokee chief, Tomochichi (Church, op. cit. 116–7, 120–1; Ettinger, op. cit. 144). HW had probably seen him at Eton on 16 Sept. 1734 when the Indians were shown the school, a visit commemorated by Richard West in some Latin verses (*Correspondence of Gray, Walpole, West and Ashton,* ed. Paget Toynbee, Oxford, 1915, ii. 303–6; *London Magazine,* 1734, iii. 494). HW here is of course referring to the Young Pretender.

4. The King had arrived in London from Hanover on 31 Aug. (*Hardwicke Corr.* i. 443).

5. Part, at least, of the King's 'indifference' was the result of the concerted attempt of Lord Granville and his friends to play down the importance of the rebellion in Scotland, as HW himself was well aware (Mann iii. 105), though he attributed most of the confusion to Newcastle in his next letter to Williams (*post* 21 Sept. 1745).

6. HW told Mann on 6 Sept. that notice had arrived on the previous day that there were 10,000 men, thirty transports, and ten men of war at Dunkirk (Mann iii. 103).

7. William Breton (d. 1773), Kt, 1761; groom of the Chamber; Privy Purse bearer; perhaps M.P. Bossiney 1746–7 (Montagu ii. 119 n. 11; Mann iii. 106 n. 18).

8. Sir Thomas Bootle (1685–1753), Kt, 1745; chancellor and keeper of the Great Seal to Frederick, P. of Wales; M.P. Liver-

Princess and Lady Middlesex[9] below in a hackney coach: they were impatient and ran up, but were met on the stairs by some Templars who would kiss them?[10]

I don't tell you anything about our journey, because I hate writing travels: all I will say about travelling is, that except I am obliged to travel off, the next journey I take shall certainly be to Coldbrook. My picture is gone down to Rigby's, but I will make him send it up to be copied for you.

You can't imagine how much I shall think myself distinguished by being mentioned in your works;[11] I know it would be right to beg you not, but I like it too much to dissemble the satisfaction it will give me.

I am ashamed of sending you such a scrap of a letter, but I have found so many that I must answer, besides a long one I am obliged to write to my brother[12] about his wife,[13] that I hope you will forgive me. Attribute any of my faults to anything rather than to my not being

Yours most sincerely,

HOR. WALPOLE

pool 1724–34, Midhurst 1734–53 (MANN i. 234 n. 30). His chambers were in the Inner Temple (*Court and City Register*, 1748, p. 53).

9. Hon. Grace Boyle (d. 1763), m. (1744) Charles Sackville, styled E. of Middlesex 1720–65, 2d D. of Dorset, 1765; Mistress of the Robes and a lady of the Bedchamber to Augusta, Ps of Wales 1743–63.

10. Henry Harris sent a somewhat different account of this incident to Williams on 6 July: 'T'other day the Prince would give his wife a jaunt in a hackney coach to Tom Bootle's chambers: but while he ran upstairs to catch his chancellor in his whole dirt and slovenliness, a pert, lewd, young Templar below made some very familiar advances to the royal incognita, proffered a whole guinea, good Burgundy, bragged of his prowess, great practice, etc.

In short, the lady had like to have seen the difference of proceedings in her own court and a court of law' (MS in Newport Public Library, Newport, Monmouth, quoted by Toynbee, *Supp.* iii. 386 n. 7).

11. Williams mentions HW in 'An Epistle to the Right Hon. Henry Fox':
'Has my young Walpole, blest with truest taste,
Adorned with learning, with politeness graced,
When I repeated, thought the moments long,
Friend to the poet, partial to his song?'
          (Williams, *Works* ii. 145)

12. His eldest brother, Lord Orford.

13. HW's letter to his brother is missing. Lady Orford had recently arrived in England (HW to Mann 6 Sept. 1745, MANN iii. 104).

To C. H. Williams, Saturday 21 September 1745

Printed from a photostat of the MS in the Newport Public Library, Newport, Monmouth. First printed, Toynbee *Supp.* iii. 387–9.

Arlington Street, Sept. 21, 1745.

My dear Williams,

IF you have been able to conceive anything that has happened on our side these two years, you may conceive how the Pretender's boy with three thousand banditti has been able to march the whole length of Scotland, and take possession of Edinborough[1] where he now is. If you can conceive how a man[2] who has betrayed all parties and ministers without deceiving any, who without any degree of parts has not only turned out ministers who had parts,[3] but has kept himself minister for twenty years together,[4] though the chief cause of every miscarriage for which they suffered; if you can conceive why old generals[5] who are past service are employed, or men who never saw any service[6] made generals in the very country of those old ones, who if they remember anything, it must be just their own spot; if, why we keep vast fleets to bully one town,[7] without doing them any damage, and that at a vast distance, while we are effectually bullied at home by a superior power; if, why we sent three thousand men to save Ostend,[8] after we thought it must be gone, and when we had not three more in England, which at that very instant we thought was going too: if you can conceive all the men of power in Scotland, posting to London[9] the moment they were wanted at home—but that I

1. On 17 Sept. (*London Gazette* No. 8468, 17–21 Sept. 1745). The news reached London on the night of 20 Sept. (*Hardwicke Corr.* i. 456).

2. Newcastle.

3. Sir Robert Walpole and Lord Carteret. See J. B. Owen, *The Rise of the Pelhams*, 1957, pp. 7–8, 127–8 for a vigorous dissent.

4. Newcastle had been secretary of state since 1724.

5. Lord Stair and Marshal Wade.

6. Sir John Cope, commander-in-chief in Scotland, who had had little military service; HW makes a similar criticism of him in a letter to Mann 27 Sept. (Mann iii. 117).

7. Mr Romney Sedgwick points out that the Mediterranean squadron had threated to bombard Naples in 1742 if Charles III refused to withdraw his troops from Lombardy (see Mann ii. 15–16). It was now patrolling off Cadiz and Genoa instead of coming home to reinforce the weak Channel squadron.

8. Two battalions numbering about 600 men had been sent to Ostend at the end of July (Mann iii. 78 and nn. 3, 4). At the same time HW estimated the number of troops in England at 'not five thousand,' a figure accepted by the French themselves (Mann iii. 79 and n. 8).

9. HW reported on 6 Sept. that the Dukes of Argyll and Athol were 'come post to town' (Mann iii. 102).

believe you can conceive, because they are Scotchmen—or why the Parliament is not called,[10] when the whole body of our acts of Parliament for above these last fifty years is attacked by the avowed enemy of all Parliaments—if you can comprehend these mysteries, you may the case of the rebels, because the same persons have suffered their progress, who in all the other instances paved the way for them.[11] You see how freely I write to you, but I am not afraid of my letters being opened—for there is a rebellion on foot, and to open letters would be to get intelligence—and that they don't know anything, is the best excuse I can find for the ministry.

The rebels are in possession of Edinborough, to the number of five or six thousand.[12] Cope[13] is at Dunbar,[14] twenty miles east, with about three thousand.[15] Some Dutch are in Burlington Bay;[16] the rest are all arrived in the River, and are marching north.[17] The rebels seem as ill-conducted as we are; we give one another time mutually.

10. Parliament was scheduled to meet on 19 Sept., but on the 18th it had been further prorogued to 17 Oct. (*Daily Adv.* 19 Sept.; *London Gazette* No. 8468, 17–21 Sept.; Owen, op. cit. 280).

11. In a letter to Mann on 20 Sept., HW distributed the blame for the rebels' progress more equitably between the inaction of the government and the success of Lord Granville and his friends in persuading the King that the rebellion was of no consequence, adding, however, that Newcastle was 'glad' when the rebels made any progress since it enabled him to confute Granville's assertions (MANN iii. 109). For the divisions in the government at this time, see Owen, op. cit. 279–84.

12. 'Old Horace' told HW on the 20th that the rebels numbered 5,000 (MANN iii. 108), but later information on the 20th reported that only 2,500 to 3,000 had entered Edinburgh (*Hardwicke Corr.* i. 456). The Jacobite army at Prestonpans on 21 Sept. actually numbered only 2,580 (W. B. Blaikie, *Itinerary of Prince Charles Edward Stuart*, Edinburgh, 1897, p. 91).

13. Sir John Cope (d. 1760), K.B., 1743; Lt-Gen., 1743; commander-in-chief in Scotland against the insurgents; M.P. Queensborough 1722–7, Liskeard 1727–34, Orford 1738–41.

14. 'On the 16th in the afternoon, Brigadier Fowkes marched to Prestonpans, six miles east of Edinburgh, with two regiments of dragoons, in order to join Sir John Cope, who was just arrived from Aberdeen, where he had embarked, and was then making a disposition to land the troops under his command at Dunbar, eighteen miles east of Edinburgh, the wind not being then fair to carry the transports up to Leith' (*London Gazette* No. 8468, 17–21 Sept. 1745).

15. The force generally attributed to him (*Hardwicke Corr.* i. 456), but Cope said at his trial that he had only about 2,000 men at the battle of Prestonpans, which was fought the day this letter was written (*Report of the . . . Examination . . . of . . . Sir John Cope*, Dublin, 1749, p. 42, confirmed by *More Culloden Papers*, ed. Duncan Warrand, Inverness, 1923–30, iv. 45). Blaikie, op. cit. 90, estimates Cope's army at 2,560.

16. Bridlington Bay, in Yorkshire, commonly pronounced Burlington. A Dutch regiment, to be commanded by Oglethorpe, arrived there 17 Sept. (Minutes of the Cabinet Council, 20 Sept., BM Add. MSS 33004, f. 83; *Daily Adv.* 21 Sept.).

17. About 2,500 Dutch arrived at Gravesend on 17 Sept. and were immediately ordered to march to Lancaster. Two more Dutch regiments arrived at Gravesend on the 20th (MANN iii. 109 n. 13; Winnington to Williams [ca 21 Sept. 1745], Williams MSS lxviii, ff. 229–30).

The general fright here has only begun since the news of their being at Edinborough: everybody now is raising regiments: the Duke of Bedford,[18] Duke of Devonshire,[19] Lord Malton,[20] Lord Halifax,[21] and some others:[22] but all that is actually raised, are addresses: the University of Cambridge presented theirs yesterday:[23] she of Oxford has only sent hers[24] to the Archbishop;[25] and I suppose a duplicate of it to Edinborough.

None of our troops from Flanders are yet come;[26] the best thing I know, is the arrival of twelve men of war from the Mediterranean,[27] who may perhaps prevent France in some degree from giving the boy the assistance which they will naturally be inclined to do,[28] on hearing he is master of the capital of one kingdom.

This is all I know; but I am persuaded I shall know a great deal more of the rebellion, before I know less. If we get over it, I shall be very happy, and flatter myself still with the prospect of an agreeable

18. John Russell (1710–71), 4th D. of Bedford. On 5 Oct. some two hundred men were sworn into his regiment, which at that time he was to clothe and pay himself (*Daily Adv.* 7 Oct.).

19. William Cavendish (1698–1755), 3d D. of Devonshire. HW told Mann on 20 Sept. that Devonshire was raising men in Derbyshire (MANN iii. 110).

20. Thomas Watson-Wentworth (1693–1750), cr. (1728) Bn and (1734) E. of Malton; cr. (1746) M. of Rockingham.

21. George Montagu (after 1741 Montagu-Dunk) (1716–71), 2d E. of Halifax.

22. HW mentions the D. of Montagu as raising a troop of horse (MANN iii. 110) and the *Daily Adv.* stated on 26 Sept. that Lord Gower had gone to his seat in Staffordshire to raise men. These regiments were commemorated in a ballad by Williams, 'The Heroes' (Williams, *Works* i. 161–6). In a note to it HW says, 'It is certain, that not six of the regiments ever were raised; not four of which were employed' (ibid. i. 161). From material in the War Office papers, however, it would appear that 13 regiments of foot and two of horse were in fact raised and that by 5 Jan. 1746 nine of the regiments of foot were on garrison duty, while four more and both regiments of horse were in the field with the Duke of Cumberland and Ligonier (C. T. Atkinson, 'Jenkins' Ear, The Austrian Succession War, and the

'Forty-Five,' *Journal of the Society for Army Historical Research,* 1943–4, xxii. 283–4, 293, 295; information kindly supplied by Mr David Erskine).

23. The Cambridge Address is printed in the *London Gazette* No. 8468, 17–21 Sept. 1745; it was presented by 'the Rev. Mr Prescot, Master of Catherine Hall, and his Grace the Duke of Newcastle, High Steward of the University of Cambridge, attended by several heads of houses, doctors in the several faculties, masters of arts, and other members of that learned body.'

24. It is printed in the *London Gazette* No. 8468, 17–21 Sept. 1745, as 'having been transmitted to his Grace the Lord Archbishop of Canterbury' and 'has by him been presented to his Majesty.'

25. John Potter (ca 1674–1747), Archbishop of Canterbury 1737–47.

26. The English troops from Holland were expected that day, but did not arrive until the 23rd, when ten battalions landed at Gravesend (*Hardwicke Corr.* i. 456, 457; *London Gazette* No. 8469, 21–24 Sept. 1745; Atkinson, op. cit. 292).

27. An exaggerated report which HW also repeated to Mann (MANN iii. 110); only four ships of the line and two smaller ships seem to have been sent from the Mediterranean at this time (Richmond, op. cit., ii. 249).

28. The French never made a serious attempt to aid the Jacobites.

winter with my dear Williams, for neither you nor I shall care one straw about the continent, when we are secure at home, though John of White's will be very angry with us, as he is already with me, for being so indifferent about the election of the Emperor,[29] which I care no more about, than for Dayrolle's[30] being of the Old Club.[31] Adieu!

Yours ever,

H. WALPOLE

PS. I hope the Pretender has not prevented your finishing all you have been about this summer, for I know I am never to see anything till it is quite done.

To Fox, Saturday 19 July 1746

Printed from the MS now WSL. First printed, Cunningham ii. 35–6; reprinted, Toynbee ii. 211–13. The MS seems to have passed to Grosvenor Bedford, HW's deputy at the Exchequer, since it was sold with letters addressed to Bedford, then in the possession of his great-niece Mrs Erskine, at Sotheby's 15 Nov. 1932, lot 485 to Maggs for WSL. Cunningham, who first printed the letter, acknowledges gratitude to the representative of the Bedfords for permission to print various unpublished letters in their possession. Cunningham and Sotheby's erroneously identify the recipient of the letter as Conway.

Endorsed by Fox: Mr H. Walpole jr, July 19, 1746. Answered.

Mistley, July 19, 1746.

Dear Harry,

WHEN I left London, I piqued myself upon paying my court to Lady Caroline[1] by some present that should make her think

29. 'John at White's rejoices that the Emperor is chose and quarrels with everybody that does not think that to be of more consequence to us than rebellions or embarkations or anything' (Rigby to Williams, 10 Sept. [1745], Williams MSS lxviii, f. 73). News of the election of Francis II, Grand Duke of Tuscany, as Holy Roman Emperor (as Francis I) on 13 Sept. NS reached London on 8 Sept. OS (*Daily Adv.* 9 Sept. 1745).

30. Solomon Teissonière, known as Dayrolles (1709–86), gentleman of the Privy Chamber, 1740; Master of the Revels, 1744; gentleman usher of the Black Rod, 1745 (MANN iii. 403 n. 7). He had been elected to White's in 1743 ([W. B. Boulton], *The History of White's*, 1892, ii pt ii. 25). For HW's opinion of him see MANN iii. 403–4 and notes.

31. The senior club at White's. It had been so called from at least 1736, but the distinction became more important after the organization of the 'Young Club at White's' in 1743 ([W. B. Boulton], op. cit. i. 34, 67–70).

———

1. Fox's wife.

me a reasonable creature, and capable of entertaining myself without music which I don't love, and without seeing a thousand people for whom I don't care a straw; but having been so unfortunate as neither to kill a brace of partridges, nor hook a dish of whitings, I am reduced to flatter her[2] in a way as extraordinary, as the other of recommending oneself by being natural and unaffected, to a woman who has been bred up in the kingdom of Herveys, Dives's and Queensburys.[3]

Lady Caroline will give me leave to wonder at her being so awkward as to like to hear Lady Emily[4] commended rather than herself; and even you who are so fond of that uncouth sense of hers, may be amazed that she thinks her sister handsomer than herself: but since she is so ungenteel, and has so many of those strange properties, called good qualities, which being out of fashion and out of character, I can't help reckoning a want of knowing the world, I have e'en humoured her in her own way, and said of her sister, what if she had been like other people, I should naturally have said of herself.[5]

I wish, my dear Harry, you loved Lady Emily as well as your wife does, and then I should have no excuses to make for sending you the enclosed lines, which I command Lady Caroline to like on pain of Dayrolle's[6] eternal displeasure: but as a fit of poetry is a distemper which I am never troubled with, but in the country, you will have no reason to apprehend much trouble of this sort: the trees at Vauxhall, and purling basins of goldfish never inspire one.

I can fairly say at least that Rigby[7] makes me send you these verses, which I have compounded to do, upon condition he lets the names stand as they are; though he contended a great while for a set of beauties of his own, who he swears by God are handsomer than any one (except Lady Emily) that I have mentioned. But as neither

---

2. By sending her his verses 'The Beauties,' which, though published with the sub-title 'An Epistle to Mr Eckardt the Painter,' were originally written for Lady Caroline. The verses, with HW's notes, are printed below, Appendix 4, from HW's copy in *MS Poems*, pp. 153–60.

3. All friends or court associates of Lady Caroline's parents during her youth.

4. Lady Emilia Mary Lennox (1731–1814), m. 1 (1747) James Fitzgerald, 20th E. of Kildare, cr. (1761) M. of Kildare and (1766) D. of Leinster; m. 2 (1774) William Ogilvie; Lady Caroline's sister. Although only fifteen she was already a celebrated beauty.

5. 'Ten queens of beauty, sure I see!
Yet sure the true is Emily (ll. 62–3).

6. According to HW, Dayrolles had been employed by the Duke of Richmond, Lady Caroline's father, at various times 'in quality of governor' to Lady Caroline and Lady Emily (*MS Poems*, p. 119; *MS Political Papers*, f. 15; Mann iii. 403–4).

7. According to HW, Rigby was the man Fox 'most loved' until Rigby snubbed him in 1763 (*Mem. Geo. III* i. 208; Jesse, *Selwyn* i. 267; *post* 11 June 1765, n. 6).

Mr Peachy[8] nor Mr Briton would reckon his ladies good company,[9] I have fought them all off, but Fanny Murray,[10] for whose sake he insists the description of Flora[11] shall at least be left doubtful by the letters F.M. in the margin, and may be wrote at length in the Covent Garden editions.[12]

I have done with excuses, and give up any merit in the lines: and will only add that Lady Caroline must forgive any private partialities in the last line.[13] As to any omission of divinities,[14] I can only say that I intended merely to mention those I think beauties, not all who are reckoned so by themselves or their court: I am no such Herculean labourer, as Tom Hervey says.[15]

Adieu! dear Sir,

Yours most sincerely,

HOR. WALPOLE

8. James Peachey (*ante* 30 May 1745, n. 11).

9. Rigby told Williams 7 Aug. 1745 that Peachey would not go to Ranelagh 'because the company is not good enough' (Williams MSS lxviii, f. 66).

10. Fanny Rudman, later Murray (ca 1729–78), m. (1757) David Ross; a celebrated courtesan, just rising to fame (Horace Bleackley, *Ladies Fair and Frail*, 1925, pp. 3–49).

11. 'How pretty Flora, wanton maid,
    By   Zephyr   woo'd   in   noon-tide
        shade,
With rosy hand coquetly throwing
Pansies, beneath her sweet touch
        blowing;
How blithe she look'd, let Fanny
        tell;
Let Zephyr own if half so well.' (ll. 103–8)

HW's note identifies the Fanny he had in mind: 'Miss Fanny Maccartney; she was a very pretty poetess; married to Fulk Greville, Esq. in 1748' (*MS Poems*, p. 157).

12. Lists that contained 'An Exact Description of the Person, Tempers, and Accomplishments of the several Ladies of Pleasure who frequent Covent Garden and other Parts of the Metropolis.'

13. 'Which   Emily   might   yield   to
        Evelyn's eyes.'
HW's note reads 'Miss Elizabeth Evelyn, married in 1750 to Peter Bathurst Esq. of Clarendon Park in Wiltshire' (*MS Poems*, p. 159). In his extra-illustrated copy of the *Des. of SH*, 1784, HW added late in life on p. 96: 'In Lord Orford's closet next to his bedchamber in the attic . . . Elizabeth Evelyn, with a book and a lamb, small life in oil from a design by Sir Godfrey Kneller, by Eckardt.' The portrait was sold SH xxii. 32 to Town and Emanuel for 30s.

14. 'The Duke of Montagu, who was in love with Miss Peggy Banks, not finding her name in this poem, added these two lines to it:
    Now ladies all, return me thanks,
    Or else I'll sing of Peggy Banks'
(HW's note, in *MS Poems*, p. 159).

15. Hervey uses the expression in *A Letter . . . to Sir Thomas Hanmer, Bart*, [1741], p. 51. HW quotes it again in a letter to Conway 2 Sept. 1758.

From Fox, Tuesday 22 July 1746

Printed from the MS now WSL. First printed, Toynbee *Supp.* ii. 85–7. The MS passed to Mrs Damer, and was bequeathed by her to Sir Wathen Waller, 1st Bt. It was bought in at the first Waller sale, Sotheby's, 5 Dec. 1921, lot 148; in the second, Christie's 15 Dec. 1947, lot 34, it was sold to Maggs for WSL.

War Office,[1] July 22, 1746.

Dear Sir,

AS many thanks as I have to give you, I think more are due to Rigby, for I have long known that it is much easier for you to write good verses than to show them when you have done. In gratitude to him, I think I shall, before you get to town, make them, as he would have everything that is beautiful be, common[2]—and when your Muse has had a week's run in the Court of Request,[3] it will be in vain for you to think of shutting her up any more; she will certainly do well there, which poor Winnington[4] used to say was the true test of a woman's beauty, and is at least as true a one of a poet's merit.

Upon my word, I never read anything more poetical and pretty than many parts of this and especially that on Fanny; Caroline commends exceedingly, but does not think there is quite enough on Emely,[5] and there is a little obscurity in the last line upon her, *but none, alas! the Goddess calls her son,*[6] which I can't clear up to her. Caroline is, I thank God, what you so obligingly describe her in prose, and as a proof of it, she admires most, and thinks Emely will best like your praise where it compares her to a village fair.[7] She hardly can allow the last line of all, even to you, but I tell her if

1. Fox had been appointed secretary at war in May 1746.
2. Despite HW's protests about circulating or publishing his verses, Fox gave them about and they were published in September; see *post* 24 July 1746, n. 2.
3. A lobby between the House of Commons and the House of Lords; *see* MANN iv. 123 n. 30.
4. Who had died 23 April 1746.
5. Eight lines in the MS; ten, in the published version.
6. HW explains this line in his reply (*post* 24 July 1746) but subsequently altered it. The MS reads:

'Whole swarms of Cupids round, yet none
Alas! the Goddess calls her Son!'
HW has crossed these out and substituted (as in the published version):
'Attracting all, indulging none,
Her beauty like the glorious Sun
Throned eminently high above,
Impartial warms the World to love!'
(ll. 66–9).

7. 'Such majesty of youth and air;
Yet modest as the village fair' (ll. 64–5).

Emely comes now so near her you like best, she may probably one day or another get before her; for that none but we plodding mere prose-writing people have any constancy in our natures.

Your letter and verses want no foil, or else they came in the midst of a dozen and half of letters, full of returns, complaints, accounts of deserters, etc., which I was forced to return to reading of, and must now go to answering, as soon as I shall have told you that the Pretender's son escaped from Sir Alexander Macdonald's[8] house in Sky in woman's clothes.[9] That we pay and are to pay Sir Alexander and his *well-affected clan* for their assistance,[10] and that the Duke[11] will now certainly be here soon, and that I am

Your infinitely obliged and faithful humble servant,

H. Fox

Pray give my affectionate service to Rigby, and ask him how he thinks you, of whose modesty at the dock-yard in Portsmouth[12] he was witness, will stand the compliments of everybody you meet, on the verses, which, seriously, do deserve all that can or will be said in praise of them. But 'tis for your good, and you won't be shy any more, and so I dare hope he'll commend me.

8. Sir Alexander Macdonald (1711–46), 7th Bt of Sleat, was only indirectly, if embarrassingly, implicated in this episode.

9. On 30 June. Fox's statement represents the prevailing opinion before Sir Alexander managed to clear himself of guilt in the escape. The Prince arrived in Skye, disguised as Flora Macdonald's female servant, on 29 June. The story from that point is told in *The Lyon in Mourning*, ed. Henry Paton, Edinburgh, 1895–6, i. 117–22, 300–2; W. B. Blaikie, *Itinerary of Prince Charles Edward Stuart*, Edinburgh, 1897, p. 53–4; *The Prisoners of the '45*, ed. Sir Bruce Gordon Seton and J. G. Arnot, Edinburgh, 1929, iii. 38–9; A. M. W. Stirling, *Macdonald of the Isles*, 1913, pp. 78–89 and DNB *sub* Flora Macdonald.

10. Sir Alexander Macdonald of Sleat and his clan adhered to the Hanoverians when France failed to aid Charles Edward with either men or money. The other Macdonald clans followed the Prince, but

through an excess of injured pride at Culloden, were partly responsible for his defeat (Stirling, op. cit. 74). Since the government did not quite trust Sir Alexander the rumour of his assisting Charles Edward's escape found ready acceptance.

11. Of Cumberland, at this time commander of the forces in Scotland. He reached London on the 25th (*Daily Adv.* 26 July).

12. HW visited Portsmouth in Aug. 1745 with Rigby on their way to Mount Edgcumbe (*ante* 6 Aug. 1745). The incident is not further explained, but whatever happened left a lasting impression on HW who wrote Bentley 9 July 1754 that he had not yet seen the tomb he erected to his mother in Westminster Abbey. 'None of my acquaintance were in town, and I literally had not courage to venture alone among the Westminster boys at the Abbey; they are as formidable to me as the ship-carpenters at Portsmouth.'

To Fox, Thursday 24 July 1746

Printed from the MS now WSL. First printed, Cunningham ii. 37–8; reprinted, Toynbee ii. 213–15. For the probable history of the MS, see *ante* 19 July 1746; it was sold Sotheby's 15 Nov. 1932, lot 491, to Maggs for WSL. Cunningham erroneously identifies the recipient as Conway, and Sotheby's as Dodsley.

Endorsed by Fox: Mr H. Walpole junior, July 24, 1746. Answered.

Mistley, July 24, 1746.

Dear Sir,

YOU frighten me out of my wits, which is indeed a fair step towards making me in earnest a poet, a title I should dread even more than that of patriot, and which I should certainly get into no wills by.[1] I will be so honest as to own that the obliging things you say to me, please me vastly: I find I have enough of the author in me to be extremely sensible to flattery; and were I far enough gone to publish a miscellany, there would certainly be one copy *To My Honoured Friend Henry Fox on His Commending my Verses.* But seriously, my dear Sir, you alarm me with talking of making those I sent you public.[2] I never thought poetry excusable, but in the manner I sent you mine, just to divert anybody one loves for half an hour —and I know I must love anybody to put myself so much in their power for their diversion. But to make anything one writes, especially poetry, public, is giving everybody leave under one's own hand to call one fool. You think me modest, but all my modesty is pride— while I am unknown, I am as great as my own imagination pleases to make me—the instant I get into that dreadful Court of Requests

1. Sarah, Duchess of Marlborough, left William Pitt £10,000 'upon account of his merit in the noble defence he has made for the support of the laws of England, and to prevent the ruin of his country,' an estate in Bucks, and property in Suffolk and Northants, on her death in 1744. She also gave him the reversion of half the large landed estate bequeathed to her grandson, John Spencer, if that family should fail. Spencer died in June 1746, having added, at his grandmother's request, the reversion of his Sunderland estates, in the event of his sickly son's death, to Pitt's prospective inheritance (Brian Tunstall, *William Pitt, Earl of Chatham,* 1938, p. 70 and references cited p. 501). HW had commemorated the last bequest in verses published in the *London Evening Post* 26 June 1746 (MS *Poems,* pp. 151–2).

2. HW comments on his MS copy of the poem: 'Some copies of this poem having got about, it was printed without the author's knowledge, and with several errors; it was reprinted more correctly, in the second volume of a miscellany of poems in three volumes published by Dodsley in 1748' (MS *Poems,* p. 153). The 1746 edition, published by M. Cooper, despite a few small errors, is in general very close to the MS copy.

you talk of, I am as silly a fellow as Thompson[3] or Glover.[4] You even reduce me to plead that foolish excuse against being published, which authors make to excuse themselves when they have published, that their compositions were made in a hurry or extempore: Rigby will assure you that what I sent you was literally wrote in less than three hours—and my dear Harry, I am not vain enough to think that I can write in three hours what would deserve to live three days. I will give you two more very material reasons for your suppressing my verses, and have done— One is, I don't care to make all the women in England my enemies but sixteen, as their resentments would probably hurt me more, than the gratitude of my goddesses would do me good, with all their charms—and the other reason is, that the conclusion of the poem is more particular, than I would choose publicly to subscribe to.

I am content with your approbation and Lady Caroline's: pray tell her the reason I said so little of Lady Emily in detail, was, what the critics, a set of gentlemen she is happily not acquainted with, say in excuse for the heroes of the epic poems, who are very little talked of in comparison with their rivals, but who are supposed to be celebrated enough, by surpassing those who are more amply commended: or you may tell her what will be more familiar to her than Homer and Virgil, that if I had said Mrs Bethel[5] was the ugliest woman in the world, I should not have specified her nose, her mouth or her complexion. For the last line on Lady Emily, which you don't understand, it only means, that it is a pity she is not as like Venus in being a mother,[6] as she is in the rest of her merits.

I beg your pardon for troubling you with a second letter so long, when I shall be in town the day after it, but I was so anxious about

---

3. James Thomson (1700–48), author of *The Seasons*. HW usually spelled his name with a *p*. For HW's low opinion of his poetry see MONTAGU i. 215; BERRY i. 353; MASON ii. 97; MANN iii. 27.

4. Richard Glover (1712–85), poet. His 'Leonidas,' first published in 1737, was taken as a 'political manifesto' against Sir Robert Walpole, so that HW had political as well as aesthetic reasons for disliking his poetry. For an even stronger condemnation of him by HW see MANN i. 353–4.

5. Not identified, though possibly either Priscilla (b. 1690) or Bridget Bethel (b.

1692), the unmarried sisters of Slingsby and Hugh Bethel, friends and correspondents of Pope (Joseph Foster, *Pedigrees of the County Families of Yorkshire*, 1874, iii. *sub* Bethel of Rise; Pope, *Correspondence*, ed. Sherburn, Oxford, 1956, *passim*). The other candidates suggested by Mrs Toynbee (ii. 215 n. 2) and Jesse, *Selwyn* i. 10, are impossible chronologically. This Mrs Bethel is mentioned several times as a sort of archetype of ugliness in HW's letters to Montagu (MONTAGU i. 41, 139, 183) and in HW to Bentley 13 April 1755.

6. She repaired this shortcoming by producing twenty-one children.

your talking of making my verses public, that I could not refrain a moment from begging you not. Rigby has left his kindest love for you; he is gone to a cricket-match, from which your letter has saved me: since you have commended me so much, he begins to look on me in a higher light, and even deigns to treat my leisure as sacred. I am dear Sir, and always shall be if you will suppress my verses,

Your most obliged humble servant,

HOR. WALPOLE

From Fox, *post* 24 July 1746

Missing. Mentioned in the endorsement of HW to Fox 24 July 1746.

To Fox, Thursday 9 October 1746

Printed from *Letters to Henry Fox* 18; reprinted, Toynbee *Supp.* i. 59. The MS of this letter, and all others printed in *Letters to Henry Fox,* are in the possession of the Earl of Ilchester.

Windsor,[1] Oct. 9, 1746.

Dear Sir,

YOU will think me very far gone, when even curiosity about this new battle[2] can't fetch me to town, but it is charity that keeps me here. Poor Mr Montagu[3] has lost his only remaining brother,[4] and I cannot bring myself to leave him and his sisters[5] in the ex-

1. HW had taken a house 'within the precincts of the Castle of Windsor' in August 1746 ('Short Notes,' GRAY i. 16).

2. Of Roucour or Rocour, near Liége, 11 Oct. NS. The first reports of the battle reached London on 8 Oct. OS (*Daily Adv.* 9 Oct.).

3. George Montagu (ca 1713–80), HW's friend and correspondent.

4. A false report. Lt-Gen. Sir Charles Montagu (d. 1777); K.B., 1771; Montagu's youngest brother, was at this time Lt-Col. in the 11th Foot (MONTAGU i. 31 n. 14; Richard Cannon, *Historical Record of the Eleventh . . . Foot,* 1845, p. 34). He was

reported killed in the first accounts of the battle, but was known to be a prisoner a few days later (*Daily Adv.* 9 Oct.; *London Gazette Extraordinary* 9 Oct.; *London Gazette* No. 8580, 14–18 Oct.). Montagu's brothers Edward and Christopher had been killed at the battle of Fontenoy in 1745 (MONTAGU i. 11 n. 2; *Daily Adv.* 17 May 1745), but his brother John (MONTAGU i. 204 n. 4) was still alive.

5. Arabella Montagu (d. 1798), m. (1750) Nathaniel Wettenhall of Hankelow, Cheshire; and Henrietta (or Harriet) Montagu (d. 1755) (MONTAGU i. 12 n. 6).

tremest distress I ever saw. Though I know writing to you is securing an answer, yet I know too how unreasonable it is to trouble you; but if you could find a moment to tell me the material particulars, I should be infinitely obliged to you, and more if you would send your friend the Duke[6] to repair this misfortune, unless one of the Grenvilles[7] should insist on the command.

I am, dear Sir,

Your obedient servant,

HOR. WALPOLE

From Fox, Thursday 9 October 1746

Printed from the MS now WSL. First printed, Toynbee *Supp.* i. 60. For the history of the MS see *ante* 22 July 1746.

October 9, 1746.

Dear Sir,

I SEND you Mr Stone's[1] letter to me[2] and will add all the particulars I know.

There were two English battalions and six Hessian and Hanoverian, in all eight, attacked, as Leg[onie]r[3] writes, by no less than 55 battalions, which they repulsed more than once.[4] One of these Hanover regiments lost every officer;[5] the two English were Graham's and Douglas's,[6] in the first of which your friend's gallant brother lost his

---

6. Of Cumberland.

7. Richard Grenville (later Grenville-Temple) (1711–79), 1st E. Temple, 1752; and his brother George Grenville (1712–70), first lord of the Treasury 1763–5. They were just rising into political prominence as allies of Pitt.

---

1. Andrew Stone (*ante* 6 Aug. 1745, n. 9).

2. Missing.

3. Gen. Sir John Louis Ligonier (1680–1770), K.B., 1743; cr. (1757) Vct and (1766) E. Ligonier; commander-in-chief of the British troops and troops in British pay in the Austrian Netherlands, 1746.

4. 'Our three villages [Liers, Warem, and Rocour, which the eight battalions were

defending] were . . . attacked by 55 battalions, in columns, by brigades; and as soon as one brigade was repulsed, another came on' (*London Gazette Extraordinary* 9 Oct.). 'The English horse repulsed the enemy continually' (Ligonier's dispatch to Lord Sandwich, quoted in DNB *sub* Ligonier).

5. Maidell's regiment (*London Gazette Extraordinary* 9 Oct.). The Hanoverians suffered 1,212 casualties in the battle (*Oesterreichischer Erbfolge-krieg 1740–1748*, Vienna, 1896–1914, ix. 910).

6. Brig.-Gen. William Graham's 11th Foot (not the 43d, as *Oesterreichischer Erbfolge-Krieg*, op. cit., ix. 435, quoted in MANN iii. 318 n. 5, erroneously states), and Brig.-Gen. William Douglas's 32d

life, and is exceedingly lamented. Major Sowle[7] was wounded and taken, and Captains Debrizé[8] and Sir Harry Nisbett,[9] and several subalterns not named were killed.[10] Of Douglas's Major Kendal[11] had his leg shot and cut off in the field.

Houghton's brigade[12] came up and was of great use in the retreat but did not lose a man.[13] The Dutch fought extremely well and suffered much,[14] being attacked on three sides. A great deal is laid to the treachery of the Bishop of Liége,[15] who admitted the French through Liége in the night,[16] and to the generalship of the Marshal Saxe[17] who kept the main of our army *en respect* whilst with advantages be-

Foot. The latter, however, was not directly engaged in defending the village of Rocour, though it suffered a few casualties in its position near the centre of the Allied line. The other regiment at Rocour was Major-Gen. the Hon. Charles Howard's 19th Foot. The confusion of regiments in this early report of the battle apparently came about because those defending the village were grouped in a brigade under the temporary field command of Brig.-Gen. Douglas, while Douglas's own regiment, like the rest of those in the centre, was under another temporary field command; see especially the several successive reports of the battle summarized in a letter from Fanny Russell to Col. Charles Russell 11 Oct. 1746, Hist. MSS Comm., *Frankland-Russell-Astley MSS*, 1900, p. 355; Richard Cannon, *Historical Record of the Eleventh . . . Foot*, 1845, pp. 33–4; and Richard Cannon, *Historical Record of the Nineteenth . . . Foot*, 1848, p. 11.

7. Marmaduke Sowle (d. 1766), Major in the 11th Foot, 1745; Lt-Col., 1748; commissioner of appeals in the Excise 1763–6; brother-in-law of 1st Bn Holmes (GM 1748, xviii. 573; 1763, xxxiii. 98; *Court and City Register*, 1749, p. 140; Robert Beatson, *Political Index*, 3d edn, 1806, ii. 376; *London Magazine*, 1748, xvii. 573; 1766, xxxii. 493; Sir John Bernard Burke, *Genealogical History of the Dormant . . . and Extinct Peerages*, 1866, p. 283). He was described as 'wounded and taken' in the *London Gazette Extraordinary* 9 Oct.; and as 'prisoner' in the casualty list a few days later (*London Gazette* No. 8580, 14–18 Oct.).

8. Not identified. 'Captain Desbrisay' is listed as 'killed or missing' in the casualty list (*London Gazette* No. 8580, 14–18 Oct.).

9. Sir Henry Nisbet (d. 11 Oct. 1746 NS), 4th Bt; Capt. in the 11th Foot. He is described as 'killed' in the *London Gazette Extraordinary*, 9 Oct.; as 'dead of his wounds' and the only certain fatality among the British officers at Rocour in the casualty list (*London Gazette* No. 8580, 14–18 Oct.).

10. A list of the officers of the 11th Foot who were casualties in one way or another is in Richard Cannon, *Historical Record of the Eleventh . . . Foot*, 1845, p. 34.

11. John Kendall (d. 1746), Ensign in the 32d Foot, 1733; Lt, 1741; Capt., 1743; Major, 1745. He apparently died of his wounds, since his successor's commission is dated 22 Oct. 1746 (information kindly supplied by Mr David Erskine from the MS Army Lists in the Public Record Office, W. O. 64/8–10).

12. The 8th, 13th, and 25th Foot, commanded by Brig.-Gen. Daniel Houghton.

13. At least five men were killed in the 8th Foot alone during the retreat (Richard Cannon, *Historical Record of the Eighth . . . Foot*, 1844, p. 58).

14. Dutch casualties were 1,791 (*Oesterreichischer Erbfolge-Krieg*, op. cit. ix. 910).

15. Prince Johann Theodor (1703–63) of Bavaria; cardinal, 1746; Bp of Liége 1744–63; son of Maximilian II, Elector of Bavaria.

16. 'What contributed greatly to our ill success in this action, was, that the people of Liége had the night before introduced the French into the town, and put them into possession of it, just in Prince Waldeck's back, whose disposi-

sides the vast superiority of numbers, he attacked our left. What the *Gazette Extraordinary* (which I'll send you) will call it;[18] I don't know. The other newspapers make a victory of it on our side,[19] however for fear of such another we are got beyond Maestricht, and on the other side of the river. No express from Lestock.[20] We have done great damage at Port L'Orient as letters from Paris through Holland say, though they got time to carry very valuable effects to Port Louis, which we are besieging.[21] If we take that place, I believe the damage will indeed be prodigious and absolute ruin to their E[ast] Ind[ia] trade.

But I am a coward—for so everybody is who is afraid of France.[22] I am, dear Sir,

Your most obedient and most humble servant,

H. Fox

Have you sent any verses to D. Edgecumbe about Nanny Day?[23] If you have, pray enclose a copy of them to me, as well as of Mr Grey's.[24]

tions were excellently made before that accident' (*London Gazette Extraordinary* 9 Oct.).

17. Hermann-Maurice, Comte de Saxe (1696–1750), Maréchal de France; commander of the French forces in Flanders.

18. 'We have certainly quitted the field with as little disadvantage as could be in a battle, if that can be called a battle, where two thirds of our Army were not engaged, the action having been wholly upon the left. The enemy did not think fit to pursue us; but not being able, for want of wood in this advanced season, to stay on the other side of the Meuse, we passed that river this morning' (*London Gazette Extraordinary* 9 Oct.).

19. The *Daily Adv.* 9 Oct., described it as a victory in one column and a defeat in another, but like the other early reports of the battle, confused a preliminary skirmish on 7 Oct. NS with the principal engagement on 11 Oct. NS. The *London Gazette Extraordinary* on the 9th unscrambled the confusion.

20. Richard Lestock (ca 1679–1746), Vice-Adm., 1743; Adm., 1746; commander of the squadron operating against Lorient. Fox had defended him against court martial in April 1745 (MANN iii. 33 and n. 10).

21. This over-sanguine report of the success of the expedition to Brittany, accepted at face value by some of the Cabinet (see Pelham to Unknown [10 Oct. 1746], BM Add. MSS 32709, f. 33), was reported at length in the *London Gazette Extraordinary* 9 Oct. 1746; but within a few days, the truth that the expedition had been a complete fiasco had sobered English spirits (MANN iii. 319 and notes).

22. Fox favoured an immediate peace with France. The Cabinet was split on the issue; Pelham and Harrington urged peace, while Newcastle, Hardwicke and the King supported the war. Fox's letters to his brother indicate the bitterness of the dispute between members of the government (Ilchester, *Henry Fox* i. 136–8; T. W. Riker, *Henry Fox*, Oxford, 1911, i. 71).

23. Mrs Ann Franks, alias Day (d. 1790), m. (ca 1761) Sir Peter Fenouilhet, Kt, Exon of the Guard; Richard Edgcumbe's mistress ('Short Notes,' GRAY i. 36 n. 242). No other mention of any such verses by HW has been found.

24. Gray's *Ode on a Distant Prospect of Eton College* which HW had recently received in MS. He sent a copy to Conway on 3 Oct.

Caroline was brought to bed of a boy[25] yesterday morning and is very well.

From C. H. WILLIAMS, 1747

Missing; mentioned *post* 27 June 1748. Written after Williams left England in April 1747.

To C. H. WILLIAMS, 1747–1748

HW says *post* 27 June 1748 that he wrote to Williams 'several times' after the latter left England; all are missing.

To Fox, ca Thursday 29 October 1747

Missing.

From Fox, Friday 30 October 1747

Printed from the MS now WSL. First printed, Toynbee *Supp.* iii. 126–7. For the history of the MS see *ante* 22 July 1746.

October 30, 1747.

Dear Sir,

WHAT you ask for Mr Montagu,[1] is in my province, but like other things that are so, not the more in my power for being so.

What I can do, I will not omit, which is to lay this request before the Duke as soon as he comes.[2] It is a reasonable one, and I think

---

25. Henry Charles Fox (8 Oct. 1746–Dec. 1746 *or* Jan. 1747), Fox's second son (Ilchester, *Henry Fox* i. 143; Collins, *Peerage*, 1812, vii. 310).

1. What HW asked for George Mon-

tagu in a missing letter has not been discovered; it probably concerned some military favour for Col. Montagu.

2. The Duke of Cumberland was still in Flanders with the army but expected to return to England very soon. He finally

likely to succeed. I am not so sure that it is a thing much worth asking.

You'll observe that I say 'lay it before the Duke' which is, because I asked the clothing of Houghton's for his widow,[3] and the King would not determine that till he had with the Duke talked over the merits of the candidates for regiments and determined whom he should give them to.

Depend upon it, dear Sir, I'll do my best for your friend, and whoever you honour with your friendship may be always surer of mine than I believe Caroline or I can easily be made of your delighting in the country,[4] though that country not being ten miles from town is no doubt a great help to it.

Cibber[5] has celebrated the sea fight[6] in his ode[7] as he tells me, and when I asked him if he had made any mention of Berg op Zoom,[8] he answered that he had talked of the French *pilfering* a few towns from us,[9] which no doubt is just the proper expression.

I received your letter in the Drawing-Room, and I answer it at dinner.

Yours ever,

H. Fox

reached London on 13 Nov. (Newcastle to Sandwich 13 Nov. 1747, BM Add. MSS 32810, f. 278; MANN iii. 446, nn. 3, 4, 5).

3. That is, Fox had asked that the widow (unidentified) of Daniel Houghton, late Col. of the 24th Foot (see *ante* 13 Sept. 1741 OS, n. 7) be allowed to supply the clothing for her late husband's regiment, so that she would continue to receive the income he had derived from this source. For the system itself, see C. M. Clode, *Military Forces of the Crown; Their Administration and Government,* 1869, i. 107–8; ii. 538–9. The first inquiry into the profits made by it was held in 1746, when several colonels appeared to be gaining over £300 a year from the privilege (*Reports from Committees of the House of Commons,* 1803–6, ii. 79–93).

4. HW had taken a lease of Strawberry Hill in June 1747 ('Short Notes,' GRAY i. 17 n. 112).

5. Colley Cibber (1671–1757), actor; dramatist; poet-laureate.

6. Adm. Hawke's victory over the escort of a French convoy off La Rochelle on 14 Oct. 1747, in which his fifteen ships had captured six of the eight French ships of the line, though the convoy itself escaped (H. W. Richmond, *The Navy in the War of 1739–48,* Cambridge, 1920, iii. 102–11). The news had been published in London on the 26th (*London Gazette Extraordinary* 26 Oct.).

7. On the King's birthday.
'What their numbers from barriers have
       pilfered on shore,
Our forts on the floods from their Indies
    restore'   (*Daily Adv.* 31 Oct.).

8. Bergen-op-Zoom had been captured by the French under Lowendal on 16 Sept. 1747 NS. The wide-spread belief that the place had fallen by treachery seems to have been ill-founded (MANN iii. 440 n. 10).

9. See above, n. 7.

All the prizes with those who took them got in safe, just before yesterday's storm began, except the *Nottingham* which, however, 'tis thought is in no danger.[10]

From Fox, Monday 28 March 1748

Printed from the MS now WSL. First printed in full, Toynbee *Supp.* iii. 128–30; printed in part, Ilchester, *Henry Fox* i. 110. For the history of the MS see *ante* 22 July 1746.

Dated by the reference to the Foxes' reconciliation with the Duke and Duchess of Richmond.

Address: To the Honourable Hor. Walpole Esquire.

Dear Hori,

ON Saturday Lady Caroline had a long and kind letter from the Duke and Duchess of Richmond[1] telling her that if I would bring her at one-half hour after seven the next evening,[2] she should be received with the utmost tenderness and affection, that they had said all they would say in the letter, and desired no mention ever might be made on either side of anything that had passed.

As this was not at all expected, (no application having been made this twelve-month)[3] it surprised and confused Lady Caroline and was that illness that made her send to put your dining here off.

We went, supped there last night, and are to dine there today.

No conditions whatever are required, nor do I know how it came

10. 'On Saturday morning [31 Oct.] came advice that Rear-Admiral Hawke, in his Majesty's ship the *Devonshire*, with the following ships of war, viz. *Kent, Lion, Defiance, Tilbury, Yarmouth, Pluto* and *Vulcan* fireships, and the six French men-of-war his prizes are arrived in Portsmouth harbor' (*Daily Adv.* 2 Nov.).

---

1. Lady Caroline's parents; they had refused to receive her or communicate with her since she had eloped with Fox in May 1744. Their letter, forgiving her and offering to receive her and Fox, is printed in Princess Marie Liechtenstein, *Holland House*, 1874, i. 69–72, and Toynbee *Supp.* iii. 128–9 n. 2. **Full accounts**

of the match, the furore it caused in London society, and the subsequent attempts at reconciliation, are in Ilchester, *Henry Fox* i. 104–10; Ilchester, *Hanbury-Williams* 80–2; and HW to Mann 29 May 1744, MANN ii. 450–1.

2. The time was not set in the letter, but was to be settled by Fox and Lady Caroline with Lord Ilchester.

3. Earlier attempts at reconciliation had been made through the Dowager Countess of Cadogan, Lady Caroline's grandmother, and Lord and Lady Kildare, her sister and brother-in-law. The Richmonds in their letter to Lady Caroline conceded that the former had had some effect, but attributed the decision principally to themselves.

into their thoughts now. And you actually are now as much apprised of it all as I am.

If you should be so good as to intend dining here on Wednesday, I think verily you won't be put off again.

Ever yours,

H. Fox

From C. H. WILLIAMS, June 1748

Missing; presumably written from Dresden where Williams had been residing as English minister since late May 1747 (Ilchester, *Hanbury-Williams* 147).

To C. H. WILLIAMS, Monday 27 June 1748

Printed for the first time from the MS now WSL. The MS was among the Williams MSS sold by Williams's great-nephew, Ferdinand Hanbury-Williams, to Sir Thomas Phillipps in 1841. The collection was bought by Messrs W. H. Robinson who sold it to WSL.

Endorsed: Strawberry Hill, June 27th 1748.

Strawberry Hill,[1] June 27th 1748.

Dear Sir Charles,

YOU must not look on my answering your letter immediately after a long silence, as a mark of my piquing myself on your being punctual with me: I don't, as you saw by my writing several times, but when you had dropped me entirely, and I had had but one letter from you since you left England,[2] I could not help concluding that you intended our correspondence should cease. I am very willing to renew it, and will say no more than that the intermission of our friendship shall never begin on my part.

You will perceive by the date of my letter that my love for London is wore out; I have got an extreme pretty place just by Twickenham,

1. This and the letter written to Conway the same day are the earliest that we have dated from 'Strawberry Hill,' though HW had referred to his new house by that name in letters to Montagu 18 May 1748 (MONTAGU i. 56) and to Mann 7 June (MANN iii. 486). See also 'Short Notes,' GRAY i. 17 and n. 115.

2. All these letters are missing.

which I am likely to be pleased with for at least some time, as I have many alterations to make. The prospect is delightful, the house very small, and till I added two or three rooms[3] scarce habitable: at present it will hold as many people as I wish to see here; when you return, I shall be extremely glad to have you of the number. Mr Fox and Lady Caroline dined here yesterday, and he has promised me to send this letter for me. He has made Holland House a very fine place;[4] Kent's[5] death has rather put a stop to much farther improvements: I think there is great danger everywhere of our relapsing into bad taste, for scarce any school retains its purity after the death of the institutor. Mr Fox told me a curious history of Colebrook:[6] he was gone into the country for the summer, when he received an express to come to his father[7] directly, who greeted him at once with this speech: 'You promised me you would never game any more nor go to White's; you have not only gamed, but gone to White's every day'— ('Did you promise this,' said Mr Fox, 'Yes')— 'You know I have settled three thousand pounds a year[8] upon you, and I have given you a large sum in my will,' (which he showed him). 'I have left your mother[9] a great sum, of which she will give you a proper part' (which she has since told Bob, but one is not very apt to believe this) 'I will not give you one shilling of all this, unless you will go and

3. 'Designed by Mr W. Robinson of the Board of Works, before there was any design of farther improvements to the house' ('Des. of SH,' *Works* ii. 421). The kitchen was moved, and probably the breakfast room was added (W. S. Lewis, 'Genesis of Strawberry Hill,' *Metropolitan Museum Studies*, 1934–6, v. 62).

4. Fox leased Holland House in the summer of 1746 when it was in disrepair and immediately began improving it. The author of *A Tour through England* in 1748 describes his alterations: 'It seems that this famous old house, the residence of the Earls of Warwick, was deserted; but the present possessor has restored it, repaired it, and beautified it, embellished the gardens, enclosed the park, and made a coach road into Acton Road, and a coach-way through his own grounds from the turnpike to the house. He is daily improving the delightful situation' (quoted in Ilchester, *Henry Fox* i. 142).

5. William Kent (1684–12 April 1748),

painter, sculptor, architect, and landscape gardener. He had been called in to advise on the new terraces at Holland House just before his death (ibid. i. 175).

6. Presumably Robert Colebrooke (1718–84) of Chilham Castle, Kent; M.P. Maldon 1741–61; minister to the Swiss cantons 1762–4; ambassador to Turkey July–Nov. 1765 (MANN i. 185 n. 15).

7. James Colebrooke (1680–1752), of Chilham Castle, Kent; citizen and mercer of London; 'a great money scrivener in Threadneedle Street' (GEC, *Baronetage* v. 116; H. C. Cardew-Rendle, 'James Colebrooke: A Forgotten Figure in Insurance,' *Notes and Queries*, 1956, cci. 26–8).

8. At Robert Colebrooke's death, his estate was estimated at £3,500 per annum (GM 1784, liv pt i. 475).

9. Mary Hudson (1689–1753), m. (1706) James Colebrooke (George Lipscomb, *History and Antiquities of the County of Buckingham*, 1847, i. 134; Sir Bernard Burke, *Peerage*, 1928, p. 566).

live at Richlieu in France for three years, and I will have you go Monday fortnight—give me a list of your debts and I will pay them, but I will have no reply'— Bob has submitted to this extempore exile, is to live on four hundred a year, and the rest of his allowance is to be stopped to reimburse what his father lays down to pay his debts. Dick Edgcumbe says the old man certainly picked out *Richlieu* for the name of the place: I wonder what significant sound he found out in Constantinople that captivated my Lord Edgcumbe.[10]

I shall be obliged to you for anything that shows me you don't quite forget me, and consequently am much obliged to you for your ode[11] which is very pretty. There is nothing new worth sending you; when there is I shall take any opportunity that I can find.

The Duchess of Kent[12] is dead, and has left her charming place[13] at Old Windsor to her mother[14] for life, and then to her daughter Lady Sophia.[15]

Just before I came out of town I heard some histories of Tom Hervey, which have such particular strokes in them that they are worth telling you. When he heard his father[16] had determined to set up Felton[17] for Bury,[18] he wrote a long letter to the Mayor and Corporation of that place, in which he recounted the long bead

10. Richard Edgcumbe (1680–1758), cr. (1742) Bn Edgcumbe of Mount Edgcumbe. From Fox's letters to Williams it appears that Lord Edgcumbe had exiled Dick to Turkey sometime in the 1730's and kept him there for seven years (letters of 7 July and 2 Aug. 1744, Williams MSS xlviii, ff. 85, 93).

11. Presumably Williams's 'An Ode on the Death of Matzel, a Favourite Bullfinch,' written for Philip Stanhope, natural son of Lord Chesterfield, in June 1748 (Williams, *Works* i. 107–10; Ilchester, *Hanbury-Williams* 129–30).

12. Lady Sophia Bentinck (d. 14 June 1748), dau. of 1st E. of Portland; m. (1729) Henry Grey, 12th E. of Kent, cr. (1706) M. and (1710) D. of Kent.

13. Remenham, or Remnam's, later Beaumont, which the Duchess of Kent purchased in 1741. It subsequently belonged to Warren Hastings, and is now the property of the Society of Jesus. The history of the house and its owners is given in T. E. Harwood, *Windsor Old and New*, 1929, pp. 187–98.

14. Jane Martha Temple (1672–1751), m. 1 (1692) John Berkeley, 3d Bn Berkeley of Stratton; m. 2 (1700) William Bentinck, 1st E. of Portland.

15. Lady Anne Sophia Grey (d. 1780) m. (1748) John Egerton, Bp of Bangor 1756–68, Lichfield and Coventry 1768–71, Durham 1771–87 (GM 1748, xviii. 524; 1780, l. 155; DNB *sub* John Egerton). She sold the property at Old Windsor to the Duke of Roxburghe in 1751 (Harwood, op. cit. 193).

16. John Hervey (1665–1751), cr. (1703) Bn Hervey of Ickworth; cr. (1714) E. of Bristol.

17. Hon. Felton Hervey (1712–73), 7th son of 1st E. of Bristol; M.P. Bury St Edmunds 1747–61; equerry to Queen Caroline (*Eton College Register 1698–1752*, ed. R. A. Austen-Leigh, Eton, 1927, p. 173).

18. Tom Hervey had been M.P. for Bury 1733–47. For a rather one-sided account of the family quarrel this contested election provoked, see *The Letter Books of John, 1st Earl of Bristol*, [ed. S. H. A. Hervey], Wells, 1894, iii. 327–35.

roll of his distresses, and concluded—to add to my misfortunes I have married a woman[19] without a shilling to prevent her running distracted or making away with herself. This has all his character in it. The other wants the delicacy of a Hervey: he had one day company to dinner: she was not ready: at last she came down extremely dressed. He looked at her, and said 'Madam, I never saw anybody so perfectly well-dressed and genteel'; and then walking up to her, and taking her by the hand, he gave her a violent twirl round and said—'but times are finely altered since I took you, when your knees came through your stockings and your elbows through your shift sleeves!'

I believe you will think me altered in more points than in the strength of my voice, when I tell you that I am this instant going downstairs to see some hurdles that I have sent for to fold my sheep[20] upon a lawn before my house: indeed my sheep are Turkish, and have four horns, and look as uncommon as if I had bought them at Margas's.[21]

Adieu! My dear sir, I shall hope to hear from you from Warsaw,[22] as you promise me; but to make your letter what I wish it, you must speak a little more feelingly than you do of returning to England; I can't help thinking a genius like yours thrown away out of your own country.

Yours most sincerely,

H. Walpole

To Fox, Thursday 20 October 1748

Printed for the first time from the MS now wsl. The MS is untraced until it was sold Sotheby's 24 Apr. 1934 (property of the late Florence, Lady Ward) lot 442 to Maggs for wsl.

Endorsed by Fox: Hori Walpole October 21, 1748.

19. Ann Coghlan (d. 1786), dau. of Francis Coghlan, counsellor-at-law in Ireland; m. (1744) Hon. Thomas Hervey (Mann iv. 103 n. 15).

20. HW's Turkish sheep, then eighteen in number, were killed by dogs in August 1763 (HW to Montagu 15 Aug. 1763, Montagu ii. 94).

21. The shop of Philip Margas (d.

1767), a tea and china importer and fashionable china dealer in Bucklersbury near Stocks Market (gm 1767, xxxvii. 331; Sir Ambrose Heale's Collection of tradesman's cards).

22. Williams had been ordered to accompany the King of Poland to Warsaw early in June 1748 (Ilchester, *Hanbury-Williams* 162).

Strawberry Hill, Oct. 20, 1748.

Dear Sir,

I CONCLUDE you are tired with being wished joy of your great prize,[1] but you must undergo one compliment more— Had I been in town, I should have been one of the first; but living in a distant county, I can only pretend to be one of the sincerest. This sounds very much like the country gentleman; I am so much so, that I tell you honestly I am too busy with my plantations[2] to call upon you and tell you how glad I am of your good fortune— Had it happened to me just now, I believe I should lay it all out in trees. My dear Sir, I am seriously happy that you are so fortunate, and whatever wishes you leave to chance, I hope will be always as successful— Those that depend on yourself, you know I am too confident to have the least doubt about.

I am yours most sincerely,

HOR. WALPOLE

From C. H. WILLIAMS, ca Tuesday 19 September 1749

Missing; mentioned in the following letter.

To ?SELWYN, Friday 22 September 1749

Printed from the MS now WSL. First printed, Wright ii. 304; reprinted Cunningham ii. 182; Toynbee ii. 411. It was presumably among the MSS that HW bequeathed to the 6th Earl Waldegrave, whose executor, the 5th Duke of Grafton, sold them to Richard Bentley, the publisher, in the 1840's (HW's *Letters Addressed to the Countess of Upper Ossory,* 1848, i. p. viii; Mitford's preface to the HW-Mason correspondence, 1851); bought by WSL, 1937, from the estate of Richard Bentley the younger.

Endorsed: No. 2.

The earlier editors identify the recipient as Chute, but a better guess would seem to be Selwyn. As far as we know, Chute and Williams, far from being on the terms of intimacy suggested by this letter, were not even acquainted.

1. Fox had won the £10,000 prize in the annual government lottery (MONTAGU i. 79 n. 2 and references cited).

2. HW's *Strawberry Hill Accounts,* ed. Paget Toynbee, Oxford, 1927, pp. 36–8, show that he was at the height of his enthusiasm for planting during the autumn of 1748.

Strawberry Hill, Sept. 22, 1749.

My dear Sir,

I EXPECT Sir Charles Williams[1] to scold me excessively; he wrote me a letter, in which he desired that I would send you word by last night's post that he expected to meet you here by Michaelmas,[2] according to your promise; I was unfortunately at London; the letter was directed hither from Lord Ilchester's where he is,[3] and so I did not receive it till this morning. I hope however this will be time enough to put you in mind of your appointment; but while I am so much afraid of Sir Charles's anger, I seem to forget the pleasure I shall have in seeing you myself; I hope you know that; but he is still more pressing, as he will stay so little time in England.[4] Adieu! believe me

Yours ever,

⟨   ⟩[5]

To C. H. WILLIAMS, Saturday 23 September 1749

Printed for the first time from the MS now WSL. For the history of the MS see *ante* 27 June 1748.

Strawberry Hill, Sept. 23, 1749.

I ENCLOSE Miss Rigby's[1] verses, and trust that they will move Mr Fox: Lady Caroline cannot help protecting the suit; if she will set such examples, of falling in love and then making such a good wife, I don't see how she can avoid patronizing distressed damsels that have a mind to be of her party.

I own myself I should scarce believe so much poetry came out of that family, if there were not that mark of Rigbyism in the ode, that

1. Who had returned to England from Dresden 3 Sept. 1749, primarily to arrange the preliminaries of the marriage of his daughter Frances to the Earl of Essex (Ilchester, *Hanbury-Williams* 177–8).

2. 29 Sept.

3. Maddington, Wilts, a house of Stephen Fox (after 1758, Fox-Strangways) (1704–76), cr. (1741) Bn and (1756) E. of Ilchester; Henry Fox's brother. HW is apparently mistaken; Williams had intended to join the Foxes at Maddington, but was detained in London (Fox to Williams 12, 17, 18 Sept. 1749, Williams MSS lii. ff. 39–41; Ilchester, *Hanbury-Williams* 177).

4. Williams did not leave England for Berlin until 5 May 1750 (ibid. 179).

5. The signature has been cut out of the MS.

———

1. Presumably Anne Rigby (ca 1717–91), the elder of Rigby's two sisters (GM 1788, lviii pt i. 371, 462; 1791, lxi pt ii. 783). The verses are missing.

hint of *sitting round the cheerful glass:* however the young lady may resemble Sappho in her numbers, I don't believe she will in her Methodism. Adieu! my dear Sir Charles,

Yours most sincerely,

Hor. Walpole

From Fox, Thursday 23 November 1752

Printed in full for the first time from the MS now WSL. First printed in part, Cunningham ii. 312; reprinted, Toynbee iii. 133 n. 3. For the history of the MS, see *ante* 22 Sept. 1749.
Dated by HW's endorsement.
Endorsed by HW: 'Mr Fox's note to me Nov. 23d 1752, returning the letter[1] I intended and did send to Mr Pelham.'

Dear Hori,

I RETURN you your very proper and genteel application[2] to Mr Pelham, which appears to me such, that I really think it will succeed so far at least, as that he will try it with the King. I have been in doubt whether mentioning the very little self-denial that his getting this for you would be, was right. But you do it very civilly and I am not sure, that without considering the matter, he may not think it a great one. Adieu, I heartily wish you success.

[PS.] Mr Harding[3] is used, or used you, ill. For you had not been gone ten minutes yesterday, before a very fair, well-bound, Milles's *Catalogues of Honour*[4] was brought me with the enclosed note.[5]

1. HW to Pelham 25 Nov. 1752.
2. HW was asking that the patent for the collectorship of the Customs be altered to run for his own life in addition to those of his elder brothers, Robert and Edward. HW desired this arrangement to secure the £1400 per annum he enjoyed from the sinecure, but Pelham refused to do more than substitute HW's name for his brother Edward's, an offer HW declined. HW misdates this application 1751 in his 'Account of My Conduct Relative to the Places I hold under Government, and towards Ministers' (*Works* ii. 366–7), written in March 1782.
3. Bookseller (HW's note). Samuel

Harding (d. 1755), bookseller and publisher at the 'Bible and Anchor on the Pavement,' St Martin's Lane ca 1726–55. (H. R. Plomer *et al., A Dictionary of the Printers and Booksellers who were at work in England, Scotland and Ireland from 1726 to 1775,* Oxford, 1932, p. 115). This is the only reference so far found to Harding as HW's bookseller.
4. *The Catalogue of Honor, or Tresury of True Nobility, Peculiar and Proper to the Isle of Great Britaine . . . Translated out of Latyne,* 1610, by Thomas Milles (ca 1550–1627).
5. Missing.

The letters of George James ('Gilly') Williams to Selwyn contain frequent references to HW. The earliest is in the summer of 1753 when he told Selwyn:

'Hor. Walpole has been in town a few days, he told me your bon mot about Lord Pomfret and the Parks [see MONTAGU i. 153]. . . . Walpole abuses you for sending him to Ashridge, he says he never saw anything more trumpery' ([26 July 1753], MS now WSL).

To SELWYN, Saturday 1 September 1753

Printed from a photostat of the MS in the Forster Collection in the Victoria and Albert Museum. First printed, Toynbee iii. 183–4. The MS was sold Puttick and Simpson's 19 Dec. 1862, lot 366, to Forster, and was bequeathed by him to the Victoria and Albert Museum at his death in 1876.

Arlington Street, Sept. 1, 1753.

Dear Sir,

NOT that I should ever put myself in competition with a death,[1] but I would flatter myself that I am going to notify two things that will neither of them be totally disagreeable to you. Poor Lord Coke is dead,[2] and if you are at Matson,[3] I propose to wait upon you there about Tuesday sennight the 11th.[4] If this is at all inconvenient to you, be so good as to send me any notice of it to Sir George Lyttelton's[5] at Hagley.[6] The death I mentioned (sorry as I really am for

1. Selwyn was notoriously fond of executions.

2. Coke died 31 Aug. 1753. News of his death would be particularly welcome to Selwyn, HW assumed, because he thought, like Selwyn's other friends, that it would mean the cancellation of a debt of at least 400 guineas that Selwyn owed Coke. Instead the money was assigned to Thomas Hervey who six months later began to press Selwyn for repayment ('Gilly' Williams to Selwyn, Sunday [2 Sept. 1753]; Sir William Maynard to Selwyn 6 Sept. 1753; Thomas Hervey to Selwyn 7 Feb., 11 Feb. 1754—MSS now WSL).

3. Selwyn's seat on Robins Wood Hill, about 2 miles SE of Gloucester; it is described and illustrated in an article by Arthur Oswald in *Country Life*, 8 Dec. 1950, cviii. 1990–4.

4. HW stayed two days at Matson (HW to Bentley Sept. 1753).

5. Sir George Lyttelton (1709–73), 5th Bt, cr. (1756) Bn Lyttelton; M.P. Okehampton 1735–56; a lord of the Treasury 1744–54; chancellor of the Exchequer 1755–6; the 'good Lord Lyttelton.'

6. Lyttelton's seat near Stourbridge, Worcestershire; HW describes his visit there in his letter to Bentley Sept. 1753.

it) will I hope prevent your succeeding Sir William Bunbury[7] at the press:[8] Mr Hervey[9] had laid so many eggs of letters to you, that I think he must have hatched some in print.

My Lady[10] is still at Tunbridge drinking the waters—merely for Mr Townshend's[11] sake, who would be miserable if she was out of order. Sir Charles Williams, who has been arrived some time,[12] has not yet seen her—however the meeting will be cordial.[13]

I beg my compliments to King Charles the First,[14] the Queen of Scots,[15] the ninth of February[16] and all friends.

Yours most truly,

Hor. Walpole

7. Rev. Sir William Bunbury (ca 1710–64), 5th Bt, of Bunbury, Cheshire, and Barton Hall, Suffolk; rector of Mildenhall, Suffolk.

8. Bunbury, as nephew and heir of Sir Thomas Hanmer (whose wife had eloped with Thomas Hervey), had been attacked by Hervey in *Mr Hervey's Letter to the Rev. Sir William Bunbury Bart, together with a Short Preface by the Author*, published in July 1753 (MONTAGU i. 152 and n. 7). Why Selwyn was likely to be the subject of Hervey's next pamphlet or why Lord Coke's death would prevent it, is not clear, though the confused debts of the three parties doubtless provide a partial explanation. Doubtless also Hervey's eccentricities provided Selwyn with subjects for ridicule. Two unpublished letters from Hervey to Selwyn, 7 Feb., 11 Feb. 1754 (now WSL), refer to the assigned debt, but neither mentions any earlier dispute. Selwyn later (in 1763) incurred Hervey's wrath by interfering in his vendetta against his wife (Jesse, *Selwyn* i. 220–2, 408), but this issue had not yet arisen.

9. Tom Hervey.

10. Lady Townshend.

11. Her son George (*ante* 30 May 1745, n. 5).

12. Williams reached London about 7 Aug. from Dresden where he was residing as envoy extraordinary to Saxony-Poland (*Daily Adv.* 7, 9 Aug. 1753; Ilchester, *Hanbury-Williams* 279–80).

13. Williams and Lady Townshend had

finally made up their quarrel of 1746 (ibid. 100–101, 196 n.; Henry Harris to Williams 7 July 1752, Fox to Williams 28 Aug. 1752, Williams MSS lxvii, ff. 41, 129).

14. Who had stayed at Matson during the siege of Gloucester by the Royal Army in 1643 (Sir Nathaniel Wraxall, *Historical Memoirs of His Own Time*, new edn, 1836, iii. 55–6; HW to Bentley Sept. 1753; *Country Life*, 1950, cviii. 1992–3 and plate 12). Selwyn later commemorated the visit by placing a bust of Charles, executed by Roubiliac in 1759, in the gallery at Matson (Mrs K. A. Esdaile, *The Life and Works of Louis François Roubiliac*, 1928, pp. 163–5 and plate xliii; GM 1788, lviii pt ii. 669). It is now in the Wallace Collection, London, presumably having passed with the rest of the contents of Matson to Maria Fagnani at Selwyn's death and then into the Hertford family through her marriage to the 3d Marquess. The fact that Charles was beheaded would increase his attractiveness to Selwyn, who was reputed to find decapitation the most interesting form of execution; see particularly MONTAGU i. 52.

15. Another royal victim of the axe, though the allusion may be to a specific portrait as well. Selwyn is known to have collected historical portraits (*Country Life*, 1950, cviii. 1994), which presumably passed to Mlle Fagnani as did the bust of Charles I, and hence into the Hertford family and the Wallace Collection,

While at Matson, HW made the acquaintance of Selwyn's friend and agent, the Rev. S. Harris, who later consulted him about a medal. HW responded, for Harris told Selwyn in November:

'Before this could go to the post I had the favour of an ingenious conjecture from Mr Walpole about the medal for which I am much indebted to him, and ashamed of giving him so much trouble' (24 Nov. [1753], MS now WSL).

To Fox, ca Tuesday 12 March 1754

Missing, described by HW in *Mem. Geo. II* i. 384–5: 'Horace Walpole, the younger, laid before him [Fox] the succession of the Duke of Newcastle's wiles and falsehoods; and being persuaded that this coalition was intended only to prejudice Mr Fox, and that he would be betrayed, mortified, disgraced, as soon as the new minister should have detached him from his connections, and prevented his strengthening them, urged him to refuse the seals [as secretary of state for the southern department].' That this advice was given in a letter is clear from HW's endorsement on the following letter and from that letter itself.

From Fox, Wednesday 13 March 1754

Printed from the MS now WSL. Previously printed, Toynbee *Supp.* iii. 136; Ilchester, *Henry Fox* i. 205–6. For the history of the MS see *ante* 22 July 1746.
Address: To the Honourable Hor. Walpole, Esquire. H. Fox.
Endorsed by HW: 'Answer to my letter, dissuading him from taking the Seals,[1] as D. of N.[2] had at setting out, broke his engagement.'[3]

where there is a copy of François Clouet's portrait of Mary of uncertain provenance (information kindly supplied by Mr Francis J. B. Watson).

16. Possibly a slightly confused reference to the date of Mary's execution, 8 Feb. 1587, but more likely to the date of the burning of John Hooper, Bishop of Gloucester, at the stake in Gloucester on 9 Feb. 1555; the house from whence Hooper was led to the stake was one of the tourist attractions of Gloucester. HW visited it a few days later (HW to Bentley Sept. 1753).

1. Fox was offered the seals as secretary of state for the southern department on 12 Mar. 1754 (*Mem. Geo. II* i. 381–2; Ilchester, *Henry Fox* i. 203; T. W. Riker, *Henry Fox*, Oxford, 1911, i. 154). The death of Henry Pelham, 6 March, required a reconstruction of the ministry.

2. Newcastle.

3. Not the reason HW had urged in his letter, since Fox acquaints him with this development in his reply. See below, n. 7.

CARICATURES OF NEWCASTLE, LYTTELTON, THE DUKE OF
CUMBERLAND, AND HENRY FOX, BY GEORGE TOWNSHEND

March 13, 1754.

Dear Hori,

I AGREE with you in almost every word of your kind letter, except as to what will follow from my union with the Duke of Newcastle, with whom you will not see me united. I do not know how I could avoid accepting,[4] if you do, tell me; would you advise me to continue secretary at war,[5] for the promise on which I accepted this[6] is notoriously broke in my first conference this morning.[7] If I am secretary of state, it is to complain from the first moment.

Yours ever,

H. Fox

I'll call on you at noon tomorrow.[8]

4. Fox did not hesitate to accept the secretaryship of state when it was offered to him 12 March. On Pelham's death he had hoped momentarily for the Treasury itself, but as soon as he realized this was impossible he indicated a willingness to accept any major office in the reconstructed ministry. His doubts began only when Newcastle revoked the terms that accompanied the offer. Fox later gave out that he had doubted the wisdom of accepting from the first (Ilchester, Henry Fox i. 203–4; Riker, op. cit. i. 155; Hist. MSS Comm., 8th Report, App., Digby MSS, 1881, pp. 220–22; Hartington to Newcastle [11 March 1754], BM Add. MSS 32734, f. 218).

5. Fox remained secretary at war at his own request, separated from Newcastle, but declaring against opposition (Ilchester, Henry Fox i. 208–9; HW to Mann 28 March 1754).

6. That he should have the management of the House of Commons along with the secretaryship of state, an exact accounting of the expenditure of the secret service money, and the disposal of some places to help in the management of the Commons (Ilchester, Henry Fox i. 203; Hist. MSS Comm., 8th Report, App., Digby MSS, 1881, pp. 220–22; Mem. Geo. II i. 381–2; HW to Bentley 17 March 1754). These additional conditions, which would have guaranteed his personal power, and not the secretaryship

itself, had been the principal reason for Fox's original acceptance.

7. When Fox waited on Newcastle on the morning of the 13th, he found that the Duke had thought better of every condition he had offered, and now proposed to deny Fox all means of effectual leadership in the Commons. He declared he had no intention of disclosing the disposal of the secret service money to anyone; that he reserved to himself the nomination to all places at the recommendation of any member of the House of Commons; and even refused to discuss arrangements for the coming elections with Fox (Mem. Geo. II i. 382–3). Newcastle, confronted by Lord Hartington who had carried the original offer, could not deny that he had broken his engagement; after asserting that he had been misunderstood, that he had never intended to offer Fox so much power, he finally admitted that he had decided not to stand by his original engagements, but intended that Fox should have no power whatever outside his own office as secretary of state (James, 2d Earl Waldegrave, Memoirs from 1754 to 1758, 1821, p. 19; Hist. MSS Comm., 8th Report, App., Digby MSS, 1881, p. 222; Mem. Geo. II i. 384).

8. When he may have told HW what passed between him and Newcastle. HW's account of the interview in Mem. Geo. II i. 382–3 is more complete than any other source.

To C. H. Williams, Wednesday ?ca March 1754

Printed for the first time from MS now wsl. For the history of the MS, see *ante* 27 June 1748.

Tentatively dated March 1754 from the concurrence of circumstances that Williams was in England during the winter of 1754; that during March 1754 Charles James Fox was very ill; and that the reference to Henry Fox's semi-retirement suggests his conduct during the political negotiations following Pelham's death 6 March 1754.

Wednesday night.

Dear Sir Charles,

I CAME to town but this morning, not having heard of Mr Fox's inoculating his son:[1] you will oblige me by letting me know how he does. If Mr Fox likes seeing people, I will wait on him, but don't mention it unless he does in general, for I would not trouble him. I return on Saturday, and if you come to London before that, I shall be very glad to see you anywhere you choose.

I am

Yours etc.,

Hor. Walpole

To Selwyn, ca 1755

Printed for the first time from the MS now wsl. It was inserted in an extra-illustrated copy of Spence's *Anecdotes* that was sold at Christie's 20 Oct. 1953 (Earl of Derby sale) lot 286, to Mr James M. Osborn who removed it and gave it to wsl.

Dated conjecturally by the hand.

Address: To George Augustus Selwyn, Esq.

Dear Sir,

I AM excessively obliged to you and send you the ballad. He must not mind my absurd interpretation: it is the last stanza that I wish particularly to have explained.

Yours ever,

H. W.

---

1. Charles James Fox (1749–1806). Lady Caroline Fox considered four to be 'the proper age' for inoculation (*Leinster Corr.* i. 215).

Two of 'Gilly' Williams's letters to Selwyn in the autumn of 1755 mention HW. In October he urges Selwyn to join him at Bath and adds:

'Try if you can't revive these intentions [of visiting Bath] in Mr Walpole, say everything of this place it deserves, and give it ten thousand things which it wants' (16 Oct. [1755], MS now WSL).

In December he writes:

'I supped with H. Walpole last night, and (don't laugh) Mr Fox's picture is taken down, and a print of Mr Pitt put up in its place, what do you infer from thence? He is this day gone to Strawberry peevish and fretful the reason of which he can't tell. . . . You will also see they have turned your Paymaster Vane into an epigram, I suspect Horry is the author' ([27 Dec. 1755], MS now WSL; see also HW to Bentley 17 Dec. 1755 and to Gray 25 Dec. 1755, GRAY ii. 87–8).

To Fox, ca June–July 1756

Printed for the first time from the MS in the possession of the Earl of Ilchester, collated by WSL.

Dated by the allusions in the anonymous verses that begin the letter. The verses have not been found elsewhere.

Endorsed by Fox: Jac. Prophecy.

The Prophecy of Prophecies
or Tamas the Rymer's prophecy for the year 1756

When Yorken name, but nae the House,
Shall rise till Lyon frae a Louse;[1]
And bind your bairns frae matrimonie,[2]

1. The rise of Philip Yorke (1690–1764), cr. (1733) Bn and (1754) E. of Hardwicke; lord chancellor 1737–56, from humble origins to a dominant position in the government. The 'House' of York is the 'legitimate' line of the Pretender; James II was Duke of York before he became King. 'Lyon' in this spelling is also used synonymously with the King of Scotland from the lion on the royal shield (as in Lyon King of Arms for the chief herald of Scotland, and in *The Lyon in Mourning*, ed. Henry Paton, Edinburgh, 1895–6, a collection of material relating to the Jacobites after Culloden).

2. Hardwicke's Marriage Act of 1753 came into force in March 1754. Fox had violently opposed the measure (Ilchester, *Henry Fox* i. 184–95).

Till it bring unco ruin on ye;
When foreign redcoats fill the lands,[3]
And clymores held frae British hands;[4]
When Britain's fleet in midland sea
Before a Frenchman's face shall flee;[5]
When Tod[6] shall strip his livery coat
'Mong Lords and commoners to vote;
And like a wizard with a wand
Raise the horn'd De'el within the land;
When round the world a chief that ganged
Shall rule the navy and be hanged;[7]
When Duke of regicide-descent[8]
Your gear shall guide till aw be spent;
And by his head shall ill atone
For death, his race brought Charles upon;
When he that does the Sceptre guide[9]
Shall have twa holes in ae backside;
When Richard's soul in Willy's breast[10]
Shall wish his nephews aw at rest;
When the white hag[11] shall ride the Lyon,
Till ev'ry honest man cry fie on!
Then shall the Eagle, Lamb, and Flower[12]

3. More than 8000 Hessians had been landed at Southampton on 15 May 1756 and 10,000 Hanoverians at Chatham on the 21st to defend England from an expected French invasion (GM 1756, xxvi. 259).

4. The Militia Bill, for a general arming of the people, had been defeated in the Lords on 24 May 1756 after a speech against it by Hardwicke (*Mem. Geo. II* ii. 201–2).

5. Byng's abandonment of Minorca, and the retreat of the English fleet to Gibraltar, after being defeated by the French on 20 May; the first reports reached London in early June (HW to Mann 14 June 1756).

6. Henry Fox himself, from the Scots for fox. The rest of the couplet refers to the humble origin of his family: his father, Sir Stephen Fox, was commonly believed to have begun life as a footman (HW to Mann 29 May 1744, MANN ii. 450 and nn. 17, 18).

7. Lord Anson, first lord of the Ad-

miralty and circumnavigator. He was much abused at this time for his share in Byng's disgrace.

8. Newcastle. His Pelham and Holles ancestors, though not technically regicides, had been active Parliamentarians during the Civil Wars.

9. Apparently George II himself; the following line could refer to his operation for an anal fistula in Oct. 1746 (MANN iii. 327 n. 6).

10. A comparison of the Duke of Cumberland with Richard III, implying that the former would like to murder his nephews so that he could ascend the throne as the latter had done.

11. Probably the Princess of Wales and the Leicester House Opposition to the government. The Princess's insistence on an appointment for Lord Bute in June 1756 is perhaps particularly alluded to.

12. A projected alliance of Austria, Spain, and France to restore the Pretender. The Eagle is Austria; the Flower, the fleur-de-lis of France; the Lamb is ob-

Restore our Royal Sovereign's power;
Peace, plenty, liberty shall reign,
And Britain anes mair rule the main.

My dear Sir,

I SEND you the Scotch verses, because I promised them, but they are really so dull, Grub-street and scurrilous, that I had a great mind not to keep my word.

Yours ever,

HOR. WALPOLE

To Fox, Saturday 31 July 1756

Printed from a pencil note by HW on the reverse of Gray to HW 30 July 1756. Previously printed, Toynbee *Supp.* i. 72; Thomas Gray, *Correspondence*, ed. Toynbee and Whibley, Oxford, 1935, ii. 469 n. 13; GRAY ii. 89.

The letter was probably never sent; on 4 Aug. Gray thanked HW for his willingness to overcome his scruples about applying to ministers, but stated that the apparent recovery of Dr Long would probably spare him the trouble of applying at this time (GRAY ii. 91–2). Mason had also told HW on 1 Aug. that an application to Fox was hardly necessary (MASON i. 1).

GREAT poets have a right to command and none are so much their subjects as great men. I know you think Mr Gr[ay] the greatest poet we have and I know he thinks you the greatest man we have;[1] judge if you can disobey him.[2]

To Fox, Wednesday 27 October 1756

Printed from *Letters to Henry Fox* 96; reprinted, Toynbee *Supp.* i. 74–5. Dated from the reference to Newcastle's intention to resign.

scure, although it may refer to the Golden Fleece, the emblem of which is used with the arms of Spain.

---

1. If Gray ever held this opinion, he had changed it by 1768 when he wrote the bitter verses on Fox's villa at Kingsgate. Other references to Fox in Gray's correspondence are not particularly complimentary (Gray, *Correspondence*, ed. Toynbee and Whibley, Oxford, 1935, i. 442; ii. 524, 526, 808; iii. 927, 1259–62).

2. Gray had written to HW on 30 July requesting that he ask Fox to support James Brown for election as Master of Pembroke Hall (GRAY ii. 89–90).

Wednesday night.

Dear Sir,

I SENT to Holland House, but they told me you dined in town and was not expected home till very late.

After what you know this morning,[1] it would be impertinent in me to tell you what I heard. I only trouble you with this, to apprise you of one thing which you certainly ought to know. The K[ing], Lady Y[armouth], and the Chancellor[2] are persuaded that you would not take the Treasury.[3] I should hope you had made no such resolution. You may depend upon this information.[4]

I know another very particular circumstance,[5] which not being immediately necessary, I should choose not to put upon paper; but if you will give me leave, I will see you in the evening and tell it you.

Is it worth your knowing that the D[uke] of N[ewcastle] yesterday (Tuesday) told my Lord Orford[6] that he was going out?[7]

I am most truly yours,

H. W.

1. As a result of an interview with the King. Fox, who had been secretary of state and leader of the House of Commons since November 1755, had announced his intention of resigning, 13 Oct. 1756, because of friction with Newcastle, thus provoking a ministerial crisis (Ilchester, *Henry Fox* i. 355–60). In the interview on the 27th the King informed Fox that Newcastle would retire; then asked him to see Pitt and try to arrange a union; and authorized him to speak to such other persons as he thought proper to cooperate in a new administration (Hist. MSS Comm., 8th Report, App., *Digby MSS*, 1881, p. 222; Ilchester, op. cit. ii. 2–3). This attempt failed because of Pitt's intransigence, and after other vain attempts at conciliation, Fox formally resigned 13 Nov. (ibid. ii. 14).

2. Lord Hardwicke.

3. Fox had every intention of taking the Treasury if he could form a ministry (John, 4th D. of Bedford, *Correspondence*, 1842–6, ii. 205), although he refused to discuss his own prospective place in his interview with the King on the morning on the 27th. He had indicated to the King his willingness to take an inferior place under Pitt earlier in the month (Ilchester, *Henry Fox* i. 359), which may have created the royal impression that he would now refuse the Treasury.

4. HW's source may have been his nephew, Lord Orford (see final paragraph).

5. Possibly the report that Bedford and Halifax were to be secretaries of state, which HW was repeating the next day (MONTAGU i. 200).

6. George Walpole (1730–91), 3d E. of Orford; HW's nephew.

7. Newcastle definitely decided to resign as first lord of the Treasury on 26 Oct., but did not actually do so until 11 Nov. (BM Add. MSS 32868, f. 431; HW to Mann 4 Nov., 13 Nov. 1756).

To Fox, Saturday 4 December 1756

Printed from a photostat of the MS in the Henry W. and Albert A. Berg Collection, New York Public Library. First printed, Toynbee *Supp.* i. 75–6. The MS passed to Mrs Damer; bequeathed by her to Sir Wathen Waller, 1st Bt; sold Sotheby's 21 Dec. 1921 (the first Waller sale) lot 28, to Hoare; subsequently acquired by Dr Berg.

Dec. 4, 1756.

Dear Sir,

TO my great surprise and concern Lord Hilsb[orough][1] has just told me that you go out of town tomorrow for a long time, giving up the House of Commons.[2] If I could have hoped to find you tonight, I should have come to you directly: I am now reduced to trouble you with a few lines.

Had you stayed, I should have had no rule for my behaviour in Parliament but in doing whatever you did. As that is not to be the case, I must entreat that you will leave me your commands. Let me but know how you wish me to act and vote, and I shall obey it. I have too mean an opinion of myself to think I can be of service to you, but I shall be proud of showing that it is the ability not the inclination that is wanting.[3]

Should you be unwilling to give me any directions in writing, I shall be as ready to obey the least hint that you send me at any time by any person that you trust most. I hope you have many friends that can do you more honour; you have none more unalterably attached to you than

Your most faithful and obedient humble servant,

H. W.

1. Wills Hill (1718–93), 2d Vct Hillsborough; cr. (1751) E. of Hillsborough, and (1789) M. of Downshire. He was a friend and political ally of Fox, who had secured the post of treasurer of the Chamber for him when he entered the Cabinet in 1755 (Ilchester, *Henry Fox* i. 276). Hillsborough followed Fox out of office, but was compensated, at the latter's request, with an English barony

(*Mem. Geo. II* ii. 274; HW to Mann 29 Nov. 1756).

2. An exaggerated report; see the following letter.

3. This profession of attachment is at variance with the account that HW gives in *Mem. Geo. II* of his attitude and conduct towards Fox during this ministerial crisis. See below, Appendix 7.

From Fox, Sunday 5 December 1756

Printed from a photostat of the MS in the Henry W. and Albert A. Berg Collection, New York Public Library. First printed, Toynbee *Supp.* i. 76 n. For the history of the MS see *ante* 4 Dec. 1756.

December 5, 1756.

My dear Hori,

I CAN never sufficiently thank you for your very kind letter, and am glad Lord Hilsborough put my journey in so much a more serious light than it deserves, since it produced it. It is true that I go two days sooner than I intended, to avoid expostulations[1] which Sir William Temple[2] observes may do well between lovers, but never between friends.[3] But my remaining out of town longer or less while, shall be determined by the occasion there may be for my appearance in the House of Commons. Indeed I foresee none, and rather think my situation when I am there will be awkward, and therefore believe I shall stay five or six weeks.[4] But no design is more changeable than this. If you have any thoughts arise against it, I beg you would oblige me with them in a letter left with the porter here. I shall move so from place to place, that unless I knew the very day you would write I can't send you my direction. The mention of Sir William Temple puts me in mind of the likelihood there is that my political life may soon end like his in total retirement. If it does I'll write memoirs too, if not frightened from it, by thinking that the just characters I should give and the true facts I should relate, would be such as might make the readers think that an uneasy and disappointed mind exaggerated them.

At the close of this letter you won't expect any wishes from me of what your conduct should be in Parliament, other than what I am

---

1. According to HW, the Duke of Devonshire had annoyed Fox by yielding too much and too readily to Pitt, while Fox, though out of office, had expected that the Duke, at the Treasury, would be more or less his 'creature' (*Mem. Geo. II* ii. 275–6; HW to Mann 8 Dec. 1756). The immediate cause of the dispute was Devonshire's refusal to give Charles Hamilton the surveyorship of woods, of which Fox had received a promise, when Pitt demanded it for his brother (Ilchester, *Henry Fox* ii. 15–17).

2. Sir William Temple (1628–99), statesman and author.

3. The passage is in Temple's *Memoirs of what passed in Christendom, from the War begun 1672 to the Peace concluded 1679,* 2d edn 1692, p. 78.

4. He stayed only a week, returning to London the 12th and resuming his place in the House on the 13th (Ilchester, *Henry Fox* ii. 18–19).

sure it will be whenever there is opportunity of showing that you are my friend, which is a very great honour and happiness, and the greater because you are not, like some men, everybody's.

Your ever obliged,

H. Fox

To Fox, Monday 20 December 1756

Printed from the MS now WSL. First printed, Toynbee *Supp.* i. 77. For the history of the MS see *ante* 22 July 1746.

Endorsed by HW: To Mr Fox.

Memoranda by HW: Best proof that people don't think want of birth a real objection, is, that no man would set his name to that objection.

Must merit have three or four descents before it can be noble? can it never be so of itself![1]

Monday night, Dec. 20, 1756.

Dear Sir,

I HAVE written out and enclose the character,[2] and have added a little preface,[3] in which, as is apt to be my case, my heart speaks. If you should order it to be printed, be so good as to let me have the proof sheet to revise: but as it is a most incorrect composition, and as you know designed for and confined to a private letter, it is most unfit I fear to appear in public. However, as it is a testimonial of my attachment to you out of power, my passionate principle, I could no more refuse my own inclination than your request, and trust that the faults of the author will be forgiven to the friend.

Yours ever,

H. WALPOLE

1. These are apparently notes for a defence of Fox, but HW does not seem to have used them elsewhere.

2. HW's character of Fox, which was written originally in 1748 as a letter to Lady Caroline Fox; it is printed below, Appendix 6, from HW's manuscript. It was published with minor changes as a *World Extraordinary* on 4 Jan. 1757 and reprinted *London Chronicle* 8–11 Jan. 1757, i. 34–5. It is also printed in HW's *Fugitive*

Pieces, SH, 1758, pp. 160–8 and in *Works* i. 192–4.

3. It is in the form of a 'covering' letter to 'Mr Fitz-Adam,' the printer of the *World;* see *Works* i. 190–1. In it, HW laments the differences between Fox and Pitt and states his desire of defending Fox's reputation, whose fame he considers 'much superior to reproach,' though he has been 'aspersed in the most injurious manner.'

From Fox, ca Wednesday 22 December 1756

Missing.

To Fox, ca Wednesday 22 December 1756

Printed from *Letters to Henry Fox* 99; reprinted, Toynbee *Supp.* i. 77–8.
The text of this letter printed in *Letters to Henry Fox* carries the date of '1756' as though it were in HW's hand, but this seems unlikely. It was, however, certainly written soon after HW's letter of 20 Dec. 1756.

Dear Sir,

BY your note I imagined that I should find you at home, and came hither[1] to prevent your having the trouble of coming to Arlington Street. I agree entirely in thinking that the paper to which you do too much honour, and which the world will certainly treat very differently, will do better in Dodsley's paper,[2] and I don't see how he can with any decency refuse it.[3] I am sensible too of the great incorrectness of it, and could easily mend it, I left it exactly as I sent it to Lady Caroline, to prove that it was, what it really was, a genuine, careless letter. It would be hard if I could not make it better, when I have known the subject eight years longer! I would call tomorrow morning on you, but my brother[4] sends his daughters[5] at twelve to breakfast[6] with me, and whatever I might think, he would not allow any engagement to be of greater consequence. I will therefore hope to have the pleasure of seeing you at eleven.

Yours ever,

H. W.

1. Presumably to Holland House.
2. *The World*, published by Robert Dodsley (1703–64), poet, dramatist, and bookseller.
3. *The World* No. 207, on the late ministerial revolution, criticized Fox and Pitt and defended Newcastle. HW alludes to this paper in the first paragraph of his preface to his character of Fox (*Works* i. 190).
4. Sir Edward Walpole.
5. Laura (ca 1734–1813), m. (1758) Hon. Frederick Keppel, Bp of Exeter; Maria (1736–1807), m. 1 (1759) James Waldegrave, 2d E. Waldegrave, m. 2 (1766) William Henry, D. of Gloucester; and Charlotte (1738–89), m. (1760) Lionel Tollemache, 5th E. of Dysart.
6. Ten seems to have been a more usual hour for breakfast, which was normally a simple meal of tea and rolls or bread and butter; see Dorothy Marshall, 'Manners, Meals, and Domestic Pastimes,' in *Johnson's England*, ed. A. S. Turberville, Oxford, 1933, i. 343–4; Arnold Palmer, *Movable Feasts*, 1952, pp. 10–11.

To Selwyn, ca 1757

Printed for the first time from the MS now wsl. The MS was given to wsl by Mr H. W. Liebert in November 1953; its earlier history is unknown.
Dated conjecturally by the hand.
Address: To Mr Selwyn.

A PARTICULAR friend of yours, one Mrs Isabella Leneve, wants extremely to be conveyed tomorrow evening to Strawberry Hill in the easiest *voiture* she can get. As there is a gentleness in everything that is Selwyn from their tempers downwards, I imagine your four-wheel chaise must be a perfect featherbed, and therefore beg to borrow it. *If it should not keep its equilibrium in Kensington Town,*[1] why, she may once or twice in her life have met with a rub or a jolt even from the soft carriages of your house, and will know the better how to bear it.

From Fox, Friday 13 May 1757

Printed for the first time from a copy made by Dr R. W. Chapman of the original in possession of Earl Stanhope at Chevening, near Sevenoaks, Kent. It is probably the letter sold SH vi. 134 to Thorpe and offered by Thorpe in his catalogues for 1843 and 1844.

Burlington Street, May 13, 1757.

Dear Sir,

I EITHER don't understand the line I have marked or it says nothing particular, vassals everywhere are vassals either of the crown or of the nobles.[1]

I think you might work more into this very pretty plan, and I wish you would, what is there being so pretty. I can have no objection to your showing this.[2] If the third and least party[3] and Lord Gawkee[4]

1. Allusion unexplained.

1. The last sentence of the first paragraph of HW's *Letter from Xo Ho* written 'in less than an hour and a half' on 12 May 1757 and published on the 17th ('Short Notes,' Gray i. 27): 'To have the country enslaved; they desire it not; were there vassals, they would be the vassals of the crown, or of the nobles; while all are free to sell their *liberty*, the richest or craftiest may purchase it' (*Works* i. 206).

2. Presumably HW had asked Fox, as he did George Grenville (HW to Grenville 13 May 1757) whether he found anything personally disagreeable in the *Letter*.

3. In the *Letter* HW refers to Pitt's friends as the 'third' and 'least' of the political factions (*Works* i. 206, 207).

4. Lord Temple, usually caricatured and satirized as 'Squire Gawkee.' HW in the

had been a little worse treated I should have liked it better. I would not have them very ill-treated neither.[5] Adieu. You may have time for any addition you please to make for by what I learn at the Emperor's country house[6] Lien Chi may answer Xoho's letter before the new ministry will be formed.[7]

Pray let me have a copy.

Yours ever,

H. Fox

To Fox, Saturday 18 June 1757

Printed from Toynbee xv. 455–6. The MS was apparently given to Gen. Giuseppe Binda by the 3d Bn Holland. Binda bequeathed it to his daughter, Mademoiselle Beatrice, an actress, who on her death ca 1875, bequeathed it to her fiancé Frank Hilton, known as Frank Harvey (d. ca 1903). In 1905 the MS was in the possession of his widow and children (information from J. W. Hilton's letters to Mrs Toynbee, now WSL).

Dated by the endorsement and by the Townshends' interview with Pitt (below, n. 3).

Endorsed by Fox: Mr H. Walpole, June 18, 1757.

Arlington Street, between 5 and 6.

Dear Sir,

AS I am going out of town[1] in less than half an hour, I cannot help telling you what I have this moment heard: the two Townshends[2] were with Mr Pitt this morning;[3] he desired their opinion; George replied, things had been carried too far without his com-

---

Letter from Xo Ho, treats Temple's failure to bow to the King as the reason for the dismissal of the ministry (*Works* i. 207). His insolence had in fact been the principal stumbling block in the late administration (Ilchester, *Henry Fox* ii. 35).

5. Fox seems to have been considering some sort of reconciliation with Pitt and Temple at this time (ibid. ii. 46–8).

6. Kensington Palace.

7. That is, it will be long enough for Lien Chi, in Peking, to reply to Xo Ho's letter from London before a new ministry is formed.

---

1. To return to SH, which he had left the evening before; see HW to Montagu 18 June 1757 (MONTAGU i. 212).

2. George Townshend and his brother Charles (1725–67), chancellor of the Exchequer 1766–7.

3. The Townshends waited on Pitt at the latter's invitation on the morning of 18 June, the first time he had communicated with them 'for about a fortnight.' George Townshend's description of the interview differs somewhat from the report given by HW: 'to our astonishment [we] heard him [Pitt] avow the ridiculous and dishonest arrangement of men which is now to take place [see below, n. 8]—not the least adoption of any public system of measures being declared or even hinted at by him. Upon this occasion I without hesitation declared my resolution to be no part of it—my brother did the same'

munication, for him to give any opinion: that now he had neither approbation nor disapprobation; he had only admiration. Pitt asked if he might tell the King he would take anything? he replied, he desired to be excused, he had a friend or two by whom he should send what he had to say to the King; but he desired that the King might not be told that he objected to *you*,[4] or any particular man. Charles said he could only repeat what his brother had said. With regard to his office,[5] he said he actually had it still; he should not kiss hands, nor would be in the *Gazette* with this administration, with which they said he had nothing to do; that they would not appear at Court with them, but would go out of town tomorrow.

Lord Halifax has, as I suppose you know, resigned.[6] Pitt protested to him this morning, that if he could have had his will, his Lordship should [have] been named one of the first[7] on this new plan.[8] Pitt, I hear, has kissed hands;[9] and that Lord Temple is to be privy seal,[10] and Lord Gower[11] Master of the Horse; is this all so? Adieu!

Yours ever,

H. WALPOLE

(Hist. MSS. Comm., 11th Report, App. iv, *Townshend MSS*, 1887, p. 393, where the dates given by G. Townshend are one day out).

4. Two days later HW reported that the inclusion of Fox in the new ministry was the 'real sore' that enraged George Townshend and made him refuse to cooperate with Pitt (MANN v. 104).

5. Charles Townshend had been appointed treasurer of the Chamber in November 1756; he retained the office during Pitt's administration 1757–61 but did not take much part in the administration (DNB *sub* Charles Townshend).

6. Halifax resigned as president of the Board of Trade 16 June 1757, on discovering that Newcastle had not proposed him to Pitt as third secretary of state (for the West Indies) as he had promised to do, and that Pitt had no intention of creating any such office. He eventually withdrew his resignation in September on being called to the Cabinet Council (Halifax to Newcastle 16 June 1757, BM Add. MSS 32871, f. 323; A. H. Basye, *The Lords Commissioners of Trade and Plantations*, New Haven, 1925, pp. 94–100).

7. Considering Pitt's reluctance until the last moment to consent even to Halifax's being called to the Cabinet as an individual, such a remark seems unlikely; several people at the time, however, had the impression that Newcastle and not Pitt had been responsible for Halifax's disappointment (Basye, op. cit., 97, 99–100 and the documents there cited).

8. The ministerial arrangement engineered by Lord Hardwicke between the 15th and 18th of June which resulted in a coalition of the Pitt, Newcastle, and Fox groups. Since Pitt's dismissal in April there had been various attempts by each of the groups separately, and in combinations of two to the exclusion of the third, to form a ministry, all of which had failed.

9. Pitt did not kiss hands as secretary of state until 29 June because of delays in legal appointments (Basil Williams, *Life of William Pitt*, 1913, i. 323).

10. The King refused to have Temple reinstated as first lord of the Admiralty, as he had been in Pitt's first administration; he became privy seal, instead, in the new administration (Williams, op. cit. i. 324–5).

11. Granville Leveson-Gower (1721–1803), 2d E. Gower, cr. (1786) M. of Staf-

PS. I forgot to tell you a particularity; yesterday or the day before Charles Townshend found Pitt at Newcastle House, who would have gone away, but being pressed by Charles to stay, he said with a sneer, 'Whom God and nature has joined, let no man put asunder.'

I fear it will be troublesome to you to write as you are at dinner; but if you have anything to say to me, if you will send a line to my nieces at my brother's in Pall Mall, or to my Lady Albemarle's,[12] her daughters[13] will bring it me tomorrow.

To Selwyn, Tuesday 6 September 1757

Printed for the first time from a photostat of the MS in the possession of Sir John Murray. On 5 Aug. 1857, J. W. Croker wrote to Peter Cunningham: 'I am afraid I am again too late for you, but I find this morning a portfolio containing a dozen and a half of original letters and notes of Horace Walpole's, of various dates from 1746 to 1787. They are mostly to George Selwyn, and some of them little more than invitations to dinner; but half a dozen are of more importance, and one of the 6th of September 1757 is peculiarly curious as it contains an admission of his consciousness of being hereditarily mad' [in the last sentence of the first paragraph].[1] A similar note giving this absurd interpretation of HW's pleasantry now accompanies the MS. The rest of Croker's description also fits the collection of HW's letters now in possession of Sir John Murray quite closely—19 letters, dated 1746 to 1784, of which ten are to Selwyn. It is possible that the MSS were already in possession of the then John Murray, with whom Croker was closely connected.

Dated 1757 in another hand (probably Croker's), but confirmed by the reference to the approaching marriage of Lord Bolingbroke and Lady Diana Spencer.

Lady Townshend's, Sept. 6th.

As I began to write at ten o'clock at night, I have not time to engrave so finely that you might at once know my pen-writing. I should have thanked you sooner, my dear Sir, for your obliging present,[1a] but did not receive it till today, and till I came to town

ford; lord privy seal 1755–7. He resigned to make way for Temple, but was appointed Master of the Horse 2 July.

12. Lady Anne Lennox (1703–89), m. (1723) William Anne van Keppel, 2d E. of Albemarle.

13. Lady Caroline Keppel (1737–69), m. (1759) Robert Adair; and Lady Elizabeth Keppel (1739–68), m. (1764) Francis Russell, styled M. of Tavistock (Collins, *Peerage*, 1812, iii. 741).

1. Cunningham i. p. xi, n. 1.

1a. Possibly the painted glass, 'the arms of Ayliffe impaling Clifford of Frampton' that HW placed in the window of the Little Parlour at SH, 'given me by Mr George Selwyn' ('Des. of SH,' *Works* ii. 418).

tonight, did not know how to direct to you. As poor *Mrs* Crawford[2] is dead, I was not sure of whom you was most fond in Scotland, I mean of those whom you never saw: but at Arthur's[3] they tell me, that *Mr* Crawford[4] will take care to convey this to you. The glass is extremely pretty, and extremely cheap—I want to want some of it. I have nothing to send you in return but a repetition of poor Perry's[5] self-murder. Does not this go on to prove what I have always said, that you and I shall live to be the least mad of all England?[6]

Frederick-Clinton-Maynard-Nevil-Douglas Viscount Bolinbroke[7] is to be married on Friday at the camp[8] to Lady Diana Hamilton West.[9] The Duke[10] is expected home with the remains of the Electorate,[11] where Marshal Richelieu[12] has been at a play and reigned

2. Perhaps Hon. Sarah Sempill (d. 1751), dau. of Hew, 12th Bn Sempill; m. (1750), as his second wife, Patrick Craufurd of Drumsoy and Auchinames, Ayrshire, the father of HW's and Selwyn's friend John ('Fish') Craufurd (*Scots Peerage* vii. 563; below n. 4). HW told Lady Ossory, 1 Sept. 1780, that he was as sorry for someone's death 'as George Selwyn was for poor Mrs Craufurd whom he had never seen.'

3. White's, frequently called Arthur's after its proprietor, Robert Arthur.

4. Probably either Patrick Craufurd (d. 1778), of Drumsoy and Auchinames, Ayrshire; M.P. Ayrshire 1741–54, Renfrewshire 1761–8 (Sir Bernard Burke, *Landed Gentry*, 4th edn, 1868, p. 305; above, n. 2); or Alexander Craufurd (ca 1729–97), cr. (1791) Bt, of Kilburney, Sterlingshire, with whom Selwyn was in correspondence after 1774. 'Fish' Craufurd was only about fifteen and at Eton in 1757 (Judd, *Members of Parliament* 163; *Eton College Register 1753–90*, ed. R. A. Austen-Leigh, Eton, 1921, p. 135).

5. George Perry (d. 1757), army officer; Col. of the 55th Foot 1755–7; friend of Selwyn, Conway, and 'Gilly' Williams. Williams described him as 'our Perry' in telling Selwyn that he had received a regiment (Williams to Selwyn 25 Dec. 1755—MS now WSL). See also [W. B. Boulton], *The History of White's*, 1892, ii pt i. 8, 9, 10, 12, 17, 32; ii pt ii. 69. News of his suicide at Halifax, Nova Scotia, reached England by packet on 29 Aug., but the newspapers did not specify the cause of his death and in-

deed went out of the way to make it appear that his 'weak constitution' could not stand the fogs of Halifax (*Daily Adv.* 31 Aug., 2 Sept. 1757; *London Chronicle* 1–3 Sept. 1757, ii. 223). But Conway to HW 3 Sept. 1757 mentions 'Col. Perry's killing himself,' and Lord Holland, in 1766, draws a parallel between Perry's death and the suicide of the Duke of Bolton (Jesse, *Selwyn* i. 381–2).

6. An echo of the gravedigger's remark to Hamlet (V. i. 170) that men in England are mad, a favourite with HW.

7. Frederick St John (1734–87), 2d Vct Bolingbroke. The four additional names refer to previous attachments, though the principal one, Lady Coventry, is not included.

8. The marriage took place on Thursday, 8 Sept. at Harbledown, Kent (GEC).

9. Lady Diana Spencer (1734–1808), m. 1 (1757) Frederick St John, 2d Vct Bolingbroke; m. 2 (1768) Topham Beauclerk. The two names refer to her previous suitors: Conway told HW when the match was first known that it would break the heart of 'my poor aide-de-camp [Hamilton] and George West's; at least the latter, for Hamilton's, indeed, stood its trial when she changed to him' (Conway to HW 29 Aug. 1757).

10. Of Cumberland; at this time in command of the army in Hanover.

11. Hanover had been overrun by the French in August. The Duke of Cumberland did not return to England until October, although the *Daily Adv.* printed a

in the King's box. The secret expedition[13] remains, and a secret. New York is in danger[14]—the greatest news besides, is, that all I have told you even in this room, is true. Adieu!

Yours ever,

H. Walpole

From Selwyn, ca 30 September 1757

Missing; mentioned *post* 2 Oct 1757 *bis*.

To Selwyn, Sunday 2 October 1757

Missing; mentioned in the following letter.

To Selwyn, Sunday 2 October 1757 *bis*

Printed from a photostat of the MS in the possession of the Carl H. Pforzheimer Library of New York. First printed, Toynbee *Supp.* i. 142, where it is assigned to 21 Sept. 1766. The MS was sold Anderson Galleries 21 Nov. 1918 (G. D. Smith sale) lot 364; in possession of Mr Pforzheimer by 1944.

Dated '1757?' in another hand; confirmed by the agreement between HW's projected dates in this letter for going to London and then to Bath and those mentioned *post* 6 Oct. 1757, which can be precisely dated by internal evidence.

Endorsed: H. Walpole.

Address: To Mr Selwyn in Curzon Street.

report on 7 Sept. (contradicted on the 9th) that he had embarked at Stade for England.

12. Louis-François-Armand Vignerot du Plessis (1696–1788), Duc and Maréchal de Richelieu; first gentleman of the Bedchamber; commander of the French forces in Germany July 1757—Feb. 1758.

13. To Rochefort (see following letters). Its departure from Portsmouth had been delayed for nearly a month by contrary winds, but it finally sailed on 7 Sept. (Con-

way to HW 11 Aug., 29 Aug., 3 Sept., 7 Sept. 1757; HW to Mann 3 Sept. 1757; *Daily Adv.* Aug.–Sept. 1757, *passim*).

14. The dispatches from America that arrived on 29 Aug. had mentioned a threat to New York (Conway to HW 3 Sept. 1757), a report magnified by rumour until the newspapers reported that 'some letters from New York advise that Mons. de Montcalm, the French general in Canada, was advancing towards Albany at the head of 9000 men' (*Daily Adv.* 5 Sept. 1757).

Strawberry Hill, Sunday night.

Dear Sir,

I WROTE to you this morning in answer to your obliging letter, but my Lady Townshend tells me that you are likely to go out of town tomorrow, and you will possibly not receive it, which makes me send you this, to say, that I will certainly wait on you at Matson in my way to Bath,[1] but cannot set out before tomorrow sennight. I would be in town myself tomorrow morning, but am engaged to dine at Kingston—if I hear you are not gone, I will be in town tomorrow night. I finish, for fear of putting any more *tomorrows* into my letter, of which I perceive it is totally composed.

Yours ever,

H. W.

To SELWYN, Thursday 6 October 1757

Printed for the first time from a photostat of the MS in the possession of Sir John Murray.

Dated in another hand; confirmed by the reference to the first reports from the secret expedition against Rochefort, although Thursday was 6, not 5, October in 1757.

Strawberry Hill, Thursday 5th[6th].

Dear Sir,

IT was impossible for me to get to town on Monday night; and I was as sorry to find you gone on Tuesday. I only write you this line, that you may not be disappointed, if you should not see me at Matson next week, where however I will be, if I am delivered from the anxiety I am in at present. In short, an account is come that the secret expedition, which now appears was against Rochfort, has taken the little Isle of Aix[1] which lies just before it. As this is all we know yet, and as the enterprise is of so desperate a nature, you may imagine what pain I am in for Mr Conway,[2] and how little I can think of amusing myself, unless I hear he is safe. If I am so happy as to know that before Mon-

1. HW did not make this trip.

———

1. On 23 Sept. An express with this intelligence reached London on 6 Oct.

(*Hardwicke Corr.* iii. 186; *Grenville Papers* i. 209).

2. Who was second in command of the secret expedition.

day, I shall certainly set out:[3] if not, I am sure you will excuse me. Be
so good, as soon as you receive this, to let me know by a line directed
to Arlington Street, when you propose being at Bath, where I will
meet you, if I cannot come to Matson in time—I mean, if I learn any
good news. Adieu! dear Sir,

Yours ever,

H. WALPOLE

To SELWYN, Saturday 8 October 1757

Printed for the first time from a photostat of the MS in the possession of Sir
John Murray.

Dated in another hand; confirmed by the references to Conway's return from
the secret expedition (Conway to HW 7 Oct. 1757; HW to Conway 8 Oct. 1757).

Arlington Street, Saturday.

Dear Sir,

YOU will conclude, when Mr C[onway] is returned, that I am
absolved from my excuse—but the return of the expedition
without doing anything, makes such a noise,[1] that I cannot think of
stirring without seeing him. We are, according to custom, very angry
that holding up our leg to piss against France, has not ruined that
country. Shall you be surprised, if that merciful and disinterested
legislator my Lord Hardwicke[2] should want to hang General Mordaunt?[3] My Lord Bath told me today[4] that this foolish and imprac-

3. HW learned of Conway's safe return
to England by the 8th, but postponed and
eventually abandoned his visit to Matson
and Bath because of the uproar caused
by the failure of the secret expedition to
accomplish its purpose (*post* 8 Oct. 1757;
Conway to HW 7 Oct. 1757; HW to Conway 8 Oct. 1757).

1. For the immediate effect of the news
of the failure of the secret expedition,
which reached London on 7 Oct., see
Hardwicke Corr. iii. 187; *Grenville Papers*
i. 212–4; and *post* 11 Oct. and 13 Oct.
1757.

2. Though Hardwicke was no longer a
member of the government, he was in

constant communication with Newcastle.

3. Gen. Sir John Mordaunt (1697–1780),
army officer; M.P. Pontefract 1730–4, Whitchurch 1735–41, Cockermouth 1741–68;
commander of the expedition against
Rochefort. Hardwicke's letters to Newcastle on the failure of the expedition,
though very critical of the conduct of the
army officers in general, betray no special
animosity to Mordaunt (Hardwicke to
Newcastle 9 Oct. 1757, BM Add. MSS
32874, ff. 489–90; 16 Oct. 1757, quoted in
Hardwicke Corr. iii. 190).

4. Probably at Lady Townshend's, where
HW had picked up other information regarding the expedition (HW to Conway
8 Oct. 1757).

ticable project costs two millions[5]—a pretty codicil, for having added Mr P[itt][6] to Newcastle, Hardwicke and Anson! We lost two men[7] in this exploit, who, they say, are the only two who don't know what fools we are. I write freely, but to tell you the truth, I grow afraid of the Bastile, not of the Tower. Adieu!

Yours ever,

H. W.

To Selwyn, Tuesday 11 October 1757

Printed for the first time from a photostat of the MS in the possession of Sir John Murray.

Strawberry Hill, Oct. 11th 1757.

My dear Sir,

BY the gladness with which I received your invitation, I trust you will believe that my disappointing you was not a matter of choice. The obliging things you say to me, make me doubly sorry. I will tell you my exact situation, and then you shall judge, how difficult it would be to me to leave this part of the world just at present, though the fleet is returned and Mr Conway well. In short, the world is so disappointed at our not taking France prisoner, that the clamour would stun anybody whose ears had not been deafened last year.[1] Gen. Mordaunt is sent for to town,[2] and I believe the late Chancellor Shylock,[3] that Jew who loves human blood better than anything but money, is whetting a cleaver—that he has borrowed; for even for murder I believe he would grudge a penny to have his own new-set. Mr Conway, who, thank God, is not blamed,[4] is ordered

---

5. Other estimates placed the cost in the vicinity of half a million (Chesterfield, *Letters*, ed. Dobrée, 1932, v. 2247; report of the Prussian embassy in London, 7 Oct. 1757, cited in Albert von Ruville, *William Pitt, Earl of Chatham*, trans. Chaytor and Morison, 1907, ii. 152).

6. Who had been secretary of state for the south, with direction of the war, since June 1757. The secret expedition had been his creation; see J. S. Corbett, *England in the Seven Years' War*, 1907, i. 187–201.

7. A 'letter from Portsmouth dated October 7,' printed in the *Daily Adv.* 10 Oct. 1757, reported 'there were two marines killed on board the *Magnanime.*'

1. During the uproar caused by the loss of Minorca.

2. He had already arrived, since he was at Court on the 10th (Newcastle to Pitt 10 Oct. 1757, BM Add. MSS 32875 f. 28).

3. Hardwicke.

4. HW enlarges on this to Mann 12 Oct. 1757 and to Conway 13 Oct. 1757.

to stay at Portsmouth,[5] and there have been great deliberations in the Cabinet whether he and the fleet should not be sent back to Rochfort,[6] with a card to desire the French would knock their brains out to retrieve our honour.

The bonfires for burning Mordaunt have extinguished those that were lighting to roast the Duke.[7] *The Honestest Man* in the world[8] is so enraged at Mordaunt for *cowardice*,[9] that he has almost forgot to sacrifice his own son for obeying him.[10]

The war between my Lord Townshend and his heir apparent[11] continues with great violence, notwithstanding all the pains my Lady takes to reconcile them. They write such scurrilous papers against one another, that she trembles lest they should cut one another's throats.

5. Conway told HW that he had gone to Bevismount on the 9th as 'a sort of volunteer' to supervise the debarkation of the troops (Conway to HW 10 Oct. 1757).

6. At a Cabinet meeting on the night of 7 Oct., Pitt proposed sending the fleet and army to take the Isle of Ré, and was supported by Lords Holdernesse and Ligonier, but when the other members opposed the idea, Pitt did not press it (Newcastle to Hardwicke 8 Oct. 1757, BM Add. MSS 32874, f. 473; J. S. Corbett, *England in the Seven Years' War*, 1907, i. 229). Conway was not specifically mentioned.

7. Of Cumberland, who had enraged the King and the mob by signing the 'disastrous' convention of Kloster-Zevern with the Duc de Richelieu on 8 Sept. 1757. It left Hanover at the mercy of the French troops, opened a corridor for the French invasion of Prussia, and provided for the dispersal of Cumberland's army (W. L. Dorn, *Competition for Empire, 1740–1763*, New York, 1940, p. 320). The effects of the Duke's action can be followed in Evan Charteris, *William Augustus, Duke of Cumberland, and the Seven Years' War,* [1925], pp. 302–17; and *Hardwicke Corr.* iii. 178–90.

8. George II, probably in allusion to HW's twice-repeated opinion that the King, far from deserving his reputation for strict honesty, might have been an honest man 'if he had never hated his father or had ever loved his son' (*Mem. Geo. II* i. 180, iii. 65; the latter passage applies the dic-

tum to the King's conduct in the affair of Kloster-Zevern).

9. The King's opinion of Mordaunt's conduct is unrecorded, though he virtually ignored the General when the latter appeared at Court on 10 Oct. (Newcastle to Pitt 10 Oct. 1757, BM Add. MSS 32875, f. 281).

10. The King had disavowed the Duke of Cumberland's action in signing the Convention of Kloster-Zevern, asserting that the Duke had exceeded his instructions. HW, on the contrary, believed that the Duke had acted on express orders to save what remained of Hanover and his army at all costs, an interpretation more in accord with the facts than the King's attempt to extricate himself from an embarrassing situation by discrediting his son's negotiation. See, in addition to the references cited above, n. 7, *Mem. Geo. II* iii. 57–65; HW to Mann 29 Sept. 1757; Richard Waddington, *La Guerre de sept ans,* 1899–1914, i. Chap. IX, and accounts of the affair in biographies of Pitt. The Newcastle Papers show that disappointment at Mordaunt's failure in no way diminished the King's determination to sacrifice the Duke of Cumberland.

11. George Townshend. They were quarrelling over the Militia Bill, which George had promoted in Parliament, while his father had raised a mob against it in Norfolk (HW to Mann 29 Sept. 1757; HW to Strafford 11 Oct. 1757). See also R. W. Ketton-Cremer, *Norfolk Assembly*, 1957, pp. 153–5.

Mrs Mennil[12] is dead suddenly.

I know no other news. My best compliments to Mr Williams. By the time I receive your next letter, I hope to be at liberty, at least that I shall know what I can do.

Yours ever,

H. W.

To Selwyn, Thursday 13 October 1757

Printed for the first time from a photostat of the MS in the possession of Sir John Murray.

Arlington Street, Oct. 13th 1757.

Dear Sir,

IT is quite impossible for me to wait on you at Matson, and I have little hopes of seeing you at Bath. I shall not see Mr Conway for some days, who stays to see the troops disembark; the clamour has brought me to town,[1] but I have the satisfaction to find that it is generally known that Mr Conway did his utmost to obtain the descent:[2] even the seamen are full of his praises.[3] The City have recommenced where they left off last year,[4] and talk in high terms of demanding redress—in short, they don't scruple to say that Sir J. Mordaunt's and the Duke's instructions were the same, lest a hair of Hanover's head should suffer.[5] You will be entertained with the ad-

12. Anne Gell (d. 1757), dau. of John Gell of Hopton, Derbyshire; m. (1754) Hugo Meynell of Bradley, Derbyshire, and Quorndon, Leics (John Nichols, *History . . . of the County of Leicester*, 1795–1815, iii pt i. 101; James Pilkington, *A View of the Present State of Derbyshire*, 1789, ii. 296). Though Nichols says she died in June, the *London Chronicle* 8–11 Oct. 1757, ii. 346, reported her death 'a few days since.'

1. HW went to London to meet the Earl of Hertford, Conway's brother (HW to Conway 13 Oct. 1757).

2. Conway had opposed a direct attack on Rochefort, but had urged 'several other plans' to enable the expedition to accomplish more than it did (Conway to HW 26 Sept., 30 Sept., 10 Oct. 1757; *Mem. Geo. II* iii. 53–6).

3. HW heard this from Lady Suffolk (HW to Conway 13 Oct. 1757).

4. During the Byng agitation in 1756–7 the City merchants had taken the lead, first in forcing the trial of the Admiral, and then in insisting on the execution of the death sentence (Brian Tunstall, *Admiral Byng and the Loss of Minorca*, 1928, pp. 179–80, 258–9, 273–5).

5. Newcastle, describing the uproar caused by the failure of the expedition, wrote to Hardwicke on 15 Oct. that the greater and most effective part of the criticism was based on the supposition 'that the fleet, etc. were recalled, to prevent the

venture of your nephew Lord Middleton,[6] who reading in the papers that Rochfort was taken,[7] ordered his chaise and sat out for the *Bureau de Bob*[8] to learn particulars. At Guildford he overtook Sir John Mordaunt changing horses, who, he concluded, had sent himself post with the news. Between impatience and politeness he could not think of letting a conqueror travel to the Capitol in a post-chaise with no company but his valet-de-chambre, but begged his Heroship to make use of his chaise as a triumphal car till his own should come home. Sir John with the utmost humility condescended to accept the offer, did not crowd my Lord at all with his laurels, and in they got together. Nothing exceeded your nephew's impatience to hear him begin, but his astonishment that so great a man should be so modest, who never offered to tap the chapter of glory. The Viscount was under a thousand perplexities whether in good manners he ought not to hope that Sir John had received no mortal wounds, which would balance the advantages that Britain had received—however the fear of being impertinent prevailed, and they arrived at Hyde Park Corner without the victory being mentioned. Middleton was as much overjoyed at the turnpike to quit his hero for news, as he had been to meet him.

I enclose two grubs,[9] very bad ones, but nonsense acquires sense by the time it has got an hundred miles from London.

Can you forgive me, can Mr Williams, for disappointing you? or can't you feel for me? When a friend one loves extremely is concerned, one can't be indifferent even to his innocence. Adieu!

Yours ever,

H. W.

French from committing further violences upon the Electoral dominions, and thus is connected with the late convention [of Kloster-Zevern]. But . . . that is without the least foundation' (BM Add. MSS 32875, f. 124). See also HW to Conway 13 Oct. 1757; *Mem. Geo. II* iii. 74; *Chatham Corr.* i. 277–8.

6. George Brodrick (1730–65), 3d Vct Midleton; M.P. Ashburton 1754–61, Shoreham 1761–5, who had m. (1752) Albinia Townshend (ca 1731–1808), dau. of Selwyn's sister Albinia.

7. The *Daily Adv.* carried this report on 7 Oct., the same day that news of the return of the expedition reached London.

8. That is, Robert Arthur's or White's. The incident that follows probably occurred on 9 Oct., since Mordaunt was at Court on the 10th (*ante* 11 Oct. 1757, n. 2).

9. That is, Grub Street verses; they are missing.

To Selwyn, Tuesday 18 October 1757

Printed for the first time from a photostat of the MS in the possession of Sir John Murray.

Dated '1757' in another hand; confirmed by the reference to the Duke of Cumberland's resignation.

Endorsed: Oct. 1757. [In a different hand] Horace Walpole.

Address: To George Augustus Selwyn, Esq. at Bath.

Postmark: 18 OC.

Arlington Street, 18th Oct. Tuesday late.

I AM but just come to town, and in the uncertainty whether and when this will find you, I write only a line to tell you both, that the Duke has resigned everything[1]—I suppose even expectations. Bath is a very pretty place when one don't know a soul in town, or in a dead autumn; but trust me you would be better diverted here. Princes of the Blood don't resign every day like Mr Doddington.[2] Adieu! I literally have barely time to write this.

Yours faithfully,

H. W.

To Selwyn, Saturday 12 August 1758

Printed from a photostat of the MS in the R. G. Shaw Library-Theatre Collection in the Harvard College Library. First printed, Toynbee *Supp.* iii. 448–9. The MS was sold Puttick and Simpson's 19 Dec. 1862, lot 364 to Roupell; probably one of the two letters erroneously described as Aug. 1788, sold Christie's 5 July 1887 (Roupell sale) lot 519 to Pearson; offered J. Pearson and Co. Catalogue 7 (n.d. but after 1887); later inserted in Augustine Daly's extra-illustrated copy of his own *Life of Peg Woffington*, Philadelphia, 1888, which was sold American Art

1. The Duke of Cumberland, immediately after his arrival in London on 11 Oct., informed the King through Lady Yarmouth of his intention to resign his command as Captain-General and his regiment of Guards. Attempts to heal the breach between father and son during the next few days failed and the Duke resigned in another audience on the 15th (*Hard-*

wicke Corr. iii. 188–91, which corrects some of the details of HW's account in *Mem. Geo. II* iii. 60–4; Evan Charteris, *William Augustus, Duke of Cumberland, and the Seven Years' War,* [1925], pp. 310–15).

2. He had lost his place of treasurer of the Navy in Nov. 1756; regained it in April 1757, and lost it again in June 1757.

Galleries 19 March 1900 (Daly sale) to George D. Smith, probably for R. G. Shaw, who presented it to Harvard on 1 August 1915.

Address: To George Augustus Selwyn, Esq., at Matson near Gloucester.

Strawberry Hill, Aug. 12, 1758.

Dear Sir,

I HAVE this instant received a note from Kensington,[1] and transcribing it will make you just as informed as I am. The troops landed on 6th six miles from Cherbourg; some force appeared, but retired on the firing of our ships, which covered the landing. General Dury[2] with the Guards marched towards the French, who again made a show of defence, and again retired. Our whole loss is not supposed to exceed 18 or 20 men. A fort was attacked by our ships and a magazine blew up.

I tell you all this, not that you will care, but because you would think you should care, if you did not know it— By the way I forgot the chief part, which is that we have actually taken Cherbourg.[3] Mr Pitt proposes to make it the headquarters of the war, the Duke of Newcastle is learning where it is situated[4]—and somebody or other is already offering to restore it, provided orders are sent to Prince Soubize[5] not to stir a step farther. Adieu!

Yours ever,

H. W.

From C. H. Williams, Tuesday 15 August 1758

Printed from the MS now wsl. First printed, Toynbee *Supp.* iii. 153–4. For the early history of the MS, see *ante* 22 July 1746; it was sold Sotheby's 5 Dec. 1921 (first Waller sale) lot 197 to Criddle; sold by Kyrle Fletcher, Nov. 1936, to wsl.

1. From Conway 11 Aug. 1758. The first paragraph of the present letter is almost a transcript of the first part of Conway's note.

2. Alexander Dury (d. 11 Sept. 1758), Major-Gen., 1757 (*Burke's . . . Landed Gentry*, 17th edn, ed. L. G. Pine, 1952, p. 722; GM 1758, xxviii. 443, 444).

3. On the 8th. HW was informed of it in a second note from Conway at five o'clock on the 11th.

4. HW gives another instance of New-castle's geographical vagueness in *Mem. Geo. II* i. 396: 'Annapolis, Annapolis! Oh! yes, Annapolis must be defended; to be sure, Annapolis should be defended—where is Annapolis?'

5. Charles de Rohan (1715–87), Prince de Soubise; commander of the French forces in Germany. His advance guard had won a considerable victory at Sandershausen on 23 July which threatened Hanover.

Colebrook, the 15th August 1758.

Dear Sir,

I HAVE a favour to beg of you which I flatter myself from our long and uninterrupted friendship you'll grant me. A friend of mine[1] to whom I can refuse nothing has begged me with great earnestness to ask you for a set of the lives of the *Royal and Noble Authors*.[2] As you are sure I would do anything of this sort to oblige you, be so good as to indulge me in this request.

As I shall soon fit up a library at this place, I should also be much obliged to you if you would order anybody (who I will willingly pay for his trouble) to make me a design of the inside of yours,[3] for I would have mine exactly the same.

I have no more to add but to tell you what I will believe will be agreeable to you, which is that by a strict regimen, much exercise, and the excellent air of this place, I have entirely recovered my health.[4] I wish I could say Lady Essex[5] was as well, but as she is prescribed the Bristol waters, I am going thither with her, and therefore beg you'd send me the books by the Bristol coach. I am, dear sir, with great regard and a true esteem,

Your most faithful and obedient humble servant,

C. HANBURY WILLIAMS

Lady Essex who I have the happiness of having with me here assures you of her sincerest services.

From SELWYN, ca 13–20 August 1758

Missing; mentioned *post* 29 Aug.; sent to HW at Ragley but not received before HW left there about 20 Aug.

1. Unindentified.

2. HW had finished printing the *Royal and Noble Authors* in April 1758 ('Short Notes,' GRAY i. 29).

3. There is no evidence that this was done.

4. Williams had returned from Russia in February 1758 in a state of mental derangement. He was confined for a time,

but was able to go to Coldbrook at the end of April. For a time he seemed better, but his health declined during the autumn until he went permanently insane in December (Ilchester, *Hanbury-Williams* 422–8).

5. His daughter, Frances Hanbury Williams (1735–59), m. (1754) William Anne Holles Capel, 4th E. of Essex (ibid. 37).

To Selwyn, Tuesday 22 August 1758

Printed for the first time from the MS now wsl. It was sold Puttick and Simpson's 19 Dec. 1862, lot 367 to Roupell; probably one of the two letters, erroneously described as Aug. 1788, sold Christie's 5 July 1887 (Roupell sale) lot 519 to Pearson; offered J. Pearson & Co. Catalogue 7 (n.d. but after 1887) lot 451; sold by Hamill and Barker, Chicago, to wsl in April 1951.

Dated by the contents.

Arlington Street, Aug. 22d.

D O you like a conquest or a defeat? do you choose an admiral[1] who is so sparing of his words that he will neither write what he is doing nor scarce what he has done, or a general[2] who is knocked on the head before he has almost ever spoken at all? Do you wish the English in France, or the French in Hanover—you have but to say; all this choice is come over within a week. Boscawen has taken Louisbourg,[3] Lord Howe and fifty other officers[4] are killed at Ticonderago, which I believe Betty[5] can no more spell, than my Lady Townshend pronounce, and the new Lord Howe[6] has entirely demolished the works at Cherbourg;[7] the fleet is off Portland,[8] and is perhaps going

1. Edward Boscawen (1711–61), admiral; M.P. Truro 1742–61; commander-in-chief of the fleet covering the siege of Louisbourg.

2. George Augustus Howe (ca 1724–6 July 1758), 3d Vct Howe; army officer; M.P. Nottingham borough 1747–58.

3. On 26 July; word of its fall reached London on 18 Aug. (*London Gazette Extraordinary* 18 Aug. 1758; GM 1758, xxviii. 392).

4. Only one other officer was killed in the skirmish in which Howe fell on 6 July, but many others were killed in an attack on Fort Ticonderoga itself on the 8th (General Abercromby to Pitt 12 July 1758, in *London Gazette Extraordinary* 22 Aug. 1758, reprinted GM 1758, xxviii. 389–90; a text supplying some omitted passages, but leaving out others printed in the contemporary version is in William Pitt, *Correspondence . . . with Colonial Governors*, ed. Kimball, New York, 1906, i. 297–302). See also L. H. Gipson, *The British Empire before the American Revolution*, New York, 1936–56, vii. 230–1. News of the battle reached England on 21 Aug. (GM 1758, xxviii. 392).

5. Elizabeth Munro (or Neale) (ca 1730–97), apple-seller (MONTAGU i. 109; MASON i. 81).

6. Richard Howe (1726–99), 4th Vct Howe; cr. an English Vct (1782) and an Earl (1788); brother of the above-mentioned; naval officer; M.P. Dartmouth 1757–82. He was in command of the attack on Cherbourg 6 Aug. 1758 and later, during the American Revolution, commander-in-chief of the British fleet in America.

7. See *ante* 12 Aug. 1758 and HW to Mann 12 Aug. 1758 for the taking of Cherbourg; further accounts 'that his Majesty's forces, after having completely demolished the basin, piers, and harbour of Cherburg, and destroyed all the batteries, forts, magazines, and stores, at that place, and along the coast, were all re-embarked, without the least opposition from the enemy, in order to pursue the further objects of his Majesty's instructions' arrived in London 19 Aug. (GM 1758, xxviii. 383). See also Gipson, op. cit. vii. 135.

8. The fleet returned to Portland for fresh supplies on 19 Aug. and after one false start on the 22d, sailed again for

on another silent enterprise. You will find the details in the *Gazettes*.[9]
I heard the news of Cape Breton at Oxford,[10] and wished for you to
invite the Vice-Chancellor[11] to drink the King's health on the occasion. Tell me exactly, if you know, your motions, for I will not de-
tain you *again* at Matson, when you want to *march*[12] somewhere else.
Adieu!

Yours ever,

H. W.[12a]

Scarlet[13] has got a sweet little picture of two of King Charles I's
younger children: he calls it Vandyke,[14] I doubt if all of it is of him;
he asks 20 guineas, I think would take fifteen. I don't tell you of what
I did not think worth buying myself, for I bid him money for it,
and had much mind to it, but having no room to spare and less
money, I resisted, and tell you of it, who I think would be glad of
it—yet I recommend it tenderly, as you was not pleased with your
last purchase there.

To Selwyn, Tuesday 29 August 1758

Printed from a photostat of the MS in the Forster Collection in the Victoria and
Albert Museum. First printed, Toynbee iv. 181. The MS was sold Puttick and

another raid on the French coast 31 Aug.
(J. S. Corbett, *England in the Seven Years'
War*, 1907, i. 296; GM 1758, xxviii. 392–3).

9. In the *London Gazette Extraordinary*
18 Aug., 22 Aug. 1758, and the *London
Gazette* No. 9818, 15–19 Aug. 1758.

10. On his way from a visit to Hertford
at Ragley, Warwickshire, between 13 and
20 Aug. (HW to Conway 21 July 1758;
HW to Mann 12 Aug. 1758; HW to Montagu 20 Aug. 1758, Montagu i. 223).

11. A reference to the Jacobitism of Oxford and to Selwyn's expulsion from Oxford in 1745 for profaning the sacrament
(*ante* 30 May 1745, 25 June 1745 and notes).

12. Apparently Selwyn had complained
to HW that HW's abandoning his proposed visit to Matson in Oct. 1757 (*ante*
2, 6, 8, 11, 13 Oct. 1757) had kept him
from making a trip with Lord March.

12a. HW has written 'Turn over' at the
bottom of this page of the MS.

13. Edward Scarlett, jr, optician and
dealer in pictures and curiosities near St
Anne's Church, Dean Street, Soho, 1724–70
(Sir Ambrose Heal's collection of trades-
men's cards; *Walpole Society*, 1933–4, xxii.
117; 1937–8, xxvi. 61 n). HW had purchased from him an enamelled standing
cup and cover after designs by Parmigiano,
signed 'Johanus Penicaudi, Junior, 1539'
(ibid.; 'Des. of SH,' *Works* ii. 410; sold
SH xii. 59).

14. No picture answering this description is mentioned in the account of Van
Dyck's portraits of the children of Charles
I in Lionel Cust, *Anthony Van Dyck*, 1900,
pp. 109–12, nor in the catalogue of his
portraits of the Royal Family, pp. 262–7.
The picture was perhaps a copy in another hand of a group from the picture of
the five children of the King now at
Windsor.

Simpson's 19 Dec. 1862, lot 365 to Forster, and by him bequeathed to the Victoria and Albert Museum at his death in 1876.

Strawberry Hill, Aug. 29, 1758.

I GUESSED right, I find: my journey to Matson would again interfere with one of yours; and as all parties of pleasure should be as much so as possible, we will defer ours if you please, till we can accommodate it to the satisfaction of both. I will deal frankly with you, which we have known one another long enough to do. I could not well set out before the tenth;[1] and I own, besides the pleasure of seeing you and Mr Williams, I did propose this time to look at Berkeley Castle,[2] Lord Ducie's,[3] Mr Morris's,[4] and finish with Bath; you see what a furious list I had prepared, and how far this would carry you towards winter; and having missed your letter at Ragley, it would be idle to return back all this way for a day or two. Now, whenever you shall really have nothing else to do, and will let me make Matson my headquarters, this will be more agreeable to me, and I shall have the satisfaction of thinking I don't constrain you. Instead of my going this year to Matson, you will come hither when you have again had enough of London and Betty; and in October, if you are still idle, we may go and fetch Mr Williams from Bath. What say you to this?

I will speak to Scarlet about the picture the first moment I am in town. Do write me a line as soon as you receive this, for I will still be at your command if you insist upon it. Adieu!

Yours ever,

H. W.

1. Probably because of the marriage of his niece, Laura Walpole, to the Rev. Hon. Frederick Keppel, later Bishop of Exeter, which was to take place on 10 Sept. (HW to Mann 9 Sept. 1758).

2. About 12 miles SW of Gloucester. HW did not visit it until 15 Aug. 1774 (Cole i. 343–4; HW's 'Journals of Visits to Country Seats,' *Walpole Society*, 1927–8, xvi. 75).

3. Presumably Tortworth Court, about 16 miles N. of Bristol, principal seat of Mathew Ducie Moreton (*ante* 1700–70), 2d Bn Ducie. The house is illustrated in Thomas Dudley Fosbrooke, *Abstracts of Records and Manuscripts respecting the County of Gloucester*, Gloucester, 1807, ii. facing p. 40; HW apparently never saw it.

4. Probably the house of John Morris (ca 1730–88), later (1782) of Barnwood, Glos; sheriff of Glos, 1782 (F. H. Fowler, *Notes on Barnwood in the County of Gloucester*, Gloucester, 1914, pp. 9, 27).

'THE OUT OF TOWN PARTY,' BY REYNOLDS, 1761

To Selwyn, ca November 1758–May 1761

Printed for the first time from the MS now WSL; it was sold Anderson Galleries 21 Nov. 1918 (Dodd sale) lot 563 to J. F. Drake; sold by the Hampshire Book Shop in 1932 to WSL.

This letter probably refers to one of the Christmas or Easter parties at SH, when HW regularly entertained Selwyn, 'Gilly' Williams, and Edgcumbe. Since the latter is called 'Lord,' it must have been written after he succeeded his father in Nov. 1758 and before his death in May 1761.

Endorsed: H. Walpole.

Dear Sir,

THOUGH I am violently angry at your disappointing me in a party you had chosen and fixed yourself; at your not saying a word to Mr Williams and Lord Edgcumbe; and at making me go out of town on purpose and break other parties I had; yet I fear my resentment does not come up to the dignity some people would require; and if it would not be a notorious prostitution of that spirit that makes inveteracy even sentimental, I would own that I had forgiven you before you asked pardon, so far from not forgiving you afterwards—but don't betray me—I shall not be thought worthy to love Mr —— if I don't hate you heartily. Adieu!

Yours, etc.

H. Walpole

To Fox, Sunday 11 March 1759

Printed from *Letters to Henry Fox* 141–2; reprinted, Toynbee *Supp.* i. 89–90.

Arlington Street, March 11th 1759.

Dear Sir,

I WILL not trouble you with an apology for sending *you* one of the enclosed volumes:[1] almost every one of the pieces in it wanted an apology so long ago, that now it would do them no service. The

---

1. HW's *Fugitive Pieces*, printed at SH April–July 1758. When HW stated in the 'Short Notes' that he did not begin to distribute copies until 17 March 1759, he had forgotten these copies and doubtless others.

best excuse for them is that they are here assembled as the last of their race, at least (for I don't trust myself with making authors' resolutions) if I write any more, it will be nothing that will appear a great while.[2] The real business of this letter is to beg you to offer one of these volumes to Lord Berkeley.[3] I cannot have the confidence to send it him myself, and am ashamed to do it even by you; but as you told me he did me the honour to order me to send him anything I should write, it would be more arrogant to decline sending than to send this. He will see by the dates that several things here were written before I could almost be expected to write well, some when I certainly ought to have written better. However I will not do still worse.

As I have printed very few copies,[4] I could wish you would not mention it to anybody. I want to depart as an author without noise or ceremony: I have taken a thorough aversion to the profession, and I will play the fool for the future in a less serious way.

Adieu! Dear Sir, I wish I could hear a better account of your son.[5]

Yours ever,

H. Walpole

To Fox, Tuesday 8 May 1759

Printed from *Letters to Henry Fox* 143–4; reprinted, Toynbee *Supp.* i. 90–1.

Arlington Street, May 8th 1759.

Dear Sir,

IT is not worth troubling Lord Marchmont[1] with a letter on purpose, and would look too officious about a trifle, as I have not

2. HW's distrust of 'author's resolutions' was justified: his next publication, the *Dialogue between Two Great Ladies,* was written in March and published in April 1760 (Hazen, *Bibl. of HW* 43–5). By that time he had also begun to write the *Anecdotes of Painting* (Hazen, *SH Bibl.* 55).

3. John Berkeley (ca 1697–1773), 5th Bn Berkeley of Stratton, courtier and political ally of Fox (HW to Mann 21 Dec. 1755, 29 Nov. 1756).

4. HW printed 200 copies (Hazen, *SH Bibl.* 39).

5. Stephen Fox (1745–74), 2d Bn Holland, 1774. He had suffered from St Vitus's dance at intervals since birth and was at the moment very seriously ill from a prolonged attack (Ilchester, *Henry Fox* i. 174; *Leinster Corr.* i. pp. xv, 191–220 *passim*).

————

1. Hugh Hume-Campbell (1708–94), 3d E. of Marchmont, politician and book-col-

the honour of knowing him, but if you see him and remember it, will you be so good to tell him, that in the new catalogue of the Harleian MSS.[2] numb. 1073.8 mention is made of the original warrant of *Charles II* for the coronets of Barons.[3] For Sir G. Mackensie, it was a blunder of my own,[4] and a very careless one, as I have the book itself.[5]

I cannot help mentioning to you another curiosity, relating to yourself. In the same Harleian collection is a book of arms and pedigrees. In numb. 1072.51 are recorded 27 different coats borne by the name of Fox.[6] I would ask any one who questions your family, whether they believe that you are not descended of any one of these twenty-seven branches? if they doubt it, their faith is as great *per contra* as that of any genealogist that ever existed! adieu!

Yours ever,

H. WALPOLE

To SELWYN, Tuesday 5 June 1759

Printed from Toynbee iv. 271–2. The MS was in the possession of Mrs Alfred Morrison in 1904; sold Sotheby's 15 April 1918 (Morrison sale) lot 892 (with another) to Maggs.

lector; friend of Pope and the Duchess of Marlborough; M.P. Berwick-on-Tweed 1734–40.

2. *A Catalogue of the Harleian Collection of Manuscripts, purchased by Authority of Parliament, for the Use of the Public: and preserved in the British Museum*, compiled by Humfrey Wanley (1672–1726) but not published until 1759; HW's copy (Hazen, *Cat. of HW's Lib.*, No. 218) is now WSL.

3. 'Warrant of King Charles II to his attorney- or solicitor-general, for preparing a bill of his signature, containing his grant to the barons of England and their heirs males, to use a red velvet cap, and a circle of gold with six pearls on the top. Dat. 6 July, A.D. 1661, fol. 364.' Presumably Marchmont had asked HW's authority for his statement in *Royal and Noble Authors*, 2d edn, 1759, i. 99n, that barons received their coronets from Charles II.

The Harleian MSS reference is added to the note in *Works* i. 300.

4. In *Royal and Noble Authors*, 2d edn, 1759, ii. 208, HW confused George Mackenzie (1669–1725), M.D., fellow of the Royal College of Surgeons in Edinburgh, and author of *The Lives and Characters of the Most Eminent Writers of the Scots Nation*, 3 vols, Edinburgh, 1708–22, with his first cousin once removed, Sir George Mackenzie (1636–91), king's advocate (HW to Dalrymple 11 July 1758, DALRYMPLE 33 and n. 10). HW was aware of his error in describing Dr Mackenzie as 'Sir George' as early as March 1759 (HW to Dalrymple 25 March 1759, DALRYMPLE 55); the error is corrected in *Works* i. 497.

5. HW's copy of *Lives and Characters* is Hazen, *Cat. of HW's Lib.*, No. 444.

6. 'Twenty-seven coats [of arms] borne by those of the surname of Fox, or Foxe, fol. 35.'

Strawberry Hill, June 5, 1759.

Dear Sir,

I CHOSE to write a word to you rather than speak to you, especially in my own house, because of all things in the world, I
would not lay you under any difficulty. If what I am going to propose
to you should be in the least disagreeable to you, another short line
in answer will save both you and me any awkwardness of civilities or
apologies: one certainly ought not to ask a favour without facilitating
all means of refusal to the person of whom one begs it. You mentioned the approaching death of your deputy,[1] and your being totally
unengaged and unprovided with a successor. You know Mr Bentley's[2]
merit, his situation, and my friendship for him; I should be happy if
he would suit you. I shall be content if he would not. He will find
what security you require; and if he is not to know what would place
him in ease, he shall not know what might even make it for a moment unpleasant to you to meet him at my house, as I hope in either
case you often will. Adieu!

Yours, etc.,

H. Walpole

To Selwyn, Tuesday 14 August 1759

Printed from a photostat of the MS in the Roberts Collection, Haverford College
Library. First printed, Toynbee iv. 292. The MS was sold Sotheby's 13 Dec. 1881
(W. M. Punshon sale) lot 73 (i.a.) to Naylor; sold Sotheby's 27 July 1885 (Naylor
sale) lot 970 (i.a.) to Barker; in the possession of Charles Roberts of Philadelphia
by 1900, and by him bequeathed to Haverford.

1. Selwyn at this time held three offices, all of them exercised by deputies:
clerk of the irons and surveyor of the
meltings at the Mint, paymaster of the
Board of Works, and clerk of the crown
and peace and registrar of the Court of
Chancery in the Island of Barbados. The
Court and City Register lists Harvey Bas-
set as his deputy at the Mint until 1761
when his name is replaced by John Jones;
the other deputies are not mentioned.

2. Richard Bentley (1708–82), artist and
miscellaneous writer; friend and correspondent of HW. Although there is no
evidence that Selwyn made Bentley his
deputy, HW later told Cole that at the
time of their quarrel, Bentley's chief sub-
sistence was a place of about £100 per
year he had procured for him, and Bentley subsequently complained that he had
lost a place by writing his Mock Patriotism (1763) and had not been recompensed
by those for whom he wrote it (Cole's
'Athenæ Cantabrigienses,' in John Nichols,
Illustrations of the Literary History of the
Eighteenth Century, 1817–58, viii. 573).

Address: To George Augustus Selwyn, Esq., at Matson near Gloucester.
Postmark: 14 AV 10.

Arlington Street, Aug. 14, 1759.

Dear Sir,

AS my journey to Ragley is put off,[1] I shall not have the pleasure of waiting on you at Matson, as I flattered myself. The whole party has disappointed the races;[2] and for my own part, I am here in daily expectation of seeing the conclusion of Mrs Leneve's sufferings. Her struggles are wonderful, but as a thrush has appeared, I should think tonight or tomorrow must end it.[3]

Pray make my compliments to Lord and Lady Coventry,[4] and my excuses for not waiting on them.

Yours ever,

H. Walpole

To Selwyn, Thursday 23 August 1759

Printed from a photostat of the MS in the Cely Trevilian collection in the Society of Antiquaries. First printed, J. H. Jesse, *Memoirs of the Life and Reign of George III,* 1867, i. 598–9; reprinted, Toynbee iv. 291–2. The MS was presented to the Society of Antiquaries in 1915 by Mrs Cely Trevilian, presumably the widow of Edwin Brooke Cely Trevilian (1833–1914), with a large collection of other letters to Selwyn.

Dated by the postmark and the references to the battle of Kunersdorf.
Endorsed: H. Walpole.
Address: To George Augustus Selwyn, Esq., at the Earl of Coventry's at Croome, Worcestershire.
Postmark: 23 AV.

Arthur's, Thursday night, 10 o'clock.

I WROTE Mr Williams a very ignorant letter[1] this evening; I just hurry a few lines to you, very little more informed, but to

1. HW had been planning for more than a month to join a house party at Ragley that was to include the Duchess of Grafton. From there he intended to visit Selwyn at Matson. A change in the Graftons' plans, together with Mrs Leneve's illness, led HW to abandon the visit (Hertford to HW 14 July, 18 July, 3 Aug., 7 Aug. 1759).
2. One object of the party at Ragley was to attend the races at Warwick on 14 Aug. (Hertford to HW 3 Aug. 1759).
3. Mrs Le Neve did not die until 19 Aug. (*Daily Adv.* 20 Aug. 1759).
4. George William Coventry (1722–1809), 6th E. of Coventry; m. (1752) Mary Gunning (1732–60), one of the beautiful Miss Gunnings.

————

1. Missing.

prepare you for some very bad Prussian news.[2] The day before yesterday Mr Yorke[3] had sent a victory over the Russians,[4] the second time such a victory has been a defeat![5] Yesterday at past three Lord Holderness[6] received a mysterious letter,[7] I don't know from whence—not a word of it was told, upon which the stocks took it into their head that the King of Prussia was killed,[8] and in their panic tumbled down a hundred pair of stairs.[9] Betty says all the Germans are in tears; my Lady Townshend has been with Hawkins[10] to know if it is possible for the King of Prussia to live after his head is shot off—but here is a little comfort—General Ellison[11] tells me that my Lord Anson

2. The defeat of Frederick the Great by the Russians at Kunersdorf, near Frankfurt-on-Oder, 12 Aug. 1759. It had first been reported in England as a 'complete victory' for Prussia; see below, n. 4.

3. Hon. Joseph Yorke (1724–92); K.B., 1761; cr. (1788) Bn Dover; army officer and diplomatist; British minister at The Hague 1751–61, ambassador 1761–80; M.P. East Grinstead 1750–61, Dover 1761–74, Grampound 1774–80.

4. 'On Tuesday evening [21 Aug.] one of General Yorke's domestics arrived at Whitehall from The Hague with a letter advising that M. de Hellen, the Prussian minister there, had received in his letter, dated at Berlin on the 13th instant, an account, that on the 12th the King of Prussia had defeated the combined armies of the Russians and Austrians at Konesdorff [sic], near Franckfort on the Oder, and had gained a complete victory. Yesterday [22 Aug.] another express arrived, with a confirmation of this victory' (London Chronicle 21–23 Aug. 1759, vi. 182; see also the announcement of the messenger's arrival, 21 Aug. 1759, 'at night,' in BM Add. MSS 32894, f. 331). That the 'victory' was really a resounding defeat was generally known by the 23d (Newcastle to Rutland 23 Aug. 1759, BM Add. MSS 32894, f. 391).

5. The first time was a report received in London on 5 Aug. that General Wedel had defeated the Russians at Paltzig on 23 July, when he had actually been defeated by them. The favourable version was published in the London Gazette No. 9919, 4–7 Aug., but mails arriving from Holland on the 11th revealed the truth about the battle (HW to Mann 8 Aug.

1759; to Strafford 9 Aug. 1759; to Conway 14 Aug. 1759; London Chronicle 11–14 Aug. 1759, vi. 146–7; Daily Adv. 13 Aug. 1759).

6. Robert Darcy (1718–78), 4th E. of Holdernesse; secretary of state for the south 1751–4, and for the north 1754–61.

7. Not recovered; but some such letters, stating the truth about the battle, were received on the 22d and forwarded by Newcastle to Speaker Onslow on the 23d (BM Add. MSS 32894, f. 400).

8. According to the London Chronicle 23–25 Aug. 1759, vi. 192, this rumour was caused by Frederick's being temporarily stunned when a horse was shot from under him.

9. 'Various reports were yesterday spread regarding the success of the King of Prussia, which were so much believed by many people, that the price of stocks fell considerably, though it's asserted very positively by some that the late expresses brought no account of any engagement, only that the King of Prussia had passed the Oder; notwithstanding, copies of a letter were handed about, said to be written by General Yorke, which mentioned the King of Prussia's being defeated' (Daily Adv. 24 Aug. 1759). The published reports of the price of stocks, however, indicate only a slight decline (GM 1759, xxix. 394).

10. Cæsar Hawkins (1711–86), cr. (1778) Bt; surgeon-general to George II and George III.

11. Cuthbert Ellison (1698–1785), Major-Gen., 1755; Gen., 1772; M.P. Shaftesbury 1747–54 (Robert Beatson, Political Index, 3d edn, 1806, ii. 118; GM 1785, lv pt ii. 836; Judd, Members of Parliament 186).

half an hour ago received a letter from a very *sensible man* (*his Lordship* says) at Ostend, which says the action was very bloody, but not decisive, except that it appeared by the consequences that the Russians had the advantage, and that this account is rather a French one—Where the goodness or sense of this account lies, General Ellison does not tell me—I suppose my Lord did not tell him. Adieu!

PS. The D[uke] of D[orset][12] carried a letter from his son[13] to the King yesterday. Townshend's Advertiser.[14]

To SELWYN, Wednesday 29 August 1759

Printed from a photostat of the MS in the Cely Trevilian collection in the Society of Antiquaries. First printed, J. H. Jesse, *Memoirs of the Life and Reign of George III*, 1867, i. 598; reprinted, Toynbee iv. 297–8.

Address: To George Augustus Selwyn, Esq., at the Earl of Coventry's at Croome, Worcestershire.

Postmark: 30 AV.

Strawberry Hill, Aug. 29, 1759.

ALL I know, you shall know, though I dare to say, not a jot more than you know already. Just as the battle turned, Prince Ferdinand[1] sent his Legonier[2] to order Lord George to bring up all the cavalry. That message was scarce delivered, before Fitzroy[3] came to order only the British cavalry. Lord George said there must be a mistake, and that he would go and ask Prince Ferdinand what he really would have. The horse were not carried up; Lord George was

---

12. Lionel Cranfield Sackville (1688–1765), 7th E. of Dorset; cr. (1720) D. of Dorset.

13. Lord George Sackville (later, 1770, Germain) (1716–85), cr. (1782) Vct Sackville; commander-in-chief of the British detachment at the battle of Minden. The public attack on him for failing to obey the commands of Prince Ferdinand of Brunswick at Minden had begun immediately after the publication of the details of the battle in the *London Gazette* No. 9920, 7–11 Aug. 1759. This particular incident, however, is not confirmed.

14. That is, HW had picked up this information at Lady Townshend's.

1. Prince Ferdinand of Brunswick (1721–92); commander of the Westphalian army in the Seven Years' War and in supreme command at the battle of Minden.

2. Edward Ligonier (1740–82), 2d Vct Ligonier, 1770; cr. (1776) E. Ligonier; army officer and aide-de-camp to Prince Ferdinand.

3. Col. Charles Fitzroy (1737–97), younger brother of the 3d D. of Grafton; cr. (1780) Bn Southampton; aide-de-camp to Prince Ferdinand at the battle of Minden; M.P. Orford 1759–61, Bury 1761–74, Thetford 1774–80.

coldly received after the battle, Lord Gr[anby][4] warmly; they all dined together, and next day came out the famous orders of thanks.[5] Lord G[eorge] was enraged, sent over for leave to resign and to return, has leave;[6] has written an explanatory letter[7] to the Duke of Richmond,[8] which I have not seen, and is not come that I know. He is as much abused as ever poor Mr Byng[9] was, and by nobody so much as by my Lord Tyrawley.[10] The Duchess[11] imputes it all to malice, the Duke sinks under it—I seriously don't know a word more, nor have been in town, except a very few hours, since Mrs Leneve's death.

The great King[12] is reduced to be King of Custrin;[13] the King of Spain[14] is dead; regiments of light horse swarm,[15] as the invasion disappears.[16] This is all your gazette knows, till Gen. Yorke[17] mistakes some other defeat for a victory. Adieu!

Yours ever,

H. W.

4. Who was second in command of the British troops at the battle of Minden.

5. Printed in *Daily Adv.* 15 Aug. 1759; reprinted GM 1759, xxix. 388. Lord George was omitted from the thanks. HW's account of the events at Minden is substantially accurate to this point, but Sackville did bring up the horse, although too late for them to engage in the battle (Louis Marlow, *Sackville of Drayton*, 1948, p. 102).

6. Sackville's request to be recalled was received in England on 11 Aug.; permission for him to return was granted on the 14th (*Letters from George III to Lord Bute, 1756–1766*, ed. Romney Sedgwick, 1939, p. 29 and MS references there cited).

7. Not found; Sackville did write explanatory letters to Bute and Col. Fitzroy, which may have been turned by report into a letter to Richmond (ibid.; Marlow, op. cit. 280–2).

8. Charles Lennox (1735–1806), 3d D. of Richmond; at this time another of Prince Ferdinand's aides-de-camp.

9. Admiral John Byng (1704–57), executed for the loss of Minorca.

10. James O'Hara (1690–1773), 2d Bn Tyrawley; diplomatist and army officer; later (1760) president of Sackville's court martial. Sackville had attempted to move a vote of censure against him in the House of Commons in 1758 for expenditures on the works at Gibraltar.

11. Elizabeth Colyear (d. 1768), m. (1709) Lionel Cranfield Sackville, 7th E. of Dorset, cr. (1720) D. of Dorset.

12. Frederick the Great.

13. Küstrin or Cüstrin, a town and fortress in Brandenberg. HW uses the same expression in his letter to Mann, 29 Aug. 1759, perhaps because the *Daily Adv.* 27 Aug. 1759 had carried two reports that Frederick was retreating toward Küstrin and had given orders to surrender Berlin as soon as it was invaded.

14. Ferdinand VI (1713–10 Aug. 1759), King of Spain 1746–59. News of his death reached England on 27 Aug. (*Daily Adv.* 28 Aug. 1759).

15. The *London Chronicle* 21–23 Aug. 1759, vi. 182, mentions reports of several regiments of foot, light infantry, and light cavalry to be raised, but the only one actually raised at the time appears to have been the 16th Light Dragoons, for which the commission was issued 8 Aug. (information kindly supplied by Mr David Erskine).

16. Owing to the English success at Minden and the effectiveness of Hawke's Channel blockade; but the French had not abandoned their projected invasion of England (HW to Mann 1 Aug., 8 Aug.

To Fox, Wednesday 6 February 1760

Printed from *Letters to Henry Fox* 144; reprinted, Toynbee *Supp.* i. 92.

Arlington Street, Feb. 6, 1760.

Dear Sir,

I TOLD you, I think, that my Lord Lyttelton had heard of a monument to be placed in the Abbey for Sir Charles Williams.[1] As I loved him, it naturally came into my head to make an epitaph[2] for him; but I don't intend it should be seen, nor were it necessary would the Dean and Chapter, I suppose, allow Semele Christian burial. Here it is; you are not obliged to like it.

> Adieu! bright genius, dangerously great!
> Like the fond Theban maid's[3] thy signal fate.
> Lightnings or inspirations are the same,
> Alike th'ambitious bard, th'ambitious dame.
> Too near to madness are fine parts allied:[4]
> Both wished the glorious blaze by which ye died!

I propose sometime or other with your leave to come to Holland House, and write a few notes to his poems;[5] and I shall in the mean time draw up a little account of him,[6] and will give it you for your manuscript. I need not say to you, that all this will be a secret to everybody else.

Adieu!

Yours ever,

H. WALPOLE

1759; Richard Waddington, *La Guerre de sept ans*, 1899–1914, iii. 364 ff.).

17. The Hon. Joseph Yorke (*ante* 23 Aug. 1759, n. 3) had been made a Major-Gen. on 18 Jan. 1758.

———

1. Williams had died 2 Nov. 1759; the generally accepted statement that he committed suicide seems to be without foundation. He was buried in the north aisle of Westminster Abbey on 10 Nov.; no monument was erected there (Ilchester, *Hanbury-Williams* 428; HW's character of Williams, printed below, Appendix 3).

2. Another copy of HW's epitaph is in his MS 'Book of Materials,' 1759, p. 57.

3. Semele, daughter of Cadmus, King of Thebes, and Hermione (or Harmonia); beloved of Zeus who was father of her son Dionysus. She was destroyed by lightning when Zeus granted her request that he appear before her in his true shape.

4. In HW's copy in 'Book of Materials,' 1759, p. 57, this line reads,
'Fine parts to madness are too near allied.'

5. These notes were purportedly published in *The Works of . . . Sir Charles Hanbury Williams*, ed. Edward Jeffrey, 3 vols, 1822, but a careful examination of the notes signed 'W' in these volumes reveals that many of them are merely quotations from published letters and other works, not originals written for the poems.

6. Presumably the account in HW's *MS Commonplace Book of Verses*, pp. 53–6, 81, printed below, Appendix 3.

From LINCOLN, Monday ?14 ?April ?1760

Printed from a photostat made in 1935 of the MS then in the Waller Collection.
First printed, Toynbee *Supp.* iii. 314. The MS was among those which passed from
HW to Mrs Damer; bequeathed by her to Sir Wathen Waller, 1st Bt; it cannot
be identified in either Waller sale. In 1947 the MS was owned by B. T. Batsford,
Ltd, who were holding it for an unknown client.

Enclosed is a ticket, 'No. 2,' with seal, signed 'Lincoln,' and endorsed by HW
'Ticket for Lord Lincoln's gallery at the trial of Lord Ferrers.'

Dated on the assumption that the letter was written on the Monday preceding
the opening of the trial of Earl Ferrers for murder 16 April 1760; see HW to
Mann 20 April 1760.

Exchequer, Monday Morning.

Sir,

I HAVE according to your desire, sent you a ticket for my gallery;
and give me leave to assure, that I am very happy it is in my power
to do anything that is agreeable to you.

I am, Sir,

Your most obedient humble servant,

LINCOLN

To SELWYN, Sunday 19 October ?1760

Printed for the first time from a photostat of the MS in the possession of Sir
John Murray.

Dated, as is the following letter, which discusses the same subjects, by the
elimination of all other possible years in which 19 Oct. fell on a Sunday.

Endorsed: H. Walpole, Oct. 19th.

Address: To George Augustus Selwyn, Esq., in Curzon Street, Mayfair, London.

Postmark: 20 OC.

Strawberry Hill, Sunday, Oct. 19th.

I DID not write an answer to you at Croome,[1] because I could not
be sure what day you was to leave it; nor can I tell you any more
yet, than that I have writ to my Lady Ailesbury[2] about the commode,
and have not heard from her.

1. Croome Court, near Severn Stoke, Worcestershire, seat of the Earl of Coventry, where Selwyn was a frequent visitor.
2. Caroline Campbell (1721–1803), m.

1 (1739) Charles Bruce, 3d E. of Ailesbury; m. 2 (1747) Hon. Henry Seymour Conway. The letter is missing.

I think of being in town on Tuesday, and hope to find you there. Adieu till then.

Yours ever,

H. Walpole

To Selwyn, Tuesday 21 October ?1760

Printed for the first time from a photostat of the MS in the possession of Sir John Murray.

For the dating, see the previous letter.

Endorsed (twice, in different hands): H. Walpole.

Address: To George Augustus Selwyn, Esq., in Curzon Street, Mayfair, London.

Postmark: 22 OC.

Strawberry Hill, Tuesday.

Dear George,

IF you are in town you had a line from me yesterday to tell you I should be there today, but I am forced to stay here for some company I expect tomorrow; and shall not see you before Saturday, unless I meet you at Holland House on Thursday, where I wish you would contrive to dine with my Lady Townshend, Lord Waldegrave[1] and me.

My Lady Ailesbury is much obliged to you, and very glad to have the commode, without seeing it, provided I approve it. I give you this hint that you may make me a handsome offer for disposing of it —I am not very mercenary; you may bribe me by a visit hither. Adieu!

Yours ever,

H. Walpole

To Selwyn, Friday 13 March 1761

Printed for the first time from a photostat of the MS in the possession of Sir John Murray.

Dated in another hand; confirmed by the reference to Lord Holdernesse's resignation.

---

1. James Waldegrave (1715–63), 2d E. Waldegrave; HW's nephew by marriage after 1759.

Arlington Street, Friday night late.

YOU desired me to send you news, and I send you more than you will like to hear—I don't mean that you are going to lose your place or your election,[1] but you will hate the latter for keeping you out of town at such a moment. To the great surprise of the world Lord Holderness resigned the Seals this morning—not, as formerly,[2] to prelude a tide of resignations— He had not the least notice of it till yesterday at two o'clock, when he received the command. Lord Bute[3] succeeds him. Mr Pitt, who knew nothing of this an hour before Lord Holderness, was very angry, but is sweetened by the offer of cofferer for Jemmy Grenville,[4] which is to be ceded by the Duke of Leeds,[5] who returns to justice in eyre. The King hoped he should be able to do something for Lord Holderness some time or other,[6] and the Duke of Newcastle is so sorry for him, that it does all but get the better of his joy for it.[7] Lord Halifax is named Lord Lieutenant of Ireland,[8] and Lord Delawar[9] has kissed hands for the earldom. They talk of promotions in the Treasury and Admiralty, but I know none certain.[10] If Lord Bute quits Groom of the Stole,[11] your

1. Selwyn was at Gloucester standing a contested election (*Letters to Henry Fox* 145).

2. Holdernesse had been the first minister to resign in June 1757 in a manœuvre which prevented the formation of a Fox-Waldegrave ministry; see HW to Mann 9 June, 14 June 1757.

3. John Stuart (1713–92), 3d E. of Bute. For the motives behind the changes described in this letter, see L. B. Namier, *England in the Age of the American Revolution*, 1930, pp. 178–93.

4. Hon. James Grenville (1715–83); M.P. Old Sarum 1742–7, Bridport 1747–54, Buckingham borough 1754–68, Horsham 1768–70; a lord of the Treasury 1756, 1757–61; cofferer of the Household 1761–3 (Collins, *Peerage*, 1812, viii. 553; Judd, *Members of Parliament* 212–13). His new office was worth an additional £1,000 a year ('Lord Holland's Memoir,' *Life and Letters of Lady Sarah Lennox*, ed. Countess of Ilchester and Lord Stavordale, 1902, i. 36).

5. Thomas Osborne (1713–89), 4th D. of Leeds; chief justice in eyre, south of Trent 1748–56; cofferer of the Household 1756–61; chief justice in eyre, north of Trent 1761–74.

6. Holdernesse was almost immediately consoled with the reversion of the wardenship of the Cinque Ports for life, worth at least £2,500 to £3,000 a year, with a pension of £4,000 a year until he succeeded to that sinecure (HW to Mann 17 March 1761; 'Lord Holland's Memoir,' op. cit. i. 37).

7. Because he and Holdernesse had quarrelled when the latter deserted the Duke for Pitt in 1757 (Montagu i. 341; 'Lord Holland's Memoir,' op. cit. i. 37).

8. Halifax was not formally appointed until 20 March (*London Gazette* No. 10088, 17–21 March 1761); he retained the post until April 1763.

9. John West (1693–1766), 7th Bn De La Warr; cr. (1761) E. De La Warr. His patent is not dated until 18 March 1761 (GEC), nor was the new peerage announced until 21 March (*London Gazette*, loc. cit.).

10. HW describes the changes made in these departments in his letter to Mann 17 March 1761.

11. On the 13th the King was still trying to persuade Bute to remain Groom of the Stole (*Letters from George III to Lord Bute, 1756–1766*, ed. Romney Sedgwick, 1939, p. 52).

cousin[12] will have the importance of being out of humour at not succeeding, as he certainly will not.

I could tell you of a civil war in Northumberland, where the mob have shot an officer and three men of the militia, and the militia have in return shot twenty-one of the mob,[13] but you have too much taste to care about such events, when the Cabinet itself is the scene of action.

The other peers[14] kiss hands on Monday—you will not want news I think while you stay in the country. Good night.

Yours ever,

Hor. Walpole

Saturday.

Poor Lady Gower[15] died this morning in her lying-in.

To Selwyn, Saturday 21 March 1761

Printed for the first time from a photostat of the MS in the possession of Sir John Murray.

Arlington Street, March 21st 1761.

I SHOULD have writ again, but Mr Fox and so many of your friends told me they should write this week, that it would only have been multiplying evening posts. The state is fixed for the pres-

12. The only cousin of Selwyn's who could have had any pretension to becoming Groom of the Stole is Lord Robert Bertie (1721–82), 2d son of the 1st D. of Ancaster by his second wife, Albinia Farrington, Selwyn's aunt; army officer; lord of the Bedchamber; M.P. Whitechurch 1751–4, Boston 1754–82 (Montagu i. 85 n. 43). HW's certainty that he would not succeed was justified: Bertie was not even mentioned in any of the extensive correspondence in the Newcastle Papers concerning the appointment; the only candidates discussed at the time of Bute's promotion were Lord Holdernesse, the Duke of Rutland, the Duke of Leeds, and Lord Talbot (BM Add. MSS 32920, passim). Lord Huntingdon, not mentioned as a

possibility at this date, was appointed to the office within a week (HW to Mann 17 March 1761).

13. The account of the riot of the miners at Hexham over balloting for the militia given in the London Chronicle 12–14 March 1761, ix. 249, 254–5, differs from HW's account in the number of casualties. Further details are ibid. 14–17 March 1761, ix. 258; and GM 1761, xxxi. 187–8. See also HW to Mann 17 March 1761.

14. HW to Mann 17 March 1761 gives a list of the new peers.

15. Lady Louisa Egerton (1723 – 14 March 1761), m. (1748) Granville Leveson-Gower, 2d E, Gower, cr. (1786) M. of Stafford.

ent, till the weathercock-Duke[1] veers about and blows north and by treachery. Everybody has kissed hands[2] (and I believe somebody something more) except the red ribbands,[3] of whom I have heard ten different lists. You lost an entertaining day on Wednesday; you might have seen virtue ravished by the impotent, and in the way the impotent always do ravish—by the offer of an annuity. In short it was the day for the Speaker's[4] adieu! Sir John Philipps[5] moved the thanks to him, but forgot his speech, and though in his hat, could not read it.[6] Legge,[7] as you may suppose, did much better, and talked, feelingly, of retreat.[8] The Speaker acted well, and contrary to my expectation, did not overact. He assured us he is going into the most close and obscure retreat.[9] Harry Archer,[10] Velters Cornwall,[11] Sir John Rushout[12] and a parcel of such fools, insisted on addressing the King for a pension to him, to which at last he submitted. I went the next day to hear him in the House of Lords,[13] but he said nothing on himself. The crowd was enormous; the House was entirely full of women,[14] who literally stood upon all the benches of the Lords.

1. Newcastle.

2. Some of the new appointments and reappointments in the reconstruction of the ministry were made on 17 and 20 March; most of them on the 21st (*London Gazette* No. 10088, 17–21 March 1761).

3. Ten Knights of the Bath were named on 23 March (W. A. Shaw, *The Knights of England*, 1906, i. 170).

4. Arthur Onslow. Much of the discussion on the motion of thanks to him turned on a subsidiary resolution to address the King to grant him an annuity (*Mem. Geo. III* i. 40; *Journals of the House of Commons* xxviii. 1108–9).

5. (ca 1701–64), 6th Bt; M.P. Carmarthen borough 1741–7, Petersfield 1754–61, Pembrokeshire 1761–4; distant cousin of HW (MONTAGU i. 69 n. 13).

6. The rules of procedure of the House forbid the overt reading of speeches (Sir Thomas Erskine May, *A Treatise on the Law, Privileges, Proceedings and Usage of Parliament*, 13th edn, 1924, pp. 303–4).

7. Hon. Henry Bilson Legge (1708–64), chancellor of the Exchequer 1754–5, 1756–Apr. 1757, July 1757–March 1761; M.P. East Looe 1740–1, Orford 1741–59, Hampshire 1759–64.

8. Legge had just been dismissed from

the chancellorship of the Exchequer for refusing to bring forward a motion in the House of Commons for the payment of a large sum of money to the Landgrave of Hesse (*Mem. Geo. III* i. 30, 34, 37).

9. Onslow's speech, incorporated verbatim into the vote of thanks to him, is printed in *Journals of the House of Commons* xxviii. 1108–9.

10. Henry Archer (1700–68), M.P. Warwick borough 1735–68 (Judd, *Members of Parliament* 106; *Notes and Queries*, 1903, 9th ser. xi. 313–14).

11. Velters Cornwall (ca 1696–1768), M.P. Herefordshire 1722–68 (Judd, *Members of Parliament* 160). HW describes his remarks on this occasion as 'one of his absurd, ill-natured speeches, which the House was always so kind as to take for humour, teasing the Speaker under pretence of complimenting him' (*Mem. Geo. III* i. 40–1).

12. (1685–1775), 4th Bt; M.P. Malmesbury 1713–22, Evesham 1722–68. He had been a prominent opponent of Sir Robert Walpole.

13. On the occasion of the prorogation of the session of Parliament.

14. 'There was the greatest number of ladies of quality and persons of distinc-

I know nothing more but what you will be sorry to hear, that Edgcumbe's dropsy is confirmed[15]— He laments not dying a fortnight ago.[16]

I rejoice that your election goes on so well;[17] I set out for mine on Tuesday;[18] consequently I must resign my place of your gazetteer; but I don't insist on your giving me a pension or getting me an Irish peerage. Adieu!

Yours ever,

H. W.

From Lincoln, Monday 15 February 1762

Printed for the first time from a transcript of the MS in the possession of Earl Waldegrave. The MS was sold SH vi. 134 (i.a.) to Thorpe; offered Thorpe's *Cat. of Autographs*, 1843, p. 234, lot 2252; subsequently bound into a volume entitled 'Walpole Papers' containing an annotated SH Catalogue, newspaper clippings, a letter from HW to Lady Browne ?Nov. 1783, and other material; purchased before 1883 by Chichester Samuel Parkinson-Fortescue, cr. (1874) Bn Carlingford, who m. (1863, as her fourth husband) Frances Elizabeth Anne, Countess Dowager Waldegrave, from whom it passed into the Waldegrave collection.

Exchequer, February 15, 1762.

LORD LINCOLN presents his compliments to Mr Walpole, and returns him his best thanks for his very kind, and as well as most entertaining present.[1]

To Selwyn, Tuesday 31 August 1762

Printed from a photostat of the MS given to WSL in 1933 by its then owner, Dr Roderick Terry, Newport, Rhode Island. First printed, Toynbee *Supp.* i.

---

tion at the House of Peers yesterday ever known on any occasion' (*London Chronicle* 19–21 March 1761, ix. 273).

15. Edgcumbe died 10 May 1761.

16. 'If Dick's health depends upon his resolution, I am afraid it is a bad tenure by which he holds his life' (Selwyn to Fox, Thursday [19 March 1761] in *Letters to Henry Fox* 145).

17. On 19 March Selwyn wrote Fox that his election would take place on the 27th; 'nothing can withstand my popularity' (ibid.).

18. To be re-elected for Lynn.

———

1. The first two volumes of the *Anecdotes of Painting*, published 15 Feb. 1762 (Hazen, *SH Bibl.* 55).

102–3. The MS was sold at the Anderson Galleries, New York, 21 Nov. 1918 (Dodd and Livingston sale) lot 559, apparently to Dr Terry, who laid it into a presentation copy of Gray's *Odes,* SH, 1757. It was resold at the American Art Association 14–15 Feb. 1935 (Terry sale) lot 149.

Dated 'Aug. 1762' in another hand; confirmed by the reference to the Queen's being almost up and the Duke of Bedford's kissing hands; mentioned as being written on the 30th in a list in HW's hand on the cover of Lady Hertford to HW 14 Aug. 1762.

Strawberry Hill, Tuesday 31st.

Dear George,

YOU, Lord March[1] and the Countess,[2] flattered me with the hopes of a visit,[3] as soon as the world was delivered of all its big events. The Queen[4] is almost up again,[5] so is scrip,[6] the Duke of Bedford kisses hands tomorrow,[7] and for the Havannah,[8] I trust you are weary of expecting it. After Friday next I have no engagement till Saturday sennight. Bed or beds will be ready as they are commanded. Only let me know a day before that I may not be abroad. If Williams is in town, perhaps he will accompany you. Adieu!

Yours ever,

H. Walpole

1. William Douglas (1725–1810), 3d E. of March; 4th D. of Queensberry, 1778; 'Old Q'; Selwyn's intimate friend.
2. The Contessa Rena, Lord March's mistress. She has not been fully identified, but some biographical details are given in Mann to HW 17 Dec. 1757 and HW to Mann 14 April 1769.
3. Lord March and the Rena spent a night at SH within the next few days (HW to Conway 9 Sept. 1762).
4. Charlotte Sophia (1744–1818) of Mecklenburg-Strelitz, m. (1761) George III.
5. After the birth of her eldest son, later George IV, on 12 Aug. 1762; she was apparently not up until 13 Sept. (*Letters from George III to Lord Bute, 1756–1766,* ed. Romney Sedgwick, 1939, p. 134).
6. Scrip had risen during Aug. from about 82¾ to a high of 94 on 26 Aug. It dropped slightly during the week, but

averaged about 88 (GM 1762, xxxii. 344). The rise was caused by the exchange of ambassadors between England and France to settle the terms of the peace.
7. It was generally believed, and even officially notified to the Lord Mayor of London, that Bedford's formal appointment as ambassador to France would take place on 1 Sept., but it was not officially announced until 4 Sept. (HW to Mann 29 Aug. 1762; GM 1762, xxxii. 389; *London Chronicle* 2–4 Sept. 1762, xii. 225; *London Gazette* No. 10240, 31 Aug.–4 Sept. 1762).
8. The British fleet, which had been besieging Havana since 6 June, finally captured it on 13 Aug. News of the victory, which had been daily expected since intelligence reached London on 18 Aug. that it probably fell on 7 July, did not reach London until the evening of 29 Sept. (GM 1762, xxxii. 447).

From Fox, Sunday 21 November 1762

Printed from a copy by the Earl of Ilchester of Fox's copy in his possession and further collated with HW's transcripts in the 'foul' and 'fair' copies of the MS of *Mem. Geo. III* in the possession of Earl Waldegrave. First printed, *Mem. Geo. III* i. 168–9; reprinted, Cunningham iv. 44–5. HW's notes are taken from the 'fair' copy; those in the 'foul' copy are less complete.

H[olland] H[ouse], November 21, 1762.

Dear Sir,

AS soon as I heard that the Parks[1] which Lord Ashburnham[2] has quitted were worth £2,200 a year (as they certainly are) I thought such an income might, if not prevent, at least procrastinate your nephew's[3] ruin. I find nobody knows his Lordship's thoughts on the present state of domestic politics.[4] Perhaps he has none.

Now are you willing, and are you the proper person, to tell Lord Orford, that I will do my best to procure this employment for him,[5] if I can soon learn that he desires it? If he does choose it, I doubt not of his and his friend Boone's[6] hearty assistance, and believe I shall

1. 'The Rangership of St James's and Hyde Parks. This post was not worth £2,200 a year by itself, but with the Bedchamber, as Lord Ashburnham had held it. Lord Orford was already lord of the Bedchamber, so, though I did not know it at that time, the offer was grossly fallacious. Fox however might be ignorant too of this circumstance' (HW). Lords of the Bedchamber received salaries of £1,000 a year (*Court and City Register*, 1761, p. 75).

2. John Ashburnham (1724–1812), 2d E. of Ashburnham. He resigned as Ranger of St James's and Hyde Parks and lord of the Bedchamber, 19 Nov. 1762, in the general secession of Newcastle's friends from office following the King's 'affronts' to the Duke of Devonshire (Newcastle to Devonshire 20 Nov. 1762, BM Add. MSS 32945, f. 92; *London Chronicle* 18–20 Nov. 1762, xii. 496).

3. 'George Walpole, third Earl of Orford, grandson of Sir Robert Walpole. Not only his grandfather and father had left great debts, but his own dissipation had involved him in many more' (HW). By 1773, when HW temporarily took over the

management of his affairs, Lord Orford's personal debts, exclusive of those of his father and grandfather, amounted to £44,-000 (HW to T. Walpole 4 Sept. 1773).

4. 'He scarce ever had any thoughts about politics, but lived almost always in the country and at Newmarket, wasting his time and fortune by carelessness, rather than in pleasures and expense. With a most engaging figure and address, he profited of no one advantage to which he was born, and without any view of advantage to himself, disgusted every friend he had by insensibility, and every friend he might have had, by insincerity' (HW).

5. Fox was engaged at the moment in an attempt to beg or buy support for Bute's ministry for the immediate purpose of carrying the preliminaries of the Treaty of Paris.

6. 'Charles Boone brought into Parliament by Lord Orford for Castlerising. Mr Fox *had already* sounded Lord Orford through his friend Mr Boone, but without receiving any answer' (HW). Charles Boone (ca 1730–1819), M.P. Castle Rising 1757–68, 1784–96; Ashburton 1768–84. For an account of him see L. B. Namier,

see you, too, much oftener in the House of Commons. This is offering you a bribe, but 'tis such a one as one honest good-natured man may without offence offer to another.

If you undertake this,[7] do it immediately, and have attention to my part in it which is delicate.

If you do not undertake it, let me know your thoughts of the proposal; whether I had better drop it entirely; or put it into other hands, and whose?

You'll believe me when I tell you that goodness of heart has as much share in this to the full as policy.

Yours ever,

H. Fox

To Fox, Sunday 21 November 1762

Printed from a copy by HW laid into the 'foul' copy of the MS of *Mem. Geo. III* in the possession of Earl Waldegrave; collated with transcripts in the texts of the 'foul' and 'fair' copies. First printed, *Mem. Geo. III* i. 170–1; reprinted, Cunningham iv. 46–7, Toynbee v. 275–6. HW's notes are taken from the 'fair' copy; those in the 'foul' copy are less complete.

Nov. 21st 1762.

Dear Sir,

AFTER having done what the world[1] knows I have done to try to retrieve the affairs of my family, and to save my nephew from ruin, I can have little hopes that any interposition of mine will tend to an end I wish so much. I cannot even flatter myself with having the least weight with my Lord Orford. In the present case I can still less indulge myself in any such hopes. You remember in the case of the Mitchell election how hardly he used me on your

---

'Charles Garth and His Connexions,' *English Historical Review*, 1939, liv. 458–62; Montagu ii. 7 n. 1.

7. HW did so; see the following letter.

1. 'This alludes to my having projected a match for Lord Orford with Miss Nicholl, an heiress worth £150,000, whom Lord Orford would not marry, and in the course of which negotiation I had a great quarrel with my uncle, old Horace Walpole, who endeavoured, though trusted with her by me, to marry her to one of his own younger sons. This quarrel had made very great noise, and many persons were engaged in it. The young lady afterwards married the Marquis of Carnarvon' (HW). See Gray ii. 193–233 for a detailed account of the affair.

HENRY FOX

account;[2] I know how much he resented last year his thinking you concerned in the contest[3] about the borough where he set up Mr Thomas Walpole,[4] and as he has not even now deigned so much as to answer Mr Boone's letter,[5] I can little expect that he will behave with more politeness to me; yet I think it so much my duty to lay before him anything for his advantage and what is by no means incompatible with his honour, that I will certainly acquaint him immediately[6] with the offer you are so good as to make him.

You see I write to you with my usual frankness and sincerity, and you will I am sure be so good as to keep to yourself the freedom with which I mention very nice family affairs. You must excuse me if I add one word more on myself. My wish is that Lord Orford should accept this offer;[7] yet I tell you truly, I shall state it to him plainly and simply, without giving any advice, not only for the reasons I have expressed above, but because I do not mean to be involved in this affair any otherwise than as a messenger. A man who is so scrupulous as not to accept any obligation for himself, cannot be allowed to accept one for another without thinking him-

2. 'Lord Orford had been much governed by George Lord Townshend, a capital enemy of Mr Fox, and very warm words had passed between my nephew and me, on my taking a different side from him, in the Mitchell election, which is mentioned in a former part of these memoirs. I shall in the appendix give a long letter which I wrote on that occasion to Lord Orford, and which will explain many parts of my conduct' (HW's note, omitted from *Mem. Geo. III*). Virtually nothing is known of HW's quarrel with Lord Orford over the affair of the contested election for St Michael in 1755. HW's account of it (*Mem. Geo. II* ii. 10–14) does not mention his personal interest in the matter; the letter to Lord Orford that he mentions in this note apparently has not survived.

3. 'Mr Fox had supported Mr Sullivan at a borough in the west against Mr T. Walpole; I forget whether it was Callington or Ashburton. Lord Orford was heir to estates in both by his mother' (HW). Laurence Sulivan (ca 1713–1786), chairman of the East India Company 1758–64, 1780; M.P. Taunton 1762–8, Ashburton 1768–74; had contested the Ashburton election in 1761. He petitioned against the return

of John Harris, Orford's step-grandfather, not of Thomas Walpole whom he admitted to be legally elected, but eventually withdrew his petition (L. S. Sutherland, *The East India Company in Eighteenth-Century Politics*, Oxford, 1952, p. 59 *et passim*; Judd, *Members of Parliament* 348; GM 1786, lvi pt i. 183; *Journals of the House of Commons* xxix. 18–19, 178, 183).

4. Hon. Thomas Walpole (1727–1803), banker in Paris; M.P. Sudbury 1754–61; Ashburton 1761–8; King's Lynn 1768–84; HW's cousin and correspondent (Judd, *Members of Parliament* 369).

5. 'Mr Boone had acquainted me with this, and Mr Fox thought I did not know it, but I chose to let him see I did' (HW). The letter is missing.

6. See HW to Lord Orford 22 Nov. 1762.

7. Lord Orford did so. 'Without preface or apology, without recollecting his long enmity to Fox . . . and without a hint of reconciliation, to Fox he went, accepted the place, and never gave that ministry one vote afterwards; continuing in the country, as he would have done if they had given him nothing' (*Mem. Geo. III* i. 172).

self bound in gratitude as much as if done to himself. The very little share I ever mean to take more in public affairs shall and must be dictated by disinterested motives. I have no one virtue to support me but that disinterestedness, and if I act with you, no man living shall have it to say that it was not by choice and by principle.[8] I am, dear Sir,

Your sincere humble servant,

HOR. WALPOLE

From Fox, Thursday 20 January 1763

Printed for the first time from a photostat of Add. MSS 23218, f. 80.
Address: To the Honourable Hor. Walpole, Esquire, Arlington Street.

Jan. 20, 1763.

Dear Hory,

IT will not happen again that you will be denied. But I was asleep it seems. I was very sorry for I have wanted much to see you, without any view however I confess, to your skill in physic.[1] I am heartily glad you have succeeded in your own case,[2] and will follow your advice if upon consultation and inquiry you do not find our complaints as different as our forms,[3] as cold to heat. But I will, as a wise man should do, tell my new physician when I see him all my symptoms without disguise. I have, and so has another friend of yours, a heavy complaint that you can cure. Lord Berkley of Stratton is mystified to the greatest degree that you have not given him your character of his friend.[4] And I think of it when I lay awake.[5]

Adieu.

8. HW asserts that these sentiments, together with his refusal to vote for the preliminaries of peace (he left the House before the division), so annoyed Fox that he used his influence to stop HW's payments from the Treasury for several months (*Mem. Geo. III* i. 167–8, 171).

1. Fox had been somewhat ill for several weeks; his wife wrote on 22 Jan: 'he thinks himself in a bad way, I flatter myself indeed without any reason; that he is far from well and very nervous is certain' (*Leinster Corr.* i. 358).

2. In December HW complained of the 'flying gout' in his stomach and breast but thought himself quite recovered, thanks in part to cold weather, by the end of January (HW to Cole 23 Dec. 1763, COLE i. 33; HW to Mann 28 Jan. 1763). HW had no doubt urged Fox to take James's powders.

3. Fox was fat while HW was excessively thin.

4. Not identified.

5. One of Fox's complaints at the time was sleeplessness (*Leinster Corr.* i. 357).

HW appears occasionally in the letters of his friends during the summer of 1763. In July 'Gilly' Williams informed Selwyn, then at Paris:

'Horry is taken up with nursing his niece [Lady Waldegrave], who bore a most painful operation on her breast very heroically' (Jesse, *Selwyn* i. 249–50).

Meanwhile Fox, now Lord Holland, at Spa, was arranging for a present to HW. He wrote to Selwyn:

'The two things I was to put you in mind of were to let Hor. Walpole know that you have the care of two pictures bespoke by me as a present for him, and to consult him what views he would have' (16 July 1763, MS in Society of Antiquaries).

Selwyn had already sent the former message to HW through Williams, who reported:

'I have notified the presents which Lord Holland is to make to my Lady and Horry. The latter is gone a progress into Northamptonshire to Lady Betty Germaine's. Is it not surprising how he moves from old Suffolk on the Thames to another old goody on the Tyne; and does not see the ridicule which he would so strongly paint in any other character?' (18 Aug. 1763, Jesse, *Selwyn* i. 252; for HW's 'progress,' see Montagu ii. 88–92, 332–47, and HW's 'Journals of Visits to Country Seats,' *Walpole Society*, 1927–8, xvi. 51–60).

To Selwyn, Wednesday 28 September 1763

Printed for the first time from the MS now wsl. The MS was sold by Miss Emily Driscoll of New York in Nov. 1950 to wsl.

Dated from the references to HW's difficulties with his printers and to Miss Hampden's legacy.

Strawberry Hill, Sept. 28th.

Dear Sir,

I AM prevented waiting on you as I intended on Sunday. There is no end of my plagues with printers. My present one,[1] like his predecessor,[2] has run in debt here, and been forced to leave me;[3] and

1. William Pratt, HW's fifth printer 1761–4 (HW's *Journal of the Printing-Office at Strawberry Hill,* ed. Toynbee, 1923, pp. 10, 13, 84–6).
2. Thomas Farmer, HW's fourth printer

1759–61; for his disappearance, see ibid. 81–2.

3. Pratt had run heavily into debt on his weekly wage of 10s. 6d. and by 26 Sept. 1763 owed his landlord £13 10s. 5¾d. for

I cannot stir, as I must have my bookseller[4] come from London and examine my printing-house, and see whether he has taken any copies away;[5] and I must get another printer, having just begun a very curious book,[6] that has been lent me,[7] and which I am very much pressed to get finished—in short, the state is not more out of order[8] than my *imprimerie*. This is very disagreeable on many accounts; on none more, than by interfering with the agreeable tour I had proposed. I don't know whether I am robbed, nor how I may have suffered by this fellow and a drunken wife, who has occasioned his extravagance. Make my compliments to Mr Williams. I don't know a word of news, but the magnificent legacy which Mr Child[9] has left to Miss Hambden,[10] which you will see in the papers, and which is true. Adieu!

Yours ever,

H. WALPOLE

Later in the autumn Williams told Selwyn:
'Our friend Horry is peevish, and retired to Strawberry till the meeting' of Parliament (Jesse, *Selwyn* i. 190).

TO LINCOLN, ? 1764

Printed for the first time from a photostat of the MS deposited in the Nottingham University Library by the Trustees of the Newcastle Estates.

cash advances and for lodging. But his departure from the SH Press was only temporary since HW settled the bill on 18 Oct. and then apparently allowed Pratt to work out the debt during the next year. HW finally discharged him in Dec. 1764 (ibid. 84–5).

4. Probably William Bathoe (d. 1768), bookseller in the Strand, who sold HW's *Anecdotes of Painting* on which Pratt had been working during most of his time at the SH Press.

5. There is no evidence that Pratt stole any copies.

6. *The Life of Edward Lord Herbert of Cherbury, Written by Himself,* which HW had begun to print on 23 Sept. 1763 (Hazen, *SH Bibl.* 68).

7. By Lady Hertford, to whom its owner, Lord Powis, had lent it; see HW to Montagu 16 July 1764 for his account of printing the book (MONTAGU ii. 129–30).

8. A ministerial crisis, resulting in the exclusion of Lord Bute, had occurred in early September.

9. Francis Child (ca 1736 – 23 Sept. 1763), banker; M.P. Bishop's Castle 1761–3 (MONTAGU ii. 103 n. 9).

10. Hon. Maria Constantia Hampden (until 1754, Trevor) (1744–67), only dau. of 4th Bn Trevor; m. (1764) Henry Howard, 12th E. of Suffolk. She was about to marry Child; he left her £50,000 (MONTAGU ii. 104 and n. 3).

Dated on the supposition that it was written shortly before Lincoln's letter of ca 15 Feb. 1764. The hand is of this period.

My dear Lord,

I HAD hoped that as you had admitted me to a renewal of our friendship, I was to have the satisfaction of sometimes seeing you; but I begin to think you only meant to tantalize me with the prospect of a happiness you did not intend I should possess. I am grown much too old to care for more than very few friends, and I have always been too sincere to say I loved those I did not. You know, I am sure you do, that my affection for you is neither counterfeit nor luke-warm. It would make me seriously happy to pass some of the remain-ing hours of my life with you. I will not be troublesome, and you may get rid of me whenever you please, as you may command me whenever you will accept of me. Nobody can be more devoted to you, or more pleased with the honour of your friendship. You may have newer servants, but none are so attached to us as those we make when we are young.

Yours most sincerely,

HOR. WALPOLE

To Lincoln, Tuesday ?1764

Printed for the first time from a photostat of the MS deposited in the Notting-ham University Library by the Trustees of the Newcastle Estates.
Dated tentatively by the hand.
Address: To the Earl of Lincoln at the Exchequer.

Strawberry Hill, Tuesday.

My dear Lord,

I WAS very unhappy to receive your commands *here* this morning too late to obey them. I shall be in town tomorrow, and will wait on your Lordship any time you will give me leave before dinner on Thursday. I have company to dine with me here on Friday and Sun-day. These are all the engagements I have, and I will make no other,

till I know your orders, being not only what you give me leave to
call myself your

Sincere friend, but most devoted servant,

HOR. WALPOLE

From LINCOLN, ca Wednesday 15 February 1764

Missing.

To LINCOLN, Friday 17 February 1764

Printed for the first time from a photostat of the MS deposited in the Nottingham University Library by the Trustees of the Newcastle Estates. There is a rough
sketch (perhaps a floor plan) on the back.

Feb. 17th 1764.

My Lord,

IT is a long time since I have had so much pleasure as your Lordship's kind note gave me. I have often told Mr Spence and poor
Mr Reade[1] how earnestly I wished that you would permit me to
wait on you. It is my duty and exceedingly my inclination to prevent
your troubling yourself to come to me, and therefore when you return to town, I flatter myself you will honour me with your orders
to come to you at any hour that is most agreeable and convenient
to you. I shall think it a great honour, and hope you will believe it
will be still a greater pleasure to me. My regard, esteem, and since
you permit me to say so, my friendship for you has been invariable,
and you will always find my heart as much yours as ever. My affection

1. Henry Reade (d. 1762), comptroller
of the tax office; Lincoln's steward and at
one time his tutor (*London Chronicle* 14–
16 Dec. 1762, xii. 577; GM 1762, xxxii. 600).
HW noted in his copy (now WSL) of Giles
Duwes, *An Introductorie for to Lerne to
Rede*, [1539?], that it was 'A present from
Mr H. Reade 1758'; see Hazen, *Cat. of
HW's Lib.*, No. 118.

is of very little consequence to anybody, but such as it is, nobody can command it more than your Lordship.

I am your Lordship's

Most obedient and most obliged humble servant

HOR. WALPOLE

To Lincoln, Monday 6 August 1764

Printed for the first time from a photostat of the MS deposited in the Nottingham University Library by the Trustees of the Newcastle Estates.

Strawberry Hill, Aug. 6, 1764.

My dear Lord,

YOU are so exceedingly good to me upon all occasions, that I flatter myself you will accept a trifling tribute of my gratitude in the volume I send you from my press.[1] I think it will amuse you for an hour, as it is one of the most extraordinary books ever published. Two hundred copies are only printed, of which Lord Powis[2] has half. Of my share could I think of disposing of one without offering it to you?

Give me leave to ask you after the Duke and Duchess of Newcastle.[3] I had the misfortune to be witness to the melancholy account his Grace received on Saturday,[4] and felt for him from my heart, and for what I was sensible the Duchess was to suffer. I need not add that whatever touches my dear Lord must affect

His very sincere and obedient humble servant,

HOR. WALPOLE

1. *The Life of Edward Lord Herbert of Cherbury,* which HW was just beginning to distribute, although the printing had been completed in January (Hazen, *SH Bibl.* 70).

2. Henry Arthur Herbert (ca 1703–72), cr. (1743) Bn Herbert of Chirbury and (1748) E. of Powis; M.P. Bletchingly 1724–7, Ludlow 1727–43.

3. Lady Henrietta Godolphin (d. 1776), m. (1717) Thomas Pelham-Holles, 1st D. of Newcastle.

4. Of the death of the Duchess of Leeds, the Duchess of Newcastle's sister; see HW to Hertford 3 Aug. 1764 for an account of the arrival of the news.

HW's publications and politics were the subject of much discussion among his friends in the autumn of 1764:

'Horry's [*Counter Address to the Public*] I have sent to Guerchy. If it is but peevish enough I shall like it. As to his argument it is a jest, and so would the government have been if it had not done exactly what it did [in dismissing Conway]. I have nothing to blame but the delay myself. *Pardonnez-nous, grandes dieux! si le peuple romain a tardé si longtemps à condamner Tarquin*' (Selwyn to Holland, 9 Sept. [1764], *Letters to Henry Fox* 201).

'Till I see you, I shall say nothing of Hume's absurdity, Horry's pamphlet, etc. . . . PS. Hor. may write another pamphlet, for I hear the Duke of Grafton has turned the Duchess out (though she is brave, and has seen service), without assigning a reason' (Holland to Selwyn 23 Sept. 1764, Jesse, *Selwyn* i. 296–7).

'I have been for two days, since I returned to town, at Strawberry. The Duke of Devonshire's illness seems to have sunk Horry's spirits prodigiously. He expects the resurrection of Mr Pitt, as the Jews do the coming of the Messiah, and, for all I can see, with as much reason. Everything political goes on as well as he could wish it. . . . Horry has published Lord Herbert's *Life,* with a very extraordinary dedication to Lord Powis. I have not read it, reserving it for the post-chaise, but I am told nothing is more odd and entertaining' (Williams to Selwyn 29 Sept. [1764], ibid. i. 301–2).

'As to your question about Don Quixote, Horry says Lord Herbert was a Don Quixote with the austere philosophy of Plato: he does not tell you Plato was a Quixote. I wish most heartily he had the managing of other old family stories. . . . I can figure no being happier than Horry. *Monstrari digito prætereuntium* has been his whole aim. For this he has wrote, printed, and built. To this we owe Lord Herbert, and I hope in future shall owe much more diversion' (Williams to Selwyn 19 Oct. [1764], ibid. i. 309–10).

'Horry told me last night, he intended to be at Paris in February. It is a d—d cold time for a patriot to leave us in, but, take my word for it, Lady Mary's [Churchill's] promotion to Windsor has had its due operation. . . . Horry Walpole dined there [?Lord Holland's] yesterday, and says his stomach is totally gone. I find the present topic of abuse, instead of Ashton, Rigby, etc. is the Woburn family. De Beaumont has breakfasted with him at Strawberry. He is now as much a curiosity to all foreigners as the tombs and lions' (Williams to Selwyn 13 Nov. [1764], ibid. i. 321–2).

'Horry Walpole whispers now and then with a Cavendish, but I think he seems rather to be ashamed of his company. He is going to make an addition to Strawberry, consisting of a Gothic museum. I think, as Bays says, "that will be a stroke," and the contents of it beyond any repository in the world' (Williams to Selwyn 12 Dec. 1764, ibid. i. 332).

'You will love the Duchess of Bedford as well as I do, for begging the old Privy Seal, which, on the delivery of the new one, is the Duke of Marlborough's perquisite. She intends to frame it, and Horry Walpole is to write the inscription for it. It is singularly circumstanced, that the same seal should have been her father's, her husband's, her brother's, and her son's! . . . . The Duke of Gloucester has professed a passion for the Dowager Waldegrave. He is never from her elbow. This flatters Horry Walpole not a little, though he pretends to dislike it. I believe we shall lose our Strawberry Christmas, for he talks of going to Woburn and Goodwood' (Williams to Selwyn [Dec. 1764], ibid. i. 333–4).

Williams wrote to Selwyn 19 March 1765:

'Horry Walpole has now postponed his journey [to Paris] till May. He procrastinates on this side of the water as much as March on the other. To tell you the truth, as I believe he has no great cordiality for his Excellency [Lord Hertford], he is not very impatient to see him. How do you think he has employed that leisure which his political frenzy has allowed of? In writing a novel, entitled the *Castle of Otranto,* and such a novel, that no boarding-school Miss of thirteen could get half through without yawning. It consists of ghosts and enchantments; pictures walk out of their frames, and are good company for half an hour together; helmets drop from the moon, and cover half a family. He says it was a dream, and I fancy one when he had some feverish disposition in him' (Jesse, *Selwyn* i. 372).

To Lincoln, Tuesday 26 March 1765

Printed for the first time from a photostat of the MS deposited in the Nottingham University Library by the Trustees of the Newcastle Estates.
Endorsed: No. 2 H. Walpole 65.

Arlington Street, March 26, 1765.

My dear Lord,

ONE always, you know, abuses the goodness of other people. You was so kind as to offer me a ticket for your gallery,[1] and the

1. Presumably for the trial of Lord Byron, held 17 April by the House of Lords, for killing William Chaworth in a duel; he was found guilty of manslaughter, but through privilege of his peerage was 'dismissed on paying his fees' (GM 1765, xxxv. 196–7).

consequence is a suit for two more! I will name the persons, and then leave them to your mercy, to refuse or not, as you think proper. They are Lady Dacre[2] and her niece, Miss Harding.[3] I could not be hard-hearted to such names; I don't know if you can.

When you have granted or denied this, I have a quarrel in bank for you, which even your compliance cannot efface. You promised you would sometimes send for me; you never have, though I think I should have come, even into Nottinghamshire.[4] I have a quarrel with Mr Spence into the bargain, with *phesoi ecneps*[5]—pray tell him, he is not the only person who can discover folks in a fairy tale. Adieu! my dearest Lord,

Yours most faithfully,

HOR. WALPOLE

This is the last letter that has been found in the HW-Lincoln correspondence. HW's final word on Lincoln seems to be the summary of his character in Mem. Geo. III i. *164–5. It appears in the* Memoirs *for November 1762, but a note in HW'S 'foul copy' shows that he finished 1762 on 30 June 1768:*

'Lord Lincoln, Newcastle's favourite nephew and heir, displayed more open ingratitude. He asked an audience of the King, called his uncle a factious old fool, and said he could not forget a message which himself had brought from his uncle to his Majesty in the year 1757, in which the Duke had signified to his then Royal Highness, that, if he would not disturb the tranquillity of the rest of his grandfather's reign, the Duke, in or out of place, though he hoped the latter, would support his measures to the utmost. It was justice to recollect this promise; but Lincoln's subsequent conduct, at the same time that it was inconsistent, was honourable neither towards the King nor his uncle. He had a second audience, in which he told the King that the Duke insisted on his resigning; "but if I must," said he, "I will show but the more warmly the next day that I remember the message, of which I have kept a copy in writing." The third time, when he went to resign, he said he must oppose. The King told him his tone was much changed since his first audience. But the Court

2. Anna Maria Pratt (d. 1806), m. (1739) Thomas Barrett-Lennard, 17th Bn Dacre of the South.

3. Probably Caroline Hardinge (1747–1826), dau. of Nicholas Hardinge, who had married Lady Dacre's sister. Her older sister Jane (b. 1740) was married to Henry Cresset Pelham of Crowhurst, Sussex, a distant cousin of Lincoln's (Collins, *Peerage*, 1812, v. 515; *Burke's . . . Peerage*, 101st edn, ed. L. G. Pine, 1956, p. 1026).

4. To Lincoln's seat at Clumber Park. Clumber does not appear in HW's visits to country houses.

5. Joseph Spence spelled backward. The incident is unexplained.

never had much reason to complain of Lord Lincoln's hostilities. His exceeding pride kept him secluded from the world, and rarely did he appear either at Court or in Parliament. For some time he fluctuated between Lord Bute and Mr Pitt, to the latter of whom he at last attached himself; but with constant derision of, and insult to, his uncle, and, whatever were the Duke of Newcastle's faults, cruel and unmerited. The truth was, Lord Lincoln's avarice was as unbounded as his haughtiness. Though possessed of two places for life, and one of them the most lucrative in England, the auditorship of the Exchequer, which never produces less than eight thousand pounds a year, and during the war had brought in at least twenty, he had resented the Duke's not bestowing on him two more places for the lives of his younger sons.'

To Selwyn, Saturday ?April ?1765

Printed for the first time from a photostat of the MS in the possession of Mrs Davy, Heckfield Place, Basingstoke, Hants. It was sold Sotheby's 21 Aug. 1872, lot 52 to Harvey; subsequently acquired by Horatio, 4th E. of Orford (n.c.) of Heckfield Place.

Dated tentatively by the reference to the Comte de Lauraguais, who visited England in April 1765 with a special recommendation to HW from Lord Hertford (Hertford to HW 10 April 1765, HW to Hertford 18 April 1765). Selwyn himself had recently returned from Paris (HW to Hertford 7 April 1765), and he, Holland, and HW were on excellent terms at the time.

Address: To George Aug. Selwyn, Esq.

Saturday.

Dear Sir,

IF you bring me any letter from Lord Holland,[1] don't leave it at my house, because, as I shall be out of town, it will be sent to me by the post, which probably he would not like. I wish you would bring both the letter and the Abbé Coyer[2] to Strawberry on Tuesday next, where you will meet Messieurs de Lauragais[3] and Sarsfeld[4] at dinner, will you?

Yours ever,

H. Walpole

1. Henry Fox had become Bn Holland in 1763.

2. Abbé Gabriel-François Coyer (1707–82), author; for HW's comments on his *De la Prédication,* 1766, see HW to Lady Hervey 10 March 1766.

3. Louis-Léon-Félicité de Brancas (1733–1824), Comte de Lauraguais, later Duc de Brancas.

4. Probably either Guy-Claude (1718–89), Comte de Sarsfield; or his brother, Jacques-Hyacinthe (1717–87), Chevalier

To HOLLAND, Tuesday 21 May 1765

Printed from *Letters to Henry Fox* 213–14; reprinted, Toynbee *Supp.* i. 106–7.
Dated by the references to the ministerial crisis.

Tuesday night. 9 o'clock.

I WAS not in the wrong, my dear Lord, on Sunday, when I told
you[1] that the reported disposition of places[2] was premature; and
I guessed as little wrong, when I doubted the accession of Mr Pitt.
He has refused almost *carte blanche*.[3]

The four ministers[4] were separately with the King that day,[5] as
you know. They told him their resolution to adhere to one another,
and that they would resign on Tuesday (today), if not dismissed
sooner.[6] This resolution however they changed.[7] George Grenville

(later Vicomte) de Sarsfield (DU DEFFAND
i. 286 n. 10; Richard Hayes, *Biographical
Dictionary of Irishmen in France*, Dublin,
1949, p. 285).

———

1. HW gives further details of his conversation with Holland in *Mem. Geo. III*
ii. 119–20. At Bute's request, Holland had
remained in town until 19 May because
of the brewing ministerial crisis, but finding he was not to be invited to take part
in forming a new ministry, he then left
for the country (Ilchester, *Henry Fox* ii.
294).

2. It was generally assumed that a New-
castle-Pitt, or a Bute-Pitt, administration
would immediately replace the Bedford-
Grenville ministry when it became known
on 16 May that negotiations for some
such arrangement were under way and
that the King intended to dismiss his ministers (*Grenville Papers* iii. 165–6; John,
4th D. of Bedford, *Correspondence*, 1842–6,
iii. 279–80). One list of a proposed distribu-
tion of places is printed in George III,
Correspondence, ed. Fortescue, 1927–8, i.
92–4; others dated 15, 16, 17 May are in
BM Add. MSS 32966, ff. 395–403, 405–8,
415–18, 424; 33000, ff. 381–4 (see L. B.
Namier, *Additions and Corrections to Sir
John Fortescue's Edition of the Correspondence of King George III (Vol. I)*,
Manchester, 1937, p. 26).

3. The Duke of Cumberland, at the
King's request, waited on Pitt at Hayes

on 19 May to sound him on joining the
proposed ministry. According to HW, the
Duke offered Pitt 'almost *carte blanche*' on
offices and constitutional points, but the
Duke's own account of the interview does
not mention so sweeping an offer nor did
Pitt understand the Duke to propose so
much. HW later described Pitt as having
been 'not . . . untractable' at the interview, but the account given here is more
accurate; everyone except Pitt himself
understood he had refused to cooperate
(HW to Hertford 20 May 1765; to Mann
25 May 1765; *Mem. Geo. III* ii. 118–9;
George Thomas, Earl of Albemarle, *Memoirs of the Marquis of Rockingham and
His Contemporaries*, 1852, i. 202–3; George
III, *Corr.* i. 103, 107; Namier, *Additions*,
op. cit. 28; *Chatham Corr.* ii. 311 n.).

4. George Grenville, first lord of the
Treasury; the Duke of Bedford, lord president of the Council; John Montagu (1718–
92), 4th E. of Sandwich, secretary of state
for the northern department; and the
Earl of Halifax, secretary of state for the
southern department.

5. Sunday, 19 May.

6. Grenville's account of the ministers'
interviews with the King does not mention a specific date for their resignation
(*Grenville Papers* iii. 170–2).

7. When Grenville saw the King on
Tuesday morning, 21 May, he clearly had
not changed his intention of resigning.
When the King pressed him to remain in

offended him much. The King ordered him to carry a message to the House to adjourn. He replied, 'Sir, would you have me cut my own throat?' 'Who must carry the message then?' 'My successor.'[8] They determined even to oppose the adjournment;[9] which intention being known, the House is only adjourned from day to day.

The Sheriffs of London[10] yesterday acquainted the Lords with intelligence they had got, that the weavers were to rise at five this morning,[11] on which Lord Halifax wrote to the King[12] to advise a commission for Lord Granby, the Duke of Richmond, and Lord Waldegrave,[13] to suppress the riot. Upon this, his Majesty resolved to name the Duke of Cumberland Captain-General, and it was even said in the House of Commons today that it was so done.[14] But your brother,[15] whom I have left this minute, tells me it was not; and I know the Duke said he would stop it if he could.[16] Lord Ilchester adds, that just as he came from Court the Duke of Gloucester[17] said it was all patched up again for a time;[18] and that he heard the Duke of

office, he said he must consult the other ministers. No further determination was reached until after HW had written this letter (ibid. iii. 177–80).

8. Grenville gives a similar account of this part of the interview (ibid. iii. 171).

9. Grenville noted in his diary on 20 May that 'the Duke of Bedford, the two secretaries, etc., are determined to oppose the adjournment' (ibid. iii. 174).

10. Brass Crosby (1725–93), sheriff of London 1764–5; lord mayor 1770–1; M.P. Honiton 1768–74 (DNB; A. B. Beaven, *The Aldermen of . . . London*, 1908–13, ii. 133); and Thomas Harris (d. 1782), Kt, 1765; apothecary; sheriff of London 1764–5 (GM 1782, lii. 312; W. A. Shaw, *The Knights of England*, 1906, ii. 292).

11. The Sheriffs reported there would be a general rising of all weavers, shoemakers, tailors and dyers, armed with cutlasses, and that these would be joined by parties of weavers already on their way from Norwich, Manchester, and other towns. They would go first to Parliament and then, if not assured no more silk would be imported from France, they would plunder all the mercers' shops in London and pull down Bedford House (Bedford, op. cit. iii. 282; *Letters to Henry Fox* 213). There had been serious riots by the weavers for several days, following the rejection of a bill for restricting the

import of foreign silks on 13 May. Since Bedford alone had spoken against the bill, the fury of the mob was directed against him; Bedford House had been saved on the 17th only by the intervention of troops (*Mem. Geo. III* ii. 110–13; HW to Hertford 20 May 1765).

12. The letter is printed in George III, *Corr.* i. 105, mistakenly described as being from the King to Halifax; see Namier, *Additions*, op. cit. 28.

13. John Waldegrave (1718–84), 3d E. Waldegrave; general; M.P. Orford 1747–54, Newcastle-under-Lyme 1754–63.

14. HW received this report from Conway at 11:00 that morning (HW to Hertford 20 May 1765; *Mem. Geo. III* ii. 121). The King did ask the Duke of Cumberland to act as Captain-General on the 20th, and the Duke replied that he would obey, although he showed no enthusiasm for the commission (George III, *Corr.* i. 106).

15. Lord Ilchester.

16. The matter was dropped when the expected riot failed to materialize, though the affair of the Captain-General played some part in the subsequent negotiations of the Bedford-Grenville ministry to remain in office (*Grenville Papers* iii. 184–5).

17. William Henry (1743–1805), D. of Gloucester; brother of George III.

18. I.e., the proposed resignation of the ministry.

Bedford say the same thing a minute afterwards, but adding, 'there is one point given us to consider of'; which your brother thinks is the affair of Captain-General.[19]

There has not been the appearance of a riot today. The two Secretaries dropped strong insinuations in the House of Lords yesterday that Lord Bute had fomented the mob,[20] which Lord Pomfret[21] took up warmly; and indeed the ministerial people have not been sparing of that language.[22]

Among these many strange events, nothing strikes more than an interview at Lord Temple's this morning between him and his brother George;[23] but as yet I know nothing of the purport or result.[24]

Good-night, my dear Lord. I hope to go in a day or two to my Kingsgate,[25] and hope still more fervently that this may be the last week of politics in which I am ever engaged. The ministers cannot be more overjoyed at recovering their power, than I shall be to recover my liberty.

Yours most sincerely,

H. WALPOLE

19. It probably was not. Bedford more likely referred to the King's order to Grenville that afternoon to consult the other ministers and bring him the terms on which they would remain in office (*Grenville Papers* iii. 180).

20. Rigby told Bedford that Halifax said, 'if there was an evil counsellor about the King, who at this time dared to advise the King to show your Grace any mark of his displeasure, he would be the detestation of every honest man in the nation, and his name be held in abomination for ever' (Bedford, op. cit. iii. 281–2). In *Mem. Geo. III* ii. 126, HW attributes the insinuations against Bute principally to Halifax. See also Egmont's notes on the debate in George III, *Corr.* i. 103. Bute actually had little part in the crisis.

21. George Fermor (1722–85), 2d E. of Pomfret; lord of the Bedchamber 1763–81. He had previously made a bitter personal

attack on Bedford in the Lords on 2 April (HW to Hertford 7 April 1765).

22. See the Duchess of Bedford's remarks to HW on Bute's supposed share in fomenting the riots in *Mem. Geo. III* ii. 113.

23. George Grenville.

24. The brothers had quarrelled over the Wilkes affair in 1763. The meeting that morning in an attempt at reconciliation did not prove 'satisfactory,' but they were reunited the following day (*Grenville Papers* iii. 42–3, 176).

25. Strawberry Hill. Kingsgate was Lord Holland's house at the edge of the cliffs near Margate, Kent. He took a long lease on the property in 1762 and began a series of fantastic 'improvements' (Ilchester, *Henry Fox* ii. 168, 279–82, and plate facing ii. 280; Hugh Honour, 'An Epic of Ruin-Building,' *Country Life*, 1953, cxiv. 1968–9).

From HOLLAND, ca Saturday 25 May 1765

Missing, but apparently written after Holland had learned of his dismissal as paymaster-general; see the following letter.

To HOLLAND, Wednesday 29 May 1765

Printed from *Letters to Henry Fox* 216–19; reprinted, Toynbee *Supp.* i. 108–12. Dated by the reference to the appointment of the D. of Ancaster as Master of the Horse to the Queen.

My dear Lord,

IF I was to write, as you bid me, all I can think of, that is, all I know of the late transactions, your curiosity, however great it may be, would be wearied before I could reduce it to any tolerable compass, even though I should methodize it like a divine under the several heads of blunders, folly, treachery, insolence, etc. Sooner or later I will give you the whole detail. At present, I will chiefly confine myself to satisfying your questions, for you know I never attempt to account for more than I understand, nor to assert more than I really know. I have learnt a great deal of these histories, but there are material points which I have not yet been able to make out.

Lord Halifax and Lord Sandwich may be as guilty to you[1] as the rest of the crew, but I cannot say that I have heard them particularly named. At Bedford House their violence against you is boasted of, and they have even been so brutal as to say it would kill you, though I thought they knew your spirit a little better. George Grenville's share in it you cannot doubt, from his own malice to you,[2] and from the new fuel which his brother Temple has supplied.[3] I was told at Richmond House that the Junto had proposed to dismiss you in some very ignominious manner; what that was to have been, I have not

1. Holland's dismissal as paymaster-general had been one of the conditions the Grenville-Bedford ministry imposed on the King as the price of remaining in office. He was informed of the decision by a letter from Halifax on 23 May (*Grenville Papers* iii. 41, 184, 186; Ilchester, *Henry Fox* ii. 292).
2. Grenville and Holland had been bitter enemies since 1761, largely because of the former's jealousy of Holland's political influence (Ilchester, *Henry Fox* ii. 151; T. W. Riker, *Henry Fox*, Oxford, 1911, ii. 218, 280; *Grenville Papers* i. 415).
3. Holland and Temple had quarrelled in 1756 over bringing Hanoverian troops to England (Riker, op. cit. ii. 105–6).

heard,[4] nor whether it went farther than the first ill-disposition. I cannot mention this dirty spite, without doing justice to the Duke of Richmond, who resents the treatment of you in the warmest, most open, and most friendly manner.[5] Lord Bute, you know, I am not acquainted with;[5a] but by what I see in his friends, he is thoroughly enraged.[6] The usage of Mr McKinsy[7] is aggravated by his having given up a place for life, on the King's promise that he should keep the privy seal for his Majesty's life.[8] Lord Frederic Campbell's acceptance of it[9] augments the injury; for Lord Bute had given him a place for life of £700 a year, and made two bitter enemies by it.[10]

The Duke[11] is taxed by Lord Temple with insincerity in the negotiation. The latter pretends that while it was depending, his R.H. advised the King to retake his old ministers.[12] But it should be remembered that in the midst of the treaty, the reconcilation of Lord T[emple] and G. Grenville happened,[13] which seems to throw the charge of insincerity upon that quarter.

---

4. No proposals for an 'ignominious' dismissal have been found.

5. See Richmond's letter to Holland, 23 May 1765, in *Letters to Henry Fox* 214–16.

5a. That is, not well enough acquainted with him to know his thoughts and plans; HW of course knew him socially and had corresponded with him.

6. Since the Bedford-Grenville ministry believed their difficulties with the King to result from Bute's secret influence, they had insisted that he be excluded from all share in the King's councils and business, and that his brother be dismissed from his post (*Grenville Papers* iii. 41, 181, 184).

7. James Stuart-Mackenzie had been dismissed as privy seal for Scotland at the insistence of the ministry merely because he was Bute's brother.

8. Mackenzie does not seem to have had 'a place for life' before he became privy seal for Scotland, but from 1761 to his appointment he enjoyed a pension of £2,000 per annum on the secret service fund. He gave this up on accepting his new office, worth £3,000 per annum, on the King's promise that, although Mackenzie did not have a patent for life, the office would never be taken from him, although the patronage might (Sir Lewis Namier, *The Structure of Politics at*

the Accession of George III, 2d edn, 1957, pp. 216 n. 2, 217, 220, 474, 479; *Letters from George III to Lord Bute, 1756–1766*, ed. Romney Sedgwick, 1939, pp. 210, 238; George III, *Correspondence*, ed. Fortescue, 1927–8 i. 113–5, 172, 173; *Mem. Geo. III* ii. 125).

9. On 24 May (*Grenville Papers* iii. 188).

10. Not identified. In *Mem. Geo. III* ii. 127–8, HW comments that Lord Frederick Campbell was nearly related to Mackenzie (he was a second cousin once removed), lived in intimacy with him and received a place of above £400 per annum from Bute 'by a preference that had made two considerable chiefs in that country the mortal enemies of the favourite.' See also *Letters to Henry Fox* 230.

11. Of Cumberland.

12. The Duke had so advised the King on the 21st and again on the 23d, in the belief that Pitt refused to take office and had broken off the negotiation (Augustus Henry, 3d D. of Grafton, *Autobiography*, ed. Anson, 1898, pp. 48–9; George III, *Corr.* i. 114–15; Albemarle to Newcastle 21 May 1765, BM Add. MSS 32966, f. 433; Newcastle's memorandum, ibid. f. 435).

13. On Wednesday 22 May (*Grenville Papers* iii. 183).

As to the Duke of Newcastle, he has been *semper idem*, busy and inconclusive, giving counsels and impediments, eager and timid. Would not accept himself;[14] yet recommended those faggots Lord Grantham[15] and Lord Hardwicke[16] for secretaries of state,[17] as if himself was in the plenitude of power.

You call the Opposition, the late Opposition, very apropos, for they declare they lay down their arms, and are attached to the King.[18] A few weeks, I think, will make them go farther, and perceive there are more detestable men than Lord Bute.

I will now answer you upon two heads more, as if you had questioned me upon them.

The King feels the outrage offered to him, with due resentment. Their behaviour to him has exceeded all bounds. Grenville had the insolence to tell him he did not know what business the Duke of Cumberland had so often at Court.[19] The Duke of Bedford went farther, and after telling him that Lord Bute had long been his bitter enemy and broke his word with him, added, that he was sorry to be forced to tax his Majesty with a like breach of promise.[20] This Lady

14. Newcastle and his friends persistently refused to accept office at this time (George III, *Corr.* i. 107, 110, 114). Newcastle himself wrote to the Bishop of Oxford on 18 May: 'I have been offered to be president of the Council, which I absolutely declined. I am most disposed, for the ease and comfort of my life, to accept no office at all; the privy seal is the only one I could take on any account. . . . The dear Duchess of Newcastle is mighty desirous that I should have the privy seal; or otherwise, I should now be determined to have nothing' (BM Add. MSS 32966, f. 426).

15. Thomas Robinson (1695–1770), cr. (1761) Bn Grantham, diplomatist; M.P. Thirsk 1727–34, Christchurch 1748–61; secretary of state for the southern department 1754–5; joint postmaster-general 1765–6 in Rockingham's administration.

16. Philip Yorke (1720–90), 2d E. of Hardwicke; M.P. Reigate 1741–7, Cambridgeshire 1747–64.

17. There is no evidence that Newcastle made any such recommendations. In his lists of proposed ministerial changes, Grantham and Hardwicke appear only as possible candidates for postmaster-general and the board of trade (BM Add. MSS 32966, ff. 393, 396, 397, 398, 402).

18. 'If he [Conway] continues in opposition, it will not be against the King, but a most abominable faction, who, having raged against the constitution and their country to pay court to Lord Bute, have even thrown off that paltry mask, and avowedly hoisted the standard of their own power' (HW to Hertford 20 May 1765).

19. HW is the only authority for this remark, which in *Mem. Geo. III* ii. 125, he assigns to 22 May. He wrote that section in July 1769 ('Short Notes,' GRAY i. 45). It may be a distorted version of Grenville's conversation with the King on the evening of 21 May: 'The King inquired whether they meant to restrain him from civility to the Duke of Cumberland. . . . Mr Grenville said that nobody could be so unreasonable as to wish to restrain any civil intercourse between his Majesty and his royal family, but that his Royal Highness must have nothing to do with the government' (*Grenville Papers* iii. 183).

20. HW refers to Bedford's conversation with the King on 16 May. Bedford described his words more mildly: 'I took the liberty to remind the King upon what conditions proposed by himself, namely, the excluding Lord Bute from his presence, and any participation in public affairs, I was called by him into his serv-

Waldegrave[21] boasted of to Lady Mary Coke,[22] and Rigby to Hamilton.[23]

The other point is Mr Pitt—never a very explicable subject, now dark indeed. Yet I think thus much is probable; that though he did not wish the reconciliation of his brothers-in-law, he is ready to profit of it. In other words, the world believes that Grenville has promised Lord Temple to get rid of the Duke of Bedford as soon as he can, possibly by fair means: that is, by persuading his Grace to retire, upon condition his friends keep their places.[24] They perhaps may accord to this, but how the Duchess[25] will like to quit victory and empire for Woburn[26] and Bath, is another question. Lord Lyttelton has dropped this inadvertently,[27] and Lord Temple told Lord Geo. Sackville he never would come in with the present ministers, but should have no objection to an administration formed from different parties;[28] meaning, I suppose, to break all parties, to govern all more easily. But that idea is seen through, and will not be so practicable as they think for, though it may to some degree.

Wednesday night [May 29].

I had writ thus far, when I hear that the King has today declared the Duke of Ancaster[29] Master of the Horse to the Queen. The Bedfords had wanted it, first for Lord Waldegrave, then for Lord Suf-

ice, and how very unfaithfully these conditions had been kept with me' (Bedford, op. cit. iii. 280).

21. Lady Elizabeth Leveson-Gower (1724–84), dau. of 1st E. Gower, m. (1751) John Waldegrave, 3d E. Waldegrave; sister of the Duchess of Bedford (Burke's . . . Peerage, 101st edn, ed. L. G. Pine, 1956, p. 2106).

22. Lady Mary Campbell (1727–1811), dau. of 2d D. of Argyll, m. (1747) Edward Coke, styled Vct Coke; HW's friend and correspondent.

23. Probably William Gerard ('Single Speech') Hamilton (1729–96), politician; M.P. Petersfield 1754–61, Pontefract 1761–8, Old Sarum 1768–74, Wareham 1774–80, Wilton 1780–90, Haslemere 1790–6.

24. There is no evidence that Grenville made any such promise, though it was generally believed, even before the reconciliation of Grenville and Temple, that Bedford intended to retire; see Letters to

Henry Fox 221; Conway to Hertford 16 May 1765, MS now WSL.

25. Lady Gertrude Leveson-Gower (1715–94), dau. of 1st E. Gower, m. (1737) John Russell, 4th D. of Bedford.

26. Woburn Abbey, Bedford's seat in Bedfordshire.

27. Lyttelton would be a sound authority for Temple's opinions; he had been offered the Treasury himself on 20 May, but refused to accept it without Pitt and Temple and had offered instead to undertake a negotiation to place Temple at the Treasury (Grenville Papers iii. 227; unpublished letters quoted in R. M. Davis, The Good Lord Lyttelton, Bethlehem, Pa., 1939, pp. 347–8).

28. This statement has not been found elsewhere.

29. Peregrine Bertie (1714–78), 3d D. of Ancaster; lord of the Bedchamber 1755–65; Master of the Horse to the Queen 29 May 1765–13 Dec. 1766; to the King 13 Dec. 1766–78.

folk.[30] I like this spirit, I only fear they should drive again too fast before they are ready. A little patience and a good deal of management, good management, would make the thing very easy. When I say good management, you will not wonder that I wish you nearer than Kingsgate. I do not believe the affront to Lord Bute has answered in the article of popularity, as they flattered themselves. The people are as hostile as ever to the Duke of Bedford; but what will surprise you, the Tories lean more to George Grenville than to Lord Bute.[32] On the other hand, one of the most violent against him, the Duke of Portland,[33] is extremely softened.[34] The Dukes of Richmond and Manchester[35] offered themselves to the Duke of Cumberland.[36] In short, if properly conducted, the machine might soon be put in motion again. There never was a fairer opportunity for a man of parts.

The ministers, as you may imagine, flew to Lord Temple with open arms. Rigby told Hamilton that both Bedford and Marlborough[37] had offered him their places;[38] but he has not even accepted a dinner. Both Secretaries[39] invited him for the Birthday.[40] He said he believed he should be out of town; if not, should dine with his brother,—not with James,[41] who is gone out of town, sulky.[42] Lord Temple carries George to Hayes tomorrow for the first time,[43]

30. Henry Howard (1739–79), 12th E. of Suffolk; deputy earl-marshal 1763–5; secretary of state for the northern department 1771–9. It was reported on the 25th that he was actually to succeed to the post (G. Onslow to Newcastle 25 May 1765, BM Add. MSS 32966, f. 468). He was a follower of Grenville (John Brooke, *The Chatham Administration 1766–1768*, 1956, pp. 137, 143, 145, 262). For the ministers' reaction to their disappointment, see Bedford, op. cit. iii. 284–5.

32. This rumour was being circulated by some of the 'King's Friends'; Lord Bateman told Lord Digby that 'they [the "Tories"] had declared for the Duke of Bedford against Lord Bute,' though Digby did not believe it (*Letters to Henry Fox* 221).

33. William Henry Cavendish Bentinck (1738–1809), 3d D. of Portland; first lord of the Treasury 5 April–Dec. 1783; 1807–9.

34. 'I hear some of the most violent in the late Opposition are much softened in

their language with regard to Lord Bute' (Digby to Holland 31 May 1765, *Letters to Henry Fox* 220).

35. George Montagu (1737–88), 4th D. of Manchester.

36. Both of them later supported the Rockingham administration.

37. George Spencer (1739–1817), 3d D. of Marlborough; lord chamberlain of the Household 1762–3; lord privy seal 1763–5.

38. It was reported in London by the 25th that Temple was to become privy seal (Newcastle to G. Onslow 25 May, to Albemarle 26 May 1765, BM Add. MSS 32966, ff. 469, 475).

39. Halifax and Sandwich.

40. The King's birthday, 4 June.

41. Hon. James Grenville (*ante* 13 March 1761, n. 4).

42. Apparently not; he accompanied his brothers to Hayes the next day (*Grenville Papers* iii. 191).

43. See *Grenville Papers* iii. 191 for an account of the visit.

a *gouty* fever[44] having prevented it hitherto. The reconciliation was negotiated by Williams,[45] and concluded by Lord Bristol and Augustus Hervey.[46]

Lord Townshend who bragged of prevailing on Charles,[47] is now I hear a little out of humour, having wanted the government of Ireland. The Irish in London are furious against the Governor[48] that is given to them.[49]

I forgot to tell you (and you will not mind my rambling, as this is rather a newspaper than a letter) that Lord G. Sackville thinks from some obscure expressions of Lord Temple, that Pitt would take a peerage and leave the House of Commons to Geo. Grenville. Were it more known that the King offered Pitt to regulate general warrants as far as was consistent with his honour, to reinstate the dismissed officers, to alleviate the cider tax, and to strengthen alliances against the House of Bourbon,[50] that, as the Duke of Cumberland made Lord Temple own,[51] they had had *carte blanche des demandes,* and that still they were not to be satisfied, I should not think it would be their popularity that would entitle one family to give law to all the world.

Friday, four o'clock [May 31].

I wish you joy of Ch. Townshend's kindness to Mr Hamilton.[52]

44. Pitt had been 'suddenly taken with the gout' earlier in the month (Conway to Hertford 16 May 1765, MS now WSL).

45. 'Gilly' Williams; he is not mentioned in any of the documents relating to the reconciliation and later denied taking any part in it (*Letters to Henry Fox* 224).

46. Augustus John Hervey (1724–79), 3d E. of Bristol, 1775; naval officer and politician; M.P. Bury 1757–63, 1768–75, Saltash 1763–8. He played the major part in the reconciliation (*Grenville Papers* iii. 39–40, 42–3, 174, 176).

47. Charles Townshend, though designated chancellor of the Exchequer by the Opposition, when they expected to come in earlier in the month, accepted the Pay Office immediately on Holland's dismissal (*Mem. Geo. III* ii. 126).

48. Thomas Thynne (1734–96), 3d Vct Weymouth, cr. (1789) M. of Bath; appointed Lord Lieutenant of Ireland 29 May (not April as in GEC; see *London*

Gazette No. 10526, 28 May–1 June 1765), but never went to Ireland.

49. For one Irishman's comments, see Edmund Burke, *Correspondence,* Vol. I, ed. T. W. Copeland, Cambridge, 1958, p. 197.

50. According to the Duke of Cumberland's account of his interview with Pitt on 19 May, Pitt insisted on three of these conditions (the cider tax is not mentioned), but there is no statement that they were conceded (George Thomas, Earl of Albemarle, *Memoirs of the Marquis of Rockingham and His Contemporaries,* 1852, i. 203, where the interview is dated a week too early).

51. HW repeats this in the *Memoirs,* but says that Pitt and his friends would never admit it (*Mem. Geo. III* ii. 123). Pitt told Charles Fitzroy on 29 May that nothing like *carte blanche* was ever hinted (Augustus Henry, 3d D. of Grafton, *Autobiography,* ed. Anson, 1898, p. 51).

52. Probably Charles Hamilton, Hol-

Lord Ilchester tells me, as I foresaw, that the Duchess and **Rigby** are against the Duke's retiring *now*.

Charles Fitzroy, by the Duke of Grafton's[53] desire, has been at Hayes, and stayed three hours and half.[54] At the conclusion he said, 'Well! Sir, then what I am to collect from all you have said, is that you are resolved to treat no more?' '*Resolved!* Mr Fitzroy! That is a strong word'; and then, after a pause, continued, 'Mr Pitt's determinations are fixed; all negotiation is at an end.'[55] Perhaps you are not great or little man enough, to see the difference between *resolved* and *determined*. I pity you; and wish you good-night.

From Holland, Tuesday 11 June 1765

Printed from the MS now WSL. First printed, Toynbee *Supp.* i. 112–14 n. For the history of the MS, see *ante* 22 July 1746.

Kingsgate, June 11, 1765.

My dear Hori,

YOUR ample and informing letter for which I can never enough thank you, leaves me still in the dark. That only is saying that what was truly unaccountable you could not account for. What have you been doing, dear Hori, these two years? Acting with men, or rather children, in the eager pursuit of what was not very likely to be attained. *Volvenda dies en attulit ultro.*[1] And then they won't take what they had been so long looking for. When I see that Grenville's ministry is now Pitt's, I don't wonder at the Tories. They must think

land's deputy paymaster; Charles Townshend retained him in the same office.

53. Augustus Henry Fitzroy (1735–1811), 3d D. of Grafton; secretary of state for the northern department in Rockingham's administration, July 1765—May 1766; first lord of the Treasury Aug. 1766—Jan. 1770. Charles Fitzroy was his brother.

54. He went to Hayes on 29 May and talked with Pitt for two hours (Grafton, op. cit. 51).

55. The exact terms used by Fitzroy in his 'formal' report of the conversation to Grafton were: 'At the end of my conversation with Mr Pitt, I asked if I should write word to you, that he was resolved

not to renew the negotiation; he said, *Resolved* was a *large* word, and desired I would express myself thus: '*Mr Pitt's determination was final, and the negotiation is at an end.* (These are his own words.)' (ibid.).

———

1. 'Turne, quod optanti divum
  promittere nemo
  auderet, volvenda dies en attulit ultro'
'Turnus, that which no god had dared to promise to thy prayers, lo, the circling hour has brought unasked' (Virgil, *Æneid* ix. 6–7).

themselves securer there than anywhere else. Your Opposition made their destruction a fundamental point; and any other might be brought to do so, but not Grenville's supported by Pitt. The King may have this comfort, that these ministers having done so much have done too little. Another opportunity must come, when I heartily wish H. M. may be better prepared. Whether he will or no I can't tell, but the occasion must come.

> Altera erit tum Tehys et altera quæ vehat Argos.
> Delectos heroas²—

That is, if you can find any. You say there never was a fairer opportunity for a man of parts.

Add, if you please, *and a little courage,* and *in the House of Commons,* and then though you abate a good deal in the article of parts, such a one could not fail. All management is at present in the Court, if it can be called management not to manage. Let but the King and Queen show the anger they must naturally have, without disguise, and that will soon bring them their revenge, in spite of the Duchess³ and Rigby, and not only make her go away, but make it intolerable to her to stay. Their revenge, if the King and Queen please, is sure upon all who have been so insolent.⁴ Farther I can say nothing.

For my part, account for it if you can, but don't dispute the fact, dear Hori! upon my word 'tis true. At the same time that I feel as much warmth as when I was a younger man to those I love and have reason to love, I can't hate. I am sure I have reason enough to hate and to be angry. And I represent it to myself as it is. But yet I am not angry. Surprised that I am not, but I am not. Horror and indignation at the usage the King, Lord Bute and Mr Mackenzie have met with, and that there was power to use them so, I really have; but for myself, no. I have this moment met in the last paragraph of Dr Hill upon sage,⁵ some *prose,* that my philosophy (natural philosophy

2.   'Alter erit tum Tiphys et altera
        quæ vehat Argo
        delectos heroas.'
'A second Tiphys shall then arise and a second Argo to carry chosen heroes' (Virgil, *Eclogues* iv. 34–5).
   3. Of Bedford.
   4. The Duke of Richmond had written to Holland: 'But as to them [the King and Queen], I know for certain that he con-

tinues very angry still, and that the Queen is so too. And you and I know, Lord Holland, that wives have influence' (*Letters to Henry Fox* 223).
   5. *On the Virtues of Sage in Lengthening Human Life, With Rules to Attain Old Age,* [1763], by Dr John Hill (ca 1716–75), miscellaneous writer and medical quack.

I suppose, for there has been no art or study I'll swear) has luckily made for me *sans le savoir*.

'Anger wastes, and even tears the frame by the disturbance it creates within us. It is not worth the *old man's* while for anything to give himself this discomposure. To live at ease is what he has to wish, and to *sum up all*. *To live at ease is the sure method to live long*.'

This is bad news for the person who prophesied at Bedford House that this would kill me. If it was Rigby, must I amidst all this wisdom, to be sincere, own this weakness that his unmerited unkindness[6] goes to my heart? I mean of two years ago, for I know of nothing new regarding him.

Before I leave off, let me beg of you to show your love to me, by expressing your sense of Mr Townshend's behaviour to me.[7] Had he seconded the rancour of others he could have made so many innocent people suffer on my account,[8] it must have vexed me heartily. But on the contrary he has continued everybody, and not only afforded protection but shown great kindness to every one of them on my account. He has amazed them; he has amazed me. My brother could not have been more obliging. And nobody can be more obliged than I am, which I beg you and every friend I have, dear Sir, to help me in expressing. Adieu. The account of the weather, place, and life here, I leave to G. Selwyn.[9] Though he should be just come from a dinner with foreigners at Lord March's, or from setting up all night at Almacks.

Yours ever most affectionately,

HOLLAND

6. During Fox's quarrel with Shelburne in 1763, Fox stopped Rigby's carriage in St James's Street and began to complain of the ill-treatment he had received. Rigby interrupted him with '*You* tell your story of Shelburne; *he* has a damned one to tell of you; I do not trouble myself which is the truth.' He pushed Fox aside and ordered the coachman to drive on (*Mem. Geo. III* i. 208; Ilchester, *Henry Fox* ii. 257; T. W. Riker, *Henry Fox*, Oxford, 1911, ii. 289–90).

7. Townshend's friendly consideration appears in his letter to Holland of 3 June 1765 (Ilchester, *Henry Fox* ii. 302–3).

8. By dismissing all of Holland's appointees at the Pay Office. Instead he dismissed no one.

9. Who had been visiting Holland and carried this letter to London. He planned to visit HW at SH on the 15th (*Letters to Henry Fox* 224).

To HOLLAND, Monday 15 July 1765

Printed from *Letters to Henry Fox* 234–5; reprinted, Toynbee *Supp*. i. 114–16.

Arlington Street, July 15th 1765.

My dear Lord,

I WISH I was as able as willing to tell you all I know of the late transactions; but for these sixteen last days I have been confined to my room, and almost the whole time to my bed, with the gout in my head, stomach, and both feet, with much fever and sharp pain.[1] You may judge what havoc, this, joined to the heat of the weather, has made in so flimsy a texture as mine! My weakness is excessive, and I am now lying at length on my couch while I write to you, and not without pain.

The dismay of the late ministers has been in proportion to their former insolence.[2] Sandwich alone has borne it well;[3] Grenville worst of all. Except the disinterested Lord Powis,[4] not a man has resigned for them that was not expected, unless you reckon Lord Charles Spencer,[5] on whom there were doubts. Lord Suffolk was so impatient to be of the number, that he carried his gold stick this morning to the King instead of the Duke of Norfolk,[6] but the King would not take it, and bade him carry it to the person he had it from.

Lord Granby, who they[6a] intended should be out of humour,[7] has

---

1. This was HW's fourth attack of gout and the sharpest so far. It began a fortnight earlier (HW to Conway 3 July 1765).

2. The King dismissed the Bedford-Grenville ministry on 10 July as soon as the first stages of forming the Rockingham administration were complete.

3. 'Jemmy Twitcher died like a cock . . . like one of the rebel lords in 'fifteen; he made only a low bow, and recommended his son to his Majesty's mercy' (Selwyn to Holland 12 [July 1765], *Letters to Henry Fox* 230).

4. Who had been treasurer of the Household since 1761. He resigned on 14 July (BM Add. MSS 32967, ff. 393, 394, 396), not out of disinterestedness but to forestall his dismissal. The Newcastle faction had never forgiven him for refusing to resign in 1762, and at Newcastle's insistence had determined to dis-

miss him (Sir Lewis Namier, *The Structure of Politics at the Accession of George III*, 2d edn, 1957, pp. 283–5, 297–8).

5. (1740–1820), politician; M.P. Oxfordshire 1761–90, 1796–1801; comptroller of the Household 1762–5. He resigned on 14 July to the disappointment of the new ministry (Duke of Cumberland to Newcastle 14 July 1765, BM Add. MSS 32967, f. 387; Rockingham to Newcastle 14 July 1765, ibid. f. 393).

6. Edward Howard (1686–1777), 9th D. of Norfolk; Earl Marshal of England. Since he was a Roman Catholic, the office had to be exercised by deputy.

6a. I.e., the late ministers.

7. HW elsewhere relates that Grenville attempted to turn Granby against the new ministry by telling him that they intended to turn out his father, the Duke of Rutland, Master of the

interceded for and saved Charles Vernon.[8] Charles Townshend makes promises to the Outs, and applications to the Ins;[9] and goes out of town tomorrow.[10] His brother, so violent two days ago,[11] has quarrelled with Lord Weymouth, who will not re-elect Lord Villiers[12] (not on that point,[13] but on the election for Tamworth),[14] and has carried Lutterel[15] down to oppose whoever is set up by Lord Weymouth. Now you are as wise about the Townshends as ever!

Horse, in order to save the Duke of Marlborough. Granby went to the King, asked if this were true, and on being informed that it was not (with the addition of a regiment for his brother) was entirely gained over from his old allies (*Mem. Geo. III* ii. 145).

8. Charles Vernon (1719–1810), Major-Gen., 1762; Gen., 1783; Lieutenant of the Tower of London 1763–1810; M.P. Tamworth 1768–74; nephew of Adm. Edward Vernon (Douglas Ford, *Admiral Vernon and the Navy*, 1907, p. 3; *Miscellanea genealogica et heraldica*, 1892, 2d ser., iv. 206; *Notes and Queries*, 1917, 12th ser. iii. 305; GM 1810, lxxx pt ii. 193; Judd, *Members of Parliament* 365). He is not mentioned in the lists of proposed changes in places at this time, but that he was being considered for removal appears from two references to Lord Townshend's intervention in his behalf in Egmont's letters to the King 13 July 1765 (George III, *Correspondence*, ed. Fortescue, 1927–8, i. 157, 160).

9. Charles Townshend's conduct had been ambiguous during the formation of the new administration. He refused Rockingham's offers of both the chancellorship of the Exchequer and a secretaryship of state, and told him 'that he neither desired nor would know of any of their transactions, that he might be able to declare in his place that he knew nothing of the plan nor ever had the least hand in it.' He even seems to have talked at one point of resigning the Pay Office, which he already held. Yet he interceded with Rockingham in an attempt to save Gilly Williams from dismissal and to secure promotion for John Buller (*Grenville Papers* iii. 207, 209, 210–11; *Letters to Henry Fox* 231, 236; J. Offley to Newcastle 12 July 1765, BM Add. MSS 32967,

f. 367; Rockingham to Newcastle 13 July 1765, ibid. f. 374).

10. He did so (*Letters to Henry Fox* 236).

11. Lord Townshend consistently refused to have any part in or to support the new administration and pressed his brother to take the same line, arguing that Newcastle did not seem inclined to forget old quarrels and had made no application to him (*Grenville Papers* iii. 209, 210–11; *Letters to Henry Fox* 233).

12. George Bussy Villiers (1735–1805), styled Vct Villiers 1742–69; 4th E. of Jersey, 1769; M.P. Tamworth 1756–65, Aldborough 1765–8, Dover 1768–9; a lord of the Admiralty 1761–2. He had been appointed vice-chamberlain of the Household on 14 July (*Daily Adv.* 15 July), so had to stand for re-election.

13. I.e., Weymouth had not refused to elect Villiers because the latter accepted office in the new ministry, but because of a previous grievance.

14. The details of the quarrel between Lords Weymouth and Townshend over the contested Tamworth election of 1761 are unknown. The borough was under their joint influence, each usually returning one member (*Journals of the House of Commons* xxix. 17–18, 140, 143–4, 147; J. C. Wedgwood, 'Staffordshire Parliamentary History' Vol II, pt ii, in *Collections for a History of Staffordshire*, 1922, pp. 280–1; [T. Oldfield], *An Entire and Complete History, Political and Personal, of the Boroughs of Great Britain*, 2d ed., 1794, ii. 101).

15. Simon Luttrell (1713–87), cr. (1768) Bn Irnham, (1781) Vct and (1785) E. of Carhampton; M.P. St Michael 1755–61, Wigan 1761–8, Weobley 1768–74, Stockbridge 1774–80. He did not represent the Townshend interest at the preliminary skirmishes for the Tamworth by-election.

Is it telling you anything, to tell you that the Duke of Newcastle is as busy as ever in teasing to have his old dishclouts new-laced![16] and in forcing people to dine at Claremont? It may be more new to acquaint you that an offer of the peerage was sent last night to Lord Chief Justice Pratt;[17] and though you know it already, I can but congratulate you on the confirmation of Lord Digby's peerage.[18]

I wish I was as well satisfied about the Duke of Richmond, who is not yet placed to his liking,[19] though it ought to have been one of the first points they thought of. I have made use of all the latitude of peevishness which the gout authorizes, to scold about him.[20] I am the more impatient about it, because I wish to see it done before I go to Strawberry, which I hope to do in two or three days,[21] and then I take my leave of politics for ever.[22] I shall go to Paris the beginning of September,[23] or sooner if I am able to bear the journey. Both my mind and body want repose, and the former to be amused with more

Townshend put up the Hon. George Shirley instead, who retired before the election. Weymouth's candidate, Edward Thurlow, was elected unopposed, 23 Dec. 1765 (Wedgwood, op. cit. 281).

16. Newcastle was importuning the new ministers with lists of suggested employments, especially urging the claims of his friends, James West, John Buller and John Offley. On 12 July he wrote to Rockingham threatening to have no part in the administration if these three were not attended to and complaining of general neglect (BM Add. MSS 32967, ff. 346–52, 371–2, 389–91, 423–8; *post* 19 July 1765, nn. 5 and 6).

17. Charles Pratt (1714–94), cr. (1765) Bn and (1786) E. Camden; Chief Justice of Common Pleas 1761–6; lord chancellor 1766–70; lord president of the Council 1782–3, 1784–94. His peerage was intended as a compliment to Pitt, a sign to the public of Pitt's support of the new administration, a seal of approval on Pratt's conduct in the Wilkes affair, and a means of rewarding him without an official promotion in order to leave the legal offices open for other candidates.

18. Henry Digby (1731–93), 7th Bn Digby, cr. (1790) E. Digby; M.P. Ludgershall 1755–61, Wells 1761–5; a lord of the Admiralty 1763–5; Lord Holland's nephew. He was promised an English barony to

lighten his dismissal on the change of ministry, but the matter was not yet completely settled (*Letters to Henry Fox* 228–9, 237). He did not receive his patent until mid-August (GEC).

19. Richmond did not yet have an office. He had been offered the post of cofferer but had declined it (according to HW) by HW's persuasion, and (by his own admission) because he did not wish an office so inferior to those of the Dukes of Portland and Grafton. He told C. J. Fox two days before that he was, however, 'perfectly satisfied' with his position as a firm supporter of the ministry out of office (*Mem. Geo. III* ii. 144; *Letters to Henry Fox* 233–4).

20. HW later asserted he had already begun to push Richmond for ambassador to France (*Mem. Geo. III* ii. 144–5); from *post* 21 July 1765 it appears that Richmond was also being considered for Lord Lieutenant of Ireland if Hertford should refuse.

21. He went on the 20th (*post* 19 July 1765).

22. HW's resolution to quit politics was strengthened by his conviction that he had been neglected, especially by Conway, in the formation of the new ministry (*Mem. Geo. III* ii. 148–52).

23. HW left for Paris on 9 Sept. ('Paris Journals,' DU DEFFAND v. 258).

agreeable nonsense than what has occupied it of late,—in short, nonsense of my own, not nonsense of other people. I rejoice that you enjoy your health so well. When I am a little stronger, if there is anything you want to know in which I can inform you, you know I am always most ready to do it. At present I am a poor creature, and write with such difficulty that I am sure you will excuse me.

Yours ever,

H. Walpole

From Holland, ca Wednesday 17 July 1765

Missing.

To Holland, Friday 19 July 1765

Printed from *Letters to Henry Fox* 240–2; reprinted, Toynbee *Supp.* i. 116–8.

Friday, July 19th.

My dear Lord,

YOU are exceedingly kind, but I certainly do not regret any pains I can take to amuse or inform you. Several things that have happened, have undoubtedly given me great satisfaction, but they cannot quiet pain, nor what, sharp as the pain was, I think worse, the fever which accompanied it. I have been lifted into a coach today to take the air, and shall be carried to Strawberry tomorrow, but the little strength I possessed does not return at all.

I doubt much whether Lord Hertford[1] will go to Ireland,[2] though I own I am singular in that opinion. He is to be here next week to make his decision.[3] You might well conclude that my journey to Paris

1. Francis Seymour Conway (1718–94), 2d Bn Conway, cr. (1750) E. and (1793) M. of Hertford; ambassador to France 1763–5; Lord Lieutenant of Ireland 1765–6; HW's cousin and correspondent.
2. He did go.
3. Hertford was offered the Lord-Lieu-tenancy immediately on the formation of the new ministry (HW to Mann 12 July 1765). He reached London 26 July (*Daily Adv.* 27 July 1765); his appointment as Lord Lieutenant was announced under date of 1 Aug. in the *London Gazette* No. 10544, 30 July–3 Aug. 1765.

was a symptom of his staying there; yet it was not. I have so long set my mind upon it, that I am now childishly eager for it. I long to go where I may hear any nonsense but what I have been so long used to, and though it is common to change one's opinion, at least one's language, when one quits Opposition, I am exactly the same I always told you I was. I am weary of politics and detest the House of Commons; and having obtained all I ever wished, the liberty of pleasing myself without being tied to a party, I shall withdraw from even the discourse of it. To be sure it would have happened a little more decently, if the gout had not come across such youthful resolutions; but why may I not go to Paris with as much propriety as the Duke of Newcastle to St James's?

Lord Barrington's[4] promotion or depression, whichever you please to call it, was I believe owing to his Grace, who wanted to parcel out the treasurer of the Navy.[5] There are few other promotions but what come from the same hand: yet he frets and scolds and sputters, and is not half satisfied,[6] and the rest are so weak as to mind him.

The Attorney-General[7] was dismissed this morning, but I do not find they have any assurance that Yorke[8] will accept his place.[9] Lord Bolingbroke,[10] Seymour,[11] and Aug. Hervey[12] have or are to resign,

4. William Wildman Barrington-Shute (1717–93), 2d Vct Barrington; M.P. Berwick-on-Tweed 1740–54, Plymouth 1754–78. He had been treasurer of the Navy since 1762, but kissed hands as secretary at war on 20 July (BM Add. MSS 32968, f. 86).

5. In an attempt to silence the complaints of Newcastle (ante 17 July 1765, n. 16, and below, n. 6), Rockingham agreed on 17 July to make his protégé James West treasurer of the Navy and to move Lord Barrington to the War Office to make room. The rumour of West's appointment caused a general outcry, but a fortunate dispute over precedence on the Navy Board enabled ministers to change their minds and appoint Lord Howe treasurer of the Navy instead. It was then suggested that West be made a lord of the Admiralty, but in the end he received no office at all (Rockingham to Newcastle 17 July 1765, BM Add. MSS 32968, f. 33; [19 July 1765], ibid. f. 84; Grafton to Newcastle [21 July 1765], ibid. f. 146; Rockingham's memorandum [21 July 1765], ibid. f. 144).

6. Newcastle had been complaining of neglect for several days. Finally, on 16 July, he sent John Roberts to Rockingham to state his grievances. Rockingham promptly appeased the Duke by an interview on the 17th in which he agreed to promote several of Newcastle's recommendations (BM Add. MSS 32968, ff. 9, 11, 33, 37, 82, 94; ante 15 July 1765).

7. Sir Fletcher Norton (1716–89), cr. (1782) Bn Grantley, attorney-general 1763–5; Speaker of the House of Commons 1770–80; M.P. Appleby 1756–61, Wigan 1761–8, Guildford 1768–82. His dismissal is discussed in Rockingham to Newcastle [19 July 1765], BM Add. MSS 32968, f. 84.

8. Hon. Charles Yorke (1722–70), solicitor-general 1756–61; attorney-general 1762–3, 1765–6; M.P. Reigate 1747–68; Cambridge University 1768–70.

9. Yorke informed Grenville on 18 July that he intended to take the place (Grenville Papers iii. 219), then changed his mind, but finally accepted 25 Aug. He had been particularly offended by Pratt's peerage; see George III, Correspondence, ed. Fortescue, 1927–8, i. 159–60.

10. Who had been a lord of the Bedchamber since 1762; he was reappointed

which I hear will shut up the list.[13] The Duke of Portland told me this morning that when Pratt went to see Pitt, after accepting his peerage, the latter took no notice about it. When Pratt told him of it, all he replied was, 'Oh! then it is true that you are made a peer.'[14] The late ministers brag of a visit Mr Pitt has made to Geo. Grenville, which lasted long enough for one of them to have made a speech in, in short, four hours.[15]

I am sorry for the charge of insincerity brought against you,[16] because the person that makes it is so great a mistress of [it] herself, that folks will think she cannot be mistaken in her own walk. But as I do not doubt but she will very soon cry up the sincerity of my Lord Temple, you may cure the wound with the scorpion's own oil.

I am heartily glad to add a new congratulation on Mr Digby's canonry;[17] it is a promotion that pleases everybody that knows his merit.

This is not written, I fear, very legibly, as I am still lying on a couch, but you must accept the intention of the writer, who is,

Ever yours,

H. WALPOLE

in 1768 and retained the post until 1780.

11. Henry Seymour (1729–1807), groom of the Bedchamber; M.P. Totnes 1763–8, Huntingdon borough 1768–74, Evesham 1774–80; half-brother of Lord Sandwich; later the lover of Mme du Barry (Bernard Falk, *The Naughty Seymours*, 1940, pp. 27–115 *passim*). 'I understood from the King today that Mr Seymour either has or will resign being groom of the Bedchamber' (Rockingham to Newcastle 17 July 1765, BM Add. MSS 32968, f. 34).

12. He was a groom of the Bedchamber but did not resign.

13. The new arrangements were not yet complete according to a list prepared by Newcastle, 21 July, of places and offices not yet settled (BM Add. MSS 32968, ff. 140–2).

14. There is no confirmation of this anecdote.

15. On 15 July. The entry in Grenville's diary reads: 'Mr Pitt and Lady Chatham came to Downing Street in the evening, stayed about an hour, and then went on to Hayes' (*Grenville Papers* iii. 218).

16. 'The Duchess of Bedford told Lord Ophaly she believed you were a very good man in your private family, but that in public life she found it was impossible to acquit you of insincerity. The Bitch' (C. J. Fox to Holland [13 July 1765], *Letters to Henry Fox* 234).

17. Rev. William Digby (1734–88), brother of 6th and 7th Barons Digby; nephew of Lord Holland; vicar of Coleshill; Canon of Christ Church 1765–9; Dean of Worcester 1769–83; Dean of Durham 1777–88 (*Record of Old Westminsters*, ed. G. F. Russell Barker and A. H. Stenning, 1928, i. 269).

From HOLLAND, ca Friday 19 July 1765

Missing. This letter arrived in London on 20 July. Holland asked HW to recommend his illegitimate son Charles Cooper as an aide-de-camp to Hertford.

To HOLLAND, Sunday 21 July 1765

Printed from *Letters to Henry Fox* 243–4; reprinted, Toynbee *Supp.* i. 118–19.

Strawberry Hill, July 21st 1765, Sunday.

My dear Lord,

I HAD sent away my letter, and left London before your last arrived there, which occasioned my not receiving it till this morning here. Lord Hertford is expected in town next Thursday. I have told you in my letter of last night[1] that I doubted his going to Ireland, but I owned at the same time that I was singular in my opinion. If he does not, it will certainly be the Duke of Richmond. However I will certainly recommend Mr Cooper[2] to Lord Hertford, though I can do it but in the second place, having promised to desire him to continue Capt. Erskine,[3] son of Lady Frances,[4] who was aide-de-camp to Lord Northumberland.[5] I should therefore, my dear Lord, advise both your Lordship and Lady Holland to write immediately, as I know of abundant solicitations. One is promised to the Duke of Grafton,[6] and Mr Conway has recommended the gentlemen that

1. HW's letter of 19 July.
2. Charles Cooper (fl. 1747–88), illegitimate son of Lord Holland; Lt, 49th Foot, 1747; 14th Foot, 1758; Capt. in the army and Lt in Goldstream Guards, 1773; retired from the army, 1776; aide-de-camp to Warren Hastings in India; comptroller of Chelsea Hospital 1761–88 (*Record of Old Westminsters*, ed. G. F. Russell Barker and A. H. Stenning, 1928, i. 211; William Hickey, *Memoirs*, ed. Spencer, 1913–25, iii. 245–6; C. G. T. Dean, *The Royal Hospital, Chelsea*, 1950, pp. 234, 315; Ilchester, *Henry Fox* ii. 277 n.). For his father's financial generosity towards him, see L. S. Sutherland and J. Binney, 'Henry Fox as Paymaster General of the Forces,' *English Historical Review*, 1955, lxx. 253.
3. John Francis Erskine (1741–1825), restored as 24th *or* 7th E. of Mar, 1824; officer in 1st Regiment of Horse 1759–70, when he resigned from the army; aide-de-camp to Northumberland when Lord Lieutenant of Ireland 1763–5; to Hertford 1765–6 (GEC *sub* Mar; GM 1765, xxxiii. 519; [Great Britain, War Office], *List of the . . . Officers*, [1761], p. 18). HW's intercession in Erskine's favour had been requested by Anne Pitt (HW to Anne Pitt 9 Aug. 1765).
4. Lady Frances Erskine (d. 1776), m. (1740) her cousin, James Erskine of Grange.
5. Hugh Smithson (after 1750, Percy) (1714 *or* 1715–86), 2d E. of Northumberland; cr. (1766) D. of Northumberland; Lord Lieutenant of Ireland 1763–5.
6. See *post* 2 Aug. 1765, n. 2.

were his aides-de-camp,[7] though they have not yet any promise. I am very minute, but when you do me the honour to consult me, it is right to tell you exactly all I know of the matter.

As I am quite alone here, I can add nothing to my last, but what I shall say very little upon. I am cool and comfortable here, which I have not been these three weeks, but not a jot stronger or less helpless than I was. Adieu! my dear Lord,

Yours most sincerely,

H. Walpole

If this affair should not succeed for Mr Cooper, you know, my dear Lord, how ready I shall be to use what little interest I have in the new ministry to serve him in any other shape. Impute this offer to my zeal, and not to any impertinent air. God knows how little that is my disposition. I have little credit with them; I have not even cultivated that little, and after trying to do what good I could in saving some, and, as they will bear me witness, speaking against none, I have left them with my good wishes, but I hope not altered myself in any point that was worth preserving.

To Holland, Friday 2 August 1765

Printed from *Letters to Henry Fox* 245–6; reprinted, Toynbee *Supp.* i. 119–20.

Arlington Street, Aug. 2, 1765.

My dear Lord,

I AM heartily concerned that you should have the smallest disappointment about Mr Cooper, but I must do justice to Lord Hertford, though at the expense of myself. He had long ago promised the younger Cunningham:[1] the Duke of Grafton recommended Mr

---

7. For the two of his three aides on whose appointment Conway 'insisted,' see *post* 2 Aug. 1765, n. 3.

---

1. James Cunninghame (d. 1788), brother of Robert Cunninghame, 1st Bn Rossmore; Capt. in 54th Foot, 1755; Lt-Col in 1st Foot, 1758; Lt-Gen. in the army, 1782; Col. of the 45th Foot, 1787; Governor of the Barbados, 1780; M.P. East Grinstead 1786–8 (Sir Bernard Burke, *Genealogical and Heraldic History of the Landed Gentry of Ireland,* 10th edn, ed. Ashworth P. Burke, 1904, p. 127; [Great Britain, War Office], *List . . . of the Officers, passim;* Robert Beatson, *Political Index,* 3d edn, 1806, ii. 122, 239; GM 1788, lviii pt ii. 840; Judd, *Members of Parliament* 166).

Fleming;[2] Mr Conway insisted on two of his three aides-de-camp,[3] and the Irish Speaker[4] could not be refused one.[5] The sixth, Lord Hertford was so good as to tell me I should recommend. You may be sure I should have had no doubt of naming Mr Cooper, if I had not, as I told you fairly, been engaged to solicit for Mr Erskine. I could not in honour waive him, when I was bound to serve him if I could, nor will you, I think, blame me. Lord Hertford has promised, and will tell you so himself, to advance Mr Cooper in the army.[6] I desire to be his remembrancer, and Lady Hertford's[7] great friendship and affection for Lady Holland[8] will more than second anything I can say. 'Tis my earnest wish that this may be satisfactory to you. I have told you the truth, and hope that will be a pledge that I shall be as zealous to serve Mr Cooper as I am ready to take the blame, if I am to blame, which however I shall be very sorry if you think me.

It is with much more pleasure I tell you that the Duke of Richmond goes ambassador to Paris;[9] for they are only agreeable things that I ever wish to be able to tell you.

I am still a prisoner to my room, and even to my couch, having had a bad return, and not yet able to wear a shoe. Adieu! my dear Lord,

Yours most sincerely,

H. Walpole

2. William Fleming (d. 1776), Major in 64th Foot, 1767; Lt-Col. in the army; Capt. in the 1st Foot Guards, 1775 ([Great Britain, War Office], *List . . . of the Officers, passim;* GM 1776, xlvi. 240).

3. Conway's appointees were George Hotham (1741–1806), entered the 1st Foot Guards, 1759, where he remained until 1776; Col. 14th Foot, 1789; Major-Gen., 1790; Gen., 1802; Conway's aide-de-camp 1761–3; later tutor and sub-governor, 1776, and treasurer and secretary to the Prince of Wales 1780–7 (*Record of Old Westminsters,* ed. G. F. Russell Barker and A. H. Stenning, 1928, i. 484); and, presumably, since the other five aides are accounted for in this letter, West Hyde (d. 1797), entered the 1st Foot Guards, 1753, where he remained until 1789; Col. 20th Foot, 1789; Major-Gen., 1782; Lt-Gen., 1793 (GM 1797, lxvii pt i. 351; Richard Cannon, *Historical Record of the Twentieth . . . Foot,* 1848, p. 69).

4. John Ponsonby (1713–89), Speaker of the Irish House of Commons 1756–71.

5. His nominee was presumably his nephew, William Henry Burton (d. 1818) who was gazetted with the other aides-de-camp. He apparently resigned from the army in 1768 (Sir Bernard Burke, op. cit. 77; [Great Britain, War Office], *List . . . of the Officers, passim; Irish Gazette* 19 Oct. 1765).

6. There is no evidence that Cooper received any promotion at this time.

7. Lady Isabella Fitzroy (1726–82), m. (1741) Francis Seymour Conway, cr. (1750) E. of Hertford.

8. Lady Holland wrote to her sister, Lady Kildare, a few months later: 'I never saw much of Lady Hertford before I lived so much with her in France; and think her very agreeable now' (*Leinster Corr.* i. 435).

9. He accepted the Paris embassy on Hertford's accepting Ireland.

BY BENJAMIN WILSON, 1766

PS. After I had written this letter, I perceived I had begun one on the other side; will you forgive my not writing it over again?[10]

Selwyn's correspondence with Holland during July and August 1765 contains several references to HW's part in the ministerial changes and his reaction to them:

'Today Horry Walpole tells me Sir W. Baker refused. Horry has suffered from the gout excessively, and is much reduced by it. . . . Horry has prepared something for our entertainment, after the settlement of these affairs. He did not tell me what it was, or that it was for anybody's entertainment but mine and his particular friends' (Selwyn to Holland 6 July [1765], *Letters to Henry Fox* 227).

'Horry has been much consulted in all this [change of administration]; has been very friendly to me about it' (Selwyn to Holland 12 [July 1765], ibid. 230).

'When Horry was confined, I was often to see him, but it was more from an attention which I owe him on all those occasions than from any curiosity. I found myself secure from the beginning: Horry told me that the things which were said to his M[ajesty] by the D[uke] of B[edford] and Mr G[renville] were incredible; I suppose they came to him from the D[uke] of C[umberland] through several other channels, chiefly the D[uke] of R[ichmond] and Harry C[onway]. I remember his saying that the K[ing] was offended in one of these conversations, that he declared that the difficulty which he had to retain his passion threw him into a profuse sweat, and that, he thought, preserved him from an illness which by that means he might otherwise have had. How true or not this might be in fact, the expression was a strong one. What the particulars were which he thought so offensive, if Horry named them, I cannot recollect them at this instant. However, as soon as I see him, I shall renew this topic, *à votre considération*. . . . Horry also told W[illiams] and me in one of these conversations, that you had wrote an extra pretty letter to Lord A[lbemarle], desiring his good offices with the D[uke] of C[umberland]: that you wished nothing more than to end your life in the friendship and good opinion of his R. H. I suppose this the D[uke] of R[ichmond] had told him, and it may be that Lord A[lbemarle] had told the D[uke] of R[ichmond] this, and mentioned it to no one else; however I did not understand this to be a secret, nor was more said of it' (Selwyn to Holland [24 Aug. 1765], ibid. 251).

10. This postscript does not appear in *Letters to Henry Fox* but was printed by Dr Toynbee.

'Poor Horri! Give my love to him. The two things he wished most have happened, for C[onway] against R[igby]; and yet I fear his own feeling must have not only deadened, but quite overcome, both the sensations those events would have inspired' (Holland to Selwyn 27 Aug. 1765, Jesse, *Selwyn* i. 407).

To Holland, Saturday 7 September 1765

Printed from *Letters to Henry Fox* 253; reprinted, Toynbee *Supp.* i. 121–2.

Arlington Street, Sept. 7, 1765.

My dear Lord,

I AM much disappointed of a pleasure I proposed, and of which perhaps Lord Digby has given you notice, as I mentioned to him my intention of calling on you at Kingsgate on Monday. But there are letters come from Lady Hertford last night,[1] which say she leaves Paris on the 14th, which will make it but just possible for me, with all the diligence I can use now, so weak and broken, to see her before she comes away,[2] which you know I have not done these two years and cannot otherwise before she returns from Ireland.

I need not say that both she and Lord Hertford will be very ready to serve Mr Cooper, and a word from Lady Holland to Lady Hertford at any time will find her a warm solicitor.

If I find I recover I shall go no further than Paris; but in truth at present I am a poor soul, and not yet able to wear my common shoes. If I can execute any command for you at Paris, you will make me very happy. I shall be impatient for our pretty Duchess[3] to follow me; though considering their bad taste about Lady Sarah,[4] they are not worthy of her.

---

1. Presumably one was to HW, but it is missing.

2. HW got to Paris on 13 Sept. and went at once to Lady Hertford. She did not leave until 22 Sept. ('Paris Journals,' DU DEFFAND v. 260, 263; HW to Conway 11 Sept. 1765).

3. Lady Mary Bruce (1740–96), m. (1757) Charles Lennox, 3d D. of Richmond; Lady Holland's sister-in-law and Conway's step-daughter.

4. Lady Sarah Lennox (1745–1826), m. 1 (1762) Sir Thomas Charles Bunbury, 6th Bt; m. 2 (1781) Hon. George Napier; Lady Holland's sister. Lady Holland wrote Lady Kildare from Paris in May 1765 that the French considered their sister Lady Louisa more beautiful than Lady Sarah, while Lady Sarah herself (then aged 20) wrote to Holland at the same time: 'If I don't tell you I am *vastly* admired you will say I am mortified, and it's very certain I can-

As you love idle French books as well as I, if there is anything amusing comes out, I shall take the liberty of sending it to you.⁵ For their dissertations on agriculture, commerce, geometry, and such wise things, which I do not understand and shall not read, I will not pretend to be your factor. I am so sick of the House of Commons, that I do not think that I shall ever peruse the remonstrances of *their* parliaments.

I heartily wish you your health, my dear Lord, and hope you will never have that great restorative the gout; I do not know anything it cures that is as bad as itself.

Yours ever,

H. Walpole

HW's triumphant visit to Paris seems to have provoked only one comment from 'Gilly' Williams:

'Has Horry wrote? You do not know how popular he is. Will they not be surprised in France to find all our wits without ——s?' (to Selwyn 17 Oct. [1765], Jesse, *Selwyn* i. 412).

From Selwyn, early November 1765

Missing; carried by Topham Beauclerk who arrived in Paris on 9 Nov. ('Paris Journals,' du Deffand v. 270).

To Selwyn, Monday 2 December 1765

Printed from Jesse, *Selwyn* ii. 4–11; reprinted, Cunningham iv. 447–9; Toynbee vi. 367–70.

Paris, December 2d 1765.

Dear George,

IN return for your kind line by Mr Beauclerk¹ I send you a whole letter, but I was in your debt before, for making over Madame du

---

not say it, but I assure you I bear my misfortune very well' (*Life and Letters of Lady Sarah Lennox*, ed. Countess of Ilchester and Lord Stavordale, 1902, i. 163; *Leinster Corr.* i. 427, 429). Holland had

perhaps passed the latter comment on to HW.

5. He did so (*post* 2 Dec. 1765).

1. Topham Beauclerk (1739–80), friend of Dr Johnson.

Deffand[2] to me, who is delicious; that is, as often as I can get her fifty years back; but she is as eager about what happens every day as I am about the last century. I sup there twice a week, and bear all her dull company for the sake of the Regent.[3] I might go to her much oftener, but my curiosity to see everybody and everything is insatiable, especially having lost so much time by my confinement.[4] I have been very ill a long time, and mending much longer, for every two days undo the ground I get. The fogs and damps which, with your leave, are greater and more frequent than in England, kill me. However, it is the country in the world to be sick and grow old in. The first step towards being in fashion is to lose an eye or a tooth. Young people I conclude there are, but where they exist I don't guess: not that I complain; it is charming to totter into vogue. If I could but run about all the morning, I should be content to limp into good company in the evening. They humour me and fondle me so, and are so good-natured, and make me keep my armed chair, and rise for nobody, and hand out nobody, and don't stare at one's being a skeleton, that I grow to like them exceedingly, and to be pleased with living here, which was far from the case at first:[5] but then there was no soul in Paris but philosophers, whom I wished in heaven, though they do not wish themselves so. They are so overbearing and so underbred!

Your old flame, the Queen,[6] was exceedingly kind to me at my presentation.[7] She has been ever since at Fontainebleau, watching her son,[8] whose death is expected every day, though it is as much the fashion not to own it, as if he was of the immortal House of Bruns-

2. Marie de Vichy-Champrond (1696–1780), m. (1718) Jean-Baptiste-Jacques-Charles du Deffand de la Lande, Marquis de Chastres. HW met her for the first time on 17 Sept. ('Paris Journals,' DU DEFFAND v. 261). Selwyn's acquaintance with her began on one of his prolonged visits to Paris between 1762 and 1765.

3. Mme du Deffand had been the mistress of Philippe de Bourbon (1674–1723), Duc d'Orléans, Regent of France, for a fortnight, probably in 1721 (GRAY ii. 144 and n. 8).

4. With the gout during most of October.

5. HW's earliest comment on Paris was that he had fallen in love with twenty things and in hate with forty (HW to Conway 11 Sept. 1765). His other early letters are quite critical of many things, particularly the dirt and the *philosophes*.

6. Marie-Catherine-Sophie-Félicité (Leszczyńska) (1703–68), m. (1725) Louis XV, K. of France. She delighted in Selwyn; see Jesse, *Selwyn* i. 272; ii. 60, 114; S. P. Kerr, *George Selwyn and the Wits*, 1909, p. 182).

7. On 1 Oct. ('Paris Journals,' DU DEFFAND v. 266). HW describes his reception by the Queen in letters to Lady Hervey 3 Oct. 1765 and to Conway 6 Oct. 1765.

8. Louis (1729–65), Dauphin. The Court had taken up residence at Fontainebleau on 5 Oct., where it remained until after the Dauphin's death on 20 Dec. (Léon Deroy, *Les Chroniques du château de Fontainebleau*, [1909], p. 170).

wick. Madame Geoffrin[9] is extremely what I had figured her, only with less wit and more sense than I expected. The Duchess d'Aiguillon[10] is delightful, frank, and jolly, and handsome and good-humoured, with dignity too. There is another set in which I live much, and to my taste, but very different from all I have named, Madame de Rochfort,[11] and the set at the Luxembourg. My newest acquaintance is Monsieur de Maurepas,[12] with whom I am much taken, though his countenance and person are so like the late Lord Hardwicke.[13] From the little I have seen of him, we have reason I believe to thank Madame de Pompadour[14] for his disgrace. At the Marquis de Brancas'[15] I dined with the Duc de Brissac,[16] in his red stockings: in short, I think my winter will be very well amused, whether Mr Garrick[17] and Mr Pitt act or not.[18]

9. Marie-Thérèse Rodet (1699–1777), m. (1713) François Geoffrin. HW had first met her on 16 Sept. and was soon praising her 'sense' ('Paris Journals,' DU DEFFAND v. 261; HW to Lady Hervey 3 Oct. 1765). She and Selwyn had been friends since 1762 (*Letters to Henry Fox* 164, 175, 193, 199, 211).

10. Anne-Charlotte de Crussol de Florensac (1700–72), m. (1718) Armand-Louis Vignerot du Plessis-Richelieu, Duc d'Aiguillon (DU DEFFAND i. 9 n. 8). HW met her for the first time on 25 Nov. ('Paris Journals,' DU DEFFAND v. 274; HW to Lady Hervey 28 Nov. 1765).

11. Marie-Thérèse de Brancas (1716–82) m. 1 (1736) Jean-Anne-Vincent de Larlan de Kercadio, Comte de Rochefort; m. 2 (1782) Louis-Jules-Barbon Mancini-Mazarini, Duc de Nivernais (DU DEFFAND i. 257 n. 10). HW met her for the first time on 30 Sept. ('Paris Journals,' DU DEFFAND v. 265; HW to Anne Pitt 8 Oct. 1765).

12. Jean-Frédéric Phélypeaux (1701–81), Comte de Maurepas; secretary of state 1715–49; minister of the marine 1723–49; minister of state 1738–49; later first minister under Louis XVI. HW had met him for the first time at the Duchesse d'Aiguillon's on 30 Nov. ('Paris Journals,' DU DEFFAND v. 278).

13. HW was much struck by the resemblance ('Paris Journals,' DU DEFFAND v. 278; *post* 31 Jan. 1766).

14. Jeanne-Antoinette Poisson (1721–64), Marquise de Pompadour; mistress of Louis XV. HW thought at this time that she had secured Maurepas's disgrace by persuading the King that he had poisoned the Duchesse de Châteauroux, an argument she did use, but the real reasons, as HW soon discovered, were satirical epigrams against her which Maurepas wrote and circulated ('Paris Journals,' DU DEFFAND v. 278, 283; *Mem. Geo. III* ii. 179; Alphonse Jobez, *La France sous Louis XV,* 1864–73, iv. 145–9; Henri Carré, *La Règne de Louis XV,* 1909, p. 223, in *Histoire de France,* ed. Ernest Lavisse, viii. pt. ii; MANN iv. 51 n. 37; NBG).

15. Louis-Paul (1718–1802), Marquis de Brancas; later Duc de Céreste (Emmanuel, Duc de Croÿ, *Journal,* 1906–7, ii. 431). HW had dined with him on 30 Nov. ('Paris Journals,' DU DEFFAND v. 277).

16. Jean-Paul-Timoléon de Cossé (1698–1784), Duc de Brissac; Maréchal de France. In the 'Paris Journals' HW described him as 'a well-bred, extravagant old man, laced down the seams and in *red* stockings' (DU DEFFAND v. 277).

17. David Garrick (1717–79).

18. Pitt's probable rôle in the approaching session of Parliament was a mystery; he had refused to cooperate with either the Rockingham ministry or the Opposition, had talked total retirement during the summer, and at the moment was confined at Bath by the gout (Brian Tunstall, *William Pitt, Earl of Chatham,* 1938, pp. 353–4). Garrick also had talked much of permanent retirement from the stage after

Pray tell Lord Holland, that I have sent him the few new things that I thought would entertain him for a moment, though none of them have much merit. I would have written to him, had I had anything to tell him, which, you perceive by what I have said, I had not. The affair of the parliament of Bretagne,[19] and the intended trial of the famous Monsieur de Chalotais,[20] by *commission*, against which the parliament of Paris strongly inveighs,[21] is the great subject in agitation; but I know little of the matter, and was too sick of our own Parliaments to interest myself about these. The Hôtel de Carnavalet[22] sends its blessings to you. I never pass it without saying an *Ave Maria de Rabutin Chantal,*[23] *gratiæ plena!* The Abbé de Malherbe[24] has given orders that I should see Livry[25] whenever I please. Pray tell me which convent was that of *Nos Sœurs de Sainte Marie,*[26]

his return to England in the spring of 1765, but he reappeared on 14 Nov. by royal command for the first time since the winter of 1763 and thereafter acted regularly until his retirement in 1776 (Margaret Barton, *Garrick*, 1948, p. 193; Percy Fitzgerald, *Life of David Garrick*, rev. edn, 1899, pp. 302–3).

19. The long-simmering crisis between the parliament of Rennes and the central administration had reached a climax in mid-November 1765 with the arrest of six members of the parliament, the exile of others, and the substitution of a commission appointed by the King for the parliament itself (Abbé Eugene Bossard, *Le Parlement de Bretagne et la royauté 1765–1769*, 1882, pp. 28–32; A. Le Moy, *Le Parlement de Bretagne et le pouvoir royal au xviiie siècle*, 1909, pp. 333–52; Marcel Marion, *La Bretagne et le Duc d'Aiguillon, 1753–1770*, 1898, pp. 353–7).

20. Louis-René de Caradeuc de la Chalotais (1701–85), procureur-général of the parliament of Rennes; champion of the Breton parliament against the central administration. He had been arrested on 11 Nov. 1765, kept in close confinement, and charged with treason. His trial by the commission that had been substituted for the parliament never reached a formal conclusion, since the process bogged down in counter-accusations; the King, however, finally (1769) cleared him of any crime but confirmed his suspension from his functions (works cited in the preced-

ing note, *passim;* and Barthélemy Pocquet, *Le Duc d'Aiguillon et la Chalotais*, 1900–1, *passim*).

21. The parliament of Paris did not protest against the impending trial of La Chalotais at this time, as HW discovered within three days of writing this letter, but it did issue a remonstrance on 8 Dec. 1765 against the substitution of a royal commission for the parliament of Rennes (E.-D. Glasson, *Le Parlement de Paris*, 1901, ii. 311–12; Jules Flammermont and Maurice Tourneux, *Remontrances du Parlement de Paris au xviiie siècle*, 1888–98, ii. 527–30; HW to Conway 5 Dec. 1765).

22. The Paris residence of Marie de Rabutin-Chantal (1626–96), m. (1644) Henri, Marquis de Sévigné. Selwyn, like HW, was one of her ardent admirers.

23. HW had said his first *ave* on 2 Oct. (HW to Lady Hervey 3 Oct. 1765).

24. Jean-Baptiste-Antoine de Malherbe (1712–71), O.S.B., had become abbé of Livry in 1759 (GRAY ii. 157 n. 55). HW had dined with him at Hénault's on 16 Nov. ('Paris Journals,' DU DEFFAND v. 272).

25. 12 miles east of Paris, where Mme de Sévigné spent her youth under the care of her uncle, the Abbé Christophe de Coulanges (ca 1607–87), prior of Notre-Dame des Anges at Livry.

26. HW visited the church of the Filles de l'Ave Maria on the Rue des Barres on 14 Dec. in the mistaken belief it was Mme

where our friend used to go on the evening that Madame de Grignan[27] set out for Provence?

My best compliments to Mr Williams: has Lord Rockingham[28] done anything for him yet?[29] or has the Duke of Newcastle his old power of dispensing with promises? I sent my Lady Townshend, as long ago as by Lady Hertford,[30] two silver knives which she desired, but cannot hear by any way that she received them. I could ask twenty other questions, but some I had better not ask, and the rest I should not care whether they were answered or not. We have swarms of English; but most of them know not Joseph, and Joseph does not desire to know them. I live with none of them but Crawford[31] and Lord Ossory,[32] the latter of whom I am extremely sorry is returning to England.[33] I recommend him to Mr Williams as one of the properest and most amiable young men I ever knew.

I beg your pardon, my dear Sir, for this idle letter; yet don't let it lie in your work-basket. When you have a quarter of an hour, awake,[34] and to spare, I wish you would bestow it on me. There are

de Sévigné's convent. The Filles de Ste Marie, however, occupied the convent of the Visitation in the Rue St-Antoine, now called the Temple Ste-Marie, which had been founded by Mme de Sévigné's grandmother ('Paris Journals,' DU DEFFAND v. 285, and ii. 183).

27. Françoise-Marguerite de Sévigné (1648–1705), dau. of Mme de Sévigné; m. (1669) François de Castellane-Adhémar de Monteil, Comte de Grignan.

28. Charles Watson-Wentworth (1730–82), 2d M. of Rockingham; first lord of the Treasury 1765–6, 1782.

29. 'Gilly' Williams had been dismissed from his post of deputy cofferer of the Household, which he had held since 1754, when the Rockingham ministry came to power in July 1765. The place, worth £450 a year, represented a great part of his income. Charles Townshend wrote 'a warm and pressing letter' to Rockingham who apparently promised to give Williams an equivalent post. The efforts of Williams's friends appear to have been unavailing (Jesse, Selwyn i. 394, 402–3, 418; Letters to Henry Fox 230–1, 245, 249; George III, Correspondence, ed. Fortescue, 1927–8, i. 144, 155; Record of Old West-

minsters, ed. G. F. Russell Barker and A. H. Stenning, 1928, ii. 998).

30. Lady Hertford had left for England on 22 Sept. She later told HW she had delivered the knives to Lady Townshend on her arrival but did not find her at home ('Paris Journals,' DU DEFFAND v. 263; Lady Hertford to HW 20 Jan. 1766).

31. John ('Fish') Craufurd (1742–1814), of Drumsoy and Auchinames in Scotland; M.P. Old Sarum 1768–74, Renfrewshire 1774–80, Glasgow burghs 1780–4, 1790; friend and correspondent of HW, Selwyn, and Mme du Deffand (DU DEFFAND i. 6 n. 21; Eton College Register 1753–1790, ed. R. A. Austen-Leigh, Eton, 1921, p. 135).

32. John Fitzpatrick (1745–1818), 2d E. of Upper Ossory; M.P. Bedfordshire 1767–94.

33. He was still in Paris on 13 Dec. ('Paris Journals,' DU DEFFAND v. 285). Cole, describing a visit Ossory paid to HW 27 Oct., mentions that he 'had been expected in England, and had fixed his departure two or three times, but a little attachment at Paris chained him there' (William Cole, Journal of My Journey to Paris in the Year 1765, ed. F. G. Stokes, 1931, p. 92).

34. Selwyn was notorious for drowsing in company.

no such things as *bons mots* here to send you, and I cannot hope that you will send me your own. Next to them, I should like Charles Townshend's, but I don't desire Betty's.[34a]

I forgot to tell you that I sometimes go to Baron d'Olbach's,[35] but I have left off his dinners,[36] as there was no bearing the authors, and philosophers, and savants, of which he has a pigeon-house full. They soon turned my head with a new system of antediluvian deluges, which they have invented to prove the eternity of matter. The Baron is persuaded that Pall Mall is paved with lava or deluge stones. In short, nonsense for nonsense, I like the Jesuits better than the philosophers. Were ever two men so like in their persons, or so unlike in their dispositions as Dr Gem[37] and Brand?[38] Almost the first time I ever saw Gem, he said to me, 'Sir, I am serious, I am of a very serious turn': yes, truly! Say a great deal for me to Lord March, and to the Rena's dog's *touffe ébourifée*.[39] The old President[40] would send his compliments to you, if he remembered you or anything else.

When we three meet again at Strawberry, I think I shall be able at least to divert Mr Williams; but till then you must keep my counsel. Madame du Deffand says I have *le fou moquer*, and I have not hurt myself a little by laughing at whisk and Richardson,[41]

34a. The apple-seller (*ante* 22 Aug. 1758, n. 5).

35. Paul-Henri Thiry (1723–89), Baron d'Holbach; encyclopædist.

36. Holbach received the literary world at large at dinners on Thursdays and Sundays, as well as smaller circles of friends on most other days; see Pierre Naville, *Paul Thiry d'Holbach*, 4th edn, 1943, pp. 35–7; 'Paris Journals,' DU DEFFAND v. 262. HW had first visited him on 19 Sept., and mentions dining with him on 22 Sept. and 6 Oct. as well as frequent visits (ibid. v. 262–304 *passim*).

37. Dr Richard Gem (ca 1716–1800), physician; HW's occasional correspondent (*Notes and Queries*, 1910, 11th ser. ii. 121–3). Cole describes him as 'a very tall awkward kind of man, of a solemn figure and no great conversation' (Cole, op. cit. 63).

38. Thomas Brand (1718–70) of The Hoo, Herts; M.P. Shoreham 1741–7, Tavistock 1747–54, Gatton 1754–68, Okehampton 1768–70; HW's 'old school fellow' and correspondent (GRAY i. 166 n. 37;

John Brooke, *The Chatham Administration 1766–1768*, 1956, p. 389).

39. 'J'embrasse Grignan et le baise à la joue droite, au-dessous de sa *touffe ébourifée*' (Madame de Sévigné, *Lettres*, ed. Monmerqué, 1862–6, iii. 62). HW was not sure what the phrase meant: see MONTAGU i. 21–2.

40. Charles - Jean - François Hénault (1685–1770), président de la première chambre des enquêtes; friend of Mme du Deffand.

41. Samuel Richardson (1689–1761), novelist. His works enjoyed an enormous reputation in France; see J. Texte, *Jean-Jacques Rousseau et les origines du cosmopolitisme littéraire*, 1895 (Eng. trans. 1899), Chap. V; B.-A. Facteau, *Les Romans de Richardson sur la scène française*, [1927]). HW, who thought them 'deplorably tedious lamentations,' found himself 'undone' when he told the French that in adopting Richardson and whist, they had chosen 'the two dullest things we had' (HW to Mann 20 Dec. 1764; HW to Brand 19 Oct. 1765).

though I have steered clear of the chapter of Mr Hume;[42] the only Trinity now in fashion here. *A propos,* I see by the papers, that the Bishop of London[43] is suppressing mass-houses.[44] When he was Bishop of Peterborough and Parson of Twickenham, he suffered one under his nose.[45] Did the Duchess of Norfolk[46] get him translated to London? I should conclude so; and that this was the first opportunity he had of being ungrateful.[47] Adieu! my dear Sir,

Yours most sincerely,

HORACE WALPOLE

From SELWYN, ca Wednesday 1 January 1766

Missing. It contained an account of Selwyn's practical joke on Lord Coventry (see following letter).

To SELWYN, Sunday 12 January 1766

Printed for the first time from a photostat of the MS in the Cely Trevilian collection in the Society of Antiquaries.

Paris, Jan. 12, 1766.

WHAT Lord William Gordon[1] was doing with my letter so long, I cannot guess; but I thank you for [your] kind answer

---

42. David Hume (1711–76), philosopher and historian, who had been the rage in Paris since his arrival with Hertford in 1763. He was appointed secretary of the Embassy in 1765.

43. Richard Terrick (1710–77), Vicar of Twickenham 1749–64; Bp of Peterborough 1757–64, of London 1764–77.

44. 'The Bishop of London has sent letters to the clergy of his diocese, requiring that they will cause diligent search to be made after private mass-houses; and to transmit to his Lordship an account of the number of Catholics in their several parishes' (*Daily Adv.* 13 Nov. 1765). A few prosecutions followed this directive; see *sub* 21 Nov. in GM 1765, xxxv. 537; *Daily Adv.* 27 Nov. 1765; and MANN vi. 394 n. 3.

45. Probably the chapel in the Earl of Shrewsbury's house at Isleworth which apparently served the Roman Catholics of Twickenham ('The Catholic Registers of Isleworth, Middlesex, 1746–1835,' *Catholic Record Society, Miscellanea* viii, 1913, pp. 299–334).

46. Mary Blount (ca 1702–73), m. (1727) Edward Howard, 9th D. of Norfolk. She was a Roman Catholic.

47. A reference to Terrick's deserting the Duke of Devonshire, who had obtained the bishopric of Peterborough for him, for Lord Bute, and to his general time-serving; see *Mem. Geo. III* i. 331, ii. 164.

---

1. (1744–1823), 2d son of 3d D. of Gordon; M.P. Elginshire 1779–84, In-

and the particulars of a story which we had heard here with many additions, and which, I own, had made me think you might as well have writ to me as to my Lord Coventry.[2] I do not quite change my opinion yet, for nothing is so dangerous as joking with a fool, because somehow or other it always wants an explanation. Neither can I help thinking but you are a little hard on laying so much blame on him. It is true, the second letter ought to have opened his eyes; but how do you know he wished to have them opened? Perhaps, the number 24[3] had opened them so far that he was glad to come [to] an explanation and retraction of his vote. It is the only way I can construe his behaviour.

It is true also, that I have a little reason to complain of your leaving me in the lurch. You know I used to foretell that you and I should live to be the two least mad in England—however I am glad this frolic has had no worse consequences. As the perfection of my wisdom is not yet arrived, I too have been writing a letter in a king's name,[4] and I freely give you leave to dismiss me his service. Mine has made some noise here, but with different effect. If I had your wit, it might have deserved it much better, and it is only from your liking anything that is fashionable at Paris, that can make it worth enclosing to you.

I will execute carefully both your commissions to Madame St Jean,[5] and Madame Geoffrin.[5a] I doubt much if the latter will go to

verness-shire 1784–90, Horsham 1790–96; vice-admiral of Scotland 1782–95 (*Scots Peerage* iv. 554). HW's previous letter to Selwyn had been sent to England by him on 4 Dec. ('Paris Journals,' DU DEFFAND v. 378).

2. Selwyn had written a letter to Coventry on 18 Dec. 1765, signed Grafton, telling him that the King had no further use for his services. Coventry, completely hoaxed, had demanded an explanation of Grafton, who in turn carried the original letter to the King. For a description of the affair, differing in a few details from that Selwyn apparently sent to HW, see Lady Hervey to HW 19 Dec. 1765. When Coventry discovered the hoax he quarrelled with Selwyn, but was reconciled to him in September 1766 (Jesse, *Selwyn* ii. 33, 35, 86).

3. The Opposition in the House of Lords

had divided only 24 to the Ministry's 80 in the vote on the amendment to the Address of Thanks on 17 Dec. 1765, despite boasts of their strength (*Mem. Geo. III* ii. 167; George III, *Correspondence*, ed. Fortescue, 1927–8, i. 203, corrected by L. B. Namier, *Additions and Corrections to Sir John Fortescue's Edition of the Correspondence of King George III* (Vol. I), Manchester, 1937, p. 42). Coventry was apparently one of the 24.

4. HW's letter from the King of Prussia to Rousseau, which he transcribes at the end of this letter; for its consequences, see *post* 17 July 1766 and n. 19.

5. Not identified; from the reference to her *post* 3 April 1766 it would appear that she was a member of a noble but impoverished family from the neighbourhood of Rennes which had apparently been connected with the Sévigné family;

England this year.[6] If you have any other commissions for me, they shall be obeyed punctually; and you will have time, for I do not think of returning before the end of March.[7] The weather is most uncommonly severe: I have no mind to venture another fit of the gout; have no disposition to your politics, and no impatience to quit Paris, where I am exceedingly pleased, and treated with the greatest kindness. The French amuse me, and the English you may swear divert me. Two nights ago I received an invitation to a ball at Lord Massareen's.[8] As I have never visited him, for I keep as clear as possible of most of my countrymen whom I certainly did not come hither to know, I could not avoid going for an hour. I went at seven; found four or five English, no Lord Massareen; was told he was not up, at least was at his *toilette*. Gentlemen arrived, ladies arrived, the Countesses of Berkeley[9] and Fife[10] etc. Still no Lord Massareen. I should tell you, that as we were in the height of the mourning for the Dauphin,[11] the ball itself was very improper. However, some English swains came in coloured frocks, satin waistcoats and breeches, and huge nosegays with bunches of ribbands. As to their flocks, they would have perished with cold, for the chimneys in that dirty *hôtel garni* smoked so much, that to save our eyes, we were forced to put out the fires and open the windows. However, to display to the French valets our victorious constitutions, both ball and cards began, though half the candles were blown out, and the fingers of the violins so frozen, that they missed every other note. In short, my athletic part of the British Constitution bore it for an hour,[12] and then I came away, before Adonis himself made his appearance.

I rejoice extremely at Mr Williams's legacy.[13] Make my best com-

see the notices of this Saint-Jean family in Vicomte Henri Frotier de la Messelière, *Filiations bretonnes*, Saint-Brieuc, 1914–25, v. 77; and Baron Henri de Woëlmont de Brumagne, *La Noblesse française subsistante*, 1928–31, ii. 420.

5a. Selwyn wanted a copy of her portrait (*post* 31 Jan. 1766).

6. She went to Poland instead; see HW to Lady Hervey 3 Feb. 1766.

7. HW did not leave Paris until 17 April ('Paris Journals,' DU DEFFAND v. 314).

8. Clotworthy Skeffington (1743–1805), 2d E. of Massareene. In 1771 he was imprisoned for debt in Paris, escaping in

1789 (GEC, q.v. for confirmation of his extravagance and foppishness).

9. Elizabeth Drax (ca 1720–92), m. 1 (1744) Augustus Berkeley, 4th E. of Berkeley; m. 2 (1757) Robert Nugent, 1st E. Nugent, 1776.

10. Hon. Dorothea Sinclair (1739–1818), m. (1759) James Duff, 2d E. Fife.

11. Who had died 20 Dec.

12. Actually two; HW arrived at seven and left at nine ('Paris Journals,' DU DEFFAND v. 294).

13. No details of this legacy have been found.

pliments to him and Lord Holland, and [I] should be glad to hear the latter was as well as I wish him.[14]

Yours ever,

H. W.

Le Roi de Prusse à Monsieur Rousseau.[15]

Mon cher Jean Jacques,

VOUS avez renoncé à Genève, votre patrie; vous vous êtes fait chasser de la Suisse, pays tant vanté dans vos écrits; la France vous a décrété: venez donc chez moi: j'admire vos talents, je m'amuse de vos rêveries, qui (soit dit en passant) vous occupent trop, et trop longtemps. Il faut à la fin être sage et heureux. Vous avez fait assez parler de vous par des singularités peu convenables à un véritable grand homme. Démontrez à vos ennemis, qui vous pouvez avoir quelquefois le sens commun: cela les fâchera, sans vous faire tort. Mes états vous offrent une retraite paisible; je vous veux du bien, et je vous en ferai, si vous le trouvez bon; mais si vous vous obstiniez à rejeter mon secours, attendez-vous que je ne le dirai à personne. Si vous persistez à vous creuser l'esprit pour trouver de nouveaux malheurs, choisissez-les tels que vous voudrez; je suis Roi, je puis vous en procurer au gré de vos souhaits; et ce qui sûrement ne vous arrivera pas vis-à-vis de vos ennemis, je cesserai de vous persécuter, quand vous cesserez de mettre votre gloire à l'être.

Votre bon ami,

FRÉDÉRIC

To SELWYN, Friday 31 January 1766

Printed from a photostat of the MS in the Cely Trevilian collection in the Society of Antiquaries. First printed J. H. Jesse, *Memoirs of the Life and Reign of George III*, 1867, i. 599–601; reprinted, Toynbee vi. 411–13.

14. HW had recently heard of Holland's illness from Lady Hervey (Lady Hervey to HW 10, 19 Dec. 1765; HW to Lady Hervey 11 Jan. 1766).

15. HW sent a copy of the letter to Conway 12 Jan. 1766, to Anne Pitt 19 Jan. 1766, to Cole 25 Feb. 1766 (COLE i. 110–11), and to Chute 3 Feb. 1766. Copies by others were circulated, and it is not surprising that the letter got into print.

Paris, Jan. 31st 1766.

I GO step by step with the British Ambassador.[1] He has achieved the payment of the Canada bills:[2] I have obtained leave from Madame Geoffrin for you to have a copy of her picture.[3] His Excellence has not demolished Dunkirk, but has made great progress towards it:[4] I have not found Mrs St John, but have found out that there are two—indeed I believe neither is the right. You must send me ampler instructions. There is an ancient Demoiselle St Jean[5] who lived with Marivaux,[6] and is above fourscore; they tell me that if she is not the right, I shall frighten her out of her no remaining senses, and that she will talk all her acquaintance out of theirs on a subject she will not comprehend. Mr Foley[7] knows a Mr and Mrs St John, but says it cannot be they. In short, I conclude yours is some old rag of the Court of St Germain's.[8] Describe exactly where she sits by the waters of Babylon,[9] crying afresh for the Pretender, and I will try to find her. Apropos, do you know that the daughter of Madame de Peyre,[10] who inhabits the Rochers,[11] is banished on the troubles in Bretagne?

I made your compliments to Madame de Bentheim.[12] I wish you would make mine to Monsieur de Guerchy[13] and say I hope he re-

1. The D. of Richmond.

2. Bills of exchange which had served as paper money in Canada before the English conquest. France had promised redemption of them in a declaration attached to the Treaty of Paris, and then refused to pay more than 20 per cent of their face value. The issue became a major source of friction between the two powers but was resolved in Jan. 1766 when Choiseul unexpectedly agreed to almost total compensation. For a further note on the Canada bills and HW's share in the settlement, see MORE 97 n. 11.

3. Nothing further has been found regarding this picture; the list of portraits of Mme Geoffrin in Pierre de Ségur, *Le Royaume de la rue Saint-Honoré*, 1898, pp. 493–6, mentions no copy of any of them.

4. Article XIII of the Treaty of Paris provided for the demolition of the fortifications of Dunkirk; the French, however, successfully evaded this obligation (*Mem. Geo. III* ii. 160–3).

5. Gabrielle-Angélique Anquetin de la

Chapelle de Saint-Jean, an old friend of Marivaux, with whom he lived during the last years of his life (Gustave Larroumet, *Marivaux, sa vie et ses œuvres*, 1882, pp. 148–53). She is described by another of his critics as 'le type même de l'inconnue' (Käthy Lüthi, *Les Femmes dans l'œuvre de Marivaux*, Bienne, 1943, p. 18).

6. Pierre Carlet de Chamblain de Marivaux (1688–1763), dramatist and novelist.

7. Robert Ralph Foley (ca 1727–82) cr. (1767) Bt; English banker in Paris.

8. Apparently not; see *ante* 12 Jan. 1766 n. 5 and *post* 3 April 1766.

9. The 137th Psalm was a favourite of HW's.

10. Unidentified.

11. Mme de Sévigné's château near Vitré in Brittany.

12. Marie-Lydie de Bournonville (1720–91), m. (1746) Friedrich Karl Philipp, Graf von Bentheim (DU DEFFAND ii. 11 n. 5).

13. Claude-Louis-François de Regnier (1715–67), Comte de Guerchy; French ambassador to England 1763–7.

ceived the letter of condolence[14] that I writ to him on the Dauphin's death; and that Madame de Guerchy[15] has received the coal-boxes[16] from Lord Barrington. I wrote to the latter[17] too, and should be sorry he did not receive my letter, but I suspect that letters sent by the post do not always arrive. As I am so punctual about your commissions, I trust you will be a little so about mine.

The French are full of the Duke of York's duel,[18] which arriving when they had nothing else to talk of, has gained entire credit. We tell them it is not true, but they think us discreet. If I regretted England ever so much, I could console myself by the exact resemblances that I find here to the most agreeable of my country-folks. The Prince of Conti[19] has all the fluent eloquence[20] of the Prince I have mentioned. The Duchess of Nivernois[21] makes amends for the instructive prattle of the Duke of Newcastle: the Princess of Ligne[22] is the very image of Mrs Askew;[23] and Monsieur de Maurepas makes one think poor dear Lord Hardwicke still alive. The Chevalier de Courte[24] came into the room one night, and I took him for my brother Cholmondeley.[25] Madame de Coislin,[26] except that her eye-

14. Missing; it was sent on 23 Dec. ('Paris Journals,' DU DEFFAND v. 378).

15. Gabrielle-Lydie d'Harcourt (b. 1722), m. (1740) Claude-Louis-François de Regnier, Comte de Guerchy.

16. Snuff-boxes made of cannel coal; see HW to Lady Hervey 1 March 1766, where HW repeats his messages to the Guerchys, because 'others . . . have not thought it worth their while to oblige me' in delivering them.

17. On 30 Dec. ('Paris Journals,' DU DEFFAND v. 378). The letter is missing.

18. Edward Augustus (1739–67), cr. (1760) D. of York and Albany. The report, as HW says, was without foundation.

19. Louis-François de Bourbon (1717–76), Prince de Conti.

20. The Duke of York was extremely garrulous; see HW to Mann 1 March 1766, and HW's reference to his 'inarticulate loquacity' in Mem. Geo. III iii. 75.

21. Hélène-Angélique-Françoise Phélypeaux de Pontchartrain (1715–82), m. (1730) Louis-Jules-Barbon Mancini-Mazarini, Duc de Nivernais. HW had made the same comparison to Lady Hervey 28 Nov. 1765.

22. Henriette-Eugénie de Béthizy de Mézières (1710–87), m. (1729) Claude-Lamoral-Hyacinthe-Ferdinand, Prince de Ligne.

23. Probably Elizabeth Holford (ca 1734–73), dau. of Robert Holford, Master in Chancery; m. (before 1758) Dr Anthony Askew, physician and book-collector; 'a woman of celestial beauty and celestial virtue' (Notes and Queries, 1891, 7th ser. xii. 64; Northumberland County History Committee, A History of Northumberland, Newcastle-upon-Tyne, 1893–1940, xi. 438; DNB sub Anthony Askew).

24. Probably Maurice (ca 1692–1766), Chevalier and Comte de Courten, a Swiss in the French service; maréchal-de-camp, 1743; HW had met him at Mme du Deffand's 3 Nov. 1765 (DU DEFFAND v. 270 and n. 89; Michael Ranfft, Fortgesetzte neue genealogisch-historische Nachrichten, Leipzig, 1762–77, vi. 19–20).

25. HW's brother-in-law, George, 3d E. of Cholmondeley.

26. Marie-Anne-Louise-Adélaïde-Mélanie-Françoise de Mailly-Rubempré (ca 1732–1817), m. (1750) Charles-George-René du Cambout, Marquis de Coislin; mistress of Louis XV (Maurice, Comte Fleury, Louis XV intime et les petites

brows are black, is as like an old Miss Bowyer[27] that you remember. Nothing that ever I saw anywhere was like the Duchess of Choiseul,[28] who has more parts, reason and agreeableness than ever met in such a delicate little figure.

As my curiosity is very active, I have almost seen everybody; but there are still two personages here that I am very impatient to see, Count Gage[29] and Lady Mary Powis,[30] who after meeting in the Asturian mines,[31] have met again at Paris: the latter is maintained by the Prince of Conti: I shall inquire after her tonight, as I sup at the Temple.

They are now acting a comic opera, called *Tom Jones;*[32] I have not seen it, but it is commended. Mr A. A.[33] is arrived here in his way to the Court of Munich. General Vernon[34] in his way I don't know whither. I hope some of the English, who are here in plenty, will carry you over the new head-dress of the men, which is exactly in a sugar-loaf, and very little lower. As the mourning checks their fancy in clothes, it is broken out on the tops of their heads. Adieu! my dear Sir; I can talk to you of nothing English, for I hear nothing but of your politics, about which I do not care a straw.

Yours ever,

H. W.

maîtresses, 4th ed., 1909, pp. 145–81, corrected by A. Révérend, *Titres, anoblissements et pairies de la Restauration,* 1901–6, ii. 429 and GM 1817, lxxxvii pt i. 189).

27. Possibly Frances Bowyer (b. 1685), dau. of Sir William Bowyer, 2d Bt, of Denham Court, Bucks (George Lipscomb, *The History and Antiquities of the County of Buckingham,* 1847, iv. 446).

28. Louise-Honorine Crozat du Châtel (1735–1801), m. (1750) Étienne-François de Choiseul-Stainville, Duc de Choiseul.

29. Joseph Edward Gage (1678–1766), Count Gage. He is confused in DNB with Jean-Bonaventure-Thierry du Mont (1682–1753), Comte de Gages; Spanish general. See DU DEFFAND v. 288 and n. 201 for HW's account of Gage and Lady Mary Herbert.

30. Lady Mary Herbert (d. 1775), dau. of 2d M. of Powis. Her obituaries called her aged 90, but this is unlikely, since her parents were not married until ca 1695.

31. 'Congenial souls! whose life one av'rice joins,
  And one fate buries in th' Asturian mines'
  (Pope, *Moral Essays* iii. 131–2).
After winning and then losing fortunes in the Mississippi speculation, both Gage and Lady Mary Herbert had operated mining concessions in Asturias.

32. By Antoine-Alexandre-Henri Poinsinet (1735–69) (NBG; Charles Brunet, *Table des pièces de théâtre décrites dans le catalogue de . . . M. de Soleinne,* 1914). HW saw it for the first time on 2 March and again on 12 Sept. 1767 ('Paris Journals,' DU DEFFAND v. 305, 319).

33. Not identified.

34. Gen. Charles Vernon; see *ante* 15 July 1765, n. 8. He had arrived in Paris on 11 Jan. ('Paris Journals,' DU DEFFAND v. 294).

From Selwyn, ca Saturday 1 March 1766

Missing; mentioned in the following letter.

To Selwyn, Friday 7 March 1766

Printed from a photostat of the MS in the Cely Trevilian collection in the Society of Antiquaries. First printed, J. H. Jesse, *Memoirs of the Life and Reign of George III*, 1867, i. 378–80; reprinted, Toynbee vi. 436–9.
Address: To George Augustus Selwyn, Esq., in Chesterfield Street, Mayfair.

Paris, March 7th 1766.

I LAUGHED till I cried at your description of Mr Pitt, hopping, crawling and dressing;[1] but I took care not to publish it here, where they believe that he is more alert, and has longer talons than the Beast of the Gévaudan.[2] They have not dared to send a man to our boisterous colonies, for fear he should skip to New York.[3] The Pope dare not acknowledge the Pretender while Mr Pitt lives.[4] Nay, one of the accusations against poor La Chalotais is, that he corresponded with Mr Pitt,[5] to whom, though no longer a minister, they conclude a conspirator would address himself. In short, they consider him as the Chinese do the East India Company, whom they call *Mr Company*. You see how true the saying is, that nobody is a hero in the eyes of his valet-de-chambre; in England you are all laughing at the flannels of a man, whose crutch keeps the rest of Europe in awe. It is now and then such a Clytus[6] as you that prevents a poor drunken mortal from passing for a god, for it does not signify whether they

1. Pitt, though badly crippled by gout, had been taking a prominent part in the repeal of the Stamp Act.

2. For descriptions of this over-sized wolf, which HW had seen at his presentation at Versailles in October, see HW to Lady Hervey 3 Oct. 1765, to Chute 3 Oct. 1765, to Conway 6 Oct. 1765, to Anne Pitt 8 Oct. 1765.

3. That is, the French were so afraid of Pitt that they did not dare fish in the troubled waters of colonial discontent with the Stamp Act for fear of bringing him back to power. See *Mem. Geo. III* ii. 163 for the effect of Pitt's name in France.

4. Sir Horace Mann had recently completed a successful negotiation to prevent papal recognition of the Young Pretender; see Mann to HW 24 Jan. 1766; HW to Mann 9 Feb. 1766.

5. This charge was widely circulated from the moment of La Chalotais's imprisonment, but played no part in his trial. It is apparently without foundation (Marcel Marion, *La Bretagne et le Duc d'Aiguillon, 1753–1770*, 1898, p. 366 n. 2).

6. Cleitus (ca 380–328 or 327 B.C.), Macedonian general who was killed by Alexander the Great because Cleitus held Philip of Macedon in higher esteem.

hiccup with Chian wine or vanity, nor whether they are adopted by Jupiter Ammon[7] or Sir William Pynsent:[8] their heads are equally turned, and so are those of the spectators. I hope the godhead will not forget that his arm *is to be* lame, and knock your brains out with his crutch. When you make so free with our great men, I wonder you are so tender of our little ones, I mean, our Princes;[9] consider that they would be still more troublesome, if they were not totally insignificant.

I will endeavour to unkennel your Madame St Jean, though by what you hint, I believe the best way would be to address myself to the *Lieutenant de Police.* I will inquire too for your Duc de Joyeuse *en Capucin*,[10] though I never heard of such a print.[11] I have a great collection of prints after Guido[12] at Strawberry, but do not remember such a head. I have bought a great quantity at the Quay de Feraille,[13] and so many other baubledoms,[14] that I should be ashamed, if I did

---

7. Alexander was saluted as the son of Zeus by the priests of the temple of Zeus Ammon in the desert of Libya in 331 B.C.

8. Sir William Pynsent (ca 1681–1765), 2d Bt. On his death in Jan. 1765 he had bequeathed Pitt his estate of Burton Pynsent, Somerset, worth £3,000 a year.

9. The King's brothers Edward Augustus, D. of York; William Henry (1743–1805), D. of Gloucester; and Henry Frederick (1745–90), D. of Cumberland. The affair hinted at here was probably the attempt of the Duke of York to arrange a coalition of Bute, Grenville and Bedford against the Rockingham ministry; see HW to Mann 1 March 1766.

10. Henri de Joyeuse (1563–1608), Comte du Bouchage, Duc de Joyeuse, 1592; Maréchal de France, 1596; a soldier who on the death of his wife in 1587 became a Capuchin monk, renounced his new vocation on succeeding to the dukedom in 1592, and again returned to the religious life in 1599 (Pierre de Vaissière, *Messieurs de Joyeuse (1560–1615)*, 1926, *passim*, esp. pp. 29–30, which revise the accepted date of the Duc's birth).

11. A portrait of the Duc de Joyeuse as a Capuchin monk appeared as the frontispiece of Jacques de Callières, *Le Courtisan prédestiné, ou le Duc de Joyeuse capucin*, new edn, 1728; this portrait, engraved by Jean Devaux (still living in 1745), is a copy of an earlier engraving by Karl or Charles Audran (1594–1674) (Ulrich Thieme and Felix Becker, *Allgemeines Lexikon der Bildenden Künstler*, Leipzig, 1907–50, ii. 237, ix. 180), reproduced from a copy in the Bibliothèque Nationale in Pierre de Vaissière, op. cit., facing p. 328. The name of the original artist, which seems to be given on the Audran engraving, is not wholly legible in the reproduction, but enough can be made out to show that the print was not, as Selwyn thought, after Guido Reni.

12. Guido Reni (1575–1642). HW's 'portfolio with leaves comprising 160 prints pasted therein, from paintings and designs of Guido Reni, of which a considerable number are etchings by his own hand, and by the most eminent of his pupils, and by celebrated engravers, from his most finished paintings' was sold London 1211.

13. On 22 Feb. at the shop of François-Charles Joullain (d. 1790), print-seller, or his father François (1697–1778) (DU DEFFAND iv. 346 and n. 8; 'Paris Journals,' ibid. v. 303).

14. HW listed his purchases in Paris, 1765–6, in 'Paris Journals' (DU DEFFAND v. 401–5). They filled 48 cases and 'a large bale of books' and cost HW more than £500; 38 of the cases contained china, chiefly Sèvres and Chantilly.

not know that *la nation anglais* is not quite *si sage* as it is reckoned here. Our stocks however are prodigiously fallen in this country, and I question, if Mr Hume was to arrive now for the first time, whether he would be thought the liveliest young fellow in the world. An unfortunate horse race, in which Lauragais's horse was poisoned, has brought great disgrace upon us[15]—it would comfort me if Madame de Sévigné was alive to write upon the subject as she did on La Brinvilliers.[16] However, though you do not know it certainly, I can assure you, that you *will* come to Paris this summer. They are determined to have races, and I do not know but· a deputation of *Parlement* (who the King intends shall have nothing else to do)[17] may not be sent to invite Lord March and Dick Vernon[18] over, as the ancients invited legislators— This will be *à la Grecque*. Madame du Deffand is much pleased with the idea of your returning: she is faithful and steady to the English, though suffering persecution on that account.

I am much concerned at what you tell me of Lord Holland,[19] and shall be sorry to find him in such a situation. I am really coming, though I divert myself well enough, and have no sort of thirst after your politics, but lilac-tide approaches, and I long as much to see a bit of green as a housemaid does that sticks a piece of mint in a dirty phial. I don't write to Mr Williams, because writing to you is the same thing, and I forget him no more than I hope he forgets me. Adieu!

Yours ever,

H. W.

PS. Have not you felt a fright lately? If you have not, there is no *sentiment* in you. Why the Queen has been in great danger,[20] re-

15. For this incident see HW to Anne Pitt 1 March and to Hertford 10 March 1766.

16. Marie-Marguerite d'Aubray (d. 1676), m. (1651) Antoine Gobelin, Marquis de Brinvilliers; poisoner. Mme de Sévigné's letters in 1676 contain many references to her (Mme de Sévigné, *Lettres*, ed. Monmerqué, 1862–6, iv. 410 ff.).

17. For the recent royal counter-offensive against the parliaments, see HW to Anne Pitt 7 March and to Hertford 10 March 1766.

18. Richard Vernon (1726–1800), 'father of the turf'; M.P. Tavistock 1754–61, Bedford borough 1761–74, Okehampton 1774–84, Newcastle-under-Lyme 1784–90.

19. Holland had been ill all winter and was apparently rather worse about the time Selwyn wrote to HW; his wife feared 'something wrong in his breast that may cause frequent returns of his disorder' (*Leinster Corr.* i. 436).

20. She had had a cold accompanied by a fever for some days; her illness became so much more serious after 1 March that

ceived the *viatique,* and had the *prières des quarante heures* said for her—but be easy. She is out of danger. La Maréchale de Luxembourg[21] saw her the night before last, and congratulating her recovery, the Queen said, 'I am too unhappy to die!'[22]

To Selwyn, Thursday 3 April 1766

Printed for the first time from a photostat of the MS in the Cely Trevilian collection in the Society of Antiquaries.

Paris, April 3d 1766.

A–COMING! a-coming! just a-coming, for nobody bids more than you: nay, there is no higher price left than what you offer, for I was yesterday at Livry,[1] and what can interest me after that? I have found your Madame St Jean, and she has sent me a tattered scrap,[2] which she says has been in Bretagne, and might have been in the Holy Land, for it is as ragged as a pilgrim, and she adds, that nobody can make anything out about it. I shall bring you this relic with proper care.

Nothing was ever more unjust and cruel than what has been said of your *old passion:*[3] she is absolutely dying of the deaths of her son and father, and you will never see her any more. *Nervous* people act grief and counterfeit not eating: she had no affectation, but has sunk under her sufferings. Hearts do not snap like a tortoise-shell snuffbox, but grief can produce a fever, and she is dying of one, though she did not pretend not to eat when she was hungry. I have heard a story of a non-eater, that is not applicable to your *passion,* but to those who have accused her of not being afflicted according to the

---

the *viaticum* was administered on the evening of the 4th by the Bp of Chartres (*Gazette d'Utrecht* 11 March 1766; *London Chronicle* 15–18 March 1766, xix. 262).

21. Madeleine-Angélique de Neufville (1707–87), m. 1 (1721) Joseph-Marie, Duc de Boufflers; m. 2 (1750) Charles-François-Frédéric de Montmorency-Luxembourg, Duc de Luxembourg, Maréchal de France. HW had supped with her at Mme de Boufflers's on 6 March when he probably heard the account of her interview with

the Queen ('Paris Journals,' du Deffand v. 306).

22. In part because of the recent deaths of her son, the Dauphin, and her father Stanislas, King of Poland and Duke of Lorraine; see the following letter.

---

1. HW describes this visit to Montagu 3 April 1766 (Montagu ii. 211–2).

2. That had presumably belonged to Mme de Sévigné.

3. The Queen of France.

rules of propriety. When the Maréchale d'Albret[4] lost her brother,[5] she would not eat. The famous Matta[6] in Grammont's *Mémoires*,[7] said to her, 'Madam, if you never intend to eat again, I have nothing to say; but if you do, you may as well eat today, as any other day.' She laughed, took his advice, and ordered a *sirloin*.[8]

I am very sorry for Lord Holland's situation:[9] not much surprised at the match,[10] though not the alliance I should have immediately expected.[11] I shall call on the Rena,[12] if I have a moment's time. Apropos, the Maréchale d'Estrées[13] has been bit by a mad dog; but they hope she will escape, and not give balls to the Hereditary Prince[14] when he arrives.

I leave Paris, I own, with regret: it is a paradise for age and wrinkles. One is never too old for a sort of society, nor neglected because one totters. Madame du Deffand has proposed to me to take an apartment in the convent where she lodges, and it tempts me for next winter, as she is much better company than Sir John Cust.[15] I played at cavagnole there two nights ago with the survivors of the last century; the youngest was Madame de Ségur,[16] a natural daughter

4. Madeleine de Guénégaud (d. 1677), m. (1645) César-Phœbus d'Albret, Comte de Miossans, Maréchal de France (La Chenaye-Desbois i. 283; Madame de Sévigné, *Lettres*, ed. Monmerqué, 1862–6, v. 348).

5. François de Guénégaud (d. 1661), Seigneur de Lonzac; councillor of the parliament of Paris; président aux enquêtes (La Chenaye-Desbois x. 2). Her other brothers survived Matta.

6. Charles de Bourdeille (1614–74), Comte de Mastas, or as it was usually spelled, Matta (*Notes and Queries*, 1854, 1st ser. x. 138–9, 157–8). He plays a prominent part in Anthony Hamilton's *Mémoires de la vie du Comte de Grammont;* see following note.

7. *Mémoires de la vie du Comte de Grammont*, by his brother-in-law, Anthony Hamilton (ca 1645–1720). The *Mémoires* were first printed in 1713; many editions followed, including one published by HW at the SH Press in 1772.

8. This anecdote is given in the biographical notes on Matta in several editions of the *Mémoires*.

9. He was actually improving, though he refused to admit it (*Leinster Corr.* i. 436, 438, 440).

10. Between the Hon. Stephen Fox, Holland's eldest son, and Lady Mary Fitzpatrick (d. 1778), eldest dau. of 1st E. of Upper Ossory. They were married 20 April 1766.

11. Because the prospective bride's mother was a sister of the Duchess of Bedford and the Bedfords and Hollands were political enemies; Lady Holland comments on the marriage in *Leinster Corr.* i. 439, 441.

12. She called on HW on 7 April ('Paris Journals,' DU DEFFAND v. 312).

13. Adélaïde-Félicité Brulart de Puisieulx de Sillery (1725–86), m. (1744) Louis-Charles-César le Tellier de Louvois, Maréchal-Duc d'Estrées.

14. Karl Wilhelm Ferdinand (1735–1806), Prince (later Duke) of Brunswick-Wolfenbüttel; George III's brother-in-law. He arrived in Paris on 20 April, three days after HW left for England (DU DEFFAND i. 13).

15. Sir John Cust (1718–70), 3d Bt; Speaker of the House of Commons 1761–70; M.P. Grantham 1743–70.

16. Philippe-Angélique de Froissy (1700–85), m. (1718) Henri-François, Comte de Ségur (DU DEFFAND iv. 424 n. 12). She seems to have been about the oldest of

of the Regent,[17] who can be no chicken, and I did not once wish myself at a debate on the Stamp Act. An old woman that cheats at berlan,[18] is to me as respectable a personage as a patriot that cheats at eloquence; and if Livy had been a matron and writ the memoirs of the Roman dowagers that played at par and impar,[19] as well as he has done the history of consuls and tribunes, I had as lief read them. Our ideas are given to us by our schoolmasters, who know nothing of the world, and we pass three[20] parts of our lives, before we discover their false judgments and our own. Adieu!

Yours ever,

H. W.

To Holland, Thursday 17 July 1766

Printed from *Letters to Henry Fox* 258–60; reprinted, Toynbee *Supp.* i. 133–5. Dated by the contents.

Arlington Street, July 17th, noon.

My dear Lord,

I HAVE not writ to you, because I did not know what to say. I could still plead the same cause of silence, for I am gaping here with the rest of the world, in total ignorance of what is to come forth.[1] Mr Pitt is at Mr Dineley's[2] at Hampstead, and has a fever.[3]

the party, except for Mme du Deffand herself, with whom HW had played cavagnole on 31 March (ibid. v. 310).

17. By Christine - Antoinette - Charlotte Desmares (1682–1753) (du Deffand iv. 424 and n. 11).

18. 'Berlan . . . is a French game . . . it's something like bray, and *quinze*, and loo' (Lady Holland to Lady Kildare 10 Aug. [1763], *Leinster Corr.* i. 384).

19. A game of odd and even, much played by the Greeks and Romans in which a person held a number of objects in his hands and his opponent guessed whether they were odd or even in number.

20. This sentence from the first comma to this point has been erased and written over, but this seems to be the reading.

1. The King sent for Pitt on 7 July to concert plans for a new administration. He notified the ministers on the 9th that he had done so, but none of the new arrangements were yet known (*Chatham Corr.* ii. 434–8; George Thomas, Earl of Albemarle, *Memoirs of the Marquis of Rockingham and His Contemporaries*, 1852, i. 362–7; *Mem. Geo. III* ii. 237–40, where the chronology is confused).

2. Charles Dingley (d. 1769) of North End House, Hampstead Heath; master of the saw mills at Limehouse (Basil Williams, *Life of William Pitt*, 1913, ii. 208; GM 1769, xxxix. 559). Pitt had retired to his house on Monday, 14 July (Williams, loc. cit.).

3. Pitt was ill when he arrived in London on 11 July; his interviews with the

Lord Temple arrived on Monday, has seen the King, and been at least three times at Hampstead.[4] Still there is nothing but rumours and guesses. If anything is known at Court today, I shall hear after the Drawing-Room, and will tell you before the post goes out.

Mr Pitt's intimates say he will not hear of Mr Grenville.[5] A friend of Lord Temple has said that *he* would not accept,[6]—is not this excellent intelligence? Nobody comes to town from any side. Rigby passed through London yesterday, on his way from Woburn to Chelmsford.[7] Not a coach or chair goes to Lord Temple's. In short, if these two monarchs reassume the throne, it may not be so unexpected, but at least it will be as silent a revolution as that in *The Rehearsal*.[8]

Lord Bute's friends assert that the measure was entirely by advice of my Lord Chancellor.[9] I can at least affirm that some of them were entirely out of the secret.

My Lady Montrath[10] is dead, and has made as drunken a will as you could expect. She has left a mortgage of forty thousand pounds on the Devonshire estate to Lord John Cavendish,[11] whom she never

King and Conway on the 12th and 13th made him worse, and his quarrel with Temple on the 16th brought his fever to a crisis (Williams, op. cit. ii. 208–9).

4. Temple came up at the King's request. He saw the King on the afternoon of Tuesday the 15th, but made only one visit to Pitt, on the 16th (*Grenville Papers* iii. 263–4; *Chatham Corr.* ii. 443–7; John Brooke, *The Chatham Administration 1766–1768*, 1956, p. 7).

5. Pitt and Grenville had quarrelled in 1761; at the present moment they were in fundamental disagreement over American policy (Williams, op. cit. ii. 109–10, 189–200).

6. Temple was determined to take office only on his own terms (*Chatham Corr.* ii. 443; George III, *Correspondence*, ed. Fortescue, 1927–8, i. 177; Brooke, op. cit. 8).

7. 'Mr Rigby left me to be at the Chelmsford Assizes tomorrow' (Bedford to Grenville, Woburn Abbey, 16 July 1766, *Grenville Papers* iii. 265).

8. In *The Rehearsal* by George Villiers (1628–87), 2d D. of Buckingham, the Gentleman Usher and the Physician usurp the thrones of the two kings of Brentford sim-

ply by announcing that they have done so (II. iv).

9. Robert Henley (ca 1708–72), cr. (1760) Bn Henley and (1764) E. of Northington; lord chancellor 1761–6. His advice alone determined the King to send for Pitt; the belief, held by nearly all the Rockingham connection, that the measure was dictated by Bute is without foundation; see George III to Bute 12 July 1766, informing him of what had been done in *Letters from George III to Lord Bute,* ed. Romney Sedgwick, 1939, pp. 250–4; *Chatham Corr.* ii. 434–5; Albemarle, op. cit., i. 359–70.

10. Lady Diana Newport (d. 14 July 1766), m. (1721) Algernon Coote, 6th E. of Mountrath, an 'anti-Walpolian Whig' (GEC). For HW's account of her drunkenness and alleged affair with Lord Hardwicke, see MONTAGU i. 135 n. 20. Similar details of her will are in HW to Lady Suffolk 17 July 1766.

11. Lord John Cavendish (1732–96), 4th son of William, 3rd D. of Devonshire; chancellor of the Exchequer 1782–3; M.P. Weymouth and Melcombe Regis 1754–61, Knaresborough 1761–8, York city 1768–84, Derbyshire 1794–6.

saw but twice. Twickenham Park[12] to Lord Frederic,[13] whom I do not know that she ever saw at all, but not till after the deaths of the Duchesses of Newcastle and Montrose;[14] an estate of a thousand pounds a year to her son;[15] another of six hundred a year to Lord Milton's youngest son;[16] and three score thousand pounds in small legacies. I do not hear of a Yorke in the number.

Rousseau has sent Mr Hume a folio of seventeen pages,[17] containing his griefs. The principal are, that when everybody had satisfied their curiosity, they troubled their heads no more about him, and that Mr Hume has been in a plot with me and D'Alembert[18] to dishonour him; that D'Alembert wrote the letter for the King of Prussia,[19] and that I fathered it, and that Mr Hume did not contradict it. I never saw D'Alembert but once,[20] and then did not speak to him, and Mr Hume never heard of the letter till he saw it here in England. You may judge of the rest by this sample. I have almost a mind to send him one of Tom Hervey's letters,[21] to show him why England is indifferent to new madmen, possessing so

12. An estate once owned by Francis Bacon, lying partly in Twickenham parish and partly in Isleworth. Lord Mountrath bought it in 1743 (Daniel Lysons, *Environs of London*, 1792–6, iii. 564–6).

13. Lord Frederick Cavendish (1729–1803), 3d son of 3d D. of Devonshire; field marshal, 1796; M. P. Derbyshire 1751–4, Derby borough 1754–80.

14. Lady Lucy Manners (ca 1717–88), m. (1742) William Graham, 2d D. of Montrose.

15. Charles Henry Coote (ca 1725–1802), 7th E. of Mountrath, 1744, to whom she left as little as she could; see Montagu i. 135 n. 20.

16. Hon. Lionel Damer (1748–1807), 3d son of Joseph Damer (1718–98), cr. (1753) Bn Milton and (1792) E. of Dorchester; M.P. Peterborough 1786–1802 (John Hutchins, *The History and Antiquities of the County of Dorset*, 3d edn, 1861–70, iv. 387; Judd, *Members of Parliament* 169).

17. Printed in Hume, *Letters*, ed. Greig, Oxford, 1932, ii. 385–401.

18. Jean le Rond d'Alembert (1717–83).

19. HW's letter; see *ante* 12 Jan. 1766. For the part played by this letter in the Rousseau-Hume quarrel, see HW's 'Narrative of What Passed Relative to the Quar-

rel of Mr David Hume and Jean-Jacques Rousseau as far as Mr Horace Walpole was Concerned in it' (*Works* iv. 247–69); Hume's *Concise and Genuine Account of the Dispute between Mr Hume and Mr Rousseau*, 1766; Hazen, *Bibl. of HW* 160–2; HW to Mme du Deffand 16 July 1766 (du Deffand i. 94–8); Hume's *Letters* ii. *passim*, esp. pp. 384–401, 407–448; F. A. Pottle, 'The Part Played by Horace Walpole and James Boswell in the Quarrel between Rousseau and Hume,' *Philological Quarterly*, 1925, iv. 351–63; M. H. Peoples, 'La Querelle Rousseau-Hume,' *Annales de la Société Jean-Jacques Rousseau*, 1927–8, xviii. 1–331; Henri Guillemin, *Les Philosophes contre Jean-Jacques: 'cette affaire infernale,' l'affaire J.-J. Rousseau-Hume, 1766*, 1942.

20. At Mme Geoffrin's, 9 April 1766 ('Paris Journals,' du Deffand v. 312; HW's 'Narrative,' *Works* iv. 252).

21. His latest public letter was *A Complaint on the Part of the Hon. Thomas Hervey, Concerning an Undue Proceeding against him at Court. Set forth in Two Letters to Her Highness the Princess of Brunswick*, 1766. HW has written 'May' on the title-page of his copy (Hazen, *Cat. of HW's Lib.*, No. 1609, vol. 14; now wsl).

much superior of her own, not forgetting our incessant revolutions.

Pray tell me how your health is.[22] George Selwyn is throwing away all his bon mots on the present occasion at Newmarket. My Lady Townshend says she has been robbed of five hundred and fifty pounds in banknotes, by her servants.[23] They have been before Fielding,[24] but I do not know how it is, nothing is discovered, and it makes no noise.

I keep the rest of my paper till after dinner.

Thursday evening.

I can tell you no more, but that Lord Temple agitated Mr Pitt so much yesterday that today he has a high fever, and the physicians have ordered him to be kept quiet.[25] The Duke of Grafton is come to town,[26] but could not see him.[27] You may depend on this, for you

22. 'Lord Holland in my opinion continues exactly as he has been for five or six weeks past; Charles thinks him mended since his arrival here' (Lady Holland to Lady Kildare 16 July 1766, *Leinster Corr.* i. 457).

23. 'Lady Townshend was robbed yesterday of five hundred and fifty pounds in bank notes. She kept them in the drawer of a little table, and in a room to which nobody had access but Molly, the niece of Dorcas, and her upper footman, who used to pay her bills, and by that means knew where she kept her money. It seems these two have kept up a constant correspondence with Draper, her old thief, who lives now in Ireland, and to whom, without the least doubt, they have remitted the money. You would like the house at this instant better than ever; Methodists, constables, Fieldings, turnkeys, etc. etc. She sleeps with one of Fielding's men in the next room. Horace Walpole has been called to the council, to apply to Lord Hertford for a *melius inquirendum* in Ireland after this Draper, who lives with a Mr Burke. He says he is glad of this *éclaircissement*, as it will deliver all those he wished well to out of a very disagreeable state of servitude; and, indeed, he has all along been in that respect very consistent' (Williams to Selwyn 10 July [1766], Jesse, *Selwyn* i. 383). A few days later Selwyn

wrote to Holland: 'My Lady has fixed the robbery almost to a certainty upon Dorcas's niece, who succeeded her aunt in the office of *femme de chambre*. She is to be stripped tomorrow before Fielding and me at eleven, and then committed to the Gatehouse for further examination. But unless she confesses, I do not see how the notes are to be recovered. She is now proved to be the second wife now living of Braber [*sic*] the butler, who robbed her Ladyship last year and fled to Ireland' (*Letters to Henry Fox* 262). For the dénouement of the affair, in which Molly was exonerated, see Selwyn to Holland 15 Sept. [1766], ibid. 271.

24. Sir John Fielding (1721–80), magistrate.

25. 'The conversation, from its length and *issue* yesterday, with Lord Temple, having been rather too much for my situation . . . my pulse quickened towards evening, so that I am advised to be peremptory with all business, and shut my door till I am quite free from fever' (Pitt to Lady Chatham 17 July 1766, *Chatham Corr.* ii. 448).

26. He came at Pitt's request (Augustus Henry, 3d D. of Grafton, *Autobiography*, ed. Anson, 1898, p. 89).

27. Pitt saw Grafton for two hours on Saturday, 19 July (*Chatham Corr.* ii. 449; *post* 19 July 1766).

know I never tell you more positively than I am sure is exactly true. Adieu!

Yours ever,

H. Walpole

To Holland, Saturday 19 July 1766

Printed from *Letters to Henry Fox* 260; reprinted, Toynbee *Supp.* i. 136.

July 19.

I SUPPOSE, my dear Lord, you will have had twenty letters by this post to tell you that Lord Temple has refused the Treasury, and is gone.[1] His creatures say Mr Pitt used him like a dog. I should not think that either was very gentle to the other before they parted.[2] Lord Temple insisted on bringing his brother Geo. too, which Pitt refused.[3] Then poor Lord Littleton; no.[4] When all was rejected the Earl recollected Almon[5] and Humphrey Cotes;[6] not for lords of

1. He returned to Stowe on the 17th after an interview with the King (*Grenville Papers* iii. 266–7).

2. The meeting appears to have been less rancourous than it was reported to have been; Pitt wrote to his wife, 17 July: 'Our dear Lord Temple returns to Stowe . . . I must do justice to the kind and affectionate behaviour which he held throughout the whole of our long talk' (*Chatham Corr.* ii. 448). The details of the conversation between Pitt and Temple which HW gives here and elsewhere, though representative of the version in general circulation, are much exaggerated; the two men do not seem to have discussed specific appointments beyond Temple's proposal of Lord Gower as secretary of state as a trial of Pitt's willingness to share power (John Brooke, *The Chatham Administration 1766–1768*, 1956, p. 8).

3. Temple told George Grenville that he did not mention him as a candidate for anything (*Grenville Papers* iii. 267).

4. 'It was thought extraordinary that I should dream of a Cabinet place for Lord Lyttelton, but as an act of special grace to

me, he might have been indulged with a place, and called to the Cabinet, as I suppose of the hanging committee' (Temple to G. Grenville 18 July 1766, *Grenville Papers* iii. 267). The report that Pitt had refused to admit him to the Cabinet was current at the time (*Grenville Papers* iii. 269; Edmund Burke, *Correspondence*, Vol. I, ed. T. W. Copeland, Cambridge, 1958, p. 261), but see above, n. 2. Temple, however, told the king that he had proposed Lyttelton as president of the Council (*George III, Correspondence*, ed. Fortescue, 1927–8, i. 177).

5. John Almon (1737–1805), bookseller and journalist. He and Cotes wrote a pamphlet for Temple, *An Inquiry into the Conduct of a late Rt. Hon. Commoner*, 1766, stating Temple's version of the interview (Basil Williams, *Life of William Pitt*, 1913, ii. 209 n.; *post* 14 Nov. 1766, n. 24).

6. Humphrey Cotes (d. 1775), politician, friend of Wilkes and Temple; wine-merchant in Mincing Lane until he went bankrupt in 1767; unsuccessful candidate for Westminster, 1774 (GM 1775, xlv. 255; *Grenville Papers* ii.–iv. *passim*; John Al-

the Treasury, but as responsible to them. He asked what Mr Pitt intended to do for Mr Mackenzie and Lord Northumberland? Considerably. This was the sum of the conference and quarrel, which in <   >[7] Billingsgate, you know, might be rolled out into a spirited dialogue of some hours. The next day his Lordship saw the King; was, I believe as well as I guess, very impertinent, was answered properly,[8] called at Lord Gower's,[9] who was not in town, left his commands for the people of England with Mr MacCartney,[10] and set out. I am so well satisfied that I am setting out too.

Mr Pitt has still much fever. The Duke of Grafton goes to him today,[11] but he himself will not, they say, be able to see the King before Wednesday.[12] I do not guess who will have the Treasury, nor care, since I know who will not.[13] Adieu! my dear Lord; I hope this charming weather will be of great service to you.

Yours ever,

H. W.

---

mon, *Correspondence of the Late John Wilkes with his Friends*, 1805, ii. 33–70, 74–103, 190–235; iii. 234–7; HW to Hertford 17 Nov. 1763; HW to Conway 27 Sept., 16 Oct. 1774; *Mem. Geo. III* ii. 245 n.; iii. 128, 137, 218; HW's *Last Journals*, ed. Steuart, 1910, i. 405).

7. According to *Letters to Henry Fox* 260 there is an illegible word here.

8. Temple himself merely stated that he saw the King on 17 July for an hour; he described the King as 'very gracious, and I believe not a little delighted with my declining' (*Grenville Papers* iii. 267). See also the King's versions of the interview in George III, *Corr.* i. 177, 377.

9. See Temple to Gower, 19 July 1766 (*Grenville Papers* iii. 272–3). Temple had suggested him to Pitt for secretary of state, but Pitt rejected him; see *post* 29 July 1766 n. 4, and above, n. 2.

10. Apparently a slip for 'Mrs Mac-

Cartney.' Lady Holland, writing to Lady Kildare a few days later, says 'to use Horace Walpole's expression, [Temple] has left his commands for the people of England with Mrs M. and Miss Gardiner' (*Leinster Corr.* i. 465, dated erroneously 25 [Aug. 1766], but clearly July). Mrs Macartney was Henrietta Gardiner, eldest dau. of Luke Gardiner, m. (1748) Francis Macartney, brother of the Fanny Macartney of HW's *The Beauties* (John Lodge and Mervyn Archdall, *Peerage of Ireland*, 1789, vii. 91). For a scandal involving her, Miss Gardiner and Lord Bateman, which resulted in a separation from her husband, see *Leinster Corr.* i. 176–7, 211.

11. An account of the interview is in Grafton, op. cit. 90–1.

12. The King expected him that day (George III, *Corr.* i. 379; *Chatham Corr.* ii. 455).

13. Temple.

To Holland, Tuesday 22 July 1766

Printed from *Letters to Henry Fox* 261; reprinted, Toynbee *Supp.* i. 137.

Arlington Street, July 22d 1766.

My dear Lord,

I AM much pleased with the good account of your health, and much satisfied that my newspaper entertains you. It will contain little tonight, for the curtain is not drawn up yet. In general, we believe that the Duke of Grafton is to be at the head of the Treasury,[1] and Charles Townshend his chancellor of the Exchequer. Certain it is that the latter was sent for, and has been at *our Palace of Hampstede.*[2] Today there is a report that Lord Camden is summoned too,[3] and that the Chancellor's[4] face is almost as long as Charles Yorke's;[5] but I have not so much as seen the truth of this.

Lord Temple demanded the place of president of the Council for Lord Lyttelton, and was flatly refused: menaced opposition, and was told by Mr Pitt that such a strong administration would be formed that he would not be able to oppose it. I question if that will deter him. Good-night.

Yours ever,

H. Walpole

---

1. Grafton had accepted the Treasury in his interview with Pitt 19 July (Grafton, op. cit. 91).

2. Pitt was still at Dingley's at Hampstead. Townshend had been sent for on 20 July, came to town at once and saw Pitt on the 21st (George III, *Corr.* i. 378; *Chatham Corr.* ii. 452, 456). After several days of indecision, he finally agreed to be chancellor of the Exchequer on the 25th (George III, op. cit. i. 380–3; Grafton, op. cit. 95–6; *post* 29 July 1766, n. 5).

3. Someone wrote to Camden before 19 July urging him to leave the circuit and come to London, but Camden declined to do so without a direct summons from Pitt (Grafton, op. cit. 93–4). He became lord chancellor in the new administration.

4. Lord Northington, who, far from being put out at the thought of being succeeded by Camden, was anxious for a less demanding post (*Chatham Corr.* ii. 450).

5. Attorney-general in the Rockingham administration; he was so piqued at the promotion of Camden that he resigned a few days later (*post* 29 July 1766, n. 9).

To Holland, Tuesday 29 July 1766

Printed from *Letters to Henry Fox* 262–3; reprinted, Toynbee *Supp.* i. 137–8.

Arlington Street, July 29, 1766.

I HAVE not writ to you, my dear Lord, for these two or three posts, because I really could not tell you what would or would not happen. There has been some confusion this last week, and much absurdity, at which you will not wonder, as you will guess the authors. I feared it would have spread farther; but though there will be a few resignations, I now think very few. The D[uke] of R[ichmond] has been hurt at his successor;[1] but has behaved sensibly and nobly, and very differently from two or three of his friends. As it is my great object not to have him dissatisfied, I have laboured to the utmost, and flatter myself I have a prospect of succeeding.[2] If the breach went farther than it will do, it would not long remain open, for there are offers of filling it from *all* quarters.[3] I trust *they* will not be wanted.

Lord Temple has endeavoured to persuade that he broke with Mr Pitt, because Lord Gower was not to be secretary of state.[4] You may judge from what you know, and from what I have hinted, whether this is believed.

Charles Townshend has contrived, as usual, to make himself more talked of than anybody in this scene, by his doing and undoing, saying and unsaying.[5] He is at last chancellor of the Exchequer.

The Duke of Grafton and Lord Shelburn, and I believe Lord Northington and Lord Camden, kiss hands tomorrow.[6] Lord John

---

1. William Petty (1737–1805), 2d E. of Shelburne; cr. (1784) M. of Lansdowne; first lord of the Treasury 1782–3. He succeeded Richmond as secretary of state for the southern department 23 July, but did not kiss hands until the 30th (below n. 6; Lord Fitzmaurice, *Life of William, Earl of Shelburne,* 2d edn, 1912, i. 280–3).

2. HW gives an account in *Mem. Geo. III* ii. 248–9 of his temporarily successful attempt to make Richmond reasonably satisfied with the new arrangements.

3. HW is presumably referring to hints from the Bedford faction that they would be glad to join the Pitt-Grafton administration; see *post* 2 Aug. 1766 and n. 4.

4. The ostensible reason for his refusal

to accept office, since it proved that Pitt had no intention of sharing power with him (*ante* 19 July 1766, n. 2).

5. Townshend's vacillations between becoming chancellor of the Exchequer and remaining Paymaster can be followed in *Chatham Corr.* ii. 456–7, 459–60, 462–6; Grafton, op. cit. 96–7; and George III, *Corr.* i. 378–83. See also John Brooke, *The Chatham Administration 1766–1768,* 1956, p. 9.

6. Pitt, now Earl of Chatham, Camden, Northington, and Shelburne kissed hands for their new offices on 30 July; Grafton on 2 Aug. (*London Gazette* No. 10646, 29 July–2 Aug. 1766).

resigns,[7] and I believe Lord Dartmouth.[8] Yorke, I am told, will not stay, but am not certain of it.[9]

I am sorry to tell you that there is a new edition of the *Bath Guide*[10] with most execrable additions. I shall adhere to the old copy.

I am going to Strawberry for two days,[11] heartily tired of all the folly I have been witness to for these three weeks.

Yours ever,

H. W.

From Holland, Thursday 31 July 1766

Printed from the MS now wsl. It is not in Holland's hand, but he has signed it and made some corrections. First printed, Toynbee *Supp.* iii. 202–3. For the history of the MS see *ante* 22 July 1746.

Memoranda (by HW in pencil for *Mem. Geo. III* i. 53–4):

Lord Granville who knew the value of rodomontade by its being his own favourite figure of speech, and who had used glory as a step to ambition, instead of making ambition the road of glory, had little esteem for <Pitt's exalted> diction or views.

7. Lord John Cavendish resigned from the Treasury Board on 30 July (*Daily Adv.* 31 July 1766). HW comments on his resignation in greater detail *post* 2 Aug. 1766.

8. William Legge (1731–1801), 2d E. of Dartmouth, secretary of state for the colonies 1772–5; lord privy seal 1775–82. He had been first lord of trade in the Rockingham administration, but resigned on 30 July (*Daily Adv.* 1 Aug. 1766) because a new post of secretary of state for the colonies was not created for him, and he was deprived of the American patronage he already exercised (Brooke, op. cit. 17; Edmund Burke, *Correspondence*, Vol. I, ed. T. W. Copeland, Cambridge, 1958, p. 262). The King had been informed of his intention as early as the 26th (George III, op. cit. i. 380).

9. Charles Yorke, piqued at not being offered the chancellorship, resigned as attorney-general on 1 Aug. (*Chatham Corr.* iii. 24; Brooke, op. cit. 17 and n. 1).

10. *The New Bath Guide: or Memoirs of the B-r-d Family*, by Christopher An-

stey (1724–1805), published 1 May. Additions, including 'A Charge to the Poets' and an 'Epilogue' in which Anstey tried to justify himself and answer certain objections to the poem, were included in the second issue of the first edition and all subsequent editions. HW probably objected particularly to the 'Epilogue,' which was 'a polemic in behalf of the author, and was hastily written after the first reports of the book's reception had reached Anstey's ears. It has none of the humour or characterization of the *Bath Guide*' (W. C. Powell, *Christopher Anstey: Bath Laureate*, Philadelphia, 1944, pp. 90–2). The day of publication of the second edition has not been found; the third is advertised as 'next week' to be published on 1 Aug. (*Daily Adv.* 1 Aug. 1766). HW's copy of the first edition (Hazen, *Cat. of HW's Lib.*, No. 3222, vol. 7), dated by him 'May' is at Harvard; his copy of the second edition (ibid., No. 1810, vol. 59) is now wsl.

11. HW apparently did not go until 3 Aug.

Kingsgate, July the 31st.

Dear Sir,

YOU act like a true friend: for what medium can there be between the D[uke] of R[ichmond] seeming content, and going
into opposition (perhaps with the base Bedfords). I don't wonder that
he is hurt at his successor,[1] but such behaviour as you prompt him
to, and flatter yourself you shall succeed in, cannot fail to please him
in the light and that soon, that we should wish to see him in; and
that his parts and birth entitle him to. Marshal Turenne[2] said that
if he could not have swallowed many *couleuvres*,[3] he had never been
the great man he was; Shelburn is a *couleuvre,* and of the most dis-
tasteful sort, but I hope his Grace won't let it have the satisfaction
of choking him. How much my Lord Temple was in earnest I won't
say, but he certainly proposed Lord Gower as if he was; for Humphry
Cotes met Tanner[4] in the street, and abused Mr Pitt with violence
for refusing my Lord Gower; he and my Lord Littleton, he said,
were the only two my Lord Temple has *insisted* upon; and as to my
Lord Gower, many years ago Mr Rigby told me, he was the most
selfish man in the world, and cared for nobody, and was ready at any
time to leave anybody for his own interest; I have had no reason to
doubt Mr Rigby's character of him.

Now my dear Mr Walpole I come to a matter which Lady Caroline and I wish exceedingly for your help in; for I don't doubt you
will approve of it; but how you will get into discoursing of it I don't
know, and must leave that to you; Lady Caroline is exceedingly
desirous of gaining, and gaining by her brother's help, an earldom
for me, or if the Duke of Richmond had rather ask it and the King,
which is probable enough, had rather give the patent to her, I shall
like it full as well. When I came from France at the end of the year
'63 the K[ing] said, giving an account of Mr Pitt's transaction with
him, that he would not have given away my place without acquaint-

1. Shelburne, with whom Holland had
quarrelled in 1763 over retaining the
pay office; the affair is fully discussed in
Ilchester, *Henry Fox* ii. 238–61.

2. Henri de la Tour d'Auvergne (1611–
75), Vicomte de Turenne; Maréchal de
France.

3. Holland seems to have had in mind
the idiomatic and literal meanings of the

word. *Couleuvre* is a generic term for non-
venomous snakes, but it is used idiomati-
cally for *affront,* as in *avaler des couleuvres,*
to receive affronts without protesting. Holland's source for attributing the phrase to
Turenne has not been found.

4. Not identified; perhaps Jonathan
Tanner (d. 1769), merchant (GM 1769,
xxxix. 367).

ing me with it and giving me what he thought I should like as well, meaning this title;[5] you know how it was taken from me last year, when the King sent me word, it was not his doing;[6] but what I wish, my dear Mr Walpole, is that the D[uke] of R[ichmond] would ask it as a parting request, and if it is granted, surely he will go out with a better grace, than if he has nothing; Lady Caroline writes to him, and is more eager about it than I ever thought I should see her, about anything of this nature. I send her letter and my own by express and the same express, shall carry this letter to Charles,[7] that he may convey it to you. When you have anything to write to me upon this or any other matter that you don't care to trust by the post send it to Charles, and he will send an express with it. I am, my dear Sir,

Your infinitely obliged humble servant,

HOLLAND

From HOLLAND, ca Friday 1 August 1766

Missing.

To HOLLAND, Saturday 2 August 1766

Printed from *Letters to Henry Fox* 266–8; reprinted, Toynbee *Supp.* i. 139–41.

Arlington Street, Aug. 2d 1766.

My dear Lord,

THE moment after I had seen your son yesterday, I went to the Duke of Richmond. He was gone to dine out of town; I called again in the evening, but he was not returned. However, as I found the Duchess alone, I spoke to her, as I could more freely even than

5. Holland does not mention this topic of his conversation with the King on 9 Nov. 1763 in his letters at the time (Ilchester, *Henry Fox* ii. 273–4); but see Richmond to Holland, 23 May 1765, mentioning a report that Holland had assurances that the loss of his place would be made up to him (*Letters to Henry Fox* 215).

6. There is no evidence of a direct message or letter from the King to Holland to this effect, though he did state more or less publicly that he had no quarrel with Holland (*Letters to Henry Fox* 223).

7. Charles James Fox.

to the Duke. I found by her that it would be impossible to persuade him to ask any favour now; and indeed I suspected so before, for Mr Conway and I have thought of and been trying everything that we thought could please him, and nothing has gone down at all. This morning I received your second letter,[1] which forbids my pushing it any farther. I thank you for having been convinced how happy I should have been to have contributed to it, and to have pleased Lady Holland. What time and absence from Lord Rockingham and Lord John[2] may do, I don't know; but at present the ill-humour promises bad effects. The Duke of Bedford, through Lord Tavistock,[3] has directly offered himself[4] to the Duke of Grafton, desiring nothing for himself, and only places for Lord Gower, Rigby, and Dick Vernon. I have told this to the Duke of Richmond, and showed him that the farther they carry their resentment, the more it will push Pitt to the Bedfords, and even facilitate his taking them; the consequence of which would be, that the Duke of Richmond would have nothing left to resort to but the two *amiable* Grenville brothers.

Lord John seems to me to have a little of the madness that has been so much in their blood. Without the smallest provocation, and living upon the best terms with the Duke of Grafton, and even before the Duke was in the Treasury, Lord John wrote to him that he concluded his Grace did not wish to see a Cavendish at the board of Treasury.[5] But Lord John is not the only person that has done mischief; Lord Albemarle[6] is not idle. Dowdswell,[7] after promising

---

1. Missing.

2. Cavendish. In September Lady Holland wrote that Lord John had governed not only Richmond, but Rockingham as well, in the late crisis (*Leinster Corr.*, i. 467).

3. Francis Russell (1739–67), styled M. of Tavistock; M.P. Bedfordshire 1761–7.

4. On 25 July Grafton learned that Tavistock had told Charles Fitzroy, Grafton's brother, that Bedford would be pleased to see Grafton at the Treasury; that he would have no post again, 'but by placing properly a few of his friends he would be perfectly satisfied with what was doing' (*Chatham Corr.* ii. 461). There were other evidences of flirtation between the Bedfords and the administration during the next few days (*Grenville Papers* iii. 288, 291),

but no such definite offer as HW states here and in *Mem. Geo. III* ii. 252.

5. Grafton mentioned this letter, though not its terms, to Pitt on 25 July (*Chatham Corr.* ii. 460), and HW expands on the incident in *Mem. Geo. III* ii. 250–1. Lord John's resignation was an unpleasant surprise to his late colleagues; see the correspondence cited in John Brooke, *The Chatham Administration 1766–1768*, 1956, p. 18; and Edmund Burke, *Correspondence*, Vol. I, ed. T. W. Copeland, Cambridge, 1958, p. 263 n. 1.

6. George Keppel (1724–72), 3d E. of Albemarle; M.P. Chichester 1746–54.

7. William Dowdeswell (1721–75), politician; chancellor of the Exchequer 1765–66; M.P. Tewkesbury 1747–54, Worcestershire 1761–75.

to accept any place not inferior to what he has had, has refused the first lord of trade.[8]

Mr Conway went early this morning to Park Place, and I go out of town tomorrow; but the moment I see him, I will ask him about Sir George Maccartney,[9] who has indeed been very cruelly treated. Stanley, but two nights ago, told Lady Hertford, that of all things in the world he disliked going to Russia, but had obtained the King's promise that whether he had finished his business or not, he should be in England that day two years.[10] He is to have six thousand pounds a year, and three thousand pounds for his equipage. I hear even that drunken porter Lord Northington is to have £4,000 a year pension, besides his appointments.[11] Lord North[12] is to have half the Paymaster's place; I don't know who the other half.[13]

Lord Temple may pretend what he pleases about my Lord Gower, but you may depend upon it that he never proposed him till he was convinced he was either not to come [in] himself, or at least with no nominations. I have reason to believe that the King thinks Lord Temple never meant to come in; and I believe too that the Bedfords are not the dupes of his professions.

8. During Charles Townshend's wavering (*ante* 29 July 1766, n. 5), Grafton and Pitt had considered leaving Dowdeswell as chancellor of the Exchequer. When Townshend finally accepted, Dowdeswell was first sounded (29 July) and then formally offered (31 July) either the first lord of trade or the joint paymastership. He refused both (*Chatham Corr.* ii. 460; iii. 22–3; George III, *Correspondence*, ed. Fortescue, 1927–8, i. 386–7; Brooke, op. cit. 18).

9. George Macartney (1737–1806), Kt, 1764; cr. (1776) Bn, (1792) Vct, and (1794) E. Macartney; diplomatist; envoy to Russia 1764–7. He had been superseded without warning by the appointment of Hans Stanley as ambassador-extraordinary to carry out Pitt's scheme of a Northern Alliance, an especially harsh treatment since he had just concluded a commercial treaty with Russia (Basil Williams, *Life of William Pitt*, 1913, ii. 224–5).

10. There is no reference to Stanley's aversion to going to Russia in his correspondence with Conway and Chatham at this time (*Chatham Corr.* iii. 15–40 *passim;* see also Pitt to the King 25 July 1766,

George III, *Corr.* i. 381). He did not take up the appointment, however, because of the King of Prussia's opposition to Pitt's scheme.

11. HW writes in *Mem. Geo. III* ii. 253, that Northington 'sold the Seals for the President's place, augmented by £5,000 a year, with the contingency of £2,000 a year if he should quit the place of President, and for the reversion of the Hanaper for two lives.'

12. Frederick North (1732–92), styled Lord North 1752–90; 2d E. of Guilford, 1790; first lord of the Treasury 1770–82; M.P. Banbury 1754–90. He accepted the joint paymastership on 29 July but was not formally appointed until 19 Aug. (*Chatham Corr.* ii. 470–1; *London Gazette* No. 10651, 16–19 Aug. 1766).

13. George Cooke (ca 1705–68), protonotary of the common pleas; M.P. Tregony 1742–7, Middlesex 1750–68; became joint paymaster-general with North on 19 Aug. (GM 1766, xxxvi. 391; 1768, xxxviii. 303; HW to Mann 9 June 1768; Judd, *Members of Parliament* 158; J. B. Owen, *The Rise of the Pelhams*, 1957, p. 324).

The Common Council are outrageous at the earldom.[14] They had given the key of the Monument to Beardmore[15] to illuminate it. On hearing of the peerage, he sent back the key.

I do not hear of one of the Duke of Newcastle's people that will resign, for which I am not sorry. The Duke of Portland, I believe, is gone out of town, and unless something new happens will not quit.[16] Lord Besborough,[17] *they say*, had a mind, but was persuaded *not*. Adm. Keppel[18] says he will not say whether he will resign or not, but thinks Mr Pitt has neglected him. Lord Albemarle is going to York races. Charles Yorke, finding how little meanness has availed him, recurs to dignity; and talks of throwing up his profession, as he will not plead under Lord Camden.[19]

This, I think, is the present state of affairs. The Duke of Richmond continues very kind to me, and you, who know how much I love him, may be sure I will do everything that depends on me to keep him from falling into the worst connections; but if his own good sense does not, I doubt nothing else will. This last busy month has deranged me so much, that I do not know when I shall be at liberty; but I will certainly endeavour to see you before you set out.[20] Pray assure my Lady Holland with what pleasure I undertook her commands, and how sorry I am, in this instance, to be so insignificant.

There seems no doubt of the strength of the new administration, but I shall never like it while the Duke of Richmond makes no part of it. Lady Holland's account of your health gives me great satisfaction.

I am most sincerely yours,

HOR. WALPOLE

14. Pitt had become Earl of Chatham on 30 July.

15. Arthur Beardmore, attorney; Lord Temple's man of business; legal advisor to Wilkes; political writer; under-sheriff of London (*Grenville Corr.* i. 459; ii. 60 and *passim*).

16. Portland remained lord chamberlain of the Household until 27 Nov. 1766 (George Thomas, Earl of Albemarle, *Memoirs of the Marquis of Rockingham and His Contemporaries*, 1852, ii. 25).

17. William Ponsonby (1704–93), 2d E. of Bessborough; joint postmaster-general

1759–62, 1765–6. He finally resigned 27 Nov. 1766 (ibid.).

18. Augustus Keppel (1725–86), cr. (1782) Vct Keppel; Rear-Adm., 1762; Adm., 1778; first lord of the Admiralty, 1782. He was a lord of the Admiralty in Rockingham's administration in 1765, and finally resigned 28 Nov. 1766 (ibid. ii. 26).

19. Yorke did virtually retire from public life.

20. Holland planned to go to Naples for the winter; he left England on 23 Sept. (Ilchester, *Henry Fox* ii. 320).

From HOLLAND, ca 28–29 September 1766

Missing; written from Reims. The Hollands were at Arras on 26 Sept. and reached Lyons on 5 Oct., having stopped half a day at Reims (*Leinster Corr.* i. 467, 469).

To HOLLAND, Friday 14 November 1766

Printed from *Letters to Henry Fox* 272–3; reprinted, Toynbee *Supp.* i. 146–8.

Arlington Street, November 14th 1766.

My dear Lord,

I HEAR with great pleasure from all hands, that you continue in the good state in which you wrote to me from Rheims. Lord Ilchester was so kind as to show me two notes[1] from Marseilles, and yesterday I had a letter[2] from my sister,[3] who speaks with great confidence of your being free from all appearance of asthma or dropsy. I have no doubt of your finding still more benefit from the sea, and surely Naples is not likely to bring back your complaints. I hope you will return as perfectly well as I am come from Bath.[4] I have not felt such health or spirits these three years. Indeed I believe the joy of leaving Bath produced half my cure, for I could not bear the place.

I waited, before I wrote to you, for the meeting of Parliament,[5] that I might have something worth telling you. I hasten away my letter now, lest I should have nothing more to tell you, for the session promises to be exceedingly unactive. The two Grenvilles proposed on the first day to issue two hundred thousand pounds from the Treasury to support the poor,[6] or hire a mob for themselves. Lord

1. Holland was at Marseilles at the end of October (*Leinster Corr* i. 476).

2. Missing.

3. Lady Mary Churchill. Lady Holland wrote to Lady Kildare from Lyons 18 Oct.: 'We had the Churchills in this town four or five days, travelling for amusement only, or rather restlessness. . . . Lady Mary is grown old, her affection worn off; you know she could always be agreeable when she pleased' (ibid. i. 471).

4. HW arrived at Bath 1 Oct. and returned to London 25 Oct. (HW to Conway 2 Oct. 1766; HW to Mann 26 Oct. 1766). He gives an account of his rapid recovery there in the letter to Mann.

5. Parliament met 11 Nov.

6. The amendment to the address of thanks moved in the House of Commons for the relief of the poor, printed in *Journals of the House of Commons* xxxi. 4, does not mention a specific sum; it was rejected without a division after a considerable debate; see Burke, op. cit. 278–9. No formal motion was made in the Lords,

Temple, with his stalking-horse Lord Lyttelton, had gone the day before to the Mayor's feast[7] to no purpose. Lord Ilchester will tell you the particulars of their debate. In our House (not that I was there), it was much more languid. Not one of the Duke of Bedford's people attended, and he himself in t'other House spoke with much moderation.[8] The history is this. At Bath, Lord Northington and Nugent[9] took great pains to negotiate between his Grace and Lord Chatham.[10] They had two or three very amicable interviews.[11] The demands were few, but very considerable.[12] However, if places could be found, I believe it would be a match.[13] George Grenville, to prevent this union and *ingratiate* himself more with the Duke, went to him the instant he came to town, and kept him above four hours; the consequence of which was that the Duke forbid all his people the next morning to oppose.[14] This will not content you,—why then, I believe the credit of the ministry at that House is very near at an end.[15] The Duchess is strong for Lord Chatham, and a person[16] who wants to come in but who does not care to leave Grenville for nothing is gone out of town and out of humour. If no bargain ensues, I suppose they will hold together a little longer. So much for that part of Opposition. The Duke of Newcastle lives at Court, and is as much at his ease there as ever. His friends declare against hostilities,[17]—

but HW mentions that Temple advanced a similar proposal, presumably in his speech on another proposed amendment (*Mem. Geo. III* ii. 263).

7. 10 Nov. See HW to Mann 13 Nov. 1766; *Mem. Geo. III* ii. 262.

8. HW makes a similar comment in *Mem. Geo. III* ii. 263. See also *Grenville Papers* iii. 383.

9. Robert Nugent (ca 1702–88), cr. (1767) Vct Clare and (1776) E. Nugent; first lord of trade 1766–8.

10. Bedford's diary of the negotiation mentions only Northington as being instrumental in the mediation, but it was widely reported that Nugent had taken a prominent part (John, 4th D. of Bedford, *Correspondence*, 1842–6, iii. 348–9; *Grenville Papers* iii. 382). For further details, see Brooke, op. cit. 38–42.

11. Three, on 24 and 31 Oct. and 1 Nov. (Bedford, op. cit. iii. 349–53).

12. 'Employments of magnitude' for Gower, Weymouth, and Rigby; the Garter for Marlborough; a peerage for Thomas

Brand; and hints of 'other applications' which would have to be considered (ibid. iii. 351; Brooke, op. cit. 40).

13. Bedford had the same impression (Bedford, op. cit. iii. 353).

14. Grenville saw Bedford the night of his arrival in town, 9 Nov., and informed him he intended to oppose the Address. Bedford replied that neither he nor his friends intended to oppose it (ibid. iii. 353–4; *Grenville Papers* iii. 381).

15. HW apparently means that Bedford's followers had ceased to defend Grenville's ministry of 1763–5, although they had been members of it.

16. Not identified.

17. Burke explained the Rockingham position at about this time: 'The consideration that a large majority of our friends were in place, and none but our worst enemies in opposition, that everything would go to pieces if we fell out with the one, or joined with the other, and that Lord Bute's game could not be

and so the Duke of Richmond is going out of town.[18] This is the single point on which I am concerned. Lord Temple goes in two days, till after Christmas. The poor Speaker will be the martyr of all this, who must sit tête-à-tête with George Grenville and hear him debate till midnight, for the latter will persist, like Dr Swift, to read prayers to his dearly beloved Roger.[19]

I am very glad I can tell you something that will give Lady Holland pleasure, and which as yet is a great secret. A patent of Duke is drawing for Lord Kildare[20]: Lord Bristol[21] obtained it, intending to guide by that interest.

I don't know a tittle of news more: of public, there is no probability till after Christmas.[22] The newspapers themselves have done with politics. Lord Temple just crawls about Almon's[23] window, in the shape of an autumnal fly[24] that a child could crush: and in the City I think there are East Indian pamphlets,[25] but I don't read what

more effectually played than by distressing even the administration which he made [determined the Rockinghams to attend the pre-session government meeting]. . . . However this support is entirely voluntary, and neither expresses nor implies any contract, but will I suppose be more or less vigorous, as my Lord Chatham shows himself better or worse inclined to the party' (Burke, op. cit. 277–8).

18. He intended to go on 19 Nov. (*Mem. Geo. III* ii. 265).

19. Swift, having been appointed to the living of Laracor, 'gave public notice to his parishioners, that he would read prayers on every Wednesday and Friday. Upon the subsequent Wednesday the bell was rung, and the Rector attended in his desk, when having sat for some time, and finding the congregation to consist only of himself, and his clerk Roger, he began with great composure and gravity, but with a turn peculiar to himself, *"Dearly beloved Roger, the Scripture moveth you and me in sundry places,"* and then proceeded regularly through the whole service' (John Boyle, 5th Earl of Cork and Orrery, *Remarks on the Life and Writings of Jonathan Swift*, 1752, pp. 31–2). HW's copy is listed in the MS catalogue of his library with the press-mark A.4.18, but it does not appear in

the SH sale catalogue (Hazen, *Cat. of HW's Lib.*, No. 43).

20. Lady Holland's brother-in-law.

21. Lord Lieutenant of Ireland since 26 Sept. The dukedom had been promised to Kildare, when he was made a Marquess in 1761, on the first creation of a duke in England or Ireland outside the royal family (Bedford, op. cit. iii. 5; HW to Mann 3 March 1761, MANN v. 485 and n. 10). When Northumberland and Cardigan were made dukes in October 1766 (the latter as Duke of Montagu) Kildare had demanded the fulfilment of the promise (*post* 15 Aug., 16 Aug. 1767).

22. Chatham's decision a few days later to dismiss Lord Edgcumbe, followed by the resignation of most of the remaining members of the Rockingham group in the administration on the 27th and 28th of November, provided plenty of news before Christmas.

23. The bookseller in Piccadilly; see *ante* 19 July 1766, n. 5.

24. Temple's pamphlet *An Inquiry into the Conduct of a late Rt Hon. Commoner*, printed for J. Almon. On the title-page of his copy (now WSL), HW has written 'supposed to be written by Lord Temple or by his direction' and, below the imprint, 'August 7th 1766' (Hazen, *Cat. of HW's Lib.*, No. 1609, vol. 15).

25. The Cabinet Council on 28 Aug.

I don't understand. When Charles Townshend is rechosen,[26] I shall go [to] the House again. Adieu! my dear Lord; I hope your whole caravan will assemble safely at Naples.

Yours ever,

Hor. Walpole

While Selwyn was in Paris in the autumn of 1766, 'Gilly' Williams kept him fully informed of HW's activities:

'Horry unluckily left this place [Bath] before I came. He is certainly better, though not in good humour; that, I think, is out of the reach of politics to occasion. He has wrote a pretty little piece on the Patagonians. When I go to town, if I can wrap it up within the compass of a letter, I'll send it to you' (Williams to Selwyn 1 Nov. 1766, Jesse, *Selwyn* ii. 61).

'Horry Walpole is quite recovered, and in tolerable humour. He says they have castrated his letter to Hume, and spoiled it. If you have read his Patagonians, I am sure you will be pleased with it' (Williams to Selwyn 11 Nov. 1766, ibid. ii. 65–6).

'I called this morning on Horry. Lord Hertford and the *beau Richard* were with him, so I had not that freedom of conversation which a tête-à-tête would have afforded. They have translated his letters. I told him you liked his Patagonians, and that half Paris were mad after it, though probably neither you nor they have read it' (Williams to Selwyn 18 Nov. [1766], ibid. ii. 73–4).

'What the deuce! do you read Horry Walpole's sterling wit in a French translation? We like it here: but *bobbing for whales* is such a characteristic of his style, that it would be impossible not to know him by it; he is in good health and spirits; no minister, but near the throne from his connection' (Williams to Selwyn 25 Nov. 1766, ibid. ii. 86–7).

'Horry Walpole is in rapture with an apposite application of a passage in relation to David Hume and Rousseau. Tell her [?Mme du Deffand] he talks of nothing else, and that about February he will make another meal in her bedroom' (Williams to Selwyn 2 Dec. [1766], ibid. ii. 91–2).

'Horry Walpole is more violent, I think, for the present arrangement than for any I have yet seen. He is forever abusing the white Cavendishes, who are whispering in every corner of White's, and declare their intention

advised the Chairman of the East India Company that Parliament would inquire into the state of their recent acquisitions in Bengal, but no definite plan had yet been forthcoming (*Mem. Geo. III* ii.

278). The hint of an inquiry produced an outburst of pamphlets.

26. He had vacated his seat for Harwich on becoming chancellor of the Exchequer; he was rechosen on 17 Nov.

of storming the Closet in a few months' (Williams to Selwyn 5 Dec. [1766], ibid. ii. 97).

'Horry Walpole is in a paper war about Rousseau and the King of Prussia's letter. There is one of the pamphlets that calls him (Horry) a "prince of cockle-shells," which I believe will hurt him more than a grave confutation' (Williams to Selwyn 26 Dec. [1766], ibid. ii. 120).

'Horry Walpole is lost in loo and politics. It is this day Conway, and the next Chatham, and he is behind them both alternately at the opera. I thought he would have been more regular in his correspondence with you, as he intends passing the next spring in that very round of foreign ecstasy which you so rapturously describe' (Williams to Selwyn 30 Dec. [1766], ibid. ii. 123).

To Selwyn, 1767

Missing; it was sold Anderson Galleries 19 April 1904 (John H. V. Arnold sale) lot 768 to an unnamed purchaser. Described as 'A.L.S. (initials), 2 pp. 4 to, 1767, to George Selwyn, giving the court and political gossip of the day.'

From Holland, January 1767

Missing; written from Naples.

To Holland, Tuesday 10 February 1767

Printed from *Letters to Henry Fox* 273–4; reprinted, Toynbee *Supp.* i. 149–51.

Arlington Street, Feb. 10, 1767.

My dear Lord,

YOUR letter to me and all your letters give me great satisfaction, as they assure me your health is so much better.[1] It is a good deal to have got rid of the imputation of two or three horrid dis-

---

1. 'Lord Holland is undoubtedly mended in the main, yet for some days past he has been as low and bad as ever' (Lady Holland to Ds of Leinster 1 Feb. 1767, *Leinster Corr.* i. 495).

orders; and I trust you will find yourself deceived too in the advance of age. Not that I think you will own that so frankly; but I will forgive your telling your friends (in hopes of being indulged in your indolence) that you are grown very old, provided you do not find the real inconveniences of it.

We are here in a most profound calm. Though Lord Chatham has been confined at Bath ever since Christmas, everything goes on in perfect quiet; nay, miraculously quietly, for even George Grenville has given over talking, and scarce goes to the House,—indeed he had talked everybody out of it first, and the last time he divided[2] had but sixteen with him. The Bedfords are not of his number, and somewhat at variance amongst themselves. Lord John[3] is reduced to his favourite empire of about half a dozen. The East India Company are all acquiescence and submission, and have at last given in their terms,[4] which I hear are very satisfactory. Lord Chatham comes in two days,[5] when I suppose that affair will be settled.

George Selwyn is come back from Paris,[6] and Lady Sarah[7] is expected. *L'amende la plus honorable*[8] has been made to her beauty: they opened their eyes and saw nothing like her. She has been exceedingly the fashion, and I dare to say is not spoiled by it.

We have just had a sad number of deaths among the young people. Lady Fortrose[9] died yesterday, but that has long been expected. Lady

2. 27 Jan., on a report presented to the House of Commons on the disposition of troops in America (*Mem. Geo. III* ii. 293–4). The *Journals of the House of Commons* give the division figures as 71–19 (xxxi. 76).

3. Lord John Cavendish.

4. The Company's proposals were submitted to the Treasury on 6 Feb.; they were acceptable to Conway and Townshend who favoured negotiation with the Company, but not to the rest of the Cabinet who followed Chatham's demand for a general inquiry into the Company. To avoid an open rupture between these two factions, the Cabinet agreed on the 14th to refer the proposals back to the Company for further explanation; see L. S. Sutherland, *The East India Company in Eighteenth-Century Politics*, Oxford, 1952, pp. 159–60; John Brooke, *The Chatham Administration 1766–1768*, 1956, pp. 99–101.

5. He collapsed at Marlborough on his

way to London and did not reach town until 2 March (ibid. 101, 110).

6. Selwyn had been in France since mid-October 1765 (Jesse, *Selwyn* ii. 47).

7. Lady Sarah Bunbury went to Paris at the end of Nov. 1766, but was back in London by 22 Feb. 1767 (*Life and Letters of Lady Sarah Lennox*, ed. Countess of Ilchester and Lord Stavordale, 1902, i. 207; Lady Mary Coke, *Letters and Journals*, ed. Home, Edinburgh, 1889–96, i. 152).

8. For their preference of her sister Lady Louisa Conolly (*ante* 7 Sept. 1765). Her sister Lady Holland described her on this trip as being 'vastly liked and much the fashion' (*Leinster Corr.* i. 500).

9. Lady Caroline Stanhope (1747–9 Feb. 1767), m. (1765) Kenneth Mackenzie, cr. (1766) Vct Fortrose and (1771) E. of Seaforth. She died of white lead poisoning; see HW to Mann 13 Feb. 1767 and Montagu ii. 137 and n. 6.

Suffolk,[10] Lord Trevor's[11] daughter, two days ago in her lying-in. Mr Howard,[12] the last remaining hope of the Norfolks, is dead of a putrid fever. He had the measles, and they were thought over; but he was seized violently at eight at night, and died in twelve hours. The title goes to Charles Howard of Greystock,[13] who is mad, is ill with the Duke[14] and Duchess, and has only one cub of a son.[15]

Lord Essex[16] is going to be married to Harriot Bladen;[17] she has twenty thousand pounds at present, and ten more on her father's[18] death. Lord Bristol has proposed himself to, and been refused by Lady Charlotte Tufton[19] and Lady Stawel;[20] but don't speak of this to my Lady Hervey,[21] as she never has to me. She has had a very good winter upon the whole, and is now pretty well.

I think I have exhausted all my news; and in truth there never were less. Pray be so good as to make my compliments to all your company, and to Mr and Mrs Hamilton[22] when you see them. How does my Twickenham neighbour, poor Lady Pococke?[23]

10. For her, see *ante* 28 Sept. 1763, n. 10.

11. Hon. Robert Hampden (until 1754, Trevor) (1706–83) 4th Bn Trevor, 1764; cr. (1776) Vct Hampden.

12. Edward Howard (1744–67), son of the Hon. Philip Howard, eldest son of Lord Thomas Howard, 2d son of 6th D. of Norfolk; nephew of the 9th D. of Norfolk and heir presumptive to the dukedom.

13. Charles Howard (1720–86), of Greystock, Cumberland; 10th D. of Norfolk, 1777; second cousin of the 9th Duke.

14. Edward Howard (1686–1777), 9th D. of Norfolk.

15. Charles Howard (1746–1815), 11th D. of Norfolk, 1786.

16. William Anne Holles Capel (1732–99), 4th E. of Essex.

17. Harriet Bladen (ca 1735–1821), m. (2 Mar. 1767, as his second wife) William Anne Holles Capel, 4th E. of Essex. 'Gilly' Williams described her and her sister as 'two of the best-bred girls I ever saw and infinitely entertaining,' and Lord March called them 'the most agreeable women in London' (Jesse, *Selwyn* ii. 50, 82).

18. Col. Thomas Bladen (ca 1698–1780), of Glastonbury Abbey, Somerset; M.P. Steyning 1727–34; Ashburton 1735–41; deputy governor of Maryland 1742–6 (GM 1780, l. 103; Judd, *Members of Parliament* 123; *Record of Old Westminsters*, ed. G. F. Russell Barker and A. H. Stenning, 1928, i. 95; *Supplementary Volume*, p. 17).

19. Lady Charlotte Tufton (1728–1803), 2d dau. of Sackville Tufton, 7th E. of Thanet. She never married (Collins, *Peerage*, 1812, iii. 446).

20. Mary Stawel (1726–80), m. 1 (1750) Henry Bilson Legge; m. 2 (1768) Wills Hill, 1st E. of Hillsborough; cr. (1760) Bns Stawel, s.j.

21. Mary Lepell (1700–68), m. (1720) John Hervey, styled Lord Hervey, cr. (1733) Bn Hervey of Ickworth; mother of the Earl of Bristol; HW's friend and correspondent.

22. William Hamilton (1730–1803), K.B., 1772; minister at Naples and archaeologist; HW's correspondent; m. (1758) Catherine Barlow (d. 1782).

23. Sophia Drake (d. 1767), dau. of George Drake, 5th son of Sir Francis Drake, 3d Bt of Buckland; m. 1 (1750) Commodore Digby Dent (d. 1761), commissioner of the navy; m. 2 (1763) Admiral Sir George Pocock, K.B. (GM 1750, xx. 428; 1763, xxxiii. 618; 1767, xxxvii. 524; Lady Eliot Drake, *The Family and Heirs of Sir Francis Drake*, 1911, ii. 248, 304 and n.).

The Duke and Duchess of Richmond came to town two days ago, very happy with the success of the Sussex election.[24] Adieu! my dear Lord,

Yours ever,

H.W.

To SELWYN, Thursday 12 March 1767

Printed from a copy by Sir Shane Leslie, Bt, of the MS in the possession (1941) of the Hon. Mrs Clive Pearson, Parham, Sussex. First printed (as 18 March) Toynbee vii. 94–5. The MS was sold Sotheby's 12 March 1903, lot 738 to Maggs; in the possession of Sir Herbert Raphael, Bt, in 1918 (Toynbee *Supp.* ii. 138), who later sold it to Vct Cowdray; bequeathed by him (1927) to his son, the Hon. Clive Pearson.

The transcript of the dateline of this letter, in the absence of the original MS, is uncertain. Mrs Toynbee, in printing the letter for the first time, read the date as 'March 18th,' but her husband, again collating the text with the original, read it as 'March 11th' (*Supp.* ii. 138). The copy from which the letter is printed below reads 'March 15th.' From internal evidence, particularly the last paragraph, the second Toynbee reading seems most likely, though Thursday was 12, not 11, March in 1767.

Thursday, March 11 [12].

Dear Sir,

IN obedience to your orders, I went to your house this morning, and found both the piece of glass and the scalloped pattern, which I carried to Betts's.[1] He had not one like the former, but has promised I shall have an exact one on Saturday or Monday at farthest. I will take care and send it away according to your directions.

I am glad to hear Lord March finds benefit from the waters;[2] pray make my compliments to him, to Raton,[3] and Ratonissa. I wish you had told me anything of Crawford; I am anxious to hear how he does.

24. The Duke's brother, Lord George Henry Lennox (1737–1805), General, was returned as M.P. for Sussex on 3 Feb. 1767 following a by-election caused by the death of John Butler ([Great Britain, Parliament, House of Commons], *Members of Parliament*, 1878, pt ii, p. 131).

1. Thomas Betts, 'At the King's Arms glass shop, Pall Mall' (Sir Ambrose Heal's collection of tradesman's cards);

mentioned in HW to Lady Mary Coke 22 Aug. 1771 and MONTAGU ii. 224.

2. Selwyn was at Bath with March who was 'much out of order' (Jesse, *Selwyn* ii. 149–53).

3. Selwyn's dog. That he was a pug seems to be clear from Reynolds's portrait of Selwyn, reproduced as a frontispiece to S. P. Kerr, *George Selwyn and the Wits*, 1909, in which Raton is sitting on Selwyn's knee.

You will have learnt the terrible accident that has happened to poor Lord Tavistock.[4] The messages one gets today say he has had a good night; but it will be a fortnight at least before his family can have the least assurance of his life. Their distress is increased by being obliged to conceal the greatness of his danger from Lady Tavistock,[5] who is six months gone with child.

I know no other news but politics. The Grenvilles and Rockinghams had conceived high hopes,[6] which have been mightily dashed by the last majority in favour of the Court.[7] The King is so warm[8] and Lord Bute's friends so active, that there can be little doubt but they will weather this storm.[9]

Charles Townshend has entertained us with another interlude: took part against Lord Chatham,[10] declared himself out of place, nobody knew whether turned out or resigning;[11] kept away on a

4. Who had fractured his skull when thrown from his horse 10 March 1767.

5. Lady Elizabeth Keppel (1739–68); she married Tavistock in 1764. Her third son, William, was born 20 Aug. 1767 (Burke's . . . Peerage, 101st edn, ed. L. G. Pine, 1956, p. 183).

6. From their success on 27 Feb. in carrying a reduction of the land tax from four shillings in the pound to three against the government by a vote of 206–188 (Mem. Geo. III ii. 296–302; HW to Mann 2 March 1767; Chatham Corr. iii. 222–4). The Grenvilles did begin to draft a shadow ministry, but the Rockinghams, at least in private, realized that this victory meant little (Grenville Papers iv. 7–8 n. 2; Edmund Burke to Charles O'Hara 28 [Feb. 1767], Edmund Burke, Correspondence, Vol. I, ed. T. W. Copeland, Cambridge, 1958, p. 297; John Brooke, The Chatham Administration 1766–1768, 1956, pp. 107–10). Both Selwyn and HW appear in the division list as voting with the Court minority on the occasion (The Debates and Proceedings of the British House of Commons from 1765 to 1768, 1772, pp. 295, 296).

7. On 9 March, when the government carried Conway's motion for a two-day adjournment of the debate on printing the East India papers by 180 to 147. The Rockingham group, contrary to HW's assumption, were more encouraged by their large numbers in the division than dispirited by their defeat, for they di-

vided 'to show how many would act against the system of the administration, totally independent of the question' and were very pleased with the result (Edmund Burke to Charles O'Hara 14 March 1767, Burke, op. cit. 299; Brooke, op. cit. 115–6).

8. For the King's reaction to the defeat, see George III, Correspondence, ed. Fortescue, 1927–8, i. 455.

9. The Chatham ministry survived this minor crisis unimpaired.

10. On 6 March, when he explained to the House of Commons the differences of opinion in the Cabinet on the negotiation with the East India Company and spoke in favour of a treaty with the Directors on the basis of their latest propositions, though Chatham wanted to wring still further concessions from the Company (Mem. Geo. III ii. 304–5; Edmund Burke to Charles O'Hara 7 March 1767, Burke, op. cit. 298; HW to Mann 8 March 1767; George III, Corr. i. 460; Brooke, op. cit. 111–14).

11. HW elsewhere describes 'the variations of Charles Townshend, who now spoke of himself as turned out, and who only spoke so because he thought himself secure of not being turned out' (Mem. Geo. III ii. 307). Townshend was undoubtedly aware, as others outside the cabinet were, that Chatham had 'exerted every nerve' to get a new and more subservient chancellor of the Exchequer on the day before the debate. Chatham's

great day of his own business,[12] hatched a quarrel with Colonel Barré,[13] returned yesterday to the House, acted as chancellor of the Exchequer, outwent the rest of the ministers,[14] made no mention of Barré, talked of his measures for the rest of the session, and probably dines with Lord Rockingham today and sups with the Duke of Grafton.[15] What he will do next, besides exposing himself, you nor I nor he can tell. Adieu!

Yours ever,

H.W.

To SELWYN, April–May 1767

Printed for the first time from the MS now wsl. The MS was sold by Tregaskis in June 1928 to wsl.

Dated by the visit of the Comte de Chabrillan in England, which lasted from 1 April to late May or very early June (GM 1767, xxxvii. 189; DU DEFFAND i. 306). *Address:* To Mr Selwyn.

Dear George,

IF you do not go to Newmarket[1] on Sunday, will you be kind enough to dine at Strawberry Hill with Messieurs du Châtelet[2] and Chabrillant?[3]

Yours, etc.,

H.W.

failure, together with the more moderate tone towards the East India Company which he adopted in the face of Townshend's and Conway's opposition to his program, explains part of Townshend's vacillation (Edmund Burke to Charles O'Hara 7 March 1767, Burke, loc. cit.; Augustus Henry, 3d D. of Grafton, *Autobiography,* ed. Anson, 1898, pp. 122–4; *Chatham Corr.* iii. 235; Brooke, op. cit. 111–12, 117–21).

12. On 9 March when two important financial resolutions were voted in the Committee of Ways and Means, besides the further debate on the East India Company affair (*The Parliamentary History of England,* ed. William Cobbett and John Wright, 1806–20, xvi. 369). His absence is mentioned in *Mem. Geo. III*

ii. 306, HW to Mann 8 March 1767, and Lady Mary Coke, *Letters and Journals,* ed. Home, Edinburgh, 1889–96, i. 170–1, 173.

13. Isaac Barré (1726–1802), at this time vice-treasurer of Ireland. No further details of his quarrel with Charles Townshend have been found; he had attacked the East India Company in the debate on the 9th (Brooke, op. cit. 115).

14. Presumably in the examination of the chairman and deputy chairman of the East India Company on 11 March; see Brooke, op. cit. 116.

15. That is, dines with the most prominent Opposition leader and sups with the first lord of the Treasury.

———

1. The first meeting in 1767 began on Monday 20 April, the second, on Monday

To Holland, Friday 7 August 1767

Printed from *Letters to Henry Fox* 276–7; reprinted, Toynbee *Supp.* i. 158–9.

Arlington Street, Aug. 7th 1767.

My dear Lord,

THOUGH you have not heard from me so soon as you might expect, I hope you will not disapprove my conduct.[1] I waited till I had made everything easy to the Duke of Grafton; and then I chose to write your request to him,[2] rather than mention it to him by word of mouth, that I might be able to show you his answer,[3] which I will do when I see you. I would send it, if it did not contain some expressions to myself above what I can deserve; but these are the very words of the rest of the answer:—'On the point of your letter, I am vain enough to say that I had previously felt its consequences, without the inconveniences which some foresee, and have not lost sight of the hopes of bringing it to bear.'

You see, my dear Lord, that I was in the right to tell you that you could not want such inconsiderable interest as mine, where your own must necessarily be much greater.[4] I have therefore no merit beyond having stated to the Duke, as strongly as I could, the attention due to you; and I am happy to find that the result is likely to be what you wish.[5] The Duke is not apt to be warm in professions, and I rely much more on what he has said than I should on a positive promise for some men.

11 May (*London Chronicle* 23–25 April, 16–19 May 1767, xxi. 400, 474).

2. Louis-Marie-Florent (1727–93), Comte (Duc 1777) du Châtelet; son of Voltaire's mistress, Mme du Châtelet; French ambassador to England June 1767–1770. Mme du Deffand's letter of 27 March makes it clear that Châtelet and Chabrillan did not leave Paris until 28 March; they reached London on 1 April (DU DEFFAND i. 278; *Répertoire . . . de la Gazette de France*, ed. de Granges de Surgères, 1902–6, i. 704; GM 1767, xxxvii. 189).

3. Jacques-Aimar-Henri de Moreton, Comte de Chabrillan; maréchal-de-camp, 1762 (La Chenaye-Desbois xiv. 556). HW had met him before the middle of May; sometime soon after his return to Paris he described SH to Mme du Deffand

(DU DEFFAND i. 295, 306, where he has been confused with his distant cousin, the Marquis de Chabrillan; see *Répertoire*, op. cit. i. 704).

———

1. Holland had requested HW to apply to Grafton for the grant of his long-coveted earldom (*Mem. Geo. III* iii. 68–9).

2. HW's letter to Grafton is missing.

3. Missing.

4. 'I told Lord Holland I would use all my interest with the Duke of Grafton to oblige him, but that I was not so vain as to think I could obtain the earldom for him, if his own importance could not' (*Mem. Geo. III* iii. 68–9).

5. Lord Holland never received his earldom.

Except the change in Ireland,[6] I think there will be no other at present. Even old Tilbury[7] is to remain, which does not appear to me quite so wise a measure.

Lady Dalkeith[8] is to have a barony; and the green ribband is to be kept for Lord Carlisle[9] till he is of age. George Selwyn has been rummaging the Herald's office for precedents of its being given to men under age, but he has not persuaded the King.[10]

The Duke of Newcastle has sent an express to Woburn, to inform the Duke of Bedford that the Parliament is to be dissolved in October,—but luckily his Grace is in no secrets.[11]

Shall you be in town, I mean at Holland House, before Monday sennight, when I shall set out for Paris?[12] My best compliments to the *Countess*.[13]

Yours ever,

H.W.

From HOLLAND, Friday 14 August 1767

Printed from the MS now WSL. First printed, Toynbee *Supp.* i. 160 n. For the history of the MS see *ante* 22 July 1746.

Dated by HW's letter of 15 Aug., which replies to this.

Address: To the Honourable Hor. Walpole, Esquire, in Arlington Street.

6. Lord Townshend had been nominated to succeed Lord Bristol as Lord Lieutenant of Ireland; he kissed hands for the appointment on 12 Aug. (Collins, *Peerage*, 1812, ii. 478).

7. The Earl of Northington, lord president of the Council, known by the nickname of 'Tom Tilbury' as early as 1764. The name was taken from that of the landlord of the Red Lion Inn at Bagshot (British Museum, *Catalogue of Prints . . . Political and Personal Satires*, 1870–, iv. 689, which see for speculation on the origin of the nickname and other examples of its use). He had expressed a wish to retire in the spring of 1767 but at the King's request remained in office until December.

8. Lady Caroline Campbell (1717–94), m. 1 (1742) Francis Scott, styled E. of Dalkeith; m. 2 (1755) Hon. Charles Townshend; cr. (19 Aug. 1767) Bns Greenwich, s.j. She and her husband had

wanted the peerage for a long time; see Brooke, op. cit. 33–4.

9. Frederick Howard (1748–1825), 5th E. of Carlisle. He was elected Knight of the Thistle 23 Dec. 1767 and installed at Turin 27 Feb. 1768.

10. Selwyn's devotion to Carlisle is shown in the hundreds of letters he wrote him that have been printed from the MSS of the Earl of Carlisle at Castle Howard (Hist. MSS Comm., 15th Report, App. vi).

11. An allusion to recent negotiations for a comprehensive administration, which broke down, in part, through the failure of the Rockingham and Bedford factions to agree on details; Newcastle had favoured more concessions to the Bedfords; see Brooke, op. cit. 295–7.

12. HW left London for Paris on 20 Aug. ('Paris Journals,' DU DEFFAND v. 315).

13. I.e., Lady Holland.

H[olland] H[ouse], Friday Night.

Dear Sir,

THE Duke[1] may have seen the K[ing] today; you may persuade him to see him on the affair on Sunday. So I beg you to write, however late, to my house in Piccadilly tomorrow night. I'll take care to have it before I attempt to go to sleep. I find, I wish, very much indeed, to be out of suspense. Either the nothing the Marquis of Ormond gave the Irishman,[2] or what I shall like much better, soon. You cannot be sorry for my impatience about what you so kindly interest yourself in. Remember my advice not to tell the Duke that silly able man's foolish behaviour.[3]

You know my going to Kingsgate or not depends on what you tell me.

Your ever obliged, at all events,

HOLLAND

To HOLLAND, Saturday 15 August 1767

Printed from *Letters to Henry Fox* 277–8; reprinted, Toynbee *Supp.* i. 160–1.

[Arlington St.], Aug. 15, 1767.

I AM but this instant arrived, and not to keep your servant, will write but three words. I took the D[uke] of Gr[afton] aside after dinner, and told him how much you was obliged to him for what he had said in the letter to me. He said, 'I am sure I shall be able to do it at the end of the session, and I know that will content him.' I replied, 'I beg your Grace's pardon, he told me but last night how earnestly he wished to have it done before he goes into the country on Monday, that he may not be obliged in his state of health to go and come two hundred miles to kiss hands.' 'Yes,' said the Duke, 'he said so to me, but I am sure he will be satisfied with a certain promise of its being done at the end of the session. There is nothing so difficult to be obtained from the King as elevation; and I know from the best authority that when Lord Bute could do most with the King, he could not get the dukedom for Lord Cardigan.'[1]

1. Grafton.
2. Allusion not found.
3. Not explained.

1. George Brudenell (after 1749, Montagu) (1712–90), 4th E. of Cardigan; cr. (1766) D. of Montagu. When Cardigan

I am sorry, my dear Lord, I could procure no more immediate promise; but from the Duke's heartiness for you, I am convinced it stops solely at the King, and yet I trust you will satisfy yourself with this assurance.

I am etc.,

H. Walpole

From HOLLAND, Sunday 16 August 1767

Printed from the MS, not in Holland's hand, now WSL. First printed, Toynbee *Supp.* i. 161 n. For the history of the MS see *ante* 22 July 1746.
Address: To the Honourable Hor. Walpole, Esquire, in Arlington Street.

H[olland] H[ouse], August the 16, 1767.

Dear Sir,

I AM very sensible (and very sorry to know) where the difficulty lies; and feel my obligation to the Duke of Grafton, for what he gets over of it. I am infinitely obliged to him, and indeed Mr Walpole, never will forget it. But may I not hope his Grace will get leave to write to me in the King's name what he told you? Till then I have nothing to trust to (especially as to the chief point, the time) if his Grace should not choose to be then about Court. The King, I am told, sent to the D[uke] of B[edford] to know whether the promise claimed by the Duke of Leinster,[1] was as he stated it, before H. M. would allow it. Luckily, the Duke of Leinster had a letter wrote by the Duke of Bedford, containing it.[2] My dear Lady Holland bids me be satisfied if I get this, and will do everything she can to make me so. Instead of thinking (if I can help it) of what I have to plead with the King for more, I'll think how little plea I have with the Duke of Grafton for this. But I am a weak old man, sensible to the jeers and taunts of Rigby etc. (some of which I heard but last week)[3] which are still more severe upon the King than me; I am only laughed at. I am ashamed of this, but I can't help it.

requested a dukedom in 1760 or 1761, all that he obtained was a promise of one whenever any were created outside the royal family (George III, *Correspondence*, ed. Fortescue, 1927–8, i. 399).

1. For Leinster's dukedom, see *ante* 14 Nov. 1766, n. 21.

2. Printed in John, 4th D. of Bedford, *Correspondence*, 1842–6, iii. 5.

3. Presumably Rigby's 'jeers and taunts' concerned Holland's interview with the King on 22 July (Ilchester, *Henry Fox* ii. 318).

We don't go till Tuesday, Lady Holland hopes to see you for she will thank you, and extremely too, for your part in this matter. By *a certain promise of its being done at the end of the sessions,* I may suppose I am to be promised to take my seat as an Earl, in the next sessions, if but the last day of it. I'll come from wherever I may be on purpose.

Good God! That Mr Grenville should have found it so easy to disgrace me[4] (which you know the Duchess of Bedford hoped would kill me)[5] and that, after two years disgrace it should be so difficult to do what I now ask! But my obligation to the Duke of Grafton is the greater.

Adieu, my dear Sir. Adieu!

Yours,

H——

From HOLLAND, ca Monday 17 August 1767

Printed for the first time from a copy by WSL of the MS in the possession of the Earl of Ilchester (Holland House MSS, Vol. XII, 2649).

Dated from the statement in the previous letter that the Hollands intended to leave London on Tuesday, 18 Aug. Holland is obviously replying to a suggestion by HW that he ask Grafton directly for the letter he mentioned in his letter to HW 16 Aug.

Address: To the Honourable Hor. Walpole, Esquire, in Arlington Street.

Dear Hory,

I DON'T wait on the D[uke] of Gr[afton] because I think he would do it now if he could, and I never loved to tease anybody that I thought wished me well (as you have taught me to think he does). I go, then, content with what his Grace told you. He was sure he could obtain for me, a *certain assurance of having it at the end of the sessions.* Mention this at your leisure, dear Sir, and get the D[uke] of Gr[afton], when he may, to write me such assurance. You may give him that of my good wishes, and of all those who in any degree have any regard for,

Yours ever,

HOLLAND

4. By securing his dismissal in May 1765; see *ante* 28 May 1765.

5. The Duchess's comments to this effect are discussed *ante* 28 May 1765.

To Selwyn, Friday 16 October 1767

Printed from the MS now wsl. First printed, Jesse, *Selwyn* ii. 188–90; reprinted Cunningham v. 68–9; Toynbee vii. 137–9. The MS was purchased from Mr T. E. O'Callaghan of New York by the Seven Gables Bookshop for wsl in Dec. 1960.

Address: À Monsieur, Monsieur Selwyn, à l'Hôtel du Duc de York, Rue Jacob, Faubourg St-Germain, à Paris.

Arlington Street, Oct. 16, 1767.

THANK you, I am as well as anybody can be that has been drowned from above and below, that was sick to death for eight hours, with the additional mortification of finding himself not invulnerable. In short, I had every affliction from my passage,[1] except in not catching cold, so that on that side I am still first cousin to Hercules.

I find London as empty as possible, and politics quite asleep—I mean in town. In the counties they are all mad about elections. The Duke of Portland, they say, carried thirty thousand pounds to Carlisle,[2] and it is all gone already. Lord Clive[3] is going before his money, and not likely to live three months.[4]

Lady Bolinbroke has declared she will come into waiting on Sunday sennight—but as the Queen is likely to be brought to bed before that time,[5] this may be only a bravade. The report is, that she intends to acknowledge all my Lord can desire.[6]

I found Lord Holland most remarkably mended in his health.[7] Lady Holland is set out today,[8] and he follows her tomorrow. I beg

1. HW had returned to London from Paris on 12 Oct. ('Paris Journals,' du Deffand v. 324; Montagu ii. 250–1).

2. Where he was engaged in a 'Homeric' contest for political control against Sir James Lowther. The figure is exaggerated; Portland's total expenditure in 1767 and 1768 for both the Carlisle and Cumberland elections was only about £20,000, but even this permanently damaged the Duke's finances (Brian Bonsal, *Sir James Lowther and Cumberland and Westmoreland Elections 1754–1775*, Manchester, 1960, pp. 104–5; A.S. Turberville, *A History of Welbeck Abbey and Its Owners*, 1938–9, ii. 103–4).

3. Robert Clive (1725–74), cr. (1762) Bn Clive; M.P. St Michael 1754–5, Shrewsbury 1761–74.

4. Clive had returned to England from India in July 1767 because of ill-health;

he had had a particularly bad seizure 'accompanied by excruciating pain' at Birmingham in early October (Sir George Forrest, *Life of Lord Clive*, 1918, ii. 345, 355–6).

5. Her fifth child, Edward Augustus (1767–1820), D. of Kent, was born 2 Nov.

6. I.e., that she was guilty of *crim. con.* with Topham Beauclerk, which would give Lord Bolingbroke grounds for divorce.

7. His wife described him as 'now as well as he has been for years' on 19 Sept. and as 'vastly well' on 8 Oct. (*Leinster Corr.* i. 520, 521). HW had called on the Hollands the night before (Lady Mary Coke, *Letters and Journals*, ed. Home, 1889–96, Edinburgh, ii. 142).

8. For Paris and, eventually, Nice, where they spent the winter because of

you will tell the Marquise de Broglie[9] (whom you will see at the President's)[10] that Lord Holland carries her a box of pimpernel seed, and will leave it at Monsieur Panchaud's,[11] whither she must send for it. I hope you will be so good as not to forget this; nor another little commission, which is to ask Madame Geoffrin where Monsieur Guibert,[12] the King's carver lives, and then to send him a guinea,[12a] for a drawing he made for me, which I will deduct from the lottery tickets[13] which I have bought for you at twelve pounds seventeen and sixpence apiece. The numbers are, 17,574, on which I have written your name and Madame de Bentheim's, and 26,442, on which I have written Wiart's.[14]

I have twice called on my Lady Townshend, but missed her; I am now going to her by appointment.

Pray tell Lord Carlisle[15] that I delivered his letters and parcels. Say a great deal for me to Madame du Deffand and Lord March, who I need not say are what I left best at Paris. Don't stay for more hurricanes and bad weather, but come away the first fine day.[16] Adieu!

Yours ever,

H.W.

Selwyn sent his opinion of HW's Historic Doubts on . . . Richard III *to Lord Carlisle, 2 February 1768:*

'Mr Walpole's book came out yesterday, but I got it from him on Saturday, and my Lord Molyneux carried it for me that morning to Sir

Lord Holland's asthma (*Leinster Corr.* i. 525–6).

9. Théodore - Élisabeth - Catherine de Besenval (d. 1777), m. (1733) Charles-Guillaume-Louis, Marquis de Broglie (*Journal de Paris*, 1777, ii. 4; La Chenaye-Desbois iv. 264).

10. Hénault's, at whose house HW had met her frequently during his visits to Paris ('Paris Journals,' DU DEFFAND v. 297–332 *passim*).

11. Probably Isaac Panchaud (1726–89), Paris banker (DU DEFFAND iv. 136 n. 7).

12. Honoré-Jean Guibert (ca 1720–91), woodcarver; brother-in-law of Joseph Vernet, the painter; 'sculpteur ordinaire des bâtiments du roi' and responsible for much of the carving executed in the royal palaces after 1760 (Emmanuel Bénézit, *Dictionnaire . . . des peintres, sculpteurs, dessinateurs et graveurs,*

1948–55, iv. 493; Ulrich Thieme and Felix Becker, *Allgemeines Lexikon der Bildenden Künstler*, Leipzig, 1907–50, xv. 269; Stanislas Lami, *Dictionnaire des sculpteurs de l'école française au dix-huitième siècle*, 1910–11, i. 392–4).

12a. HW has written 'louis' above 'guinea.'

13. For a government lottery, established by an act of Parliament in April; tickets were issued at £10, but during the middle of October were quoted at about the price HW paid for them; drawings for the prizes began 16 Nov. (GM 1767, xxxvii. 189, 526, 560).

14. Jean-François Wiart, Mme du Deffand's secretary and valet-de-chambre.

15. Selwyn was in Paris with Carlisle, who was just beginning his Grand Tour.

16. Selwyn left Paris 12 Nov. (DU DEFFAND i. 376).

John Lamb[er]t to be forwarded to your Lordship immediately. I'm confident that it will entertain you much, and, what is more extraordinary, convince you; because I have that good opinion of your understanding as not to think that ages and numbers can sanctify falsehood, and that such is your love of truth as to be glad to find it, although at the expense of quitting the prejudice of your whole precedent life. I will not forestall your judgment by saying anything more of this book, but only wish it may afford as much entertainment as it has me. This historic doubter dined with me yesterday, Williams, Lord March, Cadogan, and Fanshaw, *qui m'a demandé à dîner,* at the House.

'Horry seemed mightily pleased with the success which his new book has met with; nobody cavils at anything, but here and there an expression; his hypothesis is approved of from the most reasonable conjectures, and the most indisputable authorities. I would have had Bully [Lord Bolingbroke to] have dined with us. . . . I told him, that if he would pay his court to Horry he might give him a lick of his *vernis,* that would do his reputation no harm' (Hist. MSS Comm., 15th Report, App. vi, *Carlisle MSS,* 1897, pp. 235–6).

Carlisle, however, was skeptical:

'I have not yet received Mr Walpole's book. The Emperor Nero's character wants a little whitewashing, and so does Mrs Brownrigg's, who was hanged for murdering her apprentices the other day. I hope he will undertake them next, as they seem, next to his hero, to want it the most' (Carlisle to Selwyn 5 March 1768, Jesse, *Selwyn* ii. 286).

To Selwyn, Monday ?1768

Printed from a photostat of the MS in the possession of the Carl H. Pforzheimer Library of New York. First printed, Toynbee *Supp.* i. 175. For the history of the MS see *ante* 2 Oct. 1757 *bis.*

Dated approximately by Mme du Deffand to HW 3 March 1768, in which she consents to Selwyn's having a copy of her portrait (du Deffand ii. 35).

Address: To G. A. Selwyn, Esq.

Monday evening.

I WISH you would call on me any time tomorrow between twelve and two: I have got the two copies of Madame du Deffand's picture,[1] and you shall choose which you will.

1. These copies were after a water-colour sketch by Louis Carrogis (1717–1806), called Carmontelle, made in the autumn of 1767 for HW (du Deffand i. 392 n. 4).

To HOLLAND, Tuesday 30 August 1768

Printed from *Letters to Henry Fox* 284–5; reprinted, Toynbee *Supp.* i. 174.

Strawberry Hill, Aug. 30th 1768.

AFTER having looked so often to no purpose for the enclosed paper,[1] I found it last night by accident when I was not looking for it. I send it to you, my dear Lord, just as I found it, endorsed by yourself, and only half a sheet; the other half, if I recollect rightly, you had torn off yourself. I am exceedingly glad to have found it; though I give you my word I had twice in the summer looked, as I thought, at every single paper in the writing-box where I lighted upon it last night, as I was emptying the box against my carrying it with me today when I am going into Warwickshire and Yorkshire.[2] I shall be here or in town in a fortnight, if you have any commands for me. The best thing you can tell me, is, that you are quite well.

I passed a whole day last week with my Lady Hervey at Mr Bateman's,[3] and think I have not seen her look better for some years.[4] Her son Augustus, for fear the town should want entertainment next winter, intends to serve up some very old stories for their amusement.[5]

I am, my dear Lord,

Your faithful humble servant,

HOR. WALPOLE

To SELWYN, Thursday ?12 April 1770

Printed from the MS now WSL. First printed, Jesse, *Selwyn* ii. 392; reprinted, Toynbee vii. 374–5. The MS was sold Sotheby's 21 Aug. 1872, lot 53 to Harvey; acquired from Sotheran about 1928 by WSL.

Tentatively dated on the possibility that it was written immediately after the

1. Missing.
2. HW's account of this tour is printed in his 'Journals of Visits to Country Seats,' *Walpole Society*, 1927–8, xvi. 62–7.
3. Richard Bateman (ca 1705–73); see HW to Cole 9 March 1765, COLE i. 90 n. 11. Lady Hervey frequently visited him at Old Windsor (T. E. Harwood, *Windsor Old and New*, 1929, pp. 326–9).
4. Lady Hervey was dying; she had been

carried to London on 29 Aug. and died there on 2 Sept. (D. M. Stuart, *Molly Lepell, Lady Hervey*, 1936, pp. 340–1).
5. Augustus Hervey was preparing to divorce his 'secret' wife, Elizabeth Chudleigh (ca 1720–88), later the bigamous 'Duchess of Kingston.' For the dénouement of the affair, see HW to Mann 28 Feb. 1769.

second order for Matthew Kennedy's execution, 11 April 1770 (*Annual Register*, 1770, p. 91).

Thursday morning.

Dear George,

AFTER you was gone last night, I heard it whispered about the room that a bad representation had been made at the Q[ueen]'s House against the unhappy young man.[1] Don't mention this, as it might do hurt; but try privately, without talking of it, if you cannot get some of the ladies to mention the cruelty of the case—or what do you think of a hint by the German women,[2] if you can get at them?

Yours etc.,

H.W.

To Selwyn, Monday 9 September 1771

Printed from Jesse, *Selwyn* iii. 14–15; reprinted, Cunningham v. 331; Toynbee viii. 79–80.

Strawberry Hill, Sept. 9, 1771.

WHO would ever have thought that Raton and Rosette[1] would be talked of for one another?[2] But neither innocence nor age

1. Matthew Kennedy, a young Irishman, who, together with his brother Patrick, had been condemned to death on 23 Feb. 1770 for the murder of a watchman on Westminster Bridge. Their sister was kept by 'two young men of quality,' friends of Selwyn, who therefore interested himself in securing a pardon for the brothers. The date of his first intervention is unknown, but both brothers were temporarily reprieved on 26 Feb. and then pardoned, 22 March, on condition of being transported for life. For some reason this pardon was revoked and Matthew Kennedy was again ordered for execution on 11 April, though his brother was again reprieved. Once again Selwyn moved in, appealed directly to the King, and again got Matthew pardoned on condition of transportation. Kennedy was actually on a ship for America when Horne Tooke adopted the case

as a political weapon, got the watchman's widow to appeal against the pardon, and begin the trial over again. The widow was finally bought off for £350 and the brothers eventually transported in April 1771. For the case see *Mem. Geo. III* iv. 110–12; *Annual Register*, 1770, pp. 74–6, 84, 91, 92, 103, 109, 118, 161; Jesse, *Selwyn* ii. 384–92). The exact date of the incident mentioned in this letter is uncertain, but the day after the second order for execution seems possible.

2. The Queen's German attendants, Elizabeth Juliana Schwellenberg (or Schwellenbergen) (ca 1728–97), the domineering and supposedly influential keeper of the Robes (GM 1797, lxvii pt i. 261–2); and Mrs Hagerdorn (fl. 1761–86), also keeper of the Robes (Mason ii. 35 n. 31).

———

1. HW's spaniel.
2. According to Jesse, *Selwyn* iii. 13–4,

are secure! People say that there never is a smoke without some
fire: here is a striking proof to the contrary. Only think of the poor
dear souls having a comic opera made upon their loves! Rosette is
so shocked that she insists upon Raton's posting to Paris, and breaking the poet's bones; *sauf à les ronger après*. If he is a *preux chevalier*,
he will vindicate her character, *d'une manière éclatante*. Do not tell
me that you are lying-in and cannot spare him; I am sure you are so
fond of your little girl,[3] that you will not miss him.

Have you heard the last adventure of the *fiancée du Roi de
Garbe*?[4] She was seven years[5] and a half at sea; the captain of the
packet-boat is tall, comely enough, and a very shark on such an
occasion. He snapped her up at once as voraciously as she did John
Harding.[6] They passed a week together at Calais, and he then consigned her over to a marching regiment at Ardres.[7] Alfieri[8] told this

---

HW enclosed in this letter a copy of the
Journal des spectacles for 28 Aug. 1771,
which advertised, under *La Comédie
italienne* in Paris, 'Raton et Rosette,
parodie rémise au théâtre, avec ses
agréments.' HW had left Paris 2 Sept.
and reached London on the 6th (DU
DEFFAND v. 342).

3. Lady Isabella Caroline Howard (3
Sept. 1771–1848), eldest dau. of 5th E.
of Carlisle, m. (1789) John Campbell,
cr. (1796) Bn Cawdor. Selwyn was at
Castle Howard for her birth (Jesse,
Selwyn iii. 12–13, 16).

4. A tale by La Fontaine in which *la
fiancée* has several amatory adventures on
her way to marry *le Roi de Garbe*. HW
is referring to the Hon. Penelope Pitt
(1749—after 1792), m. 1 (1766) Edward
Ligonier, 2d Vct Ligonier, cr. (1776) E.
Ligonier; m. 2 (1784) Capt. Smith. Her
first husband was in the process of di-
vorcing her for adultery with Count
Alfieri in the spring of 1771; see below
nn. 6, 8 and HW to Nuneham ?May
1771. Contemporary references to her
frequent affairs are given in GEC vii. 656,
n. *f*.

5. Perhaps a misprint for *hours*.

6. Lord Ligonier's groom, with whom
Lady Ligonier had had an affair that
became public knowledge immediately
after her husband fought a duel with
Alfieri in May 1771. Details are in *The
Macaroni and Theatrical Magazine*, Jan.

1773, pp. 150–2; *The Life of Vittorio Alfi-
eri, Written by Himself*, trans. Sir Henry
McAnally, Lawrence, Kansas, 1953, pp.
108–9; and the *Gazetteer* and *St James's
Chronicle*, *passim*, after 15 May 1771.
None of these accounts mentions the
groom's name, but a passage in [William
Combe], *The Diabo-Lady: or a Match in
Hell. A Poem Dedicated to the Worst
Woman in Her Majesty's Dominions*, new
edn, 1777, p. 7, together with HW's letter,
supplies an identification:
'The next that rose was wanton [Ligonier]
With front assured, and dressed *en cav-
alier;*
A[lfieri] led her forth, Jack H*** fol-
lowed,
While grooms and jockeys in full chorus
hallooed.'
'Jack H***' is identified in a note as
'a postilion with whom she had her second
[public affair].'

7. The account of Lady Ligonier in
The Macaroni and Theatrical Magazine
concludes: 'After having been *legally*
separated from her Lord, she retired to
Ayre, a northern town in France; where,
instead of washing away her dishonour by the tears of repentance, her passions have taken a more ungovernable
lead; and, if fame is to be given the least
credit to, she has now no less a number of
admirers in her *suite*, than the whole of-
ficerial corps of an Irish brigade' (op. cit.
152). She was certainly behaving in some

story himself to Monsieur Francès,[9] from whom I had it fresh. Alfieri's sentiments, that had resisted so many trials, could not digest this last chapter; he has given her up. I wish, when she has run the gauntlet through all the troops on the road to Paris, she may replace Madame du Barry,[10] and prove *la fiancée du Roi de France.*

Yours ever,

H. WALPOLE

To SELWYN, Wednesday 12 August 1772

Printed from a photostat of the MS in the possession of Mr and Mrs Donald Hyde, Four Oaks Farm, Somerville, New Jersey. First printed, Jesse, *Selwyn* iii. 36–8; reprinted, Cunningham v. 403–4; Toynbee viii. 193–5. The MS was sold Sotheby's 20 May 1880 (George Manners sale) lot 111 to Harvey; in the R. B. Adam Collection, Buffalo, N.Y., by 1904; purchased by Mr and Mrs Hyde in 1948.

York, Aug. 12, 1772.

Dear George,

I LOVE to please you, when it is in my power; and how can I please you more than by commending Castle Howard?[1] for though it is not the house that Jack built, yet you love even the cow with the crumpledy horn that feeds in the meadow that belongs

such manner at Calais in 1772; see Lady Mary Coke, *Letters and Journals,* ed. Home, Edinburgh, 1889–96, iv. 83. An 'extract of a letter from Calais, dated July 24, [1771]' in the *London Chronicle* 30 July–1 Aug. 1771, xxx. 110, mentions that 'Lady L. returned here from England last Friday was a week, and is gone as a boarder into the convent of the Benedictine order at Ardres, nine miles from this place.'

8. Vittorio Alfieri (1749–1803), poet. He devotes two chapters (X and XI) of his autobiography to his affair with Lady Ligonier; see also Emilio Bertana, *Vittorio Alfieri,* 2d edn, Turin, 1904, pp. 75–85.

9. Jacques Batailhe de Francès (ca 1724–88), diplomat; French chargé d'affaires in London with character of minister plenipotentiary, 1769 (*Intermédiaire des chercheurs et curieux,* 1906, liv. 107;

London Chronicle 13–15 June 1769, xxv. 566; *Répertoire . . . de la Gazette de France,* ed. de Granges de Surgères, 1902–6, ii. 474). He had called on HW in Paris on 3 Aug. ('Paris Journals,' DU DEFFAND v. 337).

10. Jeanne Bécu (1743–93), m. (1768) Guillaume, Comte du Barry; mistress of Louis XV.

———

1. The seat of the Earl of Carlisle near Malton, Yorks, which HW had visited that day; see his 'Journals of Visits to Country Seats,' *Walpole Society,* 1927–8, xvi. 72–3. Of the many accounts of Castle Howard, see especially H. A. Tipping and Christopher Hussey, *English Homes. Period IV. Vol. II. The Work of Sir John Vanbrugh and His School 1699–1736,* 1928, pp. 1–61.

to the house that Jack's grandfather² built. Indeed I can say with exact truth that I never was so agreeably astonished in my days, as with the first vision of the whole place.³ I had heard of Vanbrugh,⁴ and how Sir Thomas Robinson⁵ and he stood spitting and swearing at one another—nay, I had heard of glorious woods—and Lord Strafford⁶ alone had told me I should see one of the finest places in Yorkshire—but nobody, no, not *votre partialité*, as Louis Quatorze would have called you,⁷ had informed me that I should at one view see a palace, a town, a fortified city, temples on high places, woods worthy of being each a metropolis of the Druids, vales connected to hills by other woods, the noblest lawn in the world fenced by half the horizon, and a mausoleum⁷ᵃ that would tempt one to be buried alive— In short, in short, I have seen gigantic places before, but never a sublime one. For the house, Vanbrugh has even shown taste in its extent and cupolas, and has mercifully remitted ponderosity. Sir Thomas's front is beautiful without; and except in one or two spots has not a bad effect, and I think, without much effort of genius or much expense, might be tolerably harmonized with the rest. The spaces within are noble, and were wanted, even the hall being too small— Now I am got into the hall, I must beg when you are in it next, to read Lord Carlisle's verses on Gray,⁸ and then write somewhere,

<hr>

2. Most of Castle Howard was built by Charles Howard (1669–1738), 3d E. of Carlisle, the 5th Earl's grandfather.

3. 'I was infinitely struck and surprised with the first view of Castle Howard from the new road, which is like a terrace opposite to it. The mass of the house, the great inn crowned with a pyramid, the noble woods crowning the hills, the woods that unite the vales to the risings, the Temple, the Mausoleum and the great pyramid and column, set off by a vast lawn and prodigious extent of country, and the park and garden embraced by a wall thick set with towers and that connects the buildings, compose the grandest scene of real magnificence I ever saw' (HW's 'Journals of Visits to Country Seats,' op. cit. 72).

4. Sir John Vanbrugh or Vanburgh (1664–1726), Kt, 1714; dramatist and architect. He built most of Castle Howard, including the famous south façade, between 1701 and his death.

5. Sir Thomas Robinson (ca 1700–77), cr. (1731) Bt; governor of Barbados and amateur architect; son-in-law of the 3d E. of Carlisle. He designed and built the west wing of Castle Howard between 1753 and 1759 in a style out of harmony with Vanbrugh's work.

6. William Wentworth (1722–91), 2d E. of Strafford; HW's friend and correspondent. HW had visited him at Wentworth Castle before going to Castle Howard (HW to Mann 3 Aug. 1772; HW's 'Journals of Visits to Country Seats,' op. cit. 71).

7. As he called Mme de Maintenon *Votre Solidité*.

7a. Designed by Nicholas Hawksmoor.

8. Carlisle's 'Ode upon the Death of Mr Gray,' first published in Carlisle's *Poems*, 1773. HW had evidently seen a private printing of the verses in May 1772 (Mason i. 34–5 and n. 2).

under the story of Phaeton[9] these lines, which I ought to have made extempore, but did not till I was halfway back hither:

> Carlisle, expunge the form of Phaeton;
> Assume the car, and grace it with thy own,
> For Phœbus owns in thee no falling son.

Oh! George, were I such a poet as your friend, and possessed such a Parnassus, I would instantly scratch my name out of the buttery-book at Almack's,[10] be admitted *ad eundem* among the Muses, and save every doit to lay out in making a Helicon, and furnishing my palace.

I found *my* Lord Northampton;[11] his name is on his picture, though they showed me his nephew Suffolk's[12] portrait, who was much fatter, for his. There is a delicious whole-length of Queen Mary[13] with all her folly in her face and her hand, and a thousand other things which I long to talk over with you. When you write to Spa,[14] pray thank Lord Carlisle for the great civilities I received there. The housekeeper showed me and told me everything, and even was so kind as to fetch Rosette a basin of water, which completed the conquest of my heart. Wine I was offered, and fruit was heaped on me, and even dinner was tendered—in short I never passed a day more to my content—I only wanted you, and I should have been as happy as I was at Sceaux[15]—you know my ecstasies when I

9. The hall at Castle Howard was decorated with paintings of the story of Phaeton by Antonio Pellegrini (1674–1741), of Padua. HW describes them as 'without force and now much faded' (HW's 'Journals of Visits to Country Seats,' op. cit. 72; Tipping, op. cit. 18 and plate 23).

10. Carlisle had been almost ruined by involvement in C. J. Fox's gambling exploits; see particularly Lord Ilchester, 'Some Pages Torn from the *Last Journals* of Horace Walpole,' in *Studies in Art and Literature for Belle da Costa Green*, ed. Dorothy Miner, 1954, pp. 454–6.

11. Henry Howard (1540–1614), cr. (1604) E. of Northampton; one of HW's authors in the *Catalogue of Royal and Noble Authors* (*Works* i. 334–40). The portrait at Castle Howard is engraved in Edmund Lodge, *Portraits of Illustrious Personages of Great Britain*, 1835, iv. plate 9, where it is erroneously attributed to Zuccaro.

12. Lord Thomas Howard (1561–1626), cr. (1597) Lord Howard de Walden; cr. (1603) E. of Suffolk. The portrait at Castle Howard is engraved in Lodge, op. cit. iv. plate 20, where it is also erroneously attributed to Zuccaro.

13. 'A very extraordinary whole length, said to be Queen Mary the First, and I think it may be, the features resembling her though not the countenance, which is very singular, vulgar, and expressive of her obstinacy and folly rather than like her other pictures of her sourness. She has a large crucifix in her right hand, and seems to triumph in exalting it; in the other, a sceptre or wand, twisted with leaves' (HW's 'Journals of Visits to Country Seats,' op. cit. 73).

14. No letters from Selwyn to Carlisle in 1772 are printed in Hist. MSS Comm., 15th Report, App. vi, *Carlisle MSS*, 1897.

15. The seat of the Duchesse du Maine which HW had visited on 25 Sept. 1767 with Mme du Deffand and Selwyn ('Paris Journals,' DU DEFFAND v. 322; vi. 114).

am really pleased. By the end of next week I shall be in town, and hope to find you there, that I may satisfy both ourselves with larger details—when I mentioned the attentions paid to me, I am ungrateful to forget the sun, who was complaisance itself, shone all day, gilt an hundred haycocks that were spread over the great lawn, and illuminated the mausoleum during my dinner—and now will you tell me that Lord Carlisle is not nearer related to him than some folks thought? Let me tell you this is much better-authenticated than his Lordship's priority to Howard of Corbie,[16] in which you are mistaken; and so good night!

Yours most cordially,

Hor. Walpole

To Selwyn, ca Monday 5 April 1773

Printed from the MS now wsl. First printed, Toynbee *Supp.* i. 214. The MS was in possession of Dodd and Livingston of New York in 1918; later in possession of John Heise, Syracuse, New York, from whom it was acquired by Mr J. T. Babb who gave it to wsl in Oct. 1933.

Dated approximately by HW to Lady Ossory 3 April 1773: 'You are to be at Strawberry Hill tomorrow sennight [Sunday 11 April].'

Address: To G. A. Selwyn Esq.

LORD and Lady Ossory[1] and some of their court are to dine at Strawberry next Sunday; will you make one of their circle? and shall I say to you, as I do to Crauford, will you come, though you say you will?[2]

In 1775, HW again mentioned to Mme du Deffand 'l'extrême félicité que je sentais avec vous à Sceaux' (ibid. iv. 145).

16. Philip Howard (1730–1810), of Corby Castle, Cumberland. He was descended from Sir Francis Howard, 2d son of Lord William Howard, and younger brother of Sir Philip Howard, ancestor of the Earl of Carlisle. It would appear that Selwyn was correct in asserting Lord Carlisle's priority to Howard of Corby in the line of succession to the dukedom of Norfolk. At this time the descendants of Lord William Howard were fourth in line of succession to the dukedom, being preceded by the Howards of Greystock, the Howards of Glossop, and the Howards, Earls of Suffolk. See the genealogical chart in gec ix, between pp. 612–13.

1. Hon. Anne Liddell (ca 1738–1804), m. 1 (1756), Augustus Henry Fitzroy, 3d D. of Grafton, 1757 (divorced, 1769); m. 2 (1769) John Fitzpatrick, 2d E. of Upper Ossory; HW's friend and correspondent.

2. 'I have asked Mr Crawfurd to meet you, but begged he would refuse me, that I might be sure of his coming' (HW to Lady Ossory 3 April 1773).

To Selwyn, Wednesday 10 August 1774

Printed from Jesse, *Selwyn* iii. 78; reprinted, Cunningham vi. 103; Toynbee ix. 26.

Dated by the references to HW's intended visit to Matson and to James Bruce. *Address:* To George Augustus Selwyn, Esq., at Matson, near Gloucester.

Strawberry Hill, Wednesday, Aug. 10th, at night.

I THINK I shall be with you on Saturday;[1] at least I know that I intend to set out tomorrow and lie at Park Place; but it is so formidable to me to begin a journey, and I have changed my mind so often about this, though I like it so much, that I beg you will not be disappointed if you do not see me. If I were juvenile enough to set off at midnight, and travel all night, you would be sure of me; but folks who do anything eagerly neither know nor care what they do. Sedate me, who deliberate, at least do not determine but on preference; therefore, if I surmount difficulties, I shall at least have some merit with you; and, if I do not, you must allow that the difficulties were prodigious, when they surmounted so much inclination.

In this wavering situation I wish you good night, and hope I shall wake tomorrow as resolute as Hercules or Mr Bruce;[2] but pray do not give me live beef[3] for supper.

Yours ever,

H.W.

1. HW arrived at Matson on Friday, the 12th. 'At night I heard that Mr Walpole was here; I was then at Gloucester; so I hurried home, and have now some person to converse with who speaks my own language. He came yesterday from Lady Ailesbury's and stays with me till Tuesday, and then I hope we shall return to London together' (Selwyn to Carlisle 13 Aug. 1774, Hist. MSS Comm., 15th Report, App. vi, *Carlisle MSS,* 1897, p. 277). HW gives an account of his visit in a letter to Cole on the 15th (Cole i. 340–5), and Selwyn, a few details in another letter to Carlisle (Hist. MSS Comm., op. cit. 278). See also HW's 'Journals of Visits to Country Seats,' *Walpole Society,* 1927–8, xvi. 75–6.

2. James Bruce (1730–94), African

traveller. He had only recently returned to England from his trip to Abyssinia, but his tales of his adventures were rapidly circulated, although they were not published until 1790. HW and Selwyn viewed his stories with scepticism (HW to Mann 10 July 1774; Mason i. 204–5, 250).

3. Bruce created a sensation with his accounts of the fondness of the Abyssinians for raw beef cut from a living creature. The first of his tales that HW mentions is that he 'breakfasted every morning with the Maids of Honour on live oxen'; Bruce later complained of the 'violent outcry' which this story caused in England (HW to Mann 10 July 1774; James Bruce, *Travels to Discover the Source of the Nile,* 2d edn, 1804–5, iv. 477).

To Selwyn, Monday ?December 1774

Printed from Jesse, *Selwyn* iii. 39 (undated); reprinted, Toynbee ix. 113.
Dated tentatively by HW's statement that his attack of the gout in Dec. 1774 settled in his chest, making it difficult and even dangerous for him to talk (HW to Mann 23 Dec. 1774, to Conway 26 Dec. 1774, 31 Dec. 1774).
Address: To G. A. Selwyn, Esq., Chesterfield Street.

Monday night, 9 o'clock.

Dear Sir,

I AM so much enjoined silence, that it is the more necessary for me to speak to *you*. I am utterly incapable of writing to Paris:[1] I have nobody to write for me, and am not allowed to dictate above two or three lines. It would oblige me infinitely if that might be to you, either at the beginning or end of your letter, if you write to-morrow.[2] One at noon, or seven in the evening, are the cleverest[3] hours for me,—but I must not choose.

Yours, etc.

H.W.

To Selwyn, Saturday 8 July 1775

Printed from the MS now wsl. First printed (misdated 15 July), Toynbee *Supp.* i. 257. The MS was in the possession of G. A. Gaskill, Worcester, Mass., in 1918; acquired from his grandson in December 1939 by wsl.
Address: To George Augustus Selwyn, Esq., in Chesterfield Street, Mayfair, London.
Postmark: 10 IY. Free. ISLEWORTH.

Strawberry Hill, July 8th 1775.

Dear Sir,

IF it will suit you to dine at your brother Townshend's[1] next Friday, and it will suit them, I will be in town on Thursday night,

1. To Mme du Deffand. HW's one surviving letter to her at this time (26 Dec.) is not in his or Selwyn's hand.
2. Selwyn's letter is missing. Mme du Deffand mentions a letter from him 4 Dec. 1774 (du Deffand iv. 116).
3. 'Convenient, suitable, agreeable' (OED *sub* clever 8. a).

1. Hon. Thomas Townshend (1701-80), 2d son of 2d Vct Townshend; m. (1730) Albinia Selwyn (ca 1715-39), Selwyn's sister. The projected dinner was apparently to be at Townshend's house, Frognal, between Chislehurst and Sidcup, Kent.

and go thither with you the next morning. Be so good as to send your answer to my house in *Arlington Street* on *Wednesday* evening.

Yours ever,

H. Walpole

From Selwyn, early September 1775

Missing.

To Selwyn, Saturday 16 September 1775

Printed from the MS now wsl. First printed, Jesse, *Selwyn* iii. 102–6; reprinted, Cunningham vi. 257–9; Toynbee ix. 256–8. The MS was sent or given to Edward S. Roscoe of Chalfont St Peter, Bucks, in 1900; sold Hodgson's 22 July 1927, lot 545; sold Sotheby's 4 May 1942, lot 261, to Maggs for wsl.

Address: To George Augustus Selwyn, Esq., in Stanhope Street, Berkeley Square, London.

Paris,[1] Sept. 16, 1775.

MR BRODERICK[2] brought me your letter yesterday, and I told him, as you may be sure, how glad I shall be to be of any use to him.[3] I shall be of little I believe, as his object is to see things not persons.[4] Madame du Deffand would have been more pleased with your message,[5] which I delivered immediately, if she had had greater faith in it—yet when Craufurd and I come so often, how can she doubt her power of attraction? If possible, she is more worth

1. HW had arrived in Paris on 19 Aug. ('Paris Journals,' du Deffand v. 343).

2. Hon. Thomas Brodrick (1756–95), 2d son of 3d Vct Midleton; Selwyn's great-nephew (Collins, *Peerage*, 1812, viii. 474; Jesse, *Selwyn* iii. 100–101; 'Paris Journals,' du Deffand v. 349).

3. Brodrick wrote to Selwyn 18 Sept., 'We lost so little time on the road that we were safely lodged at this house . . . on Thursday night [14 Sept.], and I waited on Mr Horace Walpole and Dr Gem the next morning. The first I found

at home, and was received with great civility and assurances of any services he could do me, in procuring me the sight of anything I wished' (Jesse, *Selwyn* iii. 100).

4. Selwyn had advised him not to seek introduction into society because he did not really understand or speak French (ibid.).

5. Apparently that he would visit her soon; Selwyn, however, did not go to Paris again until April 1778.

visiting than ever; and so far am I from being ashamed of coming hither at my age, that I look on myself as wiser than one of the Magi, when I travel to adore this Star in the East. The Star and I went to the opera last night, and when we came from Madame de la Valiere's[6] at one in the morning, it wanted to drive about the town because it was too early to *set*. To be sure you and I have dedicated our decline to very different occupations! you nurse a little girl of four years old,[7] and I rake with an old woman of fourscore! *N'importe;* we know many sages that take great pains to pass their time with less satisfaction.

We have both one capital mortification, have not you? That a great-granddaughter of Madame de Sévigné,[8] pretends, for it is not certain, that she has been debauched by ancient Richelieu,[9] and half the world thinks that she is more guilty of forgery.[10] The *mémoires* of the two parties[11] are half as voluminous as those of Monsieur de Guines,[12] and more are to appear.

<hr/>

6. Anne-Julie-Françoise de Crussol (1713–93), m. (1732) Louis-César de la Baume le Blanc, Duc de la Vallière.

7. Maria Emily Fagnani (1771–1856), m. (1798) Francis Charles Seymour-Conway, 3d M. of Hertford; 'Mie Mie.' She was legally the dau. of Giacomo, Marchese Fagnani, who had m. (1767) Costanza Brusati (d. 1804) (DU DEFFAND v. 77 n. 2), but in reality probably the dau. of the Marchesa and Lord March. Selwyn virtually adopted her soon after her birth and brought her up except for a brief period in 1778–9; see *post* 7 July 1779, n. 4.

8. Julie de Villeneuve (ca 1731–78), m. (1746) Jules-François de Fauris, Président de Saint-Vincent; her mother was a dau. of Mme de Grignan, Mme de Sévigné's dau. (Maurice Soulié, 'La Présidente de Saint-Vincent' in *Les Œuvres libres*, March 1928, lxxxi. 341–3, 378).

9. The Maréchal-Duc de Richelieu (*ante* 6 Sept. 1757, n. 12).

10. Richelieu had charged Mme de Saint-Vincent with forging his signature to notes-of-hand for 240,000 livres; she had replied with a suit for 300,000 livres damages and the charge of seduction. Richelieu had been instrumental in securing *la présidente's* release from the convent where she had long been con-

fined by her family for infidelity and had contributed to her support before the affair of the 'forged' notes. Although several witnesses in the case attested to the validity of his signature, the court determined in his favour in May 1777. For a full account of the whole affair, see Jean-Bernard Lafon (called Mary-Lafon), *Le Maréchal de Richelieu et Mme de Saint-Vincent*, 1863; and Soulié, op. cit. 341–79.

11. 'Pendant que la procédure suivait son cours, le plaignant et l'accusée inondaient Paris d'un déluge de factums, mémoires justificatifs, vendus chez Mazuel, sur le Pont-Neuf, à l'enseigne de la *Levrette*, et au Palais de Justice chez Rigaut à l'enseigne de la *Fleur de Lys*' (Maurice Soulié, op. cit. 370).

12. Adrien-Louis de Bonnières (1735–1806), Comte and (1776) Duc de Guines; French ambassador to England 1770–6. He was engaged in law-suits against his ex-secretary Barthélemy Tort de la Sonde and others who had used the ambassador's name in conducting secret stock-jobbing operations of their own in England; see HW's *Last Journals*, ed. Steuart, 1910, i. 517–21; DU DEFFAND iv. *passim*; HW to Mann 7 May 1775. As of the date of the present letter at least four *mémoires* in Guines's behalf had been published:

You shall have some royal prints. New fashions in dress, furniture, baubles I have seen none. Feathers are waning, and almost confined to *filles* and foreigners.[13] I found out an Englishwoman at the Opera last night by her being covered with plumes and no rouge, which made her look like a whore in a salivation, so well our countrywomen contrive to display their virtue!

I do not tell you about Monsieur Turgot's[14] regulations and reformations,[15] because you care no more about their *patrie* than your own; but you *shall* hear a bon mot of Madame du Deffand. M. Turgot has begun several reforms, and retracted them: she said, '*Dans le bon vieux temps on reculait pour mieux sauter, au lieu que Monsieur Turgot saute pour mieux reculer!*

Of the House of Harrington, I know as much as you do. Lady Barrymore[16] is here, and my Lord[17] and Lady Harriot[18] are coming: the first is excessively admired.[19] Lady Mary Coke,[20] Harry Grenville and his wife,[21] Craufurd,[22] Lord Coleraine[23] and Lord Dun-

---

Mémoire pour le Comte de Guines . . . contre les sieurs Tort et Roger . . . et le sieur Delpech, [Nov. 1774]; *Réplique pour le Comte de Guines . . . contre le sieur Roger,* [Feb. 1775]; *Réplique pour le Comte de Guines . . . au premier mémoire du sieur Tort,* [March 1775]; *Éclaircissements pour le Comte de Guines. Sur la réponse de M. Gerbier,* [1775]. These totalled nearly 400 pages, to say nothing of the *mémoires* and *contre-mémoires* of the other side.

13. 'The head-dress of the ladies here is still rather ridiculous though much less so than it was; the feathers, though not quite gone, are greatly diminished. Nobody who is reckoned genteel wears more than two, and one of them very small' (Lady Mary Coke, *MS Journals* 8 Aug. 1775).

14. Anne-Robert-Jacques Turgot (1727–81), Baron de l'Aulne, *philosophe*, economist, and statesman; controller-general of finances 1774–6.

15. Since assuming control of the finances, Turgot had been engaged in a determined though virtually fruitless attempt to reform the fiscal structure of France.

16. Lady Amelia Stanhope (1749–80), dau. of 2d E. of Harrington; m. (1767)

Richard Barry, 6th E. of Barrymore. She had arrived in Paris on 27 Aug. HW apparently saw her for the first time there at Mme du Deffand's on 30 Aug. (Lady Mary Coke, op. cit. 27 Aug. 1775; 'Paris Journals,' DU DEFFAND v. 345).

17. William Stanhope (1719–79), 2d E. of Harrington. He and his daughter were still at Spa at this time (Lady Mary Coke, op. cit. 24 Sept. 1775).

18. Lady Harriet Stanhope (1750–81), dau. of 2d E. of Harrington; m. (1776) Hon. Thomas Foley, 2d Bn Foley, 1777.

19. See also HW to Conway 8 Sept. 1775.

20. Lady Mary had been in Paris since 31 July and remained until 28 Sept. (Lady Mary Coke, op. cit. 1 Aug., 27, 30 Sept. 1775).

21. Hon. Henry Grenville (1717–84), English ambassador to Turkey 1761–5; m. (1757) Margaret Banks (d. 1793). They had arrived in Paris about 6 Sept. when HW had dined with them (Lady Mary Coke, op. cit. 7 Sept. 1775; 'Paris Journals,' DU DEFFAND v. 347).

22. He had arrived on or before 12 Sept. ('Paris Journals,' DU DEFFAND v. 348).

23. John Hanger (1743–94), 2d Bn Coleraine.

cannon[24] are here: the latter will carry this letter.[25] There are many
other English, but I did not come hither to get acquaintance of that
sort. Madame du Deffand has recruited her vacancies and given me
enough new French. With one of them you would be delighted, a
Madame de Marchais.[26] She is not perfectly young, has a face like
a Jew pedlar, her person is about four feet, her head about six, and
her coiffure about ten. Her forehead, chin and neck are whiter
than a miller's, and she wears more festoons of natural flowers than
all the *figurantes* at the opera. Her eloquence is still more abundant,
her *attentions* exuberant. She talks volumes, writes folios, I mean in
billets, presides over the Académie, inspires passions, and has not
time enough to heal a quarter of the wounds she gives. She has a
house[27] in a nutshell, that is fuller of invention than a fairy tale;
her bed stands in the middle of the room, because there is no other
space that would hold it, and is surrounded by such a perspective of
looking-glasses, that you may see all that passes on it from the first
antichambre—but you will see her if you come in spring—which
you will not do, unless you bring Mimy, and Raton, and one or two
of Lord Carlisle's children[28]—and that you will be afraid of doing,
for Madame du Deffand has got a favourite dog[29] that will bite all
their noses off, and was very near tearing out one of Lady Barrymore's eyes[30] t'other night. Adieu! I shall see you by the middle of
October.[31]

21st.

Lord Duncannon is not gone, but I can send my letter tomorrow,
and shall.

---

*When Selwyn saw HW shortly after his return from Paris, he found
him 'as peevish as a monkey' (to Carlisle [Oct. 1775], Hist. MSS Comm.,*

24. Frederick Ponsonby (1758–1844),
styled Vct Duncannon 1758–93; 3d E. of
Bessborough, 1793.

25. The letter was carried by a Mr
Morgan instead; see postscript and 'Paris
Journals,' du Deffand v. 396.

26. Élisabeth-Josèphe de la Borde (ca
1725–1808), m. 1 (1747) Gérard Binet,
Baron de Marchais; m. 2 (1781) Charles-
Claude Flahaut, Comte de la Billarderie
d'Angiviller.

27. Where HW supped on 11 Sept.
('Paris Journals,' du Deffand v. 348).

28. Three of Carlisle's nine children
had been born by this time.

29. Tonton, later bequeathed to HW.

30. HW to Conway 8 Sept. 1775 has a
fuller account of this episode.

31. HW arrived in London on 17 Oct.

15th Report, App. vi, *Carlisle MSS*, 1897, p. 298). *His next reference to HW is nearly two years later:*

'I saw Horry W[alpole] yesterday for a few minutes; *his distresses* are, Lord O[rford's] lunacy, and the Duchess of Gloucester's situation if his R. H. dies. . . . I wish these were mine, and I had no other, but we cannot choose our own misfortunes; if we could, there is nobody who would not prefer being concerned for a mad nephew whom they did not care for, or a simple Princess whom they would laugh at, *si l'orgueil ne s'en mêlait pas*' (to Carlisle [early August 1777], ibid. 321).

Carlisle agreed with him:

'Horace Walpole's distress for his royal relations flows from much the same source as Offley's for poor Munchausen, the most ridiculous of affectations. I don't wonder you wish to change afflictions with him' (Carlisle to Selwyn 8 Aug. [1777], Jesse, *Selwyn* iii. 215).

Selwyn was irritated in 1778 by HW's belief that 'Mie Mie's' parents would probably poison him when he followed them to Milan (see post 7 July 1779, n. 4). Selwyn wrote to his niece Mary Townshend:

'I hope that Lady M[idleton] has not been made to believe by Mr W[alpole] that they will poison me. Of all the ideas which ever come into a man's head, who knew the world, and me, I think that was the most absurd; upon any supposition which could have been the foundation of it. But his historic doubts, and his historic certainties, have always appeared to me to have something more singular in them than those of any other person. But the fact is, *il ne parait s'en douter désire, il n'y point de secret impénétrable pour lui*' (15 June [1778], quoted in S. P. Kerr, *George Selwyn and the Wits*, 1909, p. 235).

To Selwyn, Monday 5 July 1779

Printed from a MS copy by the Duchess of St Albans from the MS then (1904) in her possession. First printed, Jesse, *Selwyn* iv. 204–6; reprinted, Cunningham vii. 219–20; Toynbee x. 437–8.

Strawberry Hill, July 5, 1779.

I TAKE the liberty which I know you will forgive, my dear Sir, of troubling you with the enclosed,[1] begging you will add anything that is necessary to the direction, as *par la Hollande* or what-

1. HW's missing letter to Mme du Deffand 4 July 1779 (DU DEFFAND v. 156, 160).

ever else is requisite,[2] and to put it into the post as soon as you receive it. Pray tell me too what is necessary to the direction, and where my maid in town must put in my future letters to Paris, that I may not trouble you any more with them. I fear they will not go so safely and regularly as in the old way, which will vex our good old friend who cannot bear to lose any of her stated occupations.

I have just received a present of four beautiful drawings of Grignan,[3] which far exceed my ideas of its magnificence and charming situation. I had concluded that Madame de Sévigné either from partiality or to please the Seigneur had exaggerated its pomps and command. I long to show them to you and talk them over—and am glad to have anything new that may tempt you hither. Can you tell me if the Duchess of Leinster still goes to Aubigné,[4] and if she does, when: and if she is in London. I shall be much obliged to you for a true account of Lord Bolingbrooke.[5] It is not common curiosity that makes me anxious,[6] though not particularly interested about him nor is he *the husband*[7] I most wish dead.

Yours most sincerely,

H. W.

2. HW had to adopt a new channel for his correspondence with Mme du Deffand since the direct packet-boats between Dover and Calais, which had continued to run despite the war between England and France, had recently been suspended (*Daily Adv.* 29 June 1779).

3. From George Hardinge; see Hardinge to HW 21 June 1779, 1 July 1779; HW to Hardinge 4 July 1779; 'Des. of SH,' *Works* ii. 424. They were sold SH xi. 107 ('Four coloured drawings, views of the Castle of Grignan and of La Roche Courbiere, both in Provence. A present from George Hardinge, Esq.') to Lady Shelley for £2.

4. The French country seat of the Duke of Richmond, the Duchess of Leinster's brother, where the Duchess and her family had lived almost constantly since her second marriage in 1774. In the spring of 1779 she made a visit to England (*Leinster Corr.* ii. p. x, 280), but was already returning to France by the time of this letter (*post* 7 July, 20 July 1779).

5. It had been reported that Lord Bolingbroke was dying of an overdose of laudanum, but HW had heard the day before that he would live (HW to Lady Ossory 6 July 1779).

6. HW was concerned for his Twickenham neighbour, Lady Di Beauclerk, Bolingbroke's divorced wife.

7. Topham Beauclerk, Lady Di's second husband, who treated her badly; see *post* 7 July 1779, n. 5; and 21 Sept. 1779, n. 10.

To Selwyn, Wednesday 7 July 1779

Printed for the first time from a photostat of the MS in the Cely Trevilian Collection in the Society of Antiquaries.

Strawberry Hill, July 7th 1779.

I CAN only answer you, my dear Sir, in your own words and ideas, and it would be difficult indeed ever to find better, that if a friendship of 55 years will not draw me to Matson, what would? but alas! 55 years, though they have not at all lessened my affection for you, have yet left a sediment that clogs all my motions and inclinations. I have been lame for two days this last week, and blind of one eye for four,[1] and my constantly flitting gout deters me from any excursions beyond the power of returning home at night. I was last summer no farther than Ampthill and Park Place;[2] and therefore I dare not promise you a visit, which I have scarce courage to perform. If I have anything to tell you that can make my letters amusing, I shall certainly not spare such trifling pains.

For poor Madame du Deffand, I had long resigned the hope of seeing her again. You have alarmed me terribly about her increasing deafness; the new difficulty of hearing how she goes on, doubles the anxiety. I doubt she will think me guilty of neglect in not writing by the Duchess of Leinster; but Lady Ailesbury had just told me that Mrs Damer's[3] journey was laid aside, and therefore I had concluded the Duchess's was too, at least for some time.

I cannot pretend to judge but on general grounds of your longer or shorter possession of your prize.[4] My opinion is that it will never

1. See HW to Lady Ossory 6 July 1779 for more details of this attack of the gout.

2. HW had been to Park Place and Nuneham in Sept. 1778 (HW to Harcourt 17 Sept., 27 Sept. 1778); he planned to go to Ampthill, but apparently did not.

3. Anne Seymour Conway (1748–1828), dau. of H. S. Conway and Lady Ailesbury; m. (1767) Hon. John Damer. HW and her mother were both mistaken, since she did accompany the Duchess of Leinster. See the following letter and HW to Lady Ailesbury 10 July 1779.

4. Selwyn had finally succeeded in regaining possession of 'Mie Mie' after a two-year struggle. Though the Fagnanis had virtually consigned her to him after her birth, they reclaimed her in the fall of 1777 and took her back to Milan. Selwyn followed them in the spring of 1778, in an effort to persuade them to let him have her again. He succeeded in having her visit him in Paris in the spring of 1779, and, in June, permission was given for him to take her to England. They were never separated again. The story is told, primarily through Selwyn's letters to his niece Mary Townshend, in S. P. Kerr, *George Selwyn and the Wits*, 1909, pp. 203–68. HW's real feeling about

be redemanded—but as the conduct of the parents has been in my eyes inexplicable by any common rules, I may again be mistaken. There is an uniquity in your story that baffles all reasoning. I heartily wish you may be happy in your own way. I think you will: unalterable perseverance to any one point is very apt to be successful.

Lady D.'s case is melancholy indeed.[5] It is patched up for the present; but there is *an affection upon the brain*[6] in both husbands that I believe incurable. It is pity that one is not in as much danger as the other. Adieu! I do not wind up my letter in the old-fashioned way from the obstinacy of age, but because I love to assure you how much I am

Ever yours,

H. Walpole

To Selwyn, Tuesday 20 July 1779

Printed for the first time from a photostat of the MS in the Cely Trevilian Collection in the Society of Antiquaries.

The year is added in another hand; confirmed by the account of the capture of the Duchess of Leinster by the French.

Address: To George Augustus Selwyn, Esq., at Matson near Gloucester.
Postmark: 21 IY.

Strawberry Hill, July 20th, at night.

YOU desired me to write to you,[1] and I promised I would if I had any news to send. Happily all other letters, except of events or business, are exploded, together with pretty or complimentary conclusions, and services to cousins, and even, as we are an economic age, with *To* on a direction, which however I still retain, as Lord

Selwyn's attachment to 'Mie Mie' is shown in his letter to Lady Ossory 7 Aug. 1778.

5. 'I have been almost distracted these ten days with miseries of my poor sister's [Lady Di], they are patched up, and she has consented to bear a little longer; . . . Husbands are dreadful and powerful animals' (Lady Pembroke to Lord Herbert 2 July 1779, printed, with an omission as indicated, in *Henry, Eliza-*beth and George (*1734–80*), ed. Lord Herbert, 1939, p. 208).

6. Lord Bolingbroke's illness was described as 'palsy on his brain' (Lord Pembroke to Lord Herbert 9 July 1779, ibid. p. 202; Lady Mary Coke, *MS Journals* 10 July 1779).

1. Selwyn had been at Matson since 13 July (Hist. MSS Comm., 15th Report, App. vi, *Carlisle MSS*, 1897, p. 431).

Vere[2] does powder on his shoulders. Yet I am at a loss how to send you new news, for every lie is in the papers before it can reach Twickenham, though Lady Greenwich[3] sounds her horn round the parish as fast as possible. All I can do is to confirm what little truth remains in the sieve. It is fact that the Duchess of Leinster, Mrs Damer and Lady William Campbell,[4] not Lady Almeria Carpenter,[5] were taken by a privateer and carried to Dunkirk,[6] but they were treated with the romantic *delicacy* of Scipio and Lord Anson;[7] not a glove was touched, and they were told they were *padrone* to go where they pleased. Mr Oguelvit[8] was not in agonies for a moment. It is true too that Jack Townshend[9] and Mr W. Hanger[10] are gone volunteers on board the fleet[11]—not to the Fleet.

I was in town on Wednesday and called on my Lady,[12] who told me Mrs Cavendish[13] could not live till morning—but her my-

2. Lord Vere Beauclerk (1699–1781), cr. (1750) Bn Vere.

3. HW frequently alludes to Lady Greenwich's news-mongering. The post-boy's horn announced his approach.

4. Sarah Izard (d. 1784), m. (1763) Lord William Campbell, 5th son of 4th D. of Argyll (*Scots Peerage* i. 385; du Deffand iv. 63 n. 3).

5. Lady Almeria Carpenter (1752–1809), 2d dau. of 1st E. of Tyrconnel (John Lodge and Mervyn Archdall, *Peerage of Ireland*, 1789, iii. 94; John Debrett, *Peerage*, 1823, ii. 976). The false report of her capture appears in the *London Chronicle* 17–20 July 1779, xlvi. 59.

6. HW to Lady Ossory 20 July 1779 gives a similar account of this incident which occurred about 7 July; news of their capture was published in the London papers on 17 July in the form of a letter from Dover of the 15th (GM 1779, xlix. 373; *Daily Adv.* 17 July 1779; *London Chronicle* 15–17 July 1779, xlvi. 54). Lady Mary Coke's *MS Journals* 18, 19 July 1779, also contain similar accounts of their capture and release, derived from conversation with HW and Lady Ailesbury.

7. Richard Walter's edition of Anson's *Voyage Round the World*, 1748, pp. 204–5, tells how Anson had allowed a Spanish lady and her two beautiful daughters to

keep their quarters on a captured vessel without ever having seen them.

8. William Ogilvie (1740–1832), 2d husband of the Ds of Leinster; he had formerly been her children's tutor. HW is mimicking the French spelling of his name.

9. Hon. (after 1787, Lord) John Townshend (1757–1833), 2d son of 4th Vct and 1st M. Townshend; M.P. Cambridge University 1780–84, Westminster 1788–90, Knaresborough 1793–1818 (Collins, *Peerage*, 1812, ii. 478–9; Judd, *Members of Parliament* 357).

10. Hon. William Hanger (1744–1814), 3d Bn Coleraine, 1794; M.P. East Retford 1775–8, Aldborough 1778–80, St Michael 1780–4. He was deeply in debt; see HW to Mann 20 Aug. 1776.

11. Lady Mary Coke saw them at Portsmouth in their new rôle just before the fleet sailed in September (Lady Mary Coke, *MS Journals* 9 Sept. 1779).

12. Lady Townshend.

13. Elizabeth Cavendish (d. 2 Aug. 1779), dau. of Lord James Cavendish, 3d son of 1st D. of Devonshire; m. (1732) Richard Chandler, later Cavendish (Collins, *Peerage*, 1812, i. 354; Francis Bickley, *The Cavendish Family*, 1911, p. 186 n. 1). Collins gives the date of her death as 4 Aug., but see Lady Mary Coke, *MS Journals* 3 Aug. 1779, where Lady Mary recounts that she had that day

Ladyship, you know, is apt to take places for people in Charon's boat before they are ready to set out—but there is no advance money given and forfeited.

I have not received a line from Madame du Deffand since the packets were stopped.[14] It surprises me, as I concluded she would write by Holland. They cannot surely have forbidden her. They must know she abhors politics, and was not likely to write if she knew any of consequence, which she was not likely to do.

I believe Lord Shelburne was married yesterday.[15] They were to go the next day to Woburn.[16]

If your aldermen want politics, Gibraltar is thought to be besieged,[17] and it is believed the Cales squadron will be employed there[18] and not join the French. I know nothing else true or false; and I will not write again, unless I can entertain you better. This was only to prove that I am not silent from idleness.

To Selwyn, Tuesday 21 September 1779

Printed for the first time from a photostat of the MS in the Cely Trevilian Collection in the Society of Antiquaries.

Strawberry Hill, Sept. 21, 1779.

I DO not know in what style it is proper to write to you. You, who are living in a cottage on love with Pastora, may be insensible to the alarms of war, and to national disgrace, and humiliation; and at any time

> All the noise the distant world can keep
> Rolls o'er your grotto, nor disturbs your sleep.[1]

learned of Mrs Cavendish's death 'last night' from Lord Frederick Cavendish, and gives details of her will.

14. HW eventually received her letters of 27 June, 5 July, 11 July, and 12 July.

15. Shelburne married as his second wife (19 July 1779) Lady Louisa Fitzpatrick (1755–89), dau. of 1st E. of Upper Ossory.

16. Lady Shelburne was a niece of the Dowager Duchess of Bedford.

17. The blockade of Gibraltar by the French and Spanish fleets began 21 June

1779. HW had heard the first reports from letters that reached London on 17 July (HW to Lady Ossory 20 July 1779).

18. The Cadiz squadron. War between England and Spain had begun in mid-June.

———

1. 'Know, all the distant din that world can keep,
   Rolls o'er my grotto and but soothes my sleep.'
            (Pope, *Satires* i. 123-4).
Selwyn also quotes the lines in a letter

News I have none but what everybody has, and of myself I can tell you nothing that you would be glad to hear. I have not been well the whole summer, and for the last three weeks have had twenty disorders, that concluded with the gout in my left hand, which is still useless. Old age has marked me for her own; and yet taken away one of my resources, I mean, Lady Blandford's house,[2] whither I went oftenest, because I met nobody younger than myself—but I shall drop that subject, which only leads to moralizing, on which I am sure one can say nothing new.

Lord and Lady Hertford called on me last night, and were very unhappy with reason. Lord Lincoln[3] is so near death, that I expect when my servant, whom I have sent to Ditton,[4] returns, to hear he is dead. There would be another ample theme for moralizing— but I know, and therefore need not repeat, all you and I should say on that subject, if we were together. Lord Temple's death[5] is much more barren. He had outlived a fictitious importance, and was but an historic Strulbrug.[6]

Do not you come to town before the Parliament meets? You will find me in Berkeley Square.[7] Madame du Deffand has desired to know whether I have a *cour* and a *jardin*, and an *escalier honnête?*[8] To the last I answered a little uncivilly, that I should have a very clean one.[9]

I hear matters go very smoothly at Brighthelmstone[10] though I

to Lord Holland in 1765 (*Letters to Henry Fox* 210).

2. Maria Catherina de Jong (ca 1697–1779), m. 1 (1729) William Godolphin, styled M. of Blandford; m. 2 (1734) Sir William Wyndham, 3d Bt. She died at her house at Sheen 7 Sept.

3. Henry Pelham-Clinton (1777–23 Sept. 1779), styled E. of Lincoln 1778–9; grandson of Lord and Lady Hertford and, while he lived, heir to the Dukedom of Newcastle.

4. Thames Ditton, Surrey, on the Thames opposite Hampton Court. The Hertfords had recently taken a house there (HW's note to his letter to Conway 13 Sept. 1779).

5. 11 Sept.

6. An inhabitant of Luggnagg, an island in Book Four of *Gulliver's Travels*. Its people had the privilege of eternal life without immortal vigour, strength, or intellect.

7. HW's title to his new house, No. 40 (later No. 11) Berkeley Square, had been cleared on 21 July 1779; he took possession on 14 Oct. (Mason i. 453 n. 1; HW to Lady Ossory 14 Oct. 1779).

8. In Mme du Deffand to HW 20 Aug. 1779 (du Deffand v. 167).

9. Probably in his missing letter of 2 Sept. 1779, for Mme du Deffand in her reply (10 Sept.) mentions the 'détail' which he had given of his new house (du Deffand v. 173).

10. Between Topham and Lady Di Beauclerk. Lady Di's sister, Lady Pembroke, who had been with her at Brighton since 20 Sept., wrote on 28 Oct. that 'Mr B. keeps such odd hours that she does not see him above a minute in the day, and she lies in the next house, and there have been no disputes at all since they came here' (*Henry, Elizabeth and George (1734–80)*, ed. Lord Herbert, 1939, p. 301). See also ibid. 259 and *Diary and Letters*

believe the staircase is not very clean.[11] The Ossorys are at Farming Woods.[12] Where anybody else is I don't know, for I have not been in London these three weeks—I know this hash of old scraps does not deserve an answer, and yet as I shall be glad to hear of you, I think you will write.

Yours almost these 60 years,

H. W.

Tuesday [?Wednesday] morning.

Lord Lincoln is not dead, and therefore they have some faint hopes.[13]

From SELWYN, ca Friday 1 October 1779

Missing.

To SELWYN, Monday 4 October 1779

Printed for the first time from a photostat of the MS in the Cely Trevilian Collection in the Society of Antiquaries.
Endorsed: Mr Walpole.
Address: To George Augustus Selwyn, Esq., at Matson near Gloucester.
Postmark: 4 OC. ISLEWORTH. FREE.

Strawberry Hill, Oct. 4, 1779.

YOU may be perfectly easy, my dear Sir. When I said, I had nothing to tell you that you would be glad to hear,[1] I did not allude to you or your connections, but to myself, who am out of order and have been so the whole summer. Self is always uppermost or at bottom in all our thoughts: you thought I referred to you; and I concluded you would know I meant myself. This will make you smile as it did me; and we shall both agree that our con-

of Madame d'Arblay, ed. Charlotte Barrett and Austin Dobson, 1904–5, i. 282–3).
11. See the following letter, n. 18.
12. Their house in Rockingham Forest, Northants.

13. He died the following day.

———

1. *Ante* 21 Sept. 1779.

clusions were most natural for we neither of us affect to be supernatural.

I know nothing but reports. The combined fleets, they say, are to come forth again;[2] and on the other hand, they talk of the two Empresses interposing to make peace.[3] I wish heartily for the latter, as I am persuaded the longer it is deferred, the worse it will be. War is like other gaming; when one is out of luck, it is wise to leave off.

I am sorry to tell you, that Lord Maccartney,[4] who was setting out for Paris, is sent to Limoges,[5] having not learnt taciturnity in the family in which he was originally protected,[6] nor, which is much more strange, in that into which he had entered,[7] nor in his profession of ambassador.[8] I do not believe that the latter function will correct Hare,[9] who set out under some of the same auspices as Sir George.[10]

I do hear sometimes from Lady Ossory, but seldomer than usual. She, like many others, has passed an anxious summer. She is now gone, or going to Bowood.[11]

It is not probable, I think, that the sexton found anything of any kind of value in poor Prince Edward's[12] coffin at Tewksbury,[13]

2. This rumour was perhaps founded on letters from Brest of 15 Sept. reporting that orders had been received for the combined fleet to put to sea as soon as possible (*London Chronicle* 30 Sept.– 2 Oct. 1779, xlvi. 319).

3. Letters from The Hague during September carried reports of Catherine the Great's essays at mediation between the belligerent powers; it was also reported that Austria was 'not pleased' at the blockade of Gibraltar (*London Chronicle* 16–18 Sept., 30 Sept.–2 Oct. 1779, xlvi. 272, 318).

4. Sir George Macartney (*ante* 2 Aug. 1766, n. 9) had been created a baron in 1776.

5. Macartney, at this time governor of Grenada, had been captured by the French when the island fell in July 1779 and sent a prisoner to France. News of his arrival at La Rochelle on 3 Sept. reached London on the 20th, and was followed in a few days by reports that he had been refused permission to go to Paris and was being sent to Limoges instead. He had offended his captors by his language on board the ship carrying him to Europe (H. H. Robbins, *Our First Am-*

bassador to China, 1908, pp. 108–13; *London Chronicle* 18–21, 21–23, 25–28 Sept. 1779, xlvi. 280, 281, 302; DU DEFFAND v. 177, 178; HW to Lady Ossory 14 Oct. 1779).

6. Macartney began his career as a protégé of Henry Fox.

7. Lord Bute's; Macartney married Lady Jane Stuart in 1768.

8. Macartney had been envoy to Russia 1764–67, and was named ambassador there after his return to England, but did not go out again.

9. James Hare (1747–1804), wit and politician; friend of C. J. Fox; M.P. Stockbridge 1772–4; Knaresborough 1781–1804; minister plenipotentiary to Poland Oct. 1779—Jan. 1782. He sought the post as an escape from his gambling debts.

10. Particularly his intimate connection with the Foxes.

11. Wiltshire, the seat of Lord Shelburne, to visit her sister-in-law, the new Countess.

12. Edward (1453–71), Prince of Wales; son of Henry VI.

13. 'Some bones of a small skeleton, as of a youth, and a coffin were discovered by the breaking of the stone. . . . It is not

considering the moment of his catastrophe.[14] No affection could be present at his interment, nor that more bountiful mourner, pretended affection; nor those imaginary mourners, flattery and loyalty. With all his Lancastrian zeal Henry VII did not bestow so much as a tomb on the last real heir of the house; and for his coffin he would sooner have robbed, than enriched it.

I heard last night that an ancient maiden Trevor,[15] sister of Lord Hampden,[16] has left some fortune to Lady Di's two girls.[17] I most cordially hope it true, that they may have bread to eat,—if they are not eaten first, of which there is some danger, for, as modern conjurers are not greater adepts than pharaohs, and as that potent sovereign's magicians had no power over lice, I doubt the visitation is inveterate.[18]

You may be sure I am pleased with your improving Matson—I still retain partiality for the mansions of ancient families, though I have so recently swallowed a dose[19] that, one would think, would cure any man of genealogic pomps and vanities!—but, adieu! you

likely that the last remnant of a royal house, which was so completely crushed in this battle, should have had any memorial laid over him' (Richard Gough, *Sepulchral Monuments in Great Britain*, 1786–96, ii pt ii. 225).

14. He was either killed in the battle of Tewkesbury or, more probably, murdered immediately after it at the instigation of Edward IV.

15. Lord Hampden had two maiden half-sisters, Elizabeth Trevor (d. 1773) and Anne, perhaps the lady somewhat confusingly described as 'the Hon. Mrs Trevor, sister to Lord T.' who died in 1785, aged 81 (George Lipscomb, *The History and Antiquities of the County of Buckingham*, 1847, ii. 297; GM 1785, lv pt i. 236). They were great-aunts of Lady Di Beauclerk. There is no confirmation of the reported bequest.

16. For him, see *ante* 10 Feb. 1767, n. 11.

17. Mary Beauclerk (1766–1851), m. (as his 2d wife, ca 1795) Graf Franz von Jenison zu Walworth; and Elizabeth Beauclerk (ca 1767–1793), m. (1787) George Augustus Herbert, 11th E. of Pembroke and Montgomery, 1794 (MASON ii. 71 n. 22).

18. Topham Beauclerk was notoriously

lousy. 'The elegant and accomplished gentleman . . . was . . . what the French call *cynique* in his personal habits beyond what one would have thought possible in anyone but a beggar or a gipsy. He and Lady Di made part of a great Christmas party at Blenheim, where soon after the company were all met, they all found themselves as strangely annoyed as the Court of Pharaoh were of old by certain visitants—"*in all their quarters*"— It was in the days of powder and pomatum, when stiff frizzing and curling, with hot irons and black pins, made the entrance of combs extremely difficult—in short, the distress became unspeakable. Its origin being clearly traced to Mr Beauclerk, one of the gentlemen undertook to remonstrate with him, and began delicately hinting how much the ladies were inconvenienced— "What!" said Beauclerk, "Are they so nice as that comes to? Why I have enough to stock a parish"' (*Notes by Lady Louisa Stuart on George Selwyn and His Contemporaries by John Heneage Jesse*, ed. W. S. Lewis, New York, 1928, pp. 22–3 and n.).

19. The sale of the pictures at Houghton to Catherine the Great; see particularly HW to Mann 4 Aug. 1779.

will find me in town, I think, when you return, for, when I am not well, London agrees better with me than the country.

Yours ever,

H. W.

To Selwyn, ca 1780

Printed from the MS now WSL. First printed, Jesse, *Selwyn* iv. 317; reprinted, Toynbee xv. 449. The MS was sold Sotheby's 10 June 1869 (John Dillon sale) lot 155 to Dobell; sold Sotheby's 21 Aug. 1872, lot 54 to Walford; offered *The Ingatherer* (Colbeck, Radford & Co.) No. 19 (Sept. 1929) item 176; acquired by Mrs Octavia Gregory, Melville, Parkstone, Dorset; subsequently acquired by Alan G. Thomas who sold it, July 1948, to WSL.

Dated tentatively 1780 by the hand and by the reference to Berkeley Square, where HW lived after October 1779.

Address: To Mr Selwyn.

I SEND the key of the Square,[1] which you will keep as long as you please. What do I owe you for the basket of provisions?

Last night I saw a proof-piece of seven-shilling pieces, struck in 1776:[2] I know they were not uttered—but could you get me one from the Mint?[3] I had much rather be obliged to you than to my dear nephew, the Master.[4]

---

1. Presumably Berkeley Square.

2. Patterns for a seven-shilling gold piece were made in 1775 and 1776, but the coin was not issued until 1797 from a somewhat different design; the coins were introduced to supply to a certain degree the great shortage of silver money in the late eighteenth century (S. M. Leake, *An Historical Account of English Money*, 3d edn, 1793, App., pp. 3–4; H. A. Grueber, *Handbook of the Coins of Great Britain and Ireland in the British Museum*, 1899, p. 148; Sir Charles Oman, *The Coinage of England*, Oxford, 1931, p. 360). The 1776 proof, apparently very rare, is illustrated in Grueber, op. cit., plate xxxvi;

and Oman, op. cit., plate xlii (3). Selwyn presumably obtained the coin for HW, since one was sold SH x. 11 to Till (with a pattern of the 1761 guinea) for £2 12s.

3. Selwyn had held the sinecure of surveyor of the meltings and clerk of the irons at the Mint since 1740 (S. P. Kerr, *George Selwyn and the Wits*, 1909, pp. 54–5).

4. Charles Sloane Cadogan (1728–1807), 3d Bn Cadogan, cr. (1800) E. Cadogan; master of the Mint 1769–84. He had m. (1777), as his second wife, Mary Churchill, dau. of HW's half-sister Lady Mary Churchill.

To Selwyn, ca Monday 10 April 1780

Missing; described in Sotheby's Catalogue 10 April 1924 ('Property of a Lady') lot 470, as ALS 1 p. small 8vo, dated '4 o'clock' and as 'saying that he had just come to town and finds M. de Sources[1] has called; he wishes to know where he is, and the length of his stay.'

The letter was probably written about 10 April 1780, as may be deduced from DU DEFFAND V. 213, 217–8, and HW to Mann 21 March and 8 April 1780.

To Selwyn, Thursday ?27 January 1785

Printed for the first time from the MS now WSL. The MS is bound in a copy of L. B. Seeley's *Horace Walpole and His World*, 1884, extended to 12 vols by M. C. D. Borden; sold at his sale, American Art Galleries 19 Feb 1906, lot 812; sold Rains Galleries, New York, 27 Nov. 1935 (W. D. Breaker Sale), lot 628, when it was bought in by Breaker; sold by him to WSL, 1939.

Dated by HW's serious relapse of the gout in Jan. 1785. The attack began after 13 Jan. (HW to Lady Ossory 13 Jan. 1785). On the 23d, Lady Mary Coke reported that HW was 'still very ill and attended by Sir John Elliot,' on the 25th that he was 'much better,' on the 26th that he was 'worse,' but on the 30th that she had 'passed an hour with Mr Walpole this evening and was surprised to find him so much recovered' (Lady Mary Coke, *MS Journals* 23, 25, 26, 30 Jan. 1785). The summary account of this relapse that HW wrote to Mann on 2 Feb. 1785 (in which he says he has been much better 'within these few days') also corresponds with the symptoms described in this letter. The present letter, however, was probably written when he was first receiving visitors, and 27 Jan. seems the most probable date.

Address: To G. A. Selwyn, Esq., Cleveland Court.

[Berkeley Square], Thursday evening.

Dear Sir,

I WAS very sorry not to be able to see you when you was so good as to call, and when Lord Carlisle did me that honour too, for which I beg you will thank his Lordship—I have been very seriously ill indeed; and though better for these last three days, the attack on my breast was so violent, and the least talking gave me such fits of coughing, that till today Sir John Elliot[1] has allowed me to see nobody but one or two of my family, and those only for a moment. I will not ask you to call in an evening, because I know

---

1. Jean-Louis du Bouchet (1750–ca 1782), Vicomte (later Comte) de Sourches (*Journal de Paris*, 1784, i. 622).

1. Sir John Elliot or Elliott (1736–86), cr. (1778) Bt; physician.

it is not pleasant to you to go out till later than would suit me yet, for I am forced to be quite quiet till two hours before I go to bed, or I get no rest. I beg your pardon for this detail, but I profit of my first liberty to tell you I shall be happy to see you any morning.

Yours ever,

H. Walpole

To Selwyn, August–September 1785

Printed from a copy, now wsl, by an unknown transcriber.

Strawberry Hill.

Mon enfant,

I SEND you not only the Royal and Noble Authors[1] which you wanted, but another noble author of whom you may not have heard, the Duc de Nivernois.[2] There are but few printed,[3] but you are a favourite of the printer.

H. W.

To Selwyn, Wednesday 5 July 1786

Printed from a photostat of the MS in the possession (1956) of Robert H. Taylor, Yonkers, N.Y. First printed, Toynbee xiii. 395–7. The MS was bound in a volume of autographs in the collection of the Rev. John Wild of Whitehill, Newton Abbot, in 1900; by 1935 it was in possession of R. N. Carew Hunt; it passed to Mr Taylor before Feb. 1953.

Endorsed: Ho. Walpole July 1786.

Address: To George Augustus Selwyn, Esq., at Matson near Gloucester.

Postmark: 5 IY.

1. HW's *Catalogue of the Royal and Noble Authors of England,* first printed at SH in 1758.

2. Louis-Jules-Barbon Mancini-Mazarini (1716–98), Duc de Nivernais. The book was Nivernais's translation of HW's *Essay on Modern Gardening,* printed at the SH Press July–Aug. 1785, as *Essai sur l'art des jardins modernes, par M. Horace Walpole, traduit en français par M. le Duc de Nivernois, en MDCCLXXXIV.* HW was distributing copies in Sept. (Hazen, *SH Bibl.* 129–31).

3. 400 copies, of which HW sent 200 to Nivernais in Paris (ibid.). The whereabouts of Selwyn's copies are unknown.

Strawberry Hill, July 5th 1786.

I HAVE received the books[1] that you was so kind as to leave for me at Richmond,[2] and am sorry I did not know that you would have liked to have taken them with you, which I could have lent you without the least compliment as I had read them this winter; and because they amused me, though very tedious on the articles and prices of provisions, I desired Dr Gem to get them for me; and I must now beg you to put me into the way of paying him for them; for I certainly do not mean that he should make me a present.

I think you quite in the right to prefer Richmond to Gloucestershire, or rather, to live most where you find yourself most amused. Nor do I say this not merely from self-interest, though I readily own that I am very glad of your decision. I pass as many lonely hours as most men, but I choose to have company, with whom I *can* converse, within reach: and *that* company must at least be such as have lived in the same world as I have. It is too great a constraint, when one is old, to adapt one's conversation to people whose ideas are totally different, and indeed one makes a foolish figure when one attempts it. One is like my Aunt Townshend who hoped Alderman Bury was very well.[3] It is still more natural for me to rejoice in having you for my near neighbour, who have delighted in your company for above half a century, and who have outlived so many with whom I was intimate, and who have little propensity to connecting myself with new generations. The newspapers compliment me on being 'a well-preserved veteran.'[4] I, who feel myself weak, and lame, and crippled, thought everybody saw me as I see myself—but I will not believe them, nor be flattered into attempting

---

1. HW later mentions the books Dr Gem acquired for him, and which he had asked Selwyn to pay for, as *Les Mœurs des Français* (HW to T. Walpole 25 Oct. 1786). The volumes were probably *Histoire de la vie privée des français*, 3 vols. 1782, by Pierre-Jean-Baptiste Le Grand d'Aussy (1737–1800); HW's set is Hazen, *Cat. of HW's Lib.*, No. 3026.

2. Selwyn had had a house at Richmond since 1782 (S. P. Kerr, *George Selwyn and the Wits*, 1909, p. 309).

3. 'When Lord Townshend was secretary of state to George the First, some city dames came to visit his lady [Dorothy Walpole, sister of Sir Robert (1686–1726), m. (1713) Charles Townshend, 2d Vct Townshend], with whom she was little acquainted. Meaning to be mighty civil, and return their visits, she asked one of them where she lived? The other replied, near Aldermanbury. "Oh," cried Lady Townshend, "I hope the Alderman is well" ' (John Pinkerton, *Walpoliana*, [1799], i. 14).

4. This paragraph has not been found in any of the available newspapers; HW also mentions it to Lady Ossory 5 July and to Dr Burney 6 July 1786.

feats of activity; I will not leap over the back of a chair like Sir Joseph Yorke![5] On the contrary I find many comforts in being infirm; it serves me for an excuse against whatever I don't like to do. They who disguise their age and counterfeit juvenility, put themselves to an hundred tortures unnecessarily, and yet deceive nobody but themselves. Adieu! my dear Sir,

Most sincerely yours,

H. Walpole

The following undated letters are arranged tentatively in the order suggested by the handwriting and contents.

To Selwyn, n.d.

Printed from Toynbee xv. 453 from the MS in the possession of the Earl Waldegrave.

RIGBY tells me you have promised to dine with him tomorrow; as you are a sort of man not to be depended upon, I am not much surprised, but will you come on Tuesday?

Yours, etc.,

H. Walpole

To Selwyn, n.d.

Printed from Jesse, *Selwyn* iii. 39; reprinted, Toynbee xv. 447.

Dear Sir,

AS I have more gout today, and am not able to stir out of my bedchamber, which is up two pair of stairs, and where it is not proper to receive her, I must decline the honour you flattered me with of seeing Lady Holland, till I can get down stairs again; but

5. Who was now 62 years old.

I hope that will not hinder you from calling on me, whenever you have nothing better to do.

> Yours, etc.
>
> H. W.

To Selwyn, Thursday, n.d.

Printed from Toynbee xv. 447. The MS was then (1905) in possession of Mrs Alfred Morrison.

Thursday night

I HAVE not only been so very ill that I could not see anybody, but so weak that I could not have spoken to them if I had. I am a little better today, and shall be happy to see you tomorrow at one or two. I don't name the evening, because I know you do not go out early enough for me; but I hope the worst is over, and that in a few days I shall have recovered a little strength. I give you a thousand thanks for all your kindness.

To Selwyn, n.d.

Printed for the first time from a photostat of the MS in the Cely Trevilian Collection in the Society of Antiquaries.
Address: To G. Selwyn, Esq.

Young Mr Selwyn,

THERE is in the world an old gentleman that remembers you from a child and all your pretty sayings, and that foretold what you would come to. If you can bear such old-fashioned talk for half an hour, you will be very welcome in Arlington Street whenever you please, where you will find an armed chair and a good fire and your

> Very ancient friend,
>
> H. W.

To Selwyn, n.d.

Printed from a copy by John W. Ford of the MS then (1905) in his possession.
First printed, Toynbee xv. 448.
Address: To G. A. Selwyn, Esq., at Richmond.

LADY CAROLINE HOWARD, la Signorina Fagnani, and Miss in the lodging,[1] or any other three ladies, are very welcome to see Strawberry Hill any morning this week; but Mr Selwyn is not, as he has not made a visit there in form to the seneschal of the castle, since he resided at Richmond.

Your Honour,[2]
My master is going to town this evening, and will not be back till Thursday, from your Honour's

Most obedient to command,

Margaret Young

Pray be secret.

To Selwyn, n.d.

Printed from Toynbee xv. 448; the MS was then (1901) in possession of J. F. Rotton, Lockwood, Frith Hill, Godalming.

Dear Sir,

DO send me the third volume of Rousseau; take care, for a few leaves of this second are loose. I am this instant going to Strawberry Hill; I don't know how to ask you to go and dine there, but if you should like it, I will bring you back as soon as we have dined.

Yours, etc.

H. Walpole

To Selwyn, n.d.

Printed from the MS now WSL. First printed, Toynbee *Supp.* ii. 75. The MS was in the possession of W. H. Sampson of New York, 1918; sold Freeman's Auction Room, Philadelphia, 3 Nov. 1933 to the Brick Row Book Shop for WSL.

1. Not identified.
2. The rest of the letter is in the feigned   handwriting of Margaret Young (fl. 1760–85), HW's housekeeper (Toynbee).

Dear George,

IF you and Mr Williams are disposed to charity, you will find me any time this evening with a gouty foot on cushions.

Yours,

H. Walpole

To Selwyn, n.d.

Printed from Toynbee xv. 452. The MS was sold Sotheby's 3 June 1902 (Miscellaneous Sale) lot 1137 to Denham, in whose possession it was when Mrs Toynbee printed it.

Dear Sir,

DR. KING[1] has brought me this print for you. If you wish to thank him, he lives at this end of Berkeley Street close to the gateway into the stable-yard.

Yours, etc.

H. Walpole

We have records of the following missing letters to Selwyn:

Two letters sold Sotheby's 21 Aug. 1872, lot 54 (with 'a memorandum from some book dated 1788') to Walford. One of the letters is described as containing a 'notice of Lady Di.'

A letter described in *Appendix to the Rowfant Library*, 1900, p. 46, as 'autograph note of 3 lines to Selwyn on 4to,' inserted in an extra-illustrated copy of Boswell's *Life of Johnson*.

A letter sold Sotheby's 27 July 1885 (Naylor Sale) lot 969 (with HW to Unknown 22 April 1789 and HW to R. Jephson 3 Dec. 1781) to Suyster. Described as 'ALS 1 p. 4to.'

Selwyn died in Cleveland Row, St James's, 25 January 1791. On that day HW wrote to Lady Ossory, 'I am on the point of losing, or have lost, my oldest acquaintance and friend, George Selwyn . . . him I really loved, not only for his infinite wit, but for a thousand good qualities.' See Berry i. 183-4 for Selwyn's death and his will.

---

1. Not identified.

APPENDICES

APPENDIX 1

WALPOLE'S 'PATAPAN OR THE LITTLE WHITE DOG'

Printed for the first time from HW's copy in *MS Poems*, pp. 93–112. See *ante* 21 Nov. 1739 NS, n. 1; 7 July 1744, n. 38; and 19 Sept. 1744, n. 8.

HW wrote this 'tale' in the summer of 1743 ('Short Notes,' GRAY i. 14). The notes were written at various times, some of them (e.g. n. 55) as late as 1752.

Endorsed by HW: Wrote at Houghton, 1743.

Patapan[1] or the Little White Dog.
A Tale from Fontaine.[2]

When James[3] the Scot ascending Britain's throne
With ev'ry folly that debased his own;[4]
Lessened the glory of our warlike fame,
Disgraced our annals and defiled our name;
Mixed rascal Highlanders, a lawless brood
With the fair daughters of our purest blood;
In scabby hands our generals' truncheons placed;
Pedlars with ev'ry badge of greatness graced;
And gave fair Albion's brightest star to shine
On the black bosoms of each traitor line;
The gains of union these! 'Tis thus we gain
The Islays and Argyles[5] of ev'ry reign!
  Well! in that reign there lived one honest knight;
And Arthur Onslow[6] was our hero dight.

---

1. 'The name of a little Roman dog of Mr Walpole's' (HW).
2. 'See "Le Petit Chien" de Fontaine' (HW).
3. 'King James the First' (HW).
4. 'The two first lines stood originally thus;
When James the Scot succeeded good Queen Bess,
And by enlarging Britain made it less;
which the author altered on account of the quibble, which it seems had struck another author writing on the same period; "They mouthed out that *Great* Britain was become *less* than *little* England." Wilson's life of King James p. 190' (HW).

5. Notes on these two names are indicated in HW's text, but the page containing them has been torn out. On it were also HW's notes on the persons mentioned in nn. 6–10 following. The reference here is to John Campbell (1680–1743), 2d D. of Argyll, and his brother Lord Archibald Campbell (1682–1761), cr. (1706) E. of Ilay; 3d D. of Argyll, 1743. The former became a leading opponent of Sir Robert Walpole after 1733, and HW attributed his father's fall in part to the 'treachery' of Ilay.
6. The Speaker.

He was born of an ancient family that had often made a figure in their county, and had yielded notable services to the government. If they had not been present at the Battles of Cressy or Agencourt, yet they had often presided at the burning a French king in effigy, or at the ducking of a Frenchman in person. They had read the gazettes of the times to their neighbours, and drew the characters of the French noblemen that were taken prisoners.

Arthur, our hero was bred up in all the sage maxims of his ancestors; he knew every particular of their lives, and was acquainted with every accession of dignity to the family.

> But most his glory from two Speakers[7] rose,
> Who famously had gathered yeas and noes:
> Full in his view he kept their pattern fair,
> And his big soul breathed nothing but the Chair.
> For this each rising morning saw him pore
> In ev'ry hoard of senatorial lore;
> Each waning moon beheld his taper burn
> O'er Holinshed's or Glanville's[8] mould'ring urn.

He had all the rolls and records of Parliament by heart, and (to talk in the Eastern style), he had fathomed all the unsearchable depths of Gybbon,[9] and unfolded ev'ry plait of Sandys's[10] immeasurable neckcloth.

> While flocks of moths disturbed from parchment groves
> Their fav'rite authors quit and ancient loves;
> And charters, journals, legible or not,
> No longer are indulged the leave to rot.
> Long in this mouldy, musty, dusty road
> The happy knight ambitiously had trod,
> Hid from day's garish eye—

All his time was spent in making collections, and when he wanted to unbend his mind from his studies, and take a little exercise, he

---

7. Onslow's great-great-great-grandfather Richard Onslow (1528–71), speaker of the House of Commons 1566–71; and his grandfather Sir Richard Onslow (1654–1717), 2d Bt, cr. (1716) Bn Onslow, speaker of the House of Commons 1708–10.

8. Raphael Holinshed (d. ca 1580), chronicler; and Ranulf de Glanville (d. 1190), chief justiciar of England 1180–9,

supposed author of a *Treatise on the Laws and Customs of England*.

9. Phillips Gybbon (1678–1762), M.P. Rye 1707–62, lord of the Treasury, 1742 (GM 1788, lviii pt ii. 699 n., 834; MANN i. 332 n. 22, which see for some of HW's other notes on him).

10. For other notes by HW on Samuel Sandys, see MANN i. 249 n. 5.

would divert himself in tying up his notes with red tape, or in killing moths and flies, which was not only an innocent and prece-
dented[11] amusement, but contributed to the preservation of his
health and his manuscripts.

> But as for none will time his course delay,
> And learn'd or unlearn'd ev'ry head grows gray;
> As Potter's[12] head furrowed with Grecian lines
> Than Churchill's[13] untilled pate no smoother shines;
> As ev'ry parchment that neglected lies
> But sooner grows a prey for worms and flies;
> The knight reflected that with all his toil
> He did but vainly waste his vital oil;
> Nor yet had sown in wedlock's goodly bed
> A stock of Onslows and a future breed.

This consideration determined him to marry—It was no wandering
fire, no carnal appetite that prompted him to matrimony;

> —His soul was free
> From ev'ry tickling of mortality;
> Except when swelled with some diviner gust;
> He sunk into the chair, and dignified his lust.

But if he ever had had such a tickling, it was now over; and well
had it been for the blood of Onslow, if he had thought of matching
himself a little sooner.

The damsel he pitched upon was named Isabel,[14] of a suitable
family, and very handsome. The knight had been handsome him-

11. A note indicated here in HW's text
has been torn out.

12. 'John Potter [ca 1674–1747] Archbishop of Canterbury [1737–47], author of
the Grecian Antiquities [1697–8]' (HW).

13. 'For General Churchill's history, see
the "Town Eclogue" above [HW's MS
Poems, pp. 33–8]. For his illiterateness, it
will be only necessary to quote himself and
his works; he professed never having read a
whole book through in his life, and his
letters were so ill-wrote and so ill-spelled
that Sir R[obert] Walpole used to keep
them unread till he saw him, and then he
often could not read them himself.—A
good reply of his to Sir Robert, was one
day when he was soliciting him for one
Phil Anstruther [Philip Anstruther (ca

1678–1760), M.P. Anstruther Easter burghs
1715–41, 1747–54]: Sir Robert said, "Phil!
Phil! I never knew a fellow in my life that
was called by his Christian name that was
good for anything."—"Thank you Sir," said
he, "you have called me Charles all my lifetime" ' (HW).

14. 'There is no particular person meant
here; no more than any reality in the
catastrophe of the story; Mr Onslow being
married to a very homely gentlewoman to
whom he was always very faithful, and by
whom he had a son and daughter' (HW).
Onslow m. (1720) Anne Bridges (1703–63),
through whom he inherited Ember Court.
Their children were George Onslow (1731–
1814), 4th Bn Onslow, 1776, cr. (1801) E.
of Onslow; and Anne (d. 1751).

self in his youth, and was still a very comely personage. He was willing to transmit the features of the family fair to posterity as he received them—at least this was the reason he gave for his excessive jealousy: Isabel only knew whether he had any other motives. Certain it is that the strictness of her confinement did but raise the fame of her beauty: nothing was talked of in the country but the jealousy of Arthur and the charms of Isabel. There was not an old battered fox-hunter in the neighbourhood that did not toast himself in love with her; there was not a young one that did not hunt or shoot round the house. In short all arts were used by those that had or had not a mind to succeed, to get sight of her. But she who was as beautiful as Venus, and as chaste as her own husband, took no pains to distinguish between her pretended and her sincere admirers, and was equally cold to the noisy declarations of the one, and the silent propositions of the other.

During this state of inactivity, it so happened that a Parliament being summoned to meet at Westminster, our knight was pitched upon to represent his county;[15] and for his great knowledge and dignity, was elected Speaker by his brother members, and raised to the long wished-for honours of his ancestors. Before he set out for London, he thought it prudent to leave some directions with the wife of his bosom, whose frailty though he did not in the least suspect, yet were it unbecoming a person of his wisdom, not to provide against the most distant accidents. Therefore placing himself in his elbow-chair, and dilating all the awful majesty of his person and character, he summoned the submissive Isabel before him.

> [16]So have I seen an old despotic dame,
> Whom trembling virgins a school-mistress name,
> High on a seat of elbowed state, which far
> O'ertopped or Friend's or George's[17] curule chair,
> With red right hand the dreadful fasces shake,
> While stripped before her, little buttocks quake.
> With levelled spectacles she takes her aim,

15. 'Surrey' (HW).

16. 'A grand simile in the manner of Homer, so much admired by the critics, who when a simile runs out far beyond all likeness, and takes in several impertinent circumstances, say it does not run upon all fours' (HW).

17. 'Masters of Westminster and Eton Schools' (HW). Robert Freind (1667–1751), headmaster of Westminster School 1711–33; and William George (1697–1756), headmaster of Eton 1728–43; Dean of Lincoln, 1748.

While scolds and cruel cuts her wrath proclaim:
Nor pray'rs nor tears can stop th' impending switch;
She snuffs the spouting blood, and triumphs o'er the breech.

Then with the greatest gravity, he gave her the following charge:

'They part us, Isabel!—my country calls
To Westminster's high vaults, and Stephen's[18] walls—
Summoned by her, what patriot dare remain
A slave to ease, inglorious on the plain?
Who but must break from pleasure's magic charms,
And rush, like me, from his beloved's arms?
—Nay, weep not, Isabel—repress that tear,
Nor wound my soul with sighs I must not hear!
Shall gravity to urchin love give place?
Shall I a distaff grasp before the mace?
Shall I lag last—as if, like Gage,[19] they bought
My absence dearer than they would my vote?
See Sands already beckons me away,
And Rushout's forward leg[20] reproves my stay:
See Waller,[21] Sternhold-like, begins to hum

---

18. ' 'Tis well known that the House of Commons was formerly St Stephen's Chapel; I have often heard the Speaker descant with rapture on the grandeur of our ancient monarchs, when, said he, Westminster Hall was their parlour, the Abbey their Chapel, and the House of Commons a private oratory where the servants heard prayers' (HW).

19. 'Lord Gage, a remarkable person about this time. He was bred a Papist, but turned Protestant, as indeed he always turned to whatever was for his advantage. He was constantly paid by the foreign ministers for intelligence; did all kinds of jobs for Sir R[obert] Walpole in the same way; turned Patriot, declaimed in coffee-houses, and was the chief person employed in getting together the party to the House, and keeping watch at the door to prevent their going away. On the change, he was paid for staying away a whole sessions. At his house in the country, he would frequently leave his company to go and read letters from, or write them to the King and royal family. Soon after he was made

Master of the Household to the Prince' (HW).

20. 'Sir John Rushout always stepped one leg forward and looked at it while he was speaking' (HW).

21. 'A dull obscure person, of great application to figures and the revenue, which knowledge he could never communicate. He spoke with a tone, which yet was the least cause of the unintelligibility of his speeches. Lord Chesterfield went for six weeks to his country house to be instructed in the public accounts, and when he came back, said he had been *beating his head against a Waller*. On Sir R[obert] W[al-pole]'s disgrace, he was offered to be a lord of the Treasury, but would not quit his party; on Lord Granville's dismission, he joined in the coalition, and was made Cofferer, in the room of Mr Winnington, who was made Paymaster. Just at that time Mr Waller grew totally deaf, and came no more to the House' (HW). HW repeats Chesterfield's bon mot on Waller in his marginal notes to Chesterfield's *Letters to His Son*, 1774, i. 269 (now WSL), and in his

The broken notes of an imperfect sum:
See Watkyn's[22] *One of Those*, when rhet'ric fails
Gives weight to nonsense, as the Prince of *Wales:*
See Mistress Sydenham[23] hath prepared to sing
Her fear of God, and honour of the King;
And gracious Bubb[24] has deigned his coach to load
With half the trudgers of the Northern Road!
  Then press me not to wound my honour fair—
Oh! may your honour be as much your care!
'Tis there I'm hurt! 'Tis that I fear to leave:
For that my steady soul has learnt to grieve.
For say, what bus'ness has this revel rout
Of youngsters that besiege my house about?
Why all this gallantry? These ogling eyes
That mock my diligence, and 'scape my spies?
You'll tell me no success has crowned their vows;
That e'en in thought you never wronged your spouse—
Well! I'll believe it—but to be more sure,
At once my fears and their attempts to cure,
At Ember Court,[25] my love, you shall remain—

notes to Chesterfield's *Miscellaneous Works*, 1777, i. 290 (printed *Miscellanies of the Philobiblon Society*, 1867–8, xi. 44).

22. 'Sir Watkyn Williams Wynn [1692–1749, 3d Bt], a simple Welsh knight of a vast estate, and head of the Jacobites in that part of the kingdom, from whence he was called, Prince of Wales; some people think there is a double allusion in nonsense and the Prince of Wales. Sir Watkyn always began his speeches with, "Sir, *I am one of those*"' (HW).

23. 'An honest devout gentleman, who always talked out of the Common Prayer Book' (HW). Humphrey Sydenham (ca 1695–1757), M.P. Exeter 1741–54 (Judd, *Members of Parliament* 349).

24. 'George Bubb Doddington, remarkable for his wit and want of principles. He wrote the grossest panegyric in the world on Sir R[obert] W[alpole], then turned against him, on becoming favourite to the Prince of Wales, but having introduced Mr Lyttelton there, who routed him, he grew courtier again, and came into the Treas-

ury; but falling in with the Duke of Argyle, he was one of the chief persons in turning the Cornish boroughs against Sir R[obert] and was in the list for the Secret Committee but not chose. He set up for a Catiline and headed the young Patriots, and the needy Scotch Jacobites, and on the coalition was made treasurer of the Navy in the room of Sir John Rushout' (HW).

25. 'Ember Court in Surrey, a villa of the Speaker's, where he has a noble river every Sunday, it being stopped on other days to supply a mill; and a spacious wood consisting of forty fair forest trees. He one day judiciously bragged to the Queen of some compliments that had been made him on his impartiality by Sir J. Rushout and Mr Gybbon, then in the Opposition; and added, "These, Madam, are the honours I carry with me to Ember Court." She replied, "Oh, you are in the right— There was Sir Spencer Compton, who was so simple as to prefer carrying a hundred thousand pound to his Ember Court." The Speaker was Treasurer of the Navy; on the

Avoid the town and all its giddy train
Of balls, assemblies, races, sheriff's dinners,
Those pamp'ring nurseries of glutton-sinners.
To all their flatt'ries shut averse your ears,
For false are all their words, their vows, their tears;
False is each lover, though his winning eye
With truth's own colours paint the pleasing lie—
But most beware the flattery of gold;
Let not these charms, beyond all price, be sold.
To pay your constancy I'll give my all;
Reign mistress absolute of Ember Hall!
Take all the wealth this goodly seat contains;
I'll melt my maces down and coin my golden chains.
Of all your pleasures no account I ask:
Guard but one treasure, be that all your task—
Too happy if the joys of love alone
Returning I may find untouched, my own.'

Alas! Good man, that was too much for him!—He indulged her in all pleasures, except one; but without which one there can be no pleasure at all. His fair wife gave him a full promise to remember his commands, and to have neither eyes, ears, hands, nor anything else till his return, and assured him that he should not find the least traces of any lover's path.

As soon as he was departed, Isabel shut herself up in his villa, and as soon her lovers made parties to visit her. Some she would not see; and those she did, she used ill. They wearied her; they fatigued her; they made her peevish, and if she let them in again, it was only to show them how little impression they had made on her. She was so confident of her own cruelty and insensibility that she loved all opportunities of exerting it; and was never so satisfied, as when

change, his friend Mr Clutturbuck [Thomas Clutterbuck (ca 1671–1742), M.P. Liskeard 1722–34, Plympton Erle 1734–42] persuaded him to resign it, telling him that the Opposition thought he would be more impartial, if he had no place: this was his foible; he resigned, and Mr Clutturbuck immediately got the place. When Lord Orford was told of it, who had a very bad opinion of Clutturbuck, he said it put him in mind of the Duke of Rox-burgh's [John Ker (ca 1680–1741), 5th E. of Roxburghe, cr. (1707) D. of Roxburghe] persuading the Duke of Montrose [James Graham (1682–1742), 4th M. of Montrose, cr. (1707) D. of Montrose] that he had been ill-used by the Court, which made him give up his place, which was immediately given to Roxburgh' (HW). HW repeats this anecdote in a note to his letter to Mann 8 April 1742 (MANN i. 391 n. 10).

she had given proofs of her fidelity to her husband, by venturing it among all kinds of temptation.

Of all her train there was but one youth that had made the least way with her; and though he could not make all he would, he had made more than he knew. His name was Henry,[26] a young lord who had a seat not far from Ember Court. He was tall, well-made, and his complexion of a manly brown. He had every feature and limb that promised strength and vigour; and his words promised still a vast deal more. He spared no hints to woo her, nor expense to win her. His hints cost him nothing; but his entertainments were not so cheap: his estate flew away, and left him almost miserable. In this distress, he resolved to leave the fair insensible, and seek in other countries a remedy for his love. He took ship and landed in Italy. It was among those desert precipices and horrid mountains, that he sought a retirement adapted to the melancholy cast of his mind. One morning as he was wandering a prey to dismal thoughts, he met a peasant going to kill a snake. Henry, whose soul was all tenderness, interposed and saved it. The peasant marched off, and the lover and the serpent took each their several way among the rocks. Here he gave a loose to all those amorous complaints which are in use upon these occasions, and which are to be found at length in every lover's ritual. At last without knowing whither he strayed, he found himself at the foot of the Apennine, and taking his course along the banks of the Arno, which flows from among those mountains, he came in sight of the fair city of Florence. A nymph in imperial robes bright as Aurora, majestic and of heavenly dignity, presented herself to the eyes of our astonished lover. He took her of course for the Goddess of the Stream, for Venus just risen from the waves, or for any other divinity that you please; when accosting him with an air of authority, tempered with sweetness, she spoke thus:

'Henry, dispel black trouble from thy breast;
Know that I wish thee, and can make thee blest.
Fair Florence knows the wonders of my fame;
Of fairy race, Grifona[27] is my name.

26. 'Henry Clinton Earl of Lincoln, a very dark thin young nobleman, who did not look so much of the Hercules, as he said he was himself' (HW).

27. ' 'Tis said that the author, when on his travels, fell in love with a most beautiful lady at Florence, called La Signora Elizabetta Capponi Grifoni, to whom it is

Grim death o'er all our species has no pow'r,
Young and immortal from our native hour.
But hard conditions clog th'eternal boon,
And human ills deform our brightest noon. ·
Each seventh sun sees us obliged to try
Some earthly shape of frail mortality.
A servile beast we ruminate the plain,
Or grov'ling insects taint the springing grain:
A partridge now with trembling wing we shun ⎤
The captivating net or flashing gun;   ⎬
Or bask a loathsome serpent in the sun.   ⎦
Not the divinest of our sex is free;
All taste alike th' immutable decree.
See like a tow'ring swan Camilla[28] sail,
Pluming her graceful neck and downy tail:
See Brina[29] lash the waves with larger tail,
And all the goddess bloated to a whale.
A butterfly see Lindamira[30] dote   ⎤
On the gay sunbeams of a gaudy coat: ⎬
See fair Vanella[31] browse a lustful goat. ⎦
A wasp Brunella[32] brandishes her sting;   ⎤
Richelia[33] loves, a nightingale, to sing,   ⎬
Bills with each tuneful cock, and cow'rs her flutt'ring wing. ⎦

supposed he here alludes: at least there was no other apparent reason for transporting Henry into Italy, only to make him meet a fairy; especially as all kinds of supernatural beings were in vogue in England at the time he has chose for his history to happen; witness King James's act against witches' (HW). For HW's intimacy with Mme Grifoni see *ante* 31 Jan. 1741 NS and n. 16, 18 April 1741 NS and n. 5.

28. 'Lady Camilla Bennet [d. 1785], only daughter to the Earl of Tankerville' (HW). She m. 1 (1754) Gilbert Fane Fleming and 2 (1779) —— Wake (Collins, *Peerage*, 1812, iv. 131).

29. 'Any fat beauty; for instance Margaret Cecil Lady Brown, a very comely woman' (HW).

30. 'Lady Brook' (HW). Presumably Elizabeth Hamilton (ca 1720–1800), m. 1 (1742) Francis Greville, 8th Bn. Brooke, cr.

(1746) E. Brooke and (1759) E. of Warwick; m. (2) Gen. Robert Clerk.

31. 'Lady Vane. See some account of her in the "Town Eclogue" ' (HW). Frances Hawes (ca 1718–88), m. 1 (1733) Lord William Hamilton; m. 2 (1735) William Holles Vane, 2d Vct Vane; the notorious 'Lady of Quality' whose memoirs were later (1751) included in Smollett's *Peregrine Pickle*.

32. 'Mrs Brudenel, Bedchamber woman to the Queen' (HW). Susan Burton (d. 1764), m. Hon. James Brudenell; woman of the Bedchamber to Queen Caroline 1731–7; she was notoriously ill-tempered (Joan Wake, *The Brudenells of Deene*, 2d edn, 1954, pp. 258–60).

33. 'Lady Rich, a great patroness of operas' (HW). Elizabeth Griffith (ca 1692–1773), m. (1714) Sir Robert Rich, 4th Bt; see HW on her fondness for opera-singers in MANN ii. 481–2.

Myself that serpent was your pious care
Preserved, and gave again to sport in air
Etherial and inviolate—such zeal
The force of heav'nly gratitude shall feel.
All that a fairy's pow'r can grant, I grant:
Enjoy whate'er thy fondest wishes want:
Return—before two rising moons shall shine,
Thy love, thy Isabella shall be thine.
Thy flames shall warm her, and thy presents win:
Bribe, scatter, dissipate on all, begin!
Thy treasures shall in golden channels flow;
Mines inexhausted spring for me below.
Madam shall see how vast is our command:
What woman can a fairy's pow'r withstand?
But first to soften this imperious dame,
To wake her fondness and her pride to tame,
A small queer cap'ring dog[34] I will become,
And like a weary pilgrim you shall roam:
Your pipe shall soothe each haughty passion's rage,
And all my little tricks her tenderness engage.'

No sooner said than done—Henry's rich vest fell down into a pilgrim's coat, and the jetty ringlets of the august fairy blanched into the softest curls of white silk. He piped like another Orpheus, and she pranced before him like the musical beasts of old; she had an admirable ear, and did not give a frisk out of time. A cloud at the fairy's command descended to receive them, and immediately skimmed away to Ember Court. The piper and his dog soon drew a circle round them. Henry sounded away his merriest notes, Patapan capered, and the whole family danced with pleasure. Isabel heard the noise and sent her nurse to know the meaning—'Oh! Madam, the King of Spaniels! a little jewel! an angel[35] if ever there was one upon earth! the sweetest little dog! I'll warrant you he has more wit in his little finger than I have in my whole body! Your honour would dote of him! He must be yours: his master shall sell him your Ladyship whether he will or no'— The nurse goes and asks the price: the pilgrim cuts her short—

34. 'Tradition says that Patapan was given to the author, by the peerless Lady Grifoni' (HW).

35. 'This expression of the nurse's, was in reality a common one of the author's, about Patapan' (HW).

'Not to be given is my dog, nor sold;
A treasure inexhaustible of gold,
Supplies whate'er I want; whene'er I please
Shakes pearls into my hand, instead of fleas.
Small are his ears, yet each contains a store
Of orient ruby and Peruvian ore;
And from each curl of his snow-waving tail
I call forth show'rs of diamond, like hail.
—In short, a prodigy is Patapan,
Beyond what tale can tell, or fancy scan.
Yet Madam has they say a kind of ready[36]
Might pay his price—For one night with your lady—
You take me, Mistress—for one night alone,
And Patapan that moment be her own.'
'How!' quoth the nurse astonished; 'lie with Madam!
No; were you the first pilgrim, Sir, since Adam—
Lie with the Speaker's lady, saucebox, pray!
You that last night perhaps were lodged on hay!
A sweet companion, troth, to take to bed!
—Yet by our Halidame he's not ill-made:
Then for a leg so clean, and calf so plump—
Compared to his, Sir Arthur's were a stump.
Who but this youth before the knight would choose?
What could one to a mien like this refuse?
And then his dog—why that would kingdoms buy:
He for one lock with me ten nights should lie.'

While the good woman's fancy and avarice were warming themselves with the beauties of the pilgrim and the riches of his dog,
Henry pretended to whisper Patapan, who immediately scratched
his yellow ear, and out dropped ten jacobuses, which the piper immediately presented her. A diamond too strayed out, and Henry
smiling desired her to offer it with his compliments to her lady.
Away ambles the old crone, full of the wonders of the pilgrim and
his dog, of the diamonds, the gold and the message. Isabel was ready
to beat her nurse—

36. A cant term for money, now largely   *Slang and Unconventional English*, 3d edn,
obsolete (Eric Partridge, *Dictionary of*   1950, p. 690).

'How! Impudence! to me! propose to me
An act so base, such shocking infamy!
My purer soul starts at the guilty sound,
And conscious honour feels th' eternal wound.
Shall my chaste ears that shunned the voice of love,
When sighing nobles tried in vain to move—
Shall I—and pray with whom?—had he but sent,
Poor Henry, whom these eyes must still lament!
He, whom my scorn to death or exile drove—
Yet he so boldly never pushed his love:
Oh! 'twas the most respectful, decent youth,
For bashfulness renowned and am'rous truth!
Not from a monarch I th' attempt would bear—
And from a pilgrim shall I offers hear?
I who am Speaker's wife—'

'Madam,' quoth the nurse, 'if you were my Lord Mayor's wife, I tell you, this pilgrim might chance to purchase your honour— Henry, quotha, if your Henry were even what he says of himself, he were not worth a tithe of yon youngster at the gate'— 'But, dear nurse, my husband made me swear'— 'Swear! swear what? Did he make you swear more than the parson did? besides, who should tell? I know many a dame has done worse, and their husbands never the wiser—

There's Madam Bona[37] ev'ry summer can
Produce a whiteamoor, a Patapan;
Yet who more ignorant than her good man?
And pray for whom would you preserve your charms?
For poor Sir Arthur's unembracing arms?
Alack! alack! use all you can—and still
I'll warrant you his Honour finds his fill.'

These coarse arguments of the nurse's sounded so reasonable in Isabella's ears, that she gave a low consent for the calling up the pilgrim. She was still in bed— She was so lazy! The pilgrim stepped nimbly up to the bedside; he did not stand bashfully twirling his

37. 'Mrs Boothby, a mistress of General Churchill's. Her children being remarkably white, and like him, Lady Townshend called them, the little Whiteamoors' (HW). Probably Anne Clopton (ca 1699–1776), m. (1721) Thomas Boothby-Skrymsher; she was second cousin to HW's mother (MANN i. 173 n. 8).

hat and scraping his leg—but made her a bold well-turned compliment, in which the purpose made up for what it might want in delicacy. He surprised and pleased the dame— In short, she bought his dog—but how was she transported to find Henry in her arms, and to discover as marvellous and as numerous qualities in him as there were in Patapan.

Her payments were not so cautiously made, but more persons than one took notice of her expenses, and maliciously hoarded up an account of them against her husband's return. That happened sooner than the lovers wished—nay sooner than he wished himself; for scandal says, he was so enamoured of the Chair, that he preferred it to the holy bed of marriage.

The first thing he heard at his return was the dear purchase his lady had made of Patapan. Words cannot express the tempest of his person! He swelled, foamed, roared, rolled tumultuously from one side of the house to t'other—resolved to use the weapon[38] the law had put into his hand—and poor Isabel knew the terrible consequence of that— But as the bluster of his rage abated, he cooled into more bitter revenge. He determined to wipe off this stain of the Onslow name. Nothing but the blood of the offender could expiate it. He sent for his wife from the city to Ember Court, and gave command to a trusty servant to poignard her by the way, with great promises of reward for the deed done.

Isabel was soon advertised by Patapan of this bloody command: 'but,' says he, 'never fear: go along with him; I'll engage to save you from all dangers.' As they passed through a wood, the cruel executioner of his Worship's honourable commands, sent the equipage a little before, and then broke his commission to his lady, who instantly disappeared: Grifona had carried her off in a cloud. Away scampers the servant, scared out of his wits, to tell his master, who immediately went to the spot, the only way [39] he thought to be certain of what had happened. But O marvellous! O Astonishment! On the very spot he finds a most magnificent castle. Sir Arthur could not

38. 'A common expression of the Speaker's, who when any members were disorderly, threatened to *use the weapon the House had put into his hands*, which was to name them, and then they were to ask pardon on their knees at the bar; *and gentlemen know the consequence of that;* being sent to the Tower if the House voted they should. A Speaker of the Irish House of Commons on such an occasion, called out to a gentleman, "Indeed, Mr Smith, I shall be obliged to name you" ' (HW).

39. 'The common evidence of a Roman Catholic miracle' (HW).

believe his eyes— It was a palace for a god! Apartments richly fur-
nished, sumptuous hangings, gold and marble in every room! Brave
gardens, woods, fountains and cascades! The doors everywhere
open, but not a soul to be seen—at last appeared a tall, lean, dry,
swarthy giant of an Ethiopian—in short, a figure somewhat taller
and somewhat darker than our friend, Ned Finch.[40] The Speaker
took him for the chimney-sweeper in waiting to this palace, and
thinking to do him honour, cried, 'Prithee, friend, tell us to what
god does this noble edifice belong: for his Majesty, God bless him!
'twould undo him, should he think of building such an one.' The
Moor, who was somewhat dusky-eyed, putting on some half dozen
of spectacles, and poring at him, replied, ' 'Tis mine.' The Speaker
bounced back, and making a leg, asked pardon for his boldness—
'May your Infernal Godship,' said he (for he now concluded it was
Pluto before him) 'excuse my ignorance, but 'tis impossible the
world should match what I now behold.'—'What if I should make
thee a present of it!' replied the Moor: 'I will make thee master of
this enchanted habitation upon a certain condition—don't laugh:
I am in earnest—you shall be absolute lord of it, if you will only
serve me two days as page of honour—

               Say, dost thou comprehend the term? hast heard
               To what soft rites you pages are preferred?
               Dost know Jove's cup-bearer?'
Arth.   Who, Ganymede?
Moor. The same: suppose me Jove, you in his stead;
               You are not quite so handsome, nor so young,
               Though white your hand, bewitching is your tongue.
Arth. Ah! good my Lord, you joke—but pray forbear;
               Think of the years, the dignities I wear—
Moor. I joke! not I—
Arth.   My Lord!
Moor.   And so you won't?

Sir Arthur paused—and thus meditated on the strange temptation:

40. 'Edward Finch [later (1764) Finch-
Hatton (d. 1771)], brother to the [8th]
Earl of Winchelsea, ambassador in Sweden [1729], and Russia [1739] and Groom
of the Bedchamber to the King [1742].

This thought is borrowed from *le bétier*
[sic]. Mr Finch often spoke, with spectacles
on and a magnifying glass in his hand'
(HW).

'O Arthur,[41] feel thyself![42] and steady weigh
The various fates of this important day.
Be in one scale this sumptuous fabric placed;
In that, a life of glorious fame disgraced.
Wilt thou possess whate'er these walls contain,
And prostitute thy chastity for gain?
Or greatly proof to bribery, wilt go
A spotless Speaker to the shades below?
Methinks like tempted Hercules I stand,
Virtue on this, and vice on t'other hand.
Shall I, who have so long this office bore,
Whose voice confusion hears, and wild uproar,[43]
While angry parties hang upon my beck,
And as my finger points, abusive speak;
My finger, which could Pultney's self command,
Silence, or let him loose upon the land:
Whose hand impartial holds the balance right,
Unmoved by breath of courts, or party spite:
I, who great champion of St Stephen's cause,
Have bound invading lords[44] to equal laws:
Whose thunder trembling justices[45] have felt
Hurled at their heads submissive as they knelt:
Whose big remonstance[46] and emphatic form

41. 'In this speech he sums up as was frequently his custom, his mighty qualities impartiality and bullying' (HW).

42. 'One day when the Speaker had voted in the Committee against the army, Horace Walpole, brother to Sir Robert, reproved him for it: the Speaker said, "Why really Mr Walpole in some things a man must *feel himself.*" "Feel himself!" replied Mr W[alpole]. "I'll tell you a story: a gentleman married a girl with forty thousand pound. The morning after the wedding night, in which he had given his bride no reason to think herself married, he said, 'well, my dear, how do you *feel yourself?*' 'Feel myself!' replied she; 'did my father give you forty thousand pound for me to *feel myself?*' " ' (HW).

43. ' "Confusion heard his voice and wild uproar stood ruled." Milton [*Paradise Lost* iii. 710]' (HW).

44. 'He was particularly stiff in main-taining the privileges of the Commons against the Lords, who, in a famous speech against them were, he said, in respect to the Commons, but as a drop to the ocean' (HW).

45. 'A great period of Sir Arthur's glory, when on the Westminster election 1742 he was commissioned by the House to reprimand three justices of the peace on their knees, which he did [23 Jan. 1742] with ample exertion of his authority. This speech was printed and concluded with, *more might have been said;* Sir Charles Williams told him there was a false print in it, that to be sure it ought to have been, *less might* etc.' (HW). The speech is printed in *The Parliamentary History of England,* ed. William Cobbett and John Wright, 1806–20, xii. 327–8; the phrase quoted appears several lines from the end.

46. 'At the end of every sessions the Speaker makes a speech to the King on the

Have dared before the Sov'reign's self to storm;
Have taught the monarch on his throne to reign,
Taught him to conquer France and plunder Spain:
Shall I who have done thus, the mighty I
Prostrate before a lech'rous Ethiop lie?
Softened to a bardash, avert my face,
With robes tucked up, opprobrious to my place?[47]

Sand's could his dullness with his neckcloth veil;
Oh! could a neckcloth shade my injured tail!
Disgraced, abused, how shall I ever dare
To place a shameful bum in Stephen's chair?
Did all our rolls one precedent produce
To countenance or mitigate th' abuse!
Gods! that not handsome Hanmer[48] should have tried
Joys, that ne'er knew his disappointed bride!
That his fair face, and his still fairer glove
Should never tempt one lustful Ethiop's love!
Why did the gods this comely form bestow?
'Tis to my beauty I my ruin owe.
Had I, like Wilmington,[49] been born to scare ⎫
With nose protuberant the pregnant fair, ⎬
I still had filled inviolate the Chair. ⎭

How the young members can I hope to please,
While Winnington[50] will joke on ev'ry squeeze?
How shall I dare to press and wish them joy?
E'en Strange[51] will be suspected for my boy:

Throne, which opportunity Sir Arthur always took to display his pompous rhetoric' (HW).

47. ' "With robes tuck'd up, opprobrious to the King." Prior's *Solomon* [Book II, l. 898], where he speaks of King David's prancing naked before the Ark' (HW). The line refers to Solomon himself in a passage on the effects of his mistresses on him; HW has confused it with the account in 2 Sam. 6.

48. 'Sir Thomas Hanmer [1677–1746, 4th Bt, Speaker of the House of Commons 1714–5], a dainty Speaker, who was first married [1698] to the Dowager Duchess of Grafton, and afterwards espousing a young lady [Elizabeth Folkes, d. 1741], the first night he made some faint efforts towards

consummation, and then begged her pardon for her disappointment. See Mr T[homas] Hervey's letter to him [1741] on this subject. He lived long, published an edition [1743–4] of Shakespear, and always wore white gloves. In *Othello* he made this emendation, *A fellow almost damn'd in a fair phiz*, instead of fair *wife*, because he found no other mention of Cassio's being married' (HW).

49. 'Sir Spencer Compton [ca 1674–1743], was Speaker of the House of Commons [1715–27], and afterwards [1730] Earl of Wilmington' (HW).

50. 'Thomas Winnington Esq. Paymaster of the Forces, was remarkable for his wit. He died in 1746' (HW).

51. 'Lord Strange, eldest son to the [11th]

And Harding[52] leaning o'er the table nigh
Will be thought tempting to the Speaker's eye.
With artful horror Pitt[53] will paint my shame,
And Lyttelton[54] Philippicize my name:
Cotton[55] with wit the joking crew will join
And own that his Broad-Bottom yields to mine!'

These were fine reflections, but soon gave way to the tempting palace; and the poor knight consented to the performance of the mysterious articles:

But then dire omens filled th' offended sky,
And angry portents frowned his ruin nigh.
The sun[56] himself gave signs; and who so bold
To say the Delphic sun has false foretold?
He in that ugly hour withdrew his light,
With darksome clouds enwrapped his troubled sight;
And impious lawyers feared eternal night.
In that bad hour the earth and silver Thame
Gave forth their signs, and witnessed to his shame.
Owls from old offices flew forth amain,
And rolled obscene the tongue of Harry Vane.[57]
How did hot Vernon's[58] flaming tropes o'erswell
The bounds of sense and grammar! how foretell
The worst of shameful deeds on this side Hell!
Scotch members seemed to hear the clank of chains,

Earl of Derby, remarkable for his ugliness, and busy disposition' (HW). James Stanley (after 1747 Smith-Stanley) (1717–71), erroneously styled Lord Strange 1736–71, M.P. Lancashire 1741–71.

52. 'Nich[olas] Harding[e (1699–1758)], clerk of the House of Commons [1731–48], a very ugly fellow' (HW).

53. 'Mr Will[iam] Pitt, a popular young orator' (HW).

54. 'George Lyttelton, a poet; a tragic declaimer; a Patriot; a lord of the Treasury' (HW).

55. 'Sir John Hind [Hynde] Cotton [ca 1688–1752, 3d Bt, M.P. Cambridge borough 1708–22, 1727–41, Cambridgeshire 1722–7, Marlborough 1741–52], a Jacobite of great wit, and from the size of his backside, called the type of the Broad-Bottom. On

the coalition, he was made treasurer of the Chambers. He died in 1752' (HW).

56. 'This whole passage of the omens is imitated from the end of the first *Georgic*, beginning, *Sol tibi signa dabit* etc.' (HW).

57. 'Harry [Henry] Vane [ca 1705–58, 3d Bn Barnard, 1753, cr. (1754) E. of Darlington], eldest son to Lord Barnard, and a creature of the Earl of Bath's, who got him made joint vice-treasurer of Ireland [1742]. If ever he had attempted to speak, he would have been prevented by a monstrous tongue, that always lolled out of his mouth' (HW).

58. 'Admiral Vernon, a most silly noisy popular commander, who said in a speech that we were the most taxed of any country on this side Hell' (HW).

And fancied halters shook o'er Preston plains.[59]
Through the dun air a voice of deepest sound
All Westminster's lone aisles was heard around!
Pale spectres glanced along! and seemed to skim
The mighty shades of Hampden and of Pym,[60]
Indignant! Ominous! Averse!—a yell
Of screeching goblins rung a fun'ral knell!
And livid Lim'rick's[61] mischief-boding head
Looked pale to see Sir Arthur look so red![62]
Compton[63] was heard to speak!—and stranger still,
Fazakerley[64] stopped short—against his will!
Baltimore[65] would have spoke—but mangled hung
Mistaken terms, and faltered on his tongue;
Prophetic e'en in error—for before
His lips could cry, Sir Arthur is no more!
His jumbled *idioms* had pronounced, no Moor!
    Wide and more wide th' ill-omened horror spread!
Lords became prophets to avert the deed.
Tears such as statues weep from Secker[66] fell!
Tears such as he would weep, were Potter[67] ill!

59. 'The Scotch Rebellion in 1715, put an end to at Preston in Lancashire' (HW).

60. 'Hampden and Pym, two celebrated patriots in the reign of Charles I and whose portraits adorned Sir Arthur's library' (HW).

61. '[James] Hamilton [d. 1758, cr. (1719) Vct Limerick and (1756) E. of Clanbrassill] Lord Limerick, a stiletto-fellow, belonging to Lord Bath, by whose influence and his own malice, he seconded the famous *motion* [13 Feb. 1741] on Sir R[obert] W[alpole] and afterwards moved [9 March 1742] for the secret committee on him, of which he was the worthy chairman' (HW).

62. ' "And gods look pale to see us look so red." Lee.' (HW).

63. '[Hon. George] Compton [ca 1692–1758, 6th E. of Northampton, 1754], a silent gentleman' (HW).

64. '[Nicholas] Fazakerley [1684–1767, M.P. Preston 1732–67], a long-winded lawyer' (HW).

65. '[Charles] Calvert [1699–1751, 5th] Lord Baltimore, of the Bedchamber to the Prince [1731–47], and lord of the Admiralty [1742–4]; a very good-natured man,

but unhappy in his English; he always used patriarchs for patriots, area for era, idioms for ideas etc. He died in 1751' (HW).

66. '[Thomas] Secker [1693–1768] Bishop of Oxford [1737–58; Archbishop of Canterbury 1758–68], was bred a Presbyterian, commenced man-midwife, was president of an atheistical club, and lastly a popular preacher of the Church of England by which means he rose to episcopacy. He had a service of silver plate given him by Lord Chancellor Hardwicke, for matching his son to the heiress of the Duke of Kent, whose wife he directed. He afterwards married Lady Mary Gray, a most deformed daughter of the Duke's, but very rich, to Dr Gregory, a parson famous for his vigour. Sir Ch[arles] H[anbury] Williams going to see the Duchess of Kent's house at Old Windsor, the Bishop of Oxford's gown hung upon a chair in her dressing-room where he had been reading prayers; Sir Charles stepped back, and said "Oh! I see they are not up" ' (HW).

67. 'Potter Archbishop of Canterbury' (HW).

With madding torrents of unbounded wrath
Furious uprose the mighty Earl of Bath,
Pouring the monsters of his mud along,
Sea-calves, portentous cubs, an ugly throng,
Hoopers,[68] and Furneses,[69] and such-like things,
Dirt-born, and warmed to life by breath of kings:
Howling they bayed the sun; and when the priest
On the reared altar placed each mystic beast,
The frightened priest the bloody knife let fall
For they were tongueless, brainless, heartless all!

Yet even these dreadful omens could not hinder the bewitched
knight from yielding up his charms to the wanton will of the Moor.
Immediately his habit was transformed to a page's, and himself conducted by his negro-paramour to the scene of bliss, where in the
very midst of their joys, they were caught by Isabella and her lover.
Henry gave a loose to all his mirth on the pleasant adventure, and
teased the poor confounded knight with infinite humour. Isabella,
though more composedly, did not yield to him in torturing her
spouse, and with the gravest countenance in the world, apostro-
phized him thus:

'What do I see, ye gods?—behold I right,
Or do strange phantoms dance before my sight?
Is this, my dear, your senatorial trade?
And thus go Speakers clad in masquerade?
Is this soft couch your *Chair,* and boasted place?
And that same swarthy instrument your mace?
Are these the *motions* that you make? is this
The joy that you prefer to wedded bliss?
No wonder Isabella's hapless form
Ne'er knew the art to please, the pow'r to warm!
More lusty joys you love, and manlier grace,
To grapple in an Ethiop's strict embrace—
But modesty forbids me to pursue

68. 'Mr [Edward] Hooper [ca 1702–95, M.P. Christchurch 1734–48] was rewarded by Lord Bath with a place of 900 a year (Paymaster of the Pensions) for one day saying his Lordship had spoke with the tongue not of a man, but an angel' (HW).

69. 'H[enry] Furnese, was bred a mer- chant's clerk, had an estate left him, and was made secretary of the Treasury by Lord Bath, which place he resigned soon after with as little reason as it had been bestowed on him' (HW).

Th' ungrateful theme—yet tell me, Sir—was't you
Who to the death condemned and cruel steel
For an offence so slight your Isabel?
Yet what were my adulteries to yours?
No giants my gallants, my swains no Moors.
See ev'ry grace on blooming Henry shed
To tempt a yielding maiden to his bed!
See Patapan with ev'ry treasure fraught,
With which frail woman's fondness could be bought!
He won my love, and he preserved my life;
He built this dome, for which—but here our strife
Be ended! Both have failed; be pardoned both!
Here be our loves revived and here renewed our oath!'

Poor Sir Arthur was glad to accept any terms, and mutual peace and forgiveness were sealed, with a solemn promise from Isabella never to mention his Worship's having been a page. But Henry could not help sometimes when he met him, to shake him by the hand, and cry, 'Ah! Monsieur le Page!'

APPENDIX 2

WALPOLE'S 'LITTLE PEGGY'

Printed for the first time from HW's copy in *MS Poems*, pp. 119–22. See *ante* 2 July 1743, n. 5.
Endorsed by HW: Wrote in November 1743.

Little Peggy[1]
A Prophetic Eclogue,
In Imitation of Virgil's *Pollio*.

Ye nymphs of Drury, pour a nobler strain!
I like not rural themes, and scorn the plain:
I sing of courts; and when of courts I sing,
Notes worthy Lincoln flow, or Lincoln's King!
    The hour is come, by ancient dames foretold,
E'er his small cock were yet a fortnight old,
How with majestic vigour it should rise,
Strong to the sense, and tow'ring to the skies!
Women unfucked at sight of it should breed,
And other virgins teem with heav'nly seed.
    But thou, O Venus, on the newborn maid
Thy quintessence of pow'rful beauty shed,
That impious loves and barren vice may cease,
And joys of golden fucking only please.
Propitious hear, O goddess of delight!
Thy fav'rite Lincoln reigns, thy own adopted knight.
    While you, my Lord, are stallion of the age,
The graceful virgin shall the men engage;
Her little veins with warmth paternal glow;
Her monthly flow'rs, like her chaste mother's, blow!
If any traces still of sin remain,
Venereal symptoms and the secret pain;

1. 'Peggy Lee, a whore of Lord Lincoln's, had a daughter by him, whose birth was the subject of this eclogue. Sir Ch[arles] Hanbury Williams wrote another imitation of the *Pollio*, just at this time, on a report of Mother Douglas having a son by Earl Fitzwilliam' (HW). Williams's verses (which are unpublished), 'The Fourth Eclogue of Virgil Imitated and Inscribed to the . . . E. of Lincoln and H. Fox,' dated November 1743, are in Williams MSS lxx. ff. 39–43; see also below, Appendix 3. Further references to 'Mother' Douglas's son are in Fox to Williams 25 Oct. 1743, Williams MSS xlviii. f. 61.

You shall instruct her to remove the fear,
Nor but in cundum armed embrace her dear.
Oh! what celestial pleasures shall she taste!
Great as celestial, if they could but last—
The bravest heroes shall the fair enthrall,
And govern with paternal lust the ball.

Presents till then shall strew the nurs'ry floor,
And golden playthings round the cradle pour:
To gather coral admirals shall sail,[2]
And British navies seek the spicy gale,
Spice for the pap, and silver for the bells,
Whose tinkling soothes the throbbing gum that swells.
The comely nurse the tumid dug shall press,
Nor fear to tempt the mighty sire's caress.
Dayrolle[3] shall rock and o'er the cradle loll,
Present the rattle or undress the doll.
The smiling infant in her hand shall bend
The nut-brown engine of her father's friend,
Pleased shall behold the goodly member rise,
And innocently touch her titillating thighs.

But soon as manifest of hair, the maid
Conceives the praises to her beauty paid;
In at both ears her sire's exploits shall suck,
And comprehends, the mighty joy, to fuck;
The sable down its ringlets shall disclose,
And twine crisp tendrils round the pouting rose,

2. 'At this time Lord Lincoln's two uncles were at the head of the ministry; the Duke of Newcastle secretary of state, and Mr Pelham chancellor of the Exchequer etc.' (HW).

3. 'Mr Dayrolle a private gentleman, very brown of complexion: he was a led captain to the Dukes of Grafton and Richmond, Lord Chesterfield and Lord Lincoln, and often employed as governess to the Duke of Richmond's daughters. The Duke of Grafton made him Master of the Revels [1744], and Lord Chesterfield Black Rod to the Lord Lieutenant of Ireland [1745]. He was very passionate and no fool, though their Graces fancied they laughed at him: he was entrusted by Lord Lincoln with the duennaship of Peggy Lee, and was supposed to be well with her. His father was gentleman to Mr Stanhope, minister at The Hague, who lay with his wife: an honest gentleman told Mr Stanhope what scandal he gave by lying with another man's wife; he replied, "I don't; I lie with my own man's." Mr Dayrolle has since [1747] been sent Resident to The Hague' (HW). HW repeats these anecdotes in his letter to Mann 19 May 1747 (MANN iii. 403–4, which see for identifications of the persons mentioned and corrections to HW's account); and in his marginal notes to Chesterfield's *Miscellaneous Works*, 1777, printed in *Miscellanies of the Philobiblon Society*, 1867–8, xi. 17–18.

While the stiff member the glad space shall fill,
And balmy honey from each pore distill.

But still some tracks of ancient fraud shall last:
Distended cunts with alum shall be braced;
With foreign hair the circle shall be bound;
And dildoes make an imitative wound.
Another Onan shall new crimes invent,
And noble seed in selfish joys be spent:
Another Bateman[4] shall debauch the boys,
And future Sapphos practice mimic joys.

But when matured to love thy breasts shall pant,
And conscious blushes speak the tender want;
Each happy islander shall own thy sway,
Nor foreign beauties plough the British sea.
All pricks shall stand for thee: no more shall feel
Italia's sons the music-making steel.
Robust Hibernians, muscularly strong,
With well-proportioned yards, and nobly long,
Yards, that ten backs of modern beaux would sprain,
Shall *kneel* before thy throne, and vindicate thy reign.

Thus spake the Fates, as the fair thread they spun,
And bade thy years with equal tenor run.
Arise, O maid, to promised joys arise!
Linco's sweet seed, and daughter of the skies!
See joyous brothels shake their conscious beds!
See glowing pricks exalt their crimson heads!
See sportive buttocks wanton in the air!
And bawds cantharides and punch prepare!
The youth unbuttoned to thy arms advance,
And feather-tickled elders lead the lech'rous dance!

Oh! may those Fates propitious slowly twine
The thread revolving of my vital line,
That I may live thy wondrous deeds to tell,
How oft you shall be rogered, and how well!
Pope should not sweeter weave the flowing tale,
Nor Cibber's numbers o'er my verse prevail;

---

4. 'Lord Viscount Bateman, separated from his wife, by her brother Charles Spencer Duke of Marlborough, for his amours of this sort' (HW). William Bateman (d. 1744), cr. (1725) Vct Bateman; m. (1720) Lady Anne Spencer (d. 1769).

Though one has sung of Wortley's[5] loves; and this
How Pope was perch'd[6] on the soft mount of bliss.
Nay, should thy sire himself his acts repeat,
Thy sire should soon acknowledge his defeat.
    Begin, sweet babe, on thy chaste mother smile!
Ten tedious months with thee did Peggy toil.
Begin!—on whom no parent smiled, shall fall
A maid, unkissed by most, unfucked by all.

5. 'Lady Mary Wortley Montagu, often mentioned in Mr Pope's works, and famous for her wit, poems, intrigues, avarice, and dirt' (HW).

6. 'See Mr Cibber's *Letter to Mr Pope* [1742, pp. 46–9], where the latter is described in an amorous situation, and compared to a bird' (HW).

SIR CHARLES HANBURY WILLIAMS.

APPENDIX 3

WALPOLE'S ACCOUNT OF SIR CHARLES HANBURY WILLIAMS

Printed for the first time from HW's *MS Commonplace Book of Verses*, pp. 53–6, 81. Parts of this account are incorporated, with minor verbal changes, in Williams, *Works* ii. 207–11, probably from a copy HW made for Henry Fox in 1760 (see *ante* 6 Feb. 1760). The main account, through the list of Williams's writings, was apparently written about 1749 (see *post* p. 316).

Some Anecdotes Relating to Sir Charles Hanbury Williams [1708–59] and His Works

HE was a younger son of Mr Hanbury[1] of Pont[y]pool, and changed his name for an estate.[2] Bred at Eton.[3] Travelled.[4] Introduced to Sir R[obert] W[alpole].[5] Made a fine speech on the Convention,[6] which he opened; but did not practice speaking for which he thought he had no talent. Made paymaster of the Marines[7] by Sir R[obert] W[alpole] and Knight of the Bath[8] by Mr Pelham on an old promise of Sir Robert's. His great friend Mr Winnington;[9] on

1. John Hanbury (1664–1734), known as Major Hanbury; iron-master; director of the South Sea Company, M.P. Gloucester city 1701–8, Monmouthshire 1721–34 (Ilchester, *Hanbury-Williams* 23–8; William Coxe, *An Historical Tour in Monmouthshire*, 1801, pp. 236–8). Charles was his 4th son.

2. Which had been bequeathed to his father by Charles Williams (ca 1644–1720), who had amassed a fortune as a merchant in Smyrna after being forced to flee England for killing his cousin in a duel. Hanbury and Williams apparently agreed that the fortune should go to Charles, who was Charles Williams's godson. Another provision of the bequest was that the heir should take the surname of Williams, which Charles did about 1729, though he did not receive the estate until 1732 (Ilchester, *Hanbury-Williams* 25–6, 33; Coxe, op. cit. 96–7, 237, 270).

3. From 1718 until about 1724 (Ilchester, *Hanbury-Williams* 31–2; *Eton College Register 1698–1752*, ed. R. A. Austen-Leigh, Eton, 1927, p. 157).

4. Between 1724 and 1726; see Ilchester, *Hanbury-Williams* 32.

5. Apparently about 1735 by Henry Bilson Legge, Sir Robert's private secretary, with whom Williams had spent some months in Italy (ibid. 37–8).

6. Of the Pardo, 1739. HW is apparently mistaken. Williams moved the address to the King at the opening of the session, 1 Feb. 1739, which thanked the King for the Convention (William Coxe, *Memoirs of . . . Sir Robert Walpole*, 1798, iii. 515; *Parliamentary History of England*, ed. Cobbett and Wright, 1806–20, x. 940–1 and note; *Journals of the House of Commons*, xxiii. 207), but is not mentioned in the lists of speakers in the debate on the Convention itself, 8–9 March 1739 (Coxe, op. cit. iii. 517–18), nor in any reports of the debate.

7. November 1739, after an outburst of temper over the appointment of Legge, rather than himself, as secretary to the Lord Lieutenant of Ireland (Ilchester, *Hanbury-Williams* 44–6).

8. 28 May 1744 (*ante* 10 Aug. 1744, n. 5).

9. Their friendship began about 1738 (Ilchester, *Hanbury-Williams* 43).

which account often slighted and disobliged by Mr Pelh[am].[10]
Resigned his Lord Lieutenancy of Monmouthshire,[11] and soon after
the Marines,[12] upon an inquiry in the House of Commons,[13] in
which he was most unjustly censured by the world, his deputy[14]
having put the money out to interest without his knowledge; of
all men living he was the most generous, and thought the least of
money; but he had innumerable enemies; all the women, for he
had poxed his wife,[15] all the Tories for he was a steady Whig, all
fools, for he was a bitter satirist, and many sensible people, for he
was immoderately vain. Mr Winnington's unexpected death,[16] and
a foolish affair about an ode on the Duchess of Manchester's wedding with a boy,[17] which being published, she and Lady Townshend,
whom Sir Charles had broke[18] with on Winnington's death, Lord
Bath and others, some talking on the necessity of Mr Hussey's fight-
ing Sir Charles, and some telling him so, the Irish husband who had
no inclination to the duel, though Sir Charles had less, went to
Holland House the morning Sir Ch[arles] was to go into the country, but went late, and his enemy had gone early; this was blazed
about, the Irish and Sir Charles's enemies triumphed, and he let
them, one Soame Jennings[19] a paltry poet wrote an abusive parody
on Williams's ode, without his name; all these reasons concurring,

10. Winnington occasionally opposed
Pelham (twice in 1745, for example; see
J. B. Owen, *The Rise of the Pelhams*, 1957,
pp. 265, 288), but was usually one of the
leaders of his administration. Williams
also had a quarrel with Pelham in 1745
over a minor appointment at Hereford (Ilchester, *Hanbury-Williams* 89–90).

11. Williams was Lord Lieutenant of
Herefordshire (not Monmouthshire) 1741–
7 (ibid. 53).

12. At the end of Nov. 1746; the appointment of his successor is mentioned in
the *Daily Adv.* 1 Dec. 1746.

13. For the scandal in Williams's office,
see Ilchester, *Hanbury-Williams* 95–7.

14. Edmund Herbert (ibid.).

15. Lady Frances Coningsby (d. 1781),
dau. of the 1st E. of Coningsby by his
second wife, whom Williams married in
1732 (ibid. 34–5, 430). Her illness is referred to in Williams MSS lxxi, pp. 175–
80; lxxxiii, pp. 73–4; 26018, ff. 2–22; MANN
ii. 104; and Ilchester, *Hanbury-Williams*
56–7.

16. 23 April 1746; see Ilchester, *Han-*

bury-Williams 94–5 for its effect on Williams.

17. 'An Ode to the Honourable Henry
Fox,' printed in Williams, *Works* i. 90–3,
written in July 1746 and published,
through the carelessness of Lord Lincoln,
in August (GM 1746, xvi. 444; MONTAGU
i. 36, 43; Ilchester, *Hanbury-Williams* 97–
101). Williams also wrote and published
'An Ode Addressed to the Author of the
"Conquered Duchess"' on the same subject
in Sept. 1746 (GM 1746, xvi. 500), printed
Williams, *Works* i. 94–9; and an ode to
Hussey, printed ibid. i. 167–72, also published in Sept. 1746 as *H-ss-y to Sir C——
H—— W——, or, the Rural Reflections of
a Welch Poet* (GM 1746, xvi. 500). The last
ode, however, is attributed to 'Mr Nugent'
in a MS note in the Yale Library copy of
The Foundling Hospital for Wit, Part IV,
1747, p. 5.

18. For Williams's quarrel with Lady
Townshend, see Ilchester, *Hanbury-Williams* 100.

19. Soame Jenyns (1704–87), miscellaneous writer; M.P. **Cambridgeshire** 1741–54,

Sir Charles chose to go abroad, and got appointed envoy to Dresden.[20] He had wrote other things on the Duchess of Manchester,[21] the origin of which was her refusing to marry his friend Mr Fox; Lord Hervey and my Lady[22] to make their court to Lord Scarborough,[23] contracted a great intimacy with the Duchess, whom he was to marry, but shot himself a few days before the appointed day.[24] Lord Hervey then persuaded Mr Fox to make love to the Duchess, in order to betray this amour to rich Mrs Horner,[25] who kept Mr Fox: she quarrelled with Mr Fox, and flung herself and her presents into Lord Hervey's power,[26] and the Duchess refused Mr Fox, who broke with Lord Hervey;[27] he had been his second in his duel[28] with Mr Pultney. Sir Charles Williams had from a boy an inclination to be a poet and for some years wrote reams of bad verses,[29] particularly an epistle to G. Lyttelton, which was ridiculously bad and began thus;

> Since, dearest George, you're at that time of life,
> In which your friends would have you take a wife[30]—

The first thing that made him known as a poet of great genius and wit, was an ode wrote in the person of General Churchill, in imitation of *O Venus, Regina Cnidi*,[31] and soon after that appeared a dialogue between Giles Earle[32] and G. Bubb Doddington, on the latter's again breaking with Sir R[obert] W[alpole].[33] It was printed;

Dunwich 1754–8, Cambridge borough 1758–80.

20. He kissed hands for the post in mid-December 1746, but did not set out until 11 April 1747 (MANN iii. 341 n. 14, 347 n. 14).

21. Especially 'Isabella, or The Morning'; see below, n. 62.

22. Presumably Lady Townshend.

23. Richard Lumley (ca 1688–1740), 2d E. of Scarbrough.

24. He committed suicide 29 or 30 Jan. 1740; see the account in Frances, Countess of Hertford and Henrietta Louisa, Countess of Pomfret, *Correspondence*, 1805, i. 188–9.

25. For a biographical note, see *ante* 1 Oct. 1741 OS, n. 16.

26. HW mentions this affair in a note to Hervey's letter to Fox 13 Nov. 1736, printed in *Lord Hervey and His Friends 1726–38*, ed. Earl of Ilchester, 1950, p. 257 n. 1.

27. By 1742; Ilchester, *Henry Fox* i. 85,

states that the cause of their quarrel is uncertain, but that the breach was evidently serious.

28. 25 Jan. 1731.

29. The earliest ones which can be dated are from 1729 and 1730; see Ilchester, *Hanbury-Williams* 113–4.

30. These lines are quoted in Williams, *Works* i. 234 in a note attributed to HW.

31. Horace, *Odes* I. xxx. It was written in December 1739; printed GM 1741, xi. 48 and (with a number of verbal changes) Williams, *Works* i. 234–6. A copy is in Williams MSS lxix. f. 8; the verses are also transcribed in Conway to HW *ante* 23 Aug. 1740 and in HW's *MS Poems*, p. 39.

32. (ca 1678–1758), M.P. Chippenham 1715–22, Malmesbury 1722–47; lord of the Treasury 1737–42, whose defeat as chairman of the committee on elections and privileges 16 Dec. 1741 paved the way for Sir Robert Walpole's fall.

33. Written in January 1741 and published during that year by T. Taylor; re-

and a second dialogue between the same persons was afterwards published in imitation of it,[34] but wretchedly done. He wrote jointly with Mr Winnington and Sir W. Yonge[35] one or two political ballads before Lord Orford went out, and had begun some political papers, intended for a weekly journal against those of the Opposition, in one of which Lord Chesterfield was particularly satirized: but Sir R. W. who happened never to have any good writers amongst the numbers he paid, did not enough promote this scheme, and it dropped. Sir Charles then began a poem called 'The Pandæmonium,'[36] which was never finished, there being only the speeches of Lyttelton and Lord Granville done, which were admirable; the latter was entirely lost by some accident; after summing up the distresses of Europe on the breaking out of the war, which in a pathetic speech Lord Gr[anville] really said 'would be signalized with the blood of kings and tears of queens,' the speech in the poem concluded with this line,

And vizier's heads come rolling down Constantinople streets

Very soon after the change of the ministry, there appeared in the newspapers a pretty ode wrote by him, and called 'The Country Girl,'[37] it was to abuse Lord Bath; and being much liked, it was followed by an ode called 'Nova Progenies,'[38] on a great number of great men, in imitation of *Quem virum aut heroa.*[39] It had excessive wit in it and was admired extremely as it deserved to be. It was not known to be Sir Charles's, nor two or three more odes that succeeded it in the public papers. One was called 'The Capuchin,'[40]

printed Williams, *Works* i. 30–6. A copy is in Williams MSS lxix. ff. 41–4.

34. *A Second Dialogue between G—s E—l and B—b D—n,* 1743.

35. Sir William Yonge (ca 1693–1755), 4th Bt; M.P. Honiton 1715–54, Tiverton 1754–5; politician and versifier.

36. Mentioned in Fox to Williams 27 June 1741, Williams MSS xlviii. ff. 24–5. HW gives similar accounts of it in his notes to Chesterfield's *Miscellaneous Works,* 1777, printed in the *Miscellanies of the Philobiblon Society,* 1867–8, xi. 47–8, 57. He also quotes the line here quoted in his letter to Mann 20 Sept. 1770.

37. Advertised as 'this day . . . published' in the *Daily Adv.* 4 Aug. 1742; printed in *The New Ministry,* 1742, **pp. 1–**

3; Williams, *Works* i. 132–6; and transcribed by HW in his letter to Mann ca 9 Aug. 1742 (MANN ii. 22–3 and n. 11). A copy, dated July 1742, is in Williams MSS lxix. ff. 58–60.

38. 'A New Ode, to a Great Number of Great Men, Newly Made,' printed in Williams, *Works* i. 137–45; published 3 Sept. 1742. For its several contemporary printings, see MANN ii. 48 n. 12. A copy dated Aug. 1742 is in Williams MSS lxix. ff. 61–5.

39. These verses are an imitation of Virgil, *Eclogues* iv. 7ff, not of Horace, *Odes* I. xii, as HW says here. For Williams's imitation of 'Queen virum aut heroa' see below n. 42.

40. Printed in *The New Ministry,* 1742, pp. 10–12; Williams, *Works* i. 182–5; and

and another began[41]   . There
was a third which he always denied,[42] as it mentioned Lord Ilchester, Mr Fox's brother, but I am persuaded it was his; it began ['What
statesman, what hero, what king'].[43] He soon after wrote a dissertation
in prose on these two lines of Dr Young, in one of the *Night Thoughts*.

> A Wilmington go slower than the sun,
> And all mankind forget their time of day.

It was to abuse Lord Wilmington, but was never printed;[44] indeed
it was a very dull performance though Sir Charles was extremely
fond of it. There was another ode wrote on Lord Bath, equal to, if
not better than the former ones, but this too was not printed.[45] He
then published without his name a ballad on the repeal of the Gin
Act, called 'Sandys and Jekyll,'[46] and wrote another on the same
subject on Lord Hervey,[47] which was showed to very few persons.
The next summer came out, but not known as his, a 'Congratulatory Letter' in prose to Lord Bath on his missing the Treasury on
Lord Wilmington's death.[48] This and his odes were generally reck-

transcribed by HW in his letter to Mann
8 Oct. 1742 (MANN ii. 71–3). A copy, dated
Sept. 1742, is in Williams MSS lxix. ff. 66–8.

41. Blank in MS. Possibly 'An Ode,
Humbly Inscribed to the Earl of Bath,'
beginning 'Great Earl of Bath, your reign
is o'er' which HW transcribed for Mann 8
Oct. 1742 (MANN ii. 73–5). It was printed
GM 1742, xii. 544; *The New Ministry*, 1742,
pp. 12–13, and Williams, *Works* i. 146–9.
A copy, dated Nov. 1742, is in Williams
MSS lxix. ff. 69–71.

42. This ballad, which HW quotes to
Mann 23 Oct. 1742 OS (MANN ii. 90–1),
was usually called 'The Statesman' and is
printed Williams, *Works* i. 150–2; see
MANN ii. 90 n. 5 for other printings. In
his copy (now in the BM) of *A Collection
of Poems, Principally Consisting of the
Most Celebrated Pieces of Sir Charles
Hanbury Williams*, 1763, p. 29, HW has
written about this poem 'This was said to
be written by Dr King of Oxford, and
was never owned by Sir Ch. Williams, yet
I always believed it written by him.' A
MS note in the Yale Library copy of
The Foundling Hospital for Wit, Part I,
1743, p. 15, also attributes 'The Statesman' to Dr King.

43. HW has left a blank in MS.

44. It is printed Williams, *Works* ii. 102–
11, as 'A Letter to Mr Dodsley, Bookseller
in Pall Mall' and dated January 1743.

45. Perhaps 'An Ode Humbly Inscribed
to the Right Honourable William Earl of
Bath,' April 1743, printed Williams, *Works*
i. 190–3. A copy is in Williams MSS
lxix, ff. 89–90. There are 24 odes and
squibs against Bath printed in Williams,
Works.

46. Printed Williams, *Works* ii. 122–8. A
copy in Williams MSS lxix. ff. 86–7 is
dated April 1743, but it is in the GM's list
of books published in February 1743 (GM
1743, xiii. 112).

47. Printed Williams, *Works* ii. 129–35;
it is discussed in an undated letter from
Williams to Fox, printed in Ilchester, *Hanbury-Williams* 120.

48. 'A Congratulatory Letter to a Certain Right Hon. Person upon his Late Disappointment,' published in September
1743 (GM 1743, xiii. 504). That it was by
Williams seems doubtful; Fox wrote to
him 4 Oct. 1743: 'The congratulatory letter
which was sent us at Maddington, shows
how infinitely unpopular Lord Bath is, for
I think you did not much admire it, but
here it is extolled to the last degree, has
bore five editions, and is talked of by

oned Mr Doddington's, who had a great deal of wit, but I don't know that he ever wrote anything but his celebrated poem to Sir R[obert] W[alpole][49] in which is this line, mentioned by Pope,[50]

In pow'r a servant, out of pow'r a friend;

and some stanzas on the Treaty of Worms, called 'John Moore's Worm Powder.'[51] N.B. Mr Dodd[ington] has wrote this winter 1749 an 'Ode from Earl Powlett to Francis Fane Esq.'[52]

Other Poems and Pieces by Sir Charles Williams

Ode for Mr Doddington.[53] 1741.

Several little poems to Mr Winnington in the name of Mr Harris.[54]

Ditto to Mrs Woffington (whom he kept one winter) [55] under the name of Kitty Walker,[56] who was kept by Lord Loudon,[57] but was Sir Charles's mistress too.[58]

Epistle to Parson Hill.[59]

'On Legacy Hunters,'[60] in imitation of *Hoc quoque Tiresia*.[61]

everybody. Lord Chesterfield is by most people said to be the author, which I don't believe; but much less another whom I have heard named, which is yourself, but unless you are very close indeed I think I can witness for you against that report' (Williams MSS xlviii. ff. 54–5).

49. *An Epistle to the Right Honourable Sir Robert Walpole*, 1726; 4th edn, 1741.

50. *Epilogue to the Satires*, Dialogue II, l. 161.

51. *An Epistle from John Moore, Apothecary of Abchurch Lane, to L—— C—— upon his Treatise of Worms*, [1743].

52. These verses are not mentioned in HW's account of Doddington in the *Royal and Noble Authors* (*Works* i. 458, 531–2), although several others are included. This sentence is added in a later hand than the rest of the preceding paragraph.

53. 'A Grub upon Bub,' March 1741; printed Williams, *Works* i. 25–7. A copy is in Williams MSS lxix. ff. 45–6.

54. Three, at least, survive: 'To the Right Honourable Thomas Winnington from Mr Henry Harris Commissioner of the Wine Licence,' 1742 (an imitation of Horace, *Epistles* I. v), printed Williams, *Works* ii. 81–4; 'An Ode Humbly Inscribed to Thomas Winnington, Esq. by Henry Harris, Esq.' 1743, printed ibid. ii. 77–80;

and 'An Ode Supposed to have been wrote by Mr Harris to the Honourable Thomas Winnington Esq.' (an imitation of Horace *Odes* III. viii), printed Ilchester, *Hanbury-Williams* 118–9. Copies are in Williams MSS lxix. ff. 56–7, 91–2.

55. 1744; see *ante* 26 June 1744 and nn. 42–4.

56. Williams wrote two poems to Kitty Walker; one in December 1742, printed Williams, *Works* ii. 6–7 (copy in Williams MSS lxix. f. 75) and another in January 1743 (copy in Williams MSS lxix. f. 79). Four poems addressed to Mrs Woffington are in Williams, *Works* ii. 3–5, 8–15.

57. John Campbell (1705–82), 4th E. of Loudoun; army officer.

58. See the letter from Williams to Fox 27 Dec. 1742, quoted in Ilchester, *Hanbury-Williams* 65. Lord Ilchester thinks it unlikely that the verses to Kitty Walker were really addressed to Mrs Woffington.

59. 'To the Rev. Samuel Hill, Canon of Wells,' August 1744, printed Williams, *Works* ii. 57–62; copy in Williams MSS lxx. ff. 48–50.

60. 'Peter and My Lord Quidam,' August 1743, printed Williams, *Works* i. 37–60; copy in Williams MSS lxx. ff. 20–8.

61. Horace, *Satires* II. v.

The Duke of Dorset, old Horace Walpole and others were satirized in it. It has been reckoned his best: in my opinion his best was the following;

'The Toilette or the Morning';[62] it is a description of the Duchess of Manchester's levée and her lovers, Dicky Bateman, Charles Stanhope, Charles Churchill, and Lord Leicester.

'The Evening,' a soliloquy of Lady Fanny Shirley.[63]

A Dialogue between George Lyttelton and Mr Lechmere,[64] member for Leicestershire.

Ditto between Sandys and Waller.[65]

Imitation of *Donec gratus eram tibi*,[66] for Mr Winnington and Lady Townshend. Mr Winnington altered this and put in some lines on Lady Archibald Hamilton,[67] and then gave it Lord Bath, who showed it the Prince, who was extremely angry with Williams.

The same ode imitated for the Duchess of Manchester and General Churchill.[68]

'Clytemnestra to Sappho'; an Epistle for Mrs Edwin to Lady Townshend.[69]

An Imitation of *Sicelides musæ,* on a report of Mother Douglas having a son by Lord Fitzwilliam,[70] with notes. Mr H.W. wrote another imitation of the same at the same time on Lord Lincoln's having a daughter by Peggy Lee.[71] Soon after Sir Charles whose letters were not good in proportion to his other works,[71a] wrote a very good letter to Lord Lincoln on the death of Mother Hayward.[72]

62. 'Isabella or the Morning,' June 1743, printed Williams, *Works* i. 72–89; copy in Williams MSS lxx, ff. 9–19. Williams considered it his *'chef d'œuvre'* at the time of composition (to Fox 6 June 1743, quoted in Ilchester, *Hanbury-Williams* 121).

63. Lady Frances Shirley (ca 1706–78), dau. of 1st E. Ferrers. No copy of it has been found.

64. Edmund Lechmere (1710–1805), M.P. Worcestershire 1734–47 (Judd, *Members of Parliament* 252). The verses, 'A Political Eclogue,' written at the end of 1740, are printed Williams, *Works* i. 61–70.

65. 'A Dialogue between Samuel Sandys and Edmund Waller, Esquires' February 1743, printed Williams, *Works* ii. 112–20; copy in Williams MSS lxix. ff. 82–4.

66. Horace, *Odes* III. ix. It is printed Williams, *Works* i. 130–1, dated February 1740. Williams also wrote 'An Ode to Etheldreda, Viscountess Townshend,' in

September 1743; it is printed Ilchester, *Hanbury-Williams* 74–5; a copy is in Williams MSS lxx. ff. 29–30.

67. Lady Jane Hamilton (d. 1752), m. (1719) Lord Archibald Hamilton; Mistress of the Robes to the Princess of Wales and supposed mistress of the Prince (MONTAGU i. 16 and n. 19).

68. No copy of it has been found.

69. Written in July 1744; no copy of it has been found (Ilchester, *Hanbury-Williams* 86–7).

70. 'The Fourth Eclogue of Virgil Imitated and Inscribed to the Right Hon. the E. of Lincoln and H. Fox, Esquire' November, 1743; a copy is in Williams MSS lxx, ff. 39–43. See also above, Appendix 2, n. 1.

71. Printed above, Appendix 2.

71a. But see *post* n. 106.

72. 11 Dec. 1743 (*ante* 27 Dec. 1743, n. 1). The letter has apparently not survived.

Ode to Lord Lincoln,[73] with a fine compliment at the end to Mr Pelham.[74]

I think another ode to Lord Lincoln.[75]

'Prudence and Parts,' a satire to Mr Fox;[76] chiefly satirizing Mr Pelham; with the characters of Sir R.W. and Mr Winnington in opposition to his. There are many very fine lines in this poem; I remember these two,

> How Pelham would in little Lucca shine,
> And Sands be in Marino styled divine!

'Ode to Lord Chesterfield'[77] from Dresden. Soame Jennings wrote a miserable, and abusive ode on seeing this, and published it.[78]

'Stanzas on the Death of a Bullfinch killed by a Cat,'[79] wrote at Dresden and addressed to Philip Stanhope[80] Esq. natural son to Lord Chesterfield; they are very insipid, and the preceding ode to the father is little better.

None of the above have been published; the six following have.

1. 'A Simile,' in imitation of Dear Thomas of Prior.[81] On the new Treasury 1742.

2. 'Dear Betty Come Give Me Sweet Kisses';[82] a ballad from Martial,[83] for Lady Ilchester.[84]

73. Founded on a report he was to marry Lady Caroline Fitzroy (see Ilchester, *Hanbury-Williams* 117–8); printed Williams, *Works* ii. 33–5; a copy dated February 1743 is in Williams MSS lxix. ff. 80–1.

74. Williams also wrote a laudatory 'Ode to the Right Honourable Henry Pelham, Esq., On his being Appointed first Commissioner of the Treasury,' September 1743, printed Williams, *Works* ii. 71–3; a copy is in Williams MSS lxx. ff. 31–2.

75. Not discovered.

76. 'An Epistle to the Right Hon. Henry Fox,' written 1744–5, printed Williams, *Works* ii. 136–49.

77. Possibly *Tar-Water, A Ballad Inscribed to the . . . Earl of Chesterfield*, published in January 1747 (GM 1747, xvii. 52), reprinted in Williams, *Works* ii. 21–4. HW, however, has written 'not by Sir Ch. W.' on the verses in his copy of the 1763 edition of Williams's poems (now in the BM); and a MS note in the Yale Library copy of *The Foundling Hospital for Wit, Part IV*, 1747, p. 12, attributes the ode to

Soame Jenyns. Lord Ilchester (*Hanbury-Williams* 128), arguing for Williams's authorship of *Tar Water*, mentions an unfinished ode to Chesterfield on which Williams was working at Dresden in November 1747.

78. Apparently 'An Ode to Sir Charles Hanbury Williams; occasioned by seeing an ode inscribed to Lord Chesterfield,' printed Williams, *Works* ii. 30–2.

79. 'An Ode on the Death of Matzel, A Favourite Bullfinch,' June 1748, printed Williams, *Works* i. 107–10.

80. (1732–68).

81. Possibly 'A Simile: Printed in Geoffry Broadbottom's Journal; April 1743,' printed Williams, *Works* ii. 55–6.

82. Written in August 1740; printed Williams, *Works* i. 111–12; a copy is in Williams MSS lxix, f. 25.

83. *Epigrams* VI. xxxiv.

84. Elizabeth Strangways (1723–92), m. (1736) Stephen Fox, cr. (1741) Bn and (1756) E. of Ilchester.

3. 'Ode to Mr Poyntz'[85] on the suppression of the Rebellion.

4. 'Lord Bath to Ambition.'[86] On the revolution of three days 1746. An Advertisement came out in the papers on this, calling it, *Lacrymosa Poemata Puppi.*[87]

5. Speech of David Morgan[88] who was executed on Kennington Common, in prose.

6. Some lines that begin,

> Unhappy England, still in forty one
> By Scotland art thou doomed to be undone.[89]

In the winter 1749 on hearing of the debates on the bill for punishing mutiny and desertion, he sent this epigram from Dresden to Mr H. Harris;

> Why has Lord Egmont 'gainst this bill
> So much declamatory skill
> So tediously exerted?
> The reason's plain—but t'other day
> He mutinied himself for pay,
> And he has twice deserted.[90]

About the same time Mr Doddington, in hopes of being restored to the Prince's favour, resigned the treasurership of the Navy;[91] Mr Fox asked for it, but both the King and Duke pressed him not to take it, as there was nobody else whom they could like to have secretary at war:[92] upon which Mr Fox dropping his suit, the King told him, he would immediately make his friend Sir Charles Williams envoy extraordinary at Berlin, which he did.[93] Sir Charles had been trying much to be sent to Turin,[94] but his enemies had got it

---

85. Published in October 1746 (GM 1746, xvi. 560); reprinted Williams, *Works* i. 100–6.

86. *An Ode from the E— of B— to Ambition*, reprinted *The Foundling Hospital for Wit*, Part III, 1746, pp. 1–3; and Williams, *Works* i. 157–60.

87. Not found.

88. David or Thomas David Morgan, a 'poetical lawyer' who was executed 30 July 1746, with eight others, for his part in the '45; see MANN iii. 287 nn. 56 and 57. The 'speech' is printed in *The Foundling Hospital for Wit*, Part IV, 1747, pp. 37–46.

89. Written in Dec. 1741; printed Williams, *Works* i. 28–9; a copy is in Williams MSS lxix. f. 47. HW quotes them

to Mann 25 Feb. 1742 (MANN i. 346–7).

90. HW quotes these lines in his letter to Mann 3 May 1749 (MANN iv. 51).

91. 11 March 1749 (MANN iv. 39 n. 11).

92. HW mentions this incident in his letter to Mann 23 March 1749 (MANN iv. 39).

93. Williams was informed of the King's intention by Newcastle 18 April 1749; see MANN iv. 51 n. 39 for details of the appointment.

94. HW mentions that Williams had been hoping to be sent to Turin as early as December 1746; he was pressing it sharply and Fox was urging it for him throughout 1748 (MANN iii. 347, 456, and n. 5; iv. 16 and n. 2).

for Lord Rochford.[95] Before he went to Berlin, he was[96] commissioned in July 1749[97] along with Mr Anstis,[98] Garter K[ing] at Arms, to carry the blue ribband to the Margrave of Anspach.[99] Sir Ch[arles] came to London from the Hague Sept. 6, 1749.[100] Wrote an epitaph in verse for Mr Winnington's monument in Worcestershire.[101] He set out for Berlin in May 1750, and passed through Hanover when the King was there.[102] From whence he was sent to the King of Poland[103] who was holding the Diet at Warsaw,[104] to engage his vote for the Archduke Joseph to be King of the Romans. On this progress he wrote a celebrated letter[105] to the Duke of Newcastle at Hanover, which was sent over to England and much admired, as his ministerial letters were.[106] About this time he met the ministers[107] of the two Empresses of Germany and Russia, and reconciled those Princesses,[108] and then set out for Berlin,[109] where he was very coldly received, and soon grew so offensive to the King of Prussia, that he desired to have him recalled,[110] and he accordingly was again sent to Dresden, whither he went in February 1751.[111] Some of the reasons for the King of Pr[ussia]'s disgust were,

95. William Henry Nassau de Zuylestein (1717–81), 4th E. of Rochford; envoy to Sardinia 1749–55.

96. Much of the rest of this account of Williams's diplomatic career is incorporated *literatim* in the 'Account of the Embassy of the Right Hon. Sir Charles Hanbury Williams,' in Williams, *Works* ii. 208–11.

97. Actually in August 1749, on his way from Dresden to England (Ilchester, *Hanbury-Williams* 173).

98. John Anstis (ca 1709–54).

99. Karl Wilhelm (1712–57), Markgraf of Ansbach 1723–57.

100. He left Ansbach ca 28 Aug. 1749 (MANN iv. 90 n. 8), arrived at Lowestoft 3 Sept. (Ilchester, *Hanbury-Williams* 177) and reached London 5 Sept. according to the *Daily Adv.* 8 Sept. 1749.

101. Printed Williams, *Works* ii. 85–6.

102. For more details of this visit, see Ilchester, *Hanbury-Williams* 181–2.

103. Frederick Augustus II (1696–1763), K. of Poland 1733–63.

104. In August 1750.

105. Not identified. For Williams's mission, see D. B. Horn, *Sir Charles Hanbury-Williams and European Diplomacy*, 1930, pp. 55–9.

106. HW told Mann 20 Sept. 1750 that Williams's letters 'are as much admired as ever his verses were,' and on 18 Oct. that Williams and Keene were the envoys in fashion (MANN iv. 186, 198).

107. Heinrich, Freiherr Gross (d. 1765), Russian minister to Prussia 1748–50; and Anton von Portugal, Graf von Puebla (d. 1769), Imperial envoy to Prussia 1749–56 (MANN iv. 186 n. 7). Williams arrived at Berlin 7 July 1750 NS and had met Gross by the 11th and Puebla by the 15th (ibid).

108. HW makes similar comments to Mann 20 Sept. 1750 (MANN iv. 186–7), but Horn, op. cit. 57 n. 3, commenting on that passage, writes that 'there appears to be no foundation, in fact, for this sentence.'

109. Williams resided at Berlin 7 July–1 Aug. 1750 NS before going to Warsaw; he returned to Berlin from Warsaw 13 Sept. 1750 NS (Ilchester, *Hanbury-Williams* 182, 190, 200).

110. For these events, see ibid. Chap. VIII and Horn, op. cit. 60–7.

111. Williams left Berlin for Dresden 9 March 1751 NS (Ilchester, *Hanbury-Williams* 222).

that Sir Charles as soon as he came to Dresden[112] discovered that the
Saxon minister[113] there informed the Court of Berlin of all the
secrets that he learned from the Russian minister,[114] which correspondence Sir Charles broke off;[115] and that a Tartar[116] having been
sent to Berlin to get the release of one of his countrymen who was
in that army, the King of Prussia paid him the highest honours, in
order to make the Court of Russia believe that this was a minister
sent him by the Tartars who had a mind to break their union with
Russia: Sir Charles discovered the fictitiousness of this embassy. In
March 1753 he was sent to Vienna[117] to demand the assistance of
that Court, in case the King of Prussia should proceed to extremi-
ties, after stopping the Silesian Loan: here he made the following
distich on the Empress Queen

O Regina, orbis prima et pulcherrima; ridens
Es Venus, incedens Juno, Minerva loquens.[118]

He returned to Dresden,[119] and August 5th, 1753 landed at Harwich, and was soon after made a privy councillor.[120] Sept. 13. No.
37 of a paper called the *World* was published, written by Sir
Charles. In Dec. being at his own house at Coldbrook, his eldest
daughter[121] was very ill, Mr Garnier[122] and Mr Peirce[123] the surgeon
came from Bath to attend her, and on her recovery, Sir Charles
wrote an ode to them, in praise of humanity[124]—but it was a very

112. A slip for Berlin.
113. Friedrich Gotthard, Freiherr von
Bülow (1688–1768), Saxon envoy to Prussia
1746–57 (*Repertorium der diplomatischen
Vertreter aller Länder*, Vol. II, ed. Hausmann, Zurich, 1950, p. 340; *Neues Preus-
sisches Adels-Lexicon*, Leipzig, 1842–3, i.
328; Michael Ranfft, *Fortgesetzte neue genealogisch-historische Nachrichten*, Leipzig,
1762–77, viii. 639–40).
114. Gross (above, n. 107).
115. For this incident, see Ilchester,
Hanbury-Williams 184, 189; Horn, op. cit.
54 and n. 9.
116. Mustafá Aǧa, who was at Berlin on
a special mission 27 July–8 Aug. 1750
(Hausmann, op. cit. 398). For the incident,
see Ilchester, *Hanbury-Williams* 189, and
Horn, op. cit. 54–5 and n. 9.
117. On an unofficial mission; see Il-
:hester, *Hanbury-Williams* Chap. XI, and
Horn, op. cit. Chap. VIII, for details.

118. HW also quotes this in a letter to
Conway 5 May 1753.
119. 17 June 1753 (Ilchester, *Hanbury-
Williams* 278). He left for England 17 July
(ibid. 279).
120. Williams was never a privy councillor.
121. Frances (*ante* 15 Aug. 1758, n. 5).
122. George Garnier (1703–63), of
Rookesbury, Wickham, Hants; apothecary-
general to the Army 1735–63; friend of
Chesterfield and Garrick (A. E. Garnier,
*The Chronicles of the Garniers of Hamp-
shire*, 1900, pp. 21–4).
123. (d. 1768), surgeon (*London Magazine* 1768, xxxvii. 54).
124. 'To Mr Garnier and Mr Pearce of
Bath. A Grateful Ode, in return for the
extraordinary kindness and humanity they
showed to me and my eldest daughter, now
Lady Essex, 1753,' printed Williams, *Works*
i. 230–3.

middling performance—*Antoni gladios si sic!*[125] At the same time he wrote a ballad on his niece,[126] a child of five years old. He was sent for in great haste,[127] to go abroad, on the situation of affairs in Germany, but did not set out for Dresden till Aug. 7, 1754, having waited for the nuptials of his eldest daughter Frances, who was married to the Earl of Essex Aug. 1, 1754. At the end of the year he attended the King of Poland to Warsaw,[128] where he entered too warmly into the interests of the Poniatowskis,[129] in an affair called the Disposition of the Ostrog, wherein Count Brühl[130] taking the part of the enemies of that house, Sir Charles and Brühl came to an open rupture. In April 1755, Sir Charles was named ambassador to Russia; and that year concluded a subsidiary treaty with that Court, for taking a body of Russians into our pay,[131] to defend the Electorate of Hanover, in case the King of Prussia should take part with France in the war we were then entering into,[132] and which treaty produced a reconciliation and alliance with the Court of Berlin—However, Sir Charles incurred the King's anger, by letting the Russians sign both copies of the treaty first,[133] contrary to all usage.

He returned to England Feb. 26, 1758, but appearing to be disordered in his senses, was sent to Kensington and put under the care of Dr Battie,[134] a mad-doctor. Recovering in very few days, he retired to his own house of Coldbrook in Monmouthshire:[135] but relapsed in the next spring[136] and was shut up.

Oct. 31, 1759. He was seized with convulsions as he went to bed and continued in them till next day when he fell into a kind of apoplectic lethargy, and died on Friday morning Nov. 2d 1759. His eldest daughter Lady Essex died in childbed a few months before

125. Antoni gladios potuit contemnere, si sic (Juvenal, *Satires* x. 123). (Had Cicero always spoken thus, he might have laughed at the swords of Antony.)

126. 'A Song on Miss Harriet Hanbury,' printed Williams, *Works* i. 116–18.

127. For this incident, see Ilchester, *Hanbury-Williams* 283–4.

128. In September 1754 (ibid. 289).

129. For this affair, see ibid. 289ff. and Horn, op. cit. Chap. IX.

130. Heinrich von Brühl (1700–63), Graf von Brühl, prime minister of Saxony-Poland (MANN v. 2 n. 8).

131. For this treaty and its effects, see Horn, op. cit. Chaps. X and XI.

132. The Seven Years' War.

133. For somewhat contradictory accounts of this incident, see Ilchester, *Hanbury-Williams* 320–1, and Horn, op. cit. 190.

134. William Battie (1704–76), M.D., 1737.

135. By 25 April 1758 (Ilchester, *Hanbury-Williams* 424).

136. Actually by December 1758 (ibid. 427–8).

him,[137] and two days after [*sic*] her death, his other daughter[138] married Mr Boyle-Walsingham, second son of the Earl of Shannon, and Captain of a ship.

137. 19 July 1759.

138. Charlotte Hanbury-Williams (1738–90), m. (17 July 1759) Hon. Robert Boyle (later Boyle-Walsingham) (1736–80), Capt. in the Navy.

APPENDIX 4

WALPOLE'S 'THE BEAUTIES'

See *ante* 19, 22, and 24 July 1746.
Printed from HW's copy in *MS Poems,* pp. 153–60.
Endorsed by HW: Wrote in July, 1746.

The Beauties.
An Epistle to Eckardt,[1] the Painter.

[2]Desponding artist, talk no more
Of beauties of the days of yore;
Of goddesses renowned in Greece,
And Zeuxis'[3] composition piece,
Where ev'ry nymph, that could at most
Some single grace or feature boast,
Contributed her fav'rite charm
To perfect the ideal form.
'Twas Cynthia's brow, 'twas Lesbia's eye,
'Twas Chloe's cheek's vermilion dye;
Roxana lent the noble air;
Dishevelled flowed Aspasia's hair;
And Cupid much too fondly pressed
His mimic mother Thais' breast.
    Antiquity, how poor thy use,
A single Venus to produce!
Friend Eckardt, ancient story quit,
Nor mind whatever Pliny writ:
Felibien[4] and Fresnoy[5] disclaim,

1. 'He was a German and scholar to Vanloo' (HW). John Giles Eccardt (d. 1779), who painted some two dozen portraits of HW's friends and relatives for HW. His portraits of HW and Gray are now in the National Portrait Gallery.

2. 'Some copies of this poem having got about, it was printed without the author's knowledge, and with several errors: it was reprinted more correctly in the second volume of a miscellany of poems in three volumes published by Dodsley 1748 [*A Collection of Poems. By Several Hands,* 1748, ii. 321–7]' (HW). The 'errors' are greatly exaggerated.

3. (d. ca 400 B.C.). His 'composition piece,' combining the best features of five maidens, is described in Pliny's *Natural History* XXXV. xxxvi. 64 and Cicero's *De Inventione* II. ii. 1–3.

4. André Félibien (1619–95), sieur des Avaux and de Javercy, architect and author of many books, including *Entretiens sur les vies et sur les ouvrages des plus*

Who talk of Raphael's matchless fame;
Of Titian's tints, Correggio's grace;
And Carlo's[6] each Madonna-face;
As if no beauties now were made,
But Nature had forgot her trade.
'Twas beauty guided Raphael's line,
From heav'nly women styled, *divine:*
They warmed old Titian's fancy too,
And what he could not taste, he drew.
Think you devotion warmed his breast,
When Carlo with such looks expressed
His virgins, that her vot'ries feel
Emotions—not, I'm sure of zeal?

   In Britain's isle observe the fair,
And curious choose your models there:
Such patterns as shall raise your name
To rival sweet Correggio's fame:
Each single piece shall be a test,
And Zeuxis' patchwork grow a jest,
Who ransacked Greece and culled the age
To bring one goddess on the stage:
On your each canvas we'll admire
The charms of the whole heav'nly choir.
Majestic Juno shall be seen
In Hervey's[7] glorious awful mien.

   Where Fitzroy[8] moves, resplendent fair,
So warm her bloom, sublime her air,
Her ebon tresses form'd to grace,
And heighten while they shade her face;
Such troops of martial youths around,
Who court the hand that gives the wound;

excellentes peintres anciens et modernes, 1666.

5. Charles-Alphonse Dufresnoy (1611–65), painter and poet. The reference is to his *De arte graphica,* 1668, which HW considered 'a middling poem' (Mason i. 473).

6. 'Carlo Maratti' (HW).

7. 'Lepelle, eldest daughter to John Lord Hervey, and wife to Mr Phipps: see the history of their wedding in the "Fairy Tale" above' (HW). Lepell Hervey (1723–80), m. (1743) Constantine Phipps, cr. (1767) Bn Mulgrave; HW's 'Fairy Tale' is in his *MS Poems,* pp. 69–76.

8. 'Lady Caroline Fitzroy, eldest daughter to Charles Duke of Grafton, and since married to William Stanhope Lord Viscount Petersham, eldest son to the Earl of Harrington' (HW).

'Tis Pallas, Pallas stands confessed;
Though Stanhope's more than Paris blessed.
So Cleveland[9] shone in warlike pride,
By Lely's pencil deified:
So Grafton,[10] matchless dame, commands,
The fairest work of Kneller's hands:
The blood, that warmed each am'rous Court,
In veins as rich still loves to sport;
And George's age beholds restored
What William boasted, Charles adored.

    For Venus's—the Trojan ne'er
Was half so puzzled to declare—
Ten queens of beauty sure I see!
Yet sure the true is Emily![11]
Such majesty of youth and air;
Yet modest as the village fair:
Whole swarms of Cupids round, yet none
Alas! the goddess calls her son![12]

    In smiling Capel's[13] bounteous youth
Rich autumn's goddess is mistook:
With poppies and with spiky corn,
Eckardt, her nutbrown curls adorn;
And by her side in decent line
Place charming Berkeley,[14] Proserpine.

9. 'The celebrated Duchess of Cleveland, great-grandmother to Lady Caroline, is drawn like Pallas among the beauties of King Charles II's reign, at Windsor, by Sir Peter Lely' (HW). Barbara Villiers (1641–1709), m. (1659) Roger Palmer, cr. (1661) E. of Castlemaine; cr. (1670) Ds of Cleveland, s.j.; mistress of Charles II.

10. 'The Duchess of Grafton, grandmother to Lady Caroline, is among King William's beauties at Hampton Court, by Sir Godfrey Kneller' (HW). Lady Isabella Bennet (1688–1723), m. 1 (1672, remarried 1679) Henry Fitzroy, cr. (1672) E. of Euston and (1675) D. of Grafton; m. 2 (1698) Sir Thomas Hanmer, 4th Bt; Cts of Arlington, s.j.

11. 'Lady Emily Lenox, second daughter to Charles Duke of Richmond; since married to the Earl of Kildare' (HW).

12. This and the preceding line are crossed out and the following substituted by HW:
    Attracting all, indulging none,
    Her beauty like the glorious sun
    Throned eminently bright above,
    Impartial warms the world to love.
The published versions follow the revised form.

13. 'Lady Mary Capel, second daughter to the late Earl of Essex' (HW). Lady Mary Capel or Capell (1722–82), dau. of William Capel, 3d of Essex; m. (1758) Adm. the Hon. John Forbes (Collins, *Peerage*, 1812, iii. 484; GM 1782, lii. 206).

14. '[Elizabeth] daughter to Henry Drax Esq., sometime maid of honour to the Princess of Wales, and now wife to Augustus Earl Berkeley' (HW).

Mild as a summer sea, serene ⎫
In dimpled beauty, next be seen ⎬
Ailsb'ry,[15] like hoary Neptune's queen. ⎭
   With her, the light dispensing fair,
Whose beauty gilds the morning air,
And bright as her attendant sun,
The new Aurora, Lyttelton.[16]
Such Guido's[17] pencil beauty-tipped,
And in ethereal colours dipped,
In measured dance to tuneful song
Drew the sweet goddess, as along
Heav'ns azure, 'neath their light feet spread,
The frolic hours she fairest led.
The crescent on her brow displayed,
In curls of loveliest brown inlaid,
With ev'ry charm to rule the night,
Like Dian, Strafford[18] woos the sight.
The easy shape, the piercing eye,
The snowy bosom's purity;
The unaffected gentle phrase
Of native wit in all she says;
Eckardt, for these thy art's too faint;
You may admire, but cannot paint.
How Hebe smiled, what bloom divine
On the young goddess loved to shine,
From Carpenter[19] we guess, or see,
All-beauteous Manners[20] beam from thee.

15. 'Caroline daughter to General John Campbell, and second wife to old Charles Bruce Earl of Ailsbury, on whose death she was married in 1747 to Colonel Henry Conway only brother to Francis Lord Conway; now Earl of Hertford' (HW).

16. 'Lucy, sister to Hugh Fortescue Earl Clinton, and wife to George Lyttelton Esq. She was a great friend to, and like Lady Ailsbury, but still handsomer. She died in January 1747. Her husband, since Sir George Lyttelton, wrote a monody on her death' (HW).

17. 'Guido's Aurora in the Rospigliosi Palace at Rome' (HW).

18. 'Lady Anne Campbell [ca1715–85], second daughter to John late Duke of Argyle, and wife [1741] to William Wentworth Earl of Strafford' (HW).

19. '[Hon. Alicia Maria Carpenter (d. 1794)] daughter to Lord Carpenter, married to Sir Ch[arles] Windham Earl of Egremont March 1751' (HW).

20. '—— natural daughter to Lord William Manners. She since ran away with, and is married to a Capt. Hall: 1748, and died in childbed the next year' (HW).

How pretty Flora, wanton maid,
By Zephyr wooed in noontide shade,
With rosy hand coquetly throwing
Pansies, beneath her sweet touch blowing,
How blithe she looked, let Fanny[21] tell;
Let Zephyr own if half so well.

Another goddess[22] of the year,
Fair queen of summer see appear;
Her auburn locks with fruitage crowned,
Her panting bosom loosely bound;
Ethereal beauty in her face,
Rather the beauties of her race,
Whence ev'ry goddess envy-smit,
Must own each Stonehouse meets in Pitt.[23]

Exhausted all the heav'nly train,
How many mortals yet remain,
Whose eyes shall try your pencil's art,
And in my numbers claim their part.
Our sister Muses must describe
Chudleigh,[24] or name her of their tribe;
And Juliana[25] with the Nine
Shall aid the melancholy line
To weep her dear resemblance[26] gone,
Where all these beauties met in one.
Sad fate of beauty! more I see
Afflicted, lovely family!
Two beauteous nymphs here, painter, place
Lamenting o'er their sister[27] Grace;

21. 'Miss Fanny Maccartny; she was a very pretty poetess: married to Fulk Greville Esq. in 1748' (HW).

22. 'Pomona' (HW).

23. 'Miss Penelope Atkins [ca 1725–95], wife [1746] to George Pitt Esq. of Stratfieldsea, and daughter to Sir Robert Atkins [Sir Henry Atkins (ca 1707–28) 4th Bt], by [m. 1723] Miss [Penelope] Stonehouse [d. 1734], afterwards [1733] married to John Lord Gower. The Stonehouses and Dashwoods were near relations and remarkable for their beauty: in Dryden's *Miscellanies* in a poem on the then beauties, it is said

"The Dashwoods are a family of charms" ' (HW).

24. 'Miss Chudleigh, maid of honour to the Princess of Wales' (HW).

25. 'Lady Juliana Farmor [1729–1801], fourth daughter to Thomas Earl of Pomfret: married in 1751 to Mr [Thomas] Pen [1702–75], the lord of Pensilvania' (HW). For a note on her see BERRY i. 7 n. 2.

26. 'Lady Sophia Farmor, eldest daughter to Lord Pomfret, and second wife to John Earl Granville: she died in childbed at the age of 24, 1745' (HW).

27. 'Miss Mary Evelyn, died 1745' (HW).

One,[28] matron-like, with sober grief
Scarce gives her pious sighs relief;
While 'tother[29] lovely maid appears
In all the melting pow'r of tears;
The softest form, the gentlest grace,
The sweetest harmony of face;
Her snowy limbs and artless move
Contending with the Queen of Love,
While bashful beauty shuns the prize,
Which Emily might yield to Evelyn's eyes.[30]

The genealogy of the Evelyn family in *Miscellanea genealogica et heraldica* 2d ser., 1892, iv. 339 gives the date of her death as 1744.

28. '[Ann] Evelyn [1721–81], wife [1736] to Daniel Boone Esq.' (HW). For her see *Miscellanea genealogica et heraldica,* loc. cit.

29. 'Miss Elizabeth Evelyn [1723–94]; married in 1750 to Peter Bathurst Esq.

of Clarendon Park in Wiltshire' (HW). See ibid.

30. 'The Duke of Montagu, who was in love with Miss Peggy Banks, not finding her name in this poem, added these two lines to it:

Now, ladies all, return me thanks,
Or else I'll sing of Peggy Banks'
(HW).

APPENDIX 5

WALPOLE'S LETTER FROM THE KING OF THE MOHOCKS TO RICHARD RIGBY

See *ante* 25 June 1745, n. 12, and 6 Aug. 1745, n. 23.
Printed for the first time from HW's copy in *MS Poems*, pp. 175–6.
Endorsed by HW: Strawberry Hill, 1748.

Mac-Hack-Shock-Knock-O-Thunder-Blood
Late King of the Mohocks,
To Richard Rigby.[1]

Right lusty and well-beloved cousin,

DAMN our blood over again, if it is not with great satisfaction that we every day receive expresses, setting forth your great valour and high exploits. Confound our royal soul, if it does not give us damned pleasure to think that our mighty empire is likely to rise from its ruins, and again triumph over peace and law! There is not a ghost comes hither, but relates some new achievement of yours. We have heard how you encountered and vanquished in single combat a brawny priest at the ford of Bristol: how courageously you overthrew with a crystal mace charged with Burgundy an Oxonian proctor—not wont to be so overcome; and how heroically after that victory you assumed the royal dignity of Monarch of the Mohocks, and yourself declared your person sacred.[2] We have heard how in consequence of your own royal proclamation, very properly issued in a city[3] which is accustomed to set up kings in defiance of the laws of the land, you have since attacked your competitor,[4] and assaulted his guards at the very gate of his palace; an adventure not to be

1. 'Richard Rigby of Mistley Hall in Essex, born Feb. 1721 [1722]; only son of Richard Rigby Esq. [d. 1730, factor to the South Sea Company] by Anne Perry [d. 1741], was chosen member for Castle Rising in Norfolk on the death of General Churchill in 1745 (being a borough of Lord Orford's), and for Sudbury in Suffolk in the new Parliament that began in 1747' (HW).

2. 'Mr Rigby going with Sir Ch[arles] Williams into Wales, made a visit to Mr G[eorge] Selwyn at Oxford, where they supped at a tavern, and the riot here mentioned happened. The proctor threatened to commit Mr Rigby to prison, who told him he was a member of Parliament, and that his person was sacred' (HW). See *ante* 6 Aug. 1745 for further references to this incident.

3. 'Oxford' (HW).

4. 'The King. Mr Rigby, Mr George Pitt, and some other young men coming home from the tavern, got into a riot with the guard at St James's, who fired upon them' (HW).

paralleled in the annals of Mohock, in as much as the greatest victories achieved by us or our royal predecessors were only over unarmed and defenceless people. But, O wonderful youth, by God, you have far outstripped our greatest heroes, and art even a match for those Swiss champions who used to be our bodyguards, I mean the bruisers of the thrice illustrious Bear Garden; witness your ever-memorable combat in the inn at Epsom. Nor are even the renowned and laudable body of smugglers to be compared with you, who not only set law at nought, but having assumed the royal dignity yourself, are so hardy, unlike other monarchs, as to execute the duties of your high office in person; alone, unassisted you defeated a troop of rebel custom-house officers, and pressed[5] another gang without any commission. But these exploits are nothing compared to your famous campaign at Sudbury, concluded so triumphantly, and signalized so memorably by your stigmatizing with cowardice the conqueror[6] of Porto Bello.

5. 'He was sailing down the river, when some custom-house officers insisting on visiting the boat, he pretended to be a press officer, and took them prisoners' (HW).

6. 'A new Parliament being summoned in 1747, Mr Nugent carried Mr Rigby to the Prince who promised to assist him with £1,000 if he would go down and stand for Sudbury in his interest which he did, and though so populous a town, and in which he did not know one man, he carried his election [on 1 July 1747], notwithstanding the opposition of Mr [Thomas] Fonnereau [1699–1779, merchant; M.P. Sudbury 1741–68, Aldeburgh 1773–9] the old Court candidate, and the friends of Capt. [John] Robinson who lived in that country, and the interest of the Duke of Grafton who had intended to choose there his son-in-law Lord Petersham. A petition was threatened, but said to be dropped, till the very last day [30 Nov. 1747] for presenting them, when Mr Rigby having been assured there would be none, had gone out of town on business. Late in the evening before the last day, Mr H.W. had notice that a petition [printed *Journals of the House of Commons* xxv. 451–2] would be presented against Mr Rigby, on which he got a counter-petition [printed ibid. xxv. 453] drawn up by Mr Fox, and signed by what Sudbury voters he could meet with in London, and sent post for Mr Rigby. Mr Fonnereau prevailed on Admiral Vernon to present it, and Mr W. got Mr [Richard Savage] Nassau [1723–80, M.P. Colchester 1747–54, Malden 1774–80] to present that against Mr Fonnereau, and seconded it himself; and Vernon having complained of Mr Rigby's carrying the election by violence and having a body of bruisers there, Mr W. concluded his speech with saying, "They have raised up buckram-bruisers who terrified with their hands in their pockets, and now get their petition presented by an hon[ourable] gentleman of such known zeal for his country that he terrified it for a whole winter with buckram-invasions" (alluding to his behaviour during the Rebellion). Mr Rigby arrived in the House just at the conclusion, and Col. [John] Mostyn [ca 1710–79, M.P. Malton 1741–68] telling him in joke that Vernon had called him bruiser, he said in his speech, at the conclusion, "that he heard that gentleman had called him bruiser; but, Sir, there is no appellation of courage that I shall ever bestow on him."—Vernon took it quietly. The petition was put off to a long day and dropped the next year. The Prince sunk one hundred of the 1,000 he was to

On these and many other accounts we are inclined to confirm to you the act of succession to our throne and dignity, which you, like other princes, first assumed; and we shall by our ambassadors invite all other Christian princes here in Hell to guarantee this succession.

But sink us! if amidst all our joy, we have not one great cause to complain of you, for as much as we are informed by our emissaries, that with all your achievements you mix a wit and spirit, which is unprecedented in our story, no true Mohock having ever had parts or courage, or at least not both. We therefore adjure you by the eternal lake of ever-flowing brimstone not to degenerate from your great predecessors, as you hope to arrive at immortal damnation!

By his Majesty's command
MAC-ZOUNDS

PS. Alexander the Great is drinking your health in a bumper of blood out of the ghost of a skull-cap.

Given at our Court in Pluto's Round-House in the 34th year of our Damnation.

give Mr Rigby, and after having promised for two years to make him groom of the Bedchamber, his friend Mr Nugent got that place for a Mr [William] Trevanion [1728–67, M.P. Tregony 1747–67], on promise of choosing Mr Nugent's son [Edmund Nugent (ca 1731–71), army officer; M.P. Liskeard 1754–9, St Mawes 1761–70] at his own borough, where Trevanion had been opposed by the Prince, and voted in by the ministry before he was of age' (HW).

APPENDIX 6

WALPOLE'S CHARACTER OF HENRY FOX, 1748

See *ante* 20 Dec. 1756 and ca 22 Dec. 1756.
Printed from the MS now WSL.
Endorsed by HW: To Lady Caroline Fox (*and in his later hand*) Strawberry
Hill, 1748.

Madam,

I HAVE been attempting to draw a picture of one of your friends, and think I have in some degree succeeded; but as I fear natural partiality may make me flatter myself, I choose to submit to your judgment, whose prevention for the person represented is likely to balance what fondness I may have for my own performances. As I believe you love the person concerned as much as ever other people love themselves, the medium between the faults you shall find and the justness that I see in the following portrait, is likely to be an exact image.

The gentleman I am going to draw is about three and forty; as you see all the fondness, and delicacy and attention of a lover in him, perhaps your Ladyship may take him to be but three and twenty; but I, whose talent is not flattery, and who from his judgment and experience and authority should at first set him down for threescore, upon the strictest inquiry can only allow him to be in the vigour of his age and understanding. His person decides rather on my side, for though he has all the ease and amiableness of youth, yet your Ladyship must allow that it has a dignity in it which youth might aim at in vain, and will scarce ever be exchanged for. If I were like common painters, I should give him a ruddy healthful complexion, and light up his countenance with insipid smiles and unmeaning benevolence. But this would not be a faithful portrait: a florid bloom would no more give one an idea of him, than his bent brow at first lets one into the vast humanity of his temper, or than an undistinguishing smile would supply the place of his manly curiosity and penetration. To paint him with a cheerful open countenance would be a poor return of compliment for the flattery that his approbation bestows, which by not being promised, doubly satisfies one's self-love. The merit of others is degrading to their friends; Mr —— makes his open upon you, by persuading you that he discovers some in you.

Mr —— has that true characteristic of a great man, that he is superior to others in his private, social, unbended hours. I am far from meaning by this superiority that he exerts the force of his genius unnecessarily: on the contrary, you only perceive his superiority in those moments by his being more agreeably good-natured and idle with more ease than other people. He seems inquisitive as if his only business were to learn, and is unreserved as if he were only to inform; and is equally incapable of mystery in pretending to know what he does not, or in concealing what he does.

In the House of Commons he was for some time an ungraceful and unpopular speaker, the abundance of his matter overflowing his elocution: but the force of his reasoning has prevailed both over his own defects and those of his audience. He speaks with a strength and perspicuity of argument that commands the admiration of an age apt to be more cheaply pleased. But his vanity cannot satisfy itself on the terms it could satisfy others, nor would he thank any man for his approbation unless he were conscious of deserving it. But he carries this delicacy still farther, and has been at the idle labour of making himself fame and honours by pursuing a regular and steady plan, when art and eloquence would have carried him to an equal height, and made those fear him who now only love him—if a party can love a man who they see is only connected to them by principles.[1]

In another light one may discover another littleness in his conduct: in the affairs of his office he is as minute and as full of application as if he were always to remain in the same post; and as exact and knowing as if he always had been in it. He is as attentive to the solicitation and interests of others in his province as if he were making their fortune not his own; and to the great detriment of the ministry, has turned one of the best sinecures under the government into one of the most laborious employments, at the same time imagining that the ease with which he executes it will prevent the discovery of his innovation. He receives all officers who address to him with as little pride as if he were not born their equal or inferior: yet this defect of birth is a blemish which some of the greatest men have wanted to make them completely great. Tully had it,

---

1. 'Not by choice' is crossed out.

had the happiness and glory of raising himself from a private condition, but boasting of it, might as well have been noble. A patrician's daughter would have degraded herself by marrying a man who usurped that privilege of nobility, pride of what one can neither cause nor prevent.

I say nothing of his integrity, because I know nothing of it, but that it has never been breathed upon even by suspicion; it will be time enough to vindicate it when it has been impeached. He is as well-bred as those who colour over timidity with gentleness of manners, and as bravely sincere as those who take or would have brutality taken for honesty; but though his greatest freedom is polite, his greatest condescension is dignified with spirit, and he can no more court his enemies than relax in civility to his friends. But though he has more spirit than almost any man living, it is never looked upon as flowing from his passions, by the intimate connection that it always preserves with his understanding. Yet his passions are very strong; he loves play, women more, and one woman more than all. The amiableness of his behaviour to her, is only equalled by hers to him—but as your Ladyship would not know a picture of this charming woman, when drawn with all her proper graceful virtues; and as that engaging ignorance might draw you even into an uncertainty about the portrait of the gentleman, I shall lay down my pencil, and am, Madam,

Your Ladyship's most obedient humble servant,

VANDYKE

APPENDIX 7

WALPOLE AND HENRY FOX

THE criticism of Fox in Walpole's *Memoirs* and in his letters to others is in striking contrast to the friendliness of his letters to Fox. This divergence is largely accounted for by Walpole's attitude towards the events that transpired between the writing of his letters and the composition of the *Memoirs,* an interval that might be as great as four or five years. To make the divergence clear, we quote or summarize here Walpole's chief references to Fox in the *Memoirs,* comparing (when possible) his retrospective opinions with those that he had expressed in his letters when the events occurred, and indicating the intervening factors that may have led him to become more hostile to Fox. We omit most of the passages in Walpole's letters to Mann, since many of them, including the most favourable to Fox, were written while Fox was Mann's superior as secretary of state and Walpole's letters were being sent through his office.

Walpole treats Fox equally well in the letters and the *Memoirs* until the autumn of 1755. Their relations had been especially harmonious during the ministerial crisis of March 1754 when Fox had followed Walpole's advice to refuse a secretaryship of state.[1] Fox's conduct in this crisis is therefore recounted with approval in the *Memoirs* (which were written shortly after 26 December 1755); Walpole's rôle as successful adviser is noted.[2] Yet things had already begun to go wrong when Walpole wrote this passage.

In September 1755 Fox accepted the renewed offer of a secretaryship of state without consulting Walpole, who promptly informed Chute 29 September that Fox was 'all Christian charity, and forgiving everybody but himself and those who dissuaded him, for not taking the seals before.' Although he confessed to Conway 15 November that he remained silent in the House during the opening debates because he 'would not vote against Mr Fox' even though he disapproved of the measures Fox was now pledged to support, 'Gilly' Williams noted a few weeks later that Walpole had taken down Fox's picture and put up one of Pitt instead.[3] Walpole certainly did not

1. See *ante* 13 March 1754 and notes.   3. See above, p. 125.
2. *Mem. Geo. II* i. 384–5.

conceal his disapproval of Fox's conduct when he described the events of 1755 in the *Memoirs* (written apparently in 1756 or 1757), stating that in accepting office Fox 'took care not to consult his former counsellors, who had been attentive only to his honour, but listened to men far less anxious for it.'[4] A year's further reflection and observation provided an even harsher characterization of Fox as secretary of state in the *Memoirs* for 1756 (written in 1758):

He had neither the patriotism which forms a virtuous character, nor the love of fame which composes a shining one, and often supplies the place of the other. His natural bent was the love of power, with a soul generous and profuse; but growing a fond father, he became a provident father—and from a provident father to a rapacious man, the transition was but too easy.[5]

This unflattering characterization of Fox helps prepare the reader of the *Memoirs* for Walpole's account of how he frustrated Fox's scheme for a ministry without Pitt during the ministerial crisis of the autumn of 1756.

Walpole's correspondence with Fox during this crisis is the most difficult of all to reconcile with the relevant passages in the *Memoirs*, written two years later. In his letters Walpole urged Fox to take the Treasury himself if possible;[6] then later, when Fox temporarily retired from the House in December, he assured him that he would 'act and vote' as Fox directed, because he would have 'no rule for my behaviour in Parliament but in doing whatever you did';[7] and finally he told him that he was preparing for publication his character of Fox, written eight years before, as 'a testimonial of my attachment to you out of power, my passionate principle.'[8]

The account in the *Memoirs*, written in the summer of 1758, gives a totally different picture of their relations and of Walpole's political behaviour during the crisis.

Walpole had uniformly persisted in detaching himself from Fox, from the moment the latter had entered into engagements with Newcastle, with whom the other had determined never to have the most minute connection. Yet, I fear, passions of more mortal complexion had cooperated a little to his disunion (I cannot call it breach, as he never had the least

---

4. *Mem. Geo. II* ii. 42–3.
5. *Mem. Geo. II* ii. 214.
6. *Ante* 27 Oct. 1756.

7. *Ante* 4 Dec. 1756.
8. *Ante* 20 Dec. 1756.

quarrel) with Fox. Rigby, who had vast obligations to him [Walpole], was, however, grown weary of Walpole's ardour for factious intrigues, and wished a little to realize his politics. . . . This had made a breach between them; and Walpole, whose resentments were impetuous, and by no means of an accommodating mould, was little desirous of serving that league, and of breaking Fox's fall, especially by dishonourable means. It was enough to do wrong to gratify his own passions—he was not all disposed to err, only in contradiction to them. This detail would be impertinent, if a crisis, which Fox reckoned decisive, had not turned . . . on these secret springs; and if the author did not think it his duty to avow his own failings and blemishes with the same frankness which he has used on other characters.[9]

When this 'decisive' event is described by Walpole at length a few pages later,[10] the reader is left with the impression that Walpole had been one of the most determined, though secret, enemies of Fox during the entire crisis. Yet it is unjust to convict Walpole of duplicity towards Fox: Walpole had merely changed his mind about the character and political aims of his friend in the interval. He had at least two reasons for doing so, besides irritation arising from Fox's persistent disregard of his advice. Fox, as secretary of state, had once half-heartedly offered to procure the reversion of Sir Edward Walpole's place in the Customs for Walpole in return for Walpole's support of Newcastle, an offer which Walpole refused with indignation. Walpole does not mention this incident in contemporary letters, but it rankled increasingly in his mind and eventually came to form a principal item in his later criticisms of Fox.[11] Secondly, in February 1757 Fox joined the ministerial cry against Admiral Byng. Neither of these events provoked an immediate alteration in Walpole's support of Fox during the winter and spring of 1757. The letters to Mann during those months are, as usual, favourable towards Fox, and there are no hostile comments in letters to others. Walpole even relates in the *Memoirs* that he attempted himself to arrange a Pitt-Fox coalition under the nominal leadership of the Duke of Dorset in early June 1757: 'Horace Walpole saw the precipice on which Fox stood, and wished to save him from it.'[12]

Fox refused to be saved on Walpole's terms, and instead, a few days later, united his faction with Newcastle's and Pitt's to form a

9. *Mem. Geo. II* ii. 255–6.
10. Ibid. ii. 268–70.
11. *Mem. Geo. III* i. 167, iii. 69 and n. 1;

Last Journals i. 488–9; all quoted below, pp. 340, 342–3.
12. *Mem. Geo. II* iii. 28.

coalition ministry in which he abandoned high office for the immensely lucrative post of paymaster of the forces. Walpole's letters to other correspondents, even to Mann, begin for the first time to contain harsh reflections on Fox's conduct and clear indications that he and Fox are drifting apart politically. He found it 'extraordinary' that Fox should 'submit' to such an office as the paymastership under Pitt and Newcastle;[13] during the Parliamentary session he commented occasionally on Fox's 'underhand management' in stirring up opposition to bills;[14] and finally he spelled out his current attitude to Fox in a letter to Conway 17 October 1758:

It is almost impossible for *me* to find out the real destination [of the proposed secret expedition]. I avoid every one of the three factions—and though I might possibly learn the secret from the chief of one of them [Fox], if he knows it, yet I own I do not care to try; I don't think it fair to thrust myself into secrets with a man, of whose ambition and views I do not think well, and whose purposes (in those lights) I have declined and will decline to serve. Besides, I have reason just now to think that he and his court are meditating some attempt which may throw us again into confusion; and I had rather not be told what I am sure I shall not approve—besides I cannot ask secrets of this nature without hearing more with which I would not be trusted, and which, if divulged, would be imputed to me.

During the months that this critical, even hostile, attitude was forming in Walpole's mind he was writing the *Memoirs* for 1756 and 1757, reflecting upon and analysing Fox's past conduct. It would hardly be surprising if he remembered his conduct and opinions two years before to have been closer to those of 1758 than they seem to have been in fact. Nor is it surprising that Walpole thought fit to include in his letters as well as in his *Memoirs* (in a passage written between August and October 1759) some strictures on Fox among his reasons for a temporary retirement from politics in the autumn of 1758:

Fox's behaviour on the case of Mr Byng had rooted out his esteem, and the coldness discovered by Fox on Walpole's refusing to concur in all his politics, had in a manner dissolved their friendship. . . . From Mr Fox, as I have said, he had felt coldness and ingratitude.[15]

13. To Mann 20 June 1757 (MANN v. 103).

14. To Mann 21 March, 31 May 1758 (MANN v. 182, 205).

15. *Mem. Geo. II* iii. 160–1; see also HW to Montagu 24 Oct. 1758, MONTAGU i. 228, where he calls Fox 'Louvois, rash and dark.'

Only occasional letters between Walpole and Fox have been recovered for 1758–1763. They are amicable enough; the letters of their common friends indicate a continuing social intimacy, but Walpole's tone towards Fox in the *Memoirs* is now uniformly hostile: Fox is 'ambitious and exceptionable' with 'boldness and wickedness enough to undertake whatever the Court wished to compass,' and 'cruel, revengeful, daring and subtle.'[16] Walpole condemned Fox's union with Bute and censured his vindictiveness in punishing all who opposed him.[17] Here again hindsight was probably influencing Walpole: he did not begin his account of the first three years of the reign of George III until 18 August 1766 nor finish it until 2 August 1768; a temporary crisis in his personal relations with Fox had intervened in the spring of 1763. Nevertheless, Walpole was reasonably careful to exclude this later attitude from the account he gives of his own earlier relations with Fox (as an introduction to Fox's offer to Lord Orford in November 1762). Personal grievances appear, it is true, but they date from the 1750's:

I had, soon after my appearance in the world, lived in much intimacy with Fox, had warmly espoused his side when persecuted by the Duke and Duchess of Richmond, and had happened to have conferred some other little favours on him. I had carefully avoided receiving the smallest or the greatest from him. As his character opened more to the world, I declined any connection with him in politics, though determining never to have a quarrel with him, as I well knew his vindictive nature. When he united with the Duke of Newcastle, he had offered in truth slightly enough to procure the reversion of a considerable place, which I hold only for my brother's life, to be confirmed for my own, provided I would be upon good terms with the Duke. I had ever, in the most open manner, spoken of that minister with contempt: and having never to this hour received a favour from any minister, I shall be believed that I never would accept one from Fox. I answered accordingly with much scorn, 'I will not accept that reversion from the Duke.' Fox, knowing this spirit, and knowing, too, that I had declared to Lord Bute that I would receive no favour from the Court, had no hope of fixing me to his measures by any offers he could make. . . . Direct offers, or direct threats, would be vain: but to put me in mind of my dependence on my nephew, by whose interest I was chosen into Parliament, and which dependence Fox ought to have remembered I had braved for his sake [in the St Michael election

16. *Mem. Geo. III* i. 51, 196; iv. 84.   17. Ibid. i. 154–6, 187–90.

contest in 1755]; or of my dependence on the Treasury, which could hurt me severely by stopping the payments of my place in the Treasury; he wrote me the following letter.'[18]

Fox offered the Rangership of St James's and Hyde Parks to Orford, in return for which he expected Orford's and Walpole's votes for the preliminaries of the Treaty of Paris. Walpole replied guardedly that he would lay the matter before Orford, but that he considered himself involved in it only as a messenger and would not be obligated in any way by the result. Instead, he left the House of Commons before the vote on the preliminaries, stating in the *Memoirs* that, although his aversion to war forbade his voting against them, he was 'too much an Englishman to vote *for* them.'[18a] Fox's vengeance was prompt:

The consequence to me was, that by his influence with Martin, secretary of the Treasury, my payments were stopped for some months, nor made but on my writing to Lord Bute himself; which, as, notwithstanding this persecution, I would take no part with the administration, proved that the delay had not flowed from the minister himself, but from his associate, my good friend: nor did it stop there.[19]

Fox's letter of 20 January 1763 had been friendly, but by mid-March, this affair of the deferred payments inspired a new resentment towards Fox (now Lord Holland) in Walpole's letters. He wrote to Montagu 22 April: 'To my great satisfaction the new Lord Holland has not taken the least friendly, or even formal notice of me, on Lord Waldegrave's death. It dispenses me from the least farther connection with him,' and again on 16 June that he had been 'very indifferent' to a recent report of Fox's death and regretted that it had not occurred eight months before.[20] He described Fox's quarrel with Rigby and Calcraft in April 1763 as 'such a scene of ingratitude as could scarce happen but to a man who had selected his friends more for their utility than their merit.'[21]

The breach was patched up in the summer of 1763,[22] but Walpole continued to accumulate secret grievances against him—chiefly instances of enmity to Hertford and Conway.[23]

---

18. Ibid. i. 166-8, followed by the text of Fox to HW and HW to Fox 21 November 1762.

18a. Ibid. i. 167-8.

19. Ibid. i. 171.

20. MONTAGU ii. 68, 83.

21. *Mem. Geo. III* i. 207.

22. See Fox's messages to HW quoted above, p. 171.

23. *Mem. Geo. III* i. 209; see also HW to Hertford 22 Jan. 1764 and other comments on Holland in the HW-Hertford correspondence 1763-64.

Walpole also believed Fox to be an instigator of Conway's dismissal in April 1764,[24] but admits, even in the *Memoirs*, that he had resumed political conversations with Fox, as in the case of Conway's dismissal (1764), when, 'to hoodwink me to his own share in that business and to inflame my anger to Grenville, he [Fox] laid the chief blame of Conway's disgrace on the latter.'[25] Walpole gives other conversations with Fox, 1765–7,[26] indicating the greatest distrust of everything Fox told him, and making no mention of their extensive and friendly correspondence during the ministerial crises of 1765 and 1766. He also passes over his share in Fox's attempt to obtain an earldom in 1766, but describes in unflattering terms a similar request for his assistance in August 1767, when 'he supplicated me in the most flattering terms to obtain him an earldom from the Duke of Grafton. In a long intimacy, and during every period of his power, he had barely once, and that when he foresaw I should not accept it, offered me a faint attempt to serve me conditionally. I had the strongest presumption for believing that he had afterwards essentially injured me for declining to assist his bad measures. I was not at all sorry to have this opportunity of repaying both debts by forgiving both, and by endeavouring to obtain what he desired.'[27]

The same hostile attitude also appears occasionally in the *Last Journals*, although Walpole's criticisms are now directed more against Fox's paying his sons' gambling debts[28] than against personal and political relationships. Walpole, however, finds some of the old hostility still operative; when relating Conway's opposition to the Royal Marriage Act of October 1772, he mentions that 'Lord Holland, who never lost sight of injuring Conway, and who had received a recent disobligation from him, set every engine at work to hurt him.'[29] In October 1775, Walpole responded to Col. Keene's overtures about the Customs place: ' "Lord Holland, when I lived with him *in great* intimacy, offered to make my place for my own life, but I would not accept it." "No?" said Colonel Keene, "I am amazed at that! why not?" "Because, Sir," said I, "it is a greater favour than

24. *Mem. Geo. III* i. 320, 324, 329.
25. Ibid. i. 329.
26. Ibid. ii. 69–71, 119–20; iii. 49.
27. Ibid. iii. 68–9.
28. See especially a long passage, omitted by the 3d Lord Holland from the first edition of the *Last Journals*, but published by the late Earl of Ilchester as 'Some Pages Torn from the Last Journals of Horace Walpole,' in *Studies in Art and Literature for Belle da Costa Greene*, ed. Dorothy Miner, 1954, pp. 454–6.
29. *Last Journals* i. 142.

I will ever accept from any man." . . . Having refused to accept the place twenty years before from Lord Holland when he wanted to buy me to approve his measures, and rejected all overtures from Lord Bute, and withstood Grenville at the hazard of my fortune, and advised Mr Conway to resist all overtures, and offers, and threats, it was not probable that at fifty-eight I would disgrace my whole life, character, and principles.'[30]

30. Ibid. i. 488–9. HW had asked for the place twice from Pelham, once by letter (25 Nov. 1752) and once in person; he had also asked Newcastle for it in 1758. All three overtures were unsuccessful. Were HW confronted with his statements in *Last Journals* and his earlier solicitations of the Pelhams he would no doubt point out that the later offers to him of the place were made with a view to securing his political support, and that his own attempts to secure the place were entirely non-political. See MASON ii. 327 n. 4, and *Letters from George III to Lord Bute, 1756–1766*, ed. Romney Sedgwick, 1939, pp. xxix–xliii.

APPENDIX 8

WALPOLE'S WILL

Printed for the first time from the copy at Somerset House (P.C.C. 218 Exeter). We have added punctuation, normalized the spelling (except of proper names), and abbreviated the repetitious entails of the Norfolk estates and Strawberry Hill.

I, HORATIO, Earl of Orford, do make and publish this to be my last will and testament. I give and devise all those my freehold manors or lordships of Crostwight[1] otherwise Crostwick, Sloley, Honeing, Worstead Vaux otherwise East Ruston Vaux with the rights, members, and appurtenances thereof in the County of Norfolk and the advowsons of the several rectories and parish churches of Crostwight otherwise Crostwick and Sloley in the said County of Norfolk and also all that the site of my late capital mansion house called Crostwick Hall with the lands and appurtenances thereunto belonging; and also all and every my freehold and copyhold messuages, farms, lands, tenements, advowsons, mill, and hereditaments with their appurtenances situate, standing, lying, and being in the several parishes, places, townships, or territories of Crostwight otherwise Crostwick, Worsted, Honeing, Witton, Happisburgh, East Ruston, Ridlington, Sloley, Scottow, Tunsted, Stalham, Ingham, Westwick, Massingham, and Syderstone, or elsewhere in the said County of Norfolk, which descended to me as heir at law of my nephew George, late Earl of Orford, deceased, or whereof or wherein I or any person or persons in trust for me have or hath any estate of inheritance in possession, reversion, or remainder with their and every of their rights, royalties, members, and appurtenances (all which copyhold premises I have surrendered or intend to surrender to the use of my will), subject to and charged and chargeable, together with my leasehold premises held of the Bishop of Norwich and the Master

---

1. Most of the estates mentioned below, as well as those specified in the first codicil, had been purchased by Sir Robert Walpole in 1720; see J. H. Plumb, *Sir Robert Walpole*, 1956, pp. 310–12. Most of them were in the vicinity of North Walsham, north of Norwich, although some, including Massingham and Syderstone, were nearer Houghton. The descent of the Houghton estate itself had already been settled by George, 3d E. of Orford's will, although a lawsuit was underway between the Cholmondeleys and the Walpoles of Wolterton as to the right of succession; see below, n. 68.

and Fellows of Christ College, Cambridge, respectively hereinafter bequeathed with the payment of the two several principal sums of thirteen thousand five hundred pounds and four thousand pounds and interest due and owing upon two mortgages of the said manors and hereditaments hereinbefore devised, or of some part or parts thereof or so much thereof as shall remain due at my decease, and to which my personal or any other part of my real estate shall in no ways contribute or be liable; and also subject to the annuity hereinafter by me given to my servant Philip Colomb,[2] to the several uses upon the several trusts, and to and for the ends, intents, and purposes, and subject to the provisos and declarations hereinafter mentioned, expressed, and declared of and concerning the same: (that is to say) to the use and behoof of my great-nephew George James, Earl of Cholmondeley[3] and his assigns for and during the term of his natural life without impeachment of or for any manner of waste other than and except voluntary waste in pulling down houses and not rebuilding the same, and from and after the determination of that estate by forfeiture or otherwise in his lifetime to the use of His Grace Charles, Duke of Richmond and the Right Honourable George Lenox commonly called Lord George Lenox and their heirs during the life of the said George James, Earl of Cholmondeley, in trust to support and preserve the contingent uses and estates hereinafter limited from being defeated or destroyed, and for that purpose to make entries and bring actions as occasions shall require, but nevertheless to permit and suffer the said Earl of Cholmondeley and his assigns to receive and take the rents, issues, and profits thereof for his and their own use and benefit, and from and immediately after the decease of my said great-nephew, to the use and behoof of George Cholmondeley, commonly called Viscount Malpas,[4] only son and heir apparent of my said great-nephew and his assigns for and during the term of his natural life without impeachment of or for any manner of waste except such voluntary waste as aforesaid, and from and after the determination of that estate by forfeiture or other-

2. (d. 1799), HW's valet. For the annuity, see below, pp. 348–9, and for additional bequests, pp. 360, 366.

3. George James Cholmondeley (1749–1827), 4th E. of Cholmondeley, 1770; cr. (1815) M. of Cholmondeley; grandson of HW's sister Mary.

4. George Horatio Cholmondeley (1792–1870), styled Vct Malpas 1792–1815, styled E. of Rocksavage 1815–27, 2d M. of Cholmondeley, 1827.

wise in his lifetime to the use of the said Charles, Duke of Richmond and Lord George Lenox and their heirs during the life of the said Viscount Malpas in trust by the ways aforesaid to support and preserve the contingent uses and estates hereinafter limited, but nevertheless to permit and suffer the said Viscount Malpas and his assigns to receive and take the rents, issues, and profits of the said manors and premises for his and their own use and benefit during the term of his natural life, and from and after his decease to the use and behoof of the first, second, third, fourth, and all and every other son and sons of the body of the said Viscount Malpas lawfully to be begotten, severally, successively, and in remainder, one after another, in order and course as they respectively shall be in priority of birth and seniority of age, and of the several and respective heirs male of the body and bodies of all and every such son and sons lawfully issuing, the elder of such son and sons and the heirs male of his body issuing being always preferred and to take before the younger of such sons and the heirs male of his and their body and bodies issuing, and for default of such issue to the use and behoof of the second, third, fourth, and all and every other son and sons of the body of my said great-nephew George, Earl of Cholmondeley, lawfully to be begotten, severally, successively, and in remainder, one after another, in order and course as they respectively shall be in priority of birth and seniority of age and of the several and respective heirs male of the body and bodies of all and every such son and sons lawfully issuing, the elder of such son and sons and the heirs male of his body issuing being always preferred and to take before the younger of such son and sons and the heirs male of his and their body and bodies issuing, and for default of such issue to the use and behoof of my nephew the Honourable and Reverend Robert Cholmondeley[5] and his assigns for and during the term of his natural life. [The entail of the Norfolk estates continues in similar terms, vested successively in George James Cholmondeley,[6] only surviving son of Robert Cholmondeley and his heirs in tail male by primogeniture; in any other lawfully begotten sons of Robert Cholmondeley in tail male by primogeniture; and finally, in case of the failure of the Cholmondeley line in male heirs, 'to the use and behoof of my dear sister Lady Maria Churchill, her heirs and assigns for ever.']

5. (1727–1804), 2d son of HW's sister Mary.   6. (1752–1830).

Also I give and bequeath unto the said Charles, Duke of Richmond, and Lord George Lenox all that the site of the manor of Cardeston [Kerdiston] in East Ruston in the said County of Norfolk and all the lands and premises thereunto belonging or appertaining held by lease from the Bishop of Norwich; and also all that the rectory and parsonage of Darsingham [Dersingham] in the said County of Norfolk with the glebe lands, tithes, and hereditaments to the same belonging as the same are likewise held by lease from the Bishop of Norwich; and also all those lands, tenements, and hereditaments, services, liberty of fold, and fold course in Massingham and Harpley in the said County of Norfolk with all the appurtenances and commodities thereunto belonging as the same are held by lease from the Master or Keeper of Christ College in the University of Cambridge and the Fellows and Scholars of the same College. All which leasehold premises I lately purchased of the executors of the last will and testament of my said late nephew George, Earl of Orford, deceased, at and for the price or sum of three thousand eight hundred and forty-three pounds and for the payment of which I borrowed the said sum of four thousand pounds with which I have charged my said estates as aforesaid, to have and to hold the said premises last hereinbefore by me given and bequeathed unto the said Charles, Duke of Richmond and Lord George Lenox, their executors and administrators, for all such term and terms and other estate and interest as I shall have therein at the time of my death, subject to the payment of the rents and performance of the conditions reserved and contained on the lessee's part in the several indentures of lease by which the said premises are held to be paid, done, and performed, and also subject to and charged and chargeable together with the said freehold hereditaments and premises hereinbefore devised to the payment of the said principal sums and interest due and owing upon the said two mortgages of the aforesaid freehold hereditaments and premises or of some part or parts thereof as aforesaid or so much thereof as shall remain due at my decease. And I do hereby declare that the said bequest of the said leasehold premises was so made to the said Charles, Duke of Richmond, and Lord George Lenox, their executors and administrators, upon this special trust and confidence nevertheless that they and the survivor of them and the executors and adm[inistrat]ors of such survivor do and shall permit and suffer the said leasehold premises to be enjoyed, and the rents, issues, and profits thereof to be had, taken, and received from time to time by such person or persons who by virtue of and under the limitations hereinbefore contained shall be in possession of or entitled to the rents and profits of the freehold manors and premises hereinbefore by me devised. It being my will and intention that the said leasehold premises shall go and be enjoyed with the aforesaid freehold manors and premises so long and as far as the rules of law and equity will admit and for that end and purpose I do will and desire and direct, authorize, and empower my said trustees and the survivor of them and the executors or administrators of such survivor to renew the leases of the said premises from time to time at the usual and accustomed times. And I do direct that the fines, charges, and expenses of such renewal and renewals shall be borne and paid by and out of the rents and profits of the aforesaid freehold and leasehold premises. But it is my will that no person taking an estate tail by purchase in the aforesaid devised freehold premises shall be entitled to a vested or transmissible interest in my said leasehold premises unless he shall attain the age of twenty-one years or die under that age leaving issue male.

Also I give, devise, and bequeath unto my servant Philip Colomb one annuity or yearly sum of twenty-five pounds during his life to be issuing and payable out of and charged and chargeable upon the said freehold and leasehold heredit[ament]s and premises hereinbefore devised, free and clear of all Parliamentary and other taxes, rates, charges, assessments, and deductions whatsoever, by two equal half-yearly payments on Midsummer Day and Christmas Day in every year during the life of the said Philip Colomb and the first payment thereof to begin and be made on such of the said days of payment as shall first and next happen after my decease. And I do also give and grant unto the said Philip Colomb such and the like powers and remedies for recovering and receiving the said annuity by distress and entry and perception of the rents and profits of the said premises charged therewith or of a sufficient part thereof as are usual and customary in cases of grants of rent charges payable out of lands, provided always and my will is and I do hereby direct, limit, and appoint that it shall and may be lawful to and for the respective persons to whom any estate for life is hereby limited and appointed as aforesaid of and in the aforesaid manors and premises when and as they respectively shall be in the possession of the premises hereby limited to or in trust for them respectively for life as aforesaid or any part thereof by indenture or indentures under their respective hands and seals to demise, lease, and grant the same premises whereof they respectively shall be in possession unto any person or persons for any term or number of years not exceeding twenty-one years to take effect in possession and not in reversion so as there be reserved upon every such lease the best and most improved yearly rent or rents to continue payable half-yearly or quarterly during the terms in such leases to be granted that they respectively can get for the same without taking any fine, premium, or foregift and so as there be contained in every such lease a condition of re-entry for nonpayment of the rent and rents thereby respectively to be reserved and made payable and so as the respective lessees execute counterparts of all such leases and so as no clause be contained in any of the said leases giving power to any lessee to commit waste or exempting him, her or them from punishment for committing the same.

Also I give and devise all my messuages, lands, tenements, and hereditaments with their appurt[enance]s now in my own occupation situated at Strawberry Hill in the parish of Twickenham in the County of Middlesex, part of which being copyhold and held of the Manor of Isleworth Sion in the said County of Middlesex I have surrendered to the use of my will, and all other my messuages, lands, tenements, and hereditaments whatsoever whether freehold or copyhold with their appurtenances in the said Parish of Twickenham, except as hereinafter mentioned, unto and to the use of the said Charles, Duke of Richmond, Lord George Lenox and the Right Honourable Frederick Campbell, commonly called Lord Frederick Campbell, and their heirs during the life of the Honourable Ann Damer, widow, only daughter of my cousin, General Henry Seymour Conway, in trust to permit the said Ann Damer to have, hold and enjoy the same during her life to and for her own sole and separate use independent and exclusive of any husband she may marry to whose power or control, debts or engagements the same shall not be subject or liable, but the receipts and directions touching such premises of the said Anne Damer alone without any such husband shall, notwithstanding her coverture, be sufficient for all such purposes for which the same shall be given as fully and effectually as if she was sole and unmarried. And from and after the death of the said Ann Damer I give and devise all and every my said last men-

tioned freehold and copyhold messuages, lands, tenements, and hereditaments except as before excepted; and also all that my perpetual
advowson, free disposition, and right of patronage and presentation
of, in, and to the Church of Pelden [Peldon][7] in the County of Essex
to take effect from and immediately after my own decease to the uses
and purposes following: that is to say, to the use of my great-niece
Elizabeth Laura, Countess Dowager Waldegrave,[8] widow of George,
late Earl Waldegrave, deceased, and daughter of James, late Earl
Waldegrave, deceased, by my niece Her Royal Highness Maria, now
Duchess of Gloucester, and the assigns of the said Elizabeth Laura,
Countess Dowager Waldegrave, for and during her natural life, and
from and after the determination of that estate to the use of the said
Charles, Duke of Richmond, and Lord George Lenox and their
heirs during the life of the said Elizabeth Laura, Countess Dowager
Waldegrave, in trust by the ways aforesaid to support and preserve
the contingent uses and estates hereinafter limited, yet nevertheless
to permit and suffer the said Elizabeth Laura, Countess Dowager
Waldegrave, and her assigns to receive and take the rents, issues, and
profits of all and every the said last mentioned hereditaments (except
as before excepted) to her and their own use during her life, and
from and after her decease to the use of George, now Earl Waldegrave,[9] her eldest son and his assigns for and during his natural life,
and from and after the determination of that estate to the use of the
said Charles, Duke of Richmond, and Lord George Lenox and their
heirs during the life of the said George, Earl Waldegrave, in trust by
the ways aforesaid to support and preserve the contingent uses and
estates hereinafter limited, yet nevertheless to permit and suffer the
said George, Earl Waldegrave, and his assigns to receive and take the
rents, issues, and profits of the said last mentioned hereditaments
(except as before excepted) to his and their own use during his life,
and from and after his decease, to the use of the first, second, third,
fourth, and all and every other son and sons of the body of the said
George, Earl Waldegrave, lawfully to be begotten, severally, successively, and in remainder, one after another, as they and every of

7. This had been bequeathed to
Catherine Daye and the heirs of her body
in Sir Robert Walpole's will (P.C.C. 91
Seymour) with a remainder, in case of
her death without issue, to his eldest son
and his heirs and assigns for ever. For

further details about it, see below, p. 359.
8. Lady Elizabeth Laura Waldegrave
(1760–1816), m. (1782) George Waldegrave
(1751–89), 4th E. Waldegrave, 1784.
9. George James Waldegrave (1784–94),
5th E. Waldegrave, 1789.

them shall be in seniority of age or priority of birth, and the several and respective heirs male of the body and bodies of all and every such sons lawfully issuing, the elder of such sons and the heirs male of his body to be always preferred and to take before the younger of such sons and the heirs male of his and their body and bodies issuing, and for default of such issue to the use of the Honourable John James Waldegrave,[10] second son of the said Elizabeth Laura, Countess Dowager Waldegrave, and his assigns for and during his natural life. [The entail of Strawberry Hill continues in similar terms, vested successively in the male descendents of the Hon. John James Waldegrave; in the Hon. Edward Waldegrave[11] and his male heirs; in the Hon. William Waldegrave[12] and his male heirs; and in any other sons lawfully begotten of Elizabeth Laura, Countess Dowager Waldegrave, and their male heirs; then, in case of the failure of the Waldegraves in the male line, in Lady Charlotte Maria Fitzroy, styled Countess of Euston,[13] the Duchess of Gloucester's second daughter by Lord Waldegrave; in Lady Euston's eldest son, Henry Fitzroy, styled Vct Ipswich,[14] and his male heirs; in any other sons of Lady Euston and their male heirs; then, in case of the failure of the Fitzroys in the male line, in Lady Anna Horatia Seymour Conway,[15] youngest daughter of the Duchess of Gloucester by Lord Waldegrave; in her eldest son George Francis Seymour Conway[16] and his male heirs; in her second son Hugh Henry Seymour Conway[17] and his male heirs; in any other sons of Lady Horatia and their male heirs; and then finally, in case of the total failure of the male lines from the Duchess of Gloucester by Lord Waldegrave, to George, Earl of Cholmondeley, his heirs and assigns for ever.]

And I give and bequeath unto the said Duke of Richmond and Lord George Lenox all my household goods, furniture, pictures, book[s], china, jewels, and collections of curiosities and my plate, household linen, and other implements of household whatsoever and all my cattle, coaches, horses, carts, and other carriages and all my

---

10. (1785–1835), 6th E. Waldegrave, 1794.

11. (1787–1809), army officer.

12. (1788–1859), 8th E. Waldegrave, 1846.

13. Lady Charlotte Maria Waldegrave (1761–1808), m. (1784) George Henry Fitzroy, styled E. of Euston 1760–1811, 4th D. of Grafton, 1811.

14. Henry Fitzroy (1790–1863), styled Vct Ipswich 1790–1811, styled E. of Euston 1811–44; 5th D. of Grafton, 1844.

15. Lady Anna Horatia Waldegrave (1762–1801), m. (1786) Hon. Hugh Seymour Conway (later Lord Hugh Seymour).

16. (1787–1870), G.C.H.; G.C.B.; admiral.

17. (1790–1821), army officer.

other implements and utensils of all kinds whatsoever that shall be
at my death in or about the messuage, garden, lands, offices, out-
houses, and premises at Strawberry Hill aforesaid now in my own
occupation (except such part thereof as I shall otherwise dispose of
by this my will or by any other means) in trust for and to the intent
that the same chattels personal shall go and be enjoyed by the person
or persons who for the time being shall be entitled to and in possession of my said messuage, garden, lands, and premises in my own
occupation at Strawberry Hill by virtue of the aforesaid disposition
thereof and that the same shall remain and continue there and be
held therewith as heirlooms as far as the law will admit, but it is
my will that no person taking an estate tail by purchase in my said
last devised real estates shall be entitled to a vested or transmissible
interest in the chattels personal next before bequeathed unless he
shall attain the age of twenty-one years or die under that age leaving issue male. And I do desire and recommend to the person or
persons so having the enjoyment of my said household goods, furniture, pictures, books, china, curiosities, plate, implements, and other
things to keep and preserve the same entire and transmit them as
far as may be in succession to such other person or persons to whom
I intend the same shall go by my aforesaid disposition thereof, in
confidence of which I have not appointed any inventory to be taken of
the said things, provided always and it is my will that if the said
Anne Damer shall at any time dispose of her estate and interest or
any part thereof in my said messuage, garden, lands, tenements, and
hereditaments in my own occupation at Strawberry Hill in the Parish
of Twickenham aforesaid or shall charge the same with the payment
of any money or depart from the possession or occupation of the same
or any part thereof by lease, sale, exchange, loan, or otherwise howsoever to any person or persons (except to my said great-niece Elizabeth Laura, Countess Dowager Waldegrave) then and in either of
such cases the uses, estates, and trusts in this my will limited of or
concerning all and every my messuages, lands, tenements, and hereditaments in the Parish of Twickenham aforesaid unto or for the
benefit of or in trust for the said Anne Damer as well as such right
as she may have under this my will to the use of my said household
goods, furnitures, pictures, books, china, curiosities, implements, and
other things by me appointed to go as heirlooms as aforesaid shall
cease and be void to all intents and purposes and all and every my

said messuages, lands, tenements, and hereditaments and premises in the Parish of Twickenham with the use of the said things last mentioned shall thereupon immediately go over and remain to the use of or in trust for such person or persons who under this my will would be then entitled to the same in case the said Anne Damer was actually dead.

Also I give and bequeath to the said George Fitzroy, Earl of Euston, and the said Hugh Seymour Conway[18] and the Honourable George Fitzroy,[19] eldest son of the Right Honourable Charles Fitzroy, Lord Southampton, ten thousand pounds in trust to place the same out at interest in government securities and pay and apply the yearly interest or dividends thereof as the same shall become payable to my niece Her Royal Highness Maria, Duchess of Gloucester, for and during the joint lives of her and her husband His Royal Highness the Duke of Gloucester or to such person or persons as my said niece, notwithstanding her coverture with the Duke of Gloucester, shall from time to time by writing or writings under her hand direct or appoint or otherwise to empower or permit her to receive the same during the joint lives of her and the Duke of Gloucester, it being my intention that the said interest or dividends shall be for my niece the Duchess of Gloucester's sole and separate use and not to be subject to the power or control, debts or engagements of the Duke of Gloucester and that her receipts and directions alone notwithstanding her coverture shall without her husband the Duke of Gloucester be at all times a sufficient discharge for all money that shall be paid to her or her use or order in respect of such interest or dividends, and in case His Royal Highness the Duke of Gloucester shall die in the lifetime of my said niece his wife, then in trust to pay the said ten thousand pounds or transfer or assign the securities in which it shall be invested to her my said niece, her executors, administrators, and assigns for her and their own use, but if she shall die in the lifetime of the Duke of Gloucester her husband then in trust to pay the said ten thousand pounds or transfer or assign the securities in which it shall be invested to such person or persons and in such parts and proportions and manner as she by her last will and testament under her hand in writing attested by two or more witnesses or any

18. Hon. Hugh Seymour Conway (after 1794, Lord Hugh Seymour) (1759–1801), admiral.

19. George Ferdinand Fitzroy (1761–1810), 2d Bn Southampton.

codicil under her hand in writing so attested shall direct or appoint, and in default of such direction or appointment then as to all or such part of the said ten thousand pounds or the securities in which it shall be invested whereof there shall be no such direction or appointment, my will is that the same shall sink into the residue of my personal estate and be considered as part thereof.

And I desire Her Royal Highness the Duchess of Gloucester to accept the four small landscapes by Gasper Poussin[20] which are in my house in Berkeley Square and which were bequeathed to me by the late Sir Horace Mann, Knight of the Bath.

And I request Her Grace Mary, Duchess of Richmond, will accept three hundred pounds to buy her a ring.

Also I give and bequeath unto the said Ann Damer the sum of two thousand pounds to enable her to keep the premises at Strawberry Hill in good condition and repair.

Also I give to my said dear sister Lady Maria Churchill two thousand pounds and to her two daughters Maria, Lady Cadogan,[21] and Sophia Walpole[22] five hundred pounds apiece.

I give to my niece Laura Keppell, widow of the late Bishop of Exeter, five hundred pounds.

Also I give to each of her children, my great-nephew and great-nieces Frederick Keppell,[23] Anna Maria Stapleton,[24] Laura Fitzroy,[25] and Charlotte Keppell[26] five hundred pounds apiece, and if any one or more of my said last named great-nephew and great nieces shall die before me then I give the legacy or legacies of him, her or them so dying unto such of them as shall be living at my death to be equally divided between them if more than one, provided always nevertheless that if my said great-niece Laura Fitzroy shall die in my lifetime leaving her only daughter Maria Fitzroy[27] who shall survive me,

20. For these see the younger Sir Horace Mann to HW 17 Nov., 12 Dec. 1786.

21. Mary Churchill (b. 1750), m. (1777) Charles Sloan Cadogan, 3d Bn Cadogan, cr. (1800) E. Cadogan, by whom she was divorced in 1796 (MONTAGU i. 104 and n. 7). This legacy was revoked and converted to a trust in a codicil to the will (below, p. 375).

22. Sophia Churchill (d.1797), m. (1781) Hon. Horatio Walpole, styled Bn Walpole, 1806; 2d E. of Orford (n.c.), 1809.

23. (1762–1830), of Lexham Hall, Norfolk.

24. Anna Maria Keppel (1759–1836), m. (1790) William Stapleton.

25. Laura Keppel (1765–98), m. (1784) George Ferdinand Fitzroy, 2d Bn Southampton, 1797.

26. Charlotte Augusta Keppel (1771-post 1828), m. (1802) Robert Foote, of Charlton Place, Kent (William Berry, *Pedigrees of the Families in the County of Kent*, 1830, p. 27).

27. Georgiana Maria Fitzroy (d. *ante* 1834), m. (1814) John Horace Thomas Stapleton.

then and in such case I give unto the said Maria Fitzroy as well the said legacy of five hundred pounds before bequeathed to the said Laura Fitzroy as also such share or shares as she the said Laura Fitzroy would have been entitled to had she survived me of and in all or any of the said other legacies of five hundred pounds before given to my said great nephew and great nieces Frederick Keppell, Anna Maria Stapleton, and Charlotte Keppell in case of any of their deaths in my lifetime.

Also I give to my said great-niece Elizabeth Laura, Countess Dowager Waldegrave, five thousand pounds.

Also I give and bequeath all my leasehold piece of ground and the messuage or tenement thereon erected and built situate in Berkeley Street otherwise Berkeley Square in the Parish of Saint George, Hanover Square, in the County of Middlesex now in my own occupation together with the coach house, stables, edifices, offices, erections, buildings and other appurtenances thereunto belonging, and also the full and free use and enjoyment of all such of my household goods, plate, household linen, pictures, books, china, furniture, and implements of household that shall at the time of my death be in or about the same messuage or tenement and premises (my account books and such pictures that shall at my death be in the said last mentioned messuage or tenement as I shall otherwise dispose of by this my will or any codicil to the same excepted) unto the said Elizabeth Laura, Countess Dowager Waldegrave, and her assigns for and during so long of the term of years, estate, and interest which I shall have in the same leasehold premises at my death as she shall live, subject nevertheless as to the same leasehold premises to the rent and covenants under which I hold the same so far as such rent and covenants ought to be paid and performed during her life. And from and after her death then I give and bequeath my said last mentioned leasehold ground, messuage or tenement and premises with their appurtenances (subject to the rent and covenants aforesaid) and also my said household goods, plate, household linen, pictures, books, china, furniture, and implements of household that shall be in or about the same at my death (except as aforesaid) unto the said George now Earl Waldegrave, the eldest son of the said Elizabeth Laura, Countess Dowager Waldegrave, his executors, administrators, and assigns for his and their own use and benefit in case he, the said George, Earl Waldegrave, shall be living at the death of his said mother the said Elizabeth Laura, Countess Dowager Waldegrave, but not otherwise. And in case the said George, now Earl Waldegrave, shall be then dead, I give and bequeath my said leasehold ground, messuage or tenement and premises with the appurtenances (subject as aforesaid) and also my said household goods, plate, household linen, pictures, books, china, furniture, and implements of household therein (except as aforesaid) unto such other son or such grandson of the said Elizabeth Laura, Countess Dowager Waldegrave, as shall at her death be Earl Waldegrave, his executors, adm[inistrat]ors, and assigns for his and their own use and benefit. But in case the said George, Earl Waldegrave, shall die in the lifetime of his said mother and shall leave no son living at her death and there shall be no other son or grandson of her the said Countess Dowager Waldegrave living at her death who shall then be Earl Waldegrave, then and in such case I give and bequeath my said leasehold ground, messuage or tenement and premises with the appurtenances and all my right and interest therein and also my said household goods, plate, household linen, pictures, books, china, furniture, and implements of household therein (except as before excepted) unto the Right Honourable Lady Maria Waldegrave,[28] the only daughter of the said Elizabeth Laura, Countess Dowager Waldegrave, now living and the executors, administrators, and assigns of the said Lady Maria Waldegrave for her and their own use and benefit, subject nevertheless as to the same leasehold premises to such rent and covenants as aforesaid.

Also I give to my said great-niece Lady Maria Charlotte Fitzroy, commonly called Countess of Euston, five hundred pounds, and to my said great-niece the said Lady Horatia Ann Seymour Conway five hundred pounds.

Also I give to my said nephew the Honourable and Reverend Robert Cholmondeley five hundred pounds for his own use and benefit.

And I also give to his son, my great-nephew the said George James Cholmondeley five hundred pounds in trust to place the same out at interest or some or one of the public stocks, funds or securities being government securities and pay and apply the yearly interest or

28. Lady Maria Wilhelmina Waldegrave (1783–1805), m. (1804) Nathaniel Micklethwait, of Taverham, Norfolk.

dividends thereof as the same shall become payable to his mother Mary Cholmondeley[29] for and during the joint lives of her and her husband my said nephew Robert Cholmondeley or to such person or persons other than and except her said husband as she notwithstanding her coverture with him shall from time to time by writing or writings under her hand direct or appoint or otherwise to empower or permit to receive the same during the joint lives of her and her said husband, it being my intention that the said interest or dividends shall be for her sole and separate use and not to be subject to the power or control, debts or engagements of her said husband and that her receipts and directions alone notwithstanding her coverture shall without her husband be at all times a sufficient discharge for all monies that shall be paid to her or her use or order in respect of such interest or dividends, and in case the said Robert Cholmondeley shall die in the lifetime of his said wife then in trust to pay the said last mentioned five hundred pounds or transfer or assign the securities in which it shall be invested to the said Mary Cholmondeley, her executors, administrators, and assigns for her and their own use. But if she shall die in the lifetime of the said Robert Cholmondeley her husband, then in trust to pay the said five hundred pounds or transfer or assign the securities in which it shall be invested to him the same, the said Robert Cholmondeley, his executors, administrators, and assigns for his and their own use.

Also I give to my said great-nephew George James Cholmondeley five hundred pounds for his own use and benefit.

To his sister my great-niece Margaret Cholmondeley,[30] daughter of the said Robert and Mary Cholmondeley, five hundred pounds and to my great-niece Mrs Frances Bellingham,[31] daughter of the said Robert and Mary Cholmondeley, five hundred pounds.

Also I give to my great-niece the Honourable Mrs Hester Lisle,[32] sister of my said great-nephew George, Earl of Cholmondeley, five hundred pounds.

Also I give and bequeath to Sir Horace Mann[33] of Linton in

29. Mary Woffington (ca 1729–1811), m. (1746) Rev. Hon. Robert Cholmondeley.
30. Apparently an error for Henrietta Maria (or Mary Harriet) Cholmondeley (1754–1806); the Cholmondeleys had a daughter Margaret, born in 1760, but she died in infancy (Collins, *Peerage*, 1812, iv. 35).

31. Hester Frances Cholmondeley (1763–1844), m. (1783) William Bellingham, cr. (1796) Bt.
32. Hon. Hester Cholmondeley (1755–1828), m. (1773) William Clapcott Lisle.
33. (1744–1814), 2d Bt, 1786, nephew and heir of HW's correspondent.

Kent, Baronet, five thousand pounds, but if the said Sir Horace Mann shall die before me then I give the said last mentioned five thousand pounds unto all the daughters of the said Sir Horace Mann that shall be living at my death to be equally divided between them and if there then shall be but one such daughter the whole of the said five thousand pounds last mentioned shall be paid to such only daughter, her executors, and administrators for her and their own use, but if there shall be no such daughters or daughter of the said Sir Horace Mann living at my death, then my will is that the said five thousand pounds last mentioned shall go and be paid to the executors or administrators of the said Sir Horace Mann as part of his personal estate and effects.

Also I give to my brother-in-law Charles Churchill, the elder, of Grosvenor Street in the parish of Saint George, Hanover Square, in the County of Middlesex, Esquire, and to George Churchill,[34] Esquire, his son, three thousand five hundred pounds in trust that they or the survivor of them, his executors, or administrators shall place the same out at interest on such of the public stocks, funds, or securities as they or he shall think fit and pay and apply the yearly interest or dividends thereof as the same shall become due to or for the use of Elizabeth Hunter Daye and Rachel Davison Daye,[35] daughters of Carey Daye[36] of Chichester in Sussex, widow, equally to be divided between the said Elizabeth Hunter Daye and Rachael Davison Daye during their joint lives and in case of the death of either of them, whether in my lifetime or afterwards, then in trust to pay and apply the whole interest and dividends of the said stocks, funds, or securities wherein the said three thousand five hundred pounds shall be invested as the same shall become payable to or for the use of the survivor of them, the said Elizabeth Hunter Daye and Rachael Davison Daye, for and during the life of such survivor, and from and after the death of both of them in trust to pay the said three thousand five hundred pounds or transfer the securities in which the same shall be invested to my said brother-in-law Charles Churchill for his own use and to be in the mean time a vested interest in him so as to go to his executors and administrators in case of his death before the same shall be transferrable to him. And I do

34. (d. 1808), army officer (BERRY ii. 212 n. 6).

35. For these sisters, who were insane, see BERRY i. 281–2 and n. 14 and HW to Lady Ossory 2 Aug. 1793. Their mother had made HW their trustee.

36. (d. 1791).

hereby declare that the provision hereinbefore made for them, the said Elizabeth Hunter Daye and Rachael Davison Daye, is by me meant and intended to be and shall accordingly be in full satisfaction and discharge of all such claims and demands as they or either of them now have or hath or can, shall, or may have upon or against the advowson of the Church of Peldon aforesaid by virtue of or under the last will and testament of Catherine Daye,[37] late of Chichester in the County of Sussex, spinster, deceased, in respect of the several life annuities therein directed to be purchased for their respective benefits or in respect of any other legacy or legacies given by the said will with which the said advowson is or may eventually be or become subject and charged, and in or to which they, the said Elizabeth Hunter Daye and Rachael Davison Daye, or either of them, are or is or can, shall, or may be interested or entitled either as the next of kin or by virtue of the will or respective wills of any of the legatees therein named or otherwise howsoever, and upon condition also that they, the said Elizabeth Hunter Daye and Rachael Davison Daye, do and shall when thereunto required by the person or persons for the time being entitled to the said advowson under the limitations thereof in this my will contained, release all such claims and demands against the same. But in case the said Elizabeth Hunter Daye and Rachael Davison Day shall refuse or neglect so to do by the space of three calendar months next after such request, then it is my will that the said legacy or bequest of the said sum of three thousand five hundred pounds for the benefit of the said Elizabeth Hunter Daye and Rachael Davison Daye shall be void and the said sum of three thousand five hundred pounds and the securities in which the same shall be invested shall immediately go and be paid or transferred to my said brother-in-law Charles Churchill, his executors or administrators for his and their own use. And my will also is that in case there are any other subsisting charges, claims, or demands upon or against the said advowson of the Church of Peldon by virtue of the said will of the said Catherine Daye, then and in such case the same shall be paid and discharged out of my personal estate in exoneration of the said advowson.

Also I give to my deputy Charles Bedford[38] of the Exchequer two thousand pounds.

37. (ca 1724–75), an illegitimate dau. of Sir Robert Walpole. For an account of her see COLE ii. 371–2.

38. (ca 1742–1814).

To my Clerk William Harris[39] of the Exchequer one thousand five hundred pounds.

Also I give to my said servant Philip Colomb one thousand five hundred pounds and all my wearing apparel as well linen as silken and woollen or otherwise over and above the annuity hereinbefore given him.

Also I give to John Monnerat, son of my late servant Daniel otherwise David Monnerat[40] one hundred pounds, and to Mary Monnerat, daughter of the said Daniel otherwise David Monnerat one hundred pounds.

Also I give to the said William Harris the sum of three hundred pounds in trust to place the same out at interest in his name in such government security as he shall think fit and pay and apply the yearly interest or dividends thereof as the same shall become due and payable to Mary Newton *alias* Farren[41] of Chelsea, whom I have maintained from her infancy, or otherwise to permit, suffer or empower her to receive and take such yearly interest or dividends during her life which I direct shall be for her sole and separate use and at her own disposal, exclusive of and not to be intermeddled with by any husband which the said Mary Newton *alias* Farren hath married or may hereafter marry and that the same or any part thereof shall not be paid to nor be subject or liable to the power or control, debts or engagements of any such husband of the said Mary Newton *alias* Farren, but her receipts and directions alone, whether she be married or sole, shall at all times be a sufficient discharge to all intents and purposes for all sums of money that shall be paid to her or her use or order for or in respect of such interest or dividends, and after the death of the said Mary Newton *alias* Farren then if the said William Harris shall survive her in trust and to the intent that the said principal sum of three hundred pounds or the securities in which it shall be invested shall go and remain to the said William Harris, his executors and administrators for his and their own use and benefit, but if the said William Harris shall die in the lifetime of the said Mary Newton *alias* Farren then my will is that the said three hundred pounds or the securities in which it shall be invested shall after her death go and be transferred to all and every or such one or more

39. (d. *post* 1793).
40. (d. 1785).
41. Nothing further is known about this woman, who died before Dec. 1796, when HW revoked the legacy in a codicil (below, p. 375).

of the child or children of the said William Harris as shall be living at the death of the said Mary Newton *alias* Farren in such parts or proportions either absolutely or conditionally and according to such rights and interests and at such time or times after the death of the said Mary Newton *alias* Farren and with such powers and under such limitations and restrictions and in such manner and form as the said William Harris shall by his last will and testament in writing or any codicil to be by him signed and published in the presence of two or more witnesses give, direct or appoint the same or any part thereof, and in default of such gift, direction, or appointment or in case of any such, then when and so soon as the rights and interest thereby appointed shall determine and as to the whole or any part of the said three hundred pounds or the securities in which it shall be invested whereof there shall be no such direction or appointment, my will is that the same shall go and be transferred at the death of the said Mary Newton *alias* Farren to all and every the child and children of the said William Harris that shall be then living to be equally divided between them if more than one, and if but one then to such only child. But in case there shall be no child or children of the said William Harris then living, my will is the said three hundred pounds or the securities in which it shall be invested shall go and be paid, transferred, or remain after the death of the said Mary Newton *alias* Farren to the executors or administrators of the said William Harris as part of his personal estate and effects.

Also I give to my old gardener John Cowie[42] one annuity or yearly sum of twenty pounds during his life, and in case his now wife Catherine shall survive him, then from and after the death of the said John Cowie I give to the said Catherine his wife a like annuity or yearly sum of twenty pounds for and during her life and my will is that the said annuities to the said John Cowie and Catherine his wife shall be paid to them respectively free and clear of all Parliamentary and other taxes, rates, charges, assessments, and deductions whatsoever by two equal half-yearly payments on Christmas Day and Midsummer Day in every year that the same shall respectively continue and that the first payment of the said annuity to the said John Cowie shall begin and be made on the first of the said days of

---

42. (d. 1795), had been HW's gardener from about 1749 until after 1781 (BERRY ii. 179 n. 7, 183).

payment as shall happen next after my death, and the first payment of the said annuity to the said Catherine Cowie shall be made on the first of the said days of payment as shall happen after the death of the said John Cowie her husband. And my will is and I direct that my executors hereinafter named do and shall as soon as conveniently may be after my death appropriate and set apart a sufficient part of my money in the public stocks or funds to answer and pay the said annuity of twenty pounds a year to the said John Cowie and Catharine his wife.

Also I give to my printer Thomas Kirgate[43] one hundred pounds.

To my housemaid Martha Fare one hundred pounds.

To my housekeeper Ann Bransom one hundred pounds.

To my cook Elizabeth Colomb thirty pounds.

To Ann Sibley of Teddington, widow of my late footman James Sibley, one hundred pounds.

To James Colomb[44] my footman one hundred and fifty pounds.

To Christopher Vickers, my gardener, ten pounds.

To Ann Emerson, my housemaid at Strawberry Hill, five pounds, and to John Fitzwater,[45] my footman, ten pounds, which several pecuniary legacies to my printer and several servants last named shall be only paid to such of them respectively as shall be in my service at my death, and I direct that all such legacies as I have given to my servants shall be over and besides what may be due to them for wages or otherwise.

Also I give to Bartlett Reeve, who hath sometime watched my house at Strawberry Hill, ten pounds.

To [   ] Bransom, father of my said servant Ann Bransom, twenty pounds, and to Thomas Farr, my gardener's man, if he shall be so or in my service at my death, twenty pounds.

I give to Maria Colomb (the eldest daughter of the said Philip Colomb) whom I have taken into my house as a servant one annuity or yearly sum of six pounds for and during her life which is to be paid her free and clear of all taxes and deductions whatsoever by two equal half-yearly payments on Christmas Day and Midsummer Day in every year that the same shall continue and that the first payment of the said annuity to the said Maria Colomb shall begin and be made

43. (1734–1810).

44. For an additional bequest to him, see below p. 375.

45. For additional bequests to him, see below pp. 371, 377.

on the first of the said days of payment as shall happen next after my death.

And I charge all and every my messuages, lands, tenements, and heredit[ament]s which I have hereinbefore devised to the said Anne Damer for her life and after her death to the uses and purposes hereinbefore mentioned concerning the same with the payment of the said annuity of six pounds to the said Maria Colomb and I do for that purpose direct that the same shall be duly paid as it becomes due by the person or persons for the time being entitled under this my will to the possession of the said messuages, lands, tenements, and hereditaments so devised to the said Anne Damer for her life and after her death to the uses and purposes aforesaid and that all other my estate and effects, real and personal shall be freed and discharged and be exempted from the payment of the said annuity of six pounds. And I recommend the said Maria Colomb to the person who for the time being shall be entitled to the possession of my said house at Strawberry Hill to retain her there during her life in that capacity in which she shall at my death be in my service if she thinks proper to continue in that capacity, but nevertheless that the said annuity shall be paid to the said Maria Colomb in manner aforesaid whether she remains there or not.

And whereas part of my messuages, lands, tenements and hereditaments at or near Strawberry Hill aforesaid consists of a messuage or tenement and garden with the offices and appurtenances thereunto belonging heretofore in the occupation of Mrs Catherine Clive, deceased, and late of Sir Robert Goodere,[46] Baronet, and of the long meadow before the said messuage between the same and the great road leading to Teddington, now I do hereby (notwithstanding anything hereinbefore contained to the contrary) give, devise and bequeath the said messuage or tenement and garden with the appurtenances late in the occupation of the said Sir Robert Goodere and the said long meadow and also my goods, furniture, and other effects in the same messuage to the uses and purposes following: that is to say, to the use of Mary Berry[47] and Agnes Berry,[48] daughters of Robert Berry[49] of North Audley Street in the County of Middlesex, Esquire, for and during their joint lives and the life of the survivor

---

46. (ca 1720–1800), Kt (not Bt), 1762, had occupied Little SH between 1785 and Dec. 1790 (BERRY i. 124 n. 19).

47. (1763–1852).
48. (1764–1852).
49. (d. 1817).

of them if they shall both so long remain unmarried, and if it shall happen that either of them, the said Mary Berry and Agnes Berry, shall marry in the lifetime of the other of them, then to the use of such one of them, the said Mary Berry and Agnes Berry, as shall remain unmarried for her life, and from and after the death of the survivor of them, the said Mary Berry and Agnes Berry, in case they both continue unmarried or in case of the marriage of one of them only, then from and after the death of the other of them or in case both of them shall marry, then I give, devise, and bequeath the said messuage or tenement, garden and meadow with the appurtenances and the said goods, furniture, and effects therein to such person and persons and for such uses and estates and to and for such intents and purposes as I have hereinbefore given and devised or mentioned or appointed of and concerning my messuages, farms, lands, tenements, and heredit[ament]s in my own occupation at Strawberry Hill aforesaid, and the household goods and other things in or about the same or such of the said uses, estates, intents, and purposes as shall be then existing and capable of taking effect. And my will is that it shall not be lawful for the said Mary Berry and Agnes Berry or either of them to let or demise the said messuage or tenement, garden, and premises late in the occupation of the said Sir Robert Goodere and the said long meadow and the said goods, furniture, and other effects in the same messuage or any of them or any part thereof for any longer term than one year, to commence in possession from the time of every such letting or demising the same, and I trust that the said Mary Berry and Agnes Berry or either of them will not build or cause to be built any edifice, outhouse, or any other thing that may hurt or obstruct the views from Strawberry Hill, and this I am sure from their regard for me they will strictly observe. And I direct that the person or persons for the time being in possession of the said messuage and premises late in the occupation of the said Sir Robert Goodere shall pay the taxes for the same and keep the same in good and sufficient repair.

Also I give to the said Mary Berry and Agnes Berry two thousand pounds apiece.

Also I give to the vicar and churchwardens for the time being of the Parish of Twickenham in the County of Middlesex three hundred pounds to be by them placed out at interest in some or one of the public stocks or funds being government security in the names of the said vicar and such four substantial persons, parishioners of the said parish, as the said vicar and churchwardens or the major part of them shall by writing under their hands nominate and appoint. And my will is that the said vicar and such persons so to be appointed shall stand possessed of such stocks, funds, or securities in which the said three hundred pounds shall be invested in trust to pay and distribute the yearly interest or dividends arising therefrom once or oftener in every year among such poor of the said parish as the said trustees of such stocks, funds, or securities for the time being or the major part of them shall think proper objects of relief, and in such proportions as they or the major part of them shall think fit. And my will is that in case of the death of any such vicar or his removal from such vicarage, the succeeding vicar for the time being shall be a trustee of the said trust money or securities with the other trustees thereof for the time being in the room of every such vicar dying or removed. And if any or either of such other trustees shall die or cease to be parishioners of that parish or be at any time desirous to be discharged from such trust, then in every such case the said vicar and the other surviving or remaining trustees or trustee for the time being of such trust money or securities, being parishioners of the said parish and not desiring to be discharged from such trust, or the major part of them the said vicar and such other surviving or remaining trustees shall by writing under their hands nominate and appoint one or more substantial person or persons being a parishioner or parishioners of the said parish to be a trustee or trustees of the said trust money or securities together with the vicar for the time being in the room and stead of every such trustee (not being vicar of the said parish) dying or ceasing to be a parishioner of the said parish or desiring to be discharged of the said trust and as often as any of the events aforesaid respecting such last mentioned trust money or securities shall happen, a new trustee or trustees may be so appointed. And whenever the death or removal of a vicar of the said parish shall happen or any other new trustee or trustees shall be appointed as aforesaid the same trust money or securities shall be paid, assigned or transferred so as to be vested jointly in such succeeding vicar and the other trustees thereof for the time being or in the vicar and surviving or remaining trustees for the time being and such new trustee or trustees to be appointed as aforesaid as the case shall from time to time happen upon the trusts and for the purposes before mentioned concerning the said last mentioned trust money and securities.

Also I give and devise unto and to the use of my said servant Philip Colomb, his heirs and assigns for ever, over and above the several other bequests herein before made to him all that my copyhold messuage or tenement with the yard, garden, and appurtenances thereto belonging commonly called the Walnut Tree House situate in Twickenham in the County of Middlesex together also with the small messuage or tenement standing and being in the yard of the said messuage or tenement called the Walnut Tree House and the appurtenances thereto belonging, which messuage or tenement called the Walnut Tree House is one of my late three small messuages adjoining to Lord Strafford's garden in Twickenham and which being copyhold I have surrendered to the use of my will.

And I appoint the several legacies I have before given and which are not otherwise appointed to be paid, shall be paid within twelve calendar months next after my death, provided nevertheless and my will is that if any person or persons to whom I have given any pecuniary legacy or legacies (except such as I have given in trust as aforesaid) shall be under the age of twenty-one years at the time appointed by this my will for the payment thereof, then I authorize and empower my executors and executor for the time being of his, her, and their own authority in mean time and until such person or persons shall respectively attain the said age, to place out his, her, or their legacy or legacies at interest on government or other public stocks or funds and in like manner to place out the dividends or interest accruing therefrom respectively when they shall amount to a competent sum on securities of the like kind, and all money arising from such last mentioned legacies and the said stocks or funds in which the same or the interest thereof or any part thereof shall be invested shall be paid, transferred, or assigned to the person or persons from whose legacy or legacies the same shall accrue in proportion to their respective interests therein as such person or persons shall respectively attain the age of twenty-one years.

And I empower my executors and also the respective trustees for the time being of the several trust funds or securities in which any of the trust legacies or money aforesaid shall be placed out, to call in and dispose of such securities respectively or any part thereof as often as they shall respectively see occasion, and to place out the money arising therefrom as well as all money that may at any time be paid off or in discharge of any part of the principal money that may be so invested in such securities in any other securities of the like kind which other securities shall be taken in the names or name of the trustees or trustee for the time being of the security charged or paid off and shall be subject to the trusts before mentioned concerning the same respectively. And I direct that neither of my executors nor any trustee herein named nor any future trustee that may be appointed in pursuance of this my will of any of the trust money or securities aforesaid shall be answerable for any involuntary loss that may happen by the placing out or replacing the said trust money or any part thereof on any such securities as aforesaid, neither shall either of them be answerable for any money belonging to such respective trusts which did not come to his or her hands or possession notwithstanding his or her signing any receipt or receipts or other discharge for the same jointly with my other executor or the trustees or trustee of such trust money, nor shall either of them be answerable for the acts, deeds, receipts, or defaults of any other of them but each for his or her own only. And it shall be lawful for my executors and every trustee of the respective trust money or securities aforesaid to reimburse and pay himself and herself respectively and pay or allow his or her co-executor or co-trustee or co-trustees out of the said trust money, effects, or securities all costs, charges, and expenses which he or they shall respectively be put to by means of such respective trusts.

Also I give, devise, and bequeath to my cousin General Henry Seymour Conway, his heirs, executors, and administrators for his and their own use and benefit for ever all the rest and residue of my estate and effects, real and personal, freehold and copyhold, whatsoever and wheresoever and of what nature, kind or quality so ever not hereinbefore by me otherwise disposed of, which I now am or shall at my death be seized or possessed of, interested in or entitled to or over which I have a disposing power.

And lastly I appoint my said cousin General Henry Seymour Conway and his daughter the said Anne Damer executor and executrix of this my last will and testament.

And I do request that all such manuscript letters which shall be in my possession at my death that shall not concern or relate to my estate or effects and shall be written by any person who shall be living at that time may be returned to the person or persons by whom the same were written.

And I hereby revoke all former and other wills.

In witness whereof I, the said Horatio, Earl of Orford, the testator, having caused two parts of this my last will and testament of the same tenor and date to be written or engrossed, the one of such two parts upon paper and the other part upon parchment, have to this, being one of such two parts which is written and contained in twenty-two sheets of paper and fixed together at the top with my seal, set my hand to the twenty-one first sheets thereof and to this twenty-second and last sheet thereof my hand and seal. And to the other part of my said will which is written and contained in three skins of parchment also fixed together at the top with my seal, I have to the two first skins thereof set my hand and to the third or last skin thereof my hand and seal, the fifteenth day of May in the year of our Lord one thousand seven hundred and ninety-three.

Orford.   (LS)

Signed, sealed, published and declared by the said Horatio, Earl of Orford, as and for his last will and testament in the presence of us who in his presence and in the presence of each other have hereunto subscribed our names as witnesses thereof.

Robt. Blake, Essex Street.
Ja. Hall, Poultry.
Fras. Moon, clerk to Mr Hall.

I, Horatio, Earl of Orford, do make publish this to be a codicil to my last will and testament bearing date the fifteenth day of May last. Whereas in the devise contained in my said will of my Norfolk estate I have described and mentioned by name some only of the manors and advowsons, parishes, places, townships, or territories of which the same consists or in which the same is situate and have omitted the names of many other manors, advowsons, parishes, places, or townships: (that is to say) my manors of Lessingham, Costin, Roses Hill [Hall?] House and Georges, Walcott East Hall, West Hall, and Masons, Hemptons, Pentons, Stapletons, Thuxtons, Withes[?], and Heydons, Brunstead, Roses, Parkers, and Walshams, Halham [? Stalham] Hall with Brunstead, Parkers, and Walshams, East Ruston Burnells, Kerdeston, Netherhall Vaux and Marshalls in East Ruston, Great Massingham, and Syderstone; my advowsons of Great Massingham and Syderstone alias Systerne, and the parishes, townships or territories of Walcot, Dilham, Brunstead, Scarning, and Harpley wherein divers messuages, farms, lands, tenements and hereditaments, other parts of my said Norfolk estate are situate, lying, and being. Now although I am advised and fully persuaded that the said devise is sufficiently comprehensive to pass the whole of my said Norfolk estate, yet in order to prevent the possibility of any misconception of my true meaning, I do hereby declare it was and is my will and intention to comprehend and include in the said devise contained in my said will not only my manors, advowsons, messuages, farms, lands, tenements, mill, and hereditaments in the said county of Norfolk in my said will particularly mentioned and specified but also all and every other my manors and advowsons and other my messuages, farms, lands, tenements, heredit[ament]s and premises as well freehold as copyhold which I have power to devise or dispose of situate, lying, and being in the several parishes, places, townships or territories herein before in this my codicil mentioned and described or in any other parish, place, township, or territory in the said County of Norfolk, or by whatsoever other name or names the same are called or known. And that the same respectively shall go and be to the several uses upon the several trusts and to and for the several intents and purposes to, upon, and for which I have by my said will given and devised the several manors and advowsons therein specified and the messuages, farms, lands, and heredit[ament]s situate in the several parishes, places, townships, or territories therein named or elsewhere in the said County of Norfolk. And I do confirm my said will and the said devise of my Norfolk estate according to the explanation thereof I have hereby made.

In witness thereof I, the said Horatio, Earl of Orford, have hereunto and to one other part hereof set my hand and seal this fifth day of June in the year of our Lord one thousand seven hundred and ninety-three.

Orford.   (LS)

Signed, sealed, published, and declared by the testator Horatio, Earl of Orford, as and for a codicil to his last will and testament in the presence of us who in his presence and in the presence of each other have hereunto subscribed our names as witnesses thereof.

Robt. Blake, Essex Street.
Ja. Hall, Poultry.
William Slow, Millman Place, Bedford Row.

List of Pictures in London to be sent to Houghton if the law suit is decided in favour of Lord Cholmondeley; if not they are to go with the house in Berkeley Square.

The Lions very large.

Elector Palatine and Prince Rupert half lengths.

Two views of Florence by Patch.[50]

Heads
- Duchess of Gloucester by Ramsay
- Lady Monkton,[51] governess of the children of Charles I. *vide* Waller.
- Lady Whitmore,[52] by Mrs Beal,[53] was Miss Brook. *vide* Grammont.
- Mrs Middleton.[54]
- Charles I in armour
- Cromwell, ditto
- Lord Essex[55] or Sir Stephen Fox by Mrs Beale.

A fine Andrea del Sarto, much damaged.

Still life, by Roestraton.[56]

Two views of Venice, by Marieski.[57]

Two ditto of Strawberry Hill by Muntz.[58]

Two views in Jersey, by ditto.

Head of Nicolas Pasquier.[59]

Wilmot, Earl of Rochester.

Head of a Magdalen from the Head of Niobe by Guido, finished by Sassa Farrati.

Sir Robert Walpole in morning dress of nightgown and cap.

50. Thomas Patch (d. 1782).

51. An error for Morton. Anne Villiers (d. 1654), m. (1627) Robert Douglas, 8th E. of Morton, governess of the Ps Henrietta, whom she successfully spirited away to France. The incident is described in Waller's 'To My Lady Morton, on New-Year's Day, 1650' (Edmund Waller, *Poems*, ed. Drury, new edn, 1901, ii. 6–7).

52. Frances Brooke (d. 1690), m. (1) (ca 1665) Sir Thomas Whitmore, K. B.; m. (2) Matthew Harvey. She and her sisters are mentioned as court beauties in Gramont and her older sister, Margaret, who married Sir John Denham, is discussed at some length.

53. Mary Cradock (1632–97), m. Charles Beale; portrait painter.

54. Jane Needham (1645–92), m. (1660)

Charles Myddelton or Middleton, court beauty frequently mentioned in Gramont.

55. Probably Arthur Capell (1632–83), 2d Bn Capell, cr. (1661) E. of Essex.

56. Pieter van Roestraten (1627–1700), Dutch painter who worked in England most of his life. HW describes the painting he owned as 'well coloured, containing an ivory tankard, some figures in bronze, and a medal of Charles II appendent to a blue ribband' (*Anecdotes of Painting, Works* iii. 311).

57. Probably Michele Marieschi (1696–1743), Venetian landscape painter.

58. Johann Heinrich Müntz (1727–98), painter, who had lived at SH during the 1750's.

59. More probably Étienne Pasquier (1529–1615), French jurist and historian.

Francis, Earl and then Marquis of Hertford, with a dog in the hunting livery of George II by Dandridge[60] half length.

Henry Seymour Conway afterwards Field Marshal, his brother by ditto.

John Dodd, Esquire, of Swallowfield by ditto.

An old man's head with a double white beard, and ruff, in black, right hand on a book, left holding a glove, half length.

A view of Winchenton [Winchendon] House, the seat of the Lords and Duke of Wharton, whence Sir Robert Walpole bought the fine collection of Vandycks and Lelys.

An old peasant kissing a woman, with still life, a good copy of Teniers.

Men bathing, with rocks; a good copy of Polemburgh.[61]

Catherine,[62] eldest daughter of Sir Robert Walpole and Catherine Shorter, his first wife, in yellow, with a crook and a sheep half length.

Febr[uary] 9th, 1796. If anything should happen to me before I can make some additions to my will as I intend I desire my residuary legatee will pay to Mr Hudson,[63] the surgeon, who has attended me with so much skill, care, and tenderness one hundred guineas.[64] I desire twenty-five guineas may be paid to Mr Chamberlain,[65] one of the King's Librarians, who publishes the heads from Holbein,[66] as I have not yet paid him for such of those heads as I have had. I also desire that thirty pounds more than anything that I have left to him may be paid to my servant J. Fitzwilliam.[67] I declare this to be a codicil to my last will and testament. Witness my hand.

Orford.

60. Bartholomew Dandridge (fl. 1750), portrait painter.

61. Cornelis van Poelenburg (1586–1667), historical and landscape painter.

62. Catherine Walpole (1703–22) (J. H. Plumb, *Sir Robert Walpole*, 1956, pp. 117, 320).

63. A scribe's error for Huitson or Hewetson (HW spells the name both ways), who was treating HW during the spring and summer of 1796 (BERRY ii. 189–90, 194, 209). He was probably George Hewetson, admitted a member of the company of Surgeons 3 March 1785 (information from W. R. Le Farris of the Royal Company of Surgeons).

64. This sentence, from 'legatee,' is crossed out and 'I have paid him £200' substituted. A note on the margin of the copy of the will states that the original was so altered.

65. John Chamberlain (1745–1812), antiquary, keeper of the King's drawings and medals, 1791.

66. *Imitations of Original Drawings, by Hans Holbein, in the Collection of His Majesty, for the Portraits of Illustrious Persons of the Court of Henry VIII. With Biographical Tracts*, 2 vols, folio, 1792–1800.

67. Presumably a scribe's error for John Fitzwater, mentioned above, p. 362 and below p. 375.

I desire my executrix to give thirty guineas to Mrs Frances Seeman, a poor old pensioner of mine. Kirgate knows where she lodges.

May 23rd, 1796. I had directed that the two small red trunks in my bedchamber at Berkeley Square and the large one in the dining room there should on my death be delivered to Mr H. Walpole, but as the law has decided that he is not to have the estate at Houghton,[68] I now order that the said three trunks should be delivered to my great-nephew the Earl of Cholmondeley who is to succeed me in that estate and that they should be preserved in the library at Houghton as they contain material papers relating to the affairs of our family.

Hor., Earl of Orford.

I, Horatio, Earl of Orford, having already made my last will and testament bearing date the fifteenth day of May one thousand seven hundred and ninety-three with a codicil thereto bearing date the fifth day of June one thousand seven hundred and ninety-three do make this to be a further codicil to my said will. I give and devise unto my dear sister Lady Maria Churchill, wife of Charles Churchill, Esquire (over and above the legacy given to or for her use and benefit in and by my said will), the annual rent charge or yearly sum of two hundred pounds of lawful money of Great Britain during the term of her natural life to be issuing out of and charged and chargeable upon all and every my freehold manors, messuages, farms, lands, tenements, mill, heredit[ament]s, and premises in my said will mentioned to be situate, lying, and being in the County of Norfolk which descended to me as heir at law of my nephew George, late Earl of Orford, deceased, and not out of my leasehold or personal estates, or any or either of them or any part thereof, free and clear of all Parliamentary and other taxes, rates, charges, assessments, and deductions whatsoever by two equal half-yearly payments on Midsummer Day and Christmas Day in every year during the life of my said sister,

68. The case had been tried in the Court of Common Pleas, 6 May 1796, when a special jury found that a codicil added to George, Earl of Orford's will in 1776 had restored his will of 1752, vesting the descent of the Houghton estate in the Cholmondeleys after HW's death, and voided his will of 1756 which gave precedence to the Walpoles of Wolterton. Details of the trial are in *London Chronicle* 7–10 May 1796, lxxix. 445. Details of later trials in connection of the case, all of which confirmed the original judgment, are in Walpole v. Cholmondeley, 7 Term Reports 138–52, *English Reports*, 1900–32, ci. 897–904 and Walpole v. Cholmondeley, 3 Vesey Jun. 403–24, *English Reports*, 1900–32, xxx. 1076–85.

and the first payment thereof to begin and be made on such of the said days of payment as shall first and next happen after my decease. And I do also give and grant unto my said sister such and the like powers and remedies for recovering and receiving the said annual rent charge or yearly sum of two hundred pounds by distress and entry and perception of the rents and profits of the said hereditaments and premises charged therewith or of a sufficient part thereof as are usual and customary in cases of grants of rent charges payable out of lands. And it is my will and meaning that the annuity or yearly sum or twenty-five pounds which I have in and by my said will given unto my servant Philip Colomb during his life shall be issuing and payable out of and charged and chargeable upon such of my said estates in my said will charged therewith as are freehold and not out of any leasehold premises or other part of my personal estate.

And whereas I have enclosed or caused to be enclosed in a square wooden box marked with an 'O' on the outside of all such of my own literary works as have been heretofore published or have been printed or still remain in manuscript. Now I desire and my will is that immediately on my death the said square box marked 'O' with all its contents printed or manuscript be delivered to Robert Berry of North Audley Street in the County of Middlesex, Esquire. And I give the said box and all its contents and the whole and sole property of all such papers and writings as have been or may be published to the said Robert Berry and his two daughters Mary Berry and Agnes Berry to be published by the said Robert Berry and all the profits and advantages arising from such publication to be equally divided between the said Robert Berry, Mary Berry, and Agnes Berry, share and share alike.

And it is my will and desire that all the prints, books of prints, and incomplete numbers of prints with whatever else is contained in the large red exchequer trunk in the back room on the ground floor in my house in Berkeley Square, London, should be brought to my house at Strawberry Hill, Twickenham, on my death, as I do not mean that the contents of that trunk should go to the person or persons to whom I have by my said will given, devised or bequeathed my said house in Berkeley Square, but that the said prints, books of prints, and incomplete numbers of prints and all other things contained in the said trunk shall be deposited at my said house at Strawberry Hill aforesaid either in the Round Library of prints in the

Round Tower or in the wardrobe in the New Offices there and be enjoyed as heirlooms together with my household goods, furniture, and other particulars therein as mentioned in my said will, so that the persons to whom or in trust for whom I have by my said will given my said last mentioned house may, if she, he or they shall think fit, complete the books of prints in my said Round Library there as successive numbers of such works shall be published.

And whereas my cousin and dear friend Henry Seymour Conway, Field Marshal of His Majesty's Forces, the residuary legatee in my said will named, is departed this life, whereby the devise and bequest to him in my said will contained is become lapsed, now I do hereby give and bequeath unto the Right Honourable Frederick Campbell, commonly called Lord Frederick Campbell, and the Honourable Ann Damer, widow, in my said will severally named, the sum of four thousand pounds sterling in trust that they or the survivor of them, his or her executors or administrators do and shall put and place the same out at interest in some or one of the public stocks, funds or securities being government securities and pay and apply the yearly interest or dividends thereof as the same shall become due and payable to the Right Honourable Caroline, Countess Dowager of Aylesbury, the widow of the aforesaid Field Marshal and mother of the said Ann Damer, or otherwise empower or permit her the said Countess Dowager to receive the same for her own use and benefit during her natural life. And from and after her decease I give and bequeath the said sum of four thousand pounds or the securities or funds in which the same shall be invested unto her the said Ann Damer, her executors or administrators for her or their own use and benefit as a vested interest in her and them notwithstanding she the said Ann Damer may happen to die in the lifetime of the said Countess Dowager of Aylesbury.

Also I give and bequeath unto the said Ann Damer the further sum of four thousand pounds over and above the several devises, legacies and bequests I have made, given, bequeathed, or intended for her in and by my said will.

Also I give and bequeath to the aforesaid Mary Berry and Agnes Berry the sum of two thousand pounds[68a] apiece over and above the several legacies and bequests which I have given them by my said will.

68a. In the draft of this codicil (now WSL), this sum is substituted for £3000 apiece. There are no other important differences between the draft and the final will.

And I give and bequeath to my three nephews George Churchill, Henry Churchill, and Horace Churchill,[69] the younger sons of the said Charles Churchill, Esquire, and of my said sister Lady Maria Churchill the sum of five hundred pounds apiece.

And I do hereby revoke and make void the legacy or sum of five hundred pounds which I have in my said will given to my niece Maria, Lady Cadogan, one of the daughters of my said sister Lady Maria Churchill and in lieu and stead thereof I give and bequeath to my said nephew Horace Churchill the like sum of five hundred pounds in trust for the sole and separate use and benefit of his said sister Maria, Lady Cadogan, and to be applied and disposed of in such manner as she shall from time to time or at any time by writing or writings under her hand direct or appoint so as the same shall not be subject or liable to the power or control, debts or engagements of her present or any future husband, and that her receipts and directions alone, notwithstanding her coverture, shall be at all times a sufficient discharge for all money that shall be paid to her or her use or order by the said Horace Churchill, his executors or administrators for or in respect of the said legacy or sum of five hundred pounds or any part thereof or of the interest thereof or any part thereof.

Also I request His Grace the Duke of Richmond will accept of two hundred pounds for a ring and that Lord Frederick Campbell will accept of the like sum of two hundred pounds for the same purpose and for the trouble he will have as one of my executors which I entreat him to undertake the burthen of.

Also I give to James Colomb and John Fitzwater, my footman, the sum of fifty pounds apiece over and above the respective legacies given to them by my said will.

And forasmuch as Mary Newton *alias* Farren in my said will named is departed this life, I do therefore entirely frustrate, revoke, and make void the legacy or sum of three hundred pounds by my said will given to William Harris therein named in trust for the use or benefit of the said Mary Newton *alias* Farren during her life with such bequests, trusts, and limitations over, touching, and concerning the same legacy as are in my said will contained. And I direct that the same legacy shall sink into the residue of my personal estate.

And it is my will and I do hereby direct and appoint that the several legacies and bequests as well in and by my said will as here-

69. (1759–1817), army officer.

inbefore given and bequeathed and which are not directed to be paid out of any particular fund shall be paid and discharged by my executrix and executor hereinafter named within twelve calendar months next after my decease by and out of my personal estate not specifically bequeathed and by and out of the interest and dividends of my public stocks and funds and real and other securities which shall accrue and become due after my decease and before the said several legacies and bequests shall become payable.

And that all and every the pecuniary or money legacies in and by my said will and hereinbefore given and bequeathed and which are to be paid and payable by and out of my personal estate shall be paid and payable free and clear of all taxes or duties for the said legacies or any of them or for any receipts or other discharges to be given for the same, and that all such taxes or duties shall be borne or sustained by and out of the residue of my said personal estate.

And I do hereby appoint the aforesaid Ann Damer to be my residuary devisee and legatee in the room and stead of her late father the said Field Marshal Conway, deceased, and do give, devise and bequeath unto her the said Ann Damer, her heirs, executors and administrators for her and their own use and benefit for ever all the rest and residue of my estate and effects, real and personal, freehold and copyhold whatsoever and wheresoever and of what nature, kind, or quality soever not by me otherwise disposed of which I now am or shall at my death be seized or possessed of, interested in or entitled to or over which I have a disposing power in such and the same manner as and in lieu and place of the devise and bequest of the said rest and residue of my estate and effects to the said Field Marshal Conway in my said will contained.

And lastly I appoint the said Lord Frederick Campbell to be executor and the said Ann Damer to be executrix of my said will and codicils, and do hereby ratify and confirm my said last will and testament and the said codicil thereto in all other respects than as the same are altered or varied by this my codicil.

In witness whereof I, the said Horatio, Earl of Orford, have hereunto and to one other part hereof set my hand and seal this twenty-seventh day of December in the year of our Lord one thousand seven hundred and ninety-six.

Orford.   (LS)

Signed, sealed, published, and declared by the said Horatio, Earl of Orford, as and for a codicil to his last will and testament in the presence of us who in his presence and in the presence of each other have subscribed our names as witnesses thereof.

> John Dwerrihouse, 22 Berkeley Sqr.
> Ja. Hall, Poultry.
> Fras. Moon, his clerk.

I desire that my body may be opened on my death.

> Orford.

Dec. 27, 1796.

I desire to be buried very privately.

> Orford.

All the family papers in the library in Berkeley Square with those which I have lent to Mr Coxe for my father's life I would have sent to Houghton in the boxes in which they came.

> Orford.

This will was proved at London with seven codicils the thirteenth day of March in the year of our Lord one thousand seven hundred and ninety-seven before the Worshipful Samuel Pearce Parson, Doctor of Laws, Surrogate of the Right Honourable Sir William Wynne, Knight, also Doctor of Laws, Master, Keeper, or Commissary of the Prerogative Court of Canterbury, lawfully constituted by the oaths of the Right Honourable Frederick Campbell, commonly called Lord Frederick Campbell, and the Honourable Anne otherwise Ann Damer, widow, the executors named in the fourth codicil to whom administration was granted of all and singular the goods, chattels, and credits of the deceased having been first sworn duly to administer.

INDEX

The numbers in bold-face indicate biographical notes. Women are indexed under their maiden names, titled persons under their family names. London streets and buildings are indexed under their own names, Parisian streets and buildings under Paris.

[Walpole, Hon. Horatio (Horace), *continued*]
health of: Bath visit restores, 235; better,
238; blind in one eye, 268; colds rarely af-
flict, 250; constantly flitting gout, 268;
cough, 277; feels weak, lame and crippled,
279; fever, 195; good, 238; gout (1765), 192,
195, 201–2, 204; (1774), 261; (1785), 277;
(n.d.), 280–1, 283; gout made worse by heat,
192; gout makes writing difficult, 195; gout
not to be risked by winter return to England, 211; gout returns, 200; hand useless
because of gout, 272; improved by himself,
170; lameness, 268; mind and body want
repose, 194; not well, 71; poor, 80; 'quinsy,'
17; quite recovered, 238; riding necessary
for, 80; sea-sickness, 250; strength does not
return, 195; talking prohibited during attack of gout in chest, 261; too weak to
speak, 281; unwell all summer, 272, 273;
very seriously ill, 277; weak and broken,
202; weakness, 192, 199
letters from and to: complimentary close
adhered to in, 269; Edgcumbe reads super-
scription of, 37; forwarded to him by post
when he is out of town, 179; HW glad to
send amusing, to Selwyn, 268; HW has many,
to answer, 95; HW writes, to keep up his
English at Houghton, 34; must write themselves or remain unwritten, 80; 'newspapers,'
227; not to include everything that comes
into his head, 58; to be returned to writers
if living after HW's death, 367–8; to Lincoln,
contain first nonsense that comes into his
head, 76; to Lincoln, do not contain what he
feels, 72; 'To' retained in direction of, 269;
unplanned, 80
memoirs of, St Michael election discussed
in, 169n
occupations of: in decline, raking with
Mme du Deffand, 263; solitary coursing,
80–1; Williams, G. J., describes, as 'loo
and politics,' 239
papers of, bequeathed to Berrys, 373
political conduct of: at formation of Rockingham ministry, 199; explained in letter to
Orford, 169n
'political frenzy' of, 177
portraits of, Robinson's, 92–3, 95
reflections by, *see* Birth; Enthusiasm; Flattery; Grief; Heart, 'breaking' of; Merit;
Moralizing; Old age; Perseverance; Relatives;
Resentment; Self-interest; Taste, schools of;
War
relatives of, HW allowed to see, only briefly,
277
speech of, seconding Rigby's petition against
Fonnereau, 331n
strength of voice of, altered, 116
style of, Williams, G. J., quotes characteristic phrase of, 238
'unfashionable,' 62–3
verses by: 'epitaph' on Lincoln, 2; possibly

sent to Edgcumbe about Nanny Day, 109; to
Carlisle, 258; *see also under individual titles*
Williams, G. J., calls: 'as much a curiosity to
all foreigners as the tombs and lions,' 176;
'no minister but near the throne from his
connection,' 238
—— thinks pamphlet attack calling, 'prince
of cockle shells' will offend him more than
grave refutation, 239
will of, 344–77
writes, prints, and builds to attract attention, 176
writings of: account of C. H. Williams, 159,
311–23; character of Fox, 131–2, 333–5;
epitaph for C. H. Williams, 159; notes to
C. H. Williams's poems, 159; not to be
added to for a great while, 152; 'Patapan,'
287–306; 'Persian Letter' for Lincoln, 35–6;
see also under individual titles
Walpole, Hon. Horatio (1752–1822), styled
Lord Walpole 1806–9; 2d E. of Orford, n.c.,
1809:
HW revokes order to deliver family papers
to, 372
Houghton succession lawsuit lost by, 372
Walpole, Laura (ca 1734–1813), m. (1758) Hon.
Frederick Keppel, Bp of Exeter; HW's niece;
children of, 354
Fox can send letter to sisters and, for HW,
136
HW's bequest to, 354
HW to give breakfast for sisters and, **132**
Walpole, Lady Maria (Mary) (ca 1725–1801),
m. (1746) Charles Churchill; HW's half-
sister:
children of, 354, 374–5
entail of HW's Norfolk estates mentions,
346
HW informed of Fox's health by, 235
HW not to mention, 77–8
HW's bequests to: rent charge, 372; money,
354
HW's correspondence with, 235
Norfolk ladies visit, in odd costumes, 34
Windsor promotion of, influences HW's
politics, 176
Wolterton visited by, 80
Walpole, Maria (1736–1807), m. 1 (1759)
James Waldegrave, 2d E. Waldegrave; m. 2
(1766) William Henry, D. of Gloucester;
HW's niece:
Carlisle ridicules HW's concern for, 266
daughter of, 350, 351
Fox can send letter to sisters and, for HW,
136
HW cares for, after her breast operation, 171
HW distressed about situation of, if hus-
band dies, 266
HW's bequests to, 353–4
HW to give breakfast for sisters and, **132**
HW would laugh at, if pride did not in-
terfere according to Selwyn, 266